THE COMPLETE A-Z OF EVERYTHING CARRY ON

THE COMPLETE A-Z OF EVERYTHING CARRY ON

RICHARD WEBBER

HarperCollins*Entertainment*
An Imprint of HarperCollins*Publishers*

To Ian, Andy and Anna, thanks for all your help.

HarperCollins*Entertainment*
An Imprint of HarperCollins*Publishers*
77–85 Fulham Palace Road,
Hammersmith, London W6 8JB

www.harpercollins.co.uk

Published by HarperCollins*Entertainment* 2005
1 3 5 7 9 8 6 4 2

A catalogue record for this book
is available from the British Library

ISBN 0 00 718223 6

Printed and bound in Great Britain by
Butler and Tanner, Frome

CONTENTS

ILLUSTRATIONS

HarperCollins*Publishers* would like to thanks the following for providing photographs and for permission to reproduce copyright material:

Page 19, © Keith Turley; 155, © J.C. Eyer; 156, © Maidenhead Advertiser; 210–211, © Estate of Geoffrey and Nora Rodway.

All other *Carry On* film images are reproduced with the kind permission of ITV © Canal Plus (1959–1965 films) and © Granada Ventures (1966–1978 films).

Whilst every effort has been made to trace the owners of copyright material reproduced herein, the publisher would like to apologise for any omissions and will be pleased to incorporate missing acknowledgements in any future editions.

ACKNOWLEDGEMENTS

There are always plenty of people to acknowledge when compiling a book such as this. First and foremost, I'd like to thank Peter Rogers for supporting this project from day one, giving up so much of his time to answer endless questions and for allowing me to publish the 'unmade' film scripts. Thanks also to Audrey Skinner, Peter's PA, who was always more than willing to take time out of a busy schedule to encourage and help.

I'm grateful to the numerous actors, actresses, crew members, and relatives and friends of deceased cast members who made contact, gave interviews, wrote to me or simply provided their support, especially Valerie James; Liz Bresslaw; Janet Brown; Vince Powell; Nora Rodway, who has now sadly passed away; Amanda Barrie, who very kindly allowed me to quote from her autobiography, *It's Not a Rehearsal*; John Antrobus, who gave his permission to include his *Carry On Sergeant* script, and Norman Hudis, with whom I have discussed various aspects of his time working on the *Carry On*s – I enjoyed our numerous chats, Norman, and appreciate all the advice and information you've supplied.

Special thanks to a host of other people who've helped, particularly Roger Angell; Keith Turley, for allowing me to reproduce his excellent painting; Kevin Snelgrove and Dean Barker, for comparing notes on locations; Graham Walker, Brett Tremble and Paul Burton (check out Paul's *Carry On* website, www.freewebs.com/carryontribute) for helping check the various 'possible cut scenes' to determine if they'd been lost between the many VHS and DVD formats that have been released over the years or were genuinely deleted scenes; Trevor Dolby, Monica Chakraverty, Jane Bennett and Terence Caven at HarperCollins, who've been a pleasure to work with; my agent Jeffrey Simmons; Peter Boita Jnr.; Janet Moat, Vicky Hedley and Carolyne Bevan at the British Film Institute; Scotty Rothwell; John Herron; Rob Fellows; Jonathan Davidson; Charlotte Meyer; Robert Teek; Rita Eyer; and Eric Vasey. Finally, a big thank you to my niece, Anna Webber (I hope you didn't mind spending so many hours stuck in Hereford Library looking through the obituaries?); Ian Abraham, who compiled the merchandise, video, book and DVD lists, and helped select photos for this book; and Andy Davidson, whose web site, **www.carryonline.com** was a valuable source of information, and who helped in many other ways. Thanks, also, to anybody else who helped in this project. Cheers to you all.

Incidentally, if you're interested in contacting Keith Turley about his painting, call him on 01384 270143 or email at keithturleyart@aol.com

THE *CARRY ON* CHRONOLOGY

FILMS		STAGE		TELEVISION	
Sergeant	(1958)	*London!*	(1973–75)	*Christmas*	(1969)
Nurse	(1959)	*Laughing* – with The Slimming		*Again Christmas*	(1970)
Teacher	(1959)	Factory	(1976)	*Christmas*	(1972)
Constable	(1960)	*Wot A Carry On in*		*What A Carry On!*	(1973)
Regardless	(1961)	*Blackpool*	(1992)	*Christmas*	(1973)
Cruising	(1962)				
Cabby	(1963)			CARRY ON LAUGHING series . . .	
Jack	(1963)				
Spying	(1964)			*The Prisoner of Spenda*	(1975)
Cleo	(1964)			*The Baron Outlook*	(1975)
Cowboy	(1965)			*The Sobbing Cavalier*	(1975)
Screaming!	(1966)			*Orgy and Bess*	(1975)
Don't Lose Your Head	(1966)			*One in the Eye for*	
Follow That Camel	(1967)			*Harold*	(1975)
Doctor	(1968)			*The Nine Old Cobblers*	(1975)
Up The Khyber	(1968)			*The Case of the Screaming*	
Camping	(1969)			*Winkles*	(1975)
Again Doctor	(1969)			*The Case of the Coughing*	
Up the Jungle	(1970)			*Parrot*	(1975)
Loving	(1970)			*Under the Round Table*	(1975)
Henry	(1971)			*Short Knight, Long Daze*	(1975)
At Your Convenience	(1971)			*And In My Lady's*	
Matron	(1972)			*Chamber*	(1975)
Abroad	(1972)			*Who Needs Kitchener?*	(1975)
Girls	(1973)			*Lamp-posts of the*	
Dick	(1974)			*Empire*	(1975)
Behind	(1975)			*Carry On Laughing's*	
England	(1976)			*Christmas Classics*	(1983)
That's Carry On	(1977)				
Emmannuelle	(1978)				
Columbus	(1992)				
London (still in production					
at time of compiling this					
chapter)					

INTRODUCTION

Values and attitudes are not immutable, particularly as the years slip by and society evolves, yet people's views on the *Carry On* films remain seemingly constant through the generations. The unrestrainable *Carry On* franchise marches on, unaffected by changing fashions in an increasingly cynical world. Unashamed of its blatantly simplistic formula and unmoved in an atmosphere increasingly blinded by the political correctness brigade, the winning amalgam of sight gags, ludicrous plots, exaggerated characterisations and increasingly innuendo-laden scripts has entertained millions for nigh on fifty years. While other offerings from the comedy genre have become embarrassingly outdated, the antics of Sid James, Kenneth Williams, Charles Hawtrey, Hattie Jacques, Joan Sims et al. remain fresh, accessible and have now attracted cult status.

The *Carry On*s were a lean slice of British comedy: there was no fat, no unessential baggage in the scripts, performances or direction; they were never going to win an Oscar but, to be honest, no one intended them to. Each tightly packaged product didn't need to aspire to such dramatic heights because they were worth their weight in gold for what they set out to be: simple, fun and sure to pack the auditoriums around the country. They are not to everyone's liking, of course; there are those who regard the *Carry On*s as smutty and sexist, but the vast majority of the viewing public looked forward to the next instalment in the film series. Medical romps were always popular, as were historical capers, but one of the essential ingredients in the success of the movies was their predictability: audiences loved knowing they'd see their favourite actor playing the same old role, such as Hattie Jacques as an imperious matron. The films evolved but retained their charm, although later entries – *England, Emmannuelle* and *Columbus* – were pallid versions of their predecessors, lacking many of the trademarks epitomising a true *Carry On*.

Original writer Norman Hudis was able to interweave hilarious situations with moments of pathos. Take the tearjerking final scenes in *Sergeant*, when the hard taskmaster, Sergeant Grimshaw, upon retiring from the army after seeing his final intake march away as a champion platoon, is presented with a cigarette lighter by the lads. Personally, I missed these moments of gravitas once Hudis headed to the States and was replaced by Mister Double Entendre himself, Talbot Rothwell, heralding a new era in the history of the *Carry On*s and a difference in the approach. The comedy became more cheeky but was embraced with a warmth unrivalled by any series of comedy films produced. The saucy seaside-postcard humour appealed to the British masses and each production displayed an indefinable charm; nowadays, attempts to recreate the magic and atmosphere which surrounded the films would never succeed.

Despite the many other pictures Rogers and Thomas brought to the silver screen, it's the *Carry On* films with which they're most associated. When an unwanted script about the love of two ballet dancers, entitled *The Bull Boys,* landed on Rogers' desk in the mid-1950s, the success story began. The basic premise of national service was adopted and Norman Hudis employed to write a screenplay entitled *Carry On Sergeant.* Costing £74,000 to produce, it became one of the top box-office successes of 1958, and was quickly followed by *Nurse*, the highest-earning film in Britain during 1959; it also gained plaudits in America, where it played at cinemas for over two years. The success story had well and truly begun.

Richard Webber
Minehead – September 2005

ABOUT THE BOOK

Writing this book has been an exhausting, time-consuming, painstaking yet enjoyable task. The trouble is, when you set out to pen an A-Z of any series of television programmes or films, it's difficult to know when to take your fingers off the keyboard, switch off at the mains and declare the manuscript complete. Inevitably there's always more you could write, extra detail you could include, points that could be explored from a different angle; but before you know it, a manageable task – although, at times, it can appear completely unmanageable – quickly turns into an uncontrollable monster.

Compiling an A-Z is beset with headaches. As well as the aforementioned points, one always has that nagging thought in the back of one's mind that such a book has to try and include references to every minute scrap of detail concerning the subject matter – in this case, the *Carry Ons* – but to be honest, it's not feasible. Usually time constraints provide the final discipline, and if it's not time you're short of, it's the overall word count allowed by the publisher which restricts you. So, as you can see, it's not been easy deciding what qualifies for inclusion in this *A-Z of Carry On.*

One of the most challenging tasks has been tracking down some of the actors, actresses and crew members associated with the films, many of whom have long since left the profession or are now treading the boards of that great theatre in the sky. With agents, Equity or Spotlight holding no contact details, it's been virtually impossible, in some cases, to unearth relevant information about some of the actors' lives to enable me to pen a profile in the book. Occasionally I've resorted to telephone directories and cold-calling in the hope of tracing some of the profession's more elusive people. I have, therefore, included as many profiles as possible, thereby helping fans know at least a little more about the people associated with the films. If I was working to an open-ended contract in terms of delivery date for the manuscript perhaps I could take the next ten years or so and, no doubt, locate more performers, but, alas, that's not feasible.

Although I've included details of the various stage productions and television episodes over the years, I've decided to focus primarily on the films that had people guffawing – albeit to varying degrees – in cinemas around the British Isles upon their release. Although the small-screen offerings and highly successful stage shows were authorised projects and provided welcome entertainment for fans, it's the films which I regard as the stars of the *Carry On* canon. In the main body of the text, I've concentrated on the first thirty films, from *Sergeant* to *Emmannuelle*, with *Columbus* and *London* featuring in the 'Carry On' Revisited' chapter.

As mentioned earlier, I've tried to make this tome as comprehensive as I could, cramming in as much information as possible, but there are bound to be some details or areas that haven't made their way into the book. Nonetheless, I hope you find what *is* included informative, entertaining and helpful in answering all those nagging questions you have about the *Carry On* films. As well as actor and crew profiles, there are character profiles too. Even those unseen characters mentioned in the scripts have been given their rightful place in this publication, together with details of who mentioned them, in what film and the context in which their names were used.

And then there are the 'What Might Have Been' scenes. The majority, if not all, *Carry On* fans won't have seen the scenes included under this heading. Most were probably cut before the film hit the cinemas, while others could have been lost when the big-screen version was adapted either for the small screen or video format.

Then there are situations when a minor character perhaps had a little more to say before the editor's knife was sharpened, resulting in the said character's utterance extending to little more than a couple of lines. Whatever the circumstances, these selections makes interesting reading, such as the anaesthetist's scene involving John Horsley and Terence Longdon in *Nurse*.

Carry On reading – oh, and enjoy it too.

STEP-BY-STEP HISTORY
OF THE *CARRY ON* FILMS

1955

In August, Sydney Box commissioned R.F. Delderfield to write a film out-line with the working title, *National Service Story*. The treatment was delivered but the project was abandoned in September.

1956

The Rogers and Thomas film partnership, as producer and director respectively, began in earnest with the release of *Circus Friends* for the Children's Film Foundation.

1957

The National Service story was revisited and, in January, Sydney Box again commissioned Delderfield to prepare a screenplay, later titled *The Bull Boys*. When Box was unable to interest a financial backer, Rogers took the basic premise of conscription and decided to develop a comedy.

He approached Associated London Scripts for a scriptwriter to pen the screenplay. Spike Milligan and Eric Sykes turned down the chance but, in September, fellow writer John Antrobus was commissioned to complete a script for £750. Unfortunately the script didn't meet with Rogers' approval and he asked Norman Hudis, a contract scriptwriter, to pen a comedy screenplay based on national service for a fee of £1000. Hudis delivered a script blending comedy with pathos, a rich example of the style that had become one of Hudis' most coveted trademarks.

1958

Permission was granted by the War Office for the film to be shot at the Queen's Barracks, Guildford. Filming started on 24 March, initially with interior shots at Pinewood, and continued until May. The final produc-tion cost of making the film was under £78,000. By this time, Norman Hudis was already working on the next script, *Nurse*, delivering the first draft in June. Filming began on 3 November and was scheduled until 12 December. But even before the film was released, Peter Rogers was thinking ahead to *Teacher*, *Constable* and *Regardless*; for the first time, it was clear the foundations for an on-going series were being put in place. The final cost of making *Nurse* was £82,500, but before the year was out, scriptwriter Norman Hudis had already delivered the first draft of his screenplay for *Teacher*.

1959

Nurse was released in March and, like *Sergeant*, became a box-office hit in the UK: it also sold well abroad, particularly America. By March, the next production, *Teacher*, was already under way. Joan Sims, Hattie Jacques,

Kenneth Williams, Kenneth Connor, Charles Hawtrey and Leslie Phillips were back, and now the basis of a Rogers-and-Thomas' repertory company was forming.

A welcome introduction to the cast was Ted Ray, playing Mr Wakefield, the stand-in head at Maudlin Street School. Sadly, it was to be his one and only *Carry On*, much to Peter Rogers' disappointment. With the children, including Richard O'Sullivan, recruited from London's Corona Academy, location shooting took place at the Drayton Secondary School, Drayton Gardens, West Ealing, and was completed by 10 April. Filming, however, had begun back on 9 March at Pinewood with internal shots in Wakefield's study.

The film was released in August, just as Hudis put the finishing touches to the first draft of his *Constable* script, which was based on an idea by Brock Williams. Filming began on the streets of Ealing on 9 November.

While the film saw Leslie Phillips make his last appearance in a *Carry On* until, thirty-three years later, he reappeared in *Columbus*, Sid James made his debut. He became the anchor for many of the future films, a piv-otal point around which storylines revolved. Filming at Pinewood was completed by mid-December.

1960/61

Constable was released in February and Hudis began work on *Regardless*, which he'd later class as his least favourite script. A seven-week filming schedule ran from 28 November until 17 January 1961, with the film's release in March. Peter Rogers registered the title, *Carry On Cruising*, subsequently to become the sixth in the series, with the British Film Producers' Association in March 1961, by which time he'd already received a story treatment, initially entitled *Carry On At Sea*, from Eric Barker. The treatment was delivered by the sum-mer of 1961, but although Barker was to receive a credit on the clos-ing titles when the film was eventually released, it was, again, Norman Hudis who put pen to paper and wrote the screenplay, which was delivered to Rogers in December.

1962

Cruising was the first in colour and the last to be written by Hudis, who, on the back of *Nurse*'s success, would be invited to America, where he's become a prolific screen writer. Although he continued to write for the British screen, and later completed an unmade script for *Spying*, most of his subsequent work was in the States.

Filmed between 8 January and the middle of February, *Cruising* was released in April. Despite its title, no cruising on Mediterranean waters took place: instead, filming was contained within Pinewood, except for scenes of a liner leaving port which were filmed by a small camera unit. A new face to the *Carry On*s, although he'd worked for

Rogers and Thomas previously, was Lance Percival. He'd originally been considered for a more minor role, but was offered the part of Wilfred Haines when Charles Hawtrey's dispute over billing resulted in his declining a chance to appear in the film.

1963

Hawtrey was back for *Cabby*, which had a working title of *Call Me A Cab*. Talbot Rothwell delivered the final draft of his first *Carry On* screenplay in January, which was based on an original idea by S. C. Green and R. M. Hills, who'd go on to write for such shows as *The Roy Castle Show*, *Frankie and Brucie*, *Those Two Fellers*, *According to Dora*, *The Frankie Show* and, in Hills's case, latterly, *Carrott Confidential*. Sidney Green and Richard Hills had originally been commissioned to write a screenplay entitled *Call Me A Cab*, back in the summer of 1961, but by November 1962 Rothwell, who'd already completed a script for Rogers which would eventually be adapted into *Jack*, was brought in to turn the idea into a *Carry On* film. The film was shot between 25 March and 8 May, and after post-production formalities were complete, *Cabby* was released in June.

For the next *Carry On* picture, Rogers and Thomas returned to the draft script Talbot Rothwell had submitted prior to penning *Cabby*. It began life as *Poopdecker, R.N.*, before moving through other working titles, namely *Up the Armada*, *Carry On Mate*, *Carry On Sailor* and, finally, *Carry On Jack*.

Rogers explored the possibility of using library material from *Captain Horatio Hornblower R.N.* or *The Crimson Pirate*, both released during the 1950s; initially it appeared costs would be prohibitive but although a deal was arranged with Warner Brothers, no footage was ultimately used. The first of Rogers and Thomas's period pieces, the cast for *Jack* included some new faces, such as film veterans Donald Houston, Cecil Parker and Juliet Mills, all making their one and only *Carry On* appearance.

Filmed between 2 September and 26 October, *Jack* was released in the UK before the end of the year, by which time Talbot Rothwell was concentrating on *Come Spy With Me*, the working title for *Carry On Spying*, the final entry filmed in black and white. Rothwell – in collaboration with his friend Sid Colin – prepared a screenplay that was a parody of the successful spy movies, most notably the Bond pictures, that were receiving rave reviews during the period; but if events had turned out differently, a Norman Hudis script would have been developed. Hudis completed a draft screenplay in February 1963, spotlighting a group of secret agents who penetrate an atomic plant disguised as CND supporters before taking part in a CND demonstration themselves. Rogers rejected the script, but it wouldn't be the last time Hudis's work was considered for future *Carry On*s.

1964

Spying, which launched Barbara Windsor's *Carry On* career, was made between 8 February and 13 March and released in June. Within a month of hitting the big screen, the cast were back in period costume, this time in the days of Julius Caesar and Cleopatra for *Carry On Cleo*, the tenth in the series and Rogers and Thomas's twenty-first joint production. After completing the action between mid-July and the end of August, the film received its UK release in November. It was well received around the world, especially Australia, where its success was confirmed by various sources, including the managing director of Australia's Greater Union Theatres, who stated that in most cinemas it had beaten pictures such as *Lawrence of Arabia* and *El Cid*, taken more money than any other *Carry On* and broken numerous box-office records throughout the country.

1965

The first draft of Rothwell's screenplay for *Cowboy* was completed by March, but after script discussions with Rogers and Thomas, changes were made and a revised screenplay delivered by 11 May, two months before filming took place at Pinewood Studios and on location, with Surrey's Chobham Common and Buckinghamshire's Black Park replicating the Wild West. The final wrap was on 17 September, day thirty-nine in the schedule, with the film's release in November, weeks after Talbot Rothwell typed the final word of his next screenplay, *Carry On Screaming!*

1966

For *Screaming!*, Fenella Fielding returned for her second and final appearance in a *Carry On*, playing the vampish Virula Watt; Harry H. Corbett, meanwhile, earned £2000 per week playing Sidney Bung; Rogers was delighted to have Corbett in the cast, an actor he'd wanted to work with for some time. With filming completed by the end of February, *Screaming!* was a summer release.

By early autumn, production was under way on *Don't Lose Your Head*. It was originally released, as was the next production, *Follow That Camel*, without the *Carry On* moniker. When Peter Rogers left Anglo Amalgamated and teamed up with Rank, the new distributors were conscious of releasing future films from Rogers and Thomas under the brand of a competitor. It was only after takings for the two pictures were noticeably lower that the prefix was hastily reinstated.

Filming for *Don't Lose Your Head* took place between 12 September and 1 November and the picture, concerning two aristocrats who rescue their French counterparts from the guillotine during the country's revolution in the late eighteenth century, was released in time for Christmas.

1967

Although he'd become an integral part of seven *Carry On* films by 1967, the hard-working Sid James was unavailable, due to an earlier heart attack, when it came to casting *Follow That Camel*. Most of the big players, though, were free to step into period costume for the Foreign Legion adventure. After a run of successful parts, Jim Dale was once again in the thick of the action, this time playing Bo West, in a film based loosely on Percival Christopher Wren's novel, *Beau Geste*.

Rank, the new distributor, wanted an American face in the film, believing it would boost sales across the pond and Phil Silvers, alias Sergeant Bilko, was drafted in. But no longer a huge draw in the States, his inclusion did little for the film's success Stateside, while the actor's style and vaudeville background wasn't compatible with the traditional *Carry On* make-up.

Filming began on the 1 May, and in addition to utilising the back lot at Pinewood, the cast travelled, for the first time, beyond the environs of the studio – all the way to the Sussex coast, for location work at Rye and Camber Sands.

The film was released in September, just as the *Carry On* gang returned, after twelve films, to the hospital wards. Always a popular theme, *Carry On Doctor* (made between 11 September and 20 October) boasted the first of two film appearances for Frankie Howerd. With Rogers' wife, film producer Betty Box, responsible for the successful *Doctor* films, Peter Rogers sought his spouse's and John Davis's (then chief at Rank) permission to use the title.

When the film was released in December, *Carry On* fans were delighted to see the return of Sid James, albeit in a lesser capacity, as bed-bound patient Charlie Roper. After his enforced exclusion from the previous picture, James was recovering from his heart attack and accepted a less strenuous role, which he joked was the easiest he'd performed during his lengthy career.

1968

Long-distance location filming was rare in the *Carry On* world: outside of the immediate vicinity, the furthest the team had travelled was to the Sussex seaside for *Follow That Camel*. For the next film, *Up The Khyber*, they were on their travels again – this time to the mountains. But instead of the Himalayas, cold and wet Snowdonia was picked to represent the Khyber Pass. A favourite with both Rogers and Thomas, filming began on 8 April and was completed by the end of May. So realistic was the film's setting, Rogers and Thomas received letters from war veterans convinced they recognised locations at which they'd served.

There was a September release for *Up The Khyber* and an autumn shooting schedule (7 October-22 November) for *Carry On Camping*, another favourite of Rogers and Thomas – and millions of fans, too. It's become common knowledge that the adventures under canvas weren't filmed in the holiday season but October and November in the grounds of Pinewood. While the cast shivered in their summer gear, the mud was sprayed green to represent grass. Despite such hardships, the team – which included Barbara Windsor and her famous flying bikini top – turned out one of their best overall performances.

The script, once again, was supplied by Tolly Rothwell, although he'd originally embarked on a *Camping* script back in 1966, before it was postponed in favour of *Follow That Camel*.

1969

Camping was released in February and followed quickly by *Again Doctor*, the last time we'd see Jim Dale in a *Carry On* before the critically slated *Columbus*, some twenty-three years later.

Rothwell's draft script wasn't entirely satisfactory so he rewrote it and delivered the amended version by the end of January. The screenplay raised a few questions from Rank's legal adviser, Hugh J. Parton, who, realising Rothwell had written a rejected *Doctor in Clover* script for Betty Box, queried whether much of Frederick Carver's dialogue was so reminiscent of Sir Lancelot Spratt (portrayed by James Robertson Justice in the *Doctor* films) that it was an intended parody. Concern was also expressed over the Medical Mission and slimming cure sequences, which Parton thought he'd read before, perhaps in Rothwell's *Clover* script or in one of author Richard Gordon's books. Worried about copyright infringement, he raised the points with Rogers in February.

Filming began on 17 March and continued until the beginning of May, shooting on F, C and G stages at Pinewood, with location work in Maidenhead. It was released in August, by which time Rothwell had nearly finished *Up the Jungle*, which carried a working title of *Carry On Jungle Boy*. When Dale declined the chance to play Jungle Boy, the part was offered to Terry Scott, while Jacki Piper became the first performer to be placed on contract by Rogers and Thomas. Making her debut as Joan Sims's assistant, June, in the film, she'd appear in *Loving* and *At Your Convenience* before a cameo role in *Matron*. Howerd was back for his final *Carry On*, which was shot between 13 October and 24 November.

1970

Up the Jungle hit the big screen in March, and within weeks James, Hawtrey et al. were back at Pinewood filming *Carry On Loving*, which began life as *Carry On Courting*. Rothwell had started working on the script back in October 1969, but once he'd submitted the final draft, filming began on 6 April and was completed by mid-May.

Loving was released in September, while the cast were back in period costumes for *Carry On* film number twenty-one – *Henry*. With Sid James in commanding style as Henry VIII, and impressive sets and locations (including Windsor Great Park and the Long Walk) on view, this richly produced film was a welcome addition to the series. Rothwell had initially been working on *Carry On Comrade* (later changed to *Carry On At Your Convenience*, although it also carried the working title of *Carry On Working*) before the project was cancelled – albeit temporarily – and the scriptwriter was commissioned to pen this medieval romp, which was shot between 12 October and 27 November.

1971

After the release of the latest period piece in February, Talbot Rothwell returned to his lavatories and bidets for *At Your Convenience*, which reunited Richard O'Callaghan and Jacki Piper. In draft form, the script started out as *Carry On Working*, but by the time filming began on 22 March the title had changed. The cast travelled to Brighton Pier for some fun at the fair between Monday 3 and Wednesday 5 May and a good time was had by all, but when the film was released in December it met with a lukewarm response from audiences and took several years to recoup its original production costs, perhaps resulting from the way the film portrayed unions and shop stewards. But if audiences didn't rush to watch *At Your Convenience*, normal service was resumed with the next offering from the Rogers/Thomas production line because it was back to the world of starched uniforms and stethoscopes with *Carry On Matron*.

The script was the work of Talbot Rothwell again, but could easily have been original writer Norman Hudis if a proposed contract, originated in November 1969, had been executed. By then, however, Hudis was based in the States and for Rogers to have employed the writer on *Matron* while he was resident in the US would have cost his budget an additional fee, payable to the Writers' Guild to fund its pension and health benefits. Following correspondence between Rogers' office and the Guild, the contract was cancelled and Rothwell hired instead. Talbot's contract was issued in May and the script delivered in August. All the familiar faces were recruited for this enjoyable slice of traditional *Carry On* fare, filmed between 11 October and 26 November; the finished product hit the screens the following spring.

1972

By the time *Matron* was released in May, filming had begun on the twenty-fourth *Carry On*. With package holidays becoming increasingly popular in Britain, it was time for Rogers and Thomas to turn their attention to the sun-seeking adventures of a bunch of oddballs thrown together by circumstance. Filmed between 17 April and 26 May, *Abroad* became one of the genre's strongest entries and Charles Hawtrey's swan-song. It was the last time he'd appear in a *Carry On*. Meanwhile, location work, which June Whitfield, making her second appearance in the series, thought might take place in sunnier climes, ended up being in the grounds of Pinewood. The furthest the cast travelled was Slough to film scenes showing trippers climbing on to the coach taking them to the airport.

1973

It was off to Brighton again for location work on *Carry On Girls* (originally discussed as *Carry On Beauty Queen*) which went into production on 16 April. The first day's filming involved scenes where Larry (a rather green photographer played by Robin Askwith) is asked to take some snaps of busty model Dawn Brakes (Margaret Nolan) on Fircombe beach. Filming was completed by 25 May and the picture released in November. The highly successful *Carry On London!* stage production, which kicked off in the autumn, put paid to thoughts regarding a second *Carry On* that year, which had become the norm.

1974

A return to period comedy for the only big screen production in 1974. Sadly, it would be Sid James's last appearance, as well as Rothwell's final script. When the writer became ill before completing the screenplay for *Dick*, producer Peter Rogers stepped in and completed the script himself. Meanwhile, Jack Douglas, as Sergeant Jock Strapp, played his biggest role to date. The idea was based on a full-length script submitted by Lawrie Wyman and George Evans, but it was regular scriptwriter Talbot Rothwell who, for £10,000, was commissioned to write the screenplay, brought to life by the cast between early March and mid-April. The film was released in July.

1975

While the *Carry On Laughing* television series was being screened on ITV, *Carry On Behind* brought together a group of regular faces and some occasionals. With Sid James touring Australia in a play, and Barbara Windsor performing her one-woman show in New Zealand, two of the most popular performers were missing. The cast, however, still boasted such names as Kenneth Connor, Kenneth Williams, Peter Butterworth, Joan Sims, Bernard Bresslaw and Patsy Rowlands, with new faces including Windsor Davies and German-born actress Elke Sommer, delivering a well-crafted performance as renowned archaeologist, Professor Anna Vooshka.

The screenplay, written by Dave Freeman, was equally innuendo-laden as his predecessor's output; Freeman had originally submitted a script titled *Love On Wheels* back in 1973, which was later altered to *Carry On Carrying On*, before finally becoming *Behind* by the time Freeman delivered the screenplay in January 1975. The film was shot between mid-March and mid-April and released in December, and although many argue that the *Carry On* series had lost its way by this point, *Behind* was an amusing piece of work continuing in the same vein as those which had gone before.

1976

By the time the cast of *Carry On England* had fallen in during May, Sid James, the linchpin of so many films in the series, was dead. While performing in a production of Sam Cree's *The Mating Game* in Sunderland, he collapsed and died – he was sixty-two. Such a loss would inevitably cast a shadow over the production when the cast arrived at Pinewood.

Filming began on 3 May until 4 June, and despite some familiar faces in the cast, including Kenneth Connor, Joan Sims, Jack Douglas and Peter Butterworth, a clutch of new faces were placed in prominent roles, such as Patrick Mower and Judy Geeson. This, combined with a script written by David Pursall and Jack Seddon, experienced in their field yet new to the *Carry On* series, resulted in a different style of film, unfamiliar to many fans of the genre. For me, it's the most disappointing of all the *Carry On* pictures, and upon its release in October, *England* failed to satisfy the cinema-going public and was removed from the schedules by some cinemas days after receiving its initial viewing. It would be some time before the film clawed back its production costs.

1977

In *That's Carry On*, Rogers and Thomas offered a nostalgic trip back in time celebrating those golden moments from their catalogue of films. The compilation, with an original screenplay by Tony Church, was introduced by Kenneth Williams and Barbara Windsor, and contained all the classic scenes you'd ever want to see. After Gerald Thomas and editor Jack

Gardner spent nearly six weeks choosing the best sequences, they sat down in a theatre to check their selections, only to find the film ran for six hours. Eventually they streamlined the output and although it didn't initially set the world on fire, the film has over the years become a welcome and valued addition to the *Carry On* library, reminding fans of the halcyon days when Norman Hudis and Talbot Rothwell's scripts had audiences rolling in the aisles.

1978

That's Carry On was released in February, and the thirtieth film, *Emmannuelle*, went into production in April. When the original script by New Zealand-born Lance Peters was far too blue, experienced television writer Vince Powell was hired to tone it down. With many of the true *Carry On*ers entertaining audiences in the sky, and some regarding the film too smutty to be classed as a *Carry On*, Kenneth Williams, Jack Douglas, Joan Sims and Peter Butterworth were the only regulars present. Playing alongside Williams as his wife, Emmannuelle Prevert, was newcomer Suzanne Danielle, a mere fledgling in the world of film. But her portrayal was expertly executed, a performance defying her lack of big-screen experience.

Filming between 10 April and 15 May was followed by a November release, but the film's 'AA' certificate meant it was no longer classified as family viewing, thereby losing a sizeable proportion of the audience normally associated with *Carry On* films.

The absence of so many of the faces audiences had become accustomed to, and a script which, although offering innuendo and double entendres, lacked the flair of Hudis and Rothwell's work, *Emmannuelle* failed to revive the magic one had come to expect from a *Carry On*. Some critics regarded the film as pornographic, which is far from the truth, but the sexual connotations were rather more obvious and blatant than anything before, and the film lacked the feel-good factor which had pervaded its predecessors, with the exception of *England*.

1992

Fourteen years after *Emmannuelle*, the thirty-first *Carry On* went into production. The nuts and bolts of this movie are covered in a later chapter, together with details of various aborted projects in the preceding years, but *Columbus* was a pallid attempt to rekindle Britain's affections for the *Carry On*-style movie; sadly, it fell short of the markers set by the others and failed to capture the repertory-company atmosphere one came to expect, and want, from such films.

P. S.

Now, of course, yet another *Carry On* film is in the pipeline. At the time of writing, *London* is in production, but only time will tell whether it will prosper or sink without trace. Watch this space!

Illustration © Keith Turley

ABERDEEN ANGUS
Captain Crowther's favourite tipple in *Cruising*. He's distraught when Angus, the head barman responsible for the concoction, leaves the SS *Happy Wanderer* and his replacement, Sam Turner, hasn't a clue how to mix the drink.

ABLE, ALICE
Played by Marianne Stone
The wife of Bert Able, who's a patient at Haven Hospital in *Nurse*. She's seen visiting her hubby.

ABLE, BERT
Played by Cyril Chamberlain
A patient at Haven Hospital in *Nurse*, Bert lives in The Manor, a spacious house on the west side of the Common, with his wife and eleven kids. They rent the property from the local council for around twenty-two shillings a week.

ABLE PLATOON
Sergeant Grimshaw's final platoon at Heathercrest National Service Depot. In *Sergeant* the platoon, part of the twenty-ninth intake, becomes – to everyone's surprise – the champion platoon, breaking all records in the process.

ABLE, SERGEANT LEN
Played by Patrick Mower
Leonard Able is a lazy, conniving troublemaker who tries to make his captain's life hell in *England*. Together with the love of his life, Sergeant Tilly Willing, he tries anything to avoid having to work at the experimental 1313 anti-aircraft battery.

ABROAD, CARRY ON
See feature box on page 20–1.

ABULBUL, SHEIKH ABDUL
Played by Bernard Bresslaw
Leader of the Arabs, the Sheikh has twelve wives and intends making Lady Jane Ponsonby, whom he's kidnapped, number thirteen. Appears in various scenes during *Follow That Camel*, often attacking the garrison of his arch-enemies, the Foreign Legion.

ADAMS, GREGORY
Played by Kenneth Connor
This nervous, bumbling science teacher at Maudlin Street Secondary School is seen in *Teacher*. His hesitations and indecisiveness make for an ineffectual teacher, although there is no doubting his subject expertise. The arrival of Felicity Wheeler – a school inspector visiting Maudlin Street with Alistair Grigg, a child psychiatrist – becomes a major turning point in Adams's life as he finds himself, almost reluctantly at first, falling in love with Wheeler.

ADAMS, JILL
Role: WPC Harrison in *Constable*
Blonde beauty Jill Adams, who was born in London in 1931, spent her early childhood in New Zealand before returning to England. After completing her education she held several jobs, including working as a shop assistant and secretary, before becoming a model.

Her good looks and shapely figure saw her heralded as Britain's Marilyn Monroe, and it wasn't long before offers of film work came her way. Appearing as an extra in Albert Broccoli's *The Black Knight* in 1954, marked the beginning of many roles in, among others, *Forbidden Cargo*, *One Way Out*, *Out of the Clouds*, *The Green Man* and two Boulting Brothers' films, *Brothers in Law* and *Private's Progress*. Films in the Sixties include *Doctor in Distress*, *The Comedy Man* and *Promise Her Anything*. She's also made occasional appearances on television.

ADAMS, MISS
Miss Adams, whose phone number is 663 404271, is mentioned by Sidney Bliss in *Loving*. When Terence Philpot's first date with Jenny Grubb, which is arranged by Sid's company, the Wedded Bliss Agency, is a disaster, he's given Miss Adams's phone number; an extremely irate Mr Philpot soon reports back, though, that date number two was equally unsuccessful, which isn't surprising considering Miss Adams was already five months pregnant.

Able Platoon come up trumps for Sergeant Grimshaw (*Sergeant*)

CARRY ON ABROAD

Alternative titles ... *What A Package, It's All In, Swiss Hols In The Snow*

A Peter Rogers production.
Distributed through Rank Organisation.
Released as an A certificate in 1972 in colour.
Running time: 88 mins.

CAST

Sidney James .... Vic Flange
Kenneth Williams .... Stuart Farquhar
Charles Hawtrey .... Eustace Tuttle
Joan Sims .... Cora Flange
Peter Butterworth .... Pepe
Kenneth Connor .... Stanley Blunt
Hattie Jacques .... Floella
Bernard Bresslaw .... Brother Bernard
Barbara Windsor ...... Miss Sadie Tomkins
Jimmy Logan .... Bert Conway
June Whitfield .... Evelyn Blunt
Sally Geeson .... Lily
Carol Hawkins .... Marge
Gail Grainger .... Moira Plunkett
Ray Brooks .... Georgio
John Clive .... Robin Tweet
David Kernan .... Nicholas Phipps
Patsy Rowlands .... Miss Dobbs
Derek Francis .... Brother Martin
Jack Douglas .... Harry
Amelia Bayntun .... Mrs Tuttle
Alan Curtis .... Police Chief
Hugh Futcher .... Jailer

Gertan Klauber .... Postcard Seller
Brian Osborne .... Stall-Holder
Olga Lowe .... Madame Fifi

PRODUCTION TEAM

Screenplay by Talbot Rothwell
Music composed and conducted by Eric Rogers
Production Manager: Jack Swinburne
Art Director: Lionel Couch
Editor: Alfred Roome
Director of Photography: Alan Hume BSC
Camera Operator: Jimmy Devis
Continuity: Joy Mercer

Assistant Director: David Bracknell
Sound Recordists: Taffy Haines and Ken Barker
Make-up: Geoffrey Rodway
Assistant Art Director: Bill Bennison
Set Dresser: Don Picton
Hairdresser: Stella Rivers
Costume Designer: Courtenay Elliott
Dubbing Editor: Peter Best
Assistant Editor: Jack Gardner
Titles: G.S.E. Ltd
Processed by Rank Film Laboratories
Producer: Peter Rogers
Director: Gerald Thomas

Vic Flange, a pub landlord, is going on holiday; he's taking a short break to the Mediterranean resort of Elsbels without his missus, Cora, who hates flying. Not that Vic is worried because it gives him a chance to while away a few days with the flirtatious Sadie Tomkins. His plans are spoilt, though, when one of the regulars, Harry, spills the beans. Hearing that Vic's off to Elsbels, he tells Cora that Sadie is going too, which makes Vic's wife determined to overcome her aversion to flying to prevent Miss Tomkins getting her claws into her husband.

Vic, Cora and Sadie are joined by a rather disparate bunch, all taking advantage of Wundatours' £17 break in the sun, consisting of Marge and Lily, two girls looking for a holiday romance; a group of missionaries searching for the tomb of St Cecilia; Stanley Blunt and his complaining wife, Evelyn; mummy's boy Eustace Tuttle; the loud-mouthed Scot, Bert Conway and a rather gay Robin Tweet and his friend, Nicholas. In charge of the party is the inefficient courier, Stuart Farquhar, and his assistant, Moira Plunkett.

On arriving at the Elsbels Palace Hotel it looks like a holiday from hell is on the cards: it resembles a building site more than a hotel; the switchboard is soon overloaded with complaints about bottomless drawers, taps that spew out sand and backless wardrobes looking straight through into the adjoining bedroom.

Stuart Farquhar (Kenneth Williams), the world's worst courier

Under the spotlight at the Elsbels Palace Hotel

Despite the hotel only being half-built and builders causing a commotion from five in the morning, relationships blossom. While Brother Bernard, a missionary, forsakes the cloth upon taking a shine to Marge, Nicholas shakes off his camp boyfriend, Robin, to soak up the sun in the company of Lily.

When the holidaymakers head for the local village, with the exception of Evelyn Blunt who's accidentally left behind at the hotel, Mr Tuttle causes trouble in Madame Fifi's, a bawdyhouse, by asking the girls to play leapfrog; when he rushes back in brandishing a sword, others go in to help, resulting in a riot between the Brits and the police – even Brother Bernard gets involved when he spots a local bobby manhandling Marge.

As a result of the brawling, everyone spends the night in the police cells with attempts to negotiate their release with the Police Chief, who happens to be Madame Fifi's brother, falling on deaf ears – that is until Moira uses her charm – and probably her body – to persuade the chief to give them back their freedom. By the time they return to the hotel, Evelyn Blunt is a changed woman, as Stanley soon finds out. Gone is the complaining and lack of interest in sex, replaced by a woman who, after whiling away the previous evening in the arms of Georgio, is making up for all those lost years – much to Stanley's delight.

But at the evening's farewell party the mood is far from conducive to having a laugh; that is until a secret love potion, bought at the local market, is poured into the punch. Before long, the party is swinging and even Pepe, the hotel manager, and Floella, the cook, are joining in the fun, despite the ramshackle hotel collapsing around them thanks to the evening's torrential rain.

Funny Scene!

Vic and Cora Flange share their dinner table at the Elsbels Palace Hotel with Stanley and Evelyn Blunt. Sid goes to pour wine into Evelyn's glass.

EVELYN: Not for me, thank you.

VIC: No? Don't drink?

EVELYN: No, I tried it once and didn't like it.

VIC: Oh. (He gets his cigarettes out.) Have a smoke?

EVELYN: I tried it once and didn't like it.

VIC: (Turning to Cora.) Strange.

EVELYN: Not at all, my daughter is just the same.

VIC: Your only child I presume? (Laughs)

ADMIRAL
Played by Peter Butterworth

A randy old sailor in *Girls* who's been a permanent resident at Fircombe's Palace Hotel for years. He's in his element when the hotel is overrun by beauty contestants, all hoping to be crowned Miss Fircombe, many of whom become victims of his bottom-pinching tendencies.

ADMIRAL OF THE FLEET
Played by Jack Lynn

Sir John is seen dining at the French Ambassador's residence in *Emmannuelle.*

ADRIAN
Played by Julian Holloway

A highly-strung photographer who appears in *Loving.* He's in turmoil because he's looking for a big-chested lass for his next assignment and has offended his girlfriend, Gay, by suggesting she falls short of the requirements. His eyes nearly pop out of their sockets when the busty Jenny Grubb walks into the flat Gay shares with Sally Martin; he's finally found what he's been looking for and proceeds to launch Jenny's modelling career advertising body stockings.

ADVANCED CRIMINOLOGY
This book, written by A.C. Ball, is read by PC Benson in *Constable.*

ADVERTISING FILM STUDIOS, THE
Based near Long Hampton Hospital, the film studios are mentioned in *Again Doctor.* While filming a commercial there, Goldie Locks slips on an enormous packet of baby food resulting in severe bruising. She's taken to Long Hampton for examination, much to the delight of sex-mad Dr Nookey.

ADVERTISING MAN, THE
Played by Ian Wilson

Seen in the photographer's studio in *Regardless,* the pint-sized advertising man hangs around to watch Francis Courtenay model his client's beekeeping hat.

AGAIN DOCTOR, CARRY ON
See feature box on pages 26–7.

AGITATED WOMAN
Played by Hilda Fenemore

Seen in *Constable,* the agitated woman is desperate to spend a penny. When she realises she hasn't got any change for the lavatory, she stops Constable Constable in the street and borrows it off him.

AGRIPPA
Played by Francis De Wolff

This bearded sailor in *Cleo* is in charge of the ship taking Caesar to Egypt.

AJIBADI, YEMI
Role: Witch Doctor in *Up the Jungle*

Born in Otta, Nigeria, in 1929, Ajibadi worked in clerical positions before moving to Sierra Leone and working in a department store. Although originally intending to emigrate to America, he ventured to England in 1953. He studied journalism and law at evening classes but changed direction when he began acting, making his professional debut at the Lyric Theatre, Hammersmith.

He made occasional television appearances in shows such as *Armchair Theatre* and *Danger Man,* and was seen in a handful of films, including three Hammer productions, and 1966's *Naked Evil.*

Ajibadi, who returned to Nigeria in 1976 and spent four years helping establish a theatre company in Lagos, is also a playwright.

ALDERSHOT ROAD
A road mentioned in *Cabby* during the scene where Peggy and Sally are driving while held at gunpoint by crooks.

ALEXANDER, TERENCE
Role: Trevor Trelawney in *Regardless*

Despite countless film and television appearances during a long career, Terence Alexander, who was born in London in 1923, is probably best remembered for playing Jersey millionaire Charlie Hungerford in BBC's detective series, *Bergerac.*

In repertory at sixteen, he forged a career for himself, mainly on the screen; usually cast in light roles, often with upper-class tones, his early film credits include *The Woman of No Name, Death Is A Number, The Runaway Bus, Dangerous Cargo, Portrait of Alison, Danger Within* and *Breakout.* He also appeared in the Norman Wisdom comedies, *The Bulldog Breed* and *On the Beat.*

His television roles include playing Bill Dodds in 1950's *Garry Halliday,* Monty Dartie in 1960's *The Forsyte Saga,* Malcolm in 1970's *Terry and June* and Sir Greville McDonald in 1980's *The New Statesman.*

ALEXANDER, WILLIAM
Assistant Art Director on *Loving, Henry, At Your Convenience* and *Matron*

As well as his involvement with the *Carry On* films, Alexander has worked on various big and small screen productions, including the television series *Van der Valk, The Sweeney, Minder* and *Philip Marlowe – Private Eye.* Other film credits include *The Naked Runner* and *The Holcroft Covenant.*

ALF
Played by Cyril Chamberlain

For Alf, the caretaker in *Teacher,* see 'Hodgson, Alf'.

ALGERIAN GENT
Played by Derek Sydney

In *Spying,* when agents Simkins and Bind force their way into Hakim's Fun House, they end up trying to kick a door down only to find they've picked the door of the toilet, which is occupied by a rather annoyed Algerian gent.

ALICE
An unseen telephonist working at F.H. Rowse, a department store in *Constable.* A shop assistant asks Alice to put her through to management because she wants to report potential shoplifters, who turn out to be rookie cops, Benson and Gorse, working undercover.

Alf Hodgson (Cyril Chamberlain, left) kept the corridors clean at Maudlin Street (*Teacher*)

ALLBRIGHT, MR
Played by Norman Chappell

Seen in *Cabby*, Mr Allbright is a driver employed by Speedee Taxis Limited. He's also the firm's shop steward. A pedantic individual who's always consulting his union handbook to check his employer's actions are legitimate.

ALLCOCK, MR
Played by Bill Maynard

Mr Allcock, the general secretary of the union in *At Your Convenience*, is called to W. C. Boggs and Son to try and help resolve the unofficial strike. But he's a useless bureaucrat and does nothing to help the desperate Mr Boggs at a crucial time for the company's future – or that's how he would have been portrayed had he survived the final edit. (**Note: the scene was cut.**)

WHAT MIGHT HAVE BEEN

The workers at W.C. Boggs and Son are striking again and a meeting is arranged with the general secretary of the employees' union to try and resolve the dispute.

EXT. THE WORKS – DAY

The wheels are at a standstill, the chimney's dead, and there is no sign of life whatsoever.

EXT. THE WORKS YARD – DAY

A chauffeur-driven car purrs in. It comes to a stop in front of the works entrance. Vic, dressed fairly smartly and carrying papers, gets out and bows and scrapes to a large, stout, well-dressed, well-read, prosperous-looking gentleman getting out of the car. This is Mr Allcock, the general secretary of the union, who looks very sunburnt.

INT. BOGGS' OFFICE – DAY

The Board Table has been set with paper and pencils, glasses and water jug for a meeting.

Boggs, Lewis and Sid are standing waiting tensely as the door opens and Withering looks in and whispers excitedly.

WITHERING: They're here, Mr Boggs.

BOGGS: Show them in, please, Miss Withering.

(**WITHERING disappears again and LEWIS turns to BOGGS.**)

LEWIS: Now remember, Dad, be tough with them. We can't afford to lose this contract.

BOGGS: Yes, yes, I know, Lewis.

(**The door opens again and WITHERING ushers in ALLCOCK and VIC.**)

VIC: Mr Boggs – this is our union general secretary, Mr All-cock.

BOGGS: How do you do, Mr Allcock. My son Lewis and Mr Plummer, our works foreman.

ALLCOCK: Pleased to meet you, gents. And sorry if I'm a bit late, but I had another stoppage this morning.

BOGGS: I'm sorry to hear that. You want to try Epsom salts. Marvellous stuff.

(**ALLCOCK gives him a strange look.**)

ALLCOCK: Work stoppage, I mean.

BOGGS: Oh, I beg your pardon.

ALLCOCK: Yes. Well, shall we get straight down to it then?

LEWIS: Good idea. We've already lost four days' production over this.

ALLCOCK: Now, don't let's get off on the wrong foot, young feller. I've got a lot on my plate and I had to interrupt what little holiday I get to come 'ere today.

(**As they sit . . .**)

LEWIS: I'm sorry.

ALLCOCK: Not that I'm all that worried. Majorca's a bit boring after the first three weeks or so.

(**Confidentially to BOGGS.**)

ALLCOCK: I got a deal going on for some building development there, you know.

BOGGS: How nice.

ALLCOCK: Yes. Do you fancy a piece?

BOGGS: (**Shocked**) I beg your pardon?

ALLCOCK: A plot of land!

BOGGS: Oh. No, I don't think so, thank you. If we could just get down to business.

ALLCOCK: Yes, all right.

(**He takes the open file from VIC and puts it in front of him.**)

ALLCOCK: Well, I've had the basic facts from Spanner 'ere, and you know what your main trouble is, don't you?

SID: Yeah. It's the same old one about who does what job.

ALLCOCK: Ah yes, but the real *basic* trouble 'ere is – it's an *unofficial* strike.

LEWIS: What does that mean, then?

ALLCOCK: It means my 'ands are tied. I can't do a damn thing. Because it hasn't got union approval, see?

BOGGS: Well, I'm delighted to hear that, Mr Allcock.

ALLCOCK: So your first step towards getting a settlement is to make it *official*!

BOGGS: Yes, but . . . how exactly can we make it an official strike if it hasn't got union approval?

ALLCOCK: (**Chuckles indulgently.**) No, no, if you'll forgive me for saying so, Mr Boggs, you've got it arse about face.

(**BOGGS reacts coldly to this bit of crudity.**)

BOGGS: If you'd care to translate that, Mr Allcock, I don't understand these technical expressions.

ALLCOCK: What I mean is, the strike hasn't got our approval simply because it *is* unofficial.

Make it official and we'll damn soon approve it, don't you worry!

LEWIS: All right then, just tell us how we go about making it official?

ALLCOCK: Very simple. We submit all the facts of the dispute to the Union Judiciary Committee. They'll study them and pass on their recommendations to the Industrial Relations Committee. (**Pause.**) In due course of course.

LEWIS: How do you mean, in due course?

ALLCOCK: Well, the Union Judiciary Committee are over at a conference in Rio – and you know what that means, eh?

(**He chuckles dirtily, nudges old BOGGS, and makes an expressive zig-zag gesture with his hand.**)

BOGGS: Quite. Then how soon could we expect action to make it official?

ALLCOCK: Just as soon as the Industrial Relations Committee can study the recommendations and pass their findings on to the Direct Action Committee.

SID: Blimey, you seem to have more committees than the society for unmarried mothers!

ALLCOCK: Well, the Executive have got to have something to do, haven't they?

LEWIS: (**Getting angry.**) All right, then what happens after all that, Mr Allcock?

ALLCOCK: I can tell you that all right. It'll all be chucked right in my lap and I'll have to hop on another plane back from Majorca, dammit.

BOGGS: Well, pending settlement, Mr Allcock, couldn't you, as general secretary, recommend a full return to work?

ALLCOCK: *Me?* Listen, mate, if I was ever to make any clear-cut decision I'd be out on my ruddy arse!

SID: In other words, we can't win.

BOGGS: Well, there wouldn't be much point having unions if you could, would there?

(**And he laughs jovially.**)

BOGGS: This is madness, madness!

BOGGS: (**Packing up.**) You don't 'ave to worry, Mr Boggs. Let matters take the normal procedure and I can promise you a quick settlement. With the usual bit of give and take from both sides, of course.

BOGGS: Yes . . . we give and you take!

ALLCOCK: (**Getting up.**) Ha ha, that's very good, I like that. We give and you take. I'm glad you can see the funny side of all this, Mr Boggs. Well, I must be getting along now. Goodbye all, and I must say this meeting has been most useful. Most useful.

BOGGS: Goodbye, Mr Allcock.

(**As ALLCOCK and VIC go out.**)

SID: Well, all I can say is, whoever named him knew what he was doing!

CARRY ON AGAIN DOCTOR

Alternative titles . . . *Where There's A Pill There's A Way, The Bowels Are Ringing, If You Say It's Your Thermometer I'll Have To Believe You, But It's A Funny Place To Put It*

A Peter Rogers production
Distributed through Rank Organisation
Released as an A certificate in 1969 in colour
Running time: 89 mins

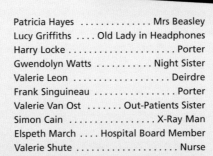

CAST

Sidney James . . . . Gladstone Screwer
Jim Dale . . . . Dr James Nookey
Kenneth Williams . . . . . Dr Frederick Carver
Charles Hawtrey . . . . . Dr Ernest Stoppidge
Joan Sims . . . . Mrs Ellen Moore
Barbara Windsor . . . . Goldie Locks
Hattie Jacques . . . . Matron
Patsy Rowlands . . . . Miss Fosdick
Peter Butterworth . . . . . . Shuffling Patient
Wilfrid Brambell . . . . Mr Pullen
Elizabeth Knight . . . . Nurse Willing
Peter Gilmore . . . . Henry
Alexandra Dane . . . . Stout Woman
Pat Coombs . . . . New Matron
William Mervyn . . . . Lord Paragon

Patricia Hayes . . . . Mrs Beasley
Lucy Griffiths . . . . Old Lady in Headphones
Harry Locke . . . . Porter
Gwendolyn Watts . . . . Night Sister
Valerie Leon . . . . Deirdre
Frank Singuineau . . . . Porter
Valerie Van Ost . . . . Out-Patients Sister
Simon Cain . . . . X-Ray Man
Elspeth March . . . . Hospital Board Member
Valerie Shute . . . . Nurse

Shakira Baksh . . . . Scrubba
Ann Lancaster . . . . Miss Armitage
Georgina Simpson . . . . . Men's Ward Nurse
Eric Rogers . . . . Bandleader
Donald Bisset . . . . Patient
Bob Todd . . . . Pump Patient
Heather Emmanuel . . . . . Plump Native Girl
Yutte Stensgaard . . . . Trolley Nurse
George Roderick . . . . Waiter
Jenny Counsell . . . . Night Nurse
Rupert Evans . . . . Stunt Orderly
Billy Cornelius . . . . Patient in Plaster
Hugh Futcher . . . . Cab Driver
Faith Kent . . Berkeley Nursing Home Matron

PRODUCTION TEAM

Screenplay by Talbot Rothwell
Music composed and conducted by Eric
     Rogers
Production Manager: Jack Swinburne
Art Director: John Blezard
Editor: Alfred Roome
Director of Photography: Ernest Steward BSC
Camera Operator: James Bawden
Assistant Editor: Jack Gardner
Continuity: Susanna Merry
Make-up: Geoffrey Rodway
Assistant Director: Ivor Powell
Sound Recordists: Bill Daniels and Ken
     Barker
Hairdresser: Stella Rivers
Costume Designer: Anna Duse
Dubbing Editor: Colin Miller
Producer: Peter Rogers
Director: Gerald Thomas

Applying the final touches to Ernest Stoppidge (Charles Hawtrey)

Down to the bare facts for
Barbara Windsor

When she asks Carver to find a replacement for the doctor's post in a medical mission she established on the far-off Beatific Islands, he thinks it's impossible to find someone daft enough to work in such an outpost, but then his mind focuses on Dr Nookey. When the young doctor, who has his drinks spiked by Dr Stoppidge, causes more mayhem at the hospital, he faces the hospital's disciplinary committee. Spotting an opportunity to fill Mrs Moore's vacancy at her mission, Dr Carver appeases the committee's concerns over Nookey by offering him a last chance to save his career. Within hours he's flying off to the Beatific Islands, tiny specks of land battered by rain and hurricanes; he soon realises his life is in the doldrums, that is until he discovers something which will make his fortune in England. Courtesy of an unsuspecting Gladstone Screwer, a serum causing drastic weight loss within days makes Nookey a millionaire when he finally returns to home shores and forms his own private clinic in partnership with none other than Ellen Moore.

At the Long Hampton Hospital, Dr Nookey seems to attract trouble, beginning with an incident in the women's washroom, which he'd mistakenly entered, frightening the highly-strung Miss Armitage out of her senses. Nookey's carefree manner isn't to everyone's liking at the hospital, with Dr Stoppidge wanting Nookey sacked for the washroom incident; there isn't any love lost between Nookey and Dr Carver either, but Carver ignores Stoppidge's request for Nookey's sacking.

Carver, meanwhile, has his sights set on his own private clinic where he can treat affluent private patients, like Ellen Moore, a lonely widow who's longing for a little romance in her life again; in Carver she sees a man who might provide that, but all he's interested in is finding a way not to her heart, but her purse; he wants her to turn his dream into reality by financing the Frederick Carver Foundation and tries to woo her, courtesy of a few chat-up lines borrowed from Dr Nookey, at the hospital's grand buffet and dance. His plans fail dismally.

Carver, meanwhile, who'd travelled to the islands to check on Dr Nookey, is lucky to escape with his life when the schooner he was travelling in, the Bella Vista, founders off the coast in a terrible storm. He faces more bad luck when he eventually returns home to find his dreams of a private clinic shattered by Nookey. Desperate to find out the constituent parts of the magic weight-losing serum, he hatches a plan to send his colleague, Dr Stoppidge, into the clinic disguised as a woman, but his scheme backfires. Dr Nookey's good luck is challenged, too, when Gladstone Screwer, realising Nookey is on to a winner exchanging the serum for 200 cigarettes, turns up for a slice of the profits.

A quick chat before the cameras roll

Funny Scene!

Dr Carver is conducting his rounds at Long Hampton Hospital when he stops at Mr Bean's bed.

```
DR CARVER:      Ah, this is the new kidney case, I
                suppose?
DR STOPPIDGE:   Oh yes, sir, Mr Bean.
DR CARVER:      Ah, kidney bean. (Laughs.). Well, Mr
                Bean, how are you? Any pain?
MR BEAN:        A bit, sir, especially when I pass
                water.
DR CARVER:      Well the best thing for you to do,
                Mr Bean, is to stop passing it.
                Every time you come to some, stop
                and turn back.
```

ALLCOCK, SARAH
Played by Joan Sims

Miss Allcock teaches PE at Maudlin Street Secondary Modern School. Seen in *Teacher*, this judo expert isn't to be messed around, as Alistair Grigg, the child psychiatrist, discovers. Before the end of term, though, she ends up falling for Grigg.

ALLEN, ANDREA
Role: Minnie in *Cowboy*

Born in Glasgow in 1946, Andrea Allen made sporadic appearances on the screen during the late 1960s and '70s, including brief roles in films such as *The Wrong Box, For Men Only, She'll Follow You Anywhere, Invasion: UFO, Vampira* and *Spanish Fly*. On television, she was seen in, among others, *Jason King*.

Allen, who's no longer in the profession, lives abroad.

ALLEN, PATRICK
Narrator on *Don't Lose Your Head, Doctor* and *Up The Khyber*

Actor Patrick Allen, born in Malawi in 1927, has one of the most recognisable voices in the business, thanks to years spent narrating films, adverts and documentaries.

After moving to Britain as a child, Allen, who's also a busy stage actor, was evacuated to Canada during World War Two, and after studying at Montreal's McGill University worked as a local radio presenter and, subsequently, appeared on television. In 1947 he returned to the UK and was cast in *The Survivors*, a series of plays for the BBC.

His first film credit, Hitchcock's *Dial M for Murder*, was the start of a busy big-screen career, which includes *The Long Haul, Dunkirk, I Was Monty's Double, Night of the Big Heat, Diamonds on Wheels, The Wild Geese, Who Dares Wins* and, more recently, *RPM*. On television he's appeared in numerous shows, including *The Return of Sherlock Holmes, Bergerac, The Protectors, The Troubleshooters* and *The Champions*, but his biggest role was playing Richard Crane in the 1960s series, *Crane*.

ALLISON, BART
Roles: Grandad in *Doctor* and Grandpa Grubb in *Loving*

Bart Allison, born in Birmingham in 1892, always wanted to act and spent his early career working in variety and the theatre. He also made occasional screen appearances from the late 1940s, with film credits including *The End of the Affair; Smashing Time; Steptoe and Son; No Sex Please, We're British* and *The Ritz*.

His television work, meanwhile, included appearances in shows such as *Dixon of Dock Green, Hadleigh, Angels* and *The Sweeney*.

He died in 1978, aged eighty-six.

AMAZON GUARDS
Played by Audrey Wilson, Vicky Smith, Jane Lumb, Marian Collins, Sally Douglas, Christine Rodgers and Maya Koumani

Clad in black cat-suits, the guards work in S.T.E.N.C.H.'s headquarters and are seen charging around in *Spying*.

AMBULANCE DRIVER
Played by Brian Osborne

The Ambulance Driver is seen in *Matron* outside the Finisham Maternity Hospital. An emergency call has been received to go and pick up Jane Darling, a film actress, who's likely to give birth any minute. A shortage of staff to hand finds Dr Prodd and Nurse Carter – who's actually Cyril Carter – roped in to help with the job.

AMBULANCE DRIVERS (1st and 2nd)
Played by Anthony Sagar and Fred Griffiths

The ambulance drivers who ferry appendicitis-stricken journalist Ted York to the Haven Hospital in *Nurse*. As it transpires, their mad dash to the hospital is motivated more by wanting to catch the horse racing than delivering a sick man.

ANAESTHETIST
Played by John Horsley

When Ted York is wheeled in on a trolley ready for his operation in *Nurse*, the anaethetist is waiting with an enormous hypodermic. (**Note: although Horsley's name appeared in the credits, the scene was cut.**)

WHAT MIGHT HAVE BEEN

When Ted York has his operation he drifts off into a dream world.

CLOSE SHOT TED

Flat on his back on moving trolley – but not quite flat out. He's still resisting the complete surrender of himself. Trolley goes in doors to:

INT. ANAESTHETIC ROOM – DAY

Ted's wheeled in beside the usual impressive equipment. He does his best to keep his eyes open. Anaesthetist is all ready. He approaches Ted.

ANAESTHETIST: (Friendly, grinning.) You look so wide awake . . .

(He injects TED, with the enormous hypo.)

ANAESTHETIST: . . . I doubt if this is going to work . . .

(TED grins back – an uncontrolled parody of a confident grin.)

TED'S EYELINE

(ANAESTHETIST blurs, spins and disappears.)

RIPPLE DISSOLVE

INT. TED'S MIND. ANAESTHESIA

Evidently Ted's a good reporter who concentrates on essentials even in his subconscious – for the f.g. of this sequence is all-important and there's no set worth speaking of, just a dark b.g. Equally evident, Ted is a regular reader of *Esquire*, for Georgie shimmies on to the screen in idealised, scant and diaphanous harem costume. Music is sinuous in accompaniment. After a self-appreciative wiggle or so on the part of Georgie, a millionaire, young, handsome and in full evening-dress, approaches her, beseechingly offering a diamond necklace, glittering in its velvet-lined case: she repulses him: sadly closing the case, he leaves. A turbaned Maharajah now approaches her, juggling with diamonds as big as potatoes: she scarcely notices the dazzlement thus created: repulses him: tearfully, he departs. A husky sunburnt prospector, magnificent in shorts and sunhat, hauls a small truck to her: it is chockful of diamonds: she hardly looks at the blinding-brilliant display, or at him: his jaw-muscles twitching in manly disappointment, he trudges off, hauling the truck behind him. Holding on to the back of the truck, like a kid scrounging a ride on a water-cart, is Ted, ludicrous in his operating-gown. He jumps off, and, apparently unaware of Georgie's presence, flexes his muscles in modest self-appreciation. Georgie clasps her hands together in delight and her expression is that of a girl who has at last Mr Right-ed herself. She strolls past him, shedding a veil. Courteously, Ted retrieves it, offers it to her. As she takes it, he kisses her hand. Chews his way, with mounting passion, up her arm. Folds her in an embrace. She's more than cooperative. Music cuts. A whip-crack O.S. Both turn. Sister's there, dressed in jodhpurs and roll-neck sweater. She cracks the whip again: Georgie, immediately re-dressed as a nurse, disentangles herself from Ted. An injections-trolley rolls towards Georgie. She grabs it and trundles it away, super-efficiently. Whip-crack. A bed rolls towards Ted. He scampers into it. Sister nods grimly, folds the whip, goes off eagle-eyed to look for more criminals.

CLOSE SHOT TED (Within dream.)

In bed, lying on his side, one eye open. Whip-crack O.S. He snaps the eye shut.

DISSOLVE

INT. WARD. NIGHT

CLOSE SHOT TED, lying on his back, eyes closed. Real background: the dream is over: he's about to emerge from the anaesthetic. His eyes flicker.

TED: (Faint) Beer . . .

(His eyes open.)

TED'S EYELINE

From his corner-bed, a night-view of the ward achieves focus after a shaky start. Six beds on the opposite side of the ward, each containing a slumbering patient. Snores are thunderous in a male ward: they can provide the background for the following.

INT. WARD. NIGHT

Ted resumed.

TED: (**Louder**) Lager. . .

(He licks his lips.)

TED: (**Normal tone**) Iced lager . . . Hey, Ethel! How about some service. . .?

(He blinks, and licks his lips again.)

TED: (**Good and loud**) How long've I gotta wait for service? I'm a good customer Ethel! Hey – (**Loudest**) – ETHEL!. . .

(Frances James, young, slim and attractive night-nurse (qualified) appears at his bedside, a firm and confident ministering angel – to begin with. He turns his head to her. Though he can now talk, he doesn't really know what he's talking about yet – or, at least, the normal defences and compromises of ordinary conversation are not in operation. His voice is strident. His ideas are uninhibited and directly expressed throughout.)

TED: 'Bout time . . . Hey – you're not Ethel . . .

FRANCES: Relax now, Mr York.

TED: (**Truculent**) Where's Ethel?

FRANCES: Fast asleep I hope – same as you should be.

TED: You know Ethel?

FRANCES: I think I know the one you mean. Barmaid at the Greyhound.

TED: That's right. Get her.

ANCIENT CARRIER
Played by Ian Wilson
Assists the Carrier in *Jack* by ferrying Midshipman Poop-Decker to his ship at Plymouth Docks.

ANCIENT GENERAL
Played by Eric Barker
Seen dining at the French Ambassador's residence in *Emmannuelle*.

ANGEL, MR (THE BOSUN)
Played by Percy Herbert
The bosun, who's been at sea fifteen years, works on the frigate Venus. He's seen in *Jack*, initially as part of the press gang scouring the streets of Plymouth for two unfortunates to join the ship's crew.

ANGELINETTA, OLGA
Hairdresser on *Teacher* and *Jack*
Olga Angelinetta, daughter of a restaurateur, was born in London in 1902. After achieving her City and Guilds in hairdressing and wig-making, she worked for leading names in the industry until being taken ill in 1943 and spending a year in hospital. Soon after recuperating, she secured a job at Pinewood Studios.

She eventually turned freelance and worked at all the top studios, including Denham and Twickenham. Her list of film credits included *The Counterfeit Plan, Make Mine Mink, One Million Years B.C., Our Mother's House* and, her final picture, *A Clockwork Orange* in 1971.

She retired in the early 1970s and died in 1995, aged ninety-three.

ANGUS
An unseen character in *Cruising*, Angus was head barman on the *Happy Wanderer* until he tied the knot and was sworn off booze. Believing a life on the ocean wave wasn't compatible with marriage, he jacked in his job. The trouble was, he was the only one capable of mixing an Aberdeen Angus, Captain Crowther's favourite tipple. Eventually, though, he passes on the details to his replacement, Sam Turner, to the relief of the captain.

ANGUS ROBERTSON & COMPANY LIMITED
The estate agent in *Cabby* who markets the yard and garages Peggy Hawkins rents for her Glamcab taxi company. The office is based at 306 Park Street.

ANTHEA
Played by Amanda Barrie
A posh-speaking Glamcab driver in *Cabby*. When Ted Watson tries infiltrating the team by posing, disastrously, as a glamour girl, she embarrasses him by asking for help out of her clothes because the staff uniforms are required for washing.

ANTONY, MARK
Played by Sid James
The courageous soldier who claims to be Julius Caesar's best friend in *Cleo*. Falls in love with Cleopatra and plots to murder Caesar but his plans are beset with unexpected difficulties.

ANTONY'S DUSKY MAIDEN
Played by Sally Douglas
A dark-haired beauty whom Mark Antony buys from a slave market in *Cleo*.

ANTROBUS, JOHN
Role: Citizen in *Constable*. Also credited for writing additional material for the screenplays of *Sergeant* and *Columbus*
Son of a sergeant-major in the army, John Antrobus was born in Woolwich Military Hospital in 1933. After leaving school he served two years in the Merchant Navy before, aged nineteen, following his father into the army. He attended Sandhurst Royal Military Academy and was progressing well until his increasing disenchantment at the thought of a military career saw him quit the Forces.

Wanting to be a writer, he was fortunate enough to meet Ray Galton and Alan Simpson, who'd established Associated London Scripts

with Spike Milligan and Eric Sykes. They agreed to read some of his work, so by day he earned his living as a waiter, supply teacher and film extra (he was in a crowd scene in *1984* and a non-speaking lab assistant in *The Man Who Never Was*), while in the evening he completed a script and sent it to the writers.

Before long he was writing with Johnny Speight and supplying material for, among others, Frankie Howerd, Arthur Haynes, Peter Sellers and Spike Milligan. He's also contributed to numerous television shows, including *That Was The Week That Was, The Army Game, Bootsie and Snudge, The Dustbinmen* and *Milligan In . . .*

Antrobus has written for all media, including the screenplays for 1959's *Idle On Parade*, starring Anthony Newley, Lionel Jeffries and William Bendix, and, a decade later, *The Bed-Sitting Room*, with Rita Tushingham and Ralph Richardson. He's also written extensively for the theatre, such as four plays for the Royal Court Theatre and the jewel in his crown, *Crete and Sergeant Pepper*.

In recent years, John has teamed up with scriptwriter Ray Galton to pen two series of *Room at the Bottom* for television and the sanatorium-based sitcom, *Get Well Soon*. They also wrote the farce, *When Did You Last See Your Trousers*, which played the Garrick Theatre for a year, and have recently written a stage version of *Steptoe and Son* which opens at the Theatre Royal, York, in the autumn of 2005.

APHRODISIA
The name of the valley beyond the mountains in Africa where the lubidubies live in *Up the Jungle*.

ARABIAN OFFICIAL
Played by Steve Plytas
Seen dining at the French Ambassador's residence in *Emmannuelle*.

ARCHIMEDES
Played by Michael Ward
Seen in *Cleo* walking the corridors of Cleopatra's abode. His official title is Chief Counsellor.

ARISTOCRATIC LADY
Played by Ambrosine Phillpotts
In *Cabby*, this snooty old girl is seen sitting in the back of a chauffeur-driven car. While waiting at a junction, Charlie Hawkins pulls up and cracks a joke, aimed at the straight-faced chauffeur, about whether he's going to a funeral, before suggesting that his passenger has got out of the box.

ARMITAGE, MISS
Played by Ann Lancaster
Appears in *Again Doctor*. Miss Armitage is a patient at the Long Hampton Hospital who's been admitted for observation. She observes more than she bargained for when Dr Nookey

CARRY ON AT YOUR CONVENIENCE

Alternative titles . . . *Down The Spout, Ladies Please Be Seated, Up The Workers, Labour Relations Are The People Who Come To See You When You're Having A Baby*

A Peter Rogers production
Distributed through Rank Organisation
Released as an A certificate in 1971 in colour
Running time: 90 mins

CAST

Sidney James . . . . Sid Plummer
Kenneth Williams . . . . W.C. Boggs
Charles Hawtrey . . . . Charles Coote
Hattie Jacques . . . . Beattie Plummer
Joan Sims . . . . Chloe Moore
Bernard Bresslaw . . . . Bernie Hulke
Kenneth Cope . . . . Vic Spanner
Jacki Piper . . . . Myrtle Plummer
Richard O'Callaghan . . . . Lewis Boggs
Patsy Rowlands . . . . . . Hortence Withering
Davy Kaye . . . . Benny
Bill Maynard . . . . Fred Moore
Renée Houston . . . . Agatha Spanner
Marianne Stone . . . . Maud
Margaret Nolan . . . . Popsy
Geoffrey Hughes . . . . Willie
Hugh Futcher . . . . Ernie

Simon Cain . . . . Barman
Amelia Bayntun . . . . Mrs Spragg
Leon Greene . . . . Chef
Harry Towb . . . . Doctor in Film
Shirley Stelfox . . . . Bunny Waitress
Peter Burton . . . . Hotel Manager
Julian Holloway . . . . Roger

Anouska Hempel . . . . New Canteen Girl
Jan Rossini . . . . Hoopla Girl
Philip Stone . . . . Mr Bulstrode

PRODUCTION TEAM

Screenplay by Talbot Rothwell
Music composed and conducted by Eric Rogers
Production Manager: Jack Swinburne
Art Director: Lionel Couch
Editor: Alfred Roome
Director of Photography: Ernest Steward BSC
Camera Operator: James Bawden
Make-up: Geoffrey Rodway
Continuity: Rita Davidson
Assistant Director: David Bracknell
Sound Recordists: Danny Daniel and Ken Barker
Hairdresser: Stella Rivers
Costume Designer: Courtenay Elliott
Set Dresser: Peter Howitt
Assistant Art Director: William Alexander
Dubbing Editor: Brian Holland
Titles: G.S.E. Ltd
Processed by Rank Film Laboratories
Toilets by Royal Doulton Sanitary Potteries
Assistant Editor: Jack Gardner
Producer: Peter Rogers
Director: Gerald Thomas

Vic Spanner (Kenneth Cope) gets an ear bashing from his mum (Renée Houston)

W.C. Boggs and Son have manufactured fine toilet ware since 1870, which is surprising considering the constant striking at the factory; Vic Spanner, the union representative, brings the workforce out at the slightest change in day-to-day procedures, such as the scrapping of drinking tea outside official breaks. When Vic broaches the subject with Lewis Boggs, the boss's son, who's still green when it comes to dealing with the union, he declines to discuss the matter, resulting in a meeting to consider yet another walk-out. No one, save Vic, is interested, though, until they're reminded that the local football team are at home that afternoon.

Meanwhile, upstairs, chief designer Charles Coote, managing director William Boggs and others watch with interest as Miss Withering, Mr Boggs's secretary, tests out a new toilet's durability. Another topic on the agenda is the making of bidets: while Lewis wants the firm to start manufacturing them to keep up with the times, his father isn't convinced.

Production at the factory grinds to a halt, though, when the latest strike takes effect. Sid Plummer returns home for the afternoon and is confronted with a pile of dirty dishes and a wife who spends all day chatting to her budgie, while Vic Spanner is berated by his loud-mouthed mother, claiming he's just like his late father; he ends up with a meagre lunch while Charles Coote, who lodges at the house, is dished up his favourite meal. Nothing seems to be going right for Vic when, en route to the football match, he spots Myrtle, the love of his life, getting into Lewis Boggs's sports car, and in a rush to follow her ends up losing his trousers.

Back at Sid Plummer's house, he discovers, to the benefit of his wallet, that the pet budgie, Joey, who hasn't tweeted a word since they bought him, has the knack of picking winners at horse racing; before placing the biggest bet of his life, Sid tests the bird on yesterday's race meetings and he comes up trumps every time. Sid soon pockets a fortune, much to his bookmaker's disgust, enabling him to help out his employer, Mr Boggs, when it's revealed the company is in financial straits, a gesture eventually repaid with the offer of a place on the

Funny Scene!

Lewis Boggs is trying to persuade his rather staid father, William, to include a bidet in their new range of products, to keep up with the times. His father isn't convinced, though.

```
WILLIAM:       I don't think that my dear grandfather
               would have approved of the name
               Boggs being associated with such an
               article.
LEWIS:         Oh, Mr Plummer, can't you persuade
               him?
SID PLUMMER:   Well quite frankly, Mr Lewis, I don't
               see the use of them; it's easy enough
               to wash your feet in the bath, innit?
LEWIS:         Bidets are not for washing your feet
               in, Mr Plummer.
SID:           What else then? Are they for dogs to
               drink out of?
LEWIS:         No. (He whispers their purpose in
               SID'S ear.)
SID:           (Smiling) Get away! Well, if it's for
               that then, you can always stand on
               your head under the shower.
```

board, which Sid is reluctant to accept because he regards himself as a shop-floor worker.

The next strike, over the fitting of a new style tap to the bidets Lewis eventually persuades his father to make, is called by Vic, but a surprise return to work the following day isn't a sign of everyone's eagerness to get back to the shop-floor, more because it's the firm's outing to Brighton. Everyone decides to enjoy the annual jolly, even Mr Boggs Senior who realises what he's been missing is a good old booze-up. A jolly time is had by all, especially Lewis Boggs, who's delighted when he eventually wins over Myrtle Plummer by producing a special marriage licence.

Back home, when Mr Coote, whose relationship with Agatha Spanner has blossomed, tells her they won't be able to marry because the strikes have brought the company to its knees, action is called for; summoning the help of other frustrated wives, Agatha and the women march to the picket line and bring the strike to an abrupt end; everything now seems rosy until Bernie Hulke tells Vic there is no loo roll in the toilet, but even the militant Vic Spanner has turned over a new leaf and dips into his own pocket to buy a new packet.

Lewis (Richard O'Callaghan) talks tough with Bernie (Bernard Bresslaw)

goes into the women's washroom by mistake and takes a shower. When he later enters her room, believing he'll find Goldie Locks in bed, it's the last straw for the eccentric Miss Armitage, who's liable to suffer the occasional fit.

ARMY OFFICER
Played by Cyril Raymond

Seen in *Regardless* struggling to squeeze by Sam Twist in the corridor of the Scotland-bound train. Twist, who's en route to the Forth Bridge in a parody of *The 39 Steps*, asks if he's got some special orders for him, annoying the officer in the process.

ARNALL, JULIA
Role: Trudy Trelawney in *Regardless*

Julia Arnall, born in Vienna, Austria, in 1931, moved to Britain in 1950 and began her career as a model before turning to acting.

During the 1950s and '60s she appeared in several films, including *Simon and Laura, House of Secrets, The Quiller Memorandum* and, most notably, *Lost*. However, when her Rank contract was terminated in 1957, her screen appearances became infrequent.

Her television credits include *Sword of Freedom, International Detective, Ghost Squad, The Saint* and *The Troubleshooters*.

ARTHUR
Played by Derek Francis

Arthur works as a security guard in the lobby of Finisham Maternity Hospital in *Matron*. A miserable-looking guy whose demeanour is remarked upon by Sid Carter, who's pretending to be an expectant father in an attempt to find out where the contraceptive pills are kept. He comments he'll christen his baby 'Happy' after him.

ASKWITH, ROBIN
Role: Larry in *Girls*

Born in Southport, Lancashire, in 1950, Robin Askwith was educated at Merchant Taylors' School, Rickmansworth. Unable to take up a place at Bristol University, where he intended reading English and drama, he happened upon a career in acting, beginning with a margarine commercial, followed by, in 1968, the part of Keating in Lindsay Anderson's film, *If*.

He's made over thirty films but is arguably best remembered for playing the lead in the *Confessions* sex comedies of the 1970s. Other film credits include *Scramble; Hide and Seek; Bless This House; Stand Up, Virgin Soldiers; Brittania Hospital*, again with Lindsay Anderson, and, in 2000, *The Asylum*. His television work over the years has seen him appear in, among others, *The Borderers, Boon, Sunburn* and *Doctors*.

In 1977 he formed The Comedy Company and toured the world with various shows. Today, he lives on the island of Gozo.

ASSISTANT MANAGER
Played by Robin Ray

The assistant manager of F.H. Rowse, a department store in *Constable*, isn't informed by his manager of PC Benson and PC Gorse's undercover work attempting to catch shoplifters in the store, which explains the confusion that ensues when they become suspects themselves.

AT YOUR CONVENIENCE, CARRY ON
See feature box on pages 30–31.

ATKINS, JOHN
Played by Paul Cole

In *Teacher*, Atkins is a leading culprit among the kids who set out to cause havoc when a school inspector and child psychiatrist visit Maudlin Street Secondary Modern School.

ATS GIRL
Played by Barbara Rosenblat

Based at the experimental 1313 anti-aircraft battery in *England*, she's one of the shirkers who suffers a severe shock to the system when the tough-speaking Captain Melly is put in charge of the unit.

ATTRACTIVE NURSE
Played by Shane Cordell

One of the nurses employed at Haven Hospital in *Nurse*.

AU PAIR GIRL
Played by Zena Clifton

When the pregnant film star, Jane Darling, is rushed off in the back of an ambulance, Mr Darling can't wait to wave his wife goodbye so he can return to the house and get his hands all over his au pair. Appears in *Matron*.

AUBREY, DIANE
Role: Honoria in *Constable*

Diane Aubrey, born in Nottingham in 1939, joined LAMDA straight from school. By the time she graduated she'd already made her acting debut, appearing in a 1957 episode of the series *The Vise* and the film *Grip of the Strangler*, a year later.

Although she worked in rep, most of her career was spent on the screen. As well as appearing in series like *Moonstrike* and *Dixon of Dock Green*, she played Sally Clarkson in *Z Cars* for several months during 1962, and Sandra in the 1963 series, *Taxi!*, with Sid James. On the big screen, her credits include *Village of the Damned; Watch it, Sailor!; Petticoat Pirates; The Wild Affair* and her last film, *The Engagement* in 1970.

She retired from acting at the age of twenty-nine after her children were born. Now based in London, she's been teaching the Alexander Technique for twenty-four years.

AUNTIE
Played by Lucy Griffiths

Named as Aunt Acid in the *Regardless* script, she's standing alongside Montgomery Infield-Hopping in the bachelor exhibit at the Ideal House Exhibition. She looks disapprovingly when Delia comes flying through the wall of the exhibit next-door, much to the delight of the raffish customer.

AVERY AVENUE

The road where Bide-a-Wee Rest Home stands in *Screaming!*

AXWELL, NURSE GEORGIE
Played by Susan Stephen

Georgie Axwell works on the ward at Haven Hospital in *Nurse*.

AZURE BAY

A region in the Beatific Islands where the Moore Medical Mission – which is nothing more than a decrepit wooden hut – stands. The bay is visited by Dr Carver and Dr Nookey in *Again Doctor*.

B

BABS
Played by Barbara Windsor
Seen in *Camping*, Babs (real name Barbara) is one of the nubile young ladies from Chayste Place, a finishing school, camping at the Paradise Camp Site. Out to enjoy herself, the mischievous Babs flirts with Sid Boggle, much to his girlfriend's chagrin, while under canvas, before heading off on the back of a lorry with other partygoers at an all-nite rave in the adjoining field. (**Note: in an early draft of the script, a character called Rosemary was due to lose her bikini top.**)

BADEN-SEMPER, NINA
Role: Girl Nosha in *Up the Jungle*
Born in the West Indies in 1945, Nina Baden-Semper first appeared on screen in the 1960s but is best known for playing Barbie Reynolds in five series of the controversial sitcom, *Love Thy Neighbour*, during the 1970s.

Other small screen credits include *Rainbow City, Counterstrike, Callan, George and Mildred* and *Children's Ward*. She appeared most recently in the revival of *Crossroads*. Her occasional film credits include *Kongi's Harvest, The Love Ban* and 1999's *Rage*.

BAGLEY, LADY EVELYN
Played by Joan Sims
Seen in *Up the Jungle* on the expedition into the jungles of Africa. Soon after her baby boy, Cecil, was born, her husband whisked her off to the African jungle for a belated honeymoon. Tragedy struck when her hubby took their son for an early morning stroll along the banks of the Limpopo River and neither were seen again. When her husband's fob watch was later discovered inside a crocodile's stomach, and her son's nappy abandoned on the riverbank, she feared the worst. Now she has returned to try and find the nappy pin, just something she can cling on to as a memory of her little boy.

When she unexpectedly meets Cecil, the Jungle Boy, and finds he has a big, silver safety pin holding his loincloth together, she suddenly realises her little baby – now a very big baby – is still alive. She's desperate to find her son

and is finally reunited by the time Lady Bagley and the other members of the party, who manage to escape the grip of the Lubidubies, a female tribe in the jungle, head home; by then, she also comes face-to-face with her long-lost husband, who's been given the title of King Tonka by the Lubidubies, and she returns to England with him in tow, too.

BAGLEY, WALTER
Played by Charles Hawtrey
It was thought that Walter Bagley, alias King Tonka in *Up the Jungle*, had been eaten by a crocodile in the African jungle. Whilst honeymooning with his wife, Evelyn, and their little baby boy, Cecil, he decided to take his son for an early morning stroll through the jungle. Nothing was seen of him, or the little boy, again; when his watch was later found inside a dead crocodile's stomach, it was assumed he'd been eaten alive.

Lady Bagley, therefore, is shocked when she's reunited with her husband, who hadn't been gobbled up at all; he's been living the life of Riley with the Lubidubies, a tribe of females, who appointed him King Tonka with the sole duty of mating with as many girls as possible. All those years ago, his watch was eaten by a warrior from the Nosha tribe, who was then eaten by a crocodile. The Noshas had captured Walter and his life was in peril until rescued by the Lubidubies.

When Lady Bagley returns home she takes Walter with her, whom the Lubidubies lose interest in once his wife appears on the scene.

BAGPIPE SOLDIER
Played by Simon Cain
A soldier of the 3rd Foot and Mouth in *Up The Khyber*.

BAGSHAW, CAPTAIN
Played by Peter Gilmore
One of Lady Jane Ponsonby's many suitors in *Follow That Camel*, Bagshaw tries his utmost to see another, Bertram West, written off by accusing him of cheating at cricket. When West is banned from ever stepping foot inside

the Ponsonbys' mansion again, Humphrey Bagshaw's conscience gets the better of him: realising he's acted despicably, he tries committing suicide.

BAILEY, ANTHONY
Role: Rider in *Dick*
Londoner Anthony Bailey was born in 1933 and trained at the City Literary Institute. Primarily a stage actor, he appeared on the screen from time to time. On television, he had a running part as Roddy Barrows in *Crossroads* and was also seen in, among others, *Arthur of the Britons, Barlow at Large, The New Avengers, The Professionals, Grange Hill* and *The Bill*. His film credits included *The Main Chance, Thunderball, The Deadly Bees* and *Hussy*.

Most recently, he was appearing at the National Theatre in London. He died in 2004, aged seventy-one.

BAILEY, JAMES
Played by Kenneth Williams
In *Sergeant*, James Bailey is a member of Sergeant Grimshaw's Able Platoon. An educated snob, he ruffles Grimshaw's feathers from day one with his supercilious manner. Eventually, though, he blends with the rest of the platoon and is instrumental in persuading them to give their utmost to become champion platoon. A graduate, his abilities are put to good use when he moves to the Education Corps after basic training.

BAIRD, ANTHONY
Role: Guard in *Spying*
Born in London in 1920, Anthony Baird has appeared in over a dozen films, including *Passport to Treason, Operation Conspiracy, Echo of Diana, The Ipcress File, Cheetah* and *Braxton*, but his most notable appearance was in Ealing's 1945 compendium, *Dead of Night*.

His television credits range from *The Count of Monte Cristo* and *The Avengers* to *Strangers* and a running role, as Mr Pearson, in *Crossroads*.

BAKER PLATOON
Sergeant Mathews' platoon at Heathercrest National Service Depot in *Sergeant*.

BAKSH, SHAKIRA

Role: Scrubba in *Again Doctor*

Crowned Miss Guyana in 1967, Shakira Baksh came third in that year's Miss World contest.

Born in 1947, she worked as a librarian and fashion model in Guyana before coming to England for the Miss World contest. She continued modelling and made a handful of screen appearances during the 1970s, including a couple of episodes of *UFO*. She was also seen in the films *Son of Dracula* and *The Man Who Would Be King*, with Michael Caine, whom she had married in 1973. Caine had first noticed Baksh in a Maxwell House coffee advert.

BALD-HEADED DOWAGER

Played by Joan Ingram

Seen at Sir Rodney Ffing's charity ball in *Don't Lose Your Head*, the bald-headed Dowager's wig is accidentally blown off her head.

BALFOUR, MICHAEL

Role: Matt in *Constable*

From *Genevieve* and *Man From Tangier* in the 1950s to *Batman* and *The Holcroft Covenant* in the 1980s, character actor Michael Balfour was regularly in demand.

Born in Kent in 1918, he appeared in films from the late 1940s, including an uncredited role in the 1948 picture, *Sleeping Car to Trieste*. Other notable credits included *Venetian Bird*, *Johnny On the Run* and *The Sea Shall Not Have Them*. On the small screen, he was seen in, among others, *Hancock's Half Hour*, *Dixon of Dock Green*, *Man from Interpol* and *Department S*.

Away from the screen, he created his own clown character and toured Europe with Gerry Cottle's Circus. He was also an accomplished sculptor and painter, opening a gallery in Spain.

He died in 1997, aged seventy-nine.

BALL, NURSE SUSAN

Played by Barbara Windsor

Employed at the Finisham Maternity Hospital in *Matron*, the even-tempered Nurse Ball shares her room – number sixteen at the nurses' home – with Nurse Carter, aka Cyril Carter. She realises he's a fella when he falls over steps and reveals his unmistakable underwear. Upon discovering the motives behind Cyril's disguise, she agrees to keep mum and ends up falling in love with her roommate.

BALL, VINCENT

Roles: Jenkins in Cruising and Ship's Officer in *Follow That Camel*

Vincent Ball, who was born in Wee Waa, New South Wales, Australia, in 1923, left school at fourteen and worked as a messenger boy until, aged eighteen, he joined the Australian Air Force. He trained in Canada and the Bahamas before completing his tour of operations in England and Scotland.

Ball returned to Australia in 1945 and decided upon a career in acting. To reach England, he secured a job on a Swedish cargo ship and spent seven months cleaning the decks en route to the UK.

He'd previously written to film studios enquiring about work and was lucky enough, upon reaching England, to complete underwater swimming scenes for non-swimmer Donald Houston in the 1949 film, *The Blue Lagoon*. After his first taste of the film industry, he trained at RADA between 1949-51 and moved into repertory theatre, beginning at Leatherhead.

His film career started in the late 1940s and encompassed a host of pictures, including *The Interrupted Journey*, *Dangerous Voyage*, *The Black Rider* and *Where Eagles Dare*. More recently he's been seen in, among others, *The Man Who Sued God* and *The Cherry Orchard*. On television, his credits include *International Detective*, *Man in a Suitcase*, *Shannon's Mob*, *The Outsiders*, *Mission Impossible* and running roles in *A Country Practice* and *Crossroads*.

Ball's recent work has mainly been in Australian television and films, which is where he's lived since 1973.

BALLET MONTPARNASSE, THE

Roles: The Dancing Girls in *Cowboy*

The ballet company was occupied in light entertainment, appearing on numerous Variety bills in the 1950s and '60s for Moss Empires, Stoll Theatres and other venues around the British Isles.

BALLS BOOK OF ENGLISH LAW

The book Bettina consults in *Henry* to check whether her marriage to King Henry VIII, a service he conducted himself, is legal; as he climbs into her bed he tries convincing her it's all above board but she later learns the truth, and it's just as well she resisted his advances because she's later whisked off across the channel by Francis, the King of France, to become the country's Queen.

BALSWORTH YOUTH HOSTEL

The youth hostel where the girls from Chayste Place stay en route to the Paradise Camp Site in Devon. The building is seen in *Camping*.

BANDLEADER

Played by Eric Rogers

Appears on stage in *Again Doctor* at the Long Hampton Hospital's grand buffet and dance. He's the bandleader of Alec and the Officers. (**Note: this is the Eric Rogers who composed and conducted the music for so many of the** ***Carry On*** **films.**)

BAND OF THE COLDSTREAM GUARDS

Played the music for *Sergeant*.

BANGOR, MISS

Played by Angela Grant

A brunette in the Miss Fircombe beauty contest who's seen in *Girls*.

BANGS THAT MADE HISTORY

A book two schoolgirls borrow from the library at Maudlin Street Secondary Modern School in *Teacher*. They wait until Mr Adams, the science teacher, is on duty before requesting the title because they want him to believe they're constructing a bomb – all part of the master plan to stop the acting head from leaving at the end of term.

BANK MANAGER

Played by Michael Nightingale

The bank manager in Stodge City is seen in *Cowboy* exasperated when the Rumpo Kid shoots yet another of his bank clerks. He explains they've been dropping like flies since the Kid arrived in town.

BANKS, EVELYN

Played by Patsy Rowlands

Sir Bernard Cutting's trustworthy secretary in *Matron*.

BANKS, PETER

Role: Gunner Thomas in *England*

Born in St Thomas, Canada, in 1943, Peter Banks studied political science at university in Ottawa, where his interest in acting escalated. His father, who worked for the Canadian government, was posted to the UK so when Banks graduated, he followed his parents in 1967, initially earning a living at a West End casino.

After a year's training at a studio theatre in Brighton, he began working in children's theatre before joining Darlington Rep. He'd gained significant stage experience by the time he made his screen debut, on television, in *The Private Thoughts of Julius Caesar*. Other small-screen credits include *The Famous Five*, *Oppenheimer* and *Seven Wonders of the Industrial World*. His film credits include *Death Wish 3*, *Highlander*, *Going Home* and *Method*.

BARKER, ERIC

Roles: Captain Potts in *Sergeant*, Inspector Mills in *Constable*, The Chief in *Spying* and Ancient General in *Emmannuelle*. Also *Cruising* was based on an idea of Barker's

Eric Barker, who made his name on radio's *Merry-Go-Round* during the Second World War, a programme in which he adopted the catchphrase, 'Steady, Barker!', was born in Thornton Heath, Surrey, in 1912.

He became one of radio's favourite stars but also found time to clock up numerous screen credits, including *Brothers in Law* (for which he won a British Film Academy Award for the most promising newcomer), *Happy Is The Bride*, *Bachelor of Hearts* and *Left, Right and Centre*.

'What's this wiggly thing?' asks Cleopatra (Amanda Barrie) (*Cleo*)

His working life began at his father's whole-sale paper business before he started writing short stories for magazines of the 1920s and '30s; he also wrote plays and novels. In 1931 he joined the Birmingham Repertory Company and, two years on, began a long association with the Windmill Theatre, subsequently becoming the venue's leading comedian. Also in this year, he made his radio debut in *First Time Here*.

During the Second World War he served in the Royal Navy after which he returned to radio to star in some of the great series between 1945-49. Although he made brief appearances on television, it was radio, film and stage work that occupied most of his career.

He died in 1990, aged seventy-eight.

BARKER, KEN

Sound Recordist on *Cowboy*, *Screaming!*, *Don't Lose Your Head*, *Follow That Camel*, *Doctor*, *Up The Khyber*, *Camping*, *Again Doctor*, *Up the Jungle*, *Loving*, *Henry*, *At Your Convenience*, *Matron*, *Abroad*, *Girls*, *Dick*, *Behind* and *That's Carry On*

During a busy career, the late Ken Barker worked on over fifty films. A sound recordist from the 1960s, his credits included *The Long Duel*, *Countess Dracula*, *Twins of Evil*, *Kidnapped*, *Doomwatch*, *Educating Rita*, *Trail of the Pink Panther* and four Bond movies: *Live and Let Die*, *The Man With the Golden Gun*, *For Your Eyes Only*

and *Octopussy*. His television work included the sci-fi series *UFO* and *Born to Run*.

BARMAN
Played by Bill Pertwee

Works at the cocktail bar in the Parkway Hotel and is on duty when Bertie Muffet arrives to meet Esme Crowfoot in *Loving*. A case of mis-taken identity sees Muffet walk out with Sally Martin, a model, who's supposed to be waiting for a photographer.

BARMAN
Played by Simon Cain

Works at the Brighton hotel frequented by the staff of William Boggs and Son, a toilet ware manufacturer, whilst on their annual jolly. He's seen in *At Your Convenience*.

BARMAN
Played by Kenneth Waller

Works behind the bar at the Riverside Caravan Site's clubhouse during the cabaret evening in *Behind*.

BARNES, DAPHNE
Played by Joan Sims

Linda Upmore's interfering mother is seen in *Behind*, making a nuisance of herself while ac-companying her daughter and son-in-law on a caravan holiday to the Riverside Caravan Site. It's hardly surprising she hasn't seen her

husband, Henry, for ten years, given her manner and constant complaining. She ran a pub until her hubby sold it, and claims she did all the work while he lazed around. She receives a big shock when she bumps into her former spouse at the caravan site, where he works as an odd-job man. Before the holiday is over, they've reignited the flame and plan on giving their marriage another try.

BARNES, HENRY
Played by Peter Butterworth

In *Behind*, Henry Barnes works as an odd-job man for Major Leep at the Riverside Caravan Site. Although he's paid peanuts, he boasts around twenty grand in his bank account thanks to a win on the pools. He hasn't seen his wife, Daphne, for ten years, ever since selling the pub they used to run, a decision which didn't go down too well with his missus, who always claimed Henry was a lazy individual. He can't believe his eyes when he bumps into his ex-wife at the caravan site, and before long they're reliv-ing old times and planning a future together.

BARRIE, AMANDA
Roles: Anthea in *Cabby* and Cleopatra in *Cleo*

Born in Ashton-under-Lyne, Lancashire, in 1939, Amanda Barrie started dancing and singing in her grandfather's theatre in Ashton at the age of three. A trained dancer, Barrie was only thirteen when she became a chorus girl in London, debuting in *Babes in the Wood*, and in 1956 became a regular at London's Winston's Club.

She broke into the film world playing small parts in, among others, 1959's *Operation Bullshine*, *A Pair of Briefs* a year later and 1963's *Doctor in Distress* before the first of two *Carry On* appearances.

She's probably best known, however, for her television work. As well as appearances in shows such as *The Seven Faces of Jim*, *Danger Man*, *Are You Being Served?*, *L for Lester* and, in recent years, *Doctors* and *Hell's Kitchen*, she'll always be remembered for playing Alma in *Coronation Street* and Bev in *Bad Girls*.

BARRON, MR
Played by Charles Hawtrey

Seen in *Doctor*, Mr Barron spends much of his time asleep on Fosdick Ward. When his wife, Mildred, told him she was expecting, he went into deep shock and was admitted to Borough County Hospital suffering a phantom pregnancy. Deciding to play along with his nonsense, Dr Tinkle sends him to pre-natal classes, which he finds humiliating, but by the end of his spell in hospital his wife gives birth and he becomes the proud father of a little boy.

BARRON, MRS
Played by Gwendolyn Watts

Mildred Barron is the pregnant wife of Mr Barron. When she told her husband they were expecting, he went into shock and was admitted to Borough County Hospital suffering a phantom pregnancy. Seen in *Doctor* visiting her hubby.

BARRY, HILDA
Role: Grandma Grubb in *Loving*

Born in California in 1896, Hilda Barry spent her early career in the theatre before becoming a regular face on the screen from the mid-1950s.

On television she made several appearances in *Dixon of Dock Green* as well as *The Flying Doctor*, *The Prisoner*, *Special Branch*, *Quatermass* and, latterly, *Angels*. Her film credits included *The Drayton Case*, *John of the Fair*, *Never Back Losers*, *Poor Cow*, *On the Buses*, *Steptoe and Son Ride Again* and her last picture, *The Confessional*.

She died in 1977, aged eighty.

BARRY, MR & MRS
Unseen characters in *Constable*, the Barries live at 35 Nathaniel Road. While they're away visiting their first grandchild in Canada, their neighbour, Miss Horton, reports an intruder entering their property, but it's a false alarm because it's only their daughter, Sally, returning early from a trip to Cornwall.

BARRY, SALLY
Played by Shirley Eaton

Befriended by PC Potter in *Constable*, Sally is an attractive blonde whom Potter encounters while investigating a possible break-in at 35 Nathaniel Road. Upset, Sally had been visiting her fiancé's family in Cornwall when she rowed with her beloved Eric.

BARTLETT, RICHARD
Role: Gunner Drury in *England*

Richard Bartlett, who's semi-retired from the industry, spent many years performing on stage, while appearing sporadically on television and in films during the 1970s.

On the small screen he was seen in *Robin's Nest* and *Minder*, as well as playing Nigel in 1977's *Follow Me* and General Vishishmou in *The Tomorrow People*. Other film credits

include *Loving Feeling* and *The Pink Panther Strikes Again*.

BASIC JAPANESE
The book, written by R. Morrison, is read by Francis Courtenay during an idle moment in *Regardless*.

BATT, BERT
Assistant Director on *Teacher* and *Matron*

Born in Islington, London, in 1930, Bert Batt entered the film industry straight from elementary school. Taking the advice of his father, he wrote to Gainsborough Studios, two miles down the road from where he lived, and within weeks was hired as a gofer, earning twenty-five shillings a week.

In 1946 he became a third assistant but his career was interrupted two years later by National Service. Back in civvies in 1950, he joined Pinewood Studios and completed ten years' service under contract before going freelance. His long career has encompassed over seventy films, including *True As A Turtle*, *Rockets Galore!*, *Make Mine Mink*, *Zulu*, *The Dirty Dozen*, *The Spiral Staircase*, *The Man Who Would Be King*, *The Sea Wolves* and, in 1998, *Les Misérables*.

Batt has also worked in television, including the 1990 *Jeeves and Wooster* comedy series.

BATTLEAXE
Played by Judith Furse

Seen in *Cabby*, this aggressive woman – who's a widow – is picked up by Charlie Hawkins in his taxi. As Charlie piles her suitcases into the car, it looks like she's taking everything but the kitchen sink.

BAWDEN, JAMES
Camera Operator on *Doctor*, *Up The Khyber*, *Camping*, *Again Doctor*, *Up the Jungle*, *Loving*, *At Your Convenience* and *Matron*

James Bawden, who was born in the Scottish town of Motherwell in 1920, began working as a camera operator in the early 1950s on films such as *The Long Memory*, *Desperate Moment* and *The Million Pound Note*.

Apart from a period working on the popular cult television series *The Avengers*, he's worked primarily in films with other credits including *The Square Peg*, *Doctor in Love*, *Crooks Anonymous*, *Quest for Love*, *The Eagle Has Landed*, *The Wild Geese* and, in 1982, *Witness for the Prosecution*.

BAXTER, JOE
Played by Ian Lavender

Goes on holiday to the Riverside Caravan Site with his wife, Norma, and her huge pet dog, Ollie, which is the bane of his life. Seen in *Behind*.

BAXTER, NORMA
Played by Adrienne Posta

With her frizzy blonde hairdo, Norma is the wife of Joe Baxter. Seen in *Behind* holidaying at

'First and foremost for me was Peter Rogers and Gerry Thomas, two of the nicest men you could wish to meet. The shooting was tough, a rigid budget and a six-week shoot with no overtime. It was non-stop but a continual laugh and some of the days were hysterical.

'The cast were great. Kenneth Williams never stopped talking, much of it deliciously outrageous. One day, on *Matron*, he slipped off a rostrum and fell to the floor. Gladys Goldsmith, the continuity girl, sat puce at her typewriter as he regaled her, loudly as ever, with the pain he was suffering from his sexual organs that had found contact with the rostrum on his descent and what the consequences might be. It was utter rubbish, of course.

'There were so many funny moments that they all blur into each other and it's difficult after all these years to remember them. One other I recall was on *Teacher*. Ken Connor had to walk down a corridor, enter the science class, take the stopper off a large glass jar, sniff it and make a face. It was a tracking shot with a low camera, awkward for the camera operator, Alan Hume. We put a stink bomb in the jar and on the first take Alan was shaking so much with anticipatory laughter in his hunched position that he fell off the dolly. I think all of us who saw that can still see Ken's face as he sniffed the jar.

'I worked on so many films that unless you keep a list, which I never did, some of them get forgotten, but the one thing you don't forget is having worked on the *Carry On*s with the crazy cast.'

BERT BATT

the Riverside Caravan Site with her spouse and their huge pet dog, Ollie, who seems more important to her than Joe.

BAYNTUN, AMELIA
Roles: Mrs Fussey in *Camping*, Corset Lady in *Loving*, Mrs Spragg in *At Your Convenience*, Mrs Jenkins in *Matron* and Mrs Tuttle in *Abroad*
A busy stage actress, Amelia Bayntun, born in 1919, also occasionally appeared on the screen. On television, her credits included *Dixon of Dock Green*, *Adamant Lives!*, *On the Buses* and her biggest role, two series as Ada Bissel in Thames Television's *Dear Mother . . . Love Albert*.
She died in 1988, aged sixty-eight.

BBC NEWSCASTER
Played by Tim Brinton
During *Emmannuelle* he's seen on the box reporting on the numerous affairs of Emmannuelle, the French Ambassador's sex-mad wife.

BEACH PHOTOGRAPHER
Played by Alec Bregonzi
On Brighton Pier in *At Your Convenience*, the Beach Photographer is earning a living taking photos of happy tourists. (**Note: the scene was cut.**)

EXT. PHOTOGRAPHIC BOOTH. DAY

It has several of those stands with cut-outs to put the face through. Start with a C.S. of Vic, with his eye to a small camera, Myrtle standing bored beside him.

VIC: Hold it!

(And now we see his shot. The stand has a garish painting of a Caveman and a

Cavewoman, the latter with large bare breasts. Bernie has his face above the Cavewoman and Popsy has hers above the Caveman.)

VIC: (OVER.) Lovely!

(A click. Bernie and Popsy come out from behind the cut-out, giggling. Bernie points over.)

BERNIE: Here, get a load of them.

(They look that way. This time the painting is of a man and woman in profile, holding hands with their face-slots placed close together. The woman has ridiculously large pert breasts sticking straight out and straining her bikini top. She also has a very pert bottom in a pair of tight red shorts. The man is ridiculously skinny and dressed in a bright blue striped blazer with a pair of shorts down to his knees. A man and a woman have their faces through the holes, and are smiling at the photographer.)

PHOTOGRAPHER: Thank you.

(The man and the woman come out from behind the screens and the joke is that they are dressed like and have exactly the same figures as the cartoon painting. Bernie, Vic and Popsy roar with laughter and even Myrtle has to smile.)

BEALE, JACK
The script for *Nurse* was based on an idea supplied by Jack Beale and Patrick Cargill, stemming from their stage play, *Ring for Catty*.

BEAMISH, LEONARD
Played by Ian Curry
Mr Beamish phones Togetherness Marriage Agency in *Regardless*. He wants a wife in time for a tea party he's giving his aunt in two weeks so asks the agency for help. But a mix-up finds Delia King arriving at his doorstep, believing she's been hired to do some housekeeping.

BEAN, MICHAEL
Played by Charles Hawtrey
The French and music teacher at Maudlin Street Secondary Modern School, Mr Bean is seen in *Teacher*. His other duties include organising and conducting the school orchestra, as well as writing the mournful tunes heard at the school's annual play.

BEAN, MR
Played by Donald Bisset
A patient at the Long Hampton Hospital, Mr Bean, who's hospitalised with a kidney stone, is seen in *Again Doctor*, talking to Dr Carver about his condition.

BEAR CREEK
When Big Heap announces inside Rumpo's Place that there has been a gold strike at Bear Creek, the hostelry clears within seconds, which is just what the Indian wanted because he aims to pinch some liquor without being shot. It's not long, though, before the would-be gold diggers realise there isn't such a place as Bear Creek and head back to the bar. The fictitious place is mentioned in *Cowboy*.

BEAR PASS
The pass is mentioned in *Cowboy* and is situated near Stodge City and Sam Houston's ranch.

BEARDED MAN IN AUDIENCE
Played by Ron Tarr
Seen in *Girls* this uncredited character is spotted laughing uncontrollably while watching the beauty contest fiasco.

BEASLEY, MRS
Played by Patricia Hayes
In *Again Doctor* this chatty, loud-speaking woman sees Dr Nookey in the outpatients department about constant ringing in her ears. Mrs Beasley, who's a hypochondriac, is a regular at the hospital.

BEATIFIC ISLANDS
Sounds like a tropical paradise but far from it, as Dr Nookey and Dr Carver find out in *Again Doctor*. These far-flung islands are battered by hurricanes for three months of the year and drenched by rain for the remaining nine. Locals call their islands, 'All rain and wind'. The rich widow, Ellen Moore, established a medical mission there in memory of her husband, who was cared for by the islanders.

BEAUMONT, SUSAN
Role: Frances James in *Nurse*
Born in London in 1936, Susan Beaumont, daughter of musical comedy actress Roma Beaumont and theatre producer Alfred Black, enrolled at RADA but left after just one term. She soon found employment in pantomime before going on to dance in a Norman Wisdom show at the London Palladium and in a *Limelight* show on television.

Upon being offered a Rank contract, aged nineteen, she became a leading lady in the 1950s, appearing in a clutch of films, such as *Man of the Moment, Simon and Laura, Jumping for Joy, On the Run, No Safety Ahead, Innocent Sinners* and *The Man Who Liked Funerals*.

BECK, JAMES
Role: Mr Roxby in *Loving* (Note: the scene was cut.)
Born in Islington, London, in 1929, James Beck – who'll forever be remembered for playing the spiv, Private Walker, in *Dad's Army* – graduated from art school and worked as a commercial artist until being called up for National Service.

Upon leaving military life, he pursued a career in the theatre, beginning as a student actor on one pound a week with a small repertory company in Ramsgate. Stints at various reps followed before he moved to London to further his career.

Soon he was appearing on stage and screen, with television credits including *Fabian of the Yard, Coronation Street, Romany Jones* (playing the lead role), *Z Cars, The Troubleshooters, Counterstrike, Beggar My Neighbour, The Motorway Men, Here's Harry* and *Taxi*.

He died in 1973, aged forty-four.

'BED OF THE CENTURY'
In *Regardless*, Sam Twist demonstrates the 'Bed of the Century' at the Ideal House Exhibition. Unfortunately it has a few teething problems and Twist gets into a right mess.

BED OF NAILS NATIVE
Played by Hugh Futcher
Seen in Algiers during *Spying*, he chides Simkins for treading on his bed of nails.

BEDSOP, JAMES
Played by Charles Hawtrey
A private enquiry agent hired in *Loving* by Sophie Bliss to keep an eye on Sidney, whom she suspects of having affairs with many of the female clients registered with the Wedded Bliss Agency.

Mr Bedsop begins his surveillance in the cocktail bar of the Parkway Hotel where Sophie believes Sidney is planning to meet Esme Crowfoot; he's hardly subtle in his methods of work, though, making it blatantly obvious later that he's following Sidney up the road.

He eventually finds himself under arrest: after donning an artificial beard as disguise, he follows Bliss into a public lavatory and begins acting suspiciously by getting down on his hands and knees and peeping under the cubicle doors. Chased out by the attendant, he tells a waiting policeman that he's looking for a man, which doesn't go down too well with the bobby.

BEEVERS, DIANA
Role: Penny Lee in *Teacher*
Born in London in 1944, Diana Beevers joined the Corona Academy at the age of eleven and was soon appearing in the BBC children's television serial, *The Thompson Family*, as Susan Thompson, in the late 1950s. She enjoyed other screen work while at the Academy, lastly in *Venture*, an Associated Rediffusion production.

Upon leaving the Corona at fifteen she went straight into *The Visit* in the West End; in addition to furthering her acting career, she began studying for O and A-levels and finally, in the 1980s, earning a degree with the Open University.

During the 1960s and '70s, Beevers appeared in a handful of television and film productions, including *Public Eye, Within These Walls* and *Rumpole of the Bailey*. She also had a running part in the '60s series, *Compact*, playing Michelle Donnelly. On the big screen, she was seen as a WRNS officer in 1968's *Submarine X-1* and Disney's *Escape to the Dark*.

Her last theatre appearance was in the Noël Coward trilogy, *Tonight at Eight*, in 1971, after which she left the profession to raise her daughter, thereafter only making the occasional television appearance. She returned in the 1980s and directed in various London fringe theatres.

In recent years she ran her own mail order company, selling classical CDs, but has since closed the business and returned to directing professional, amateur and youth theatre groups on the Isle of Wight, where she now resides.

BEHIND, CARRY ON
See feature box on pages 40-41.

BELCHER, BROTHER
Played by Peter Butterworth
Seen in *Up The Khyber*, Brother Belcher, a missionary, arrives in India's Himalayan region to preach, claiming, 'Sinners welcome with open arms'. When a guide is needed for a military operation across the border in Afghanistan, Belcher is blackmailed into taking the job.

BELL, JACK
Played by Leslie Phillips
In *Nurse* the likeable Jack Bell is admitted to Haven Hospital for a bunion operation. His admission couldn't have come at a worse time because he was hoping to sneak away for a few days with his girlfriend, Meg, staying at private hotels along the coast. After his operation is cancelled, Jack – while under the influence of champagne his girlfriend sneaked in – asks fellow patient Oliver Reckitt to perform the op, but soon changes his mind when Reckitt and other patients play along with his request and he nearly ends up being put under the knife by a student studying nuclear physics.

BELLA VISTA
The name of the schooner in *Again Doctor* which sank off the Beatific Islands during a terrible storm. As reported by the Long Hampton Advertiser, one of the schooner's passengers was Dr Carver, who was returning from the islands at the time. He was a lucky survivor.

BELLE
Played by Joan Sims
Belle, whose intimate friends call her 'Ding-Dong', is the respectable owner of Belle's Place in Stodge City. Seen in *Cowboy*, she loses her establishment to the ruthless Rumpo Kid when he swaggers into town.

BELLE'S PLACE
A saloon-cum-hotel in Stodge City that is run by Belle until the Rumpo Kid saunters into town and gains control, turning it from a respectable meeting place into a gambling den where the beer flows, fights break out and dancing girls entertain. Seen in *Cowboy*.

BELLE PARISIENNE
The magazine Professor Tinkle reads in his tent during *Up the Jungle* while his assistant, Claude Chumley, goes birdwatching.

BELTON, PETE
A corn dealer in Stodge City. He's not seen in *Cowboy* but his establishment is.

BENHAM, JOAN
Role: Cynical Lady in *Emmannuelle*
Born in London in 1918, Joan Benham is probably best known for playing Lady Prudence in the period drama, *Upstairs, Downstairs*, despite experiencing all media during her long career.

Other television credits included *The Troubleshooters, Doctor On the Go, Doctor in Charge, The Duchess of Duke Street, The Sun Trap* and *Terry and June*. On the big screen she was seen in, among others, *The Man Who Loved Redheads, It's Great to be Young, Child in the House, The Bridal Path* and *Murder Ahoy*.

She died in 1981, aged sixty-two.

BENNETT, PETER
Role: Thief in *Constable*
Born in London in 1917, Peter Bennett appeared in small roles in several films, including *Quatermass and the Pit* and *Lady Chatterley's Lover*, as well as the occasional meatier part, such as the Master of the Otter Hounds in *Tarka the Otter*.

His television credits ranged from *Man in a Suitcase* and *The Buccaneers* to *William Tell* and several appearances in the 1950s series, *The Adventures of Robin Hood*. He died in 1989, aged seventy-two.

BENNISON, BILL
Assistant Art Director on *Abroad*
Other productions Bill Bennison has worked on in the capacity of assistant art director are the films *Cromwell* and *Bless This House*, both during the 1970s, as well as *The Man in the Iron*

Mask, a production for the small screen. Promoted to art director, his credits include 1982's *The Hunchback of Notre Dame*.

BENNY
Played by Davy Kaye
The diminutive, cigar-puffing bookmaker has to restrict Sid Plummer's bets when – with the help of his little budgie, Joey – he nearly bankrupts the bookie. Appears in *At Your Convenience*.

BENSON, PC STANLEY
Played by Kenneth Williams
A snooty young policeman who's just graduated from police college when sent to help out at a station where the workforce is severely affected by the ravages of flu. A former Boy Scout, he regards himself as intellectual and an expert in criminology. Believing he can spot a criminal a mile off, he's embarrassed on more than one occasion, including being taken in by Herbert Hall, the confidence trickster, and accusing a detective-sergeant in the CID of attempting to steal a car.

BENTLEY, MRS
Played by Juliet Harmer
In *Matron*, Mrs Bentley is informed by Dr Prodd that she's pregnant before she admits that her husband isn't the father. (**Note: the scene was cut.**)

WHAT MIGHT HAVE BEEN

INT. EXAMINATION ROOM. DAY
The doors open and another YOUNG WOMAN comes in.

PRODD: Ah, Mrs Bentley, isn't it?

WOMAN: That's right.

PRODD: Well, Mrs Bentley. (He now has her card.) Our suspicions have been confirmed. You are definitely and there's no doubt about it, you are definitely a teeny, weeny bit pregnant.

WOMAN: Oh, dear.

PRODD: Aren't you pleased?

WOMAN: I don't know.

PRODD: It's nothing to worry about, you know. And you don't need to feel alone. We're all with you, you know. We're all in the same boat in this place. Like peas in a pod. All in the same pod, as you might say.

WOMAN: It's not that. You're all very kind, I'm sure. But . . .

PRODD: Why, if it will make you feel better you can have the father with you during the birth.

WOMAN: Oh, I don't think that would be very wise.

PRODD: Why not?

WOMAN: I don't think my husband would like him to be there.

PRODD: What? Oh.

WOMAN: Well thank you, Doctor. When do you want to see me again?

PRODD: Some time next week suit you?

WOMAN: Yes, fine.

PRODD: See you then. And . . . good luck.

WOMAN: Thanks.

(She goes. PRODD again speaks to the intercom.)

PRODD: Next, please.

BERKELEY NURSING HOME
Mentioned in *Again Doctor*, the wealthy Mrs Moore, a private patient of Dr Carver's, convalesces at the nursing home after having her appendix removed.

BERKELEY NURSING HOME MATRON
Played by Faith Kent
Seen briefly in *Again Doctor*, the Matron employed at the Berkeley Nursing Home ushers Dr Carver along to Ellen Moore's private room.

BERNARD, BROTHER
Played by Bernard Bresslaw
In *Abroad*, Bernard has just joined an Order, which was founded by St Cecilia, when he heads off to the Mediterranean resort of Elsbels with Wundatours. The Order he belongs to comprises missionaries, travelling the world doing good deeds, but Bernard realises it's not the life for him when he falls in love with Marge while on the trip.

BESPECTACLED BUSINESS MAN
Played by Norman Mitchell
Seen in *Cabby* preparing to jump into a Speedee Taxi until a Glamcab pulls up nearby and he opts for the leggy lovely driver instead, leaving a disgruntled Speedee driver without a fare.

BEST, GLORIA
Roles: Funhouse Girl in *Spying*, Hand Maiden in *Cleo* and Bridget in *Cowboy*.

BEST, PETER
Dubbing Editor on *Matron*, *Dick* and *Emmannuelle*
Other films that the late Peter Best worked on include *Kidnapped*, *Diamonds on Wheels*, *Tomorrow Never Comes*, *Nate and Hayes* and *Second Best*.

BETTINA
Played by Barbara Windsor
When Henry VIII first sets eyes on the blonde Bettina at a do he's arranged, he's soon drooling over her. He's in the middle of arrangements to annul his wedding to Queen Marie of Normandy and has his sights set on making Bettina his next bride. When he can't wait any longer, he performs the marriage ceremony himself and prepares for his wedding night, but while he's out of the bedroom Bettina, who's the daughter of Charles, the Earl of Bristol, consults *Balls Book of English Law* to check the legitimacy of their marriage; Henry tries convincing her it's all above board as he climbs into bed but she later learns the truth; it's just as well she resisted his advances because she ends up being whisked off across the channel by Francis, the King of France, to become the country's Queen. Seen in *Henry*.

BETTY
Played by Jackie Poole
In *Camping*, Betty is one of the girls from Chayste Place Finishing School who head for a summer break at the Paradise Camp in Devon.

BEVIS, FRANK
Production Manager on *Sergeant*, *Nurse*, *Teacher*, *Constable*, *Cabby*, *Jack*, *Spying*, *Cleo* and *Cowboy*. Associate producer on *Screaming!*
Born in Gosport, Hampshire, in 1907, into a naval family, Bevis was educated on HMS Conway, the cadet-training ship, before serving two years in the Royal Navy. After returning to civvy street, he was soon back at sea, working as a navigating officer for Canadian Pacific Steamships. He left the ocean wave behind in his early twenties and found work with a tin-canning company as a trainee production manager until being made redundant when the company was taken over.

He followed friends involved in crowd work in films and gradually forged a new career in the industry. Eventually switching to behind the camera, he gained experience via a host of jobs, including production manager on, among others, *The October Man*, *Odd Man Out* and *The Way To The Stars*. He progressed to associate producer and worked on several films in this capacity, including *Cromwell* and *Nicholas and Alexandra*, before retiring in 1980. He died in 2003.

BIDDLE, KEN
Played by Bernard Bresslaw
A patient in Fosdick Ward at the Borough County Hospital, Mr Biddle is seen in *Doctor*. He was originally admitted to have his appendix removed but fell off the operating table and hurt his leg, prolonging his stay. Falls in love with Mavis Winkle, a patient in Caffin Ward, while he's hospitalised.

BIDE-A-WEE REST HOME
The home of Dr Olando Watt and his sister, Virula, is seen in *Screaming!*. It's situated on Avery Avenue, in the middle of Hocombe Woods.

BIDET
Played by Gertan Klauber
One of the soldiers who arrives in England with Francis, the King of France. Seen in *Henry*.

CARRY ON BEHIND

A Peter Rogers production
Distributed through Fox / Rank
Distribution Ltd
Released as an A certificate in 1975
in colour
Running time: 90 mins

CAST

Kenneth Williams . . . . Professor Roland Crump
Elke Sommer . . . . Professor Anna Vooshka
Bernard Bresslaw . . . . Arthur Upmore
Kenneth Connor . . . . Major Leep
Joan Sims . . . . Daphne Barnes
Windsor Davies . . . . Fred Ramsden
Jack Douglas . . . . Ernie Bragg
Peter Butterworth . . . . Henry Barnes
Carol Hawkins . . . . Sandra
Sherrie Hewson . . . . Carol
Liz Fraser . . . . Sylvia Ramsden
Patsy Rowlands . . . . Linda Upmore
Ian Lavender . . . . Joe Baxter
Adrienne Posta . . . . Norma Baxter
Patricia Franklin . . . . Vera Bragg
David Lodge . . . . Landlord
Marianne Stone . . . . Mrs Rowan
George Layton . . . . Doctor
Brian Osborne . . . . Bob
Larry Dann . . . . Clive
Georgina Moon . . . . Sally
Diana Darvey . . . . Maureen

Jenny Cox . . . . Veronica
Larry Martyn . . . . Electrician
Linda Hooks . . . . Nurse
Kenneth Waller . . . . Barman
Billy Cornelius . . . . Man with Salad
Melita Manger . . . . Woman with Salad
Hugh Futcher . . . . Painter
Helli Louise Jacobson . . . . Nudist
Jeremy Connor . . . Student with Ice-cream
Alexandra Dane . . . . Lady in Low-cut Dress
Sam Kelly . . . . Projectionist
Johnny Briggs . . . . Plasterer

Lucy Griffiths . . . . Lady with Hat
Stanley McGeagh . . . . . Short-sighted Man
Brenda Cowling . . . . Wife
Sidney Johnson . . . . Man in Glasses
Drina Pavlovic . . . . Courting Girl
Caroline Whitaker . . . . Student
Ray Edwards . . . . Man with Water
Donald Hewlett . . . . Dean

PRODUCTION TEAM

Screenplay by Dave Freeman
Music composed and conducted by Eric Rogers
Production Manager: Roy Goddard
Art Director: Lionel Couch
Editor: Alfred Roome
Director of Photography: Ernest Steward BSC
Camera Operator: Neil Binney
Assistant Director: David Bracknell
Make-up: Geoffrey Rodway
Continuity: Marjorie Lavelly
Sound Recordists: Danny Daniel and Ken Barker
Hairdresser: Stella Rivers
Costume Design: Courtenay Elliott
Set Dresser: Charles Bishop
Dubbing Editor: Pat Foster
Titles: G.S.E. Ltd
Processed by Rank Film Laboratories
Assistant Editor: Jack Gardner
Caravans supplied by C I Caravans Limited
Producer: Peter Rogers
Director: Gerald Thomas

Elke Sommer and Gerald Thomas chat before filming

Let the cameras roll

The esteemed archaeologist, Professor Crump, is off on an archaeological dig to Templeton where a Roman encampment has been unearthed next to a caravan site. Assisting him on his dig are a group of eager students from the University of Kidburn and Professor Vooshka, an attractive woman whose mispronunciations of the English language are in danger of landing her in all sorts of trouble, especially when she greets everyone with the phrase, 'How are your doings?'

Other people heading to this quiet corner of England include Fred Ramsden and his mate, Ernie Bragg, two middle-aged men who tell their wives they're off on a fishing trip, but it's birds – and not the feathery kind – rather than fish that Fred's hoping to catch. Arthur Upmore, meanwhile, is looking forward to a break with his wife, Linda, until he discovers his nagging mother-in-law is joining them. But it's not the mother-in-law who'll be causing problems in the Baxters' caravan, but their enormous dog.

Two late arrivals at the Riverside Caravan Site, which is normally restricted to caravans, are Sandra and Carol, two leggy girls who are hoping to camp. Although Major Leep, the site owner, points out no tents are allowed, he's quick to bend the rules when Sandra shows a bit of thigh, claims she's got a bad leg and will need it massaged later. Their cunning gets them through the gates and they pitch their tent next to Fred and Ernie's caravan, who are soon eyeing them up.

In the Lipmores' van, Arthur is already fed up to the back teeth with the moaning Daphne Barnes, his mother-in-law; he's soon getting the blame for the expletives pouring out of the beak of Daphne's myna bird, and is somewhat relieved when it later escapes from its cage. But Daphne becomes a changed woman when she stumbles across her ex-husband, Henry, who's working at the site as an odd-job man. Now with nearly £20,000 in the bank, thanks to a win on the Pools, they rekindle their love after ten years apart.

A lack of progress on the girl front sees Fred and Ernie head for a pint at the local where they learn from the landlord that the caravan site is riddled with holes caused by Roman mining; they take little notice but their ignorace comes back to haunt them later.

To liven up the site, Major Leep is planning a cabaret evening and contacts a theatrical agent for a singer. When he interrupts the conversation to talk to his caretaker about paint stripper, the agent gets the wrong end of the stick and thinks he's after a stripper. Everyone is shocked when the dancer arrives and starts her erotic act, but while the men are lapping it up, the women aren't so pleased. When some decide to leave they find they're stuck to the recently painted chairs, tearing their trousers and skirts in the process.

Before the holiday is over, the old Roman mines reveal themselves, swallowing the caravans, just as it's time to go home.

Funny Scene!

Fred Ramsden and Ernie Bragg are inside Professor Crump's caravan. When an explosion caused his caravan to tip to one side, tomato ketchup spilled out of a bottle from an overhead cupboard and splattered all over his face, making him believe he's badly injured. Ramsden and Bragg rush in to try and assess the situation. To check if he's still alive, they place a mirror, still attached to the wardrobe door, over his face to see if he's breathing. When the glass doesn't mist up, Fred announces that he's dead.

```
CRUMP:     (Frightened.) Uh! No I'm not, I'm not, am I?
RAMSDEN:   He must have been holding his breath.
           (Moves mirror off CRUMP.) It's all right,
           lovely boy, you're in good hands.
CRUMP:     (Staring at RAMSDEN.) What are you?
RAMSDEN:   A butcher.
CRUMP:     Oh no! (Screams.)
RAMSDEN:   It's all right, I know what I'm doing.
CRUMP:     Haven't they got any real doctors?
RAMSDEN:   Just relax. Tell me where it hurts, I'll
           start with your left . . .
CRUMP:     (Groans and screams.) That hurts.
           (Screams more.) Oh it hurts all over.
RAMSDEN:   (Talking to Bragg.) I suspect it's multiple
           fractures, we need splints.
CRUMP:     Oh no! (Screams.)
RAMSDEN:   (Shouts.) Relax! (Bragg breaks what he
           thinks is a bit of wood. They start putting
           the wooden strips up Crump's trouser legs.)
CRUMP:     Oh! My theodolite is broken.
BRAGG:     What will we do?
RAMSDEN:   We'd better put a splint on that as well.
```

MEMORIES

'Some times I would dress the sets and other times just be on the floor as a standby, ready to do whatever was needed. I remember working on *Behind* and in the scene where Kenneth Williams and Elke Sommer are in a caravan that is leaking, I controlled the drips with the use of intravenous drip feeds, like you have in hospitals. We made little holes in the ceiling of the caravan and had the drips coming through.

'In another film, I remember having to drop ice-cream down one of the actress's cleavage. While standing on a lamp stand, hanging over her breasts with a pair of tongs holding a dollop of ice-cream, I waited for Gerald [Thomas] to say: "Action with the cornet", at which point I dropped it straight down into her breasts. Working on the *Carry Ons* was certainly great fun.'

WALLY HILL – Standby Chargehand

BIDET, CITIZEN
Played by Peter Butterworth
Seen in *Don't Lose Your Head*, Citizen Bidet is the assistant of Citizen Camembert, chief of the secret police. His incompetence drives Camembert mad at times as they set out to stop the Black Fingernail, alias Sir Rodney Ffing, from rescuing the aristocracy from the guillotine.

BIG HEAP
Played by Charles Hawtrey
Chief of a tribe of Indians in *Cowboy*, Big Heap is an accommodating, well-spoken man who agrees to help Rumpo Kid prevent the new marshal arriving at Stodge City by attacking the stagecoach he's travelling in. The attack fails, though, when sharpshooter Annie Oakley, who's also travelling in the coach, puts up strong resistance, shooting several Indians in the process.

BIGGER, FRANCIS
Played by Frankie Howerd
A charlatan spiritualist, Francis Bigger is a firm believer in positive thinking and preaches his message around the country. With his motto, 'Learn to think the Bigger way', he tries teaching the power of thinking is the way to health and happiness. Accompanied by his lifeless assistant, Chloe Gibson, he's telling everyone that nothing will happen to them if they think positive, then falls off a stage and ends up in the Borough County Hospital with a bruised coccyx. When he mishears Dr Tinkle talking to Miss Gibson he thinks he's only got days to live and deciding to make his loyal assistant happy for the last few days of his life, marries her, only to discover later, to his horror, that his days aren't numbered at all. Seen in *Doctor*.

BILIUS
Played by David Davenport
Seen in *Cleo*, Bilius stands alongside Julius Caesar, acting as his bodyguard. Champion gladiator of Rome, he's soon ousted from his position by Hengist Pod who's classed as a hero after inadvertently stumbling across Bilius's attempts to dispose of the Roman leader.

BILKINGTON RESEARCH ESTABLISHMENT
The top secret base in *Spying* where Professor Stark was developing a secret formula before being blown up while carrying out his duty.

BIND, CHARLIE
Played by Charles Hawtrey
One of the rather green agents who are sent to recover the top secret formula stolen by Milchmann for the detestable Dr Crow in *Spying*. His codename is Yellow Peril and his agent's number, 00 – 0.

BINDER, LADY
Played by Elspeth March
Seen in *Don't Lose Your Head*, Lady Binder congratulates Sir Rodney Ffing on the charity ball he's organised at his home, Ffing Hall.

BINN, DR ARTHUR
Played by Kenneth Connor
Binn is the new ship's doctor on the *Happy Wanderer*. Seen in *Cruising*, he joined the vessel from Consolidated Marmalade where he worked as the factory's medical officer. Falls in love with Flo Castle, one of the passengers, and although his early advances are spurned, finally ties the knot with the blonde, despite his timidity.

BINNEY, NEIL
Camera Operator for Khyber location work on *Up The Khyber*, and *Behind*

Born in Borehamwood, Hertfordshire, in 1931, Neil Binney followed his parents into the film industry (his father was a projectionist at Pinewood, his mother a wardrobe mistress) by working as a clapperboy on the 1946 Sydney Box-produced *The Years Between*.

After completing National Service – he served two years as a photographer in the RAF – he joined the London Studios of Technicolor, as assistant cameraman, and stayed ten years. Among the many films he worked on were Hollywood classics such as *The Man Who Knew Too Much*; he also spent time working in Italy.

He left Technicolor in the 1960s and turned freelance, clocking up numerous credits as a camera operator, including *Billy Liar*, *This Sporting Life*, *The Vampire Lovers*, *On the Buses*, *Conan the Destroyer*, *Shanghai Surprise* and

Charlie Bind (Charles Hawtrey) dons his cycling gear (*Spying*)

A Fish Called Wanda. On television he was behind the camera for, among others, *Minder* and *Space Precinct*.

His final job was on the 1997 picture, *Fierce Creatures*, after which he retired from the profession.

BINNING, TANYA
Role: Virginia in *Cleo*
Born in Newcastle, New South Wales, Australia, in 1946, Tanya Binning was a successful model and television personality by the time she arrived in the UK. Although her early ambition was to be a florist, she was chosen for a part in the controversial 1962 film, *Mondo Cane*, leading to her rapid rise to top cover-girl for Australian magazines. A handful of other films followed, all produced in New Zealand, including *Runaway, Don't Let It Get You* and *Funny Things Happen Down Under*.

BIRD, HARRY
Played by Roy Hines
In *Teacher*, Bird is one of the main culprits among the school kids who set out to cause havoc when a school inspector and a child psychiatrist visit Maudlin Street Secondary Modern School. He's also interviewed by Mr Wakefield when he's found out of bounds in the school's storeroom.

BIRD OWNER
Played by Molly Weir
Seen in *Regardless,* the woman calls Helping Hands when she wants someone to look after her collection of birds. However, a mix-up sees Mike Weston, who was expecting to be working as a bouncer at a strip club, turn up by mistake.

'BIRDS OF PARADISE, THE'
Played by Laraine Humphrys, Linda Hooks, Penny Irving and Eva Reuber-Staier
The girls entertain the patrons of the Old Cock Inn in *Dick*. The group is run by Madame Desiree, a Cockney by birth who's adopted a French accent over the years.

BISHOP
Played by Derek Francis
Shares a train compartment with Terence Philpot in *Loving*. He can't believe his ears when Philpot tells his friend, with whom he's been staying, that his wife makes love beautifully. When he broaches the subject with Philpot, he's much relieved to hear that Philpot was only thinking of his friend's best interests because to tell him the truth, that he didn't enjoy bedding his wife, might offend.

BISHOP, BERNIE
Played by Kenneth Connor
In the fourth round of an eliminating contest, boxer Bernie Bishop breaks his hand. He's admitted to Haven Hospital in *Nurse* and faces the prospect of never fighting again. It looks as if his son, Jeremy, will be following in his father's footsteps, though, because he's already practising on the family cat.

BISHOP, CHARLES
Set Dresser on *Dick* and *Behind*
Charles Bishop, who's now an art director, has built up a lengthy list of film and television credits. His television work covers productions such as *Interpol Calling, The Persuaders!* and *The Champions*, while his film credits include *Nearly A Nasty Accident, Mystery Submarine, The Eagle Has Landed, Moonraker, Superman II, Supergirl, Return to Oz* and *Empire of the Sun*.

BISHOP, JANE
Played by Susan Shaw
Boxer Bernie Bishop's attractive wife is seen in *Nurse*, visiting her husband at Haven Hospital.

BISHOP, JEREMY
Played by Jeremy Connor
Seen in *Nurse*, Jeremy is Bernie Bishop's little boy. He arrives at Haven Hospital the day his father is discharged, greeting him with a slap across the face.

BISSET, DONALD
Role: Patient in *Again Doctor*
Donald Bisset, born in London in 1911, was a veteran of stage and screen. His television work included appearances in *Crane, Doctor Who, Doctor in the House, The Professionals, Pollyanna, Love for Lydia* and *The Old Curiosity Shop* during the 1960s and '70s. By this time, he'd already cut his teeth in films, having been cast in productions such as *Murder in the Cathedral, Little Red Monkey, The Brain Machine, Up the Creek* and *The Headless Ghost*.

He remained busy in the profession until his death in 1995, with later assignments seeing him play Mr Morgan in 1993's *The Black Velvet Gown*, a manservant in *The Hound of the Baskervilles* and Trafford Simcox in *Paradise Postponed*. He was also a published children's writer.

BLACK FINGERNAIL, THE
For 'The Black Fingernail' in *Don't Lose Your Head*, see 'Ffing, Sir Rodney'.

BLACKLER, GEORGE
Make-up designer on *Nurse, Teacher, Constable, Regardless* and *Cruising*
George Blackler began working as a make-up artist in the 1940s with such classics as *The Life and Death of Colonel Blimp, A Canterbury Tale* and *A Matter of Life and Death*. He remained busy throughout the '50s and '60s, notching up a host of credits, ranging from *The Long Memory, Above Us the Waves* and *A Town Like Alice* to *Follow A Star, Raising the Wind* and *A Pair of Briefs*. His television work, meanwhile, included various episodes of *The Avengers* and *The Saint*.

He was still working in the industry during the 1970s on such films as *Lust for a Vampire, Twins of Evil, The Satanic Rites of Dracula* and *Stand Up, Virgin Soldiers*.

BLACKSMITH
Played by Tom Clegg
When the incompetent Marshall P. Knutt locks himself in his own cell in *Cowboy*, the blacksmith uses a crowbar to break open the door.

BLAIN, JOSEPHINE
Role: Hospitality Girl in *Up The Khyber*.

BLAKE, DENIS
Role: Rubbatiti in *Screaming!*
The late Denis Blake worked on various film and television productions during his career, including *Casino Royale*.

BLASTED OAK, THE
A local landmark on the London Road in the parish of Upper Dencher, it's where Harriett tells Captain Fancey and Sergeant Strapp, of the Bow Street Runners, to meet Dick Turpin. Seen in *Dick*.

BLEZARD, JOHN
Art Director on *Again Doctor*
Born in Kendal in 1927, John Blezard graduated from the Old Vic Theatre School and initially worked in television. During the 1960s he started in films as art director on such pictures as *The City of the Dead, Mary Had A Little, Reach for Glory, That Riviera Touch, When Dinosaurs Ruled the Earth* and *Hoffman*.

As a production designer his films include *Firepower, The Wicked Lady* and *Bullseye!*. Among the television productions he worked on in this capacity are *The Adventures of Black Beauty, Peter the Great, Heidi* and *The Whipping Boy*.

Most recently, he was assistant producer on Michael Winner's 1999 production, *Parting Shots*.

BLISS, SIDNEY
Played by Sidney James
Co-owns the Wedded Bliss Agency with Sophie Bliss. Seen in *Loving*, Sidney and Sophie claim they've been happily married ten years but it's all a front; their lies are for the benefit of the company – how can they run a successful marriage agency having never tied the knot themselves? The trouble is, Sidney Bliss is one for the girls and continually dismisses talk of getting married when Sophie raises the subject. The love of his life is Esme Crowfoot but she drops out of circulation when she becomes engaged to Gripper Burke. It's only when a frustrated Sophie plans to leave the Wedded Bliss Agency for good that Sidney comes to his senses and realises he can't manage without his long-term partner.

BLISS, SOPHIE
Played by Hattie Jacques
One half of the Wedded Bliss Agency, a marriage bureau run with her partner of ten years,

Sidney Bliss. Seen in *Loving*, Sophie – whose real name is Sophie Plummet – and Sidney claim they've been happily married for a decade but it's all a lie for the benefit of the company. The neglected Sophie Bliss ends up doing most of the donkey work around the office whilst Sidney goes off vetting all the attractive females who happen to walk through the door of their fourth-floor office.

When she can't take any more, Sophie tries her luck with Mr Snooper, a bachelor working as a marriage guidance counsellor who's told by his boss to find a wife if he wants to save his job, but it doesn't work out; fortunately for her, Sidney realises how much he actually needs her in his business and personal life and they tie the knot in front of all the happy – or not so happy in most cases – couples they've united over the years.

BLOGGS, MURIEL
Played by Barbara Windsor
For Muriel Bloggs in *Girls*, see 'Springs, Hope'.

BLONDE IN PUB
Played by Claire Davenport
Known as the Closet Queen of Camden Town because she can only make love standing up inside a closet, the corpulent blonde is seen in *Emmannuelle* during Leyland's flashback sequence. She takes the chauffeur back to her flat in Mayfair and it isn't long before they're undressed and heading for the closet; even the return of the blonde's drunk husband doesn't deter them.

BLOOMER, SERGEANT MAJOR 'TIGER'
Played by Windsor Davies
The loud-mouthed sergeant major, christened Tiger by his admirer, Private Ffoukes-Sharpe, shouts his way through *England* in a vain attempt to inject some order and discipline into experimental 1313 anti-aircraft battery.

BLUNT, EVELYN
Played by June Whitfield
Evelyn, who's seen in *Abroad,* is a member of the party which travels to the Mediterranean resort of Elsbels with Wundatours Limited. It's certainly a holiday to remember because she goes through a complete transformation, thanks to Georgio, the hotel barman, who makes her realise what she's been missing over the years in her sexless marriage. Her constant henpecking and whinging disappear, much to the delight of her sexually frustrated hubby, Stanley. The Blunts have one daughter, though we learn nothing about her other than that she has many of her mother's traits.

BLUNT, STANLEY
Played by Kenneth Connor
A member of the party which travels to Elsbels with Wundatours Limited in *Abroad*, Mr Blunt

is henpecked and denied the carnal pleasures he expects from his marriage by a wife who thinks even the word 'sex' is vulgar let alone the actual activity. While away, he sees in Cora Flange everything he'd like his wife to be, but by the time the holiday comes to an end, he finds his own wife, Evelyn, is a changed woman, thanks to a little help from Georgio, the hotel barman.

BLUTHAL, JOHN
Roles: The Headwaiter in *Spying*, Corporal Clotski in *Follow That Camel* and the Royal Tailor in *Henry*
John Bluthal, born in Galicja, southeast Poland, in 1929, emigrated to Australia with his family in 1938, where he later studied at Melbourne University. He came to England in the mid-1950s, worked initially in theatre before television and film offers came his way.

Since the 1960s he's been a regular on the screen. His film credits include *The Mouse on the Moon; Doctor in Distress; Father Came Too!; Help!; Casino Royale; Doctor in Trouble; Digby, the Biggest Dog in the World; The Return of the Pink Panther; Superman III* and, most recently, *Love's Brother.*

On television, Bluthal, who frequently works in Australia, has been seen in, among others, *Sykes, The Saint, The Goodies, Bergerac, Inspector Morse, It's A Square World, Q5, The Pathfinders* and *Vicar of Dibley*, playing Frank Pickle.

BOA, BRUCE
Role: US Ambassador in *Emmannuelle*
Forever remembered as Mr Hamilton, the American guest in classic sitcom *Fawlty Towers*, Bruce Boa was born in England in 1930 but raised in Calgary, Canada, where he later played professional football.

After moving to England in the 1950s he was soon appearing on television and screen, with television credits including *Out of this World, The Avengers, Special Branch, The Champions, Dempsey and Makepeace* and *Kavanagh QC*. In 1969 he had a running part in *The Troubleshooters*, playing Bill Douglas.

He appeared in various films, such as *Man in the Moon, The Cherry Picker, The Omen, Superman, The Empire Strikes Back, Octopussy, Riders of the Storm, Full Metal Jacket* and *Screamers.*

He died in 2004, aged seventy-three.

BOB
Played by Brian Osborne
A student from the University of Kidburn's archaeological department who helps Professor Crump at the dig in *Behind*. While staying at the Riverside Caravan Site, next-door to where they're digging, Bob and his mate befriend two girls, Carol and Sandra, who are camping.

BODDEY, MARTIN
Roles: 6th Specialist in *Sergeant* and Perkins in *Nurse*
Born in the Scottish town of Stirling in 1907, Martin Boddey was a busy character actor in film, television and theatre. On the big screen, where he was often seen playing policemen, his lengthy list of credits included *Cage of Gold, Seven Days to Noon, The Franchise Affair, Laughter in Paradise, The Magic Box, Chain of Events, Girl in the Headlines* and *Tales from the Crypt.*

On television, he was seen in shows such as *The Troubleshooters, Brett, The Cheaters, The Champions, Dr Who, Ivanhoe* and *The Naked Civil Servant,* his final job.

He died in 1975, aged sixty-eight.

BODKIN
Played by Bill Maynard
The barman at the Old Cock Inn, which is regularly frequented by local criminals, is seen in *Dick*.

BOGGINS, MAUDE
Played by Barbara Windsor
Maude Boggins is the real name of Goldie Locks, alias Melody Madder, the actress-cum-model who sets Dr Nookey's pulse racing in *Again Doctor*.

BOGGLE AND LUGG
A firm of plumbing and sanitation engineers, whose company van is a grey Vauxhall, registration FVB 352D. The vehicle and the partners, Sid Boggle and Bernie Lugg, are seen in *Camping.*

BOGGLE, SID
Played by Sidney James
Seen in *Camping*, Sid Boggle is one half of Boggle and Lugg, plumbing and sanitation engineers. As well as workmates, Sid and Bernie Lugg are best friends; they date Joan Fussey and Anthea Meeks respectively but are frustrated at the progress they're making towards the bedroom, so Sid suggests they visit a nudist camp, featured in a film at the local cinema. Unfortunately for Sid and Bernie, they pick the wrong site and end up in a mudpit in Devon. Possessing an eye for the girls, Sid becomes interested in the nubile Babs, who's camping with other girls from the Chayste Place Finishing School, before eventually realising that Joan is the one for him.

BOGGS, LEWIS
Played by Richard O'Callaghan
William Boggs's son who works at the family firm, W.C. Boggs and Son, manufacturers of quality toilet ware since 1870. Lewis, who's impatient at times, feels that the company's business philosophy is stuck in the nineteenth century. He's desperate to modernise not just

the company's product range, such as selling bidets like its competitors, but attitudes of those working for the company, including his father's. His approach, however, occasionally leaves much to be desired; still inexperienced in the field of work relations, he antagonises the union representative, Vic Plummer, and is to blame for some of the industrial disputes that have blighted the company for years.

Away from work, the sports-car-driving young executive (car registration VOP 436J) is smitten with Myrtle Plummer, the canteen girl who happens to be daughter of the works foreman; his determination in the race to secure a place in Myrtle's heart eventually pays off when he buys a special marriage licence and they tie the knot.

BOGGS, WILLIAM C.
Played by Kenneth Williams

The managing director of W.C. Boggs and Son, makers of fine toilet ware. The company has been in the family since it was established in 1870, and heading it nowadays is William, supported by his son, Lewis. Their views on how the company should operate differ considerably, causing friction from time to time. While the forward-thinking Lewis wants the firm to keep up with the times, William prefers the cautious approach, sticking with the tried and tested styles and designs that have served the company well for years. Lewis eventually gets his way, though, over the long-disputed issue of whether Boggs should sell bidets in its range; but even with customers queueing up to order, William takes some convincing that it's right for the firm's image.

While he's ably assisted in the office by the devoted Miss Withering, he conducts his personal life without the support of his wife, whom he refers to while testing a newly designed loo. He tells others attending the meeting during *At Your Convenience* how she had a terrible experience of what happens when a toilet cracks because it can't take the weight.

BOITA, PETER
Editor on *Sergeant* and *Emmannuelle*

Born in London in 1924, Peter Boita completed his education at the Westminster City School and worked in a factory before joining the RAF in 1942. During his five years' service he was posted to Singapore and Hong Kong.

Back on civvy street, a friend of his father's landed Boita a job at Islington Studios, assisting the dubbing editor. When the studio closed, he moved to Shepherd's Bush Studio and assisted film editor, Jimmy Needs, on a host of pictures, such as *Jassy* and *Snowbound*. He later followed Needs to Pinewood and continued working as his assistant until eventually branching out and working for other editors, including Gerald Thomas, who was responsible for giving Boita his big break.

When commissioned to direct a film, *Circus Friends*, for the Children's Film Foundation, Boita was offered the chance to edit the picture, the first of many in a long and distinguished career. His credits include *The Horsemasters* and *Third Man On the Mountain* for Disney, *The Duke Wore Jeans*, *The Traitors*, *Jane Eyre*, *Doctor in Trouble* and *The Jewel of the Nile*. For television, he edited such productions as *The Far Pavilions* and *Lace*.

He died in 1997.

BOLTON, PETER
Assistant Director on *Cabby*, *Spying*, *Cleo*, *Cowboy* and *Screaming!*

Born in Bradford in 1914, Peter Bolton spent the lion's share of his career as an assistant director, working variously on comedies, documentaries and dramas, primarily for the big screen. His credits in this medium include *Hungry Hill*, *Sleeping Car to Trieste*, *Tottie True*, *A Day to Remember*, *Saint Joan*, *Left Right and Centre*, *The Big Job*, *A Severed Head* and, in 1972, *Pope Joan*.

BOOKS
See page 275.

BOON, ERIC
Roles: Shorty in *Constable* and Second in *Regardless*

Born in Chatteris, Cambridgeshire, in 1920, Eric Boon reigned as British lightweight boxing champion between 1938-44. Just eighteen when crowned champion, Boon served in the RAF during the war and went on to box in Canada, Australia and America before retiring from the ring.

He made a handful of television and film appearances, including playing Clinker in 1944's *Champagne Charlie*. He died in 1981, aged sixty-one.

BOOSEY, BILL
Played by Sid James

Bill 'Rattlesnake' Boosey leads the expedition into the African jungle in *Up the Jungle*. Not the bravest of men: upon hearing the drums of the infamous Nosha tribe reverberating around the jungle, he wants to head back, but Lady Bagley's and Professor Tinkle's insistence leaves him little option but to continue. When he later finds himself in the hands of the all-female Lubidubies tribe, he's soon glad he continued with the expedition.

BOROUGH COUNTY HOSPITAL
The setting for *Doctor*, where the likes of Doctor Tinkle and Doctor Kilmore are employed.

BOROUGH COUNTY TIMES
A newspaper in *Again Doctor* carrying news of the mayhem Dr Nookey causes at the Long Hampton Hospital.

BORTHWICK HECK
A firm of estate agents based in Chiswick, London, whose 'For Sale' board is seen in *Constable* outside a property in Church Road where the criminals involved in a wages snatch dump their car.

BOTTOMLEY, MRS
An unseen character in *Constable*, Mrs Bottomley, who's referred to as living at number twenty-four, asks the police to call around because she's concerned about suspicious activities in the rear of her premises. Mentioned by Sergeant Wilkins, who asks one of the policemen to investigate.

BOURNE AND JONES
A milliner's shop in *Screaming!*.

BOWLER
Played by Edmund Pegge

Seen in the opening scenes of *Follow That Camel* bowling to Captain Bagshaw at the cricket match.

BOY
Played by Larry Dann

In *Teacher* the bespectacled, sallow-faced boy puts his hand up in class because he's desperate to use the loo, just when Alistair Grigg and Felicity Wheeler, two important visitors at the school, have popped in to the class to observe. He's later seen pounding away at the drum in the school play.

BOY LOVER
Played by Mike Grady

For the 'Boy Lover' in *Loving*, see 'Girl Lover'.

BRACKNELL, DAVID
Assistant Director on *Follow That Camel*, *Loving*, *Henry*, *At Your Convenience*, *Abroad* and *Dick*

David Bracknell has been working as an assistant director since the early 1960s, with credits including *The Boys*, *Serena*, *A Shot in the Dark*, *Funeral in Berlin*, *Lust for a Vampire*, *Bless This House*, *Swallows and Amazons*, *Indiana Jones and the Temple of Doom* and *Murrow*.

BRADLEY, C.
The unseen Second Assistant Purser on the *Happy Wanderer* in *Cruising*. His name is seen on the crew list.

BRADLEY, JOSIE
Role: Pianist in *Loving*

Josie Bradley's other work includes an appearance as Freda in the 1947 film, *The Mysterious Mr Nicholson*, and Mildred Knottage in a 1969 episode of the television series *Detective*.

BRAGG, ERNIE
Played by Bernard Bresslaw

One of Sid Carter's gang in *Matron*, the gormless Ernie Bragg was born on top of the number seventy-three bus in the middle of Brixton High Street.

BRAGG, ERNIE
Played by Jack Douglas

An electrician who holidays with his friend, Fred Ramsden, in *Behind*. When their respective wives decide on a break in a health farm, Fred persuades the easily-led Ernie to accompany him to the Riverside Caravan Site under the guise of a fishing trip. What Fred hopes they will catch, though, is a couple of birds – and not the feathery kind! They're out of luck, although not through lack of trying, which is just as well because their wives eventually turn up at the camp site. Although they'd sent a telegram to inform their husbands of their arrival, the message never reached Fred and Ernie.

BRAGG, VERA
Played by Patricia Franklin

When her husband, Ernie, heads off in a caravan to the Riverside Caravan Site with his close friend, Fred Ramsden, Vera opts for a health farm with Fred's wife, Sylvia. They eventually surprise their husbands by turning up at the caravan site unannounced. They had sent a telegram informing their husbands of their impending arrival, but the message never reached Fred and Ernie.

BRAKES, DAWN
Played by Margaret Nolan

The former Miss Dairy Queen is one of the contestants in the Miss Fircombe beauty contest in *Girls*. First seen sharing the same train compartment as Peter Potter, who's also travelling to Fircombe to organise publicity for the event; just before the train moves out of the station the carriage jolts forward and Peter accidentally rips Dawn's skimpy top, revealing her ample bosom, much to his fiancée's disgust. A model by profession, she poses for dirty mags, and asks Lawrence, the rather green local photographer, to take some snaps of her naked on the beach.

BRAMBELL, WILFRID
Role: Mr Pullen in *Again Doctor*

Wilfrid Brambell, born in Dublin in 1912, will forever be remembered for his fine portrayal of Albert Steptoe in fifty-nine episodes of BBC's classic sitcom. Brambell's father worked in a brewery while his mother was an opera singer. His first performance was as a two-year-old entertaining wounded troops during the Great War.

Upon leaving school he worked as a cub reporter for *The Irish Times* during the day and part-time actor at the Abbey Theatre in the evenings. He later took the plunge and turned professional after securing a job at Dublin's Gate Theatre.

During the Second World War he toured with ENSA, and afterwards appeared in numerous reps including Bristol, Bromley and Chesterfield, before working in the West End and on Broadway.

His television work included *Life with the Lyons*, the 1950s sci-fi series, *The Quatermass Experiment* and *No Fixed Abode*, while his film credits include *The 39 Steps*, *The Three Lives of Thomasina*, *A Hard Day's Night*, *Where the Bullets Fly* and *Holiday on the Buses*.

He died in 1985.

BRAY, HENRY
Played by Brian Oulton

Bray is rather ostentatious with his claims of grandeur. During his stay at the Haven Hospital in *Nurse*, he tells fellow patients a pack of lies, such as owning a house on the expensive west side of the Common. It's only when his wife, Rhoda, visits that we learn the truth, although Henry is constantly trying to shut her up in case she's overheard.

BRAY, KEN
Stills Cameraman on *England* and *Emmannuelle*

Ken Bray's other credits as a stills cameraman include the 1978 film, *The Playbirds*.

BRAY, RHODA
Played by Hilda Fenemore

Seen in *Nurse*, Rhoda visits her husband, Henry, while he's recuperating at Haven Hospital, but spends the entire visiting period embarrassing her beloved who's trying to make out he's something he isn't.

BRAYSHAW, DEBORAH
Role: French Buxom Blonde in *Emmannuelle*

An occasional actress during the 1970s, she was seen playing a technician in an episode of *Doctor Who*, as well as an episode of *Special Branch*. On the big screen, she appeared as a go-cart girl in *Confessions from a Holiday Camp*.

BREGONZI, ALEC
Role: 1st Storeman in *Sergeant*. (Note: Also played a Beach Photographer in *At Your Convenience* but the scene was cut.)

London-born Alec Bregonzi's professional acting career began, like many of his contemporaries', in repertory theatre in the mid-1950s. In venues at Farnham, York, Bromley and Leatherhead he learnt the ropes of the profession before West End opportunities came his way, including parts in *Camino Real* and understudying Ronnie Barker.

While his theatre career progressed, offers to appear on television came his way, including parts in the small-screen version of *Hancock's Half Hour*. During the 1970s and '80s, he worked with a host of comedians, including Cannon and Ball, Kenny Everett and Little and Large. Other credits during this period range from *The Two Ronnies*, *Filthy Rich and Catflap* and *London's Burning* to *The Barchester Chronicles*, *Great Expectations* and *The Recruiting Officer*. For four years he read viewers' letters on BBC's *Points of View*, presented by Barry Took, which spawned a radio series, *Joke by Joke*. More recently, he supplied many voices for the 1990s animated children's series, *The Treacle People*.

Bregonzi has also appeared in a handful of films, such as *Face of a Stranger*, *Ricochet*, *Downfall* from the Edgar Wallace series, and *Revenge of the Pink Panther*. Sadly, one of his best parts was in a French film, *L'Etincelle*, which has never been screened in Britain. He's also done a lot of theatre work, including several plays for the Royal Shakespeare Company.

BRENNAN, J.

The unseen Second Officer on the *Happy Wanderer* in *Cruising*. His name is seen on the crew list.

MEMORIES

'Alas, my memories of *Carry On Sergeant* are few and not happy ones. I was one of the storemen who had a little scene with most of the principals. Mine was with Gerald Campion, with whom I'd worked in a stage version of *Billy Bunter* at the Victoria Palace.

'We rehearsed the scene in *Sergeant*, which was a two-shot, and as the director walked away Gerry told me to change position slightly, which would have meant he would be favoured more by the camera and my ear and nose would be more prominent than my face. Gerald Thomas overheard this and said: "We'll do it exactly as rehearsed!" So we did. The scene was cut, though, probably at the last minute because my billing in the credits is much too good for an – ultimately – non-speaking character. I was very disappointed, as you can imagine, especially after the good credit and then just a glorified walk-on part.

'Later, I played a beach photographer, where people put their heads through funny cut-outs, at Brighton in *At Your Convenience*. This time all of me ended on the cutting-room floor. I asked Peter Rogers at a *Carry On* do once why I was always cut and he said Eleanor Summerfield had suffered the same fate, only more so!'

ALEC BREGONZI

BRESSLAW, BERNARD

Roles: Little Heap in *Cowboy*, Sockett in *Screaming!*, Sheikh Abdul Abulbul in *Follow That Camel*, Ken Biddle in *Doctor*, Bunghit Din in *Up The Khyber*, Bernie Lugg in *Camping*, Upsidasi in *Up the Jungle*, Gripper Burke in *Loving*, Bernie Hulke in *At Your Convenience*, Ernie Bragg in *Matron*, Brother Bernard in *Abroad*, Peter Potter in *Girls*, Sir Roger Daley in *Dick* and Arthur Upmore in *Behind*

TV: *Christmas* (69), *Christmas* (70), *What a Carry On!*, *Christmas* (73), *Under the Round Table*, *Short Knight*, *Long Daze*, *And In My Lady's Chamber*, *Who Needs Kitchener?* and *Lamp Posts of the Empire*

STAGE: *London!* and *Wot a Carry On in Blackpool*

Bernard Bresslaw was born in London in 1934. His mother, who was fascinated by the theatre, was keen for her son to become a tap dancer and enrolled him at local dancing classes, which didn't last long.

While at school – he attended Coopers School, Mile End – his English master recognised Bresslaw's love and talent for English Literature and drama and coached him ready for his drama entrance exam. He studied at RADA after winning one of two annual London County Council Awards, and was awarded the respected Emile Littler Award for Most Promising Actor.

After graduating, one of his first jobs was appearing as an Irish wrestler in *MacRoary Whirl*, a production staged by Laurence Olivier. He later asked Bresslaw to replace him in *Home and Beauty*, when Olivier was in need of a break.

Bresslaw was gaining valuable experience at various repertory theatres and as part of a touring company playing RAF camps, Borstals and even mental institutions, and before long he received offers to appear on television and in films. Credits on the big screen included *Men of Sherwood Forest*, *Up in the World*, *Blood of the Vampire*, *Too Many Crooks*, *It's All Happening*, *Up Pompeii* and *Krull*, while on television he was seen in, among others, *The Adventures of Robin Hood*, *The Vise*, *Danger Man*, *Arthur of the Britons*, *The Goodies*, *Sykes* and, what he's best remembered for on television, *The Army Game*. National Service as a driver-clerk in the Royal Army Service Corps had provided an insight into life in the services and he used it to good effect in the long-running series.

Playing Private Popplewell in the highly successful comedy series, *The Army Game*, propelled him to national prominence but saw him typecast in goofy roles, which continued throughout his time with the *Carry On* series. But Bernard, who was proud of his classical training, possessed the talent to turn his hand to any job he was offered, and was particularly proud of his time in, among others, Shakespeare's *Two Gentlemen of Verona* and *Much Ado About Nothing*. It was whilst appearing at Regent's Park in *Taming of the Shrew*, in 1993, that he collapsed and died, aged fifty-nine, after suffering a heart attack.

Although people will always remember him for his screen work, Bernard's preferred medium was the theatre, and he never declined the chance to return to the stage.

BRIDE

Played by Marian Collins

Celebrates her honeymoon with a cruise on the *Happy Wanderer*. Seen in *Cruising*, occupying room 309.

BRIDE

Played by Marian Collins

Seen in *Cabby*, Charlie Hawkins takes newly-weds to the airport; by the time he arrives, they're hugging and kissing in the back seat.

BRIDEGROOM

Played by Evan David

In *Cruising*, he's seen celebrating his honeymoon with a cruise on the *Happy Wanderer*. Occupies room 309.

BRIDEGROOM

Played by Peter Byrne

Seen in *Cabby*, Charlie Hawkins takes newly-weds to the airport; by the time he arrives, they're hugging and kissing in the back seat.

BRIDGET

Played by Gloria Best

One of the saloon girls seen at Rumpo's Place in *Cowboy*.

BRIGADIER

Played by Peter Jones

The wisecracking brigadier is seen in *England*. After assigning Captain Melly the task of trying to instil some discipline into the experimental

1313 anti-aircraft battery, he later heads down to the base to see how Melly is managing.

BRIGGS, JOHNNY
Roles: Sporran Soldier in *Up The Khyber*, Plasterer in *Behind* and Melly's Driver in *England*
TV: *The Case of the Coughing Parrot*
Johnny Briggs, born in London in 1935, is best known as Mike Baldwin in *Coronation Street*, a role he's been playing since 1976, but his career stretches back to 1947 when, as a boy soprano, he was engaged at the Cambridge Theatre.

Aged twelve, he won a scholarship to the Italia Conti Stage School and, four years later, began working in rep before completing National Service. Returning to civvy street, his career took off and he became a regular screen actor, whose films have included *Quartet, Helter Skelter, The Bulldog Breed, A Stitch in Time, 633 Squadron, Au Pair Girls* and *The Office Party*.

Other television roles include playing Detective Sergeant Russell for two years in the long-running series, *No Hiding Place*.

BRINTON, TIM
Role: BBC Newscaster in *Emmannuelle*
Tim Brinton, born in London in 1929, left school and completed National Service in the army before training for the stage at the Central School of Drama where he gained the London University Diploma of Dramatic Art. Before finishing his course he was offered a post at the BBC as a general trainee, starting as a radio news reader/announcer but, later, progressing to become a television director/producer.

In the late 1950s he was seconded by the BBC to Radio Hong Kong as head of English programmes, followed by a spell as one of the early BBC television newsreaders at Alexandra Palace in 1959. He later transferred to ITN as a senior newscaster/reporter and presented other ITV shows, including the sports programme *Let's Go* and ITN's *Roving Report*.

He's presented many commercials and was also the voice of short cinema films, such as

---

MEMORIES

'I was but a small-bit player in *Carry On Emmannuelle*, going to the studios for an hour or so to film a piece of about twenty seconds in the role of a TV newscaster, which in reality I'd been between 1959 and 1962. To save on the budget, the director, Gerald Thomas, filmed me looking through the frame of a TV screen. Nowadays they do it electronically – or should I write digitally?'

TIM BRINTON

Pathé Pictorial and *Look At Life*. Other work saw him host BBC Radio 2's *Roundabout* and he was, briefly, a DJ on Radio Luxembourg. He's coached executives of business and industry for TV and radio, and during the 1970s was media consultant to Conservative Central Office.

In 1979 he was elected MP for Gravesend, Kent, and became a member of the House of Commons Select Committee for Education, Science and the Arts. He left Parliament in 1987 to return to presentation and media coaching for business executives.

During the 1960s and '70s he played news-readers and interviewers in several films and television programmes, including *The Avengers, Doctor in Charge* and *Dixon of Dock Green* for the small screen and *Information Received, Bunny Lake Is Missing* and *Man At The Top* in films.

He retired from full-time work in 1998.

BRISTOL'S BOUNCING BABY FOOD
The model Goldie Locks was filming a commercial for the baby food company when she slipped at the Advertising Film Studios and badly bruised herself. Mentioned in *Again Doctor*.

BRODY, RONNIE
Roles: Little Man in *Don't Lose Your Head* and Henry in *Loving*. (Note: was also cast to play the pier photographer in *At Your Convenience* but released from his contract. Alec Bregonzi was his replacement but scene eventually cut.)
TV: *The Prisoner of Spenda* and *Under the Round Table*
Bristolian Ronnie Brody, born in 1918, was the son of music hall artistes Bourne and Lester. He joined the Merchant Navy at fifteen before serving with the RAF in North Africa during the Second World War.

After demob he spent several years in Variety and rep but by the 1950s, his career was dominated by both the big and small screen. Over the years he became one of the most instantly recognisable comedy character actors in the business.

During his career he worked with many top comedians in shows such as *Dave Allen at Large, The Dick Emery Show, Rising Damp, Bless This House, Home James, The Lenny Henry Show* and *The 19th Hole*. Among the films he appeared in were *Help!, A Funny Thing Happened on the Way to the Forum* and *Superman III*. Although often cast in comedy roles, he did occasionally appear in television dramas.

He died of a heart attack in 1991.

BROMLEY, SYDNEY
Role: Sam Houston in *Cowboy*
The bearded Sydney Bromley was a character actor who ran the gamut of roles on stage and

---

screen for decades without ever being the leading man. He played over one hundred Shakespearian roles for numerous companies, and performed in venues around the world, including Broadway.

Born in London in 1909, he was only twelve when he appeared in *Quality Street*. Three years later, he was part of the original production of *St Joan*, with Sybil Thorndike, the beginning of a fruitful stage career.

He was cast in many top television shows, usually one-off roles, including *Z Cars, The Pallisers, No Hiding Place, Dixon of Dock Green*, as well as films such as *Brief Encounter, Dark Road, A Date With A Dream, Operation Third Form, Half a Sixpence* and *Crystalstone*.

He died in 1987, aged seventy-eight.

BROOK, OLGA
Continuity on *Cleo*
Olga Brook began working in continuity from the mid-1930s and was assigned to some memorable films. During a career lasting more than three decades, her film credits included *Sleeping Car to Trieste, Morning Departure, Private's Progress, The Green Man, I'm All Right Jack* and *Smokescreen*.

BROOKING, JOHN
Role: 3rd Sealord in *Jack*
Supporting artist John Brooking, born in London in 1911, began a steady film and television career in the 1950s, appearing in such pictures as *Innocents in Paris, The Gift Horse, The Two-Headed Spy, An Honourable Murder* and *The Loneliness of the Long-Distance Runner*.

He was seen in various television programmes, such as *The Vise, The Cheaters* and *Danger Man*, and had a running part, Dr Stephen Brooks, in *Emergency – Ward 10*.

He died in 1966.

BROOKS, RAY
Role: Georgio in *Abroad*
Born in Brighton in 1939, Ray Brooks became an assistant stage manager at the age of sixteen and went on to appear many times in the West End in such productions as *Snap* and *Absent Friends*.

The voice behind the classic children's character Mr Benn, Brooks's other television work includes *Gideon's Way, Danger Man, Doomwatch, Coronation Street, Big Deal, Cathy Come Home, Growing Pains* and the recent BBC series, *Two Thousand Acres of Sky*.

He began working in films in 1961's *Girl on a Roof*, with other credits including *The Last Grenade, Tiffany Jones* and *House of Whipcord*.

BROOKS, SUSAN
Played by Zena Clifton
One of the beauty contestants eager to win the Miss Fircombe crown in *Girls*. A Scottish lass who embarrassingly slips on the catwalk

when the event's saboteurs, members of the Fircombe Women's Lib Movement who are against the contest, pour slippery liquid over the stage.

BROWNE, DEREK
Camera Operator on *Henry*

Born in Kenton, Middlesex, in 1927, Derek Browne left school at fourteen and began his career in the film industry at Denham Studios, working as a clapper boy on 1944's *On Approval* with Googie Withers and Clive Brook. Before he was called up for National Service, serving with the RAF in Palestine, he worked on and made an uncredited appearance in the 1940s classic, *A Canterbury Tale*.

He returned to civvy street and joined Pinewood in 1947, initially as a focus puller, but left after a year to work freelance, which he continued doing until retiring in the late 1990s after five decades in the business.

Promoted to camera operator in 1960, his first film in this capacity was Michael Powell's *The Queen's Guards*. Other credits include *The Bedford Incident*, *Zeppelin*, *For the Love of Ada*, *Omen II*, *Trail of the Pink Panther*, *Indiana Jones and the Last Crusade* and *Memphis Belle*.

BROWN, HERBERT
Played by Norman Rossington

A dimwit in *Sergeant* who's become part of the furniture around Heathercrest National Service Depot after failing to graduate from three different intakes. Just when it seems as if he'll never have the aptitude to pass out, he receives additional tuition from James Bailey and steps in to replace a sick member of Able Platoon for their final day of tests. It may be a shock to everyone's system but Brown joins up as a regular.

BROWN, MRS

Not seen at the Finisham Maternity Hospital in *Matron* but her specimen is! It's collected by Nurse Ball from Dr Prodd's consulting room.

BROWNING
Played by Brian Osborne

One of the Bow Street Runners in *Dick*.

BRUTUS
Played by Brian Oulton

Julius Caesar's political ally is seen in the senate during *Cleo*.

BRYAN, DORA
Role: Norah in *Sergeant*

Born in Parbold, Lancashire, in 1923, Dora Bryan made her name playing character parts in British movies during the 1940s and '50s, and for her long-running stage portrayal of Dolly Levi in the hit musical *Hello, Dolly!*, clocking up over 800 appearances in two years at Drury Lane.

Daughter of a director in a local cotton bobbin mill, she began her acting career at Oldham Repertory Theatre and by the time war was declared in 1939, she was leading lady. During hostilities, she joined ENSA, and made her West End debut shortly after.

By the 1950s she was a recognisable face on the screen, regularly cast as maids, waitresses, shop assistants and cooks in a host of films, including *Once Upon A Dream*, *Adam and Evelyne*, *The Interrupted Journey*, *Something in the City*, *No Highway* and *The Fake*. Excepting the role as Rita Tushingham's sluttish mother in *A Taste of Honey*, which Bryan regarded as her most important and won her a BAFTA for Best Actress, typecasting meant the scope of screen roles offered was limited.

She continued to act on the stage in countless productions and has made frequent excursions onto the television screen, including roles in *Last of the Summer Wine*, *Dinnerladies* and *Heartbeat*. (**Note: Bryan used to own the Clarges Hotel in Brighton, used as the location for the hotels in *At Your Convenience* and at Fircombe in *Girls*.**)

BUCK, JANE
Continuity on *Dick*

Jane Buck began her career in continuity during the 1950s. Among the films she worked on over the years are *Shadow of a Man*, *The Angry Hills*, *The Break*, *Clash By Night*, *Porridge*, *Chariots of Fire*, *Quartet* and latterly, in 1983, *Heat and Dust*.

BULL, CAPTAIN
Played by David Lodge

The captain was unsuccessful in trying to instil discipline into the experimental mixed-sex anti-aircraft battery 1313 in *England*. He was eventually driven to the bottle by the antics of the rabble he tried in vain to lead, relinquishing command, much to his delight, to Captain Melly, who arrives with hopes and aspirations, many of which are quashed within days.

BULLOCK
Played by David Lodge

One of the Bow Street Runners in *Dick*.

BULSTRODE, MISS

An unseen patient mentioned in *Again Doctor*. She's staying at Dr Nookey's private clinic for the weight-loss treatment which has secured him fame and fortune.

BULSTRODE, MR
Played by Philip Stone

The bank manager in *Convenience* whom Boggs goes to see about a loan to fulfil the large bidet order. (**Note: the scene was cut from the film.**)

WHAT MIGHT HAVE BEEN

INT. BANK MANAGER'S OFFICE. DAY

C.S. of door, as Boggs is shown in.

CASHIER: Mr Boggs, sir.

(As Boggs comes in, carrying a briefcase, the manager gets up and comes into shot to greet him and we now see that it is the man who was in the football ground stand with a hearing aid. His name is Bulstrode and (like most bank managers these days) he treats his caller very warily at first.)

BULSTRODE: My dear Mr Boggs, how good to see you again. Do sit down, sit down.

BOGGS: Thank you, Mr Bulstrode. And how have you been?

BULSTRODE: Oh, not too bad. But you know how trying this business is these days. Credit squeezes . . . bank rate . . . overdrafts . . . it's all very worrying.

BOGGS: Yes, yes, of course. In the circumstances, it must be a relief to know that it's other people's money you're gambling with?

BULSTRODE: (**Not sure about this.**) Yes . . . well, and what can I do for you?

BOGGS: (**Producing it.**) I thought you'd like to see this contract we've just taken on. (**Hands it over.**) For nineteen thousand odd, as you'll see . . .

BULSTRODE: Very good, Mr Boggs. Congratulations. This should put you well in credit again.

BOGGS: Thank you, Mr Bulstrode.

BULSTRODE: Yes, indeed. (**Producing box.**) A cigarette?

BOGGS: Thank you.

BULSTRODE: Just help yourself.

(Leaves open box in front of BOGGS and picks up telephone.)

BULSTRODE: Coffees please for myself and Mr Boggs.

(Replaces telephone.)

BULSTRODE: Well, this is very good news. Very good indeed.

BOGGS: I thought you'd be pleased.

BULSTRODE: I'm delighted, Mr Boggs. I don't mind telling you I've always had complete confidence in the ability of your firm.

BOGGS: You're too kind. Naturally there are one or two difficulties to be overcome yet.

BULSTRODE: (**Getting wary again.**) Yes?

BOGGS: As this is to be a completely new line for us, we'll have to invest in new moulds and various other things which I won't bother you with.

BULSTRODE: I understand, yes . . .

BOGGS: But a short term loan of . . . oh, fifteen hundred should cover it.

(BULSTRODE starts fiddling with his hearing aid.)

BULSTRODE: I don't seem to be hearing you, Mr Boggs.

BOGGS: (**Louder.**) I shall require a short term loan of fifteen hundred pounds!

BULSTRODE: That's what I thought you said! That's quite impossible, Mr Boggs. You're already in debt to us for too much as it is!

(He grabs the cigarette box, snaps lid shut and puts it back in his drawer.)

BULSTRODE: I cannot authorise any more. I hate to appear mean, Mr Boggs, but I'm sorry.

(And he picks up telephone again.)

BULSTRODE: Cancel that coffee!

BUMBLE, MAYOR FREDERICK
Played by Kenneth Connor

The mayor of Fircombe is seen in *Girls*. An ineffectual man who's regarded as a joke around the streets of this seaside town, he's booed off the stage while preparing to say a few words at the Miss Fircombe beauty contest. Married to Mildred, a slovenly woman who does little for his status in the town.

BUMBLE, MILDRED
Played by Patsy Rowlands

The frumpish wife of Frederick Bumble does little to improve her husband's standing as mayor of Fircombe, a seaside town in desperate need of a makeover. A heavy smoker, who spends much of her time in the lavatory or slouching around in her slippers and dressing-gown, much to Frederick's disgust, who classes her as an 'old compost heap'. When she can't take her husband's pomposity any more, she joins Augusta Prodworthy's women's lib movement. Seen in *Girls*.

BUNG, DETECTIVE SERGEANT SIDNEY
Played by Harry H. Corbett

In charge of investigations into the disappearance of Doris Mann, the sixth woman to vanish from Hocombe Woods within the year. Unhappily married to Emily, he accepts any chance to return to work, and ends up leaving his wife to be looked after by Virula Watt, whom he meets while sorting out the Mann case. He appears in *Screaming!*

BUNG, EMILY
Played by Joan Sims

The miserable, nagging wife of Detective Sergeant Sidney Bung who ends up being turned into a mannequin in *Screaming!* Just to prove there was not the slightest whiff of romance left in their relationship, Sidney decided to leave her as a dummy when he had the chance to return her to normality, preferring the charms of Virula Watt instead.

BUNGHIT DIN
Played by Bernard Bresslaw

The leader of the Burpas who's based in the hill town of Jacksi in Afghanistan. Seen in *Up The Khyber* causing confusion and mayhem for the men of the 3rd Foot and Mouth company.

BUNGHIT'S SERVANT
Played by David Spenser

As the Khasi and Bunghit are lounging, whilst Jelhi plays and sings in *Up The Khyber*, the servant enters and announces that the chiefs have arrived, opening their eyes to the fact that the ones they've been entertaining are impostors.

BUNN WARD
A ward in Finisham Maternity Hospital. Seen in *Matron*.

BUNNY WAITRESS
Played by Shirley Stelfox

Works at the Whippit Inn in *At Your Convenience*. While serving Lewis Boggs and Myrtle Plummer, who are dining out at the inn, Lewis doesn't know where to look when she leans over in her low-cut bunny outfit.

BUREAU OF INTERNAL AFFAIRS
Based in Washington, the Commissioner of the Bureau is seen in *Cowboy*, initially enjoying a bit of fun with a woman in his office until interrupted by Perkins, his assistant. A former janitor at the law school Judge Burke attended, he responds to Burke's request for a peace marshal at Stodge City but can't find anyone to fill the position until Marshall P. Knutt walks in looking for a job. Assuming he's actually a marshal, he packs him off to Stodge City.

BURGER, COMMANDANT
Played by Kenneth Williams

In charge of the Foreign Legion unit in *Follow That Camel*, Maximillion Burger used to teach fencing at a Viennese finishing school before donning the legion's uniform. While working in Vienna he met and fell in love with Lady Jane Ponsonby; when their relationship ended he found solace in escaping city life for the openness of the Sahara. Can't believe his eyes, though, when his old girlfriend turns up in the middle of the desert.

BURKE, GRIPPER
Played by Bernard Bresslaw

A professional wrestler who's been fighting in America for years before returning home to his previous girlfriend, Esme Crowfoot. Seen in *Loving*, this man-mountain acts like an animal and isn't to be messed around with, which Sidney Bliss – who fancied his chances with Esme before Gripper appeared on the scene – finds out. After rekindling their relationship, Gripper and Esme get engaged.

BURKE, JUDGE
Played by Kenneth Williams

An attorney by profession, Judge Burke is also mayor of Stodge City; he has strict views regarding how the place should be run, preventing impropriety by demanding no shooting, fighting, boozing, gambling and 'no

nothing'. His influence vanishes, though, the moment Johnny Finger, alias the Rumpo Kid, rides into town.

The Burke family has been resident in the area ever since his great-grandfather sailed to America on the Mayflower, married into the Wright family and became a 'Wright Burke'. Seen in *Cowboy*.

BURKE, SIR EDMUND
Played by Derek Francis

The irascible chairman of the Borough County Hospital's committee, he presides over Dr Kilmore's disciplinary hearing in *Doctor*. He says he's prepared to listen to Kilmore's case fairly despite the young doctor having bumped into his Jag, but doesn't seem to live up to his word when he quickly asks Kilmore if he's a sex maniac.

BURPA AT DOOR-GRID
Played by Larry Taylor

Seen in *Up The Khyber* guarding the door at Bunghit Din's house in Jacksi.

BURPA GUARD
Played by Steven Scott

In *Up The Khyber*, the Burpa Guard gets knocked out by Lady Joan Ruff-Diamond. Tasked with guarding the jailed British soldiers who tried to recover the embarrassing photo of the Devils in Skirts wearing underpants.

BURPA IN CROWD
Played by Patrick Westwood

Seen in *Up The Khyber*, the Burpa shouts from a crowd which has gathered to hear the Khasi of Kalabar's cries of help in his planned uprising against the British. The Burpa isn't confident that they could topple the Brits.

BURPA ON ROOFTOP
Played by John Hallam

Just as the Burpas prepare to attack the British governor's residency in *Up The Khyber*, Bunghit Din and the Khasi of Kalabar hear music drifting through the air. Bunghit asks the Burpa what he can see and reports back that the British have sat for dinner, despite shells and bullets flying around them.

BURT
Played by George Mossman

For Burt in *Cowboy*, see 'Stage Coach Driver'.

BURTON, LOUISE
Roles: Private Evans in *England* and Girl at Zoo in *Emmannuelle*

Brighton-born Louise Burton began acting professionally at the age of thirteen, working on commercials and a special *Jackanory* series. After studying at Italia Conti upon leaving school, she appeared on stage and screen, including *The Dick Emery Show* and *Mind Your Language* for television.

She quit acting in 1988 when her first child was born, at which point she'd been a regular for seven years on an afternoon show, *That's My Dog*.

BURTON, PETER

Role: Hotel Manager in *At Your Convenience*

Peter Burton, born in Bromley, Kent, in 1921, had been working on stage for several years when he entered the film industry in 1950's prisoner-of-war title, *The Wooden Horse*. Other early credits include *What the Butler Saw, The Tall Headlines, They Who Dare, The Green Scarf, The Long Arm* and *Sink the Bismarck!*.

Burton appeared as Major Boothroyd (the character was later known as Q) in the first Bond movie, *Dr No*, in 1962, but when he was unavailable for the second film, *From Russia With Love*, Desmond Llewelyn replaced him. Other big screen credits include *A Clockwork Orange, The Bitch, The Jigsaw Man* and, his last film, *The Doctor and the Devils*.

On television he's appeared in programmes ranging from *The Avengers* and *The Saint* to *The Professionals* and *UFO*.

BUS CONDUCTOR

Played by Anthony Sagar

The bus conductor is seen in *Regardless* refusing permission for Francis Courtenay to bring Yoki, a pet monkey he's been asked to exercise, on the bus.

BUS CONDUCTOR

Played by Kenny Lynch

The Bus Conductor is seen climbing the steps of the double-decker in *Loving*. He asks for fares from Bertie Muffet and the young lovers who can't stop kissing each other.

BUSINESS MAN

Played by Michael Nightingale

In *Cabby*, the Business Man enters the cab drivers' café and asks if someone will take him to the Station Hotel. He's more than happy to accept a ride from Anthea, one of the glamour girls from Glamcabs, even though protocol among the taxi-driving fraternity means one of the men, who'd been waiting longer for a customer, should have had the job.

BUSTI

Played by Alexandra Dane

One of the Khasi of Kalabar's wives seen in *Up The Khyber*, Busti becomes a volunteer when the Fakir entertains.

BUTCHER, MAJOR

Played by Julian Holloway

Based at the experimental 1313 anti-aircraft battery and seen in *England*. Ably assisted by his nurse, he examines the long line of slackers who report to sick bay when the new unit commander, Captain Melly, gets tough with the men and women in the battery. His answer to every ailment reported is to dish out a couple of Aspirin and send them on their way.

BUTTERWORTH, PETER

Roles: Doc in *Cowboy*, Detective Constable Slobotham in *Screaming!*,Citizen Bidet in *Don't Lose Your Head*, Simpson in *Follow That Camel*, Mr Smith in *Doctor*, Brother Belcher in *Up The Khyber*, Josh Fiddler in *Camping*, Shuffling Patient in *Again Doctor*, Sinister Client in *Loving*, Charles, Earl of Bristol in *Henry*, Pepe in *Abroad*, Admiral in *Girls*, Tom in *Dick*, Henry Barnes in *Behind*, Major Carstairs in *England* and Richmond in *Emmannuelle*

TV: *Christmas* (69), *Christmas* (72), *What a Carry On!*, *Christmas* (73), *The Prisoner of Spenda, The Baron Outlook, The Sobbing Cavalier, The Case of the Screaming Winkles, The Case of the Coughing Parrot, Under the Round Table, Short Knight, Long Daze, And in My Lady's Chamber* and *Lamp Posts of the Empire*

STAGE: *London!* and *Laughing*

Peter Butterworth didn't join the *Carry On* outfit until Peter Rogers and Co. headed west in *Cowboy*, the eleventh in the series, but quickly became one of the mainstays. His characterisations often possessed a diffidence and dithering nature, highlighted by his portrayal of Detective Constable Slobotham in *Screaming!* Far from assisting his superior, his incompetency simply compounds the lack of progress being made on the case of the missing Doris Mann.

Born in Bramhall, Greater Manchester, in 1919, Butterworth was approaching thirty

Peter Butterworth appeared in 16 *Carry On* films

> ### MEMORIES
>
> 'The thing about Peter is that he was one of the few people in this theatrical world who never talked about his work; he never spoke about himself outside to other actors. I never saw him studying scripts, including the *Carry Ons*, but I know he loved the camaraderie on the films.'
>
> **JANET BROWN –**
> Peter Butterworth's widow

before he turned to acting professionally. It looked as if a military career beckoned and when war broke out, he joined the Fleet Air Arm, but his flying days were shortlived when his plane was shot down off the Dutch coast in 1941 and he was taken to a POW camp where he spent the remaining war years.

While at the camp he met a fellow prisoner, none other than writer Talbot Rothwell, who would help change his life for ever. They struck up a friendship and Rothwell cajoled Butterworth into taking part in a camp concert, the primary objective being to prevent the German soldiers from hearing the noise of fellow prisoners desperately trying to escape.

When the war ended, Butterworth returned to England and pursued an acting career. Before long he was appearing in summer shows, revues and repertory theatre, before branching out into television, initially in children's programmes. As his career developed, he started being offered more than just comedy roles in shows such as *Emergency – Ward 10*, *Public Eye* and a 1964 episode of *Danger Man*.

As well as small-screen success, he was kept busy on the stage and from the late 1940s onwards, in films too, including *Murder at the Windmill*, *Night and the City*, *Blow Your Own Trumpet*, *Murder She Said*, *A Home of Your Own* and *The Day the Earth Caught Fire*.

Married to comedienne and impressionist Janet Brown, Butterworth died of a heart attack in 1979, shortly before he was due to appear in a matinee performance of *Aladdin* at the Coventry Theatre.

BUXOM LASS
Played by Margaret Nolan
The buxom beauty is chased like an animal across the fields by Henry VIII and his men in *Henry*.

MEMORIES

'I did lots of bits and pieces for Peter Rogers and Gerald Thomas, including brief roles in *Watch Your Stern*, *Raising the Wind* and *The Iron Maiden*. I had a similar small part in *Cabby*, just a few lines, yet I receive fan mail – can you believe that?

'I remember I was running from one set to another and got lost while driving over to the location near Pinewood. Eventually I turned up and we got on with the scene. I'd never met the girl [Marion Collins] who played my bride but we were introduced, went into the clinch, said "goodbye" and that was the last I saw of her – that's showbusiness. It was very pleasant, though.

'When I was in *Raising the Wind*, I was in a sequence involving the orchestra. Although it wasn't a *Carry On* film there were a lot of the same faces, including Ken Williams and Leslie Phillips, and one of the press officers came in with a group of Japanese journalists. I couldn't get over it because they treated Ken and Leslie as if they were Robert Redford and Cary Grant! They went absolutely barmy when they saw the pair of them. It was the first indication, in my view, how big they'd become worldwide.'

PETER BYRNE

When she hides in a barn, Henry follows and tries forcing himself on her until the girl's father, who hates royalty, arrives on the scene.

BYRNE, PETER
Role: Bridegroom in *Cabby*
Born in London in 1928, Peter Byrne left school and worked in a theatrical agent's office for several months while waiting for a place at the Italia Conti Stage School. He joined the drama school in 1944 but was soon working professionally, beginning with a propaganda documentary for Lewis Gilbert titled *Sailors Do Care*.

In 1945 he joined the Will Hay act on radio and, later, performed in the Jack Hylton revue, *Crying Out Loud*, before, in 1946, being called up for National Service. After leaving the army two years later, Byrne worked in various repertory theatres, including Farnham, Margate and Worthing, where he appeared in the stage adaptation of *The Blue Lamp*. He remained with the show when it moved to Blackpool and the West End.

Later, in 1955, he joined the cast of *Dixon of Dock Green* as Andy Crawford and stayed twenty years, by which time his character was a detective inspector. Other television credits include *The Pattern of Marriage* (his small-screen debut), *The Jazz Age*, *Blake's 7* and, lastly, Derek in the successful sitcom, *Bread*.

In films he played small parts in first features as well as meatier roles in second features but bowed out of this side of the business to concentrate on television and theatre. He's appeared in numerous West End roles in such shows as *There's A Girl In My Soup*, *September Tide* and, most recently, *The Mousetrap*, which he now directs.

CAB DRIVER
Played by Hugh Futcher

Pulls up in his taxi during *Again Doctor*. He drops Gladstone Screwer off at Dr Nookey's posh clinic but doesn't expect to be paid in cigarettes!

CABBY
Played by Norman Mitchell

Seen in *Screaming!* driving Emily Bung and Mrs Parker around in his taxi when Emily, suspecting her husband of having an affair, wants to keep her beady eye on him.

CABBY, CARRY ON
See feature box on pages 54–5.

CADMAN, TOM
Stills Cameraman on *Dick*

CAESAR, JULIUS
Played by Kenneth Williams

In *Cleo*, the leader of the Roman Empire, or that's what he likes to believe, is a weak-kneed individual hanging on to power by the skin of his teeth.

CAFÉ EL ZIGZIG
Seen in *Spying*, the café in Algiers is situated in the Street of A Thousand Artisans and where the British agents spot the Fat Man sitting outside wearing a fez.

CAFÉ MOZART
The café in Vienna where the British agent, Carstairs, arranges to meet Simkins and his team of trainee agents in *Spying*.

CAFÉ ZIGAZIG
Owned by Zig-Zig, this busy café is seen in *Follow That Camel*.

CAFFIN WARD
In *Doctor*, this is a women's ward at the Borough County Hospital.

CAFFIN, YVONNE
Costume Designer on *Constable*, *Spying*, *Doctor* and *Camping*

Born in Johannesburg, South Africa, in 1904, Yvonne Caffin trained at RADA and then worked in research at the Academy before entering the film industry before the war, working for Gaumont-British and Mayflower. She later joined Islington Studios and Rank, where she spent the lion's share of her career.

Films she worked on over the years include *Miranda*, *The Astonished Heart*, *The Browning Version*, *To Paris With Love*, *Hell Drivers*, *Doctor in Clover*, *A Night to Remember*, *Tiara Tahiti*, *The Big Job* and, finally, *The Executioner*.

She died in 1985, aged eighty-one.

CAIN, SIMON
Roles: Short in *Cowboy*, Riff at Abdul's Tent in *Follow That Camel*, Tea Orderly in *Doctor*, Bagpipe Soldier in *Up The Khyber*, X-Ray Man in *Again Doctor* and Barman in *At Your Convenience*

Born in Orpington, Kent, Simon Cain, while attending Banstead Residential School, volunteered to go to Australia at the age of eleven. At Kingsley Fairbridge Farm School in Western Australia he was taught about life in the outback. At sixteen, he set off on a six-year trip around Australia, moving between jobs, including sheep shearer and motorbike mechanic.

While living in Perth in 1960, earning a living selling television sets, he became interested in amateur dramatics and, later, moved to Sydney where he began appearing in small parts on stage and in films, as well as making the occasional commercial. Other offers soon came his way and he appeared in several episodes of the Australian television Western, *Whiplash*, and films such as *Summer of the Seventeenth Doll*, *The Sundowners* and *Coast Watchers*. Additional credits during the early 1960s included television adaptations of *The Merchant of Venice* and the stage plays *Show Boat* and *Once Upon a Mattress*.

He returned to England in 1964 and while working for Schweppes secured a part in a play for the Little Theatre Club at London's St Martin's Theatre, paving the way for a string of television roles in shows such as *Gideon's Way*.

Other television work has seen him in shows such as *Doctor Who*, *Ryan International*, *Manhunt* and *Doomwatch*, while his film credits include *The Blood Beast Terror*, *School for Love*, *The Chairman* and, in 1969, *The Most Dangerous Man in the World*.

CAKE, FRANCIS
Played by Mavise Fyson

One of the beauty contestants seen in *Girls*.

CALPURNIA
Played by Joan Sims

The cantankerous wife of Julius Caesar is seen in *Cleo*, tired of being left at home while her husband roams the world conquering nations.

CAMEMBERT, CITIZEN
Played by Kenneth Williams

The most feared man in France, although it's hard to see why, Citizen Camembert is chief of the secret police and is seen in *Don't Lose Your Head*. The finest pistol shot in France, Camembert is a key player in the French Revolution, taking great pleasure in sending the aristocracy to the guillotine. When the Black Fingernail, alias Sir Rodney Ffing, arrives from England and causes havoc by saving people from the chop, Camembert is instructed to stop him at all costs, leading him to England in his pursuit.

CAMPING, CARRY ON
See feature box on pages 58–9,

CAMPION, GERALD
Role: Andy Galloway in *Sergeant*

Born in London in 1921, at the age of fifteen Campion trained at RADA before working for BBC radio and acting on the stage in shows such as *French Without Tears* and *Goodbye Mr Chips*.

He was posted to Kenya during World War Two, serving as an RAF wireless operator, after which he returned to England and, due to lack of acting work, opened a club, The Buckstone.

In 1952 he was offered the title role in the BBC series *Billy Bunter of Greyfriars School*, which ran for ten years and brought him widespread recognition. He went on to appear in, among others, *Doctor Who*, *Minder*, *Sherlock Holmes* and *The Kenny Everett Show* and

CARRY ON CABBY

An Anglo Amalgamated film
A Peter Rogers production
Distributed by the Rank Organisation
Based on an original idea by S.C. Green and R.M. Hills
Released as a U certificate in 1963 in black & white
Running time: 91 mins

CAST

Sidney James . . . . Charlie Hawkins
Hattie Jacques . . . . Peggy Hawkins
Charles Hawtrey . . . Terry 'Pintpot' Tankard
Kenneth Connor . . . . Ted Watson
Esma Cannon . . . . Flo Sims
Liz Fraser . . . . Sally
Bill Owen . . . . Smiley
Milo O'Shea . . . . Len
Jim Dale . . . . Expectant Father
Judith Furse . . . . Battleaxe
Renée Houston . . . . Molly
Ambrosine Phillpotts . . . . Aristocratic Lady
Amanda Barrie . . . . Anthea
Carole Shelley . . . . Dumb Driver
Cyril Chamberlain . . . . Sarge
Norman Chappell . . . . Allbright
Peter Gilmore . . . . Dancy

Michael Ward . . . . Man in Tweeds
Noel Dyson . . . . District Nurse
Norman Mitchell . . . Bespectacled Business Man
Michael Nightingale . . . . Business Man
Ian Wilson . . . . Clerk
Peter Byrne . . . . Bridegroom
Darryl Kavann . . . . Punchy
Don McCorkindale . . . . Tubby
Charles Stanley . . . . Geoff
Marion Collins . . . . Bride

Peter Jesson . . . . Car Salesman
Frank Forsyth . . . . Chauffeur
Marian Horton
Valerie Van Ost . . . . Glamcab Drivers
(Uncredited Glamcab drivers: Elizabeth Kent, Dominique Don, Carole Cole, Anabella MacCartney, Audrey Wilson, Beverly Bennett, Heather Downham, Jean Hamilton, Christine Rodgers, Sally Ann Shaw and Maris Tant.)

PRODUCTION TEAM

Screenplay by Talbot Rothwell
Music composed and conducted by Eric Rogers
Associate Producer: Frank Bevis
Art Director: Jack Stephens
Editor: Archie Ludski
Director of Photography: Alan Hume BSC
Camera Operator: Godfrey Godar
Unit Manager: Donald Toms
Assistant Director: Peter Bolton
Sound Editor: Arthur Ridout
Sound Recordists: Bill Daniels and Gordon K. McCallum
Hairdressing: Biddy Chrystal
Make-up Artists: Geoffrey Rodway and Jim Hydes
Continuity: Penny Daniels
Costume Designer: Joan Ellacott
The Producers acknowledged the assistance of The London General Cab Co. Ltd and The Ford Motor Company Limited in the making of the film.
Producer: Peter Rogers
Director: Gerald Thomas

Charlie Hawkins has his work cut out training his new drivers

Flo (Esma Cannon) is prevented from earning a few extra pennies by Allbright (Norman Chappell)

Charlie Hawkins is the proud owner of Speedee Taxis, dedicating so much time to his work that his relationship with his wife, Peggy, who feels neglected and unloved, suffers. The final straw comes when Charlie, who'd forgotten their wedding anniversary until reminded by his wife, fails to arrive home in time to take her out for a meal. A last-minute cabbing job had turned into a nightmare, ferrying an expectant woman and her husband back and forth to the hospital.

Feeling increasingly depressed, coupled with the knowledge that her dream of starting a family and settling into a quiet country-cottage lifestyle seems increasingly remote, Peggy decides it's time for revenge. Speedee Taxis have been unhindered by competition in the district since the company was established, so she forms a rival taxi firm and gives her uncaring husband a run for his money. After buying a fleet of new Ford Cortinas and employing a team of leggy lovelies to drive them, Glamcabs opens for business, without Charlie knowing that the driving force behind his competitor is none other than his own wife. Before long, the company is the most popular taxi firm in town, hitting Charlie Hawkins where it hurts the most – in his pocket. Customers, particularly men, opt for Glamcabs every time: new motors and attractive drivers have much more pulling power than crusty old men driving antiquated wrecks.

Charlie reaches for the bottle as business hits rock bottom; attempts to sabotage his rival's vehicles and to pinch their business by intercepting their radio messages fail. Unable to muster any more ideas to see off Glamcabs, Charlie realises there is no option but to reluctantly meet Mrs Glam and discuss a merger, but nothing prepares him for the shock when he discovers that Mrs Glam is none other than his wife.

It looks as if irreparable damage has been done to the Hawkins's marriage, but when Peggy and her closest friend, Sally, run into trouble, it's Charlie who comes to the rescue. While the girls are heading for the bank with their takings, two crooks jump in their Glamcab and force them at gunpoint to drive out of town; with their lives in peril, Charlie coordinates a bold rescue using his fleet of taxis. After eventually catching the criminals and freeing his beloved, Charlie receives further good news when he hears he's going to be a father.

Funny Scene!

Ted Watson enters the canteen at Speedee Taxis and walks over to his girlfriend, Sally, who works there.

```
TED:    I think I'll have a fourpenny roll with you.
SALLY:  That's enough sauce out of you, Ted Watson.
        (Embarrassed.) If you don't shut up . . .
TED:    Well, give us a kiss, then.
SALLY:  No, I won't!
        (Ted grabs Sally and kisses her forcefully.)
SALLY:  (Struggling free.) Oh, I wish I had a nice big
        spanner handy.
TED:    (Smiling.) Oh, so do I. I'd get you loosened up
        a bit.
```

Flo (Esma Cannon) and Peggy (Hattie Jacques) consult (*Cabby*)

accrued a number of film credits including *School for Scoundrels*, *Those Magnificent Men In Their Flying Machines*, *Chitty Chitty Bang Bang* and *Half A Sixpence*.

His screen work was also combined with a fruitful career as a hotelier, restaurateur and club owner. He retired eleven years before his death in 2002, aged eighty-one.

CAMPLING, DAVID
Dubbing Editor on *Doctor*

Working in films as a sound editor from the mid-1960s, David Campling's credits include films such as *The Magnificent Two*, *To Catch A Spy*, *The Terminator*, *Platoon!*, *A Tiger's Tale*, *The Bounty Hunter*, *Thieves of Fortune*, *Flamingo Dreams* and *Wild Turkey*.

His television work covers programmes such as *Knot's Landing: Back to the Cul-de-Sac*, a mini-series revisiting the successful American show, and many films specially for the genre.

CANNON, ESMA
Roles: Deaf Old Lady in *Constable*; Miss Cooling in *Regardless*, Bridget Madderley in *Cruising* and Flo Sims in *Cabby*

Born in Sydney, Australia, in 1896, the diminutive Esma Cannon, who was adept at playing twitchy, nervous, forgetful spinsters and maids, travelled to England in the early 1930s to pursue an acting career.

Beginning in theatre, she entered films in the late 1930s with productions such as *The £5 Man*, *The Last Adventurers* and *Ladies in Love*. She took a seven-year break from acting, due to a shortage of suitable parts on offer, and worked in stage management.

In just under three decades she clocked up over sixty films, including *Contraband*, *Quiet Wedding*, *Asking for Trouble*, *A Canterbury Tale*, *Jassy*, *Here Come the Huggetts*, *Out of the Clouds*, *Nurse On Wheels* and her last film, in 1963, *Hide and Seek*. She appeared infrequently on the small screen, her most notable role being Lily in the 1960s comedy, *The Rag Trade*.

She died in 1972, aged seventy-six.

CAPTAIN HOOK
The cheeky parrot is owned by the Bird Owner in *Regardless*.

CAPTAIN OF SOLDIERS
Played by Richard Shaw

Seen in *Don't Lose Your Head*, the Captain is instructed by Citizen Camembert to guard Jacqueline night and day.

CAR SALESMAN
Played by Peter Jesson

The salesman at Peacocks of Balham sells fifteen Ford Cortinas to Peggy Hawkins when she launches the Glamcab taxi business.

CARDEW, JANE
Role: Henry's 2nd Wife in *Henry* (Note: scene was cut.)

Born in Redhill, Surrey, in 1944, Jane Cardew left school and headed for Paris to study French at college before returning to England in 1966 and starting a career in the theatre, initially as an acting assistant stage manager at Hornchurch Rep. She completed summer seasons and worked as stage manager at Chichester Festival Theatre and three years at the Greenwich

Theatre. Later, she worked as stage manager for various opera companies.

During her twenties she accepted modelling assignments between acting jobs, and later in her career television and film roles came her way including episodes of *Jason King* and *The Bill*.

She retired from acting in 1983 to look after her children but now works as a freelance proof reader and copy editor.

CARGILL, PATRICK
Roles: Raffish Customer in *Regardless* and Spanish Governor in *Jack*. Also, the script for *Nurse* was based on an idea submitted by Cargill and Jack Beale

Born in London in 1918, Patrick Cargill trained at Sandhurst for a military career and went to India to work as an officer in the Indian Army before returning to England to pursue an acting career.

During World War Two he travelled again to India, this time as an entertainments officer after which, back in Britain, he acted in repertory theatre and wrote plays and scripts, staging comedies including *Time On Their Hands* and *Ring for Catty* in the mid-1950s.

In the 1960s, Patrick moved into roles in television and film, with parts in television programmes *Top Secret*, *The Avengers*, *The Prisoner* and *The Georges Feydeau Farces* and then his own comedy show *Father, Dear Father* which ran for six years and was followed by another successful show *The Many Wives of Patrick*.

His film credits included *Around the World in Eighty Days*, *Up the Creek*, the Beatles' film *Help*, *A Countess from Hong Kong*, *Up Pompeii* and *Barnet*.

During the 1980s and '90s, Cargill, who still acted occasionally in the West End alongside his screen work, returned to the stage wholeheartedly, performing in productions such as *Key For Two*, *HMS Pinafore* and *Captain Beaky* and writing and touring with the play *Don't Misunderstand Me*.

He died in 1996, aged seventy-seven.

CARLIN, JOHN
Roles: Officer in *England* and French Parson in *Emmannuelle*

TV: *The Baron Outlook*, *Orgy and Bess*, *One in the Eye for Harold*, *The Nine Old Cobblers*, *The Case of the Screaming Winkles* and *Lamp Posts of the Empire*

John Carlin, now retired, worked in television and films from the 1950s, appearing in shows such as *Dixon of Dock Green*, *The Troubleshooters*, *Hadleigh* and *Nanny*. He had semi-regular roles as the barman in *Man About the House*, the House of Commons Speaker in *The New Statesman* and Reverend Spink in *The Darling Buds of May*. His film work includes the 1977 production, *Holocaust 2000*.

The Spanish Governor (Patrick Cargill) has his hands full (*Jack*)

CAROL

Played by Sherrie Hewson

In *Behind* she arrives at the Riverside Caravan Site by bike with her friend, Sandra. They hoped to camp at the site but are disappointed to find only caravans are allowed, that is until Sandra shows a bit of leg to the owner, Major Leep, and suggests she might need a massage later to aid her aching leg; the sight of flesh sees the Major bending the rules to accommodate the girls. Others who take a fancy to the girls include Fred and Ernie, two middle-aged men enjoying a short break away from their wives, but the girls are more interested in the students from the University of Kidburn who are helping Professor Crump with his archaeological dig.

CARON, SANDRA

Role: Fanny in *Camping*

Sister of popular British singer Alma Cogan, actress Sandra Caron has worked both sides of the Atlantic during a career which began on stage. She entered television in the 1950s and appeared in various programmes, including *Dixon of Dock Green* and *Suspense*. In the '70s she was seen in America working on shows such as *Charlie's Angels* and *The Odd Couple*, but her longest-running role saw her playing Mumsie/Auntie Sabrina for three years in

Channel 4's *The Crystal Maze*. One of her more recent jobs was playing a farmer's wife in the 1992 TV movie, *To Be the Best*.

Her film career, which started in the late 1950s, includes credits such as *Sea Wife*; *The Leather Boys*; *The Bliss of Mrs Blossom*; *Digby, the Biggest Dog in the World* and *The Dicktator*.

CARRIER

Played by Jim Dale

In *Jack*, the Carrier takes Midshipman Poop-Decker to the docks in Plymouth; he also recommends visiting Dirty Dick's if Poop-Decker is in need of entertainment.

CARROLL, EDWINA

Role: Nerda in *Up the Jungle*

Edwina Carroll entered films and television in the 1950s. Her TV work includes appearances in *White Hunter, The Troubleshooters, Department S, Paul Temple* and *UFO*. On the big screen, she's been seen in films such as *A Town Like Alice, Yesterday's Enemy, Genghis Khan* and *2001: A Space Odyssey*.

CARRYOONS, THE

In production at the time of writing, the idea behind the Carryoons was conceived in 1999 when Ken Burns approached Peter Rogers with an idea to produce twenty-six half-hour cartoons based around the legendary characters in

the films. With Rogers' backing, Burns – who'd edited ITV's documentary, *What's A Carry On?*, celebrating forty years of the film canon – began working on a pilot episode. Although the idea wasn't to remake the films, it was agreed to kick-off by basing the pilot around a familiar premise – *Camping*.

Once the pilot, titled *Carryoon Camping*, was complete, it was taken to the MIP COM 2001, Europe's biggest TV market, in Cannes to try and attract interest from within the industry. Although, as yet, the pilot has yet to be transmitted, further episodes in the series are currently being made. For further information, visit the official website, www.carryoons.com

CARSON, MR

The unseen headmaster at Maudlin Street Secondary Modern School. While he's absent from the school, his deputy, Mr Wakefield, steps into the breach. His name is mentioned in *Teacher*.

CARSTAIRS

Played by Jim Dale

In *Spying*, Carstairs is the Vienna-based agent who sends a coded message to the Director of Security Operations explaining that Milchmann, a wanted man since blowing up Professor Stark and stealing a secret formula, has arrived in the

CARRY ON CAMPING

Alternative title . . . *Let Sleeping Bags Lie*

A Peter Rogers production
Distributed through Rank Organisation
Released as an A certificate in 1969 in colour
Running time: 88 mins

CAST

Sidney James . . . . Sid Boggle
Kenneth Williams . . . . . Dr Kenneth Soaper
Joan Sims . . . . Joan Fussey
Charles Hawtrey . . . . Charlie Muggins
Terry Scott . . . . Peter Potter
Barbara Windsor . . . . Babs
Bernard Bresslaw . . . . Bernie Lugg
Hattie Jacques . . . . Miss Haggerd
Peter Butterworth . . . . Josh Fiddler
Julian Holloway . . . . Jim Tanner
Dilys Laye . . . . Anthea Meeks
Betty Marsden . . . . Harriet Potter
Trisha Noble . . . . Sally
Amelia Bayntun . . . . Mrs Fussey
Brian Oulton . . . . Store Manager
Patricia Franklin . . . . Farmer's Daughter
Derek Francis . . . . Farmer
Michael Nightingale . . . . . . Man in Cinema
Sandra Caron . . . . Fanny
George Moon . . . . Scrawny Man
Valerie Shute . . . . Pat
Elizabeth Knight . . . . Jane
Georgina Moon . . . . Joy
Vivien Lloyd . . . . Verna
Jennifer Pyle . . . . Hilda
Lesley Duff . . . . Norma
Jackie Poole . . . . Betty
Anna Karen . . . . Hefty Girl
Sally Kemp . . . . Girl with Cow
Valerie Leon . . . . Store Assistant
Peter Cockburn . . . . Commentator
Gilly Grant . . . . Sally G-String
Michael Low
Mike Lucas . . . . Lusty Youths

PRODUCTION TEAM

Screenplay by Talbot Rothwell
Music composed and conducted by Eric
    Rogers
Production Manager: Jack Swinburne
Art Director: Lionel Couch
Editor: Alfred Roome
Director of Photography: Ernest Steward
    BSC

Assistant Editor: Jack Gardner
Camera Operator: James Bawden
Assistant Director: Jack Causey
Continuity: Doreen Dernley
Sound Recordists: Bill Daniels and
    Ken Barker
Make-up: Geoffrey Rodway
Hairdresser: Stella Rivers
Costume Designer: Yvonne
    Caffin
Dubbing Editor: Colin Miller
Title sketches by 'Larry'
Producer: Peter Rogers
Director: Gerald Thomas

Charles Hawtrey on set with his mother

Sid Boggle and Bernie Lugg take their girlfriends, Joan and Anthea, to the cinema to watch a film about nudists at a holiday camp; the girls are not amused and find the film offensive but it doesn't stop Sid and Bernie secretly planning to take them there on holiday.

They decide the best course of action is to remain tight-lipped about the destination chosen for the camping holiday, but by the time they arrive at the site in Devon, the girls have twigged where they've heard the name Paradise Camp and want to head home; but after driving for hours, Sid tells them they're going in. He's soon disappointed, though, when everyone is walking around fully-clothed and he realises he's picked the wrong site.

Other campers at the site include the Potters, who arrive on their tandem for yet another stint in the muddy fields of Paradise, much to the reluctance of Peter, who's not only fed up with camping but with his wife, too. Charlie Muggins, meanwhile, is an irritant who's forever scrounging off fellow campers, while a coachload of girls from Chayste Place, a finishing school, bring smiles to the faces of Sid Boggins and Bernie Lugg, who feel they're not making much progress with their girlfriends. They begin flirting with Babs and Fanny, but attempts to lure them into their tents are continually scuppered.

Meanwhile, Peter Potter becomes a changed man. After turning to the bottle through sheer frustration with life, a chance encounter sees him invited to the tent of the promiscuous Jane, one of the schoolgirls; the experience works wonders and he asserts himself on his domineering wife; after throwing Charlie Muggins out of the tent, which he's been sharing since arriving at the camp site, he drags his wife inside for a bit of nooky.

Sid (Sid James) and Jim (Julian Holloway) don hippy gear and wreak havoc with the electrics

Over in Sid and Bernie's tent, they're waiting for Babs and Fanny to arrive, but when loud music is heard in the adjoining field, they rush to investigate and find the girls enjoying themselves at an all-nite rave. Eventually the campers drive the hippies away, but the girls go, too. Sid and Bernie, however, realise they don't need Babs and Fanny when they've got Joan and Anthea, but first they have to deal with the arrival of Mrs Fussey, who's worried about her daughter's well-being.

Kenneth Williams was a crucial part of the *Carry Ons*

Funny Scene!

At the Picture Playhouse, Sid Boggle has taken his girlfriend, Joan Fussey, and friends Bernie Lugg and Anthea Meeks, to see a film, but they didn't realise it was called *Nudist Paradise*. Anthea says she wants to go home.

JOAN: I know just how she feels. It's disgusting, that's what it is, disgusting.

SID: What are you talking about, disgusting? It's artistic, that's what it is.

JOAN: Artistic?

SID: Certainly.

JOAN: What, with all those big bottoms bobbling about all over the screen?

SID: No, you wouldn't think anything of it if we were walking around like that all of the time — free, unfettered, unashamed.

JOAN: Oh no, I suppose you'd rather we sat here all stark naked?

SID: Wouldn't bother me.

JOAN: It would if your ice lolly fell in your lap.

SID: You know what's a matter with you? You're a prude.

MAN BEHIND: (Annoyed at them constantly talking during the film.) If you don't mind, we're trying to hear back here.

SID: Oh, sorry, mate, if I'd known that I'd have spoken a bit louder.

city. Carstairs later follows him to Algiers but attempts to retrieve the formula are foiled by the bumbling Simkins and his team.

CARSTAIRS, MAJOR
Played by Peter Butterworth
Accompanies the Brigadier when he visits the experimental 1313 anti-aircraft battery to see how Captain Melly, who's recently taken charge of the base in *England*, is surviving.

CARTER, CYRIL
Played by Kenneth Cope
Cyril, who's seen in *Matron*, was only six when his mother, Gertie, died. He promised her he'd follow in his father's footsteps by becoming a small-time crook, but later claims he hardly knew what he wanted from life at that stage because he was only a kid. When offered a job in insurance, he seriously considers accepting until his father makes him feel guilty about breaking the promise made to his mother.

When his father believes he can earn a packet selling the Pill abroad, Cyril reluctantly agrees to don a nurse's outfit and pretend to be a student at the Finisham Maternity Hospital in order to find plans of the building. Whilst there, he rooms with Susan Ball, a nurse who eventually realises what he's up to. When the plan fails, he decides to settle down with Susan and quit his life of crime.

CARTER, GERTIE
Gertie died when her son, Cyril, was just six. Her name is mentioned by Sid, her husband, in *Matron* when he's trying to persuade Cyril to help with a job involving stealing pills from Finisham Maternity Hospital.

CARTER, PRIVATE
Played by Barbara Hampshire
Based at the experimental 1313 anti-aircraft battery featured in *England*, she's one of the shirkers who suffers a severe shock to the system when the tough-speaking Captain Melly is placed in charge of the unit.

CARTER, SID
Played by Sidney James
Leader of a small group of criminals who decides to steal contraceptive pills from Finisham Maternity Hospital and sell them overseas. Sid, who's seen in *Matron*, has been a widower since the death of his wife, Gertie. Their son, Cyril, is a reluctant member of Sid's gang.

CARVER, DR FREDERICK
Played by Kenneth Williams
A top surgeon in *Again Doctor* who's employed at the Long Hampton Hospital. Rather haughty, he longs for a private clinic of his own and dreams of one day running the Frederick Carver Foundation, where he can milk his rich private patients of all their money. He deviously

turns his attention to Ellen Moore, a lonely widow who's swimming in money, to finance his dream; the trouble is, she's looking for more than just a business partnership. Inexperienced in matters of courtship, Carver turns to the sex-mad Dr Nookey for help with some chat-up lines ready for the hospital's grand buffet and dance, but the evening is anything but a success for Carver in his pursuit of Moore's purse.

To satisfy Mrs Moore, Carver finds an ideal candidate – Dr Nookey – to take up the post of doctor at her medical mission in the distant Beatific Islands, but when Gladstone Screwer, the mission orderly, later reports that Nookey is failing in his duty, Carver placates Ellen by agreeing to visit the islands and establish what's going on; in doing so, he nearly loses his life when the schooner, *Bella Vista*, founders off the islands during a torrential storm. By the time he returns home, life has moved on and Mrs Moore is in partnership with none other than Dr Nookey, who's rolling in dosh since returning from the Beatific Islands with a cure for obesity, earning him millions.

At first jealous, Carver dreams up an idea, utilising his colleague Dr Stoppidge in disguise as a woman, to unearth the actual ingredients of the serum used by Nookey at his clinic. His plans backfire big-time but it's not long before he's a partner in the Moore-Nookey-Gladstone-Carver Clinic offering not just a miracle cure for obesity but sex change treatment, too.

CASLEY, ALAN
Role: Kindly Seaman in *Cruising*
Alan Casley's other screen credits saw him play a barman in a 1962 episode of *The Avengers*.

CASTLE, FLO
Played by Dilys Laye
A passenger on the *Happy Wanderer* in *Cruising*. She's on the cruise with her friend, Glad Trimble, and is hoping, with her mate's help, to net a husband. She hopes it will be the ship's PT instructor, Mr Jenkins, but knows that is wishful thinking. Eventually she falls in love with the vessel's doctor, Arthur Binn.

CASTLE, ROY
Role: Captain Keene in *Up The Khyber*
The multi-talented Roy Castle, son of an insurance agent, was born in Scholes, West Yorkshire, in 1932. He harboured dreams of playing cricket for Yorkshire, but gave them up for a career in entertainment, initially learning to dance and play instruments.

After completing national service in the RAF, he tried his luck as an entertainer, joining a musical troupe of clowns. He moved on to work with Jimmy Clitheroe and Jimmy James, both popular performers from the era, before

going it alone and entertaining at music halls, primarily on the northern club circuit.

By the 1960s, Castle was regarded as one of the nation's top all-round entertainers. He also did occasional acting, appearing on Broadway in *Pickwick* and, later, at the Palladium in *Singing in the Rain*. On the big screen he was seen in, among others, *Dr Who and the Daleks* and *Dr Terror's House of Horrors,* while on television his credits included *The Roy Castle Show* and *Record Breakers.*

In 1992 he was diagnosed with lung cancer, despite never having smoked. He died in 1994, aged sixty-two.

CAUSEY, JACK
Assistant Director on *Regardless, Cruising, Don't Lose Your Head, Camping, Up the Jungle, Girls* and *England*
Jack Causey began working as an assistant director in the 1950s on films such as *Innocents in Paris, The Captain's Paradise, Third Party Risk, Conflict of Wings, The Baby and the Battleship, The Silent Enemy, Sink the Bismarck!, Sands of the Kalahari, At the Earth's Core* and his final film, 1976's *The Slipper and the Rose.* As a production manager he was assigned to, among others, *The Magnificent Seven Deadly Sins, For the Love of Ada* and the big screen version of *Doomwatch*.

CAUSEY, J.
The unseen Third Officer on the *Happy Wanderer* in *Cruising*. His name is seen on the crew list and is obviously a reference to the film's assistant director.

CAVEMAN
Played by Michael Nightingale
Seen in *Cleo* warning other cavemen, including Horsa and Hengist who are chatting outside their caves, that the Romans are coming.

CECIL, THE JUNGLE BOY
Played by Terry Scott
Seen in *Up the Jungle*, Cecil spends his formative years living in the jungle, just like Tarzan. Soon after he was born, his father took his wife on a belated honeymoon to the African jungle. Tragedy struck when Walter Bagley took Cecil for an early morning walk along the banks of the Limpopo River and neither were seen again. When her husband's fob watch was discovered inside a crocodile's stomach, and an abandoned nappy found on the riverbank, Mrs Bagley feared the worst.

Years later, desperate to find her baby's missing nappy pin as something to remember him by, she returns to the jungle; what she doesn't realise is that Cecil is alive, and although he can only grunt, he's fit and healthy. When the Jungle Boy happens to enter her tent one night, Lady Bagley discovers he has a big, silver safety pin holding his loincloth together; suddenly realising it's her long-lost boy, she's desperate to bring him home, and after various ordeals manages to achieve her goal. The trouble is, he's unable to rid himself of his jungle habits: although he's a quick learner and soon holding down a respectable job in the City, he never wears shoes or socks and prefers living in a treehouse in London with his wife, June, formerly Lady Bagley's maid, and their new-born child.

CHAMBERLAIN, CYRIL

Roles: Gun Sergeant in *Sergeant*, Bert Able in *Nurse*, Alf in *Teacher*, Thurston in *Constable*, Policeman in *Regardless*, Tom Tree in *Cruising* and Sarge in *Cabby*

A veteran of stage and screen, Cyril Chamberlain was born in London in 1909 and became a busy character actor for over four decades.

Often cast in small parts, he always made full use of his screen time, acting with a presence befitting much larger roles. Frequently seen playing policemen or middle-ranked soldiers, he entered films in the late 1930s, notching up over a hundred credits, including *A Stolen Life, Poison Pen, My Brother's Keeper, London Belongs to Me, Once a Jolly Swagman, Quartet, Stop Press Girl, Lady Godiva Rides Again, Above Us the Waves* and *Operation Bullshine*. He also appeared in several Norman Wisdom and St Trinian's films.

He occasionally worked on television in such productions as *Stryker of the Yard, Ivanhoe, William Tell, The Saint* and *Danger Man*.

He died in 1974, aged sixty-five.

CHAPLAIN

Played by Peter Jones

Seen in *Doctor*. Sporting a hearing aid, he conducts the wedding ceremony for Francis Bigger and the equally deaf Chloe Gibson, which makes for a frustrating affair.

CHAPPELL, NORMAN

Roles: Allbright in *Cabby* and 1st Plotter in *Henry*. (Note: also cast as Mr Thrush in *Loving* but scene cut.)

TV: *Orgy and Bess; One in the Eye for Harold; The Case of the Screaming Winkles; The Case of the Coughing Parrot; Under the Round Table; Short Knight, Long Daze* and *Lamp Posts of the Empire*

Norman Chappell, who was born in the Indian city of Lucknow, arrived in the UK aged four. Son of a professional soldier, he broke with tradition and pursued a theatrical career, but not before serving for a time with the RAF, and holding down various jobs, including cook in a police canteen.

His first taste of acting was during his RAF days; upon deciding it was the career for him, he enrolled at the Italia Conti Stage School. Circumstances, however, forced him to leave prematurely, but it never affected his progress in the profession, which saw him work in all media.

On television he was seen playing several characters in *The Avengers*, and appeared in *Bless This House, Mr Aitch, Mr Digby Darling, Whoops Baghdad!, Sez Les, Danger UXB* and *Doctor's Daughters*, while on the big screen he popped up in several films during the 1960s

and '70s, such as *Jigsaw, Crooks in Cloisters, How I Won the War, Up the Creek, Nearest and Dearest, Love Thy Neighbour, The Four Musketeers* and *Intimate Games*.

He died of a heart attack in 1983.

CHARLES (EARL OF BRISTOL)

Played by Peter Butterworth

The Earl of Bristol has been ambassador at the Spanish court for some time before returning with his two attractive daughters, one of whom is blonde Bettina. He's seen briefly in *Henry* arriving with his girls at Henry VIII's do.

CHARLIE

Played by Percy Herbert

A barman at Belle's Place, he remains in the job when Johnny Finger arrives in Stodge City and starts throwing his weight around, including taking over the hotel-cum-bar and renaming it Rumpo's Place. He soon becomes Rumpo's sidekick but ends up being shot accidentally by Annie Oakley. Seen in *Cowboy*.

CHARLIE PLATOON

Sergeant O'Brien's platoon at Heathercrest National Service Depot in *Sergeant*.

CHAUFFEUR

Played by Frank Forsyth

This miserable-looking chauffeur is seen in *Cabby* waiting at a junction. Charlie Hawkins turns up in his cab, spots the sour-faced driver and asks him where the funeral is.

CHAYSTE PLACE

A finishing school, set in a sumptuous building, for young ladies. Seen in *Camping*, its principal is Dr Kenneth Soaper while the headmistress is Miss Haggerd.

CHEF

Played by Leon Greene

A monster of a man, the chef works at the Brighton hotel where the employees of W. C. Boggs and Son, out on their annual jolly, were intending to eat lunch. A strike, though, puts paid to their plans, infuriating, ironically, Vic Spanner, one of the most troublesome shop stewards around. He confronts the chef, who towers over him, and soon wishes he hadn't.

CHERRILL, ROGER

Sound Editor on *Nurse*

Roger Cherrill entered films in the early 1940s, working as a production runner on 1943's *The Life and Death of Colonel Blimp*. He was working as an assistant editor a year later on *A Canterbury Tale* and, from the 1950s, as a sound editor on films such as *A Day to Remember, Always a Bride, Doctor at Sea, Lost, Tiger in the Smoke* and *Rooney*. As an editor his credits include *Make Mine Mink, In the Doghouse, A Kind of Loving, Billy Liar, The Naked Prey* and the television series, *Interpol Calling*.

Cyril Chamberlain (far left) was a reliable character actor of stage and screen (*Constable*)

CHIEF, THE
Played by Eric Barker
The Director of Security Operations seen in *Spying* is alarmed to hear that Professor Stark has been murdered and a secret formula stolen. He assembles a team of agents and sends them off to retrieve the formula at all costs; the trouble is the team is made up of a bunch of incompetents.

CHIEF CONSTABLE
(Voice only)
Heard in *Constable*, the Chief Constable phones to congratulate Inspector Mills on catching thieves who recently snatched some wages in the district.

CHILDS, GUNNER
Played by Billy J. Mitchell
Based at the experimental 1313 anti-aircraft battery featured in *England*, he's one of the shirkers who suffers a severe shock to the system when the tough-speaking Captain Melly is put in charge of the unit.

CHINDI
Played by Michael Mellinger
Seen during the famous dinner-party scene in *Up The Khyber*, Chindi works for Sir Sidney Ruff-Diamond, the British governor in the northwest province of India.

CHINESE LADY
Played by Madame Yang
In *Regardless*, the Chinese Lady hired an interpreter from Helping Hands but a mix-up finds Sam Twist calling instead of Francis Courtenay.

CHIPPING SODBURY LADIES' GUILD
The Guild presented drainage, sanitation and garbage disposal engineer, Marshall Knutt, with a sink plunger in recognition of services rendered in *Cowboy*. He carries it with him when he visits the Bureau of Internal Affairs looking for a job, but probably wishes he hadn't when it sticks so hard to a clerk's desk that Knutt ends up tearing the tabletop off trying to release it.

CHIPPING SODBURY TECHNICAL COLLEGE
The college from which Marshall P. Knutt graduated as a drainage, sanitation and garbage disposal engineer. Mentioned in *Cowboy*.

CHRYSTAL, BIDDY
Hairdresser on *Regardless*, *Cruising*, *Cabby*, and *Spying*
Biddy Chrystal, head of Pinewood's hairdressing department for many years, began her film career in the 1940s and proceeded to work on a multitude of films, including *Blanche Fury*, *London Belongs to Me*, *Prelude to Fame*, *The Browning Version*, *Lost* and *The Early Bird*.
She turned freelance and worked through until the 1970s, latterly on productions such as

Young Winston, *Alice's Adventures in Wonderland* and, in 1974, *11 Harrowhouse*. Eventually moved to America and died in 1995.

CHUMLEY, CLAUDE
Played by Kenneth Connor
Professor Tinkle's assistant in *Up the Jungle*, Chumley follows the highly respected ornithologist on his expeditions, including recent visits to the Virgin Isles and, now, the jungles of Africa. While on the trip, he has to fight his unbridled passion for Lady Bagley, another member of the jungle expedition.

CHURCH ROAD
The street in *Constable* where the criminals involved in the wages snatch abandoned their car, registration RGT 547.

CHURCH, TONY
Wrote the screenplay for *That's Carry On*

C I CARAVANS
The company which supplied the caravans used in *Behind*.

CIGARETTE GIRL
Played by Jill Mai Meredith
Employed at the Café Mozart in Vienna, the Cigarette Girl is seen in *Spying*, taking a secret message concerning a rendezvous, which is concealed in a cigarette, from the Fat Man to Milchmann. But a mix-up sees Simkins take the cigarette instead.

CITIZENS
Played by Tom Gill, Frank Forsyth, Anthony Sagar, Eric Corrie and John Antrobus
The group of men is seen in *Constable*, complaining in the police station about various issues.

CITY GENT ON TUBE
Played by Michael Nightingale
You have to feel sorry for this guy, who's seen in *Girls* standing reading his paper on his way to work. He's just minding his own business when Paula Perkins, standing next to him, notices a photo of her fiancé, Peter Potter, on the front of the paper, showing her beloved apparently cavorting with some of the beauty contestants down in Fircombe, an event he's been asked to promote. Paula makes a comment and the rest of the commuters turn to the City Gent in disgust, thinking he's guilty of something improper towards Paula.

CLARK, CAPTAIN
Played by Hattie Jacques
Seen in *Sergeant*, the doctor is based at Heathercrest National Service Depot. Her patience is severely tested by the arrival of Horace Strong, the world's worst hypochondriac. When she can take no more, she refers him to a team of specialists who examine every inch of his body, and in doing so help him realise that he's actually in love.

CLARKE, NURSE
Played by Anita Harris
In *Doctor*, Nurse Clarke is a member of Borough County Hospital's efficient nursing staff, and just one of the many admirers of Dr Kilmore.

CLARKE, RONALD
Role: 6th Storeman in *Sergeant*
Ronald Clarke's other appearances include several roles over the years in *Dixon of Dock Green*, *Gazette* and *The Gold Robbers*. His film credits range from *The Battle of the River Plate* and *Hell Drivers* to *Up the Junction* and *The Mackintosh Man*.

CLEANER
Played by an uncredited actor
Seen briefly in *Regardless*, the cleaner at Helping Hands knocks the job allocation cards onto the floor causing chaos when the assignments are dished out the following day.

CLEGG, TERRY
Location Manager on *Follow That Camel* and Assistant Director on *Doctor*
Sheffield-born Terry Clegg worked as location manager on *A Clockwork Orange* and *The Mackintosh Man*, while as assistant director he's worked on television series like *The Saint* and, among others, the films *Lucky Lady* and *Circle of Friends*. As a production manager and executive in charge of production his list of credits include *A Bridge Too Far*, *The Elephant Man*, *Gandhi*, *Shadowlands* and *Yaadein*. More recently he worked as producer on such films as *Cry Freedom*, *Gorillas in the Mist* and *Breathtaking*.

CLEGG, TOM
Roles: Massive Micky McGee in *Regardless*, Doorman in *Spying*, Sosages in *Cleo*, Blacksmith in *Cowboy*, Odbodd in *Screaming!* and Trainer in *Loving*
A stuntman and bit-part actor, Tom Clegg's other credits include jobs in television shows *Quatermass II* and *The Sweeney*, as well as films like *The Fake*, *The Extra Day* and *Raising the Wind*. He was employed as a stuntman on numerous productions, including the films *Ivanhoe* and *Thunderball*.

CLEO, CARRY ON
See feature box on pages 64–5.

CLEOPATRA
Played by Amanda Barrie
Ruler of Egypt, the Queen of the Nile bathes in milk all day, making many men's hearts flutter, especially Mark Antony's in *Cleo*. She plots with Antony to topple Caesar but it takes several attempts before they finally see the back of Caesar and the blossoming of their relationship.

CLEOPATRA
The donkey who's led into the lounge of the Palace Hotel in Fircombe. Seen in *Girls*, the

animal is used to promote the beauty contest being held in the town; Peter Potter, a friend of Sidney Fiddler, who's tasked with organising publicity for the event plans to photograph the girls with the donkey, using the promotional line, 'Beauty and the Beast'. The donkey does little to ingratiate himself with hotel owner Connie Philpotts when it excretes all over the floor.

CLERK
Played by Ian Wilson
In *Cabby* the Clerk works at Stevens and Son, a printing firm. He speaks to Charlie Hawkins when he enters the office wanting some leaflets printed.

CLERK
Played by Lionel Murton
In *Cowboy* the Clerk works on the reception desk at Washington and briefly interviews the drainage, sanitation and garbage engineer Marshall P. Knutt when he arrives on the scene job-hunting. He soon wishes he hadn't set eyes on the accident-prone Mr Knutt, though, when Knutt gets his plunger stuck on the clerk's desk and ends up ripping the wooden top off.

CLIFF
Played by Jack Taylor
In *Constable*, Cliff is one of the robbers involved in the wages snatch.

CLIFTON, PHILIP
Role: Injured Footballer in *Emmannuelle*
Other television work saw Philip Clifton appearing in an episode of the Australian series, *Delta*, in 1970.

CLIFTON, ZENA
Roles: Au Pair Girl in *Matron* and Susan Clifton in *Girls*
As well as acting, Zena Clifton made a living as a dancer on many of Britain's top television shows, such as *Sez Les* and *The Benny Hill Show*.

CLIFFORD, PEGGY ANN
Role: Willa Claudia in *Cleo*
Born in Bournemouth in 1919, Peggy Ann Clifford worked in rep before establishing herself as a supporting actress, normally cast as a jolly character on film and television. She was particularly busy during the 1950s, and appeared in many films, including *Kind Hearts and Coronets, Man of the Moment, Brothers in Law, Doctor at Large* and *Under Milk Wood*.

On television she was seen in, among others, *Hancock's Half Hour, Fawlty Towers, Man About the House, Bless This House, Dawson's Weekly, George and Mildred, Are You Being Served?* and *Hi-de-Hi!*.

She once sold a block of flats in Fulham in order to buy a grocery shop in Chelsea, which she ran for three years while not acting. She died in 1984, aged sixty-five.

CLIVE
Played by Larry Dann
A student from the University of Kidburn's archaeological department who helps Professor Crump at the dig. While staying at the Riverside Caravan Site in *Behind*, next-door to where they are digging, Clive and his mate get friendly with two campers, Carol and Sandra.

CLIVE, JOHN
Roles: Robin Tweet in *Abroad* and Isaak the Tailor in *Dick*. **(Note: also cast as the Dandy in *Henry* but scene cut.)**
Born in 1938, Londoner John Clive began acting in rep as a child, appearing in plays like *The Winslow Boy* and *Life with Father*. His break arrived while working as a pageboy at a theatre. Hearing about auditions for a children's show, he submitted his name and was accepted as a boy singer, as well as assisting the resident comic in sketches.

His face has since become familiar from more than a hundred film and television performances. On the big screen he's appeared as a car manager in *The Italian Job*, as well as *Clockwork Orange, Great Expectations* and *Revenge of the Pink Panther*. On television his credits include *The Sweeney, Wear A Very Big Hat, How Green Was My Valley, The Government Inspector, The Saint, Man in a Suitcase, Casualty, Perils of Pendragon,* and the lead (Professor Sommerby) in the children's series, *Robert's Robots*. He's also appeared with most of the great comedy performers including Dick Emery, Tommy Cooper, John Cleese and Peter Sellers.

Today, most of Clive's time is dedicated to writing screenplays and novels – he's written six to date – although he still acts if the right part comes along. Now divides his time between homes in England and Spain.

CLOAKROOM ATTENDANT
Played by Elsie Winsor
In *Girls* the Cloakroom Attendant works at the Pier Theatre and reminds Sidney Fiddler that he's in the ladies' toilets when he's caught kissing Hope Springs just before she takes part in the Miss Fircombe beauty contest.

CLOAKROOM GIRL
Played by Angela Ellison
The Cloakroom Girl takes Simkins's hat, coat and false beard when he arrives at the Café Mozart in *Spying*.

CLOTSKI, CORPORAL
Played by John Bluthal
A corporal in the Foreign Legion, he reports to Sergeant Nocker in *Follow That Camel*.

CLUB RECEPTIONIST
Played by George Street
Works at the Philosophers' Club and is seen in *Regardless*. Speaks to Sam Twist when he arrives

'You did the *Carry On* films and enjoyed them for what they were, never thinking, of course, that they'd become enormously successful cult movies. It's quite remarkable.

'My first role was playing Robin in *Abroad*. There was one thing that David, whom I knew prior to filming, and I couldn't understand. Kenneth Williams and Charles Hawtrey were both camping it up madly and we didn't know why they wanted us to come in and do the same sort of thing. You know what actors are with everybody worried about their own positions and I didn't want Kenneth or Charles to think we were seeking to take over their roles in the film – that was the last thing in our minds.

'I liked Kenneth Williams enormously and thought he was a fabulously funny guy, so I was a little bit careful with him and waited to see how we'd get on, whether he was sharp with me but I'm glad to say he wasn't. In fact, after he'd seen the rushes he came over personally to congratulate me, patting me on the shoulder and saying: "That was terrific, you two boys are going to be great in this." Another time I was in make-up and Sid James said virtually the same thing.

'Trying to create the Mediterranean in the freezing cold of Pinewood was difficult but you just had to put up with it, but I have to say that we were blue with the cold in those bathing costumes because there was a chill wind round the place that day. We had to have body make-up plastered all over us because everybody was freezing. When we filmed the scene involving the rainstorm, everyone got soaked. Luckily I wasn't caught in it but poor old David was. It was good fun filming *Abroad*. It was one-take and on to the next.

'*Carry On Dick* was only a small part and, if I remember right, just one day's filming. It was always good fun and easy comedy. I want to pay compliment to the regulars. The only reason anyone talks to anyone else about the *Carry On* films is because of the regulars, not the script, directing or the producing. They were superb comedy actors of their generations and knew exactly where to go, how far to go and when not to cross that line from pun and innuendo into crude comedy.'

JOHN CLIVE

CARRY ON CLEO

An Anglo Amalgamated film
A Peter Rogers production
Distributed through Warner-Pathe Distribution Ltd
Released as an A certificate in 1964 in colour
Running time: 92 mins

CAST

Sidney James	Mark Antony
Kenneth Williams	Julius Caesar
Charles Hawtrey	Seneca
Kenneth Connor	Hengist Pod
Joan Sims	Calpurnia
Jim Dale	Horsa
Amanda Barrie	Cleopatra
Victor Maddern	Sergeant Major
Julie Stevens	Gloria
Sheila Hancock	Senna Pod
Jon Pertwee	Soothsayer
Brian Oulton	Brutus
Michael Ward	Archimedes
Francis de Wolff	Agrippa
Tom Clegg	Sosages
Tanya Binning	Virginia
David Davenport	Bilius
Peter Gilmore	Galley Master
Ian Wilson	Messenger
Norman Mitchell	Heckler
Brian Rawlinson	Hessian Driver
Gertan Klauber	Marcus
Warren Mitchell	Spencius
Peter Jesson	Companion
Michael Nightingale	Caveman
Judi Johnson	Gloria's Bridesmaid
Thelma Taylor	Seneca's Servant
Sally Douglas	Antony's Dusky Maiden
Wanda Ventham	Pretty Bidder
Peggy Ann Clifford	Willa Claudia
Mark Hardy	Guard at Caesar's Palace
E.V.H. Emmett	Narrator
Christine Rodgers	
Gloria Best	
Virginia Tyler	Hand Maidens
Gloria Johnson	
Joanna Ford	
Donna White	
Jane Lumb	
Vicki Smith	Vestal Virgins

(Uncredited 'Companions': Stuart Monro, Forbes Douglas, Billy Cornelius, Peter Fraser, Frederick Beauman and Keith Buckley.)

PRODUCTION TEAM

Screenplay by Talbot Rothwell
Music composed and conducted by Eric
    Rogers
Associate Producer: Frank Bevis
Art Director: Bert Davey
Director of Photography: Alan Hume
Editor: Archie Ludski
Camera Operator: Godfrey Godar
Assistant Director: Peter Bolton
Unit Manager: Donald Toms
Continuity: Olga Brook
Make-up: Geoffrey Rodway
Sound Editor: Christopher Lancaster
Sound Recordists: Bill Daniels and Gordon
    K. McCallum
Hairdressing: Ann Fordyce
Costume Designer: Julie Harris
Producer: Peter Rogers
Director: Gerald Thomas

Left: Caesar (Kenneth Williams) looks to the heavens for inspiration

Right: Amanda Barrie in fine form as Cleo

Hengist Pod's simple life as a wheelmaker specialising in making square wheels is forever changed when the Romans arrive and ransack his village. While his new neighbour, Horsa, stays with the rest of the villagers to try and fight off the Romans, Hengist jumps on his square-wheeled contraption and heads off to seek help. He hasn't gone far before his fragile vehicle collapses and he ends up thumbing a lift; when he gratefully accepts a ride in a wagon, he jumps in the back only to find he's in the company of his fellow cavemen, including Horsa, who've been taken prisoner by the Romans.

As they head for Rome, Julius Caesar is anxious to leave the damp British climate behind for sunnier skies back home; when a message arrives warning that Brutus might be planning to take over the throne in his absence, he rushes back to be met by a less than rapturous welcome.

Caesar has become so unpopular that even his father-in-law, Seneca, is having premonitions about his impending doom. Caesar consults the Vestal Virgins but as he enters the Temple of Vesta, Bilius, his personal bodyguard, takes out his sword with the intention of slaying his leader. Unbeknown to Caesar, Horsa and Hengist Pod have escaped from the slave market and are hiding with the Vestal Virgins, and a mix-up leaves numerous Roman soldiers dead and Hengist hailed as the hero by Caesar who, believing he saved his life, makes him a centurion and personal bodyguard.

Treachery is rife. When Mark Antony is sent by Caesar to see Cleopatra, the Queen of the Nile, he succumbs to her charm and beauty; when Cleopatra mentions how good they could be together if Mark Anthony was emperor of Rome, he plans to topple Caesar. Upon returning to Rome, he tells the Roman leader that Cleopatra wants to meet him, although the plan is for Caesar to be killed en route. The Roman soldiers on the ship who intend murdering Caesar are all killed by the galley slaves who manage to escape; Caesar, however, doesn't know this and, thinking the soldiers are out to get him, pushes Hengist

Funny Scene!

Julius Caesar is at the Temple of Vesta when Bilius takes out his sword with the intention of murdering Caesar.

CAESAR: What are you doing with your thing?
BILIUS: (Withdrawing his sword.) I'm sorry, sir, but for the good of Rome you must die.
CAESAR: But you're my personal bodyguard and champion gladiator — I don't want to die. I might not be a very good live emperor but I'd be a worse one dead. Treachery, infamy, infamy, they've all got it in for me.

out to deal with the rebels. A quivering wreck, Hengist soon perks up when he finds the soldiers already dead, so pretends to have killed them himself, thereby gaining even more respect from his new boss.

When Mark Antony's plans to kill Caesar at sea are thwarted, he hatches another one with Cleopatra inviting him to her bedchamber. But when he's told of a premonition depicting his death, Caesar decides against going and sends Hengist Pod instead. When he climbs on the bed with Cleopatra it collapses on top of Mark Antony, who was waiting underneath to kill Caesar. Before long, Horsa and the other galley slaves, who've entered the palace in search of food, come to Hengist's rescue again.

Despite surviving all the failed murder attempts, it isn't long before Caesar bites the dust, leaving Mark Antony free to team up with Cleopatra, Horsa to marry his long-lost love, Gloria, and Hengist to become a new man and father plenty of kids.

to replace Old Lou, who's ill. Doesn't believe Twist will be up to the job and is proved right when he has to escort him off the premises because he can't refrain from laughing at some of the geriatrics at the club.

CLULOW, JENNIFER
Role: 1st Lady in *Don't Lose Your Head*

Born in Grimsby, Humberside, in 1942, Jennifer Clulow trained at the Rose Bruford College of Speech and Drama before beginning her career on a world tour of the Royal Shakespeare Company's *King Lear* and *Comedy of Errors*. Further West End work followed including a leading role in the musical *4000 Brass Halfpennies*, as well as repertory work.

She began appearing on screen from the mid-1960s. She presented the children's series, *Disney Wonderland*, a cookery series for ATV and read the news for Westward Television. When TVS opened its doors, Clulow – who played Catherine in the famous Cointreau adverts – worked as an announcer.

Other television credits include *The Baron, The Avengers, Department S, Lovejoy, Bergerac* and, in 1993, *Keeping Up Appearances*. For two years she played Claire Clarkson in *The Troubleshooters* and Jessica Dalton in Granada's series, *Mr Rose*.

COACH AND HORSES, THE
A pub mentioned by WPC Passworthy in *Constable*. It's where she arrested the infamous Mrs May for smashing a bottle over a barman's head just because he asked her to leave.

Marian Collins played a bride in two *Carry Ons* (Cabby)

COACH DRIVER
Played by Barrie Gosney

Seen sitting on top of a stagecoach in *Jack,* this cheeky chappie tells Albert Poop-Decker to hurry up when he's alighting from the coach at Plymouth.

COBLEY
Played by Richard Wattis

This bespectacled official reports to the Director of Security Operations in *Spying*.

COBURN, BRIAN
Roles: Trapper in *Cowboy* and Highwayman in *Dick*

Born in Scotland in 1936, Brian Coburn's hefty frame meant he was instantly recognisable on stage and screen. He worked throughout the world during his career and clocked up over 200 television appearances, his favourite show being BBC's *God's Wonderful Railway*, in which he played the lead.

A steady supply of theatrical and film work came his way: among his credits on the big screen were *Octopussy, Trenchcoat, Trial by Combat, Love and Death* and *Fiddler On the Roof.*

Coburn was returning to the Royal Shakespeare Company when illness caused him to cancel the engagement. He died in 1989, aged fifty-three, from a diabetic-related illness.

COCCIUM-IN-CORNOVII
Hengist's and Horsa's home town in *Cleo*.

COCKBURN, PETER
Role: Commentator in *Camping*

He was also seen as a commentator in 1971 episodes of *Paul Temple* and *On the Buses*, while his voice was heard on Marillion's 1983 album, *Script for a Jester's Tear.*

COCK INN
The inn is mentioned by James Bedsop, the ineffective private investigator hired by Sophie Bliss to spy on Sidney, who, she feels, is seeing women behind her back. In *Loving*, Sidney was spotted in the establishment's saloon bar by Bedsop who then followed him back to his office.

CODE CLERK
Played by Gertan Klauber

Seen in *Spying* the Code Clerk brings a message to the Director of Security Operations (alias The Chief). It's from Carstairs, the Vienna-based agent, reporting the arrival of Milchmann, a wanted criminal. The Chief questions the validity of appointing foreign subjects in the decoding department.

COE, CAPTAIN
This captain's epic journey is mentioned by Captain Fearless in *Jack*. In an open boat, six sailors set out and were at sea for seventy-three days. Only three reached home shores, having survived by eating the three comrades that didn't make it. Fearless refers to the event when, together with some of his crew, he's hopelessly lost in a rowing boat, miles from anywhere. The captain isn't seen in the film.

COLE, PAUL
Role: Atkins in *Teacher*

As a child actor, Paul Cole appeared in a handful of productions between 1959 and '63, including, on television, *The Four Just Men* and *The Pursuers*, as well as the films *Dracula, Next To No Time, Please Turn Over* and *The Mouse on the Moon.*

COLETTE
Played by Suzanna East

Seen in Richmond's flashback sequence in *Emmannuelle* in which he describes his most amorous experience. Colette is the niece of the French parson who takes pity on Richmond and provides him with shelter when a German soldier chases him. Colette, though, is the reason Richmond didn't return to England until eight years after the war ended.

COLIN, SID
Co-wrote the screenplay for *Spying*
TV: Co-wrote *Christmas* (70)

Born in London in 1915, screenwriter Sid Colin specialised in comedy for screen and radio, but upon leaving school pursued a musical career. He taught himself the banjo and joined a touring group, playing and singing around the country.

During the war, he served six years in The Squadronnaires, the RAF's dance orchestra, playing guitar and writing shows, during which time he met Denis Norden and Frank Muir with whom he'd later work on numerous occasions.

After the war, he quit touring and began concentrating on his writing career, but not before he tried making a living as an artist. Colin painted, drew and sculpted all his life and eventually found work designing covers for sheet music. But his future lay in scriptwriting and he soon began writing for radio, film and, later, television.

Among his writing credits for radio are *Life With the Lyons*, while on television his output includes the series *How Do You View?*, *Before Your Very Eyes*, *The Army Game* and *Love Thy Neighbour*. His film work included *One Good Turn*, *I Only Arsked!*, and the Frankie Howerd films *Up the Chastity Belt*, *Up Pompeii* and *Up the Front*. One of his last screenplays was 1982's *The Boys in Blue*. Also a lyricist, he penned songs for films such as *Up the Front* and *Bottoms Up*.

He died in 1989, aged seventy-four.

COLLEANO, GARRY
Role: Slim in *Cowboy*
Other screen credits include a 1960 episode of *International Detective* and the 1961 film *Follow That Man*.

COLLINGS, JEANNIE
Role: Private Edwards in *England*
Born in 1952, Liverpudlian Jeannie Collings started her career as a model for the Moroccan government. After gaining success in this field, she turned her attention to acting. Among her television credits are appearances on *The Benny Hill Show*, *The Generation Game*, *The Golden Shot*, *Dixon of Dock Green* and *Armchair Theatre*. In films she's been seen in *Emily*, *Confessions of a Window Cleaner*, *Percy's Progress*, *I'm Not Feeling Myself Tonight* and *Cruel Passion*.

COLLINS, LAURA
Role: Nurse in *Matron*

COLLINS, MARIAN
Roles: Bride in *Cruising*, Bride in *Cabby*, Girl at Dirty Dick's in *Jack* and Amazon Guard in *Spying*
On screen from the 1950s, Marian Collins was also seen in the television shows *Dixon of Dock Green* and *Frankie Howerd*, as well as films such as *Behind the Headlines*, *The Desperate Man*, *Jungle Street* and an uncredited role as Goldfinger's girlfriend in the Bond movie, *Goldfinger*.

COLONEL, THE
Played by Wilfrid Hyde-White
From his own private room at the Haven Hospital, the Colonel drives the nurses mad in *Nurse* with his incessant demands. His good nature, though, is reciprocated and everyone bends over backwards to help, especially Mick, the ward orderly, who's forever placing bets on the horses for the Colonel. The staff get their own back in the end, courtesy of a strategically placed daffodil!

COMMENTATOR
Played by Peter Cockburn
In *Camping* he commentates on the film, *Nudist Paradise*, which is shown at the Picture Playhouse.

COMMISSIONER
Played by Alan Gifford
Based in Washington, the Commissioner works in the Bureau of Internal Affairs. In *Cowboy* he's first seen having a little fun with a woman in his office until interrupted by Perkins, his assistant. A former janitor at the law school Judge Burke, of Stodge City, attended, he responds to Burke's request for a peace marshal but can't find anyone to fill the position until Marshall P. Knutt walks in looking for a job. Assuming he's actually a marshal when he's actually a drainage, sanitation and garbage disposal engineer, he packs him off to Stodge City.

COMPANION
Played by Peter Jesson
One of seven companions originally seen in *Cleo*.

CONCORDE STEWARD
Played by James Fagan
Gets more than he bargained for when he attends to Emmanuelle 'Straying Hands' Prevert, the French Ambassador's wife, during a London-bound flight on Concorde. Seen in *Emmannuelle*.

CONNOISSEURS DE LONDRES
The organisation holds a wine-tasting session at the Ruby Room in *Regardless*.

CONNOISSEUR
Played by David Lodge
Seen in *Regardless*, the Connoisseur attends the wine-tasting session at the Ruby Room organised for the Connoisseurs de Londres. He helps a drunk Lily Duveen, who was hired from Helping Hands to collect invitations, to her feet when she collapses on the floor, only to be accused of having straying hands.

CONNOR, JEREMY
Roles: Jeremy Bishop in Nurse, Willy in *Constable*, Footpad in *Dick*, Student with Ice-cream in *Behind* and Gunner Hiscocks in *England*
Son of Kenneth, Jeremy Connor was born in 1955 and made occasional screen appearances as an actor. He now lives in New Zealand.

CONNOR, KENNETH
Roles: Horace Strong in *Sergeant*, Bernie Bishop in *Nurse*, Gregory Adams in *Teacher*, Constable Charlie Constable in *Constable*, Sam Twist in *Regardless*, Dr Arthur Binn in *Cruising*, Ted Watson in *Cabby*, Hengist Pod in *Cleo*, Claude Chumley in *Up the Jungle*, Lord Hampton of Wick in *Henry*, Mr Tidey in *Matron*, Stanley Blunt in *Abroad*, Mayor Frederick Bumble in *Girls*, Constable in *Dick*, Major Leep in *Behind*, Captain S. Melly in *England* and Leyland in *Emmannuelle*
TV: *Christmas* ('70); *Christmas* ('72); *What a Carry On!*; *Christmas* ('73); *The Prisoner of Spenda*; *The Baron Outlook*; *Orgy and Bess*; *One in the Eye for Harold*; *The Nine Old Cobblers*; *The Case of the Screaming Winkles*; *The Case of the Coughing Parrot*; *Under the Round Table*; *Short Knight, Long Daze*; *And in My Lady's Chamber*; *Who Needs Kitchener?* and *Lamp Posts of the Empire*
STAGE: *London!* and *Laughing*
A sublime piece of casting saw Kenneth Connor play Horace Strong, the hypochondriac who's horrified to be passed fit for national service in *Sergeant* and set the tone for the diminutive actor's *Carry On* career. If ever someone was required to play a dithering, nervous, angst-ridden little man, chances are Connor would be top of the list. He portrayed such characters with aplomb and quickly became an essential part of the gang.

Born in London in 1918, Kenneth Connor made his stage debut at the age of two and by the time he was eleven was performing various acts with his brother in revue shows. Deciding that he wanted to concentrate on becoming a 'serious' actor, he attended the Central School of Drama. Upon graduating his first professional job was as Boy David at His Majesty's Theatre, London, in 1936.

He went on to act in numerous repertory theatres, later becoming a member of the Bristol Old Vic Company; although the outbreak of war in 1939, during which he served with the army's Middlesex Regiment as a gunner, put a temporary halt to his career, he was for part of the time attached to George Black's company, Stars in Battledress, touring the Mediterranean.

After demob he returned to acting in a West End play at the Strand Theatre and, before long, a role in the television soap, *The Huggetts*; but he made his name for the array of character voices he created on radio shows such as *Just William* and *Ray's A Laugh* with Ted Ray, the start of a long and lasting association with the comedian. His success in *Ray's A Laugh* saw Ted Ray engage him as his top supporting player in the television series, *The Ted Ray Show*.

He went on to feature in the 1955 comedy, *The Ladykillers*, before appearing in the first of many *Carry On* roles. Other film credits include *Poison Pen*, *The Black Rider*, *Davy*, *Make Mine a Million*, *Watch Your Stern*, *Nearly A*

CARRY ON CONSTABLE

An Anglo Amalgamated release
A Peter Rogers production
Based on an idea by Brock Williams
Released as a U certificate in 1960 in black & white
Running time: 86 mins

CAST

Sidney James . . . . . . Sergeant Frank Wilkins
Eric Barker . . . . Inspector Mills
Kenneth Connor . . . . Constable Charlie Constable
Charles Hawtrey . . . . PC Timothy Gorse
Kenneth Williams . . . . . . PC Stanley Benson
Leslie Phillips . . . . PC Tom Potter
Joan Sims . . . . WPC Gloria Passworthy
Hattie Jacques . . . . Sgt Laura Moon
Cyril Chamberlain . . . . Thurston
Shirley Eaton . . . . Sally Barry
Joan Hickson . . . . Mrs May
Irene Handl . . . . Distraught Woman
Terence Longdon . . . . Herbert Hall
Freddie Mills . . . . Crook
Jill Adams . . . . WPC Harrison
Brian Oulton . . . . Store Manager
Victor Maddern . . . . Criminal Type
Joan Young . . . . Suspect
Esma Cannon . . . . Deaf Old Lady
Hilda Fenemore . . . . Agitated Woman
Noel Dyson . . . . Vague Woman
Robin Ray . . . . Assistant Manager
Michael Balfour . . . . Matt
Diane Aubrey . . . . Honoria
Ian Curry . . . . Eric
Mary Law . . . . 1st Shop Assistant
Lucy Griffiths . . . . Miss Horton
Peter Bennett . . . . Thief
Jack Taylor . . . . Cliff
Eric Boon . . . . Shorty
Janetta Lake . . . . Girl with dog
Dorinda Stevens . . . . Young Woman
Ken Kennedy . . . . Wall-eyed Man
Jeremy Connor . . . . Willy
Tom Gill
Frank Forsyth
John Antrobus
Eric Corrie
Anthony Sagar . . . . Citizens

Art Director: Carmen Dillon
Director of Photography: Ted Scaife
Editor: John Shirley
Production Manager: Frank Bevis
Camera Operator: Alan Hume
Assistant Director: Peter Manley
Sound Editor: Leslie Wiggins
Sound Recordists: Robert T. MacPhee and Bill Daniels
Continuity: Joan Davis
Make-up: George Blackler
Hairdressing: Stella Rivers
Dress Designer: Yvonne Caffin
Set Dressing: Vernon Dixon
Casting Director: Betty White
Producer: Peter Rogers
Director: Gerald Thomas

PRODUCTION TEAM

Screenplay by Norman Hudis
Music composed and directed by Bruce Montgomery

Sgt. Moon (Hattie Jacques) and Sgt. Wilkins (Sid James) make the perfect partnership

Benson (Kenneth Williams) and Potter (Leslie Phillips) patrol their beat

A flu epidemic sweeps Britain, affecting every industry, including the police force. With constables dropping like flies, raw recruits just out of training school are thrown into the thick of the action, as well as the incorrigible Timothy Gorse, a special constable whose services are only called upon as a last resort.

Before long, the new faces, except for the efficient WPC Passworthy, are causing chaos wherever they tread. After coming to the assistance of a distraught mother who thinks she's lost her little boy, Gorse decides to play around on the boy's scooter, only to find himself bumping into PC Benson, who's out walking Lady, a police dog. As they crash down some steps, the dog runs off.

Benson regards himself as an expert in the physiology of the criminal mind, claiming he can spot a crook a mile off. When a man bumps into him in the street, Benson doesn't regard the man as anything but a law-abiding member of the public, that is until his trousers fall to the ground because the passer-by has stolen his braces. Another example of his ineptness sees him trying to persuade a supposed car thief from committing a crime, only to discover that embarrassingly he's accusing a detective sergeant from the CID.

With the threat of suspension hanging over their heads, the new recruits pound their beats in pairs. Potter and Benson spot the getaway car involved in a recent robbery, and identifying a way of redeeming themselves for the earlier fiascos, try and find the robbers themselves. Eventually assisted by Gorse, they manage to catch the crooks in an abandoned house but it's the lazy, inefficient Inspector Mills who takes all the credit and is transferred to an area college where, ironically, he'll be in charge of morale and discipline, with Sergeant Wilkins taking over the running of the station after his long-overdue promotion to inspector.

Funny Scene!

New recruits, Constables Benson, Potter and Constable, arrive on the scene, ready to help the beleaguered station through its flu crisis.

SGT WILKINS: (A relieved smile.) Welcome, WELCOME! What a lovely sight, eh Thurston?

THURSTON: Not 'arf, Sergeant.

WILKINS: (Addressing the new recruits.) At ease, at ease.

BENSON: I'm Benson, Sergeant, (Introducing the others.) this is Constable Potter and this is Constable Constable.

WILKINS: (Puzzled, he looks at Thurston.) Who?

CONSTABLE: Charlie Constable.

WILKINS: Oh, I get it, that's your name?

CONSTABLE: Yeah, and I'm fed up with it. Everybody keeps taking the mickey.

WILKINS: Nobody will do that 'ere, Constable Constable.

CONSTABLE: I'm very pleased to hear it, Sergeant Sergeant.

Nasty Accident, Dentist on the Job, What a Carve Up and *Rhubarb*.

On television, he appeared in, among others, *A Show Called Fred*, *Blackadder the Third*, *You Rang, M'Lord?*, *Rentaghost* and provided the voices for the popular children's show, *Torchy the Battery Boy*. But he's probably best remembered in this medium for his performances as Monsieur Alfonse, the undertaker, in the sitcom *'Allo, 'Allo!* and as Uncle Sammy Morris in the holiday camp sitcom, *Hi-de-Hi!*.

Awarded an MBE in 1991 for services to showbusiness, Connor was entertaining on BBC's *Noel's House Party* just two days before he died in 1993, aged seventy-five.

CONSTABLE
Played by Billy Cornelius

The police constable appears in *Girls* alongside the police inspector at the Palace Hotel investigating reports that Patricia Potter, who's suspected of being a man, is back at the hotel.

CONSTABLE
Played by Kenneth Connor

The Parish Constable in *Dick* attempts to catch the elusive criminal, Dick Turpin. He's way past his best-before date, though, and is rather hopeless when it comes to capturing the legendary highwayman.

CONSTABLE, CARRY ON
See feature box on pages 68–9.

CONSTABLE, CONSTABLE CHARLIE
Played by Kenneth Connor

One of the newly-graduated police constables who arrives on the scene in *Constable*. A nervous, highly superstitious man who can't even attempt to develop a relationship with WPC Passworthy until he knows whether her birthday lands under the correct planetary sign, such is his reliance on astrology.

CONTE FILLIPO DI PISA
Played by Alan Curtis

Arrives in *Henry* to talk to Cardinal Wolsey about King Henry's application for an annulment of his wedding to Queen Marie of Normandy. He's employed by the Pope and travels as the emissary of the Vatican to explain that the Pope is both outraged and morally shocked but will overlook his concerns in return for 5000 pieces of gold.

CONWAY, BERT
Played by Jimmy Logan

A loud-mouthed Scot who joins the Wundatours party travelling to the Mediterranean resort of Elsbels in *Abroad*. He jokes to Stuart Farquhar, the courier, about heading off for a dirty weekend, but it's clear that is what he hopes the trip turns out like, especially when he eyes up Sadie Tomkins from the moment she climbs into the coach, even though he's competing with Vic Flange for her affections. Makes his living as a bookmaker.

COOK
Played by Anthony Sagar

In *Cruising*, the Cook is concerned when he realises his boss, Wilfred Haines, is suffering seasickness despite only just leaving port. When Haines makes a hasty dash for the toilets, he pushes into the Cook squashing a creamy dessert all over his face. Seen again, later, being accused by the chef of taking too long cracking open a pile of eggs.

COOK
Played by Mario Fabrizi

A Cook on the *Happy Wanderer*, he's seen in *Cruising* confirming to Wilfred Haines that the ship is actually sailing.

COOK, CORPORAL
Played by Patricia Franklin

In *England* seen dishing out the so-called food in the NAAFI at the experimental 1313 anti-aircraft battery.

COOKING FAT
In *Loving*, Jenny Grubb thinks the porter's unseen black cat is called Cooking Fat in the flats where she lives.

COOKSON
For Cookson, the constable in *Girls*, see 'Constable'.

COOLING, MISS
Played by Esma Cannon

The dithering, nervous old lady with a heart of gold tries her best as Bert Handy's secretary in *Regardless*. Not the most reliable person in the world, she gets messages confused, which explains why Sam Twist, one of the employees, has a wasted journey to the Forth Bridge, instead of providing a fourth at a game of bridge.

COOMBS, PAT
Roles: Patient in *Doctor* and New Matron in *Again Doctor*

Born in London in 1926, Pat Coombs started her working life as a nursery school assistant, trained at LAMDA and began working on stage before establishing herself as a familiar face on television, primarily playing comedy parts or working as a foil for well-known comedians.

Her early credits included Lana Butt in the pilot of *Beggar My Neighbour* and the three subsequent series transmitted in 1967-68. She

Bert Conway (Jimmy Logan, right) chats up Sadie Tomkins (Barbara Windsor) in the Med (*Abroad*)

also appeared as Violet Robinson in *Lollipop Loves Mr Mole* in 1971 and the series, *Lollipop*, the following year. Other series in which she was cast included two runs of *Don't Drink the Water!*, four series of *You're Only Young Twice*, *In Sickness and in Health*, *Birds of a Feather* and *EastEnders*.

Coombs, who died at Denville Hall, the retirement home for actors, in 2002, made a handful of film appearances in productions such as *Adolf Hitler – My Part In His Downfall* and *Ooh! You Are Awful*. In the mid-1990s she was diagnosed with the bone disease osteoporosis but continued working until her final days, recording an episode of the radio series, *Like They've Never Been Gone*, with June Whitfield and Roy Hudd, just months before her death.

COOPER, JUNE
Roles: Girl in *Don't Lose Your Head* and Hospitality Girl in *Up The Khyber*
Other screen credits include playing a stewardess in an episode of 1970's *Mister Jerico*.

COOTE, CHARLES
Played by Charles Hawtrey
Chief designer at W.C. Boggs, manufacturers of quality toilet ware, the foppish Charles Coote is seen in *At Your Convenience*. He lodges with Agatha Spanner, with whom he strikes up a relationship and intends to marry. Agatha's devotion to Charles rankles with her son, Vic, who happens to be the union representative at the toilet ware company.

COPE, KENNETH
Roles: Vic Spanner in *At Your Convenience* and Cyril Carter in *Matron*
Born in Liverpool in 1934, Kenneth Cope is probably best known for his television appearances in shows such as *That Was The Week That Was*, *Randall and Hopkirk (Deceased)*, *Coronation Street* and, more recently, *Brookside*, in which he played Ray Hilton.

Son of an engineer, he trained at Bristol's Old Vic Theatre School after giving up his job in the drawing office at the Automatic Telephone Company. While at Bristol, he made his screen debut when a production of *The Duenna* in which he was appearing was recorded.

After graduating, he worked in repertory theatre, initially at Cromer, before moving to London, earning money as a part-time garage attendant in-between acting jobs; eventually television work came his way with early credits being episodes of *The Adventures of Robin Hood*, *Ivanhoe* and *Dixon of Dock Green*.

His big break came with the role of Jed Stone in *Coronation Street*, which led to appearances on *That Was The Week That Was*. But for many people, he'll always be remembered as Marty Hopkirk, the helpful ghost in the detective series, *Randall and Hopkirk (Deceased)*.

He's also chalked up a lot of film credits, including *X the Unknown*, *The Yangtse Incident*, *Dunkirk*, *Naked Fury*, *Father Came Too*, *A Twist of Sand* and *Juggernaut*.

COPPING, CORPORAL BILL
Played by Bill Owen
Sergeant Grimshaw's trusty old corporal. Seen in *Sergeant*, he helps turn Able Platoon from a bunch of no-hopers into the champion platoon during their ten-week training course.

CORBETT, HARRY H.
Role: Detective Sergeant Sidney Bung in *Screaming!*
Born in Burma in 1925, the son of an army officer, Harry H. Corbett moved to Manchester as a child and served as a Royal Marine during World War Two, before training as a radiographer.

He was then drawn to the stage, first working as an understudy for the Chorlton Repertory Company and, from 1951, acting with the Theatre Workshop at the Theatre Royal, Stratford. He went on to roles at the Royal Court Theatre and the West End in productions such as *Hamlet*, *The Power and the Glory* and *The Way of the World*.

In 1955 Corbett began his big screen career, acting in films such as *Nowhere To Go* before going on to play Harold Steptoe in the television comedy series *Steptoe and Son* in 1962, a role which was the catalyst to his becoming a household name.

He continued acting in films, adding *Sammy Going South*, *The Bargee*, *Rattle of a Simple Man*, and *The Magnificent Seven Deadly Sins* to his lengthening list of credits, as well as appearing in other television series, including *Grundy* and *Potter*, while on the stage he was seen playing the lead in *Macbeth* at the Globe Theatre in 1973.

He was made OBE in 1976, before his death in 1982, aged fifty-seven.

CORDELL, SHANE
Role: Attractive Nurse in *Nurse*
Shane Cordell was seen in a 1957 episode of *Dixon of Dock Green*, as well as a handful of films during the '50s, including *Three Men in a Boat*, *The Good Companions*, *Fiend Without A Face* and *Girls At Sea*.

CORKTIP
Played by Anita Harris
A belly dancer-cum-fortune teller in *Follow That Camel* who's first seen entertaining customers at the Café ZigaZig. Sergeant Nocker takes a shine to her and although she initially works with Sheikh Abdul Abulbul to entrap Nocker and Bertram West, she ends up being employed as Nocker's batman when he's eventually promoted to commandant.

CORNELIUS, BILLY
Roles: Odbodd Junior in *Screaming!*, Soldier in *Don't Lose Your Head*, Patient in Plaster in *Again Doctor*, Guard in *Henry*, Constable in *Girls*, Tough Man in *Dick*, Man with Salad in *Behind*. Also uncredited roles in *Cleo* (Companion/escaped slave) and *Cowboy* (cowboy shot in opening scenes). He doubled for Terry Scott in *Up the Jungle*
TV: *Christmas ('72)*, *One in the Eye for Harold*, *Under the Round Table* and *Short Knight, Long Daze*
Billy Cornelius, born in London in 1934, entered the printing trade upon leaving school. Always a keen amateur boxer, he turned professional in the mid-1950s and fought competitively for five years.

When he quit the ring, he followed a friend's suggestion and began doing extra work and

---

MEMORIES

'One scene in *At Your Convenience* involved a motorbike sequence with my character and Bernard Bresslaw's. That was very memorable because Bernard couldn't ride and was terrified. I think he'd told the production team that he could.

'On the set at Pinewood, he had to come round this corner to my front door, switch off the engine, park it, leave it on its stand and come up the steps to my character's house. Well, we could hear the bike revving up around the corner and then the bike would stall. He didn't appear for about six or seven takes. Eventually he managed to get it around the corner but then drove too far past the mark, so that was no good. This went on for what seemed like all day. What made it even more funnier was that poor old Bernie's visor was misted up and he couldn't see anything either. In the end, a couple of fellas pushed the bike into the shot.

'*Matron* was a lot of fun, too. Playing Cyril Carter was a lovely part. I had some say in the costume and went for suspenders because I thought they'd be funnier than tights. At lunchtime, you couldn't get changed else you'd lose about fifteen minutes off your break, so I kept my costume on and walked over to get some lunch, wearing my full make-up, wig, the lot. I used to love going down the corridors in Pinewood because the high heels would make a hell of a noise on the floor. One day I passed three guys in the corridor, dressed like a nurse, and went straight into the gents. That didn't half make them look!'

KENNETH COPE

CARRY ON COWBOY

An Anglo Amalgamated film
A Peter Rogers production
Distributed through Warner-Pathe Distribution Ltd
Songs: 'Carry On Cowboy' and 'This is the Night for Love' – music by Eric Rogers Lyrics by Alan Rogers
Sung by Anon
Released as an A certificate in 1965 in colour
Running time: 95 mins

CAST

Sidney James	Johnny Finger / The Rumpo Kid
Kenneth Williams	Judge Burke
Jim Dale	Marshall P. Knutt
Charles Hawtrey	Big Heap
Joan Sims	Belle
Peter Butterworth	Doc
Bernard Bresslaw	Little Heap
Angela Douglas	Annie Oakley
Jon Pertwee	Sheriff Albert Earp
Percy Herbert	Charlie
Sydney Bromley	Sam Houston
Edina Ronay	Dolores
Lionel Murton	Clerk
Peter Gilmore	Curly
Davy Kaye	Josh the Undertaker
Alan Gifford	Commissioner
Brian Rawlinson	Stagecoach Guard
Michael Nightingale	Bank Manager
Simon Cain	Short
Sally Douglas	Kitkata
Cal McCord	Mex
Garry Colleano	Slim
Arthur Lovegrove	Old Cowhand
Margaret Nolan	Miss Jones
Tom Clegg	Blacksmith
Larry Cross	Perkins
Brian Coburn	Trapper
The Ballet Montparnasse	Dancing Girls
Hal Galili	Cowhand
Norman Stanley	Drunk
Carmen Dene	Mexican Girl
Andrea Allen	Minnie
Vicki Smith	Polly
Audrey Wilson	Jane
Donna White	Jenny
Lisa Thomas	Sally
Gloria Best	Bridget
George Mossman	Stagecoach Driver
Richard O'Brien	Rider
Eric Rogers	Pianist

PRODUCTION TEAM

Screenplay by Talbot Rothwell
Music composed and conducted by Eric Rogers
Associate Producer: Frank Bevis
Art Director: Bert Davey
Editor: Rod Keys
Director of Photography: Alan Hume
Camera Operator: Godfrey Godar
Assistant Director: Peter Bolton
Unit Manager: Ron Jackson
Make-up: Geoffrey Rodway
Sound Editor: Jim Groom
Sound Recordists: Robert T. MacPhee and Ken Barker
Hairdressing: Stella Rivers
Costume Designer: Cynthia Tingey
Assistant Editor: Jack Gardner
Master of Horse: Jeremy Taylor
Continuity: Gladys Goldsmith
Producer: Peter Rogers
Director: Gerald Thomas

Judge Burke (Kenneth Williams) lives up to his name

Stodge City is a sleepy Western town where people live in peace and harmony, that is until Johnny Finger, alias the Rumpo Kid, arrives on the scene and starts throwing his weight, and his bullets, around. He cuts a frightening figure and is soon running the place; even Belle's Place, an inn which only served soft drinks, is renamed Rumpo's Place and becomes a rowdy, alcohol-swilling gambling house, with dancing girls, fights and goodness knows what as part of the scene. It's a far cry from the days when Judge Burke tried banishing impropriety by declaring shooting, fighting, boozing and gambling were banned from Stodge, or as he put it so bluntly, 'no nothing'.

No one has the strength or guts to stand up to the Rumpo Kid and his growing band of followers; the last person to try, Albert Earp, the sheriff, ended up with a chestful of bullets. His dying words were for his folks to be told what happened in the hope they might try and even the score; his wish was heard and heading for Stodge is Earp's daughter, Annie Oakley, a fine shot who's determined to track down the man who killed her father. Sharing the stagecoach with her is Marshall Knutt, a drainage, sanitation and garbage disposal engineer, who's been involved in a terrible mix-up; desperate to recruit a peace marshal to sort things out in Stodge City, the local government take Marshall's Christian name as meaning he's a qualified marshal and send him to clean up Stodge City; Knutt, meanwhile, thinks he's been appointed to clear out the town's drains.

En route to Stodge, Annie has the chance to show off her prowess with the gun. Worried about the arrival of a new marshal, the Rumpo Kid, not wanting to be implicated himself, seeks the help of a local Indian tribe to try and prevent Knutt reaching Stodge. When they attack the travelling stagecoach carrying Knutt and Oakley, they didn't

Funny Scene!

The Rumpo Kid and Charlie have travelled to seek help from Big Heap, the leader of the local Indians, in stopping the new marshal from reaching Stodge City.

BIG HEAP: Son (Looks at his son, Little Heap.), tell my squaw to fetch the peace pipe.

LITTLE HEAP: Uh.

BIG HEAP: You'd care for a piece of pipe, wouldn't you?

RUMPO: Be glad to, Chief. Once talked peace with the Sioux but you can't trust them. One moment it was peace on, the next peace off.

expect to be facing a crack shot. Surviving the attack, Knutt thinks he was the one who successfully saw off the Indian threat.

Still desperate to find a way of ridding the town of Marshall P. Knutt, Johnny Finger hatches a plot whereby the marshal is tipped off about cattle-rustling taking place that night. The judge tells Marshall to take a posse out with him but he has trouble recruiting anyone, so Johnny gives him two of his own men. Arriving at the ranch, he's accused of horse-rustling and finds himself with a hangman's noose over his head. It looks like it's curtains for Marshall Knutt until Annie Oakley comes to the rescue.

Back in Stodge City, Annie entices Johnny Finger up to her bedroom and finds a way of getting him to admit to killing her father; she invites him back later and in preparation for his visit rigs up her gun to shoot him when he opens the door. Fortunately for Johnny Finger, his sidekick, Charlie, enters her room first and is killed.

Later, when the judge lets on to the Rumpo Kid that the marshal isn't actually a marshal, but an engineer sent to the town by mistake, he vows to kill him. Annie Oakley tries to persuade Marshall to leave town, revealing that she was the one who shot the Indians. Marshall isn't going to run, though, and has a plan he's confident will work if she can help him become a crack shot in the two hours remaining before the Rumpo Kid's arrival in town.

He may not know his way around a gun, but Marshall P. Knutt is an expert when it comes to drains and sets about nailing the Rumpo Kid once and for all.

The Rumpo Kid (Sid James) meets his match in the unlikely shape of Marshall Knutt (Jim Dale)

stunt work in film and television, which he combined with running pubs around the London area. His screen credits include *The Avengers, Doctor Who, Callan, Ace of Wands* and three episodes of *Carry On Laughing* for television, as well as *When Dinosaurs Ruled the Earth, Bless This House, The Mind of Mr Soames* and, his last film, *The Long Good Friday*.

Nowadays, he can be found helping his son run fruit stalls at Putney and Clapham Junction.

CORNELIUS, JOE
Role: Second in *Loving*
Born in London in 1928, Joe Cornelius started his working life, aged fourteen, in the printing trade. A keen amateur wrestler, by the time he was twenty-two he'd decided to turn pro and travelled to Berlin for his first bout. During a career spanning two decades, he fought around the world, including China and Japan, and was crowned Southern Area heavyweight champion and runner-up in the nationals.

He made occasional television and film appearances, including *Adam Adamant Lives!* and *The Befrienders* for the small screen and *The File of the Golden Goose, Trog* and *The Dirty Dozen* for the big screen.

After quitting wrestling in 1973, he managed various pubs in London before retiring to Lanzarote, where he remained for six years. Now lives in Spain.

CORRIE, ERIC
Role: Citizen in *Constable*
On screen since the 1950s, his television work included *The Scarlet Pimpernel, The Adventures of Sir Lancelot* and *Doomwatch*, while his film credits ranged from *The Colditz Story* and *A Hill in Korea* to *The Quatermass Xperiment* and *The Iron Maiden*.

CORSET LADY
Played by Amelia Bayntun
Seen in *Loving*, the woman is desperately being squeezed into a corset by Esme Crowfoot when Sidney Bliss calls to set up a date for Bertie Muffet.

COUCH, LIONEL
Art Director on *Teacher, Regardless, Don't Lose Your Head, Camping, Loving, Henry, At Your Convenience, Matron, Abroad, Dick, Behind* and *England*
Educated at Dulwich College, Lionel Couch trained at Camberwell Art School and was intending to become an architect before the outbreak of war saw him serve in the army.

After demob he quickly found employment as an assistant art director at Gainsborough Studios before transferring to Pinewood. His CV boasts such pictures as *Nurse On Wheels, Night Must Fall, Casino Royale, Anne of the Thousand Days* (for which he received an

Academy Award nomination), *Assault, Bless This House, The Satanic Rites of Dracula* and, his last picture as art director, *The Awakening*.

COULTER, PHIL
Co-wrote the song, *'Don't Lose Your Head'*, heard in the film of the same name
Born in Londonderry, Northern Ireland, in 1942, composer, pianist and arranger Phil Coulter graduated from Belfast's Queen's University and went on to write music for films such as *A Man Called Sledge* and *The Water Babies* as well as television series, including 1980's *Metal Mickey*.

He's also made the occasional appearance as an actor, such as in the 1999 film *Black Eyed Dog* and the television series, *You're A Star*, hosted his own show, *Coulter and Company* for RTE in Ireland, and released many albums.

COUNSELL, JENNY
Role: Night Nurse in *Again Doctor*

COURTAULDS
The company which supplied all the nurses' uniforms for *Nurse*.

COURTENAY, FRANCIS
Played by Kenneth Williams
Seen in *Regardless*, Francis is an intellectual who's fluent in sixteen languages, including gobbledygook, which helps when the landlord comes calling. Fancies himself as a model and is delighted when a modelling assignment is given to him – that is until discovering he's been hired to model hats for beekeepers.

COURTING GIRL
Played by Drina Pavlovic
The Courting Girl, who's sneaked into the bushes with a boy, is disturbed when Henry Barnes throws a stick into the shrubs during *Behind*.

COURTS
The shop in *Camping* which Sid Boggle and Bernie Lugg visit hoping to find a leaflet on the nudist camp they plan visiting with their girlfriends. Unfortunately they pick up the wrong one and end up in a mudpit in Devon. The shop is also visited by Charlie Muggins who causes a commotion before buying some camping gear.

COWBOY, CARRY ON
See feature box on pages 72–3.

COWHAND
Played by Hal Galili
In *Cowboy* the Cowhand is sitting beside a camp fire with his colleague, Joe, keeping an eye on his herd when he's attacked by Rumpo's men.

COWLING, BRENDA
Roles: Matron in *Girls* and Wife in *Behind*

London-born Brenda Cowling wanted to be a film star as early as her childhood, but after leaving school trained as a shorthand typist before eventually changing direction and joining RADA. While studying at the Academy she made a brief appearance as a drama student in Hitchcock's *Stage Fright*.

Plenty of rep work followed before Cowling made her television debut. Early small screen appearances include several series of an afternoon keep-fit show and *The Forsyte Saga*. Her career has focused mainly on television but she has occasionally appeared on stage and in films, such as *The Railway Children, International Velvet* and a small part in the Bond movie, *Octopussy*.

Television credits include *Dad's Army; It Ain't Half Hot, Mum, Hi-de-Hi!; Fawlty Towers; The Pallisers; Only When I Laugh;* three series of *Potter;* four series of *You Rang, M'Lord?; The Last Detective; Casualty; Murder in Suburbia; Doctors and Nurses* and *Holby City*.

COX, IAN
Technical Advisor on *Jack*
Lieutenant Commander Ian Cox supplied his naval expertise for other films, such as 1970's *Hell Boats*.

COX, JENNY
Role: Veronica in *Behind*
Born in Abervale, South Wales, Jenny Cox completed her education at Watford Grammar School and joined the local rep, making her debut as a prostitute in *The Hostage*. She moved on to begin her acting career in earnest at the Oxford Playhouse.

Her stage career has included a host of productions, including *The Dirtiest Show in Town* and *Pyjama Tops*, while her occasional small-screen appearances during the 1970s and '80s include, among others, *Steptoe and Son, Rings On Their Fingers, Shoestring, The Chinese Detective* and Thames Television's *Spasms* in 1977. She also played Dr Livingstone in the 1974 film, *Can You Keep It Up for a Week?*.

C. R. & J. BRAY
The establishment, which is next-door to D.L. Randall's, is a tobacconist and newsagent. The front of the property is seen in *Behind*.

CRIBBINS, BERNARD
Roles: Midshipman Albert Poop-Decker in *Jack*, Harold Crump in *Spying* and Mordecai Mendoza in *Columbus*
Born in Oldham, Lancashire, in 1928, Bernard Cribbins began acting at the age of fourteen upon joining his local repertory company as an assistant stage manager. By the 1950s, he was playing leading roles on the West End stage and featuring in his own revue.

He began appearing on the screen in the late-1950s, with one-off roles in series like *The*

Vise and small parts in films such as *The Yangtse Incident* and *Davy*, but it was the 1960s in which he attained national recognition. As well as releasing three novelty records, including *Hole in the Ground*, which climbed to number nine in 1962, he appeared in a string of films and television shows. His big-screen credits include *Two Way Stretch*, *The Wrong Arm of the Law*, *Crooks in Cloisters*, *The Sandwich Man*, *The Railway Children* and *Dangerous Davies – The Last Detective*. On television, he's appeared in programmes such as *The Troubleshooters*, *Fawlty Towers*, *Tales of the Unexpected*, *Barbara*, *High and Dry* and, most recently, *Coronation Street*, as Wally Bannister. He's also remembered for providing the voices to the Wombles on television.

CRIMINAL TYPE
Played by Victor Maddern
When PC Benson steps in and stops someone who he thinks is about to steal a car, he doesn't realise he's just stopped Detective Sergeant Liddell from CID.

CROMWELL, THOMAS
Played by Kenneth Williams
Henry VIII's chancellor is seen in *Henry* rushing around trying to satisfy his employer's every need. When money needs to be raised to pay for the King's annulment, Cromwell comes up with the bright idea for taxing sex, called Sex Enjoyment Tax.

CROOK
Played by Freddie Mills
Seen in *Constable*, the crook and his accomplices have just robbed a jewellery shop when PC Potter, a callow new police constable, taps him on the shoulder as he climbs into the getaway car and asks for directions to the police station, totally oblivious to the fact that he's just committed a crime.

CROSS, LARRY
Role: Perkins in *Cowboy*
Larry Cross, who died in 1976, appeared on television from the 1950s, and among his credits were roles in *Sailor of Fortune*, *International Detective*, *The Saint*, *Man of the World*, *Man in*

a *Suitcase*, *Callan*, *The Troubleshooters*, *Thriller* and *Hadleigh*. In films he was seen in, among others, *Time Lock*, *The Mouse on the Moon*, *Battle Beneath the Earth* and his last film, 1975's *The Wind and the Lion*.

CROW, DR
Played by Judith Furse
In charge of the subversive organisation STENCH, Dr Crow is seen in *Spying*. A threat to all mankind, Crow is responsible for the murder of Professor Stark and the stealing of a top-secret formula.

CROWFOOT, ESME
Played by Joan Sims
A client of the Wedded Bliss Agency who's personally vetted – on a regular basis to the disgust of Sophie – by Sidney Bliss, who fancies her rotten. The thirty-five-year-old corset specialist lives in a flat at 32 Rogerham Mansions, Dunham Road, London W23, and used to date a man-mountain of a wrestler, Gripper Burke, until he went to fight in America. When he returns, they rekindle their relationship and end up getting engaged.

Bernard Cribbins (right) makes the first of three *Carry On* appearances (*Jack*)

CARRY ON CRUISING

An Anglo Amalgamated film
A Peter Rogers production
Distributed through Warner-Pathe
Distribution Ltd
From a story by Eric Barker
Released as a U certificate in 1962
in colour
Running time: 89 mins

CAST

Sidney James . . . . Captain Wellington Crowther
Kenneth Williams . . . Leonard Marjoribanks
Kenneth Connor . . . . Dr Arthur Binn
Liz Fraser . . . . Glad Trimble
Dilys Laye . . . . Flo Castle
Esma Cannon . . . . Bridget Madderley
Lance Percival . . . . Wilfred Haines
Jimmy Thompson . . . . Sam Turner
Ronnie Stevens . . . . Drunk
Vincent Ball . . . . Jenkins
Cyril Chamberlain . . . . Tom Tree
Willoughby Goddard . . . . Very Fat Man

Ed Devereaux . . . . Young Officer
Brian Rawlinson . . . . Steward
Anton Rodgers . . . . Young Man
Anthony Sagar . . . . Cook
Terence Holland . . . . Passer-by
Mario Fabrizi . . . . Cook
Evan David . . . . Bridegroom

Marian Collins . . . . Bride
Jill Mai Meredith . . . . Shapely Miss
Alan Casley . . . . Kindly Seaman
(Note: the song sung by Dr Binn while attempting to serenade Flo was recorded by Roberto Cardinali, for a fee of £75.)

PRODUCTION TEAM

Screenplay by Norman Hudis
Music composed and conducted by Bruce Montgomery and Douglas Gamley
Director of Photography: Alan Hume
Art Director: Carmen Dillon
Editor: John Shirley
Production Manager: Bill Hill
Camera Operator: Dudley Lovell
Assistant Director: Jack Causey
Sound Editors: Arthur Ridout and Archie Ludski
Sound Recordists: Robert T. MacPhee and Bill Daniels
Continuity: Penny Daniels
Make-up: George Blackler and Geoffrey Rodway
Hairdressing: Biddy Chrystal
Costume Designer: Joan Ellacott
Casting Director: Betty White
Beachwear for Miss Fraser and Miss Laye by 'Silhouette'
The producers acknowledged the assistance of P&O – ORIENT LINES in the making of the film.
Producer: Peter Rogers
Director: Gerald Thomas

Capt. Crowther (Sid James) presides over a host of new faces

Doctor Binn (Kenneth Connor) is smitten with Flo (Dilys Laye, left)

Ready for another cruise, this time an April run around the sunny Mediterranean, Captain Crowther, who's at the helm of the S.S. *Happy Wanderer*, is horrified to see new faces among his crew. Changes in personnel make him nervous because he believes they could spell disaster, thereby killing off any hope he has of taking over the captaincy of the company's new trans-Atlantic liner.

Among the passengers embarking on the journey is an eccentric old lady, a drunk who spends his entire time propping up the bar and two girls, Flo and Glad. Flo hopes that during the cruise, with her friend's help, she'll find herself a husband. Dr Binn, the ship's doctor,

is attracted to her but it's clear that feelings aren't mutual, particularly as she's already got her eye on Mr Jenkins, the PT instructor.

Meanwhile, Leonard Marjoribanks, the new first officer, happens to pop into the captain's cabin when he's mixing up various drinks. Unbeknown to Marjoribanks, Captain Crowther is trying to find the right combination for an Aberdeen Angus, his favourite tipple. The only person who knew how to mix the drink was Angus, the head barman, who resigned from his job without passing details on to his replacement. Marjoribanks believes the captain is drunk and convenes a meeting with the rest of the crew to inform them that he's taking over the ship; everyone is, therefore, understandably shocked when a completely sober Captain Crowther strides into the room.

Flo Castle's search for a husband, meanwhile, continues. Suddenly realising she needs a mature man, she only has eyes for the captain, but attempts to woo him fail. To help her friend, Glad Trimble secures the help of the first officer to bring Dr Binn and Flo together, and it's not long before the ship's doctor overcomes his timidity and proposes to Miss Castle.

As the cruise comes to an end, a party is thrown to celebrate ten years since the captain took charge of the *Happy Wanderer*; the captain is soon the recipient of good news when a cable arrives informing him he's got the new job, but he declines the offer in order to stay with his beloved *Happy Wanderer*.

Funny Scene!

Captain Crowther inspects his crew before the voyage, but he's in for a surprise because there are a few unfamiliar faces.

CROWTHER: Well, gentlemen, here we are just about to set sail on another cruise. For ten years we've run this ship together, steadily increasing our reputation as the most efficient crew afloat. Together, that's the word. We know each other. Ten solid years of mutual knowledge, and that in itself makes for efficiency and enables me as I look at all your familiar faces to come straight to the point and say . . . (Sees a new face in the line-up.) Who are you?

MARJORIBANKS: Your first officer, sir.

CROWTHER: You're not, Foxton is. What's happened to Foxton, is he ill? What's he got?

MARJORIBANKS: Eight draws, sir.

CROWTHER: I should be so sick.

MARJORIBANKS: I'm your emergency replacement, sir.

CROWTHER: (Looks at his clipboard and reads out the name of the first officer.) Marjoribanks. (Sarcastically.) On transfer from the WRENS?

MARJORIBANKS: They told me you were a pretty wit, sir. It's pronounced Marchbanks — at your service, sir!

CROWTHER: (Upon hearing the man standing next to him, another unfamiliar face, snigger.) What are you laughing at?

DR BINN: Nothing. (Can't hold back his laughter.)

CROWTHER: Who are you?

BINN: Marjori . . . ship's doctor.

CROWTHER: Impossible.

BINN: Not impossible at all. I have certificates to prove it, have I not? (Looks at Marjoribanks.) I am certified, I am.

CROWTHER: You look it.

CROWTHER, CAPTAIN WELLINGTON
Played by Sid James

Captain Crowther has been at the helm of the *Happy Wanderer* for ten years. He served in the navy during the war, sailing Arctic waters, but has spent the last few decades ferrying passengers around the Mediterranean. Has hopes of being offered the captaincy of the company's spanking new trans-Atlantic liner but realises it's not a foregone conclusion, especially with several board members disliking him. Such an inferiority complex explains why he becomes incredibly nervous and worried when new faces join the crew of the *Happy Wanderer*, splitting up the loyal, reliable team he's established over the years.

Despite problems endured during the April cruise to the Med in *Cruising*, the trip turns out successful and Crowther is offered his dream job, only to turn it down in order to stay with the *Happy Wanderer*.

Away from the wheelhouse, he's green-fingered; his garden is the envy of everyone associated with the various horticultural societies to which he belongs.

CRUISING, CARRY ON
See feature box on pages 76–7.

CRUMP, HAROLD
Played by Bernard Cribbins

Agent 04733, whose codename is Blue Bottle, is one of the callow agents reporting to Simkins in *Spying*. A Southern Counties champion in ludo for four years, he's recruited to the team whose job is to retrieve a stolen formula. While doing so, he falls in love with fellow agent, Daphne Honeybutt.

CRUMP, PROFESSOR ROLAND
Played by Kenneth Williams

The distinguished archaeologist, who lectures at the University of Kidburn, heads to Templeton where a Roman encampment has been unearthed next to a caravan site. He's joined on his dig by a bunch of enthusiastic students and an expert in Roman remains, Professor Vooshka, who, surprisingly, takes quite a fancy to the professor, although his in-experience with the opposite sex is plain to see.

CUMMINGS, BILL
Role: Thug in *Spying*

As a stuntman, Bill Cummings worked on such films as *Willow* and ten James Bond movies, ranging from *Dr No* and *From Russia with Love* to *The Spy Who Loved Me* and *For Your Eyes Only*. On television he carried out stunts on *Randall and Hopkirk (Deceased)* and *The Prisoner*.

Cummings appeared in small parts in *The Champions* and *The Avengers* on television, as well as *Heavenly Bodies!* and *The Pink Panther Strikes Again* on the big screen.

CURLY
Played by Peter Gilmore

One of the Rumpo Kid's men who run Stodge City to their own game plan. Seen in *Cowboy*.

CURRY, IAN
Roles: Eric in *Constable* and Leonard Beamish in *Regardless*

Born in Rhodesia in 1930, Ian Curry was seen only occasionally on screen during the early 1960s. His television credits include *Richard the Lionheart*, *The Avengers* and *Zero One*, while he appeared in a few films, such as *Underground* and *The Dock Brief*.

CURTIS, ALAN
Roles: Conte di Pisa in *Henry* and Police Chief in *Abroad*

Born in Coulsdon, Surrey, in 1930, Alan Curtis left school and immediately entered the business at the Croydon Grand, appearing as a village boy in *Great Day*. Apart from a brief spell working for Anglo-American Oil, he's remained in the industry ever since. In 1947, he secured his first break with a repertory company in Gloucester, helping construct the sets, followed by a six-month spell with a small film company in Reigate, making short, animated religious films.

In 1948 he mixed acting with work behind the scenes, including a stint at Colwyn Bay, and by the mid-1950s was appearing on the screen. His film credits include *Die Screaming*, *Marianne*, *Four Dimensions of Greta*, *The Flesh and Blood Show*, *Tiffany Jones* and *The Vision*, while on television he's been seen in, among others, *The Saint*, *Paul Temple*, *Whoops Baghdad!*, *Last of the Summer Wine*, *The Corridor People*, *Crossroads* and *Duty Free*. His busy stage career, meanwhile, has seen him make just under a thousand appearances at the London Palladium.

In 1995 he suffered a stroke which restricted work opportunities for a while but has since returned to acting and, in 2003, was seen in the popular drama, *Footballers' Wives*.

CUSTOMS OFFICER
Played by David Hart

Searches Emmannuelle Prevert's baggage in *Emmannuelle* when she first arrives in the UK, paying particular attention to her underwear. (**Note: the scene was cut from the film.**)

WHAT MIGHT HAVE BEEN

When Emmannuelle first arrives in the UK she gets more than she bargained for at the Customs desk, and in an earlier draft of the script, a female customs officer was involved, too.

INT. CUSTOMS BAGGAGE AREA, AIRPORT – DAY

Emmannuelle is standing at a Customs bench watching a large, brutish, sarcastic Customs officer go through the contents of her two big suitcases. He pulls out some of her frilly underthings and feels them suggestively, grinning at her, daring her to complain.

EMMANNUELLE: You won't find anything in there.

CUSTOMS OFFICER: Pity. (Laughs like a hyena at his own cleverness.)

(The CUSTOMS OFFICER, still rifling through the suitcase, focuses his gaze on the front of EMMANNUELLE's wrap-around dress.)

EMMANNUELLE: (With a challenge.) Nor in there.

(Theodore, wheeling his luggage by on a trolley, unhampered by a customs inspection, stops behind Emmannuelle. He clears his throat to attract her attention. Emmannuelle turns, gives Theodore just a cursory glance, then turns back to the Customs officer.)

(Theodore looks hurt, hesitates, then wheels his trolley towards the exit.)

CUSTOMS OFFICER: Ever been caught smugglin' have you, darlin'?

EMMANNUELLE: I have nothing to declare and nothing to hide!

CUSTOMS OFFICER: (Still gaping at her.) That so?

(The Customs officer turns and gives a silent signal to a woman Customs official, who starts to walk towards them.)

INT. CUSTOMS INSPECTION ROOM, AIRPORT – DAY

(The uniformed woman Customs official is alone with Emmannuelle. The room is very small and as bare as a betting shop.)

CUSTOMS OFFICER: I have to ask you to remove all your clothing, if you don't mind.

EMMANNUELLE: What for?

CUSTOMS OFFICER: We have reason to suspect you may be secreting something on your person.

EMMANNUELLE: What – something?

CUSTOMS OFFICER: That's what we're going to find out!

EMMANNUELLE: (Indignantly.) I am not a smooggler!

CUSTOMS OFFICER: Then you have nothing to worry about, do you?

(Emmannuelle's mood switches from indignation to cunning. She stares at the Custom official's body.)

EMMANNUELLE: I will, if you will.

CUSTOMS OFFICER: What?

EMMANNUELLE: I said – I will, if you will.

CUSTOMS OFFICER: (Trying to take her eyes off EMMANNUELLE's body.) That's not in the regulations.

EMMANNUELLE: Who cares about regulations?

INT. OUTSIDE CUSTOMS INSPECTION ROOM, AIRPORT – DAY

(The large brutish Customs officer is covertly peeping through the knothole in the wall. His expression is incredulous.)

INT. CUSTOMS INSPECTION ROOM, AIRPORT – DAY

(From Customs officer's P.O.V. through knothole: Emmannuelle is undressed for inspection. So is the woman Customs official.)

CUTTING, SIR BERNARD
Played by Kenneth Williams

A top surgeon at Finisham Maternity Hospital in *Matron*, Sir Bernard spends most of his time worrying about his own ailments. A hypochondriac who one minute thinks he's got Asian flu, the next believes he's changing sex. Respected by many of his peers as well as those reporting to him, including Matron, whose feelings for Cutting go far beyond the line of duty. She's smitten with Cutting but the feeling isn't reciprocated, that is until Dr Goode convinces him that his worries regarding changing sex are due to an urgent desire to prove his masculinity.

From that moment, Cutting tries to develop a relationship with Matron, ending in the sound of wedding bells.

CYNICAL LADY
Played by Joan Benham

Seen in *Emmannuelle* sitting at Emile Prevert's dining-table, the Cynical Lady is a guest of the French Ambassador.

CYRIL

The cameraman who arrives at the Palace Hotel with Cecil Gaybody and the rest of the team working on the television programme, *Women's Things*. Seen but not heard in *Girls*.

D

DALE, JIM

Roles: Expectant Father in *Cabby*, Carrier in *Jack*, Carstairs in *Spying*, Horsa in *Cleo*, Marshall P. Knutt in *Cowboy*, Albert Potter in *Screaming!*, Lord Darcy de Pue in *Don't Lose Your Head*, Bertram Oliphant 'Bo' West in *Follow That Camel*, Dr Jim Kilmore in *Doctor*, Dr James Nookey in *Again Doctor* and Columbus in *Columbus*

Jim Dale, who was born in Rothwell, Northants, in 1935, imbued his characterisations with a vulnerability and naïvety, with no finer example than his beautifully portrayed Marshall P. Knutt in *Cowboy*. But he was equally adept at adopting a cheeky grin and have-a-laugh manner, which he used to great effect when crafting a medical persona for *Doctor* and *Again Doctor*.

A man of many talents, from singer and songwriter to comic and actor, Dale began to show an inclination towards a future life on the stage when, aged nine, he began studying dance and started performing in local amateur shows.

After leaving school he worked in a shoe factory but began developing a comedy act which he later toured around Variety music halls before having to interrupt his career to complete National Service in the RAF.

Moving into his twenties, he diversified and enjoyed success as a pop singer; four of his singles charted with his biggest hit, 'Be My Girl', climbing to number two in October 1957. As well as appearing on the popular music show, *Six-Five Special*, he later hosted the show, by which time his face was instantly recognisable to the viewing public. His popularity also led to a spell spinning discs on a BBC radio show for a year.

His stage career started in earnest when he was offered the chance to play Autolycus in Shakespeare's *The Winter's Tale*, followed by the part of Bottom in *A Midsummer Night's Dream*. By the beginning of the 1970s, when he'd made ten of his eleven *Carry On* appearances, he joined the National Theatre and proceeded to clock up numerous West End credits, including such productions as *The Merchant of Venice*, *The Good Natured Man*, *The Burglar* and *The Card*. It was his stage success that led to him settling in America. His impressive performances playing the lead in an adaptation of Molière's *Scapino* in San Francisco and Broadway earned him several awards and plenty of job offers.

His screen career has mainly been in films, with credits including *Raising the Wind*, *The Iron Maiden*, *Nurse on Wheels*, *The Big Job*, *The Plank*, *Lock Up Your Daughters!*, *Pete's Dragon* and *Scandalous*. His television roles, meanwhile, include appearances in *The Equaliser* and *Cosby*.

More recently, he's recorded the Harry Potter audiobooks and picked up many awards for his efforts.

Albert Potter (Jim Dale) thinks he's lost the love of his life (*Screaming!*)

DALE ROAD

A road mentioned in *Cabby* during the scene where Peggy and Sally are held at gunpoint by crooks while driving one of the Glamcabs.

DALE, SHEILA

Played by Carol White

In *Teacher*, Dale is one of the ringleaders among the schoolkids who wreak havoc when a school inspector and child psychiatrist visit Maudlin Street Secondary Modern School.

DALEY, LADY
Played by Margaret Nolan
The busty wife of Sir Roger Daley appears in *Dick*.

DALEY, SIR ROGER
Played by Bernard Bresslaw
Sir Roger is a member of the landed gentry who's tasked with running the Bow Street Runners, a special police unit formed to stop the upsurge in crime. Seen in *Dick*, his main objective is to catch the master villain himself: highwayman Dick Turpin, who happens to rob Sir Roger of all his possessions, including clothes, on two occasions. Although Sir Roger is married to the delectable Lady Daley, he still likes a little fun on the side.

DANCING GIRLS
Played by The Ballet Montparnesse
When the Rumpo Kid takes over Belle's Place in *Cowboy*, he transforms Stodge City's hostelry into a rowdy, smoky establishment full of debauched customers, with entertainment provided by the dancing girls performing the cancan.

DANCY
Played by Peter Gilmore
One of the crooks in *Cabby* who hold Peggy and Sally at gunpoint.

DANDY
Played by Guy Ward
In *Emmannuelle* the effeminate dandy wanders by a sentry, makes a comment and receives a wink in return.

DANDY
Played by John Clive
In *Henry* a crowd at Speakers' Corner gather to debate the new Sex Enjoyment Tax being imposed by the King. The Dandy, however, turns to his friend and remarks that it won't affect them! (**Note: the scene was cut.**)

WHAT MIGHT HAVE BEEN

The Heckler, Young Man and a Dandy are standing at Speakers' Corner, listening to debate about the newly proposed Sex Enjoyment Tax (S.E.T.).

EXT. 'SPEAKERS' CORNER' OF THE TIME – DAY

Hampton is addressing an at-the-moment rather apathetic little crowd of men.

HAMPTON: I tell you, citizens, we've had some cruel taxes thrust upon us but this is one of the most infamous of them all! Are we going to take it lying down? No, let's stand up to it!

HECKLER: Don't matter which way you have it, you'll still have to pay!

(**This gets a laugh from the crowd.**)

HAMPTON: You might find it amusing at the moment, friend, but will you still feel like going home and taking your wife in your arms regularly?

HECKLER: Yes.

HAMPTON: And afford it?

HECKLER: Yes. I'm knocking it off her house-keeping!

(**This gets another laugh.**)

HAMPTON: All right, all right. That may be all right for you friend, but what of you unmarried younger men? You, lad!

(**He points to a YOUNG MAN in the crowd.**)

HAMPTON: Are you married?

YOUNG MAN: No, fear.

HAMPTON: Ah! Well, do you ever take a young maid into the fields for a bit of dalliance?

YOUNG MAN: I'm going tonight.

HAMPTON: Knowing that with S.E.T. you've got to pay up for every little kiss and cuddle? No! Let's have it off, I say!

YOUNG MAN: I intend to!

(**Another laugh.**)

HAMPTON: Then you're a fool! Friends, I appeal to you! If the basic simple pleasures of life are to be taxed where's it going to end? Soon we'll be paying just to have a good scratch! We've got to put a stop to S.E.T. now!

HECKLER: How?

HAMPTON: Simple! Keep away from the women! Go on strike! Down tools!

(**There are some 'Hear hears' and murmurs of approval from the crowd now.**)

(**C.S. of two dandies, looking on dispassionately. One looks to the other petulantly.**)

DANDY: Oh come on, Cedric. It doesn't affect us.

DANDY DESMOND
A fictitious name Captain Fancey adopts while travelling incognito trying to track down Dick Turpin in *Dick*.

DANE, ALEXANDRA
Roles: Female Instructor in *Doctor*, Busti in *Up The Khyber*, Stout Woman in *Again Doctor*, Emily in *Loving* and Lady in Low-cut Dress in *Behind*. (**Note: Also had uncredited role in *At Your Convenience* but scene cut.**)

Born in Bethlehem, South Africa, in 1946, Alexandra Dane always wanted to be a ballerina but her mother steered her towards an acting career. After graduating from Cape Town University with a degree and diploma in drama, she headed for England in the mid-1960s to begin her acting career.

Her first post was assistant stage manager at Bognor Regis, before progressing to juvenile lead and moving on to other reps. Theatre has dominated Dane's career and during the 1960s she formed her own company, the Cambridge Shakespeare Group, and toured South Africa, affording her the chance to direct.

MEMORIES

'My first role was playing an instructor in *Doctor*, running antenatal classes. I was told to improvise but didn't know anything about pre-natal in those days so I got them lifting their legs up and down. I've had children since then and know it's one of the last things you'd do at antenatal class; any medical person would have been going mad!

'One of the nice things about the *Carry On* films is that when they'd used you once, if they liked you it could lead to other parts, which is what happened to me. Along came *Up the Khyber* and I was offered the part of Busti.

'I'll always remember Nora Rodway, who was helping her husband, Geoff, with the make-up. I had to use a lot of body make-up but in those days you didn't have these quick-tan methods, so Nora had to put it on with a sponge and water, and she had to do it every morning because I had so much of my body showing in *Up the Khyber*. I'll always remember her saying: "This is like distempering a small room!" She pleaded with me not to bath each evening because I'd keep washing this water-based liquid off and she'd have to go through the job each morning.

'In *Again Doctor* I had a nasty accident and suffered back problems for some time after. I was leaning back on a machine made to look like it was out of control and it came out of the floor resulting in me going to hospital.

'Working on the *Carry On*s was the happiest, happiest experience. Even when thinking about all the other bits and pieces I did in movies and on tele, I can't remember being happier because everyone was so sweet to you. I adored them all, it was like being part of a big family. It's extraordinary that after appearing in Shakespeare and rep, which I was doing when I appeared in the *Carry On*s, I'm remembered for small parts in those films; I'd never have believed it. They were lovely films to work on.'

ALEXANDRA DANE

Her screen career has seen her appear in films such as *Corruption, Confessions of a Handyman* and, in 1977, *Jabberwocky*, while her small-screen credits include *The Saint, Hazell* and *The Tripods,* as well as semi-regular characters in *Not On Your Nellie, Alas Smith and Jones* and *The Doctors.*

In 1981, she formed her own puppet company, Pom Pom Puppets, and performed around the world, including Tenerife and India. After recently buying a farm in Spain, Dane, who's retired from acting, is considering relaunching her puppet shows in the country.

DANGLE, MRS
Played by Joan Sims

Emile Prevert's housekeeper-cum-cook in *Emmannuelle.* A widow since the death of her husband, Henry, Mrs Dangle takes care of the French Ambassador's culinary needs.

DANIEL, DANNY
Sound Recordist on *Henry, At Your Convenience, Matron, Dick, Behind, England, That's Carry On* and *Emmannuelle*

Working as a sound recordist from the late 1960s, his various screen credits include *Kidnapped, Nothing But the Night, Diamonds On Wheels* and, in 1985, *Murder Elite.*

DANIEL, J. W. N.
Sound Recordist on *Loving*

Working as a boom operator on the 1957 film, *Miracle in Soho,* J. W. N. Daniel was credited as a sound recordist from the 1970s on films such as *The Private Life of Sherlock Holmes* and *Revenge.*

DANIELLE, SUZANNE
Role: Emmannuelle Prevert in *Emmannuelle*

Born in London in 1955, Suzanne Danielle grew up in Romford, Essex, where she attended the famous Bush Davies School between the age of seven and sixteen; it was here that she nurtured not only her love of acting but dancing, too. She gained experience of the stage at Hornchurch Rep before joining the cast of *Billy,* starring Michael Crawford. After four weeks in Manchester, the play moved into the West End.

Soon after appearing in *Billy,* Danielle was seen on the big screen in *The Prince and the Pauper,* while other credits include *The Wild Geese, Golden Lady, Long Shot, The Stud, Flash Gordon, Arabian Adventure* (as a dancer) and, one of her last films, *The Boys in Blue,* in 1987.

On the small screen, meanwhile, she enjoyed a busy period between the late 1970s and late '80s when she was seen in several television series, such as *The Professionals, The Generation Game, Doctor Who, Hammer House of Horror, Tales of the Unexpected, Strangers* and the *Morecambe and Wise Show.*

In the late 1980s she married golfer Sam Torrance and quit showbusiness.

DANIELS, BILL
Sound recordist on *Nurse, Constable, Cruising, Cabby, Jack, Spying, Cleo, Camping* and *Again Doctor*

Bill Daniels began working as a sound recordist from the mid-1950s, with early films including *The Secret Place, Hell Drivers, Rockets Galore!, A Tale of Two Cities* and *Too Many Crooks.* He worked regularly until the mid-70s, with later credits such as the big-screen version of hit sitcom *Bless This House* and in 1976, his last film, *The Slipper and the Rose.*

DANIELS, DANNY
Role: Nosha Chief in *Up the Jungle*

Other screen credits for Danny Daniels include the television shows *White Hunter, The Saint* and *Man in a Suitcase* as well as films such as *Passionate Summer, Murder Club, Prehistoric Women* and *The Oblong Box.*

DANIELS, PENNY
Continuity on *Nurse, Cruising, Cabby, Jack, Spying* and *Screaming!*

Working in continuity from the 1950s, Penny Daniels' long list of film credits include *Tiger in the Smoke, A Night to Remember, The Captain's Table, The League of Gentlemen, Whistle Down the Wind, Séance on a Wet Afternoon, Where Eagles Dare, The Medusa Touch* and two Bond movies, *Octopussy* and *A View to a Kill.*

DANN, DAN
Played by Charles Hawtrey

Works as a lavatory attendant at the public conveniences outside the entrance to Hocombe Park. Formerly employed at the Bide-a-Wee Rest Home, near Hocombe Woods, as a gardener before securing the job which comes with free accommodation! He sadly meets an unfortunate end when he's drowned in one of his own toilets. Olando and Virula Watt, the residents of Bide-a-Wee Rest Home, become concerned that he'll spill the beans to the police about the goings-on at their eerie house, so they despatch Odbodd to do their dirty deeds. **(Note: in an early version of the script, Dan was to be Doris Mann's father.)**

DANN, LARRY
Roles: Boy in *Teacher,* Clive in *Behind,* Gunner Shaw in *England* and Theodore Valentine in *Emmannuelle*

Born in London in 1941, Larry Dann joined the Corona Stage School from the age of eleven. Just like his opening performance in the *Carry Ons,* his screen debut, back in 1949, saw him cast as a schoolboy in Rank's movie, *Adam and Evelyn,* with Stewart Granger and Jean Simmons. While studying at stage school he appeared as an extra in several pictures, including *The Million Pound Note, Trouble in Store* and *The Bulldog Breed.*

He left Corona aged twenty-one and joined Joan Littlewood's Theatre Workshop in London's Stratford East, appearing in the original production of *Oh What A Lovely War,* marking the beginning of a fruitful stage career. Over the years he's performed with numerous repertory companies and in plenty of West End productions, while his small screen work includes playing Elsie Tanner's son, Dennis, in *Florizel Street,* the pilot episode of *Coronation Street* and Sergeant Alec Peters in *The Bill* for eight years.

DARCY DE PUE, LORD
Played by Jim Dale

A friend of Sir Rodney Ffing, he is saddened to hear of the plight of so many French men and women; since the revolution across the channel, the aristocracy are losing their heads to the guillotine at an alarming rate and the brave Darcy, accompanied by Ffing, sets out to snatch the victims from the brink of death via a series of audacious ruses and artful disguises. Seen in *Don't Lose Your Head.*

DARCY, MAUREEN
Played by Carol Wyler

One of the beauty contestants rushed on stage during the itching powder fiasco in *Girls.*

D

DARK, GREGORY
Assistant Director on *Emmannuelle*

DARLING, JANE
Played by Valerie Leon
The film star gives birth to triplets in the back of the ambulance during *Matron*. Even more remarkable, though, is that Cyril Carter, dressed up as a nurse, administered the delivery because Dr Prodd, who should have been doing the job, was knocked out after having an injection accidentally pushed into his backside.

DARLING, MR
Played by Robin Hunter
Jane Darling's husband who waves his wife goodbye during *Matron* before heading back inside his house for a bit of fun with the shapely au pair.

DARVEY, DIANA
Role: Maureen in *Behind*
Born in Richmond, Surrey, in 1945, Diana Darvey followed her mother – who topped the bill at the Windmill Theatre during the war years – into showbusiness. Originally starting out as a singer and dancer, her early career was spent working with Miss Joan Baron's Ballet in Madrid; spotted by former musical revue artist Celia Gomez, who groomed her to become England's first female star in Spanish light entertainment. She later won more plaudits as leading lady to Spanish revue artistes Luis Cuenca and Pedro Pena in Barcelona. Three years later, she returned to Madrid's Teatro Alcazar as the star attraction.

In the 1970s she was working on British television, making occasional appearances in shows such as sitcom *And Mother Makes Five*, starring Wendy Craig. She also played various character roles in several series of *The Benny Hill Show*. For many years continued to lead a successful career in cabaret at the Savoy and other top venues.

She died in 2000, aged fifty-four.

DAVENPORT, CLAIRE
Role: Blonde in Pub in *Emmannuelle*
Born in Sale, Cheshire, in 1933, Claire Davenport was the archetypal character actress, often seen playing a host of battleaxes, from fearsome traffic wardens to overbearing wives.

After grammar school she trained as a teacher at Liverpool's St Catherine's College and subsequently taught at a school in Salford. Always a keen amateur actress, she spent her evenings performing with various local companies before, in 1960, deciding to swap careers.

She studied at RADA for two years before making her professional debut in the stage version of television sitcom, *The Rag Trade*; the following year, she played Myrtle in the final series of the TV show.

Hers quickly became a regular face on television, mostly in comedies such as *George and the Dragon, Love Thy Neighbour, Fawlty Towers, Robin's Nest, George and Mildred* and *On the Buses*. On the big screen she played a masseuse in *The Return of the Pink Panther*, a fat lady in *The Elephant Man* and a six-breasted dancer in *Return of the Jedi*. She subsequently popped up in various low-budget sex comedies, including *The Bawdy Adventures of Tom Jones* and *Rosie Dixon – Night Nurse*.

A series of strokes in the 1990s stopped her working. She died in 2002, aged sixty-eight.

DAVENPORT, DAVID
Roles: Bilius in *Cleo*, Sergeant in *Don't Lose Your Head* and Major-domo in *Henry*
Born in Hertfordshire in 1921, David Davenport moved to London at the age of thirteen to attend the Cone Ripman ballet school, before joining the Lydia Kyasht Russian ballet at seventeen. Four years later, he was invited to join the Royal Ballet.

His career as a dancer was suspended for four years whilst he worked as an RAF wireless operator during World War Two, but he continued after the war with parts in *Sleeping Beauty* at the Royal Opera House in 1946 and *Annie Get Your Gun* in 1948. During the 1950s, he moved into musical stage work, playing in many productions including *The King and I* and *Oklahoma!* He also began choreographing ballets for the Joanna Denise Classical Dance Group and made the transition into acting, in films and television.

His small-screen credits include playing the nationally hated Malcolm Ryder in *Crossroads* and frequently appearing in *All Creatures Great and Small*. He also acted in numerous films including *King's Rhapsody* and *84, Charing Cross Road*.

He died in 1994, aged seventy-three.

DAVEY, BERT
Art Director on *Cleo, Cowboy* and *Screaming!*
Began as an art director in the 1950s and went on to spend the next three decades working on such films as *Time Is My Enemy, On the Beat, A Stitch in Time, Battle of Britain, At the Earth's Core, The People That Time Forgot, Eye of the Needle* and, in 1986, his last film, *Aliens*.

DAVID, EVAN
Role: Bridegroom in *Cruising*

DAVIES, WINDSOR
Roles: Fred Ramsden in *Behind* and Sergeant Major 'Tiger' Bloomer in *England*
Born in London in 1930, Windsor Davies is probably best known for playing loud-mouthed

Windsor Davis struck gold by playing Sgt. Major Williams in the sitcom *It Ain't Half Hot Mum* as well as appearing in two *Carry Ons*.

Sergeant Major Williams in Perry and Croft's 70's sitcom, *It Ain't Half Hot, Mum*.

He worked as a teacher and miner before completing a drama course at Richmond College in 1961 and turning his attention to acting. His screen career had begun by the mid-60s with early credits including television shows *Dixon of Dock Green*, *Redcap*, *The Corridor People* and *Probation Officer*, playing Bill Morgan. His film work covers the likes of *Murder Most Foul*, *The Alphabet Murders*, *Drop Dead Darling* and *Endless Night*.

More recent credits include small-screen productions *2point4Children*, *Sunburn*, *Casualty*, *Vanity Fair*, *My Family* and *Cor Blimey!*

DAVIS, JOAN
Continuity on *Sergeant* and *Constable*
Her other credits in continuity, dating back to the 1940s, include *Candles at Night*, *Turn the Key Softly*, *A Town Like Alice*, *The Iron Petticoat*, *The Spanish Gardener*, *Campbell's Kingdom*, *The 39 Steps*, *Victim* and two Bond movies, *Thunderball* and *On Her Majesty's Secret Service*.

DAVISON, RITA
Continuity on *Don't Lose Your Head*, *Henry* and *At Your Convenience*
Rita Davison began working in continuity in the 1950s and proceeded to clock up a host of film credits. She joined the production team of films such as *Innocents in Paris*, *The Vicious Circle*, *Tunes of Glory*, *Tom Jones*, *Help!*, *Petulia* and her last film, 1981's *Dragonslayer*. She also worked on the ITC drama series, *The Saint*.

DAWE, CEDRIC
Art Director on *Doctor*
Born in London in 1906, Cedric Dawe was designing for the US stage for several years before entering the British film industry. Other than the war years, during which he served in the army, he was regularly in employment.

His film credits included *Black Limelight*, *Traveller's Joy*, *Freedom of the Seas*, *Easy Money*, *So Long at the Fair*, *Street Corner*, *Star of India*, *Up in the World*, *A Hill in Korea* and his penultimate film, *The Day of the Triffids*. He also worked on the 50s television series, *Colonel March of Scotland Yard*.

He died in 1996.

DAWES ROAD
Mentioned in *Cabby* during the scene where Peggy and Sally are driving along while being held at gunpoint by crooks.

DAWSON, NURSE STELLA
Played by Joan Sims
The accident-prone student nurse is seen in *Nurse*, working at the Haven Hospital. She's so green she even thinks suppositories should be administered orally. Thankfully for poor old Ted York, the patient, she discovers her mistake before it's too late.

DAY, TILLY
Continuity on *Teacher*
From the 1930s, when she worked on films such as *The Mystery of the Marie Celeste*, Tilly Day's lengthy list of credits include *The Rocking Horse Winner*, *The Malta Story*, *Lost*, *Too Many Crooks*, *Futtock's End*, *Up the Front* and, in 1974, *Diamonds On Wheels*.

DE WOLFF, FRANCIS
Role: Agrippa in *Cleo*
Born in Southminster, Essex, in 1913, Francis De Wolff graduated from RADA and made a living playing character parts on stage and screen. His television work saw him in shows such as *Disneyland*, *Interpol Calling*, *The Cheaters* and running roles as Leopold of Austria in *Richard the Lionheart* and Jedikiah in 1970's sci-fi series, *The Tomorrow People*.

He was working in films from the 1930s, and among his credits are *Flame in the Heather*, *Adam and Evelyne*, *Tom Brown's Schooldays*, *The Diamond*, *The Smallest Show on Earth* and *The Three Musketeers*.

He died in 1984, aged seventy-one.

DEAF OLD LADY
Played by Esma Cannon
Seen in *Constable*, the old lady has just diced with death and managed to cross a busy main road when along comes interfering PC Benson who shepherds her back across, much to her annoyance.

DEAN
Played by Donald Hewlett
The Dean of the University of Kidburn is seen in *Behind*. He informs Professor Crump that he'll be assisted on the archaeological dig by Professor Vooshka.

DEARLOVE MODEL LAUNDRY (DRY CLEANING)
One of their vans is seen chugging into Heathercrest National Service Depot in *Sergeant* carrying an extra piece of cargo in the shape of Mary Sage, the newlywed who wants to be near her hubby, who was called up on their wedding day.

DEBRA
Played by Sally Geeson
With her enormous specs, Debra is Cecil Gaybody's assistant on the television programme, *Women's Things*. Seen in *Girls* when the TV crew arrive at the Palace Hotel in Fircombe to film the beauty contest.

DEIRDRE
Played by Valerie Leon
Deirdre Philkington-Battermore is employed as Dr Nookey's secretary in *Again Doctor*. With her short, low-cut dresses she's obviously willing to satisfy her boss in every conceivable way.

DELLING, HELEN
Played by Carol Shelley
Mr Delling's wife is seen in *Regardless*. She returns to the family house unexpectedly, just as her husband has arranged for Delia King, from Helping Hands, to model some new clothes, including underwear, he wanted to buy his wife as a surprise anniversary present.

Nurse Dawson (Joan Sims) is a liability at Haven Hospital (*Nurse*)

Helen has quite a shock when she hangs her coat up in the bedroom cupboard only to find Delia, disguised as a workman, clambering out.

DELLING, MR
Played by Jimmy Thompson

Appears in *Regardless*. A smart, dark-haired man who hires Delia King to model a set of outfits he's bought his wife as a surprise anniversary present. When his beloved, Helen, arrives home early, Mr Delling panics and pushes Delia into the cupboard.

DEMPSEY, MISS
Played by Patsy Rowlands

For years, the dowdy Miss Dempsey has been Mr Snooper's housekeeper, taking care of his every need, so she's understandably jealous when Sophie Bliss appears on the scene, albeit temporarily. Seen in *Loving*, she makes sure Sophie doesn't get her claws into Mr Snooper by dressing seductively – or as seductive as Miss Dempsey can be – and coming out with plenty of outrageous comments about her relationship with her boss.

DEMPSTER, JEREMY
Role: Recruit in *Sergeant*

DENBY, EILEEN
Played by Laraine Humphrys

One of the beauty contestants eager to win the Miss Fircombe crown in *Girls*.

DENE, CARMEN
Roles: Mexican Girl in *Cowboy* and Hospitality Girl in *Up The Khyber*

Between the mid-1960s and early 70s, Carmen Dene was offered small parts in a handful of films, such as *Genghis Khan*, *Cuckoo Patrol* and *Subterfuge*, as well as television shows including *The Avengers* and *The Benny Hill Show*.

DENTON, NURSE DOROTHY
Played by Shirley Eaton

A staff nurse at the Haven Hospital who's infatuated with Dr Stephens. Seen in *Nurse*, she carries out her job efficiently and effectively, but when she realises her chances of romance with Stephens, who seems to like every young and pretty nurse in the entire hospital, are slim, she considers applying for a job in America. Her plans change, however, when she falls for journalist Ted York.

DERNLEY, DOREEN
Continuity on *Camping*

She began working in films in the 1950s and established a list of credits which included such pictures as *Shadow of a Man*, *Dracula*, *Cairo*, *Up the Junction*, *Get Carter*, *On the Buses* and one of the sequels, *Mutiny on the Buses*.

DESIREE, MADAME
Played by Joan Sims

In *Dick*, Madame Desiree tours the country with a group of girls entertaining at pubs, like the Old Cock Inn, as Madame Desiree et ses Oiseaux des Paradis, or Birds of Paradise. A cockney by birth, she's adopted a French accent over the years to go with her act.

DESK SERGEANT
Played by Frank Forsyth

Seen in *Screaming!* telling Detective Sergeant Sidney Bung that he's wanted when Albert Potter causes mayhem at a milliner's.

DESMONDE, JERRY
Role: Martin Paul in *Regardless*

Born in Middlesbrough in 1908, Jerry Desmonde was always cast as the straight man, including a long-standing relationship alongside Sid Field and, later, Norman Wisdom in his films of the 1950s.

Adroit at playing haughty roles, such as Major Willoughby in Wisdom's *Up in the World*, Desmonde's other film credits included *The Perfect Woman*, *The Malta Story*, *Ramsbottom Rides Again*, *A Kind of Loving* and *Gonks Go Beat*. On television he was a regular panellist on *What's My Line*.

He died in 1967, aged fifty-eight, after committing suicide.

DEVEREAUX, ED
Roles: Sergeant Russell in *Sergeant*, Alec Lawrence in *Nurse*, Mr Panting in *Regardless*, Young Officer in *Cruising* and Hook in *Jack*

Born in Sydney, Australia, in 1925, Ed Devereaux's greatest screen success was playing Matt Hammond, a park ranger in the television series, *Skippy*, about a pet kangaroo, which sold around the world.

Prior to this success, he was a regular face in British films during the 1950s and '60s, appearing in such pictures as *The Captain's Table*, *Watch Your Stern*, *Man in the Moon*, *Very Important Person*, *The Bargee* and *Money Movers*. He was also regularly seen on television.

After leaving school he undertook a succession of jobs, including taxi-driving, before breaking into radio and films in Australia. He moved to England in the early 1950s and began appearing on the stage. An accomplished singer, he had starring roles in musicals such as *Guys and Dolls*, *West Side Story*, *Damn Yankees*, *Pyjama Game* as well as Variety and cabaret acts.

He returned Down Under in 1964 but contined appearing on British screens, including an appearance in an episode of *Absolutely Fabulous*.

He died in 2003, aged seventy-eight.

DEVIS, JIMMY
Camera Operator on *Don't Lose Your Head*, *Abroad*, *Girls* and *Dick*

Jimmy Devis, born in London in 1931, followed his brother into the film industry in 1946, joining Gaumont-British, based at Lime Grove, as a mail boy. He spent a short spell in the cutting room and, later, joined the camera department.

After the studios closed, Devis completed his National Service in the RAF, before returning home and, in 1952, working as a freelance clapper-loader. It wasn't long until he was offered a contract at Pinewood, where he worked between 1952-60, before returning to a freelance status.

He retired in 2001, by which time he was working as a director of photography for second units and directing action units. His long list of credits include *Return to Oz*, *Wild Geese II*, *Labyrinth*, *Christopher Columbus: The Discovery*, *Avalanche*, *Superman*, *For Your Eyes Only*, *Empire of the Sun* and *Daylight*.

DIAMOND, ARNOLD
Role: 5th Specialist in *Sergeant*

Born in London in 1915, Arnold Diamond started his working life as a librarian, acting as an amateur during the evenings, until he was called up for the Second World War. During hostilities he was wounded and transported to an Italian hospital for POWs, where upon recovering he wrote and directed plays for fellow prisoners.

CARRY ON DICK

A Peter Rogers production
Distributed through Fox / Rank
Distribution Ltd
Released as an A certificate in 1974
in colour
Running time: 91 mins

CAST

Sidney James . . . . Dick Turpin /
The Rev. Flasher
Kenneth Williams . . . . Captain Desmond
Fancey
Barbara Windsor . . . . Harriett
Hattie Jacques . . . . Martha Hoggett
Bernard Bresslaw . . . . . . Sir Roger Daley
Joan Sims . . . . Madame Desiree
Peter Butterworth . . . . Tom
Kenneth Connor . . . . Constable
Jack Douglas . . . . Sgt Jock Strapp
Patsy Rowlands . . . . Mrs Giles
Bill Maynard . . . . Bodkin
Margaret Nolan . . . . Lady Daley
John Clive . . . . Isaak the Tailor
David Lodge . . . . Bullock
Marianne Stone . . . . Maggie
Patrick Durkin . . . . William
Sam Kelly . . . . Sir Roger's Coachman
George Moon . . . . Mr Giles
Michael Nightingale . . Squire Trelawney
Brian Osborne . . . . Browning
Anthony Bailey . . . . Rider
Brian Coburn and Max
Faulkner . . . . Highwaymen
Jeremy Connor and Nosher
Powell . . . . Footpads
Joy Harrington . . . . Lady
Larry Taylor and Billy
Cornelius . . . . Tough Men
Laraine Humphrys
Linda Hooks
Penny Irving
Eva Reuber-Staier . . . 'The Birds of Paradise'

PRODUCTION TEAM

Screenplay by Talbot Rothwell
Based on a treatment by Lawrie Wyman
and George Evans
Music composed and conducted by Eric
Rogers
Production Manager: Roy Goddard
Art Director: Lionel Couch
Editor: Alfred Roome
Director of Photography: Ernest Steward

Camera Operator: Jimmy Devis
Continuity: Jane Buck
Assistant Director: David Bracknell
Sound Recordists: Danny Daniel and Ken
Barker
Make-up: Geoffrey Rodway
Hairdresser: Stella Rivers
Costume Design: Courtenay Elliott
Set Dresser: Charles Bishop
Dubbing Editor: Peter Best
Master of Horse: Gerry Wain

Assistant Editor: Jack Gardner
Casting Director: John Owen
Stills Cameraman: Tom Cadman
Wardrobe Mistresses: Vi Murray and
Maggie Lewin
Coach and Horses supplied by George
Mossman
Titles: G.S.E. Ltd
Processed by Rank Film Laboratories
Producer: Peter Rogers
Director: Gerald Thomas

Sgt. Strapp (Jack Douglas) took a peep once too often

It's 1750 and England is rife with crime. Highwaymen are a constant threat on the roads, and none more so than Richard Turpin, better known as Big Dick due to the extraordinary size of his weapon. To help wipe out the tidal wave of crime, a special police force, the Bow Street Runners, is set up by King George and run by Sir Roger Daley, who himself becomes a victim of the elusive Dick Turpin, leaving him and his wife, Lady Daley, naked and embarrassed.

Just when the Bow Street Runners believe they're closing in on the criminal, he slips out of their hands into the darkness. Unbeknown to the police, by day Dick Turpin dons a cassock and dog collar and becomes the Reverend Flasher. When the attacks continue, Captain Fancey and Sergeant Jock Strapp of the Bow Street Runners take personal responsibility for tracking down the dastardly villain.

They head for the Old Cock Inn, a well-known watering hole amongst the criminal fraternity, pretending to be crooks in search of some clues to help capture Turpin; when an old woman, Maggie, the local midwife, tells them that Turpin has a birthmark on his 'diddler', Jock Strapp is given the unenviable task of following every man into the toilet to check for the birthmark, but it's a pointless task and results in Strapp almost being attacked for being a Peeping Tom.

Fancey makes out he's a criminal wanting to bring Turpin in on a job he's planning, so a meeting is arranged between them, but Turpin, who's no fool, tips off the local parish policeman about the meeting and enjoys the last laugh when Fancey and Strapp are arrested and thrown in the stocks suspected of being highwaymen. A relieved Sir Roger is informed of the supposed arrest of Turpin and travels to see the legendary highwayman behind bars, but when history repeats itself and his coach is robbed en route, he knows the dastardly villain is still at large.

But Turpin's game is soon up, or so everyone thinks, when one of his sidekicks, Harriett, is captured and held as bait. Fancey, Strapp and the

Funny Scene!

Sergeant Strapp and Captain Fancey of the Bow Street Runners await Dick Turpin at the Blasted Oak. A stagecoach draws near.

STRAPP: It sounds like a coach.

FANCEY: What would he be doing in a coach?

STRAPP: I don't know but it's bang on ten o'clock so it must be him.

FANCEY: All right, all right, don't panic.

STRAPP: Pistol? (Tries to pass gun to Fancey who's misheard him.)

FANCEY: What? I haven't had a drop!

STRAPP: No, pistol!

parish constable await Turpin's arrival, knowing that he'll try rescuing his loyal friend and would-be lover, but yet again they're fooled by the highwayman as he enters the local jail with his colleague, Tom, disguised as women; they end up freeing Harriett and tying up Fancey and Strapp.

Next day, Fancey realises he recognised Turpin's face while disguised as a woman, and when it transpires that the Reverend Flasher was the only person who knew of his plans to lure Turpin, it's clear that the clergyman is the wanted highwayman. They burst in on his sermon but out of respect decide to wait until the service is over before making their arrest, but before long Turpin is on the run again, crossing the border into Bonnie Scotland.

Capt. Fancey (Kenneth Williams) is entertained by the 'Birds of Paradise'

After demob he decided to try his luck professionally, studying at RADA, before working in various reps around the country, including Bolton and Southwold. He later worked with the Royal Shakespeare Company in Stratford.

Many years in rep followed before television work began to dominate. He appeared in, among others, *The Borgias, Randall & Hopkirk (Deceased), Citizen Smith, Dad's Army, Crossroads* and *Master Spy*. His final appearance in a series was *In Sickness and In Health*. Among his sixty-plus films are favourites such as *The Constant Husband, Zeppelin, The Frightened City* and *The Italian Job*.

Although most of his roles were small, his services were in demand in every aspect of the entertainment business, including theatre and radio, particularly playing suave official types. He died in 1992 after being hit by a car, aged seventy-seven.

DICK
A photographer in *Matron* who accompanies the reporter to the Finisham Maternity Hospital to cover the story of film actress Jane Darling giving birth.

DICK, CARRY ON
See feature box on pages 86–7.

DICKENSON, TERRY
Role: Recruit in *Sergeant*

DIETRICH, MONICA
Role: Girl in *Don't Lose Your Head* and Katherine Howard in *Henry*
For a short period around the time of her *Carry On* appearances, Monica Dietrich made a few screen appearances, in television shows such as *Department S* and *Jason King*, and films like *A Dandy in Aspic* and *For Men Only*.

DIGNAM, BASIL
Role: 3rd Specialist in *Sergeant*
Once a lumberjack in Canada, Basil Dignam, who was born in Sheffield in 1905, came to the screen in the 1950s and established himself as a reliable, adaptable character actor. Regularly in demand, his long list of credits included the films *The Lady With A Lamp, His Excellency, Reach for the Sky, Carlton-Browne of the F.O., Gorgo, Life for Ruth, The Jokers* and *Young Winston*.

Equally busy on television, he was seen in, among others, *Sword of Freedom, Top Secret, Crane, The Adventurer, The Sweeney, War and Peace, The Pallisers* and the 1975 mini-series, *Edward the King*.

He died in 1979, aged seventy-three.

DILLON
Unseen in *Cowboy*, his name is mentioned by the Commissioner at the Bureau of Internal Affairs when a peace marshal is required in Stodge City. When Judge Burke, the mayor of Stodge, requests a marshal, the commissioner wonders whether a man called Dillon would be suitable, before his assistant, Perkins, reminds him that he's serving six months.

DILLON, CARMEN
Art Director on *Constable* and *Cruising*
Born in London in 1908, Carmen Dillon qualified as an architect and worked within the profession briefly, before being offered the chance to assist a colleague designing film sets. His subsequent illness saw Dillon take command as art director on *The Five Pound Man* in 1937, the beginning of a fruitful career which saw her join Pinewood Studios, where she worked on a host of films throughout her long career, including *French Without Tears, The Importance of Being Earnest, Hamlet* (which won her an Oscar), *Henry V, Richard III, Accident, The Go-Between, Lady Caroline Lamb, A Bequest to the Nation, Julia* and *The Omen*.

She died in 1991, aged eighty-three.

DIMPLE, GABRIEL
Played by Charles Hawtrey
In *Regardless*, Gabriel is employed by Helping Hands Limited and is soon given a myriad of jobs, including being a bouncer at a strip club, a job originally assigned to Mike Weston before a mix-up.

DIRECTOR OF SECURITY OPERATIONS
For the 'Director of Security Operations' in *Spying*, see 'Chief, The'.

DIRTY DICK'S
A disreputable establishment in Plymouth, visited by Midshipman Poop-Decker in *Jack*. The inn is full of drunk, loud-mouthed punters and women of ill repute, who will do anything for a gold sovereign. It's also where Sally, who's desperate to flee to Spain to try and trace her long-lost boyfriend, is employed.

DISTRAUGHT MANAGER
Played by David Stoll
The manager of Michele, a beauty salon in *Regardless*. He's organised a demonstration of the salon's latest beautification routine and invited the cream of the beauty trade. Lily Duveen, of Helping Hands, was supposed to arrive as the guinea pig for the demonstration, but a mix-up sees Montgomery Infield-Hopping turn up instead, and before long he ends up in a right mess!

DISTRAUGHT WOMAN
Played by Irene Handl
Seen in *Constable*, the distressed woman thinks she's lost her little boy, Willy, until he comes racing up the road on his scooter straight into the back of PC Gorse, who'd arrived on the scene to help.

DISTRICT NURSE
Played by Noel Dyson
While cycling peacefully along a country lane, an expectant father called Jeremy, rushes up to the nurse because his wife, who's in the back of Charlie Hawkins's taxi, has gone into labour. In the middle of the countryside, during the early hours of the morning, a baby's cries are heard, much to everyone's delight. The District Nurse, who delivers the baby, is seen in *Cabby*.

DIXON, VERNON
Set Dresser on *Constable*
Vernon Dixon began working as a set dresser back in the 1950s on films such as *The Spanish Gardener, The Secret Place, Doctor at Large* and the Norman Wisdom comedies, *Follow A Star* and *The Square Peg*.

He was working until the late 1970s, by which time he'd added, among others, *Oliver!, Barry Lyndon, Shout At the Devil* and *The Greek Tycoon* to his long list of credits.

D. L. RANDALL LIMITED
This establishment next-door to Fred Ramsden's butcher's shop sells domestic appliances and electrical goods. The front of the property is seen in *Behind*.

DOBBIN, MISS
Played by Valerie Leon
For Miss Dobbin in *Camping*, see 'Store Assistant'.

DOBBS, MISS
Played by Patsy Rowlands
The miserable desk clerk at Wundatours, the travel company organising the long weekend trip to the Mediterranean resort of Elsbels, appears in *Abroad*.

DOC
Played by Peter Butterworth
The doctor in Stodge City is seen in *Cowboy*.

DOCTOR
Played by Julian Orchard
The Doctor has the unfortunate task of calling at the Ponsonbys' mansion when Captain Bagshaw commits suicide upon hearing that his lying has led to Bertram West fleeing the country.

DOCTOR
Played by George Layton
Examines Professor Crump at the hospital in *Behind*.

DOCTOR
Played by Albert Moses
Examines the French Ambassador, Emile Prevert, because he's having trouble making love to his wife, Emmannuelle, during *Emmannuelle*. The doc believes it's a psychological problem rather than physical.

DOCTOR, CARRY ON
See feature box on pages 90–1.

DOCTOR IN FILM
Played by Harry Towb

In *At Your Convenience*, Lewis Boggs takes Myrtle Plummer to the cinema but she wasn't expecting the film to be sexually explicit. Introducing *The Sweet Glory of Love* is a doctor who, judging by his manner, appears to be getting excited himself by the movie's content.

DOLORES
Played by Edina Ronay

The good-time girl in *Cowboy* is asked by the Rumpo Kid to entertain the marshal for half an hour, giving the Kid sufficient time to get Big Heap out of jail.

DON, DOMINIQUE
Roles: Girl at Dirty Dick's in *Jack*, Harem Girl in *Follow That Camel* and MacNutt's Lure in *Up The Khyber*. Also uncredited role as Glamcab Driver in *Cabby*

Parisienne-born Dominique Don, born in 1944, made her film appearance in the 1962 rock 'n' roll film, *Play it Cool*, directed by Michael Winner. Other screen credits include playing a concubine in the 1965 film *Genghis Khan* and a customer in Jeremy Lloyd and David Croft's department store sitcom, *Are You Being Served?*.

DON'T LOSE YOUR HEAD, CARRY ON
See feature box on pages 94–5.

DOORMAN
Played by Tom Clegg

In *Spying* the aggressive doorman guards the entrance to Hakim's Fun House in the back streets of Algiers. When Simkins, Honeybutt, Crump and Bind come calling, he threatens to slit their throats unless they clear off. He finally gets his comeuppance when he's cracked over the head by Simkins.

DORNING, ROBERT
Role: Prime Minister in *Emmannuelle*

Born in St Helens in 1913, Robert Dorning trained as a ballet dancer before turning to musical comedy prior to the war. Following demob from the RAF, he resumed his career in musical comedies and moved increasingly into acting.

He worked for three years with Arthur Lowe in Granada's *Pardon the Expression* playing Walter Hunt, although he'd previously appeared with him in *Coronation Street*. A well-known face on television, he also spent four years in *Bootsie and Snudge* (1960-64) and appeared in countless other comedies and dramas, including *Bergerac*.

Robert made over twenty-five films including 1940's *They Came By Night*, *The Secret Man*, *No*

Safety Ahead, *Company of Fools*, *Dreamhouse*, *Man Accused* and *The Black Windmill*. His career encompassed all facets of the entertainment world.

He died in 1989, aged seventy-five.

DOUGLAS, ANGELA
Roles: Annie Oakley in *Cowboy*, Doris Mann in *Screaming!*, Lady Jane Ponsonby in *Follow That Camel* and Princess Jelhi in *Up The Khyber*

Angela Douglas, who was married to film actor Kenneth More, was born in Gerrards Cross, Buckinghamshire, in 1940. Her parents enrolled her at Aida Foster's Stage School in London, but she left before completing the course determined that if she was going to succeed as an actress, it was something she'd have to achieve on her own.

Before long, she'd secured an agent and was being offered small parts in films and on television, such as an episode of *Dixon of Dock Green* and *Sunday Night Theatre*. Early film credits include *The Shakedown*, *Feet of Clay*, *Murder in Eden* and *The Gentle Terror*. She became equally busy on stage, working in repertory theatre before offers in West End productions came her way.

In more recent years, she's been seen in television shows ranging from *Soldier Soldier*, *Peak Practice* and *Third Time Lucky* to *Heartbeat*, *Holby City* and *Cardiac Arrest*. She also appeared in the *Doctor Who* story, 'Battlefield', playing the Brigadier's oft-mentioned but never previously seen wife, Doris.

Other films, meanwhile, include *South Kensington*, *The Four Feathers* and *The Baby Juice Express*.

DOUGLAS, JACK
Roles: Twitching Father in *Matron*, Harry in *Abroad*, William in *Girls*, Sergeant Jock Strapp in *Dick*, Ernie Bragg in *Behind*, Bombardier Ready in *England*, Lyons in *Emmannuelle* and Marco the Cereal Killer in *Columbus*
TV: *Christmas* ('72); *What a Carry On!*; *The Prisoner of Spenda*; *The Sobbing Cavalier*; *Orgy and Bess*; *One in the Eye for Harold*; *The Nine Old Cobblers*; *The Case of the Screaming Winkles*; *The Case of the Coughing Parrot*; *Under the Round Table*; *Short Knight, Long Daze*; *And in My Lady's Chamber*; *Who Needs Kitchener?* and *Lamp Posts of the Empire*
STAGE: *London!* and *Laughing*

Jack Douglas, who's probably best known for his famous twitching character Alf, was born in Newcastle upon Tyne in 1927, the son of a

---

MEMORIES

'I was in bed when I received the call from my agent asking whether I could go to the Dorchester Hotel to meet Gerald Thomas and Peter Rogers. I remember I had a big spot on my chin, probably because I was very young in those days – about twenty-six – and used to get stressed. So I had to hide my spot before going over to meet them. They offered me an opening in *Carry On Cowboy*.

'Playing Annie Oakley was great fun and my favourite part in the *Carry On*s I did. Working with Jimmy Dale was enjoyable because he was so sweet and helpful. I remember filming the scene in the horse-drawn carriage where we're coming down a rocky road, with the horse running for dear life, galloping away and being thrown all over the place – it was just enormous fun.

'I remember having to do my singing number. Jimmy had worked with me on it, but I'm not a singer and was very shy. I was never very confident being glamorously dressed, showing bosoms, etc. My costume was fantastic; specially made and beautifully tailored. There I was in my diamanté and my tights. I was so nervous I think I was given a double brandy and pushed on. I was the baby of the scene and everyone was so nice to me.

'I can remember every day just laughing and laughing, like the time we were filming *Up The Khyber*. At the dinner party scene where the plaster, ceiling and chandelier are all over the place, there isn't one shot of my face because none of them could shoot me because I couldn't stop laughing. Tears were rolling down my face. Just watching Peter Butterworth – he was brilliant, so clever. He was my absolute favourite, a darling.

'In *Screaming!* I remember they had to take a body cast. The cast was placed on the floor for a couple of days and they didn't bother to put its clothes on, so you can imagine the scribbles and markings, with arrows in various directions. Because they put the body cast lying down, it gave me a huge ball neck, but from the neck down it looked pretty terrific – I wouldn't mind looking like that now!

'They were golden days. I think I could have gone on being the juvenile in the team for maybe another three or four movies, but I said goodbye because I wanted to have a baby. But they were happy memories.'

ANGELA DOUGLAS

CARRY ON DOCTOR

Alternative titles . . . *Nurse Carries On Again,*
Death of a Daffodil, Life Is A Four-letter Ward
and *A Bed Panorama of Hospital Life*

A Peter Rogers production
Distributed through Rank Organisation
Released as an A certificate in 1967 in colour
Running time: 94 mins

CAST

Frankie Howerd	. . . .	Francis Bigger
Kenneth Williams	. . . . . .	Dr Kenneth Tinkle
Sidney James	. . . .	Charlie Roper
Charles Hawtrey	. . . .	Mr Barron
Jim Dale	. . . .	Dr Jim Kilmore
Hattie Jacques	. . . .	Matron
Peter Butterworth	. . . .	Mr Smith
Bernard Bresslaw	. . . .	Ken Biddle
Barbara Windsor	. . . . . .	Nurse Sandra May
Joan Sims	. . . .	Chloe Gibson
Anita Harris	. . . .	Nurse Clarke
June Jago	. . . .	Sister Hoggett
Derek Francis	. . . .	Sir Edmund Francis
Dandy Nichols	. . . .	Mrs Roper
Peter Jones	. . . .	Chaplain
Deryck Guyler	. . . .	Surgeon Hardcastle
Gwendolyn Watts	. . . .	Mrs Barron
Dilys Laye	. . . .	Mavis
Peter Gilmore	. . . .	Henry
Harry Locke	. . . .	Sam
Marianne Stone	. . . .	Mum
Jean St. Clair	. . . .	Mrs Smith
Valerie Van Ost	. . . .	Nurse Parkin
Julian Orchard	. . . .	Fred
Brian Wilde	. . . . .	Man from Cox and Carter
Lucy Griffiths	. . . .	Patient
Pat Coombs	. . . .	Patient
Gertan Klauber	. . . .	Wash Orderly
Julian Holloway	. . . .	Simmons
Jenny White	. . . .	Nurse in Bath,
Helen Ford	. . . .	Nurse in Nursing Home
Gordon Rollings	. . . .	Night Porter
Simon Cain	. . . .	Tea Orderly
Cheryl Molineaux	. . .	Women's Ward Nurse
Alexandra Dane	. . . .	Female Instructor
Bart Allison	. . . .	Granddad
Jane Murdoch	. . . .	Nurse
Stephen Garlick	. . . .	Small Boy
Uncredited actor	. . .	Mr Wrigley, Bandaged
		Man
Patrick Allen	. . . .	Narrator

**(Note: Jasmin Broughton was hired as a
stunt double for Barbara Windsor.)**

PRODUCTION TEAM

Screenplay by Talbot Rothwell
Music composed and conducted by Eric
   Rogers
Production Manager: Jack Swinburne
Art Director: Cedric Dawe
Editor: Alfred Roome
Director of Photography: Alan Hume
Assistant Editor: Jack Gardner
Continuity: Joy Mercer
Assistant Director: Terry Clegg
Camera Operator: Jim Bawden
Make-up: Geoffrey Rodway
Sound Recordists: Dudley Messenger
   and Ken Barker
Hairdressing: Stella Rivers
Dubbing Editor: David Campling
Costume Designer: Yvonne Caffin
Title sketches by 'Larry'
Producer: Peter Rogers
Director: Gerald Thomas

Francis Bigger (Frankie Howerd) and his colourful underpants

Getting ready for action in Fosdick Ward

Francis Bigger is a believer in positive thinking and many people follow his doctrine as he tours the country expounding his views. The power of thinking is the way to health and happiness, claims Bigger, but it doesn't help when he slips off a stage, bruises his coccyx and ends up a patient at the Borough County Hospital.

The occupants of Fosdick Ward are a mixed bunch. Ken Biddle, who had his appendix removed before falling off the operating table and hurting his leg, has fallen for Mavis, a woman in Caffin Ward; when his friend, Fred, visits, he asks him to pass on a note not knowing that she's been moved to a different part of the ward and her place has been taken by the elderly Miss Morrison. Next time, when Biddle wants to see Mavis himself, he swaps clothes with Fred and heads off to the ward; unfortunately for Fred, who jumps into Biddle's bed, he ends up being forced to drink castor oil by a nurse as treatment for his supposed constipation.

Other patients include the work-shy Charlie Roper and Mr Barron, who's suffering a phantom pregnancy, all of whom are entertained by the jovial Dr Kilmore, an unorthodox doctor who eyes up the nurses and fraternizes with the patients; while the patients and certain nurses, particularly Nurse Clarke, are fond of Kilmore, he's disliked by Matron and Dr Tinkle who would grasp any opportunity to see him sacked.

A golden opportunity arises when he's caught hanging precariously from the roof of the nurses' home. Spotting Nurse May on the roof, Kilmore thought she was going to jump so raced up to try and coax her to safety, but his good intentions are misconstrued and he's accused of being a sex maniac, particularly when he ends up falling into another nurse's bath. Kilmore sees no other option but to resign.

When the patients hear of Kilmore's impending departure, they decide to do something about it; everyone, including Mr Bigger, who feels cheated because he misheard Dr Tinkle talking, thought he only had days left and decided to cheer up his deaf, miserable-looking assistant, Chloe Gibson, by marrying her, is keen to take action. While the

women take care of Matron, the men take Tinkle to the operating theatre and sharpen the scalpels.

When the patients win the day and Kilmore is reinstated with a fawning Tinkle now his subordinate, Borough County Hospital is a brighter place.

Funny Scene!

Nurse May is infatuated with Dr Tinkle whom she regards as her saviour. She believes he saved her life although he was only operating on her tonsils; when she arrives at Borough County Hospital as a student nurse and finds out that Tinkle works there, she heads off to his room to see him. Tinkle is using some exercise equipment, which is connected to the door, when Nurse May knocks.

TINKLE: What is it?

(NURSE MAY opens the door, sending Dr TINKLE flying across the room. He holds his chest in pain.)

MAY: Oh, Kenneth, (She rushes over to his assistance.) darling, are you all right?

TINKLE: Yeah . . . (Looks at MAY.) You? But it was you in the sluice room; I was hoping it was hallucinations.

MAY: Lucy who?

TINKLE: Lucy Nation, you remember her — the girl . . . what am I talking about?

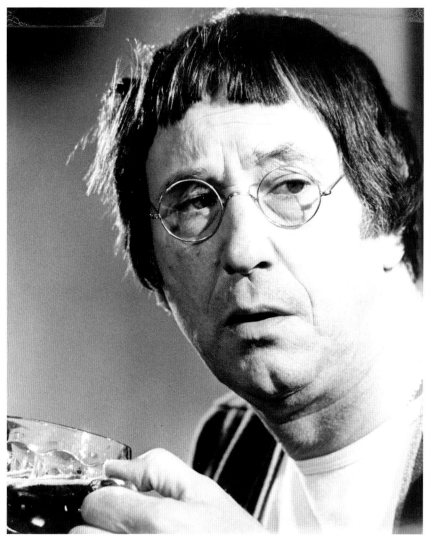

Jack Douglas brought a twitching element to the *Carry Ons*

theatre producer who staged pantomimes and summer shows. Devoted to showbusiness from a young age, he was soon acting and directing, but his big break came in the pantomime *Dick Whittington* at the Kingston Empire, Surrey, when the straight man alongside comic Joe Baker was taken ill during the dress rehearsal, and Baker persuaded Douglas, who was directing, to step in. The act was such a success it wasn't long before they had been signed by a top agent and were operating as a double-act, working all around the world.

Their big break was in *Crackerjack* with Eamonn Andrews, the first of many appearances in film and television, before the double-act split when Baker left for America. Douglas worked as a straight man with other top comics, including Bruce Forsyth, Arthur Haynes and Des O'Connor.

Small-screen credits include *Jokers Wild, The Goodies, The Shillingbury Tales, Cuffy* and *Not On Your Nellie*, while on the big screen *Nearly A*

Nasty Accident, Bloody Kids and *What's Up Nurse!*.

Nowadays, Douglas is a regular in pantomimes each year and still does occasional television work.

DOUGLAS, SALLY

Roles: Girl at Dirty Dick's in *Jack*, Amazon Guard in *Spying*, Antony's Dusky Maiden in *Cleo*, Kitkata in *Cowboy*, Girl in *Screaming!* and Harem Girl in *Follow That Camel*
At the age of fifteen, Sally Douglas, who was born in 1942, decided her ambition was to become an actress. She contacted an agent only to be told she was too young and to try again in two years. Upon leaving school she worked as a secretary in an iron foundry before approaching the agent when she was seventeen. Although he tried dissuading her from joining the profession, she was intent on pursuing her dream and finally achieved her aim by making a living from acting.

Douglas appeared in several films and various television shows, such as *Weekend with Lulu*, playing a can-can girl. Other small-screen appearances included an appearance as a stripper in an episode of *Doctor in the House*, Susie in a 1970 episode of *On the Buses* and a rent-a-girl in *Up Pompeii*. On the big screen, as well as her *Carry On* appearances, she popped up in, among others, the 1968 picture *Witchfinder General* and the strangely titled, *Can Hieronymus Merkin Ever Forget Mercy Humppe and Find True Happiness?* a year later, *The Alphabet Murders, That Riviera Touch, Mister Ten Per Cent* and *A Study in Terror*.

She died in 1992.

DOWNE, IDA
Played by Wendy Richard
The contestant in the Miss Fircombe beauty contest is seen in *Girls*.

DREERY, MR and MRS
Played by Bill Maynard and Patricia Franklin
A cantankerous man and his long-suffering wife seen in *Loving*. They meet Mr Snooper, the marriage guidance counsellor at the Citizens' Advice Bureau, to discuss their marital problems, which stem from a lack of intimacy in the bedroom. Mr Dreery doesn't like Snooper's attitude, though, especially when he makes a joke at the couple's expense.

DREW, MISS
Played by Marianne Stone
The bespectacled Miss Drew, who appears in *Girls*, is seen scribbling down the minutes at the Fircombe Town Council meeting.

DRUNK
Played by Ronnie Stevens
In *Cruising* he spends his entire Mediterranean cruise propping up the bar on the *Happy Wanderer*. We never discover his name, and he tells Dr Binn that he's drunk in order to forget a girl, not that he can remember which one.

DRUNK
Played by Norman Stanley
At Rumpo's Place in *Cowboy* the drunk man turns to Belle, who's just been rejected by the Rumpo Kid, and tells her jokingly that she can always satisfy his carnal desires.

DRUNKEN HUSBAND
Played by Norman Mitchell
Arrives back at his Mayfair flat in *Emmannuelle* at an inopportune moment because his portly wife is entertaining Leyland in the closet. He's so drunk, however, that he just collapses on the bed unaware of what's going on around him. Seen during Leyland's flashback sequence.

DRURY, GUNNER
Played by Richard Bartlett
Based at the experimental 1313 anti-aircraft

INTERVIEW WITH JACK DOUGLAS

How did you develop the twitching character which became your trademark?

A hundred years ago – it seems like it – Joe Baker and I, as young men, appeared at Butlin's at Clacton. I used to do this character called Alf but without the twitch. I played a conjuror who'd ask someone in the audience to come up on stage to help, which was Joe's cue, dressed as a little boy, to come up.

One evening, no one volunteered. There were about 1500 people in the audience but no Joe, who'd been locked out because the theatre was full. I was supposed to be the straight man and had a twenty-minute slot to fill. So I said: 'In the meantime, I'll show you . . .', my mind was going seventy miles per hour, so I picked up a tray and put lots of bits and pieces that I happened to have on stage with me on to it. I happened to notice two members of Eric Winston's band watching by the stage entrance. I suddenly remembered that Eric, the famous band leader, had a little twitch, so in desperation I said: 'I shall now make these articles disappear.' I did a twitch and all the articles went up in the air before falling all over the floor. I just picked the items up and ignored the fact that I'd done it. By this time, Joe had managed to get into the theatre and couldn't understand why all these people were falling about laughing at me – the straight man! That's how Alf was born.

How did your involvement with the *Carry On*s begin?

My agent at the time, Michael Sullivan, rang and asked if I wanted the good news or the bad news? I asked for the good news and he told me I was in the next *Carry On* picture, which pleased me, of course. I then asked what the bad news was and he told me I wasn't getting paid.* I asked him to explain, so he told me that he'd persuaded Peter Rogers to put me in a little scene in the maternity ward in *Matron*, and if it worked I'd be in the next film.

I turned up at Pinewood and went into the rehearsal room, petrified. You had a team which was so successful and had worked together in so many pictures, and suddenly here is this newcomer. I thought they could resent me immediately, but suddenly over came Sid James and introduced himself and asked if I fancied a coffee. Then Kenneth Williams got me some biscuits. It wasn't long before I felt as if I'd been part of the team from the word 'go'. They were, without doubt, the most unselfish comedy team I'd ever worked with.

A few days after I'd made my first appearance, a black Rolls Royce turned up at my house in Thames Ditton. The chauffeur brought a box up the garden (I was pruning roses at the time) and handed me a note and the box. The note read: 'Welcome to the Carry On team – here is your first week's wages.' It was from Peter Rogers and Gerald Thomas. I opened the box and it was a dozen bottles of Dom Pérignon champagne.

How did you get on with Peter Rogers and Gerald Thomas?

As a businessman, I don't think there is anybody to touch Peter Rogers. He was brilliant. He cast the pictures and didn't spend money in any wrong direction. As for Gerald, who I had the honour to work with for so long, he had this amazing gift. When we got to rehearsals we were like a lot of naughty boys and girls, joking and laughing. But as soon as Gerald clapped his hands, that was it, we went straight to work. We had minimum rehearsals, and if you made a mistake you couldn't put your hand up as they do now and say: 'Can we take that again, please?' You had to keep going.

Did you ever adlib when it came to the twitching?

Yes. Gerald would always say to me: 'If you want to do something, do it. If it doesn't work, I'll cut it out.' So I did. In *Girls* I said to Sid James, 'By the way, we'll do a little bit of adlibbing.' He replied: 'I don't adlib.' I couldn't believe it, but he said, 'I'm an actor. You'll get the same performance from me – you can set your watch by me if you like. But if you give me a line that I don't know I'm dead.' He was happy for me to do whatever I wanted and we agreed that I'd look him straight in the eye and say 'pardon' when I'd finished.

Your performance with Windsor Davies in *Behind* seemed to work well?

Yes. There are times in showbusiness when you have a magic and Windsor and I had that. We'd only just met, but from the moment we started working together it was like Laurel and Hardy bouncing off each other. He's a lovely man.

What did you think of *England*?

There is a golden rule in showbusiness: if you have something that is successful don't change it. They did on *England* and it didn't work. There were a lot of different faces and the approach to the film was different. The scene where all the girls are lined up with bare busts – when we did it with Barbara Windsor it was done like an accident and that was fine. But the way it happened on *England* wasn't. We lost a magic when Tolly Rothwell, the writer, died. He just had a magic that seemed to work. The *Carry On*s had worked because the humour was naughty but not filthy.

Then, of course, along came *Emmannuelle*.

Yes, that was a strange one for me because Gerald asked me to play it as myself. I'd done all the others in my character, which meant I was in disguise and could do whatever I liked. I don't think it had the magic that a lot of the other pictures had.

There was one embarrassing moment when I was seen taking the phone into Suzanne Danielle and handed it to her. What I didn't realise is that the wire had got caught around my neck, so when I handed the phone she took it and pulled it towards her, and me with it. I went straight into her bust and she didn't have a bra on. So we acted through all of that and when we'd finished, I asked Gerald if it was all right, which it was, and then I said: 'Can we try it another six or seven times?'

Have the *Carry On* films been the highlight of your career?

Without doubt. It was an honour to work with such top professional people, which they all were. I learnt so much from all of them.

Do you have a favourite that you appeared in?

Carry On Dick because I think the *Carry On*s lent themselves to costume and period. The film also had a certain edge to it.

JACK DOUGLAS

---

* The production files held at the British Film Institute show that a payment of £25 was made to Douglas for his appearance in the film. Jack, however, believes this could have been to cover expenses.

CARRY ON DON'T LOSE YOUR HEAD

A Peter Rogers production distributed through Rank Organisation
Song: 'Don't Lose Your Head' by Bill Martin and Phil Coulter
Sung by The Michael Sammes Singers
Released as an A certificate in 1966 in colour
Running time: 90 mins
(Note: the film was originally released without the *Carry On* moniker but it was later reinstated.)

CAST

Sidney James . . . . .Sir Rodney Ffing / The Black Fingernail
Kenneth Williams . . . . . Citizen Camembert
Jim Dale . . . . Lord Darcy de Pue
Charles Hawtrey . . . . Duc de Pommfrit
Joan Sims . . . . Desiree Dubarry
Peter Butterworth . . . . Citizen Bidet
Dany Robin . . . . Jacqueline
Peter Gilmore . . . . Robespierre
Marianne Stone . . . . Landlady
Michael Ward . . . . Henri
Leon Greene . . . . Malabonce
Hugh Futcher . . . . Guard
Richard Shaw . . . . Captain of Soldiers

David Davenport . . . . Sergeant
Jennifer Clulow . . . . 1st Lady
Valerie Van Ost . . . . 2nd Lady
Jacqueline Pearce . . . . 3rd Lady
Nikki Van Der Zyl . . . . Messenger
Julian Orchard . . . . Rake
Elspeth March . . . . Lady Binder
Joan Ingram . . . . Bald-headed Dowager

Michael Nightingale . . 'What Locket?' Man
Diana MacNamara . . . . . Princess Stephanie
Ronnie Brody . . . . Little Man
Billy Cornelius . . . . Soldier
Patrick Allen . . . . Narrator
Monica Dietrich
Anna Willoughby
Penny Keen
June Cooper
Christine Pryor
Karen Young . . . . Girls

PRODUCTION TEAM

Screenplay by Talbot Rothwell
Music composed and conducted by Eric Rogers
Production Manager: Jack Swinburne
Director of Photography: Alan Hume
Editor: Rod Keys
Art Director: Lionel Couch
Camera Operator: Jimmy Devis
Assistant Director: Jack Causey
Sound Editor: W. Nelson
Sound Recordists: Dudley Messenger and Ken Barker
Continuity: Rita Davison
Make-up: Geoffrey Rodway
Hairdressing: Stella Rivers
Costume Designer: Emma Selby-Walker
Choreographer: Terry Gilbert
Master of Horse: Jeremy Taylor
Producer: Peter Rogers
Director: Gerald Thomas

An aerial shot of the guillotine set

Sir Rodney (Sid James) and Lord Darcy (Jim Dale) saved many heads from the chop

It's Paris in 1789 and the French Revolution is in full swing with the aristocrats losing their heads like there's no tomorrow. Citizen Camembert, head of the secret police and the most feared man in France, oversees proceedings at the guillotine, a source of enjoyment for the blood-thirsty Parisians.

Meanwhile in England, aristocrats, unaware of events across the Channel, go about their lives as normal, but when Henri, a wigmaker, tells Sir Rodney Ffing and his friend Lord Darcy de Pue of the goings-on in his beloved France, where women also face the chop, the two bravehearts decide it's time they launched a rescue mission to save as many heads as possible.

They travel to France and through a series of audacious ruses and artful disguises, rescue the aristocrats from the jaws of the guillotine, angering Citizen Camembert in the process. Pressurised into capturing Sir Rodney, alias the Black Fingernail, by his boss, Citizen Robespierre, no easy task considering the array of disguises he uses, Camembert keeps a close eye out for the English; the last straw for Camembert's boss, though, is when the Duc de Pommfrit, a prominent leader of the Royalists, is whisked away just seconds from the blade.

Humiliated and angry, Camembert is sent to England to find the Black Fingernail. Disguised as an escaped French aristocrat, he ends up attending a charity ball hosted by Sir Rodney Ffing himself. Unaware of the Black Fingernail's true identity, he takes along Desiree Dubarry, who's wearing a locket the Black Fingernail had given to a French girl he'd met on one of his recent visits to France; it's hoped that the locket will attract the attention of Camembert's target. The trick works and ends up with a duel being arranged between Camembert and the Black Fingernail, but the elusive Englishman escapes again and heads for France upon hearing that the woman to whom he presented the locket has been imprisoned.

After much drama, Ffing eventually escapes with his girl and Camembert and Bidet, the secret policeman's assistant, get their come-uppance courtesy of the guillotine.

Funny Scene!

The Duc de Pommfrit's turn for the guillotine has arrived and Citizen Bidet goes to collect him.

POMMFRIT: Take your filthy hands off me, peasant.

BIDET: Peasant am I? Let me tell you that my blood is as good as yours.

POMMFRIT: Nonsense, everyone knows that your father was a basket maker.

BIDET: Aha, that's where you're wrong, see, because no one knows who my father was, not even my mother.
(POMMFRIT joins in the laughter of the crowd. BIDET sees him laughing.) You'll laugh on the other side of your face when your head comes off — come on.

POMMFRIT: Thank you, I'm quite capable of making my own way.
(POMMFRIT climbs the steps to the guillotine, laughing all the way. He gets himself comfy with his head through the machine. Then, a lady runs up with a message.)

MESSENGER: Your Grace, there's an urgent letter for you.

POMMFRIT: Oh, drop it in the basket (The basket collects the severed heads.), I'll read it later.

battery featured in *England*, he's one of the shirkers who suffers a severe shock to the system when the tough-speaking Captain Melly is put in charge of the unit.

DESIREE DUBARRY
Played by Joan Sims

Desiree Dubarry is a courtesan who spends most of her time with Citizen Camembert in *Don't Lose Your Head*. Her days usually involve lounging around eating fruit, that is until she accompanies Camembert to England in the hunt for the Black Fingernail.

DUC DE POMMFRIT
Played by Charles Hawtrey

Seen in *Don't Lose Your Head*, he's just about to be beheaded courtesy of the guillotine when he's whisked away by the Black Fingernail and his companion, Lord Darcy, who are both out to save the French aristocracy from death. The Duc De Pommfrit is a prominent leader of the Royalists, and an enemy of the revolutionaries.

DUC DE PONCENAY
Played by Julian Orchard

In *Henry* the French Ambassador arrives at Henry VIII's abode to pass on the King of France's best wishes upon hearing that Queen Marie of Normandy, Henry's current wife, is expecting. When the Ambassador announces the French monarch intends giving 50,000 gold coins, Henry has second thoughts about trying to obtain an annulment of his marriage.

DUFF, LESLEY
Role: Norma in *Camping*

Born in London in 1952, Lesley Duff worked for an insurance company to appease her father who believed she should secure a 'proper job', but after just seven weeks she left to pursue a career in showbusiness, initially trying her hand at singing. She released a single, 'The Boy from Chelsea', which failed to chart. Soon after she secured a theatrical agent and began working on the stage, initially in *Peter Pan* at London's Scala Theatre followed by a production of *Murder at the Vicarage*.

Her stage experience included spending nine months in Malta before returning to the UK and securing the part of Norma in *Camping*. Most of her screen work, though, has been on television, with early credits including Andrea in ATV's sitcom from the 1970s, *Up the Workers!*. Other work has seen her in *The Bill, Boon, Doctor's Daughters, Pie in the Sky, Westbeach, Castles, Wycliffe, Casualty* and *Heartbeat*.

She gave up acting in 1997 and co-runs Diamond Management, an actors' agency in London.

DUKES, MRS
Played by Joan Hickson

The rather eccentric Mrs Dukes, who's seen in *Girls*, believes every man is after her, which might explain why she loses her knickers and later finds them hanging from a flag pole on the esplanade. (**Note: the role was originally going to be played by Renée Houston but her contract was cancelled due to ill-health.**)

DUMB DRIVER
Played by Carol Shelley

In *Cabby* this giggly Glamcab driver is a member of Peggy Hawkins's glam team.

DURKIN, PATRICK
Roles: Recruit in *Sergeant*, Jackson in *Nurse*, Guard in *Spying* and William in *Dick*

Born in Middlesbrough in 1935, Patrick Durkin began his working life at his father's building firm, but having a penchant for acting, applied to LAMDA. He was offered a place at the academy and deferred his National Service to undertake the course.

After graduating, he joined the RAF and completed National Service before kicking off his acting career with *Carry On Sergeant*. As well as several stints in the West End he worked extensively on the screen, with other credits including television shows such as *Gideon's Way, Colditz, Timeslip, Menace, The Pathfinders* and *When the Boat Comes In*. Film work includes appearances in *Please Turn Over, Nightmare, The Big Sleep, Britannia Hospital* and *Lionheart*.

In the late 1960s, he was employed by Tommy Cooper as his straight man. He recorded a television series and spent four months with the comedian at the Winter Gardens, Blackpool, during 1968. Enjoying the experience so much, he formed his own act and became a popular London comic.

He continued working until suffering a stroke in 2002.

DURHAM, MARCEL
Dubbing Editor on *Loving*

His earliest credits saw him working as a sound editor on the 1959 film, *The Shakedown*, but subsequently employed on films such as *A Man for All Seasons, Oliver!, The Day of the Jackal* and *The Odessa File*, while his television work includes *The Martian Chronicles* and *Lace II*.

DUSE, ANNA
Costume Designer on *Again Doctor*

Born in Wilmslow, Cheshire, in 1908, Anna Duse was busy in the film industry after the Second World War, working on films such as *The Deep Blue Sea, Happy Go Lovely, Lady Godiva Rides Again, The Belles of St Trinian's*,

The Green Man, That Riviera Touch and, in 1969, *The Chairman*. She died in Lauzerte, France, in 1992.

DUVEEN, LILY
Played by Joan Sims

Seen in *Regardless*, Lily is an employee of Helping Hands Limited. Her first job turns out to be the most memorable because she ends up getting drunk at a wine-tasting session and starts throwing her weight around.

DVD RELEASES
See 'DVD releases' on page 279.

DYNAMITE DAN
Played by Joe Robinson

For the boxer in *Regardless*, see 'Grimsby, Dynamite Dan'.

DYSON, NOEL
Roles: Vague Woman in *Constable* and District Nurse in *Cabby*

Noel Dyson, born in Newton Heath, Manchester, in 1916, is well known for her role as Nanny in *Father, Dear Father* and Aileen Potter in the BBC sitcom, *Potter*. She trained as a secretary upon leaving school, but realising her interests lay elsewhere, quit to attend RADA in 1936, despite strong opposition from her father.

Her first professional engagement was at Frinton-on-Sea in a pre-war farce, before securing other small jobs around the country, but a thyroid problem forced her to retire from the business for four years, during which time she served as a nurse at a RAF convalescent home in Torquay.

During the war she worked for ENSA, performing around the country at hospitals and nursing homes. She continued working for the Association after the war, embarking on a tour of European cities. Returning to home soil she appeared at Oxford Rep, before further appearances in the West End and moving into films and television. But it wasn't until her 1960 appearance in *Coronation Street* as Ida, Ken Barlow's mother, that she became a recognisable face. Other small-screen credits included *Bergerac, Executive Stress, May To December, Prime Suspect, Never The Twain, Z Cars, Casualty, The Randall Touch, The Ronnie Barker Yearbook* and *Joan & Leslie*. She also spent six months down-under in the late 1970s, recording an Australian version of *Father, Dear Father*.

Dyson made over twenty films, including *Press for Time, Please Turn Over* and *Three Crooked Men*. She died of liver cancer in 1995, aged seventy-nine.

EAGLES, LEON
Role: Recruit in *Sergeant*
Born in Cardiff in 1932, Leon Eagles played a wide range of character parts during his career. After treading the boards around the country, he began appearing on the screen in the late 1950s. His television credits included *The Avengers, Public Eye, Crossroads, Special Branch, Doctor Who, Target, The Tomorrow People, The Squad* and *Bergerac*. His last small-screen appearances were in an episode of *Poirot* and the television movie, *Heading Home*, playing Mr Ashcroft. He also made the occasional film. He died in 1997, aged sixty-five.

EARL OF BRISTOL, THE
Played by Peter Butterworth
For the Earl of Bristol in *Henry,* see 'Charles, Earl of Bristol'.

EARP, SHERIFF ALBERT
Played by Jon Pertwee
The deaf, shortsighted Stodge City sheriff is seen in *Cowboy*. Way past his 'best by' date, Earp is killed by the Rumpo Kid, prompting the arrival of Annie Oakley, his daughter, seeking revenge.

EAST, SUZANNA
Role: Colette in *Emmannuelle*
Suzanna East was first seen on the screen in 1970, appearing in an episode of *Paul Temple* and the film *Permissive*. On television, her later credits include *The Rivals of Sherlock Holmes* and *The Survivors*.

Her film work includes *Beware My Brethren, Savage Messiah, Captain Kronos: Vampire Hunter*, all during the 1970s. In 1999, she returned to the screen to play the role of a mother in the short comedy, *Tumbled*.

EASY, PRIVATE ALICE
Played by Diane Langton
Based at the experimental 1313 anti-aircraft battery featured in *England*, she's one of the shirkers who suffers a severe shock to the system when the tough-speaking Captain Melly is put in charge of the unit.

EATON, SHIRLEY
Roles: Mary Sage in *Sergeant*, Nurse Dorothy Denton in *Nurse* and Sally Barry in *Constable*
Born in London in 1937, Shirley Eaton is remembered by many for her role in the 1964 James Bond movie, *Goldfinger,* but by then she was already a prominent screen actress, mainly in comedy roles.

A student at the Aida Foster School, she began acting at the age of twelve, debuting in a stage play, *Set To Partners*, and followed by an appearance in Sir Benjamin Britten's *Let's Make An Opera*. Her first taste of the West End came in a 1954 pantomime, *Mother Goose*, at the Palladium with Max Bygraves.

At sixteen, she was offered her first film role, playing a woman on a ferry in *A Day to Remember* followed by the part of Milly, alongside Dirk Bogarde, in *Doctor in the House*. Other film credits include *The Love Match, Charley Moon, Doctor at Large, Nearly A Nasty Accident, The Girl Hunters* and *Kiss and Kill*. On television, she popped up several times in *The Saint*.

Eaton retired from the business in the late 1960s, soon after her second child was born. She moved to the South of France in 1987 but after the death of her husband in 1994, she sold up and returned to the UK.

EDEN, EVE
Role: Khasi's Wife in *Up The Khyber*
Born in Bath in 1940, Eve Eden appeared in a handful of films and television shows from the late 1950s through to the end of the 60s, including *Young, Willing and Eager; Operation Bullshine; The Frightened City; The Contest Girl* and the Beatles' film, *Help!*.

EDWARDS, PRIVATE
Played by Jeannie Collings
Based at the experimental 1313 anti-aircraft battery featured in *England*, she's one of the shirkers who suffers a severe shock to the system when the tough-speaking Captain Melly is put in charge of the unit.

EDWARDS, RAY
Role: Man with Water in *Behind*
A busy stage actor, Ray Edwards's other screen

work includes episodes of *Softly Softly, Codename, Paul Temple, The New Avengers, Casualty* and *The Woman in White* as well as films such as *Oh! What a Lovely War, The Last House on the Left* and *Alice's Adventures in Wonderland*.

ELDERLY RESIDENT
Played by Edward Palmer
A long-term resident at the Palace Hotel in *Girls* before the beauty contestants arrive. The shapely girls stay in the hotel for the duration of the competition but their presence is too much for the gentleman's pulse so he hands in his key before his health suffers.

ELECTRICIAN
Played by Larry Martyn
The electrician appears in *Behind* installing the public address system at the Riverside Caravan Site.

ELIZABETH WARD
A ward at the Long Hampton Hospital seen in *Again Doctor*.

ELLACOTT, JOAN
Costume designer on *Sergeant, Nurse, Regardless, Cruising, Cabby* and *Jack*
Joan Ellacott's early schooling occurred in the American state of Ohio, where her father was working, before eventually completing her education back in England, at the Bromley County School for Girls.

Deciding she wanted to become a dress designer in the rag trade, she enrolled at the Bromley School of Arts and Crafts. Upon graduating after two years, she joined Worths in 1938, but after making button loops for a dress worn by actress Wendy Hiller in the film *Pygmalion,* she knew her future lay in designing and making costumes for the film world.

After serving in the WAAF during the Second World War, she returned to Worths temporarily until a speculative letter to Gainsborough Studios saw her being offered the post of assistant costume designer. Later promoted to costume designer, she spent over five decades in the business, working on myriad

CARRY ON EMMANNUELLE

Cleves Investments Ltd presents A Peter Rogers Production
A Gerald Thomas film distributed by Hemdale
Song: 'Love Crazy' by Kenny Lynch
Sung by Masterplan
Released as an AA certificate in 1978 in colour
Running time: 88 mins

CAST

Kenneth Williams	Emile Prevert
Suzanne Danielle	Emmannuelle Prevert
Kenneth Connor	Leyland
Jack Douglas	Lyons
Joan Sims	Mrs Dangle
Peter Butterworth	Richmond
Larry Dann	Theodore Valentine
Beryl Reid	Mrs Valentine
Tricia Newby	Nurse in Surgery
Albert Moses	Doctor
Henry McGee	Harold Hump
Howard Nelson	Harry Hernia
Claire Davenport	Blonde in Pub
Tim Brinton	BBC Newscaster
Corbett Woodall	ITN Newscaster
Robert Dorning	Prime Minister
Bruce Boa	US Ambassador
Eric Barker	Ancient General
Victor Maddern	Man in Launderette
Norman Mitchell	Drunken Husband
Jack Lynn	Admiral of the Fleet
Michael Nightingale	Police Commissioner
Llewellyn Rees	Lord Chief Justice
Steve Plytas	Arabian Official
Joan Benham	Cynical Lady
Marianne Maskell	Nurse in Hospital
Louise Burton	Girl at Zoo
Dino Shafeek	Immigration Officer
David Hart	Customs Officer
Gertan Klauber	German Soldier
Malcolm Johns	Sentry
John Carlin	French Parson
Guy Ward	Dandy
James Fagan	Concorde Steward
John Hallett	Substitute Football Player
Deborah Brayshaw	French Buxom Blonde
Suzanna East	Colette
Bruce Wyllie	Football Referee
Philip Clifton	Injured Footballer
Stanley McGeagh	Fleet Street Journalist
Bill Hutchinson	1st Reporter
Neville Ware	2nd Reporter
Jane Norman	3rd Reporter
Nick White	Sent-off Footballer

PRODUCTION TEAM

Original Screenplay by Lance Peters
Music composed and conducted by Eric Rogers
Director of Photography: Alan Hume
Editor: Peter Boita
Art Director: Jack Shampan
Production Manager: Roy Goddard
Camera Operator: Godfrey Godar
Make-up: Robin Grantham
Production Executive for Cleves Investments Ltd: Donald Langdon
Assistant Director: Gregory Dark
Sound Recordists: Danny Daniel and Otto Snel
Continuity: Marjorie Lavelly
Wardrobe: Margaret Lewin
Stills Cameraman: Ken Bray
Hairdresser: Betty Sherriff
Costume Designer: Courtenay Elliott
Set Dresser: John Hoesli
Assistant Editor: Jack Gardner
Dubbing Editor: Peter Best
Titles & Opticals: G.S.E. Ltd
Processed by: Technicolor Ltd
Producer: Peter Rogers
Director: Gerald Thomas

Joan Sims and Peter Butterworth play workers in the Prevert household

Flying into London on Concorde is Emmannuelle Prevert, whose husband, Emile, is the French Ambassador in London. She's a nymphomaniac and forever throwing herself at men, whether they are the steward on the plane or the gormless-looking Theodore Valentine whom she takes into the aircraft's toilet compartment to help satisfy her insatiable sexual appetite.

For Emmannuelle the toilet escapade was just a moment of lust, while for Theodore it was the defining point of his life; the mollycoddled, bespectacled guy has been living a sheltered life with his domineering mother, but now he's declared his love for Emmannuelle and sets out in the forlorn hope that he'll win her heart.

During a dinner party at the French Ambassador's residence, a casual comment about how easy it would be to assassinate the Ambassador sees Emmannuelle, who cares deeply for her husband despite her numerous flings, make it her duty to get to know the male guests a little more intimately to check if any of them is out to kill Emile.

Theodore, meanwhile, is getting desperate as his pursuit of Emmannuelle is getting him nowhere fast. He phones and asks her to marry him, warning her that if she turns him down and doesn't move in with him and his mother, he'll do something drastic. He tricks her

Emile and Emmannuelle get cosy

into meeting him so he can kidnap her but it's all in vain; he vows to cause trouble and, armed with a bundle of photographs he'd secretly taken of her with various lovers, sells them to a newspaper; Emmannuelle, however, isn't fazed by the subsequent publicity her affairs create.

Eventually her husband, Emile Prevert, who had been more interested in his ambassadorial duties and his attempts to turn his puny body into the bulging biceps of bodybuilder Harry Hernia, decides to give it all up in favour of his wife. Swapping her contraceptive pills for fertility pills, it's not long before she's pregnant, but she ends up with more than she bargained for.

Suzanne Danielle makes her one and only *Carry On* appearance

Funny Scene!

Emmannuelle has just arrived in the country and is trying to get through passport control, but an immigration officer is attempting to establish her reasons for visiting the UK.

```
OFFICER:        What is your husband's occupation?
EMMANNUELLE:    I am.
OFFICER:        (Realising this will take some time.)
                Oh, deary me, how does he earn his
                living?
EMM:            Ah, oui. In the service of his country.
OFFICER:        Would you be more explicit, please?
EMM:            Oui, monsieur, I can be very
                explicit!
OFFICER:        (Embarrassed.) About your husband.
EMM:            He is a very — how you say — 'igh
                up man.
OFFICER:        Is he important?
EMM:            (Cross.) Not impotent! He has . . .
                other interests.
OFFICER:        What is his position?
EMM:            It varies.
```

television productions and films, including *Snowbound, Helter Skelter, Forbidden Cargo, Campbell's Kingdom, The Iron Maiden* for the big screen, and *Pride and Prejudice* and *The Black Tower* for television.

ELLIOTT, COURTENAY

Costume Designer on *Up the Jungle, Loving, Henry, At Your Convenience, Matron, Abroad, Girls, Dick, Behind, England* and *Emmannuelle*

Born in Gunwalloe, Cornwall, in 1918, Courtenay Elliott moved to Old Colwyn, North Wales, where she completed her schooling. She studied ballet at Chester and worked as a dancer and in modelling before making a living as a stand-in at Pinewood. Among the films she worked on were 1958's *The Truth About Women*. Dubbed 'Miss Pinewood – No. 1 Stand-in', she was also seen doubling for many top actresses, including Ingrid Bergman in 1964's *The Yellow Rolls Royce* and Julie Christie in '67's *Far From The Madding Crowd*. Other films she worked on include *A Night to Remember, Checkpoint, Conspiracy of Hearts* and *The Whisperer*.

In 1966, aged forty-eight, she switched careers and quickly established herself as a costume designer, working initially on the 1967-released film, *The Double Man*. Other credits include *Assault, Revenge, The Limbo Line, Doctor in Trouble, Inn of the Frightened People, In the Devil's Garden* and *Bless This House*. She retired from the industry in 1978, after working on *Emmannuelle*, by which time she'd already been living on the island of Gozo for two years.

She died in 2001, aged eighty-three.

ELLISON, ANGELA

Role: Cloakroom Girl in *Spying*

Other credits include the 1964 film, *One More to Hell*.

ELSBELS

A Mediterranean resort visited by Vic and Cora Flange et al in *Abroad*. Wundatours Limited have organised a short-break in the sun for £17 per person, but inclement weather puts paid to the resort's so-called reputation for reliable sunshine hours.

ELSBELS PALACE HOTEL

This building site passed off as a hotel is where the Wundatours party stay on their short break to the Med resort of Elsbels in *Abroad*. With several floors still incomplete, work is seriously behind schedule, but that doesn't stop Pepe, who owns the hotel, trying to accommodate the visitors. Pepe runs the hotel with his son Georgio, the barman, and the bad-tempered cook, Floella.

ELSIE

Played by Marianne Stone

For Elsie in *Behind*, see 'Rowan, Mrs'.

EMILY

Played by Alexandra Dane

A tall, busty blonde who seems ill-suited to her partner, Henry. Seen exiting the Citizens' Advice Bureau in *Loving* after seeking advice from Mr Snooper, although the mind boggles regarding the nature of their problem.

EMMA

A cow Captain Fearless takes on board his frigate, *Venus*, when he sets sail for Spanish waters in *Jack*. Even when troubled times find him confined to a rowing boat, he doesn't forget his animal.

EMMANNUELLE, CARRY ON

See feature box on pages 98-9.

EMMANUEL, HEATHER

Roles: Plump Native Girl in *Again Doctor* and Pregnant Lubi in *Up the Jungle*

Born in the Malaysian capital, Kuala Lumpur, Heather Emmanuel's parents were killed when she was just nine months, at which point she was taken to Sri Lanka and brought up in a Roman Catholic convent.

She came to England in 1958, trained at RADA and spent the first six months after graduation working at the Old Vic. Soon after, she made her small-screen appearance in *Dixon of Dock Green* and was heard on radio for a year in *The Dales*. Her first film role, meanwhile, was in Hammer's *Secret of Blood Island*.

Although she's made infrequent appearances in films, she's been seen in many television shows, particularly during the '60s and '70s, including *Secret Agent, Doctor in Charge, Within These Walls, Doctor Who, Angels, Survivors, General Hospital, Play School, Prime Suspect* and *The Professionals*.

EMMETT, E.V.H.

Role: Narrator on *Cleo*

A former journalist, Edward Emmett, born in London in 1902, joined Gaumont Sound News as a cutter before becoming the voice of Gaumont-British News between 1934-1944. He became a producer/writer for GB Instructional in 1944 and, later in the decade, associate producer at Ealing.

During his career, he was heard on many films, including *Three Cockeyed Sailors, World of Plenty, Easy Money* and *The Arsenal Stadium Mystery*. He was associate producer on several movies, among them *Passport to Pimlico* and *Dance Hall*. He also contributed to many screenplays, such as *Sabotage* and *The Ware Case*.

He died in 1971, aged sixty-eight.

ENGLAND, CARRY ON

See feature box on pages 102–3.

ERIC

Played by Ian Curry

Eric is Sally Barry's fiancé in *Constable*. While

visiting Eric's parents in Cornwall, they have a row and Sally returns home, but Eric follows and they patch up their differences.

ERNIE

Played by Hugh Futcher

Works at Boggs and Son and appears in *At Your Convenience*.

ESSEX, DAVID

Role: Young Man in *Henry* (Note: the scene was cut.)

Singer David Essex was born in London in 1947. Rooted in poverty, he and his mother lived in a workhouse while his father struggled to earn enough money for a home of their own.

Although he dreamt of being a professional footballer, the purchase of his first drum kit and joining a local band set him on course for a long-standing career in music; over three decades in the business, his enduring success has included twenty-three top twenty hits and annual tours performing in front of over a quarter of a million fans. A man of many talents, he's also appeared in musicals, films and plays.

EVANS, BARBARA

Role: Khasi's Wife in *Up The Khyber*

From the early 1960s to the mid-'70s, Barbara Evans was seen on television in, among others, *Ghost Squad, The Third Man, The Man in Room 17* and an episode of *Bless This House*.

EVANS, GEORGE

Co-wrote the treatment with Lawrie Wyman on which *Dick* was based

Born in Cardiff in 1924, George Evans left school and worked as a cost clerk in the wagon-building industry in South Wales before serving with the RAF during the Second World War.

Demobbed after four years service, he rejoined the wagon-building company before eventually breaking into the world of entertainment via a radio series for BBC Wales. When comedy actor Jon Pertwee noticed Evans' work, he suggested the writer moved to London to try and make a career from writing, which he did in 1958. Evans went on to write for Pertwee's cabaret, radio and TV slots for the next forty years; he also wrote for other top comics, such as Dick Emery, Tommy Cooper and Leslie Crowther.

Evans' partnership with Lawrie Wyman began on *The Navy Lark* and lasted until the late 1970s. During his career, his work included writing for shows such as *Broaden Your Mind, Bless This House* and *Love Thy Neighbour,* as well as writing screenplays *Confessions from the David Galazy Affair* and *Queen of the Blues.*

Evans, who's now registered blind, has also taught creative writing at Sutton College of Arts and co-launched a correspondence course with fellow writer Vince Powell for five years before retiring in the late 1990s.

EVANS, PRIVATE
Played by Louise Burton

Based at the experimental 1313 anti-aircraft battery featured in *England,* she's one of the shirkers who suffers a severe shock to the system when the tough-speaking Captain Melly is put in charge of the unit.

EVANS, RUPERT
Role: Stunt Orderly in *Again Doctor*
TV: *The Prisoner of Spenda*

From the 1950s Rupert Evans was employed as a stunt artist on film and television productions, but was also given the occasional small part. On television his credits include *The Buccaneers,* while on the big screen he appeared in *The Sword and the Rose*; *Rob Roy, the Highland Rogue*; *Radio Cab Murder* and the Beatles' movie, *Help!.*

EXPECTANT FATHER
Played by Jim Dale

For the 'Expectant Father' in *Cabby,* see 'Jeremy'.

EXPRESS DAIRY
The dairy's milk float, registration 235 HLC, is spotted in *Spying.* Driven to the top-secret Bilkington Research Establishment by the crook, Milchmann, who proceeds to plant a bomb in Professor Stark's laboratory before stealing the secret formula he was working on.

CARRY ON ENGLAND

A Peter Rogers Production
Distributed by Fox / Rank Distributors Ltd
Released as an A certificate in 1976 in colour
Running time: 89 mins

CAST

Kenneth Connor .... Captain S. Melly
Windsor Davies .... Sergeant Major 'Tiger' Bloomer
Patrick Mower .... Sergeant Len Able
Judy Geeson .... Sergeant Tilly Willing
Jack Douglas .... Bombardier Ready
Peter Jones .... Brigadier
Diana Langton .... Pte Alice Easy
Melvyn Hayes .... Gunner Shorthouse
Peter Butterworth .... Major Carstairs
Joan Sims .... Pte Jennifer Ffoukes-Sharpe
Julian Holloway .... Major Butcher
David Lodge .... Captain Bull
Larry Dann .... Gunner Shaw
Brian Osborne .... Gunner Owen
Johnny Briggs .... Melly's Driver
Patricia Franklin .... Corporal Cook
Linda Hooks .... Nurse
John Carlin .... Officer
Vivienne Johnson .... Freda
Michael Nightingale .... Officer
Jeremy Connor .... Gunner Hiscocks
Richard Olley .... Gunner Parker
Peter Banks .... Gunner Thomas
Richard Bartlett .... Gunner Drury
Billy J. Mitchell .... Gunner Childs
Peter Quince .... Gunner Sharpe
Paul Toothill .... Gunner Gale
Tricia Newby .... Pte Murray
Louise Burton .... Pte Evans
Jeannie Collings .... Pte Edwards
Barbara Hampshire .... Pte Carter
Linda Regan .... Pte Taylor
Barbara Rosenblat .... ATS Girl

PRODUCTION TEAM

Screenplay by David Pursall and Jack Seddon
Music composed and conducted by Max Harris
Production Manager: Roy Goddard
Art Director: Lionel Couch
Editor: Richard Marden
Director of Photography: Ernest Steward
Camera Operator: Godfrey Godar
Wardrobe: Vi Murray and Don Mothersill
Casting Director: John Owen
Stills Cameraman: Ken Bray
Make-up: Geoffrey Rodway
Sound Recordists: Danny Daniel and Gordon McCallum
Continuity: Marjorie Lavelly
Hairdresser: Stella Rivers
Costume Design: Courtenay Elliott
Set Dresser: Donald Picton
Dubbing Editor: Pat Foster
Assistant Editor: Jack Gardner
Assistant Director: Jack Causey
Titles: G.S.E. Ltd
Processed by Rank Film Laboratories
Grateful thanks were given to the Imperial War Museum for the loan of the gun
Producer: Peter Rogers
Director: Gerald Thomas

From left to right: Peter Butterworth, Kenneth Connor and Jack Douglas in khaki

Peter Rogers checks out proceedings at the anti-aircraft battery

Funny Scene!

Captain Melly is addressing members of the battery who have fallen in in front of him.

MELLY: Now you dozy lot. When I say 'man the gun', I want you to double off to the emplacement. Now, man the gun!
(All the male soldiers run off, leaving the women lined up. Windsor whispers in the captain's ear.)

MELLY: Oh for heaven's sake, all right, woman the gun as well.

It's 1940 and every man and woman is doing their bit for the nation – well almost. The guys and gals posted to the experimental 1313 anti-aircraft battery are living the life of Riley, shunning discipline and their duties, driving their captain to the bottle and loving every minute of it; that is until Captain Bull is replaced by Captain S. Melly, a midget of a man who makes up for his lack of height by tough-talking rhetoric. But even Melly didn't bargain on seeing male soldiers with lipstick on their faces and women's underwear on the washing line as he's driven into the camp for his first day of duty.

He begins his war of attrition by faking an air raid, but can't believe his eyes when the soldiers run for the shelters instead of the gun emplacement. Unimpressed, Captain Melly decides it's time to run the unit into the ground in an attempt to get them into shape. But when all the soldiers gang up on him, he ends up putting them all on a charge and confining them to barracks, much to the soldiers' delight because being a mixed unit, it gives them more time for frolicking

When a barbed wire fence is erected to segregate the men and women, they decide the only answer is to dig a Tunnel of Love, which doesn't last long because when the battery receives an up-to-date gun, the ground – which has been severely weakened by the tunnelling – collapses under its weight. Such antics don't bode well for the Brigadier's impending visit, leaving the soldiers ample opportunity to get their own back for the gruelling programme inflicted upon them by Captain Melly.

Two new faces to the *Carry On* team were Judy Geeson (far left) and Patrick Mower (2nd left)

F

FABRIZI, MARIO
Role: Cook in *Cruising*
Mario Fabrizi was born in London, of Italian parents, in 1925. He became a seaside photographer for a while before the opportunity to play small parts in films and television came his way, including the 1957 film, *The Naked Truth*, and 1960's *Two Way Stretch*. Other big screen credits included *Operation Snatch*, *Village of Daughters*, *Postman's Knock*, *On the Beat*, *The Wrong Arm of the Law* and both of Tony Hancock's films, *The Rebel* and *The Punch and Judy Man*. Fabrizi became good friends with Tony Hancock and lived with him and Cicely for a while before he married.

He also appeared in many television episodes of *Hancock's Half Hour*. The highlight of his career, however, was playing Lance Corporal Merryweather in *The Army Game*. After appearing in two series of this highly successful series, Fabrizi struggled to find work; money was short, and with a new baby to provide for he quit acting and secured a job in advertising with a London firm.

He died of a heart attack in 1962.

FAGAN, JAMES
Role: Concorde Steward in *Emmannuelle*
In the mid-1970s, James Fagan appeared occasionally on television, including several episodes of *Space: 1999* and an instalment of *The Sweeney*, as a hotel receptionist.

FAKIR, THE
Played by Cardew Robinson
Seen in *Up The Khyber*, the Fakir provides entertainment for the Khasi of Kalabar and Bunghit Din, not that he impresses with his series of acts. (Note: the role was reportedly intended for Tommy Cooper and would have been more prominent in the film had the casting taken place.)

FANATIC PATIENT
Played by Douglas Ives
In *Regardless* the Fanatic Patient is a keen punter who we see lying in a hospital bed studying his paper, deciding who to back for that day's horse racing. When Bert Handy – who's mistaken for Sir Theodore, an important visitor – is taken on a tour of the hospital, he wanders up to the patient and offers his opinion on the horses.

FANCEY, CAPTAIN DESMOND
Played by Kenneth Williams
Reports to Sir Roger Daley in *Dick* and is responsible for day-to-day control of the Bow Street Runners. An incompetent who's constantly being fooled by the master criminal, Dick Turpin.

FANNY
Played by Sandra Caron
Fanny is one of the girls from Chayste Place, a finishing school run by Dr Soaper and Miss Haggerd, who spends a few nights under canvas at the Paradise Camp Site in Devon. Seen in *Camping*, she's best mates with Barbara, and they end up flirting with Sid Boggle and Bernie Lugg during their time at the site.

FANNY, AUNTIE
A nude painting of the Rumpo Kid's aunt, who's not actually seen in *Cowboy*, is displayed above the bar in Rumpo's Place. She worked as an artist's model for a time.

FANNY FUSSPOT, THE CALORIE QUEEN
Not seen in *Cruising*, but mentioned by Wilfred Haines, the ship's chef. He's accused of arranging a special diet and cooking meals for the lady from Cabin 73.

FARMER
Played by Derek Francis
Seen in *Camping*, the farmer is on the warpath, desperate to find the man who made his daughter pregnant. He ends up accusing everyone who arrives at the house, including Charlie Muggins and Peter Potter when they come calling for milk; a misunderstanding sees the farmer thinking Potter is his man so he deposits a barrel-load of gunshot into the poor man's backside.

FARMER
Played by Derek Francis
An anti-Royalist who appears in *Henry*. When the King chases a buxom lass into a barn, he hopes to have some fun but is stopped in his tracks by the girl's father, the farmer who owns the barn.

FARMER'S DAUGHTER
Played by Patricia Franklin
Appears in *Camping*, knitting in a farmhouse. She's pregnant but doesn't know the name of the father, which infuriates her old man who ends up accusing every innocent guy who comes calling.

FARQUHAR, STUART
Played by Kenneth Williams
The Wundatours courier in *Abroad* is placed in charge of the short break to Elsbels, a Med resort boasting an unchallenged sunshine record – that is until Farquhar's party arrives. Inefficient and ineffectual, the trip is far from successful and Stuart Farquhar pays for it with his job. Vic and Cora Flange, who were on the trip, take him under their wing, though, with the offer of a job, washing glasses at their pub. While away in Elsbels, he struck up a relationship with his assistant, Moira, which they resume back on home soil.

FARRAR, SONNY
Role: Violinist in *Loving*
Together with his band, Sonny Farrar, who was born in 1908, performed around the world. He also appeared in a few films, such as *She Shall Have Music*, *The Counterfeit Constable* and *Half A Sixpence*; he was also seen on the big screen with his band in *Talking Feet*.

FAT MAID
Played by Christine Ozanne
Seen in *Nurse* the Fat Maid works at Haven Hospital and is rather perturbed when she's accidentally belted on the behind by Mick, the ward orderly, while carrying his broom out to sweep the verandah, ready for matron's rounds.

FAT MAN, THE
Played by Eric Pohlmann
Real name Emile Fauzak, this cigar-puffing man is first seen at the Café Mozart in Vienna

during *Spying*. He's involved in the plot to transport the secret formula to Dr Crow. His job is to arrange a meeting with Milchmann and to obtain the formula before disposing of him. His extra-curricular antics at Hakim's Fun House see him lose the formula to British agents, but he's given a final chance to redeem himself by chasing Simkins and his team across Europe.

FAULKNER, MAX
Role: Highwayman in *Dick*

In a long career, Max Faulkner has often combined small parts in films and on television with his duties as a stuntman/stunt coordinator. On screen since the 1950s, he's worked on films such as *The Silent Invasion*, *The Ipcress File*, *Far from the Madding Crowd*, *Where Eagles Dare*, *The Day of the Jackal*, *Willow* and the Bond movies, *From Russia With Love* and *GoldenEye*. On television, his credits cover such shows as *The Adventures of Robin Hood*, *The Saint*, *Robin's Nest*, *Blake's 7*, *The Prisoner*, *Doctor Who*, *The Day of the Triffids* and *Poldark*.

FAUZAK, EMILE
For Emile Fauzak in *Spying*, see 'Fat Man, The'.

FAWKES, GUY
Played by Bill Maynard

A friend of Lord Hampton of Wick who's involved in the plot to overthrow King Henry VIII. Seen in *Henry*.

FEARLESS, CAPTAIN
Played by Kenneth Williams

The cowardly captain of the frigate Venus in *Jack*. On doctor's orders, he tries avoiding any form of excitement, including ignoring confrontation whenever possible. He drinks milk, suffers seasickness and is firmly against any kind of brutality, making him an unsuitable character leading a ship into battle against the Spanish Armada. An ineffectual leader, who's bullied and pushed into decisions by his subordinates.

FEENEY, PAT
Role: 4th Storeman in *Sergeant*

FEMALE INSTRUCTOR
Played by Alexandra Dane

In charge of pre-natal classes at the Borough County Hospital, the female instructor is tasked with putting Mr Barron, who's suffering a phantom pregnancy, through his paces when he's told to attend the classes by Dr Tinkle. Seen in *Doctor*.

FENEMORE, HILDA
Roles: Rhoda Bray in *Nurse* and Agitated Woman in *Constable*

Hilda Fenemore, born in London in 1919, was a veteran character actress of film, television and stage. Although her most famous screen role was arguably Jennie Wren, Jack Warner's affable neighbour in *Dixon of Dock Green*, a role she played for four years, her long list of

jobs included *Are You Being Served?*, *Goodnight Sweetheart*, *Crown Court*, *Duchess of Duke Street*, *Minder*, *Brookside*, *French and Saunders* and *Gone to Seed*.

Fenemore always wanted to become an actress and when, as an amateur, she impressed everyone with her performance in a play directed by the late Bill Owen, she decided to make it her career. In over four decades in the profession, Fenemore appeared in ninety films, including *Room in the House*, *The Tommy Steele Story*, *Clash by Night* and *The Offence*. She died in 2004.

FETTLE, DR
Played by Jon Pertwee

The bespectacled police doctor in *Screaming!* examines the finger found in Hocombe Woods, the spot where Doris Mann mysteriously vanished. An eccentric sporting a goatee, he sends an electric current through the finger and ends up seeing a monster appear before his eyes. Sadly, the monster doesn't thank the doctor for bringing him to life and ends up killing him.

FFING HALL
The palatial home of Sir Rodney Ffing is the venue for a charity ball in *Don't Lose Your Head*.

FFING, SIR RODNEY
Played by Sid James

A friend of Lord Darcy de Pue, Sir Rodney, alias the Black Fingernail, is saddened to hear of the plight of so many French men and women; since the revolution across the channel, the aristocracy are losing their heads at the gallows

at an alarming rate and the brave Ffing, accompanied by Lord Darcy, sets out to snatch the victims from the brink of death via a series of audacious ruses and artful disguises. Seen in *Don't Lose Your Head*.

FFOUKES-SHARPE, PRIVATE JENNIFER
Played by Joan Sims

Based at the experimental 1313 anti-aircraft battery featured in *England*, she fancies the unit's sergeant major something rotten, and isn't afraid of letting him know her feelings. An influential member of the unit who's able to rouse the rabble when Sergeant Major Bloomer's screaming and bawling have failed.

F.H. ROWSE
A department store seen in *Constable*. Sales figures are being affected by shoplifting, so PC Benson and PC Gorse agree with the manager to work undercover, dressed as women, to try and solve the problem. The trouble is, no one tells the assistant manager who later accuses them of acting suspiciously.

FIDDLER, JOSH
Played by Peter Butterworth

The owner of the Paradise Camp Site in Devon who's seen in *Camping*. His name certainly suits him, as campers can confirm when they arrive at his mudpit of a site.

FIDDLER, MR
Played by Bill Maynard

The boss of Wundatours, the travel firm running the weekend trip to Elsbels in *Abroad*,

Mr Fiddler (Bill Maynard, far right) never made it onto the big screen (*Abroad*)

he was to appear in a scene with Stuart Farquhar and Moira Plunkett, briefing them before they head off to the sunny Med. (**Note: the scene was cut.**)

EXT. THE MAIN OFFICE OF 'WUNDATOURS LTD' – DAY

A typical shop-fronted travel agency in the London area. The window display features most prominently:

NEW NEW NEW! TRY OUR FABULOUS NEW FOUR-DAY ALL-IN HOLIDAY TO THE FABULOUS COSTA BOMM!!! ONLY £19!!!!!!!

We pick up Stuart Farquhar as he approaches the shop entrance. He is dressed in blue blazer and slacks and carries a hold-all, and in his lapel (or on his blazer pocket perhaps) is a badge saying 'WUNDA-TOURS'.

As he turns into the shop . . .

INT. BOOKING ROOM, WUNDATOURS – DAY

There is a Reception Desk, with an attractive receptionist behind it, covered with the usual travel brochures (the desk, not the receptionist), and a large date thing which tells us that this is 'FRIDAY, 4 MAY'. There are a couple of desks with chairs where the actual booking is done, and a door at the end leading to the Manager's Office.

(STUART breezes in and up to the reception desk.)

STUART: Good afternoon, Miss Dobbs. Nice day for it.

DOBBS: (**Looking up.**) I hope it keeps that way, Mr Farquhar. Mr Fiddler wants to see you before you go.

(This is said rather ominously and STUART loses his jaunty manner.)

STUART: Oh. Well, I'd better go in right away then.

(He puts his bag down by the counter and goes to the door at the rear, arranges his appearance rather nervously, then tentatively knocks at the door. We hear a bawl of 'Yes?' from inside and he opens the door.)

INT. FIDDLER'S OFFICE – DAY

(Fiddler, a large florid-faced gentleman, is standing beside his desk. Seated on the front of the desk is Moira Plunkett, an attractive 'deb' type in her late twenties, with a very outstanding figure, which the 'Hostess' mini-skirted uniform shows off to great advantage. Fiddler has one arm around Moira's waist and the other hand rests familiarly on her thigh, but neither one of them seems particularly concerned about this as Stuart enters and comes to an embarrassed stop.)

STUART: Oh I say, I'm terribly sorry, sir. I'll come back later.

FIDDLER: What for?

STUART: I mean, if you're busy . . .

FIDDLER: If you think this is busy you should have been here ten minutes ago.

(And gives MOIRA a knowing leer and slaps her thigh.)

STUART: Why? What happened, sir?

FIDDLER: Oh, don't be more of a fool than you can help, Farquhar. Sit down, I want to talk to you.

(He indicates chair in front of the desk and takes his own chair behind it.)

STUART: Yes of course, sir.

(He takes the chair which is very close to MOIRA, still sitting on the desk. As he does so, she crosses her legs bringing one knee embarrassingly close to his face.)

FIDDLER: Right. This Elsbels trip. As you know, this is our first venture into the weekend package deal lark, so I don't want any boobs!

STUART: I beg your pardon, sir?

FIDDLER: Boobs! You know what they are, don't you?

(STUART is uncomfortably aware of the proximity of MOIRA's as he answers.)

STUART: Oh yes, of course, sir.

FIDDLER: You should do. You've made enough of them in the past.

STUART: I can promise you, sir . . . this time I shall do everything in my power to make this a holiday they'll never forget.

FIDDLER: That's what I'm afraid of! We're still getting compaints from the last lot you took.

(MOIRA speaks for the first time. She has a very debby drawl, not unattractive.)

MOIRA: Oh, Mister Fiddler, that's not quite fair. If you mean the Venice trip, you know it wasn't Mr Farquhar's fault really.

(And gives STUART a terrible warm smile. Can she possibly like this chap? STUART smiles gratefully back at her.)

STUART: That's true, sir. There was that airport strike on and I had to make some very hurried alternative arrangements.

FIDDLER: I know, and look where you all finished up.

STUART: Well, I thought Littlehampton would be better than nothing, sir.

FIDDLER: But hardly a substitute for Venice!

STUART: Well . . . it is rather short on canals, I agree . . .

FIDDLER: Which girl did you have on that trip?

STUART: Oh, none, sir. If that was one of the complaints . . .

FIDDLER: I mean, which hostess, you fool!

STUART: Oh, it was Miss Fosdick, sir. A charming girl, but the trouble was that she'd never done it before.

FIDDLER: Well, you'll have Miss Plunkett here this time. She can do it backwards.

STUART: Oh. That should be most helpful, sir.

FIDDLER: Right, off you go then and for God's sake let's have no foul-ups. It would be a pity if your last trip for us was a fiasco.

STUART: Oh, I'm not leaving the agency, sir.

FIDDLER: You will be if anything goes wrong!

(And, on STUART's worried face . . .)

FIDDLER, SIDNEY
Played by Sid James
An outspoken member of Fircombe's town council, Sid Fiddler owns an amusement arcade in the seaside resort. Seen in *Girls*, he's keen to attract more tourists to the town, hence his suggestion for a beauty contest which is vehemently opposed by women's libber Augusta Prodworthy. Sid finds a way of getting the idea accepted and calls in his old pal, Peter Potter, to deal with publicity, while housing all the girls in the Palace Hotel, run by his girl-friend Connie Philpotts; Connie, though, isn't pleased: not only are the contestants being given complimentary accommodation at the hotel, but she's having to watch her would-be hubby ogling all the gorgeous beauties.

FIELD, GEORGE
Played by Graham Stewart
A character in *Nurse*.

FIELDING, FENELLA
Roles: Penny Panting in *Regardless* and Virula Watt in *Screaming!*
Born in London in 1934, Fenella Fielding left school and for a time worked as a typist for various companies, including a theatrical agent. But she harboured dreams of treading the boards herself and joined amateur companies until finally deciding to try her luck professionally, initially working backstage at a theatre club in South Kensington, London.

After six months, she moved on and held a succession of acting jobs until getting her big break in the musical, *Valmouth*, followed soon after by her appearance alongside Kenneth Williams in the revue, *Pieces of Eight*. The exposure in these two productions helped open doors to the world of television and film, which to date had consisted of one-liners in productions such as *Charley Moon* and *Sapphire*.

Other film credits include *Doctor in Love, No Love for Johnnie, The Old Dark House, Doctor in Distress, Road to St Tropez, Doctor in Clover, Lock Up Your Daughters!* and *Beginner's Luck*. On television, she's been seen in, among others, *Ooh La La!, Destination Downing Street, International Detective, The Morecambe and Wise Show* and *The Ed Sullivan Show*.

Fielding remains busy, particularly on stage, where she's recently finished touring with *The Vagina Monologues*.

FIFI, MADAME
Played by Olga Lowe
Runs a bawdy house in *Abroad*. Happens to be sister of the local police chief, which doesn't help when Mr Tuttle and the rest of the party staying at the Elsbels Palace Hotel get into a brawl with some of the girls and the police.

FINGER, JOHNNY
Played by Sidney James
In *Cowboy* this ruthless bandit, who's also known as the Rumpo Kid, turns the sleepy town of Stodge City on its head when he swaggers into town. He cuts a frightening figure as he takes over the running of this outpost, that is until Marshall Knutt – or rather his travelling companion, Annie Oakley – arrives on the scene.

FINISHAM MATERNITY HOSPITAL
The setting for *Matron*.

FINLAY, DR
Played by William Mervyn
A physician seen in *Henry*. See 'Physician'.

FIRBANK, ANN
Role: Helen Lloyd in *Nurse*
Born in Secunderabad, India, in 1933, Ann Firbank, daughter of a military man, came to the UK aged twelve to attend boarding school. After completing her education she undertook a secretarial course and worked at a doctor's surgery in Colchester before following her dream of becoming an actress by enrolling at RADA.

She left the Academy early to accept a position in rep at Manchester before moving to Stratford. A film contract with Ealing and plenty of television work soon followed, although she's never stopped working in theatre throughout her career.

Her small-screen credits include *The Adventures of Robin Hood*, *Danger Man*, *Emergency – Ward 10*, *Out of the Unknown*, *The Lotus Eaters*, *Bergerac*, *Heartbeat* and *Kavanagh QC*. In the medium of films, she's been seen in, among others, *The Servant*, *Darling*, *Accident*, *A Passage to India* and *Anna and the King*.

She remains busy in the profession.

FIRCOMBE
The fictitious seaside resort in *Girls* has seen better days. A run-down esplanade, tacky souvenir shops and more than its fair share of amusement arcades, Fircombe has seen a decline in the number of mugs prepared to hand over their hard-earned cash for a week's stay in this crumby town; the local council seems oblivious to this blindingly obvious fact, except for Sid Fiddler, who happens to run one of the amusement arcades. Sid regards the town as a 'dump' and wants to encourage anything that will bring more tourists to the town, such as a beauty contest, even though the event will gratify his own sexual desires.

FIRCOMBE WOMEN'S LIB MOVEMENT
Led by local councillor, Augusta Prodworthy, the Movement takes great pleasure in standing up for women's rights in the town of Fircombe. Its members launch Operation Spoilsport in order to ruin the Miss Fircombe beauty contest in *Girls*, a competition Prodworthy opposed strongly before the decision to hold the event was taken behind her back.

FIRE CHIEF
Played by Bill Pertwee
In *Girls* the Fire Chief shows the mayor of Fircombe the town's new fire engine.

5 WILBUR PLACE
In *Cabby*, Flo asks Gladys, one of the Glamcab drivers, to go to the address and pick up a fare; unbeknown to Charlie and Sarge, who intercept the message in an attempt to sabotage the business, it's the address for the town's mortuary at Westford, which means Pintpot wastes his time when he heads there.

FLANGE, CORA
Played by Joan Sims
Runs the local pub in *Abroad* with her husband, Vic. Her phobia of flying means her hubby holidays alone, but when Cora hears that Sadie Tomkins, who Sid has taken a fancy to, is booked on the same trip to the Med resort of Elsbels, she decides to put aside her fear of flying in order to keep an eye on her hubby. By the end of the break, thanks to a little help from a local love potion poured into the punch at the farewell party, Cora is delighted to find her husband, once again, only has eyes for her.

FLANGE, VIC
Played by Sidney James
The local landlord runs the pub with his wife, Cora, but fancies his chances with busty blonde, Sadie Tomkins, who likes to flash her assets around. Knowing his wife doesn't like flying, Vic decides to book a £17 short break with Wundatours to the Med resort of Elsbels, not telling his wife that Sadie has booked the same trip. Their chance of a few days together is shattered, though, when Cora finds out Sadie is on the trip; she puts aside her aversion to flying in order to keep an eye on her hubby.

At first, Vic has a miserable time abroad, watching Sadie befriend the loudmouthed Scot, Bert Conway, but by the end of the break, with more than a little help from a local love potion poured into the punch at the farewell party, he's rediscovered his love for Cora. Appears in *Abroad*.

FLASHER, THE REVEREND
Played by Sid James
For the Reverend Flasher in *Dick* see 'Turpin, Dick'.

FLEET STREET JOURNALIST
Played by Stanley McGeagh
The journalist appears in *Emmannuelle* and is intrigued by the various trysts involving Emmannuelle Prevert, the French Ambassador's wife.

FLOELLA
Played by Hattie Jacques
The grumpy cook at the Elsbels Palace Hotel appears in *Abroad*, taking her bad moods out on the temperamental stove as well as Pepe, who runs the hotel.

FLOWERBUDS, THE
The hippy group providing the entertainment at the all-nite rave in Farmer Giles's field, next-door to the Paradise Camp Site. Seen in *Camping*.

FLUFF
The Vague Woman's black cat gets stuck in the belfry of a church in *Constable*.

FLUNKEY
Played by William McGuirk
Seen in *Henry* the flunkey announces the arrival of the Conte di Pisa and later helps Henry with his coat and crown.

FOGGETT, ALF
The landlord of the Royal Oak in Fircombe is one of the judges at the Miss Fircombe beauty contest. Seen but not heard in *Girls*.

FOGGETT, MRS
The name Sid Carter gives to Ernie Bragg, who's dressed up as a pregnant woman, when they arrive at the Finisham Maternity Hospital in *Matron*.

FOLLOW THAT CAMEL, CARRY ON
See feature box on pages 108–9.

FONTWELL PARK
In *Nurse*, Fontwell Park is one of the racing venues listed in the Colonel's newspaper.

FOOTBALL REFEREE
Played by Bruce Wyllie
Seen in *Emmannuelle* Prevert's flashback sequence in which she describes her most amorous experience. Appears in *Emmannuelle*.

FOOTPADS
Played by Jeremy Connor and Nosher Powell
The Footpads are seen in *Dick*.

FORD, HELEN
Role: Ward Cleaner in *Doctor*

FORD, JOANNA
Role: Vestal Virgin in *Cleo*

CARRY ON FOLLOW THAT CAMEL

A Peter Rogers production
Distributed through Rank Organisation
Released as an A certificate in 1967 in colour
Running time: 95 mins
(Note: the film was originally released without the Carry On moniker but this was later reinstated.)

CAST

Phil Silvers . . . . Sergeant Ernie Nocker
Jim Dale . . . . . . Bertram Oliphant 'Bo' West
Peter Butterworth . . . . Simpson
Kenneth Williams . . . . Commandant Burger
Charles Hawtrey . . . . Captain Le Pice
Joan Sims . . . . Zig-Zig
Angela Douglas . . . . . . Lady Jane Ponsonby
Bernard Bresslaw . . . Sheikh Abdul Abulbul
Anita Harris . . . . Corktip
John Bluthal . . . . Corporal Clotski
Peter Gilmore . . . . Captain Bagshaw
William Mervyn . . . . Sir Cyril Ponsonby
Julian Holloway . . . . Ticket Collector
David Glover . . . . Hotel Manager
Larry Taylor . . . . Riff
William Hurndell . . . . Riff
Julian Orchard . . . . Doctor

Vincent Ball . . . . Ship's Officer
Peter Jesson . . . . Lawrence
Gertan Klauber . . . . Spiv
Michael Nightingale . . . . . . Nightingale the
Butler
Richard Montez
Frank Singuineau
Simon Cain . . . . Riffs at Abdul's Tent
Harold Kasket . . . . Hotel Gentleman

Edmund Pegge . . . . Bowler
Carol Sloan
Gina Gianelli
Dominique Don
Anne Scott
Patsy Snell
Zorenah Osborne
Margot Maxine
Sally Douglas
Angie Grant
Gina Warwick
Karen Young
Helga Jones . . . . Harem Girls

PRODUCTION TEAM

Screenplay by Talbot Rothwell
Music composed and conducted by Eric Rogers
Production Manager: Jack Swinburne
Director of Photography: Alan Hume
Editor: Alfred Roome
Art Director: Alex Vetchinsky
Camera Operator: Alan Hall
Assistant Director: David Bracknell
Continuity: Joy Mercer
Assistant Editor: Jack Gardner
Make-up: Geoffrey Rodway
Sound Recordists: Dudley Messenger and Ken Barker
Hairdresser: Stella Rivers
Costume Designer: Emma Selby-Walker
Dubbing Editor: Wally Nelson
Location Manager: Terry Clegg
Producer: Peter Rogers
Director: Gerald Thomas

Phil Silvers, of Sgt Bilko fame, plays Sgt. Nocker

All smile for the camera, please!

It's 1906 and pretty Lady Jane Ponsonby has many suitors, including Bertram West and Humphrey Bagshaw, who are batting for the same cricket team in the grounds of the Ponsonby mansion. When Bagshaw, desperate to blot West's copybook, falls over and accuses his competitor of tripping him on purpose, it's just not cricket and Lady Jane's father, Sir Cyril, bans West from not only the team but from setting foot on his land again.

Believing he's lost Lady Jane for good, West rushes off to join the Foreign Legion. Before long, though, it's discovered that Bagshaw's claims were false, leaving Lady Jane no option but to set forth and find Bertram West to tell him his name has been cleared.

West, who's taken along his butler, Simpson, is completely out of place at the garrison, still acting the English gentleman. Sergeant Nocker is looking forward to knocking them into shape and it's not long before they're punished by being buried up to their necks in sand. But when the sergeant discovers that they saw him with a woman at a local café and worries that they'll blackmail him, he starts treating them like royalty: nothing is too much trouble, including delivering a morning cup of tea to the two soldiers.

Lady Jane arrives at the garrison and meets Commandant Burger, who turns out to be an old flame she met whilst at finishing school in Vienna, before continuing her search for West; when she looks for him at a local café and encounters Sheikh Abdul Abulbul, who drugs her, she's soon in trouble. So are West and Nocker, who are also captured.

Nocker eventually escapes and heads back to the garrison for help, but at first Commandant Burger doesn't believe him, especially as he recalls a previous occasion when he said he'd been attacked while out on patrol when he'd actually been shacked up with Zig-Zig, who owns the local café.

Later, when he hears that Nocker's latest story involved an English woman, Burger realises he's telling the truth and sets out to find them. West and Simpson are found pegged out in the desert, but there is no sign of Lady Jane, who remains a captive of the Arabs who are on their way to attack Fort Zuassantneuf. Burger is distraught, but by the time he reaches the fort the Foreign Legion personnel have been killed; to make matters worse, Sheikh Abdul Abulbul is planning his marriage to wife number thirteen, who happens to be Lady Jane. Before the wedding can be consummated, a switch of identity for Abdul's new wife, thanks to the help of the ever-reliable Simpson, gives a chance for Lady Jane to escape.

Funny Scene!

Commandant Burger and Sergeant Nocker are out in the desert trying to find Lady Jane Ponsonby, an old girlfriend of Burger's, who went missing with Bertram West and his loyal butler, Simpson. They discover the men pegged down in the sand.

NOCKER: (Looking at WEST.) It's all right, sir, he's alive, he's still breathing.

BURGER: I don't care about them, where's meine Liebchen? (He spots a skull in the sand and picks it up.) Uh — alas poor Jane, I knew her well.

NOCKER: Ah, come on, sir, that's a skull of a man.

BURGER: How can you tell?

NOCKER: By the jawbone: a woman's gets more worn down, you know, by the constant yaketty, yaketty, yaketty.

FORDYCE, ANN
Hairdresser on *Cleo*

Ann Fordyce first started working as a hair stylist in the 1950s on films such as *Folly To Be Wise, The Last Appointment, The Leather Boys, Devil Doll, The Crimson Cult, School for Unclaimed Girls* and *Perfect Friday*.

FORMIDABLE LADY, THE
Played by Judith Furse

A schoolteacher in *Regardless*, she's in charge of some girls who've just alighted from a train. Francis Courtenay meets her at the station but what he doesn't know is that a mix-up back at the Helping Hands office has meant he's been sent on the wrong job and is subsequently arrested for suggestive behaviour.

FORSYTH, FRANK
Roles: 2nd Specialist in *Sergeant*, John Gray in *Nurse*, Citizen in *Constable*, Chauffeur in *Cabby*, 2nd Sealord in *Jack*, Professor Stark in *Spying* and Desk Sergeant in *Screaming!*

Born in London in 1905, Frank Forsyth forged a successful career for himself playing character parts on stage and screen.

In films from the early 1950s, appearing in such titles as *The Lavender Hill Mob, The Embezzler, No Smoking, The Solitary Child, Twice Round the Daffodils, Devils of Darkness* and *They Came From Beyond Space*.

He was seen in plenty of television series, including *The Vise, Glencannon, The Flying Doctor, International Detective, Man in a Suitcase, Journey to the Unknown* and *The Carnforth Practice*. He died in 1984, aged seventy-eight.

FORT ZUASSANTNEUF
When, in *Follow that Camel*, Commandant Burger hears Sheikh Abdul Abulbul and his men are planning to attack the Saharan fort, and that he has forced Lady Jane Ponsonby to go with him, he heads off to try and protect the garrison and to retrieve Lady Jane.

FOSDICK, MISS
Played by Patsy Rowlands

Secretary to Dr Carver, Miss Fosdick is seen in *Again Doctor*. She travels with Carver to the Beatific Islands when a progress report is required on Dr Nookey, who had been forced into accepting a post at the islands' medical mission. When Carver returns, Miss Fosdick stays on the windswept islands and becomes Saturday, Gladstone Screwer's sixth wife.

FOSDICK WARD
In *Doctor* this is a men's ward at the Borough County Hospital.

FOSDYKE, AMELIA
An unseen character in *Behind* who was supposed to have appeared in the film Professor Crump was showing in his lecture, 'Getting to the Bottom of Things'. The female archaeologist, who trained under Professor Schwindlehoffer of Utrecht, was filmed uncovering an archaeological site, but the audience didn't get to see it, not that anyone minds because the film that is accidentally shown is of a woman stripping!

FOSTER, PATRICK
Dubbing Editor on *Girls, Behind* and *England*

Born in Essex in 1949, Patrick Foster, who was nominated for a BAFTA in 1978 for his work on *Superman*, has worked as a sound/dubbing editor on many films, including *Romeo and Juliet, The Magnificent Seven Deadly Sins, Bless This House, Diversions* and *Intimate Games*.

FOTHERGILL, FRUITY
Unseen in *Constable*, but the character is mentioned by Honoria while chatting to PC Potter. It was at Fruity's pyjama party that she last saw Potter.

FOXTON
An unseen character mentioned by Captain Crowther in *Cruising*, Foxton was the previous first officer who quit his job upon winning the football pools. His emergency replacement is Leonard Marjoribanks.

F. RAMSDEN
A butcher's shop in *Behind*.

FRANCIS, DEREK
Roles: Sir Edmund Burke in *Doctor*, Farmer in *Camping*, Bishop in *Loving*, Farmer in *Henry*, Arthur in *Matron* and Brother Martin in *Abroad*

Derek Francis, born in Brighton in 1923, built up an impressive list of theatre, television and film credits during a long career in showbusiness. On television he appeared in shows including *Ghost Squad, Jango, Undermind, Doctor Who* and *Man in a Suitcase* during the 1960s, *Jason King, The Sweeney, Whoops Baghdad!, Nicholas Nickleby, Oh Father* and *The Professionals* in the '70s and an episode of *Keep It In the Family* in 1980, playing the Non-Mechanical Man.

On the big screen he was seen in over forty films, such as *The Criminal, Ring of Spies, The Hijackers, Press for Time, Scrooge* and *Man of Violence*.

He died in 1984, aged sixty.

FRANCIS, KING OF FRANCE
Played by Peter Gilmore

Arrives on the scene in *Henry*, together with his sizeable army, when he hears rumours that his cousin, Marie of Normandy, is imprisoned in the Tower of London. The much-feared King of France eventually leaves England for home shores happy that his cousin is being taken care of; he's also found his future wife, Bettina, on the trip.

FRANK
Unseen character mentioned by Sam Twist in *Regardless*. When the 'Bed of the Century' goes wrong at the Ideal House Exhibition, Twist – who's demonstrating the product – calls for Frank's help.

FRANKLIN, PATRICIA
Roles: Farmer's Daughter in *Camping*, Mrs Dreery in *Loving*, Rosemary in *Girls*, Vera Bragg in *Behind* and Corporal Cook in *England*

Born in London in 1942, Patricia Franklin worked as a receptionist upon leaving school, supplementing her income with modelling assignments. Always keen on the theatre, she performed with the local amateur dramatic group until, in 1965, she joined RADA.

Graduating in 1967, she went straight into the West End production of *Uproar in the House*, beginning an extensive theatre career which has included spells at the National and Royal Court. She's also worked with the Young Vic and appeared in many West End shows.

Her big screen career began with *Camping* and has included films such as *Bless This House* and, in 2004, *Shaun of the Dead*, while she kicked off her television work in the 1971 play, *Mr Mouse, Are You Within?*. She's also appeared in, among others, *The Sweeney, Hazell, The Bill, Black Books, Joe's Ark* (which was shown in the *Play for Today* series), *Brief Encounter* and the 1977 series, *Holding On*.

Patricia Franklin, who took a break from acting between 1984-94 while her children were growing up, continues to act with a recent job being BBC2's *Look Around You*.

FRASER, LIZ
Roles: Delia King in *Regardless*, Glad Trimble in *Cruising*, Sally in *Cabby* and Sylvia Ramsden in *Behind*
STAGE: *Laughing*

Liz Fraser, born in London in 1935, studied at the London School of Dramatic Art before beginning a successful career, particularly in the medium of film where she's built up over twenty credits. Appearing mainly in comedy pictures, she's been seen in, among others, *I'm All Right, Jack* with Ian Carmichael and Peter Sellers, *The Smallest Show on Earth, The Night We Dropped A Clanger, Two Way Stretch* and *The Bulldog Breed*.

On television, one of her first jobs was in the 1955 serial, *Sixpenny Corner*, but she's also played such roles as matron in *Whack-O!*, Delilah in *Minder*, Edith in 1993's *Demob* and been seen in *The Bill, Robin's Nest* and two series of *Fairly Secret Army*.

FRED
Played by Julian Orchard

A friend of Ken Biddle who visits him at the Borough County Hospital; short of conversation, Fred is only too pleased to help his mate in *Doctor* because it will pass a bit of time during visiting hours, so he heads off to the women's ward to find out where Mavis Winkle, to whom Ken has taken a fancy, has been moved. Another favour sees him swapping clothes with Ken and jumping into his bed while his mate wanders off to talk to Mavis; he soon wishes he hadn't, though, when a nurse forces him to drink castor oil.

FRED
Played by Bill Maynard
One of Sid Carter's gang in *Matron*.

FREDA
Played by Vivienne Johnson
In *England*, Freda, an ATS, assists in the mess. (Note: her lines were cut but she's still seen standing to attention in the mess when Captain Melly is lecturing the soldiers.)

WHAT MIGHT HAVE BEEN

Sergeants Able and Tilly are getting some food at the mess and talking about their new Major causing the lazy bunch of khaki trouble.

ABLE: That three-pipsqueaker! Too little to be awkward. We'll stamp him into the ground. I'm not worried about him.

(An unidentifiable object is slammed down on his plate.)

ABLE: More worried about this. (To Cook.) What're we supposed to do with it, eat it or rub it in?

COOK: Y'can bounce it off the ceiling for all I care.

ABLE: Well, what is it then?

COOK: What d'you think?

ABLE: I'm asking the question.

COOK: Well, it's – er – it's – (Turns to an even more evil-looking ATS ASSISTANT.) Here, Freda – what is it?

FREDA: Well, obvious, it's – er – well, it's like –

(She breaks off, calls down to the other ATS ASSISTANT.)

FREDA: Here, Lill, what's on today, then?

LILL: (Calls back.) Liver, what's it look like?

(ABLE looks down at the object.)

ABLE: I'd hate to tell you.

FREDERICK CARVER FOUNDATION, THE
In *Again Doctor*, Dr Carver dreams of opening a private clinic and hopes that by buttering up the wealthy Ellen Moore she'll finance the project.

FREDERICK BUMBLE NURSERY, THE
Named after the local mayor, the nursery is found at the maternity hospital in Fircombe.

At its official opening in *Girls*, the mayor unveils a plaque only to find, to his horror, someone has pinned an enlarged photo of him with his trousers down, a regular occurrence it seems in the life of the mayor, on the plaque. The mayor's understandable outrage soon has all the babies wailing.

FREEMAN, DAVE
Wrote the screenplay for *Behind* and *Columbus*
TV: Wrote *The Prisoner of Spenda*, *The Baron Outlook*, *The Sobbing Cavalier*, *The Nine Old Cobblers*, *The Case of the Screaming Winkles* and *The Case of the Coughing Parrot*. His material was also used in *Laughing's Christmas Classics*
STAGE: Co-wrote *London!*
Born in London in 1922, scriptwriter Dave Freeman left school at fourteen and became an apprentice electrician. His trade took him into the theatre, working for Strand Electrics as a stage electrician.

He began writing in the navy, which he joined in 1940. While serving in the Indian Ocean where the sailors had to organise their own entertainment, he began writing for the ship's concert as well as performing in his own solo act.

Returning to civvy street in 1947, he tried breaking into showbusiness but failed so joined the police instead. After five years he left the force and accepted the chance to work at the American Officers' Club as the club officer, booking cabaret acts. One of the performers he hired was Benny Hill, and while talking to the comedian after the show, Freeman mentioned he enjoyed writing. It wasn't long before he was penning sketches for Hill on a regular basis, many for his BBC series, *The Benny Hill Show*; he was soon supplying work to Charlie Drake, Tommy Cooper and Arthur Askey.

He also wrote plays, including two that ran in the West End: *Bed Full of Foreigners* and *Tea for Two*.

He died in 2005, aged eighty-two.

FRENCH BUXOM BLONDE
Played by Deborah Brayshaw
Seen in Richmond's flashback sequence in *Emmannuelle* during which he describes his most amorous experience.

FRENCH PARSON
Played by John Carlin
During Richmond's flashback sequence in *Emmannuelle* the French Parson provides him with shelter in the church, away from the German soldier chasing him. Despite the war ending in 1945, Richmond stayed until 1953, no doubt attracted by the charms of the parson's young niece, Colette.

FRISCO FREDDIE
Not seen in *Nurse*, but Ginger – Bernie Bishop's boxing manager – refers to him while visiting his fighter at Haven Hospital. He uses Freddie as an example of a boxer with a gimmick, something he believes Bishop needs.

FROWSI OF ASLAM, KING
Not seen in *At Your Convenience* but the King from the Middle East places a large order for 1000 bidets, worth £90,000, with W. C. Boggs and Son. He must have an enormous harem because he wants to give one to each of his wives in time for the Feast of Abanibel.

FU KUNG SEX
The book Emmannuelle, the French Ambassador's wife, reads while lying on the sun bed in *Emmannuelle*.

FUNHOUSE GIRLS, THE
Played by Virginia Tyler, Judi Johnson and Gloria Best
In *Spying* the three girls walk past the hapless British agents and enter Hakim's Fun House, sparking off an idea which sees Harold Crump dress up in drag and accompany Daphne Honeybutt into the Fun House in an attempt to retrieve the top-secret formula.

FURSE, JUDITH
Roles: Formidable Lady in *Regardless*, Battleaxe in *Cabby* and Dr Crow in *Spying*
Born in Camberley, Surrey, in 1912, Judith Furse was a supporting actress who first appeared on stage at the age of twelve. She later trained at the Old Vic and made her professional debut walking on in *King John* at Sadler's Wells in 1931.

She proceeded to work regularly in theatre (as actress and director), television and in films. Among her numerous big-screen credits are *Goodbye Mr Chips!*, *A Canterbury Tale*, *Quiet Weekend*, *Helter Skelter*, *The Browning Version*, *A Day to Remember*, *Doctor at Large*, *In the Doghouse*, *The Iron Maiden* and *Man in the Wilderness*.

She died in 1974, aged sixty-two.

FUSSEY, JOAN
Played by Joan Sims
Seen in *Camping*, Joan Fussey is Sid Boggle's girlfriend who goes on a camping holiday with him and their friends, Bernie Lugg and Anthea Meeks. Sid's and Joan's relationship is hindered, however, by Joan's over-protective mother who can't stand the sight of Sid.

FUSSEY, MRS
Played by Amelia Bayntun
Joan Fussey's mother in *Camping*. She hates her daughter's boyfriend, Sid Boggle, thinking he's got just one thing on his mind when he whisks Joan off on a camping holiday. A cantankerous woman who lost her husband years

Playing the Battleaxe in *Cabby*, Judith Furse became well known for playing stern roles

ago, therefore we can assume he's probably dead; Mrs Fussey claims she only married him because she got pregnant.

FUTCHER, HUGH

Roles: Bed of Nails Native in *Spying*, Guard in *Don't Lose Your Head*, Cab Driver in *Again Doctor*, Ernie in *At Your Convenience*, Jailer in *Abroad*, 'There's Fiddler' Citizen in *Girls* and Painter in *Behind*

Born in Portsmouth in 1937, Hugh Futcher began his working life in a John Lewis department store, before his elocution teacher (he was studying in the evenings) put him forward for

an audition at RADA, for which he won a scholarship in 1959.

After graduating he was recruited to the original cast of *Chips With Everything* at the Royal Court for a year, and soon after made his film debut in 1961's *Invasion Quartet* playing an ambulance driver. Among his numerous film credits are appearances in *Quatermass and the Pit*, *Before Winter Comes*, *Journey to Murder* and *102 Dalmatians*. On television he's been seen in, among others, *Jason King, Minder* and *Nanny*. His preferred medium, though, is theatre and one of his most enduring roles was in David Merrick's *42nd Street* in the mid-1980s.

FYSON, MAVISE

Role: Francis Cake in *Girls*

Born in 1949, Mavise Fyson's good looks had seen her become a finalist in various beauty contests including Miss England, Miss United Kingdom and Miss Great Britain. A professional beauty queen from the age of seventeen, she spent the next six years touring the major competitions before her agent suggested turning her attention to acting. As well as minor roles in a handful of films, she was seen in television programmes like *The Avengers* and *The Saint*.

GALE, GUNNER
Played by Paul Toothill
Based at the experimental 1313 anti-aircraft battery featured in *England*, he's one of the shirkers who suffers a severe shock to the system when the tough-speaking Captain Melly is put in charge of the unit.

GALILI, HAL
Role: Cowhand in *Cowboy*
On screen since the early 1960s, Hal Galili's other credits included the television shows *Suspense*; *The Saint*; *The Troubleshooters*; *Department S*; *It Ain't Half Hot, Mum*; *The Tomorrow People* and *The Professionals*. He's appeared in films such as *The Girl Hunters*, *Goldfinger*, *Promise Her Anything*, *Loot*, *The Pink Panther Strikes Again*, *Superman II* and *Ragtime*.
He died in 1984.

GALLEY MASTER
Played by Peter Gilmore
A real slave-driver, the Galley Master bullies the poor souls who have to row the boat transporting Caesar to Egypt in *Cleo*. Before reaching their destination he's murdered by Horsa.

GALLOWAY, ANDY
Played by Gerald Campion
Andy is a guitar-strumming recruit in *Sergeant*. A member of Able Platoon at Heathercrest National Service Depot which, under the leadership of Sergeant Grimshaw, surprises everyone by becoming the champion platoon of the twenty-ninth intake.

GAMLEY, DOUGLAS
Credited on *Cruising* as partly responsible for composing the music and conducting
Born in Melbourne, Australia, in 1924, Douglas Gamley was a skilled writer, composer, conductor and music arranger. He began working in the film industry in the 1950s, building up a list of credits which included composing for such films as *Fire Down Below*, *The Admirable Crichton*, *Gideon's Day*, *Beyond This Place*, *Light Up the Sky!*, *The Land That Time Forgot* and 1974's *The Little Prince*, for which he was nominated for the Music Scoring Awards.
He died in 1998, aged seventy-three.

GARDEN OF FRAGRANCE, THE
This garden in Sir Rodney Ffing's mansion is the venue for the duel between Citizen Camembert and Sir Rodney in *Don't Lose Your Head*.

GARDNER, JACK
Assistant Editor on *Cowboy*, *Follow That Camel*, *Doctor*, *Up The Khyber*, *Camping*, *Again Doctor*, *Up the Jungle*, *Loving*, *Henry*, *At Your Convenience*, *Matron*, *Abroad*, *Girls*, *Dick*, *Behind*, *England* and *Emmannuelle*.
Editor on *That's Carry On*
TV: Editor on *Laughing's Christmas Classics*
Jack Gardner was born in Ruislip, Middlesex, in 1932. When he heard about vacancies for messenger boys at Denham Studios, his careers advisor at school arranged an interview. He was fourteen when offered a position at the studios in 1946. Two years later, he'd transferred to the sound effects film library where he spent six years, during which time he was moved to Pinewood.
In 1954 he graduated to second assistant film editor for the Norman Wisdom picture,

One Good Turn, and was promoted to first assistant editor on the 1956 picture, *The Black Tent*. His first film for Rogers and Thomas was 1962's *Twice Round the Daffodils*, followed by *The Big Job*. He was introduced to the *Carry Ons* on *Cowboy* and worked on a further seventeen, including the compilation film, *That's Carry On*.
He retired from the industry in 1996.

GARLICK, STEPHEN
Role: Small Boy in *Doctor*
Started working as a child actor in the mid-1960s, appearing in films such as *Headline Hunters*, *Crossplot*, *Scrooge*, *The Hostages* and, in 1982, providing the voice of Jen in *The Dark Crystal*. His television work ranges from *The Tomorrow People* and *Doctor Who* to *Minder* and *Lovejoy*.

GASTON ET FILS NOUVEAUTÉS
The name is seen on the side of the wagon which whisks the Duc de Pommfrit away from the guillotine moments after the Black Fingernail has saved his life. Seen in *Don't Lose Your Head*.

Editor Jack Gardner busy working on a *Carry On* film

GATRELL, JOHN

Role: 4th Specialist in *Sergeant*

Born in 1907, John Gatrell had already established a busy stage career when, in the early 1950s, he began appearing on screen. His television work included *The Buccaneers*, *The Adventures of Robin Hood*, *Adam Adamant Lives!*, *Crossroads*, *The Baron* and *Lillie*, a miniseries in 1978. In films he was seen in, among others, *Blueprint for Danger* and *Games That Lovers Play*.

He died in 1981, aged seventy-four.

GAY

Played by Janet Mahoney

The flat-chested model is seen in *Loving*. She's offended when her boyfriend, Adrian, a fashion photographer, rejects her for his latest assignment, modelling body stockings, because the brief is for bosoms.

GAYBODY, CECIL

Played by Jimmy Logan

This effeminate presenter hosts the daily television magazine show, *Women's Things*, and is seen in *Girls* when the television station he works for pays £5000 for exclusive rights to the Miss Fircombe beauty contest.

GAZETTE, THE

In *Constable*, the paper carries headlines regarding the flu epidemic sweeping the nation and, later, that shoplifting is a grave problem in the local area.

GEESON, JUDY

Role: Sergeant Tilly Willing in *England*

Born in Arundel, Sussex, in 1948, Judy Geeson, who's now based in America, made an impact when, still a teenager, she appeared alongside Sidney Poitier in the 1966 film *To Sir, With Love*, the first of over fifty big screen appearances.

She attended the Corona Academy in London and has gone on to grace the screen in films such as *Here We Go Round the Mulberry Bush*, *Berserk!*, *Two Gentlemen Sharing*, *Doomwatch*, *The Eagle Has Landed*, *Everything Put Together* and *Spanish Fly*.

Her many television credits include *Cluff*, *Hotel*, *Tracey Takes On . . .*, *George and Leo*, *The Newcomers*, *Danger UXB*, *Breakaway* and *Poldark*, playing Caroline Penvenen.

GEESON, SALLY

Roles: Lily in *Abroad* and Debra in *Girls*

Born in Cuckfield, Sussex, in 1950, Sally Geeson, younger sister of actress Judy Geeson, attended the Corona Academy in London at the age of seven. While still at drama school, she made her film debut in Cliff Richard's 1959 film, *Expresso Bongo*, and appeared in small parts on screen as well as television commercials.

Upon graduating from Corona, she began working in the theatre but it wasn't long before she was offered other roles in film and on television, such as a 1967 episode of *Boy Meets Girl*, playing a debutante. Before the decade was out, she'd gone on to appear in, among others, *Man in a Suitcase*, *Detective* and *Strange Report*, but she'll always be remembered as Sally Abbott in the classic sitcom, *Bless This House*. Other film credits include *The Oblong Box*, *What's Good for the Goose*, *Cry of the Banshee* and *Mr Forbush and the Penguins*.

Now retired from acting, Sally Geeson, who lived in Australia for a while, is a special needs teacher in a primary school, a profession she entered in 1993.

GEOFF

Played by Charles Stanley

One of the new drivers hired by Charlie Hawkins for his Speedee Taxis business. Seen in *Cabby*.

GEORGE

Seen but not heard in *Again Doctor*, George is employed by Dr Nookey as his chauffeur when the money starts rolling in upon his return from the Beatific Islands with a cure for obesity. Seen driving Nookey's white Roller.

GEORGE BRISTOW LIMITED

Based at Manorgate Road, Kingston upon Thames, the firm's lorry is spotted in Rigby Road when drivers from Speedee Taxis attempt to stop some crooks, who are holding Peggy and Sally at gunpoint. Seen in *Cabby*.

GEORGIO

Played by Ray Brooks

In *Abroad*, Georgio works behind the bar at the Elsbels Palace Hotel. Epitomising the laid-back manner of the locals in the Med resort, when Evelyn Blunt misses the coach trip to a nearby village, he entertains her with champagne, soft music and goodness knows what else! By the time her husband returns the following day, after an unplanned stopover in a local jail, Evelyn is a changed woman thanks to Georgio!

GERMAN SOLDIER

Played by Gertan Klauber

During Richmond's flashback sequence in *Emmannuelle* the German Soldier is seen on patrol. He takes a liking to a Fräulein, who happens to be Richmond in disguise, which he soon discovers when he tries forcing him into the bushes.

'GETTING TO THE BOTTOM OF THINGS'

The title of the farcical lecture and film show

Evelyn Blunt (June Whitfield) is seduced by Georgio (Ray Brooks) (*Abroad*)

given by Professor Roland Crump, the distinguished archaeologist, in *Behind*. He certainly gets to the bottom of it when his film turns out to show a stripper revealing all, much to the delight of the audience.

GIANELLI, GINA

Role: Harem Girl in *Follow That Camel*
Made sporadic appearances on the big screen during the mid-1960s, appearing in such films as *The Psychopath* and *The Deadly Bees*.

GIBSON, CHLOE

Played by Joan Sims
Seen in *Doctor*, the lifeless Chloe Gibson traipses around the country supposedly assisting Francis Bigger, who advocates positive thinking. Partially deaf, she follows Bigger to the Borough County Hospital when he falls off a stage and bruises his coccyx. When Bigger mistakenly thinks he's only got days to live, he decides to make his loyal assistant happy for the last few days of his life by marrying her, only to discover later, to his horror, that his days aren't numbered at all, and Gibson is already laying down the law.

GIFFORD, ALAN

Role: Commissioner in *Cowboy*
A busy character actor, Alan Gifford was born in Taunton, Massachusetts, in 1911, but spent the lion's share of his career in the UK. He was seen on the screen from the 1950s, appearing in the likes of *The Kangaroo Kid*, *It Started in Paradise*, *No Smoking*, *The Iron Petticoat* and *Time Lock*. Later films included *2001: A Space Odyssey*, *Ragtime* and *Who Dares Wins*.

He was regularly seen on the small screen in, among others, *Gunsmoke*, *Jango*, *Top Secret*, *Suspense*, *The Champions*, *Duchess of Duke Street*, *Champion House* and *Nancy Astor*.

He died in 1989, aged seventy-eight.

GILBERT, TERRY

Choreographer on *Don't Lose Your Head*
Dancer, writer and choreographer Terry Gilbert was born in Bond's Main, Derbyshire, in 1932. He was seen dancing in several films from the 1960s, including the two Cliff Richard movies, *The Young Ones* and *Summer Holiday*.

As a choreographer, his credits included such films as *Women in Love* and *The Devils* for Ken Russell, as well as *The Music Lovers*, *Alice's Adventures in Wonderland*, *The Bounty* and *Aria*.

He died in 2001, aged sixty-eight.

GILES, FARMER

An unseen farmer mentioned by Josh Fiddler in *Camping*. Giles owns the field next to the Paradise Camp Site and rents it out for an all-nite rave with music provided by The Flowerbuds.

GILES, MR

Played by George Moon
The husband of Mrs Giles accompanies his wife to the grand jumble sale in *Dick*.

GILES, MRS

Played by Patsy Rowlands
Mrs Giles attends the grand jumble sale in *Dick* with her husband. A conversation she has with Miss Hoggett reveals that perhaps the Reverend Flasher isn't all he makes out to be. Flasher told Hoggett that his recent late nights were due to his visits to Mrs Giles who has been very poorly, partly because her husband treats her shamefully. As Martha Hoggett discovers, there has been nothing wrong with Mrs Giles, which sets her doubting other stories the Reverend has been telling.

GILL, TOM

Role: Citizen in *Constable*
Born in Newcastle upon Tyne in 1916, he began his career in the mid-1930s and went on to notch up over fifty film appearances, including *Midshipman Easy*, *The High Command*, *Meet Mr Penny*, *The First Gentleman*, *Lady Godiva Rides Again*, *Simon and Laura*, *The Navy Lark*, *Echo of Diana* and *A Nice Girl Like Me*.

On television from the '50s, his credits include *The Third Man*, *Danger Man*, *The Rat Catchers* and *Journey to the Unknown*.

He died in 1971, aged fifty-four.

GILMORE, PETER

Roles: Dancy in *Cabby*, Patch in *Jack*, Galley Master in *Cleo*, Curly in *Cowboy*, Robespierre in *Don't Lose Your Head*, Captain Bagshaw in *Follow That Camel*, Henry in *Doctor*, Private Ginger Hale in *Up The Khyber*, Henry in *Again Doctor*, Francis (King of France) in *Henry* and the Governor of the Canaries in *Columbus*
Born in Leipzig, Germany, in 1931, Peter Gilmore arrived in England at the age of six and was raised by relatives in Yorkshire. Although he fancied working in agriculture, he pursued a career in entertainment, studying at RADA until lack of funds forced him to quit.

During a spell in the army he discovered a talent for singing and upon demob in 1952, joined the George Mitchell Singers. Before long he was performing in West End musicals and, later, offered a recording contract.

Gradually acting began dominating his career, although in periods of unemployment he was found earning a living in factories and garages. His film work includes credits such as *You Must be Joking!*, *Every Day's A Holiday*, *Doctor in Clover*, *The Great St Trinian's Train Robbery*, *The Jokers*, *Oh! What A Lovely War* and *Warlords of Atlantis*, filmed in Malta. On

Peter Gilmore notched up eleven appearances in the *Carry On* films

television he was seen in *Ivanhoe*, *The Persuaders!* and *Doctor Who* but will forever be remembered as James Onedin in *The Onedin Line*.

He retired due to ill-health in the early 1990s. Some of his last jobs were in *The Bill*, *Casualty* and *Heartbeat*.

GINGER
Played by Michael Medwin
Bernie Bishop's loud-mouthed boxing manager visits his fighter at Haven Hospital in *Nurse*. He's accompanied by Bishop's punch-drunk former sparring partner, Norm.

GIPSY ROSE
Gipsy Rose, who's not seen in *At Your Convenience*, plies her trade as a fortune-teller on Brighton pier. She's popped out for lunch when Sid and Chloe decide it's time for a laugh. Cajoling William Boggs into having his fortune told, Sid dresses up as Gipsy Rose and gives him an insight into his future, which fills him with horror.

GIRL
Played by Sally Douglas
In *Screaming!*, Odbodd's latest acquisition is seen lying on a slab in the cellar of the Bide-a-Wee Rest Home awaiting vitrification.

GIRL AT ZOO
Played by Louise Burton
The girl appears in Lyons's flashback sequence in *Emmannuelle*, in which he recalls his most amorous experience. After meeting at the zoo, they end up rolling in the hay inside the gorilla's cage.

GIRL LOVER
Played by Valerie Shute
Seen throughout *Loving* in various locations, the girl and her partner are certainly in love because they can't keep their hands off each other.

GIRL NOSHA
Played by Nina Baden-Semper
In Walter Bagley's flashback sequence in *Up the Jungle*, the Girl Nosha is seen behind a tree kissing and cuddling her lover. Bagley disturbs them when he spots a butterfly resting on the bark and goes over for a peep. It was an unwise move because Bagley is captured by the Nosha tribe and faces almost certain death until rescued by the Lubidubies.

GIRL WITH COW
Played by Sally Kemp
Seen in a country lane in *Camping*, the girl, who's taking her cow to a bull, gives Charlie Muggins directions to Salisbury.

GIRL WITH DOG
Played by Janetta Lake
In *Constable* the girl is out walking her Old English Sheepdog when she bumps into Constable Constable outside the park; after she's walked away, Constable realises the dog has left its mark all over his trouser leg.

GIRLS
Played by Monica Dietrich, Anna Willoughby, Penny Keen, June Cooper, Christine Pryor and Karen Young
In *Don't Lose Your Head* the Girls are seen frolicking with two of English society's most distinguished layabouts: Sir Rodney Ffing and Lord Darcy de Pue.

GIRLS AT DIRTY DICK'S
Played by Marianne Stone, Sally Douglas, Dorina Stevens, Jennifer Hill, Rosemary Manley, Dominique Don, Marian Collins and Jean Hamilton
The women of ill repute appear in *Jack*. When the gullible Midshipman Poop-Decker enters Dirty Dick's holding aloft a gold sovereign, he's nearly involved in a stampede as the girls rush to greet him.

GIRLS, CARRY ON
See feature box on pages 118–9.

GLADYS
An unseen Glamcab driver in *Cabby*, whose name is mentioned by Flo over the radio when she instructs her to pick up a fare at 5 Wilbur Place in Westford, which turns out to be a mortuary and is part of a scheme to teach Speedee Taxis a lesson for having the nerve to intercept the Glamcabs' messages.

GLAMCABS
The taxi firm Peggy Hawkins establishes in *Cabby*. When she can't take her husband's neglect any longer, she takes revenge by setting up a rival company. With a fleet of fifteen spanking new Ford Cortinas, and a bevy of beautiful girls to drive them, Peggy Hawkins is soon running the most popular taxi firm in town.

GLAMCAB DRIVERS
Played by Valerie Van Ost and Marian Horton
The girls enter the cab drivers' café in *Cabby* for a snack, opting for cheese rolls and tea. While they're eating, Charlie Hawkins and Terry Tankard tamper with the ladies' taxis in an attempt to stop them plying their trade.

GLORIA
Played by Julie Stevens
This shapely blonde, who's seen in *Cleo* wearing nothing but animal furs, was captured in Bristol by the Romans. She's given the job of looking after the pampered Julius Caesar, who's so impressed that he decides to take her back to Rome for his wife, the battleaxe Calpurnia. Gloria shared her life back in Bristol with Horsa, who sets out to find her. Eventually they're reunited and exchanging wedding vows.

GLORIA'S BRIDESMAID
Played by Judi Johnson
Gloria's bridesmaid appears in the closing scenes of *Cleo* attending the wedding of Gloria and her beloved, Horsa.

GLOVER, DAVID
Role: Hotel Manager in *Follow That Camel*

GODAR, GODFREY
Camera Operator on *Cabby*, *Jack*, *Spying*, *Cleo*, *Cowboy*, *Screaming!*, *England* and *Emmannuelle*
Godfrey Godar, born in Hampstead, London, in 1924, decided he wanted to be a cameraman after watching his mother, a wardrobe mistress who later became a casting director for Alexander Korda, working on a film set.

He started his career with London Films in 1946, initially as a clapper boy, before moving into the camera team as a focus puller for producer, Herbert Wilcox. Films he worked on included *Spring in Park Lane*, *Odette* and *The Courtneys of Curzon Street*. He became a camera operator when Alan Hume, who'd been promoted to director of photography on the *Carry On* films, invited him to join the team. Godar, who also worked on the cult television series *The Avengers*, made his *Carry On* debut on *Cabby*.

He retired from the industry in 1988 and now lives in Spain.

GODDARD, ROY
Production Manager on *Girls*, *Dick*, *Behind*, *England*, *That's Carry On* and *Emmannuelle*
Roy Goddard was working as a second unit assistant director from the 1930s on films such as *Love From A Stranger*, *The Mark of Cain* and *Trio* but from the '50s onwards was a production manager on, among others, *Morning Departure*, *Appointment with Venus*, *The Importance of Being Earnest*, *Passage Home*, *Jacqueline* and *Bless This House*.

The success of Glamcabs nearly forced Speedee Taxis into bankruptcy (*Cabby*)

GODDARD, WILLOUGHBY
Role: Very Fat Man in *Cruising*

Born in Bicester, Oxfordshire, in 1926, Willoughby Goddard left school and joined the Oxford Playhouse. After many years in rep, he began appearing in character parts on screen from the early '50s. His film credits include *Bait, The Green Man, The Millionairess, Inn for Trouble, Double Bunk, The Charge of the Light Brigade* and *God's Outlaw*.

On television, he made many appearances in shows such as *The Buccaneers, The Invisible Man, Zero One, The Baron, Nearest and Dearest, Ace of Wands, The Sweeney, The Black Adder* and the 1987 mini-series, *Porterhouse Blue*, playing Professor Siblington. But the lion's share of his career was spent treading the boards around Britain, including many West End performances.

Ill-health forced his retirement from the profession in 1991.

GOLD, LIZ
Role: Khasi's Wife in *Up The Khyber*

Other credits include the films *Stop the World: I Want To Get Off* and *Up the Front*.

GOLDSMITH, GLADYS
Continuity on *Regardless* and *Cowboy*

Involved with continuity from the 1950s, Gladys Goldsmith worked on films such as *Let's Have A Murder, Conflict of Wings, Checkpoint, Doctor in Love, One Million Years BC, Crooks and Coronets, The Passage* and *Moonraker*. She was also in charge of continuity for many episodes of *The Avengers*.

GOLIGHTLY, PETER
Played by Charles Hawtrey

This fey example of a man is seen in *Sergeant*, just one of the many weak links in Able Platoon. Not cut out for a life in khaki, even if it's only National Service, Golightly stumbles from one aptitude test to the next. But he turns over a new leaf, just like the rest of his comrades, when he marches out of Heathercrest as a member of the champion platoon.

GONG LUBI
Played by Verna Lucille Mackenzie

She bashes the gong in *Up the Jungle* as Leda and her Lieutenant appear.

GOODE, DR FRANCIS A.
Played by Charles Hawtrey

A specialist in psychiatry, Francis Goode, who calls his wife Hamlet because she thinks she's a Great Dane, works at the Finisham Maternity Hospital in *Matron*. Gives advice to Sir Bernard Cutting when he's worried he's turning into a woman. Away from work, Goode is addicted to the hospital-based television series, *The Surgeons*; because his wife doesn't like the show, he watches it with his close friend, Matron, rousing Sir Bernard's suspicions when he finds Goode in Matron's room.

GORDON, NORAH
Role: Elderly Woman in *Spying*

Veteran character actress Norah Gordon was born in West Hartlepool in 1893. She was a regular on the stage before branching out into television and films.

During the 1950s, in particular, she was seen in numerous productions, usually in one-off roles. On the small screen her credits included *Paul Temple, The Adventures of Robin Hood, Dixon of Dock Green* and several episodes of *The Vise*.

CARRY ON GIRLS

*A Peter Rogers production
Distributed through Fox / Rank
Distribution Ltd
Released as an A certificate in 1973 in
colour
Running time: 88 mins*

CAST

Sidney James . . . . Sidney Fiddler
Barbara Windsor . . . . Hope Springs
Joan Sims . . . . Connie Philpotts
Kenneth Connor . . . Mayor Frederick Bumble
Bernard Bresslaw . . . . Peter Potter
Peter Butterworth . . . . Admiral
June Whitfield . . . . . . Augusta Prodworthy
Jack Douglas . . . . William
Patsy Rowlands . . . . Mildred Bumble
Joan Hickson . . . . Mrs Dukes
David Lodge . . . . Police Inspector
Valerie Leon . . . . Paula Perkins
Margaret Nolan . . . . Dawn Brakes
Angela Grant . . . . Miss Bangor
Sally Geeson . . . . Debra
Wendy Richard . . . . Ida Downe
Jimmy Logan . . . . Cecil Gaybody
Arnold Ridley . . . . Alderman Pratt
Robin Askwith . . . . Larry
Patricia Franklin . . . . Rosemary
Brian Osborne . . . . 'Half a Quid' Citizen

Bill Pertwee . . . . Fire Chief
Marianne Stone . . . . Miss Drew
Brenda Cowling . . . . Matron
Zena Clifton . . . . Susan Brooks
Laraine Humphrys . . . . Eileene Denby
Pauline Peart . . . . Gloria Winch
Caroline Whitaker . . . . Mary Parker
Barbara Wise . . . . Julia Oates
Carol Wyler . . . . Maureen Darcy
Mavise Fyson . . . . Francis Cake

Billy Cornelius . . . . Constable
Edward Palmer . . . . Elderly Resident
Michael Nightingale . . . . City Gent on Tube
Hugh Futcher . . . . . 'There's Fiddler' Citizen
Elsie Winsor . . . . Cloakroom Attendant
Nick Hobbs . . . . Stunt Double
Ron Tarr . . . . Bearded Man in Audience

PRODUCTION TEAM

Screenplay by Talbot Rothwell
Music composed and conducted by
    Eric Rogers
Production Manager: Roy Goddard
Art Director: Robert Jones
Director of Photography: Alan Hume
Editor: Alfred Roome
Camera Operator: Jimmy Devis
Assistant Director: Jack Causey
Sound Recordists: Paul Lemare
    and Ken Barker
Continuity: Marjorie Lavelly
Make-up: Geoffrey Rodway
Hairdresser: Stella Rivers
Costume Design: Courtenay Elliott
Set Dresser: Kenneth McCallum Tait
Dubbing Editor: Patrick Foster
Assistant Editor: Jack Gardner
Title Sketches by 'Larry'
Titles: G.S.E. Ltd
Processed by Rank Film Laboratories
Producer: Peter Rogers
Director: Gerald Thomas

It's the broom cupboard for Hope Springs (Barbara Windsor) when she checks in at the
Palace Hotel

Dawn Brakes (Margaret Nolan) hopes to be crowned Miss Fircombe

The Fircombe Town Council is meeting to discuss ways of putting the tired old seaside resort on the map. Sidney Fiddler, who owns a local amusement arcade, classes Fircombe as a dump and can understand why people don't want to visit the town; he feels they should liven up the place and suggests a Miss Fircombe beauty contest, an idea that fails to impress local women's libber, Augusta Prodworthy. But when she leaves the meeting early, Fiddler persuades the mayor, Frederick Bumble, to put the proposal to the vote and the beauty contest is approved.

When Augusta Prodworthy hears the shocking news, she vows to do something about it. Summoning up other members of the Fircombe Women's Lib Movement, she devises Operation Spoilsport, which promises to have the contest, which is being staged at the Pier Theatre, in chaos.

Sidney Fiddler, meanwhile, is busy arranging the event, calling in his pal, Peter Potter, to coordinate publicity. Sid is lapping up the chance to work so closely with all the 36-24-36s running around the Palace Hotel, which is owned by his long-term girlfriend, Connie Philpotts. She isn't so excited about the event, though, especially as the beauty contestants are given free accommodation, her elderly residents are leaving like there's no tomorrow and she isn't getting the attention she craves from Sid.

When a publicity stunt involving a donkey goes wrong, resulting in a cat fight between two of the contestants and the mayor losing his trousers, local photographer Lawrence Prodworthy, who happens to be Augusta's son, takes a snap which ends up on the front page of the daily papers. When Peter Potter's fiancée, Paula Perkins, spots Peter in the photo apparently cavorting with the girls, she rushes down to Fircombe to see what he's up to and ends up entering the contest herself.

A television company buys the rights to the contest, so Sid Fiddler puts his thinking cap on to see how they can exploit the TV coverage; with the help of Hope Springs, a contestant whom Sid has taken a fancy to, they come up with the idea of one of the entrants being a man. While Peter, his pal, is conned into donning a wig and dress, Augusta Prodworthy is tipped off and rushes to the hotel to expose the impostor; the whole escapade brings much-needed publicity to the event, and before long the seaside town's hotel trade is booming.

The time finally arrives for the beauty contest at the Pier Theatre but as far as Connie Philpotts is concerned, it's payback time; she puts on a smile and agrees to take charge of entrance fees, determined to run off with the money. The women's libbers, meanwhile, launch Operation Spoilsport by shaking itching powder into the contestants' costumes, pouring slippery liquid on the catwalk and setting off the water sprinklers in the theatre, ruining the contest in the process.

Funny Scene!

The lecherous Admiral comes out of his room at the Palace Hotel and sees Hope Springs bending over while waiting for the lift. Spotting an opportunity for a bit of fun, he rushes over.

ADMIRAL: (Clears his throat.) Excuse me, mind
                if I join you?

HOPE SPRINGS: Oh, help yourself, it's big enough
                isn't it?

ADMIRAL: (Looks at Hope's chest.) By jove,
                yes, yes. (Gets twitchy with
                excitement.)
                (They enter the lift and Hope
                Springs presses the floor button.)

HOPE: I won't ask how far you want to go,
                I might get the wrong answer.

ADMIRAL: Only to the bottom, my dear (Pinches
                her bottom.)

Her film work covered more than thirty pictures, such as *Danny Boy, Old Mother Riley's Circus, Death in High Heels, Circle of Danger, Woman in a Dressing Gown* and, one of her last films, *The Nanny*, playing the school matron.

She died in 1970, aged seventy-six.

GORDON, PAT
Played by Jacqueline Lewis
In *Teacher*, Pat is one of the main culprits among the schoolkids who set out to cause havoc when a school inspector and child psychiatrist visit Maudlin Street Secondary Modern School.

GORILLA
Played by Reuben Martin
The furry creature creeps through the undergrowth in *Up the Jungle* and during the night enters the tents occupied by Lady Bagley and her travelling companion, June, leading to all sorts of confusion.

GORSE, PC TIMOTHY
Played by Charles Hawtrey
A special constable who's called upon by his local police station whenever an extra pair of hands is required, Gorse is seen in *Constable* helping out when a flu epidemic causes a shortage of regulars. Travels everywhere with Bobby, his little budgie, and although he means well, is more trouble than he's worth.

GOSNEY, BARRIE
Role: Coach Driver in *Jack*
Born in Woking, Surrey, in 1926, Barrie Gosney joined the local dancing school at the age of seven before progressing to Cone Ripman's School of Dancing in London's Oxford Street.

He kicked off his career in entertainment by joining the cast of *Dancing Years* at the Adelphi for two and a half years, followed by the musical *Alice in Wonderland*. Acting jobs came his way, including a small role in his first film, *Dead Man's Shoes*. Other film credits include *Futtock's End, Three Hats for Lisa, Up the Chastity Belt* and *Up the Front*, while his television work includes *Doctor in the House, Menace, Don't Wait Up, Casualty, Last of the Summer Wine* and playing Uncle Barrie in *Time Gentlemen, Please*.

GOSS, HELEN
Role: Mary's Mum in *Sergeant*
Born in London in 1903, Helen Goss appeared in over thirty films during a long career which also saw her run the Rank Charm School. Her credits, beginning in the 1930s, include *Hail and Farewell, Chance of a Lifetime, Fanny By Gaslight, The Wicked Lady, Cheer the Brave, The Hound of the Baskervilles, Half a Sixpence* and *Jane Eyre*.

GOULD, GRAYDON
Role: Recruit in *Sergeant*
Born in Saskatchewan, Canada, in 1937, Graydon Gould arrived in the UK at the age of nineteen. He began his acting career in repertory theatre, working at Bromley and, later, Liverpool before screen work started being offered.

He returned to his homeland in 1962 and played the lead, George Keeley, in a television series, *The Forest Ranger*, which extended to over a hundred episodes. Moving to California, he was cast in many shows, such as *The High Chaparral, The Big Valley* and *Dynasty*. Other small-screen credits include *The Saint, Secret Agent, Matlock* and *Ultimate Imposter*. He also provided the voice of Mike Mercury in *Supercar*.

He's also appeared in films such as *On the Run, Floods of Fear, The Enforcer, The Victors, Links of Justice, All Night Long* and *Riding the Edge*.

Over a period of twenty-five years, he completed over 200 voiceovers for television commericals and documentaries in the States. Now semi-retired, he's based back in the UK.

GRADY, MIKE
Role: Boy Lover in *Loving*
Born in Cheltenham, Gloucester, in 1946, Mike

Grady is probably best known for playing put-upon Barry in the perennial sitcom, *Last of the Summer Wine*, but his screen career, which began in the late 1960s, has covered other comedies like *Doctor in the House, Citizen Smith* and *Colin's Sandwich* to dramas such as *Bergerac, Wycliffe* and *Casualty*. His film credits include *Up the Front, The Return of the Pink Panther* and *Brittania Hospital*.

GRAINGER, GAIL
Role: Moira Plunkett in *Abroad*

GRANDAD
Played by Bart Allison
Seen in *Doctor*, Grandad arrives at Borough County Hospital with a chamber pot stuck on his head, thanks to his mischievous grandson.

GRANT, ANGELA
Roles: Harem Girl in *Follow That Camel*, Hospitality Girl in *Up The Khyber* and Miss Bangor in *Girls*
Angela Grant was born in Scarborough but moved to Leeds at the age of two. Her mother was a fashion buyer and Angela soon became fascinated with the world of glamour. At fifteen, she attended the Michael Whitaker School of Modelling in Leeds and graduated to

Moira Plunkett (Gail Grainger) is employed by Wundatours on the ill-fated Elsbels trip (*Abroad*)

teenage modelling work at fashion shows, chiefly in the north of England.

When Michael Whitaker became her agent, she moved to London at nineteen and her first assignment was in New York. Soon she was being offered photographic modelling jobs and commercials. Keen to diversify, she enrolled on a one-year evening course in acting; the tutor was Nina Finburgh, ex-RADA, who gave private tuition; before long she was cast in *Follow That Camel*. Stage and other screen work quickly followed, including television appearances in, among others, the *Morecambe and Wise Show*.

She took a break from the profession during the 1980s but has since returned. She balances her acting career with her involvement in interior design and property development, a business interest which also led to her taking a year out during the '70s.

GRANT, GILLY
Role: Sally G-String in *Camping* and Nurse in Bath in *Matron*

Other film credits during the late 1960s and early '70s include *The Big Switch*, *Zeta One*, *Clegg* and *Harry and the Hookers*.

GRANT, MR
Played by an uncredited actor

Seen in the waiting room at Finisham Maternity Hospital during *Matron*, Mr Grant is given the good news that his wife has just given birth to a baby boy.

GRANTHAM, ROBIN
Make-up Designer on *Emmannuelle*

Born in Beckenham, Kent, in 1942, Robin Grantham began his working life as an art teacher in grammar schools and comprehensives before teaching at Twickenham Art School. He taught the son of make-up artist Harry Frampton and through the father secured his membership of BECTU, resulting in a change of career and his first job, assisting on 1969's *Anne of the Thousand Days* at Shepperton Studios. By the end of the '70s, Grantham had been promoted to chief make-up artist.

His film credits include *Young Winston*, *At the Earth's Core*, *The Man in the Iron Mask*, *The People That Time Forgot*, *Are You Being Served?*, *Raise the Titanic*, *Never Say Never Again* and television productions such as *A Question of Guilt* and the lion's share of the *Inspector Morse* episodes.

He left the industry in 1996 and now works as a customer service executive within the service industry.

GRAY, JOHN
Played by Frank Forsyth

In *Nurse*, Mr Gray is a patient at Haven Hospital whose main scene finds him telling Mr Stephens, a doctor, that he's not feeling well.

GREEN, S.C.
Cabby was based on an original idea from S.C. Green and R.M. Hills.

GREENE, LEON
Roles: Malabonce in *Don't Lose Your Head*, Torturer in *Henry* and Chef in *At Your Convenience*

GREYHOUND EXPRESS, THE
A newspaper read by Bert Handy during a quiet moment in *Regardless*.

GRIFFITHS, FRED
Roles: 2nd Ambulance Driver in *Nurse*, Taxi Driver in *Regardless* and Taxi Driver in *Loving*

Fred Griffiths, born in Ludlow, Shropshire, in 1912, made a living out of character parts, appearing in hundreds of film and television productions during his career. A former London fireman, he moved into acting by accident and became a regular face in British movies, especially during the 1950s, in cameo roles.

His film credits included *Steptoe and Son*, *Perfect Friday*, *Billion Dollar Brain*, *There Was a Crooked Man* and *John and Julie*. He was also seen in, amongst others, *To Sir, with Love*; *Light Up the Sky*; *I Believe in You*; *I'm All Right, Jack* and *Dunkirk*.

He died in 1994 after a long career which had seen him play a taxi driver on more than twenty occasions.

GRIFFITHS, LUCY
Roles: Trolley Lady in *Nurse*, Miss Horton in *Constable*, Auntie in *Regardless*, Patient in *Doctor*, Old Lady in Headphones in *Again Doctor*, Woman in *Loving* (Note: scene cut.) and Woman with Hat in *Behind*

Born in Birley, Herefordshire, in 1919, Lucy Griffiths combined a busy screen career with stage work. Entering films in 1953, she'd appeared in such titles as *Will Any Gentleman . . . ?*, *Children Galore*, *The Green Man* and *Gideon's Day* before making her *Carry On* debut in *Nurse*. Other titles she worked on range from *Murder She Said* and *Murder Ahoy* to *Under Milk Wood* and *One of Our Dinosaurs is Missing*. Her last big-screen appearance was in 1981's *Dangerous Davies – The Last Detective*.

Among her numerous television credits are *Z Cars*, *Adam Adamant Lives!*, *The Prisoner*, *The Troubleshooters*, *Ace of Wands*, *On the Buses*, *All Creatures Great and Small* and '70s sitcom, *Mind Your Language*.

She died in 1982, aged sixty-three.

GRIGG, ALISTAIR
Played by Leslie Phillips

The noted child psychiatrist pays a visit to Maudlin Street Secondary Modern School in *Teacher* to conduct research for his new book, *Contemporary Juvenile Behaviour Patterns*. While he's there, he falls for Sarah Allcock, the butch PE teacher. After studying in Vienna, he made a

name for himself in psychiatry and has penned several books on the subject, including *Free Expression*, *The Angel Behind the Cosh* and his recent publication, *The Child is Always Right*.

GRIMSBY, DYNAMITE DAN
Played by Joe Robinson

Lefty Vincent's new boxer is seen in *Regardless*. This blond-haired fighter doesn't look ready to challenge the likes of gruesome Massive Micky, though, which explains why he exaggerates how much his little finger is hurting after accidentally falling off a stool.

GRIMSHAW, SERGEANT
Played by William Hartnell

Nicknamed Grimmy, this veteran soldier has spent the last six years of his career employed as a training sergeant at Heathercrest National Service Depot. In all that time he's failed to assemble a champion platoon, that is until Able Platoon of the twenty-ninth intake. Although the dishevelled bunch of characters in *Sergeant* look as if they'll pass out as the worst ever in the history of Heathercrest, they rally behind their sergeant to claim top spot – a fine retirement present as he leaves his service days behind.

GROOM, JIM
Sound Editor on *Cowboy*

A sound editor whose career began in earnest in the mid-1950s, his film credits include *Jumping for Joy*, *Up in the World*, *Jacqueline*, *Hell Drivers*, *The Brides of Dracula*, *Johnny Nobody*, *French Dressing*, *Oliver!*, *Country Dance* and *The Little Prince*.

GRUBB, JENNY
Played by Imogen Hassall

Jenny, who's twenty-four, lives with her extended family in Fulham in a house so devoid of life that it resembles a morgue more than a family home; with little or no experience of men, she has led a very sheltered life, shackled by her domineering, straitlaced mother. When we meet her in *Loving* she works in a sausage factory but that soon changes when she finally flies the nest and begins renting a flat with Sally Martin and her friend, Gay. The big-chested brunette catches the eye of Adrian, a photographer, and before long she's modelling, wearing the latest High-Street fashions and dating Terence Philpot.

GRUBB, MRS
Played by Joan Hickson

Jenny Grubb's austere mother is seen in *Loving*, dominating her daughter's life, that is until she leaves home and begins making her own decisions.

GRUBBS, THE
(Aunt Victoria, Uncle Ernest, Grandma, Grandpa, Aunt Beatrice and Wilberforce)

Played by Ann Way, Gordon Richardson, Hilda Barry, Bart Allison, Dorothea Phillips and Colin Vancao respectively

The extended family is seen in *Loving* when Terence Philpot arrives at their house, which is so quiet it could double as a morgue, to meet Jenny; they're a bunch of oddballs who sit motionless, staring at the world going on around them.

G.S.E. LIMITED
General Screen Enterprises Limited produced the titles for *Up the Jungle, Loving, Henry, At Your Convenience, Matron, Abroad, Girls, Dick, Behind, England, That's Carry On* and *Emmannuelle*.

GUARD
Played by Hugh Futcher

In *Don't Lose Your Head* the guard is seen at a roadblock, being told by Citizen Camembert to keep his eyes peeled for two Englishmen, one of whom is the Black Fingernail.

GUARD
Played by Billy Cornelius

Seen outside Cromwell's office in *Henry* when Queen Marie comes to visit.

GUARD AT CAESAR'S PALACE
Played by Mark Hardy

The Guard is seen in *Cleo*, just one of many employed by Caesar.

GUARDS
Played by Anthony Baird and Patrick Durkin

Seen at S.T.E.N.C.H.'s headquarters in *Spying*, the Guards end up killing each other while trying to capture Simkins and his motley crew.

GUN SERGEANT
Played by Cyril Chamberlain

In *Sergeant* the stern-looking Gun Sergeant delivers a lecture on everything you need to know about the Bren gun.

GUYLER, DERYCK
Role: Surgeon Hardcastle in *Doctor*

Born in Cheshire in 1914, Deryck Guyler left home to train as an Anglican minister but later became involved with theatrical work in Liverpool. His time on stage was cut short when he joined the RAF police during World War Two, but when he was invalided out in 1942, he found work at the BBC Repertory Company, where his acting roles included playing Macduff in *Macbeth*. He subsequently joined the radio comedy show, *It's That Man Again*, in 1947, playing Frisby Dyke, a part which brought instant fame.

During the 1960s and '70s, Guyler made his name on television in the sitcoms *Please, Sir!* and *Sykes* and throughout his career also appeared in films, including *A Day to Remember, The Fast Lady, Nurse on Wheels* and *One of Our Dinosaurs Is Missing*.

He died in 1999, aged eighty-five.

H

HAGGERD, MISS
Played by Hattie Jacques
Headmistress at Chayste Place, a finishing school for girls, Miss Haggerd admits she's lived a sheltered life and lacks confidence with the opposite sex. This is exemplified by her reactions when Babs and Fanny, two of the mischievous schoolgirls, cause mayhem at Balsworth Youth Hostel, where the school is staying en route to a camp site in Devon. Because they have concealed the signs on the shower rooms, Dr Soaper nearly walks in on Miss Haggerd while she's taking a shower; later he accidentally ends up in bed with her after the girls mess around with the room numbers. But after she's had time to recover from the shock, Miss Haggerd, a former hospital matron, believes Soaper is struck on her, much to his horror.

HAIG, BILLY
Played by George Howell
In *Teacher*, bespectacled Haig is one of the main culprits among the schoolkids who set out to cause havoc when a school inspector and child psychiatrist visit Maudlin Street Secondary Modern School.

HAINE, GEOFFREY
Assistant Director on *Sergeant*
During the late 1950s he worked as assistant director on second units for films such as *Bachelor of Hearts*, *The Wind Cannot Read* and *The 39 Steps*. During the '60s he was credited as production manager on numerous films, including *Night of the Eagle*, *This Sporting Life*, *Accident*, *The Hunting Party* and *Tales That Witness Murder*. He also occasionally worked on television, most notably on such '60s classics as *The Champions* and *The Avengers*.

HAINES, TAFFY
Sound Recordist on *Abroad*
Taffy Haines's credits, dating back to the 1970s, include some noteworthy films including *Gandhi*, *Indiana Jones and the Temple of Doom*, *Cry Freedom*, *Mountains of the Moon*, *Shadowlands* and, most recently, 1998's *Lost in Space*. He also worked on the James Bond movie, *Never Say Never Again*.

HAINES, WILFRED
Played by Lance Percival
The *Happy Wanderer*'s new chef in *Cruising*, replacing a guy called Norrington. Not used to life on the ocean wave, despite following in his father's footsteps, Haines suffers seasickness even before the ship has lost sight of land. He blames it on not being able to see the sky or sea from the kitchens, which are situated in the belly of the boat. A man of unusual taste when it comes to cooking, he makes a celebratory cake for the captain containing plenty of unexpected ingredients, including spaghetti.

HAKIM'S FUN HOUSE
Seen in *Spying*, Hakim's Fun House in the backstreets of Algiers is where the Fat Man goes to unwind, with the help of the harem he's assembled there.

HALE, PRIVATE GINGER
Played by Peter Gilmore
Seen during the final moments of his life in *Up the Khyber*, Ginger Hale – a friend of Private Widdle – is wounded during a battle with the Burpas. With half a dozen bullet holes littering his body, he was a victim when the Burpas wiped out an entire garrison.

'HALF A QUID' CITIZEN
Played by Brian Osborne
Queues up to buy a ticket for the Miss Fircombe beauty contest in *Girls* but complains when he learns the entrance fee is fifty pence. Becomes one of the loudest dissenting voices in the audience, bringing the mayor's speech to an abrupt end, even before it's really started!

HALL, ALAN
Camera Operator on *Follow That Camel*
Alan Hall entered films in the 1960s, initially working as camera operator on the second unit for *The Fast Lady*. On main productions he worked on the likes of *Repulsion*, *The Birthday Party*, *The Executioner*, *Hyper Sapien* and, in 1988, *Yellow Pages*.

Wilfred Haines (Lance Percival, left) creates a birthday cake to remember (*Cruising*)

HALL, HERBERT
Played by Terence Longdon

Seen in *Constable,* Hall is a well-known confidence trickster who fools new recruit PC Benson, which isn't difficult, even though he classes himself as a dab hand at identifying criminal types.

HALLAM, JOHN
Role: Burpa on Rooftop in *Up The Khyber*

RADA-trained John Hallam, born in Lisburn, Northern Ireland, in 1941, has led a busy career across all media. His stage work has seen him appear at the National Theatre and with the Royal Shakespeare Company, while his film credits range from *The Charge of the Light Brigade, Nicholas and Alexandra* and *Antony and Cleopatra* to *The People That Time Forgot, Flash Gordon* and *Robin Hood: Prince of Thieves.*

On television he's been seen in numerous shows. He's played one-off parts in such shows as *Department S, Jason King, Raffles, Minder, Casualty, Black Adder* and *Wycliffe,* as well as semi-regular roles as Terry Prince in *Emmerdale Farm,* Lord Chiltern in *The Pallisers,* Thomas Mallen in *The Mallens* and 'Barnsey' Barnes in *EastEnders.*

More recent credits include *Arabian Nights* and *The 10th Kingdom,* both for television.

HALLETT, JOHN
Role: Substitute Football Player in *Emmannuelle*

One of John Hallett's earliest screen appearances was in the 1960s series *Suspense.* Often seen as policemen, he donned uniform to play a constable in an episode of *All Creatures Great and Small* and an unfinished *Doctor Who* story, 'Shada', from 1980. Filming was interrupted by a BBC strike and the programme was never completed. Other credits include *Oil Strike North, The Regiment, Survivors* and *Call Me Mister.*

HAMILTON, JEAN
Role: Girl at Dirty Dick's in *Jack*

HAMILTON, JOHN
Role: A Nosha in *Up the Jungle*

HAMPSHIRE, BARBARA
Role: Private Carter in *England*

Londoner Barbara Hampshire studied at the North London School of Speech and Drama before emigrating to Canada for a time. Returning to England, she was working in advertising when her boss cast her as a dancer in a commercial. She then took on the guise and head of Mickey Mouse in a series of presentations around the country in youth clubs, children's theatre and hospital visits.

Small screen roles started coming her way, including parts in the 1973 film, *Penny Gold,* while on television her credits include *The Sweeney* and two episodes (*Hostage* and *Pressure Point*) of *Blake's 7* in 1979.

HAMPTON OF WICK, LORD
Played by Kenneth Connor

He's supposed to be a loyal supporter of Henry VIII but is plotting with Guy Fawkes and a couple of other cronies to kill the King; he can't believe his luck when Thomas Cromwell asks him, for the good of England, to pretend to abduct Henry in order to help the monarch in his attempts to annul his marriage. By agreeing, it gives him the ideal opportunity to carry out his plan. Unfortunately Lord Hampton's attempts fail when he and his men are defeated by sheer aggression at the hands of Queen Marie.

HANCOCK, SHEILA
Role: Senna Pod in *Cleo*

Sheila Hancock, born in Blackgang, Isle of Wight, in 1933, completed her education at Dartford County Grammar School before training at RADA. She first appeared on the London stage in 1958, replacing Joan Sims in *Breath of Spring,* the start of a long association with the stage.

Early television appearances include *The Wednesday Thriller, Thirty-Minute Theatre* and *Detective,* but she's gone on to appear in, among others, *Doctor Who, Menace, Detective, EastEnders* as well as *Home to Roost* and *Kavanagh QC,* both alongside her late husband, John Thaw. Other more substantial roles included playing Carol in *The Rag Trade,* Mag in 1992's *Gone to Seed,* Frances in 1993's *Brighton Belles* and Gwendolen Hartley in 2003's *Fortysomething.*

Her film credits include *Doctor in Love, Light Up the Sky!, The Bulldog Breed, The Anniversary, Take A Girl Like You, The Wildcats of St Trinian's, Buster* and *Hold Back the Night.*

HAND MAIDENS
Played by Christine Rodgers, Gloria Best and Virginia Tyler

Seen in *Cleo,* the Hand Maidens attend to Cleopatra's needs.

HANDL, IRENE
Roles: Madge Hickson in *Nurse* and Distraught Woman in *Constable*

Irene Handl, daughter of a banker, was born in London in 1901. Usually cast in kind-hearted Cockney roles, she was nearly forty before trying her luck as an actress.

When her mother died, Irene chose to stay at home and care for her father until, at an advanced age, she joined the Embassy School in London and began training for a career on stage and screen.

Parts were soon on offer, most notably the Cockney charmaid in the West End show, *Goodnight Mrs Puffin,* which ran for three years in the early 1960s, at which point in her career she was already a national figure courtesy of numerous film credits including *Spellbound,*

Girl in the News, Millions Like Us and *The Shop at Sly Corner.*

One of the busiest character actresses around, she made occasional appearances on television, most notably as Ada Bingley in *For The Love of Ada,* which ran to four series.

She died in 1987, aged eighty-five.

HANDY, BERT
Played by Sid James

Ex-boxer Bert runs Helping Hands Limited from a basement office in London's Denver Street, and it isn't long before the work piles in. Seen in *Regardless.*

HAPPY WANDERER, SS
In *Cruising* the *Happy Wanderer* heads off for an April cruise around the Mediterranean, captained by Wellington Crowther, who's been at the helm for ten years.

HARDCASTLE, SURGEON
Played by Deryck Guyler

A shaky-handed surgeon who's seen briefly in the operating theatre of the Borough County Hospital in *Doctor.* (Note: the character was originally going to be called MacKenzie.)

HARDY
Played by Anton Rodgers

In the opening scene of *Jack,* Hardy is a sailor who's asked by a dying Nelson to kiss him.

HARDY, MARK
Role: Guard at Caesar's Palace in *Cleo*

Mark Hardy's other television credits include two appearances in *Doctor Who* during the 1980s. He entered films in 1961, appearing that year in *Mary Had A Little* and *Very Important Person.* During the '80s he was seen in *Orchard End* and his most recent film work includes appearances in *I'll Sleep When I'm Dead* and *Bright Young Things,* both released in 2003.

HAREM GIRLS
Played by Carol Sloan, Gina Gianelli, Dominique Don, Anne Scott, Patsy Snell, Zorenah Osborne, Margot Maxine, Sally Douglas, Angie Grant, Gina Warwick, Karen Young and Helga Jones

In *Follow That Camel,* Sergeant Nocker, Bo West and Simpson stumble across the Harem Girls while attempting to escape the clutches of the evil Sheikh Abdul Abulbul.

HARMER, JULIET
Role: Mrs Bentley in *Matron* (Note: the scene was cut.)

Juliet Harmer, who's best known for her role as Georgina Jones in BBC's 1960s series, *Adam Adamant Lives!,* was a screen regular during the '60s and early '70s, appearing in shows such as *The Avengers, Danger Man, Department S, Bless This House, The Persuaders!* and *Jason King.* Her film work, meanwhile, includes roles in *Just Like*

A Woman, The Engagement, Quest for Love, Home Before Midnight and, in 1988, *Paris By Night*.

She began acting in various revues while studying at Homerton College, Cambridge, but started her working life as a teacher, before turning to acting. Nowadays, she concentrates on painting and writing/illustrating children's books.

HARPER, ROSE

Played by Marita Stanton
The character Rose Harper is spotted in *Nurse*.

HARRIETT

Played by Barbara Windsor
One of Dick Turpin's sidekicks in *Dick*, Harriett also assists Turpin with his day job as softly-spoken Reverend Flasher by working as his housemaid.

HARRINGTON, JOY

Role: Lady in *Dick*
Born in London in 1914, Joy Harrington went straight into rep from drama school. In her early career she spent a season at Stratford, making her professional debut in 1933, and worked in America. For a while she was employed by Paramount film studios in Hollywood. In addition to script editing, she made thirteen films and directed dialogue for nine others, including *National Velvet*, with a young Elizabeth Taylor.

Between 1951–61 she worked for the BBC, producing children's drama. She was responsible for the original screening of *Heidi*, *Treasure Island*, *Billy Bunter* and *Vice Versa*, among others. But she's best remembered for *Jesus of Nazareth*, for which she won a BAFTA Award, the first to be given for a children's serial.

After retiring from the Beeb in 1970, she returned to acting, one of her roles being a neighbour in *Sykes*. She toured the Far East with Jimmy Edwards, Hattie Jacques and Eric Sykes in *Big Bad Mouse*, and appeared as the housekeeper in *The Moon Stallion*.

She died in 1991, aged seventy-seven.

HARRINGTON, MISS V.

The unseen Children's Hostess on the *Happy Wanderer* in *Cruising*. Her name is spotted on the crew list.

HARRIS, ANITA

Roles: Corktip in *Follow That Camel* and Nurse Clarke in *Doctor*
The multi-talented Anita Harris, who was born in Midsomer Norton, Somerset, in 1942, has forged a career as a singer, actress and dancer. Her initial expectation was to become a dancer and she left England in the 1950s to train as a choreographed skater in Las Vegas.

Her first major engagement back in the UK, however, was as a singer, performing with the Cliff Adams Singers. She made her first recording – with the John Barry Seven – while still a teenager. Although the song wasn't a huge hit, she later released a myriad of singles, most notably 'Just Loving You', which reached number six in the British charts, and remains busy in the industry today.

In addition to the *Carry On* films, she's also made occasional appearances in other films and television shows.

HARRIS, JULIE

Costume Designer on *Cleo*
Born in London in 1921, Julie Harris studied at art school, hoping to become a fashion artist. After graduating, she worked at a dressmaking house until war broke out when she was called up into the ATS. Keen to pursue a career in the film industry when she finally returned to civvy street, she sent sketches she'd completed to various film studios. She achieved her ambition upon being recruited as an assistant in 1945, and by the 1948 film, *Holiday Camp*, had been promoted to costume designer.

Other credits include *The Clouded Yellow*, *The Net*, *Simon and Laura*, *The Fast Lady*, *A Hard Day's Night*, *Live and Let Die* and *Dracula*. Her last job as a costume designer was the 1992 television series, *A Perfect Hero*, for London Weekend.

Now retired, she spends her time oil-painting and regularly exhibits her work. She has sold pictures to, among others, the Sultan of Oman, Michael Caine and Bryan Forbes.

HARRIS, MAX

Composed and conducted the music for *England*
TV: Composed music for *Under the Round Table*; *Short Knight, Long Daze* and *And in My Lady's Chamber*
Born in Bournemouth in 1918, Max Harris, son of a tailor, played the piano with a number of prominent dance bands in the 1930s before serving with the Royal Army Service Corps in the Middle East during World War Two.

After the war, he returned to London, getting his big break in 1951 when he joined the pit band for the West End show *Fancy Free*. The band later became a popular touring act and Harris wrote music and arranged for them until 1954, when he left to become part of the BBC Show Band.

He went on to direct music for television and radio programmes, conduct his own band, score a number of films including *Baby Love*, *One of Our Dinosaurs is Missing* and *On the Buses*, as well as orchestrate music for high-profile figures like Frank Sinatra and compose a variety of now famous theme tunes for shows such as *Porridge*, *Open All Hours*, *On the Buses* and *Poldark*.

He later wrote and arranged for television, but also embraced his enduring love of jazz with a tribute to Jelly Roll Morton in 1974, a collaboration with Australian jazz musician Bob Barnard.

He continued to play jazz until retiring, two years before his death, in 2004, at the age of eighty-five.

HARRISON, WPC

Played by Jill Adams
This attractive blonde policewoman works at the station in *Constable*. PC Potter takes a liking to her but before he can fix up a date she joins the growing list of people who succumb to the virulent flu bug sweeping the country.

HARRY

Played by Jack Douglas
The man with a million nervous tics is a regular at Vic and Cora Flange's pub in *Abroad*. He crushes the bread rolls with his arm, throws his

---

MEMORIES

'By 1967 I had "Just Loving You" in the charts and a hit record opens the floodgates to a great deal of work. I then got a phone call which led to *Follow That Camel*. The *Carry On* team was like a repertory company and for me to be introduced into that company was a huge honour. It was a role quite out of character from what I was doing at the time.

'Because of the time schedules of the *Carry On*s there was an element of push – it was almost the speed of theatre. I loved working with that team. Being the new girl, and having Phil Silvers around – it was his first film, too – meant we hit it off as the "new guys". He realised he was in a different medium but he was bringing to it the extraordinary experience of what he had created so there was an element of great cultures coming together with great respect for each other, and I think it worked wonderfully. I don't think it was one of the most successful but it has grown over the years.

'I also loved playing Nurse Clarke in *Doctor*. I had my first screen kiss in that one. Then, of course, there was the famous scene where Jim Dale rips my skirt off while we were climbing on the roof of the nurses' home. Believe it or not, my knickers had to be auditioned! I went shopping with the wardrobe lady and then they had to be vetted by Mr Rogers and Mr Thomas. When it came to losing the skirt, the Velcro was too strong at first. Jim was tugging away but it was sewn on too well and had to be loosened. It was a delightful film.'

ANITA HARRIS

beer all over the place and has a tendency to put his foot in it, like the time he told Cora that the flirtatious Sadie Tomkins was booked on the same holiday as her husband.

HART, DAVID
Role: Customs Officer in *Emmannuelle* (Note: scene was cut from film.)
David Hart's other credits include playing Mr White in *Crossroads*.

HARTNELL, WILLIAM
Role: Sergeant Grimshaw in *Sergeant*
Born in London in 1908, William Hartnell is probably best remembered for playing the first Doctor in the long-running *Doctor Who* series, although he'd been plying his trade on stage and screen since 1924. But it wasn't until he was invalided out of the Royal Tank Corps during the Second World War that he received his big break on screen, appearing in Carol Reed's war film, *The Way Ahead*.

Playing sergeant and other middle-ranking military positions became Hartnell's trademark, particularly in films. But such adroitness was also exploited on television where he played Sergeant-Major Bullimore in *The Army Game*.

His numerous film credits included *Private's Progress*, *Hell Drivers*, *Piccadilly Third Stop*,

Heavens Above!, *Tomorrow At Ten* and *This Sporting Life*.

He died in 1975, aged sixty-seven, after a series of strokes.

HARVEY, MISS B.
The unseen female Purser's Clerk on the *Happy Wanderer* in *Cruising*. Her name is seen on the crew list.

HASLAM PAWNBROKERS
A shop seen in *Screaming!*.

HASSALL, IMOGEN
Role: Jenny Grubb in *Loving*
Born in Woking in 1942, Imogen Hassall's brief life came to a tragic end at the age of thirty-eight. In 1980 she was found dead at her London home from a large overdose of drugs. The daughter of a composer, she worked with the Royal Shakespeare Company but was best known for minor roles in a handful of films and television shows during the 1960s.

Often tagged 'The Countess of Cleavages', she appeared in films such as *Position of Trust*, *The Early Bird*, *The Long Duel*, *The Virgin and the Gypsy*, *White Cargo* and *No: 1 Licensed to Love and Kill*, and several television productions, including *The Champions*, *The Saint*, *The Troubleshooters* and *The Sentimental Agent*.

HAVEN HOSPITAL
The hospital is the setting for *Nurse*.

HAWKINS, CAROL
Roles: Marge in *Abroad* and Sandra in *Behind*
TV: *And in My Lady's Chamber* and *Who Needs Kitchener?*
Carol Hawkins, who was born in Barnet, Hertfordshire, in 1949, studied shorthand and typing at Pitman's College in London for two years. She worked as a secretary at a cotton factory for eight months before deciding to temp. When she met a model, she decided to try her luck in the industry and sent a selection of photos to an agency specialising in promotional work. Offers for photo-shoots and walk-on work for television soon followed.

Deciding she wanted to pursue an acting career, she enrolled at the Corona Stage School for a year. Soon after leaving drama school she attended a mass audition for the film version of the successful school-based sitcom, *Please, Sir!*. By then she'd already appeared in a couple of minor film roles but being cast as Sharon in the big-screen version of *Please, Sir!* was an important break because she reprised the role in the off-shoot television series, *The Fenn Street Gang*.

Hawkins became busy in all media, particularly the stage. She worked a lot in the Theatre of Comedy with Ray Cooney, and toured Australia and Canada in *Run For Your Wife*. On television, recent credits include *Trial and Retribution II*, *Rides*, *All At Number 20*, *My Husband and I* and *Doctors*.

For seven years she ran her own string of shops, Human Nature, selling ethnic clothing and New Age gifts in Dorking, Haywards Heath and Horsham. She still operates the Dorking store.

Nowadays, divides her time between homes in Spain and England. She continues to act and run her businesses. A new venture she's

Jenny Grubb (Imogen Hassall) went through a transformation for this appearance (*Loving*)

> ### MEMORIES
> 'Appearing in *Abroad* was wonderful. It was great fun filming the scene where the hotel collapsed – we should have got danger money! All the scenes were filmed on the back lot at Pinewood. In one sequence we were in our bikinis and swimwear and all these firemen were spraying water to make it look like there was a thunderstorm. We were given strict instructions not to move until we got our cue. You could see the firemen ready with the hoses, then the water being sprayed but we couldn't move at all. My cue seemed like an eternity.'
>
> CAROL HAWKINS

currently investigating is the opening of an animal rescue centre in Spain.

HAWKINS, CHARLIE
Played by Sidney James

The owner of Speedee Taxis Limited in *Cabby*, Charlie lives for his cabs and his neglected wife suffers as a result. Established the first taxi firm in the area with forty cars, employing twenty full-time drivers. Ex-army, Hawkins likes to employ fellow soldiers who've returned to civvy street, a situation that rankles with Mr Allbright, the firm's shop steward. With a new intake, he increases his number of drivers to forty and is riding high until a rival firm, Glamcabs, opens up in the district, employing a group of leggy girls. Little does he know that the owner of the firm which almost ruins him is none other than his frustrated wife, out for revenge after years of neglect. But true love shines through in the end with Peggy announcing she's expecting a baby, and plans are afoot to move to the country cottage she craves.

HAWKINS, PEGGY
Played by Hattie Jacques

Charlie Hawkins's wife in *Cabby*. With her husband dedicating so much time to his beloved taxi firm, Speedee Taxis Limited, it's hardly surprising she feels frustrated and neglected. All she dreams of is buying a cottage in the country and raising a family, while all her hubby thinks of is big ends, sumps and grabbing a few more quid. When she can't take any more, especially when Charlie fails to arrive home in time to take her for an anniversary meal, she seeks revenge by opening a rival taxi firm, Glamcabs, and employing a host of leggy beauties. Before long, she's beating Charlie at his own game, and when he eventually discovers Mrs Glam's identity, divorce looks on the cards. But real love shines through when Peggy, together with her close friend, Sally, become caught up with crooks and Charlie uses his taxis to catch the villains.

HAWTREY, CHARLES
Roles: Peter Golightly in *Sergeant*, Humphrey Hinton in *Nurse*, Michael Bean in *Teacher*, PC Timothy Gorse in *Constable*, Gabriel Dimple in *Regardless*, Terry 'Pintpot' Tankard in *Cabby*, Walter Sweetley in *Jack*, Charlie Bind in *Spying*, Seneca in *Cleo*, Big Heap in *Cowboy*, Dan Dann in *Screaming!*, Duc de Pommfrit in *Don't Lose Your Head*, Captain Le Pice in *Follow That Camel*, Mr Barron in *Doctor*; Private Jimmy Widdle in *Up The Khyber*, Charlie Muggins in *Camping*, Dr Ernest Stoppidge in *Again Doctor*, Walter Bagley (King Tonka) in *Up the Jungle*, James Bedsop in *Loving*, Sir Roger de Lodgerley in *Henry*, Charles Coote in *At Your Convenience*, Dr Francis A. Goode in *Matron* and Eustace Tuttle in *Abroad*

TV: *Christmas* (69) and *Christmas* (70)

One of the most popular *Carry On* faces for punters and critics alike was that of bespectacled Charles Hawtrey. Whatever role he was given, from Humphrey Hinton in *Nurse* and Timothy Gorse in *Constable* to Big Heap in *Cowboy* and Charles Coote in *At Your Convenience*, you could guarantee the interpretation would be the same – the wiry Charles Hawtrey didn't play it any other way, and that's what endeared him to his fans.

Born in Middlesex in 1914, Hawtrey began performing at an early age. Initially a boy soprano – as a youngster he made recordings for Columbia and Regal Gramophone Records and was labelled 'the angel-faced choir boy' – he performed his stage debut at eleven before training at the Italia Conti School.

At the age of eighteen he acted in the musical *Marry Me* and also began producing plays for the London stage before beginning his film career in the 1930s with parts in *Good Morning Boys* and numerous other Will Hay films such as *Where's That Fire?*, *The Ghost of St Michael's* and *The Goose Steps Out*. He also acted in, among others, the films *You're Only Young Once* and *A Canterbury Tale*: he later gained experience in other media, working with Patricia Hayes in a number of radio plays for BBC's *Children's Hour*, and subsequently appearing in the popular television comedy *The Army Game* in 1957. A year later he joined the cast of the first *Carry On* film, the first of many which would see him become a household name.

He had returned to the stage before his death in 1987, aged seventy-three. During his latter years he'd become reclusive and was rarely seen on the screen, but despite his sad decline, fuelled partly by alcohol, he'll forever be immortalised as a comic genius who'd only have to appear on the screen in a *Carry On* and utter 'Oh, hello!' to raise a laugh in the audiences who adored him.

HAYES, MELVYN
Role: Gunner Shorthouse in *England*
TV: *The Case of the Screaming Winkles*

Melvyn Hayes, who was born in London in 1935, was appearing at London's Comedy Theatre in *Maskelyne's Mysteries* at the age of fifteen, before answering an advert in *The Stage* newspaper and joining Terry's Juveniles troupe.

The next decade was dominated by films, theatre and television, but his big break came in 1960 when he signed a seven-year film contract

Charles Hawtrey wearing his familiar specs

with ABPC and starred in movies such as *No Trees In The Street, Crooks in Cloisters,* as well as the Cliff Richard movies, *The Young Ones, Summer Holiday* and *Wonderful Life.*

Early work for the BBC included the title role in the award-winning drama documentary *The Unloved,* playing the Artful Dodger in *Oliver Twist* and Edik in *The Silver Sword,* but he's probably best remembered as Gunner Beaumont in the '70s sitcom, *It Ain't Half Hot, Mum.*

HAYES, PATRICIA
Role: Mrs Beasley in *Again Doctor*
Born in London in 1909, Patricia made her acting debut, aged twelve, in *The Great Big World* at the Royal Court. She continued acting on stage throughout her teens, and at eighteen, trained at RADA. Upon graduating, she performed in a string of West End productions, including *Night Must Fall, George and Margaret, When We Are Married* and *Goodnight Children.*

During the Second World War, Hayes moved into radio, working with Ted Ray in *Ray's A Laugh,* before making the transition into television. She later became a familiar figure in the medium with parts in *Edna, the Inebriate Woman; The Corn is Green* and others. She also accumulated many film credits such as *Candles at Nine, Nicholas Nickleby, The Deep Blue Sea, The Battle of the Sexes, Goodbye Mr. Chips* and *Little Dorrit.*

Later returned to the stage and continued acting until reaching her eighties. She died in 1999, aged eighty-nine.

HEADWAITER, THE
Played by John Bluthal
Seen in *Spying* the Headwaiter ushers Simkins to a table at the Café Mozart in Vienna.

HEATHERCREST NATIONAL SERVICE DEPOT
The fictitious army training camp, supposedly near Leighton Buzzard, which is the setting for *Sergeant.*

HECKLER
Played by Norman Mitchell
When Caesar returns to Rome in *Cleo* after years away slaying foreign tribes, he talks to the waiting crowds; events soon turn nasty when the Heckler pipes up which precipitates the throwing of rocks at the leader.

HECKLER
Played by Anthony Sagar
In *Henry* a crowd at Speakers' Corner gathers to debate the new Sex Enjoyment Tax being imposed by the King. The Heckler plays an active part in the discussion. (**Note: the scene was cut. See 'Dandy' entry.**)

HEFTY GIRL
Played by Anna Karen
One of the girls from Chayste Place Finishing School, she's seen in *Camping* brawling with Babs.

HELPING HANDS LIMITED
Bert Handy's company in *Regardless.* From his basement office in London's Denver Street, Bert runs his agency offering help for all and sundry. The company's motto is 'The organisation that's always ready to lend a hand', which means its employees are prepared to do anything from walking pet monkeys and translating heated conversations to modelling underwear and collecting invitations at social functions. Assisted, although hindered is a better description, by the aged Miss Cooling, Bert enploys seven members of staff.

HEMPEL, ANOUSKA
Role: New Canteen Girl in *At Your Convenience*

HENNESSY, PETER
Director of Photography on *Sergeant*
The late Peter Hennessy began camera operating in the 1940s, with films such as *The Huggetts Abroad* and *Crofters.* During the '50s his credits included *The Planter's Wife, Forbidden Cargo, Seven Years in Tibet, Chain of Events, Life in Danger* and, latterly, *The Eyes of Annie Jones.*

HENRI
Played by Michael Ward
A wigmaker seen in *Don't Lose Your Head* attending to Sir Rodney Ffing and Lord Darcy de Pue. He's upset because of the state of affairs in his beloved France, and when he explains to Ffing and Darcy de Pue that men and women of the aristocracy are losing their heads at the guillotine, the two brave Englishmen decide it's about time they did something about it.

The staff at Helping Hands were always willing to lend one (*Regardless*)

HENRY
Played by Peter Gilmore

An ambulance man in *Doctor*. He's employed by the Borough County Hospital and works alongside his colleague, Sam. His erratic driving is to blame for Francis Bigger's abrupt arrival at the hospital, crashing through the entrance doors after flying out of the back of the ambulance.

HENRY
Played by Peter Gilmore

The bespectacled colleague of Dr Nookey in *Again Doctor*, Henry idles away a spare moment with Nookey playing a game of diagnosis.

HENRY
Played by Ronnie Brody

A diminutive guy seen exiting the Citizens' Advice Bureau with Emily, his tall, busty blonde partner in *Loving*. They seem ill-suited which might explain why they've been consulting Mr Snooper, a marriage guidance counsellor, although the mind boggles regarding the actual nature of their problem.

HENRY
Unseen in *Emmannuelle*, he's the late husband of Mrs Dangle, the French Ambassador's housekeeper-cum-cook.

HENRY, CARRY ON
See feature box on pages 130–1.

HENRY STREET
A road mentioned in *Cabby* during the scene where Peggy and Sally are forced to drive at gunpoint by crooks.

HENRY VIII, KING
Played by Sidney James

The King in *Henry* has a succession of wives and keeps Cardinal Wolsey and Thomas Cromwell busy by asking them to arrange an annulment when he finds himself lumbered with the garlic-loving Marie of Normandy. He can't keep his eyes, or hands for that matter, off any pretty girl he spots.

HENRY'S COURTIERS
Played by Peter Rigby, Trevor Roberts and Peter Munt

In *Henry* the Courtiers are seen riding with the King when he's chasing the Buxom Lass across the fields. Henry finally catches his exhausted prey in a barn.

HENRY'S SECOND WIFE
Played by Jane Cardew

In *Henry* the King's second wife became a disappointment to the monarch when he discovered that her oversized chest was, in fact, false, which quickly led to divorce. (**Note: the scene was cut.**)

WHAT MIGHT HAVE BEEN

Sick of the taste of garlic, Henry is in search of a new wife and takes a fancy to a woman who turns out to have been his second wife. He's had so many, he's forgotten.

INT. THE THRONE ROOM – NIGHT

This acts as the reception room also. There are two thrones on a low dais at one end, with drapes behind and the coat of arms. This should be a phoney one with regal-looking symbols, and a motto underneath which we will see, in due course, to be:

NON CRAPITO SUUM JANUUM. Henry is sitting slumped on his throne, with Cromwell and Wolsey in attendance. The ladies and gentlemen of the court are all at the other end of the room, whispering amongst themselves, obviously affected by the sombre atmosphere.

CROMWELL: The thing to do, sire, is to play for time. Act like a loving husband . . .

HENRY: Impossible.

CROMWELL: Oh, you don't have to *enjoy* it, sire. Just go through the motions.

HENRY: How can I go through the motions without *doing* anything?

CROMWELL: Yes . . . it would seem that the Queen has you by the well-known chandeliers.

HENRY: Exactly. 'Cause if I *do* bed her, Wolsey won't be able to get the annulment, will he?

WOLSEY: (**Cagily.**) Yes . . . well, that's liable to take time, your majesty.

HENRY: I haven't got time! I need another wife!

WOLSEY: Yes . . . well, perhaps in the meantime you could make other arrangements, sire.

HENRY: What other arrangements?

WOLSEY: Well . . . like taking a mistress.

HENRY: Well, that's nice, I must say! You, a respectably married man and head of the church, advising me to take a mistress.

WOLSEY: (**Petulantly.**) Well, that's what I have to do.

HENRY: It's different for you! I'm the King! With a proud family motto to uphold! (**Points at the coat-of-arms.**)

(C.S. of motto.)

CROMWELL: But my lord cardinal is right, sire. We must step cautiously.

HENRY: Don't tell me. How do you think we got the motto?

CROMWELL: A hasty divorce would be disastrous. And, after all, there's no immediate hurry for you to marry, is there?

HENRY: Well . . . no. Tomorrow will do, I suppose.

CROMWELL: Tomorrow! Then your grace already has a new Queen in mind?

HENRY: Well, I've hardly had time to look round yet, have I?

(Looks the people over at the other end of the room.)

HENRY: Can't see anything likely in that lot. Oh, I don't know though. (**He leers at someone and points her out to CROMWELL.**)Who's that one over there with the big . . . (**Makes chest illustration.**)

(CROMWELL looks over in her direction.)

(REVERSE SHOT: To see a rather attractive big-bosomed woman, seated, smiling sexily at them.)

HENRY: (**Over.**) Very nice. Who is she?

(Resume CROMWELL and HENRY.)

CROMWELL: (**Wearily.**) That, sire, was your second wife.

HENRY: (**Genuinely surprised.**) Get away! What was wrong with her then?

CROMWELL: They turned out to be false, sire.

HENRY: Oh yes, that's right. I remember now. I fell over them getting into bed. She should've hung them up. I can't stand untidiness.

HERBERT, PERCY
Roles: Mr Angel the Bosun in *Jack* and Charlie in *Cowboy*

Percy Herbert, born in London in 1920, was regularly cast in cockney roles after breaking into acting via the offices of Dame Sybil Thorndike.

He became a staple of the British cinema but retained his links with the theatre. His big-screen credits included *The Night My Number Came Up*, *A Hill in Korea*, *Child in the House*, *The Bridge on the River Kwai*, *Sea Fury*, *The Guns of Navarone*, *Casino Royale* and his last picture, 1987's *The Love Child*. On television he was seen in shows such as *Police Surgeon*, *The Saint*, *The Troubleshooters* and *The Tomorrow People*.

Herbert, who travelled to America during the late 1960s to appear in the TV western series *Cimarron Strip*, died in 1992, aged seventy-two.

HERNIA, HARRY
Played by Howard Nelson

The bodybuilder inspires the French Ambassador, Emile Prevert, to pick up the chest expander but bulging biceps fail to materialise during *Emmannuelle*. Upon seeing Harry in a video, the Ambassador's sex-mad wife, Emmannuelle, takes an interest and gets her husband to introduce her to the bodybuilder. But with Hernia desperate to win the Mr Muscles competition for a third time before retiring, he's not interested in trying to satisfy Emmannuelle's sexual desires.

HESSIAN DRIVER
Played by Brian Rawlinson

The driver of a wagon who picks up captives for the Romans and escorts them back to Rome in *Cleo*.

CARRY ON HENRY

Alternative title ... *Mind My Chopper*

A Peter Rogers production
Distributed through Rank Organisation
Released as an A certificate in 1971 in colour
Running time: 89 mins

CAST

Sidney James .... King Henry VIII
Kenneth Williams ...... Thomas Cromwell
Charles Hawtrey ... Sir Roger de Lodgerley
Joan Sims ..... Queen Marie of Normandy
Terry Scott .... Cardinal Wolsey
Barbara Windsor .... Bettina
Kenneth Connor ... Lord Hampton of Wick
Julian Holloway .... Sir Thomas
Peter Gilmore ..... Francis, King of France
Peter Butterworth .... Charles, Earl of Bristol
Julian Orchard .... Duc de Poncenay
Gertan Klauber .... Bidet
David Davenport .... Major-domo
Margaret Nolan .... Buxom Lass

William Mervyn .... Physician
Norman Chappell .... 1st Plotter
Derek Francis .... Farmer
Bill Maynard .... Guy Fawkes
Douglas Ridley .... 2nd Plotter
Leon Greene
Dave Prowse .... Torturers

Monica Dietrich .... Katherine Howard
Billy Cornelius .... Guard
Marjie Lawrence .... Serving Maid
Patsy Rowlands .... Queen
Alan Curtis .... Conte di Pisa
John Bluthal .... Royal Tailor
William McGuirck .... Flunkey
Jane Cardew .... Henry's 2nd Wife
Valerie Shute .... Maid
Peter Rigby
Trevor Roberts
Peter Munt .... Henry's Courtiers

PRODUCTION TEAM

Screenplay by Talbot Rothwell
Music composed and conducted by
   Eric Rogers
Production Manager: Jack Swinburne
Art Director: Lionel Couch
Editor: Alfred Roome
Director of Photography: Alan Hume
Camera Operator: Derek Browne
Continuity: Rita Davison
Assistant Editor: Jack Gardner
Assistant Director: David Bracknell
Make-up: Geoffrey Rodway
Sound Recordists: Danny Daniel and
   Ken Barker
Hairdresser: Stella Rivers
Set Dresser: Peter Howitt
Costume Designer: Courtenay Elliott
Costumes: L. & H. Nathan Ltd
Assistant Art Director: William Alexander
Dubbing Editor: Brian Holland
Titles: G.S.E. Ltd
Processed by Rank Film Laboratories
Producer: Peter Rogers
Director: Gerald Thomas

Henry (Sid James) got through wives like there was no tomorrow

Gerald Thomas (centre) joins in the fun

Moments after King Henry VIII sees his wife of six months sent off to her death, he's tying the knot with Marie of Normandy and can't wait to consummate the marriage – that is until he realises she reeks of garlic. When she refuses to give up eating the plant, Henry decides it's time to annul the marriage and asks Cardinal Wolsey and Thomas Cromwell to arrange it; both men, though, are desperate to keep the marriage together because they fear antagonising the King of France will inevitably lead to war.

Henry is infuriated further when the Queen insists all food is cooked with garlic, but heeds Cromwell's advice that the best way forward is to find a way for him to be apart from Marie until the annulment comes through, suggesting a fake abduction. Cromwell has just the man to help: Lord Hampton of Wick. The offer of the job couldn't have come at a better time for Hampton because he was actually planning a real attack on the King. But their attempts to abduct Henry are thwarted when Marie gets tough, sending Hampton and his men scampering away.

Meanwhile, the Pope's envoy arrives to confirm the price of the annulment is going to cost Henry dear, so much so that Cromwell, who also tries making something out of it himself, introduces a new sex tax to help pay the fee. But any plans for a split are complicated when it's discovered the Queen is pregnant; initially excited, the King's smile rapidly evaporates when he realises he hasn't, as yet, consummated the marriage. Unbeknown to him, his equerry, Sir Roger, who talked his way into the Queen's bed by claiming he has to try everything first for the King, is the guilty party; when he eventually finds out, the Queen and Sir Roger are placed behind bars in the Tower of London. To speed through his divorce, Henry uses the threat of the torture chamber to persuade Sir Roger to sign a confession of his wrongdoing, but it's only when he's stretched beyond belief on the rack that he gives in.

Marie persuades the Cardinal to sneak a letter out of the Tower and to send it to the King of France, who despatches a messenger, the Duc de Poncenay, to congratulate Henry on the news of the pregnancy and to offer a monetary gift of 50,000 gold crowns. Queen Marie is quickly retrieved from her cell to give the impression their marriage is rosy, but when she tells the Duc she's been banished to the Tower and that the baby isn't Henry's, the King tries his best to cover up, as well as ordering Cromwell to seek a retraction from Sir Roger.

With the Duc returning to France, life returns to a sense of normality with the King taking a fancy to Bettina, a young woman whom he employs as the Queen's lady-in-waiting; but when she's only interested in a relationship with a man she'll eventually marry, the King decides to forfeit the French money in order to marry Bettina, for which he asks the exasperated Cromwell to force Sir Roger to sign yet another confession.

Having obtained the confession, the King decides to conduct his own wedding ceremony because he's eager to get Bettina into bed, but when King Francis arrives with a 20,000-strong army ready for war if the rumours he's heard concerning the Queen's banishment to the Tower of London and the legitimacy of the baby are confirmed; while Henry tries to placate Francis by rushing off to get Marie, the Frenchman becomes impatient and heads to her bedchamber only to find the pretty Bettina, who confirms the Queen's predicament. With Francis declaring war, the returning King Henry tries to patch things up by suggesting that a plot to abduct the Queen left him with no option but to send her to the Tower for her own safety.

Amid the chaotic scenes, the Cardinal arrives and claims the Queen has actually been abducted, before she turns up with Lord Hampton who's just about to spill the beans when his silence is bought with cash; the Queen, meanwhile, restrains from revealing all to her cousin, the King of France, so long as Henry agrees to convert to garlic; so everyone is happy, including Francis, who arranges – much to Henry's regret – to take Bettina home with him to become his Queen.

Marie gives birth and the King pledges his devotion to his beloved wife, but just when it looks as if everyone will live happily ever after, Henry spots the Queen's new lady-in-waiting.

Funny Scene!

Henry VIII is trying to arrange an annulment of his marriage to Marie of Normandy but it's going to cost. What Henry doesn't know is that both Cardinal Wolsey and Thomas Cromwell are making money out of it.

```
CROMWELL:  Of course it will entail a certain
           amount of expenditure.
HENRY:     How much?
CROMWELL:  If you could let me have twenty
           thousand.
HENRY:     Twenty thousand!
CROMWELL:  Well, rather more than usual I know, but
           little enough if you have it.
HENRY:     That's just the point, I haven't had it.
CROMWELL:  The money, I mean.
HENRY:     I should have to tell you that speaking
           royally, my mint has a hole in it.
```

HEWLETT, DONALD

Role: Dean in *Behind*

Born in Manchester in 1922, Donald Hewlett was studying meteorology and geography at Cambridge when the Second World War broke out. Although unable to complete his degree, he joined the navy as a meteorologist, based in the Orkneys where he helped establish an arts club in Kirkwall. He was later drafted to Singapore where his responsibilities included taking charge of Japanese POWs and helping with the entertainments.

After demob he studied at RADA and went on to work in rep at Oxford with Ronnie Barker. Several years of stage work followed before his small-screen debut in *Mick and Montmorency* in the early 1950s. Preferring television work, Hewlett has appeared in many shows, including playing Carstairs in *Come Back, Mrs Noah*, Colonel Reynolds in *It Ain't Half Hot, Mum* and Lord Meldrum in *You Rang, M'Lord?*.

He's also appeared in a few films, such as *Saving Grace*, with Tom Conti, *Bottoms Up* and *Moments*.

HEWSON, SHERRIE

Role: Carol in *Behind*

TV: *The Case of the Screaming Winkles, The Case of the Coughing Parrot, And in My Lady's Chamber* and *Who Needs Kitchener?*

Born in Burton Joyce, Nottingham, in 1950, Sherrie Hewson was performing from the age of six, tap-dancing and singing. She progressed to all strands of the profession, appearing in the original production of *Stepping Out*, and featuring in a handful of films.

It is, however, her television work for which she's best remembered. Credits include *Z Cars, Within These Walls, Juliet Bravo, Flickers, Radio Phoenix, In Loving Memory*, two series of *Home James!* and *The Russ Abbot Show*. For four years she played Maureen in *Coronation Street*.

HEYWOOD, MILES

Played by Terence Longdon

A member of the infamous Able Platoon in *Sergeant*, the plummy-voiced Miles Heywood comes from a long line of military men but has no desire to follow suit. He claims he's not a leader of men, which disappoints Sergeant Grimshaw, who'd hoped to win some brownie points recommending him as an officer cadet in his drive for the champion platoon. Heywood provides much needed level-headedness in a platoon full of oddballs.

HICKSON, JOAN

Roles: Sister in *Nurse*, Mrs May in *Constable*, Matron in *Regardless*, Mrs Grubb in *Loving* and Mrs Dukes in *Girls*

Born in Northampton in 1906, Joan Hickson popped up in so many British post-war movies that it seemed a film wasn't made without her presence. But for many people she'll always be remembered for her portrayal of Agatha Christie's detective, Miss Marple, whom she played for eight years.

Hickson wanted to act from childhood after seeing a production of *Cinderella*. She got her first taste of the entertainment world during the Great War when she sang for wounded soldiers at home, while her mother played the piano. Although she faced resistance from her family, she pursued her dream of becoming an actress, attending RADA at the age of nineteen.

She made her first appearance on the London stage in *The Tragic Muse*, followed by two years in numerous West End comedies and three seasons in rep at Oxford. By the mid-1930s she was appearing in movies, with early credits including *Widow's Might, Love from a Stranger, Freedom Radio, This Was a Woman* and *The Guinea Pig*. During a career spanning nearly six decades, she notched up over a hundred film appearances. Other notable credits included *Seven Days To Noon, Doctor in the House, The Man Who Never Was, Angels One Five, Murder She Said* and *Clockwise*.

On television she appeared as Mrs Pugsley in BBC's sitcom, *Bachelor Father*, ITV's *Confidentially*, Mrs Morrow in *Good Girl, Mincemeat*, Mrs Pearce in the sitcom *Our Man At St Mark's, Sinister Street, A Policeman's Lot, A Ferry Ride Away* and Lady Harriet in Granada's *Poor Little Rich Girls*.

She worked until her death in 1998, aged ninety-two.

HICKSON, MADGE

Played by Irene Handl

The wife of patient Percy Hickson in *Nurse*, Madge visits her husband at Haven Hospital. A timid lady, she tries to help her beloved complete a compensation form regarding his injury at work, but ends up becoming flustered and bursting into tears.

HICKSON, PERCY

Played by Bill Owen

After falling off scaffolding and breaking his leg at work, Hickson becomes a patient of Haven Hospital in *Nurse*.

HIGHWAYMEN

Played by Brian Coburn and Max Faulkner

The Highwaymen are seen in the closing scene of *Dick* stopping Dick Turpin's coach as it crosses the border into bonnie Scotland.

HILDA

Played by Jennifer Pyle

Hilda is one of the girls from the Chayste Place Finishing School who braves the cold in *Camping*.

HILDA, AUNTIE

The unseen auntie of Theodore Valentine is mentioned in *Emmannuelle* during a conversation between Mrs Valentine and her molly-coddled son, Theodore.

HILL, BILL

Production Manager on *Cruising*

As a production manager, Bill Hill began working on films in the 1960s, with credits including *Swiss Family Robinson, Taste of Fear, Raising the Wind, Twice Round the Daffodils, Hot Enough for June* and the Bond movie, *From Russia With Love*.

He also produced the 1964 film, *The Curse of the Mummy's Tomb* and, the same year, the television series, *Court Martial*.

HILL, JENNIFER

Role: Girl at Dirty Dick's in *Jack*

Jennifer Hill's other screen credits include a 1977 episode of *Z Cars* playing a chorus lady.

HILLS, R.M.

Cabby was based on an original idea from R.M. Hills and S.C. Green.

HINES, ROY

Role: Harry Bird in *Teacher*

Roy Hines appeared in a handful of screen productions during the 1950s, such as television shows *The Vise, When In Rome* and *Huntingtower*.

HINTON, HUMPHREY

Played by Charles Hawtrey

Hinton is a patient at Haven Hospital in *Nurse*. He spends his entire waking hours listening to the radio via headphones, frequently resorting to frenzied bouts of animated gestures when a piece of invigorating music is played.

HISCOCKS, GUNNER

Played by Jeremy Connor

Based at the experimental 1313 anti-aircraft battery featured in *England*, he's one of the shirkers who suffers a severe shock to the system when the tough-speaking Captain Melly is put in charge of the unit.

HITLER

Captain Melly's enormous dog in *England*.

HOBBS, NICK

Stunt Double in *Girls*

Stunt artist Nick Hobbs has also been cast in small-screen parts, mainly in television shows such as *Doctor Who, Space: 1999, Dempsey and Makepeace, Rumpole of the Bailey* and *The Darling Buds of May*.

He's carried out stunts and stunt coordination on, among others, *An American Werewolf in London, Krull, Wild Geese II, Superman IV, The Three Musketeers, Billy Elliot, The 51st State* and *24 Hour Party People*. For television, he's worked on the likes of *Heartbeat, London's Burning, Murder in Mind* and *The Worst Week of My Life*.

HOCOMBE PARK

The entrance to the park is seen in *Screaming!*. Outside is the toilet block in which Dan Dann works as the attendant.

HOCOMBE WOODS

The infamous woods in *Screaming!* where six women have vanished within a year.

HODGSON, ALF
Played by Cyril Chamberlain

In *Teacher*, Alf is caretaker at Maudlin Street Secondary Modern School.

HOESLI, JOHN
Set Dresser on *Emmannuelle*

As set decorator, John Hoesli has worked on the 1963 films *Stolen Hours* and *I Could Go On Singing*, and as assistant art director on, among others, *Sea Wife*, *Swiss Family Robinson*, *Satan Never Sleeps* and 1985's *Lifeforce*.

He was promoted to art director and in this capacity has worked on various films, including *The Adventurers*, *The Wilby Conspiracy*, *Eye of the Needle* and, most recently, *Santa Claus*.

HOGGETT, MARTHA
Played by Hattie Jacques

The Reverend Flasher's housekeeper in *Dick* also plays the church organ during his church services. She's looked after him for ten years but longs to be his wife; what she doesn't know, though, is that the softly-spoken rector is, in fact, the legendary highwayman, Dick Turpin.

HOGGETT, SISTER
Played by June Jago

A starchy employee of the Borough County Hospital in *Doctor*.

HOLDEN, KATHERINA
Role: Khasi's Wife in *Up The Khyber*

During the 1960s, Katherina Holden appeared in a few other productions, such as a 1966 episode of *The Saint*, playing a nurse, and the 1966 film, *Stop the World: I Want To Get Off*.

HOLLAND, BRIAN
Dubbing Editor on *Henry* and *At Your Convenience*

HOLLAND, TERENCE
Role: Passer-by in *Cruising* (**Note: the scene was cut from the film.**)

Terence Holland also made a brief appearance in another Rogers/Thomas production, the 1961 music school comedy, *Raising the Wind*, playing the uncredited part of '1st Trombone'.

HOLLOWAY, JULIAN
Roles: Ticket Collector in *Follow That Camel*, Simmons in *Doctor*, Major Shorthouse in *Up The Khyber*, Jim Tanner in *Camping*, Adrian in *Loving*, Sir Thomas in *Henry*, Roger in *At Your Convenience* and Major Butcher in *England*
TV: *Christmas* (73)

Julian Holloway, son of distinguished actor Stanley Holloway, was born in Watlington, Oxfordshire, in 1944. Following his father into the business, he graduated from RADA and was offered, in 1963, a part in *All Square*, a West End review with Beryl Reid. Over the next five years, Holloway was hardly out of the West End, gaining vital stage experience.

By the time he made his debut on British television in a 1963 episode of *The Saint*, he'd already appeared on American screens in *Fair Exchange* and *Our Man Higgins*, a year earlier. During his career he's made over 200 television appearances, but restricted his stage work to just a handful of roles before returning in a 1992 revival of *My Fair Lady*.

He moved to California in 1990 but returned to England in 2000 to play Uncle George in *My Uncle Silas* and, later, *My Uncle Silas II*, but resides permanently in the States. One of his most recent jobs was the voice of Siegfried for NBC's animated sitcom, *Father Of The Pride*.

HONEYBUTT, DAPHNE
Played by Barbara Windsor

An agent with a photographic memory in *Spying*, which comes in useful on her first mission when she's sent as part of a team to retrieve a stolen formula. Agent 4711, whose code name is Brown Cow, used to sing in a rock 'n' roll band.

HONORIA
Played by Diane Aubrey

Turns up in *Constable* driving a Triumph sports car (registration YDU 212). She pulls up at the pavement upon seeing PC Potter on his beat, much to his sergeant's disgust. An old friend of Potter's, the last time they met was at a pyjama party.

HOOK
Played by Ed Devereaux

A pirate who reports to Patch in *Jack*.

HOOKS, LINDA
Roles: A 'Bird of Paradise' in *Dick*, Nurse in *Behind* and Nurse in *England*
TV: *The Baron Outlook* and *One in the Eye for Harold*
STAGE: *Laughing*

Born in Liverpool in 1952, Linda Hooks first came to prominence as a beauty queen, being crowned Miss Bournemouth in 1971 and Miss Great Britain the following year. She then travelled to Japan where she picked up honours as Miss International and Miss Photogenic; two years later, after being named Miss Southampton 1974, she quit to focus on a career in television.

During the 1970s she appeared in several television shows, playing an Alien Girl in a 1976 episode of *Space: 1999* and Ivy in a 1978 instalment of *The Sweeney*. She also appeared

in two episodes of *Carry On Laughing* and became known to millions as the hostess on *Sale Of The Century*.

HOOPLA GIRL
Played by Jan Rossini

The staff of W.C. Boggs and Son let their hair down and enjoy their annual jolly to the seaside in *At Your Convenience*. One of the pier's attractions is the hoopla stand, where Charles Coote scores a bull's-eye by throwing the hoop onto the Hoopla Girl's chest. (**Note: the scene was cut from the film.**)

WHAT MIGHT HAVE BEEN

INT. HOOPLA STALL – DAY
One with fairly large prizes and rings. C.S. of Notice saying: WHATEVER YOU RING YOU CAN HAVE! C.S. Coote, as he gets rings from a girl attendant with a very pert sweatered chest. Coote looks up at the sign and takes aim and throws. We hear a surprised exclamation from the girl attendant. C.S. girl: The ring is round one of her breasts. C.S. Coote, beaming, as he holds out his hand hopefully . . .

HORSA
Played by Jim Dale

In *Cleo*, Horsa moves into the cave next to Hengist and Senna Pod. He was living in Bristol with his sweetheart, Gloria, until the Romans ransacked their settlement, taking Gloria captive. Eventually he finds her, administering to Caesar's many whims, and they're reunited and married.

HORSLEY, JOHN
Role: Anaesthetist in *Nurse* (**Note: scene cut from film.**)

Character actor John Horsley, born in Westcliff-on-Sea, Essex, in 1920, made his name playing professional and military types in countless movies during the halcyon days of the film industry, and for his small-screen portrayal of Doc Morrissey in David Nobbs's sitcom, *The Fall and Rise of Reginald Perrin*.

Son of a doctor, Horsley launched his acting career at Bournemouth's Theatre Royal in 1938. Stints with various repertory companies followed before he was conscripted into the army in 1940.

After the war, he returned to the theatre, but by the beginning of the 1950s was working in films, starting with 1950's *Highly Dangerous*. Other film credits include *Appointment with Venus*, *The Long Memory*, *The Runaway Bus*, *Forbidden Cargo*, *Jigsaw*, *Hell Drivers* and *Ben-Hur*, but his big-screen career was dominated by numerous war movies, such as *Above Us the Waves*, *Dunkirk*, *Sink the Bismarck!* and *Operation Amsterdam*.

Whereas his film roles were predominantly

serious, he's been seen in comedies as well as dramas on television, including *The Avengers*, *Out of this World*, *The Champions*, *Doomwatch*, *The Professionals*, *Robin of Sherwood*, *Hi-De-Hi!*, *Terry and June*, *Lovejoy*, *Rumpole of the Bailey*, *Hot Metal*, *My Husband and I* and as Sir Ralph Shawcross in several episodes of *You Rang, M'Lord?*. More recently he was seen playing a judge in *Kavanagh QC* and a butler in *Rebecca*.

HORTON, MARIAN
Role: Glamcab Driver in *Cabby*
Born in Brighouse, West Yorkshire, in 1938, Marian Horton began her career in entertainment by appearing as a dancer at the Palladium for two and a half years. She'd also worked as a photographic model and cabaret artiste before making her film debut in 1963's *Ricochet*, an instalment in the *Edgar Wallace Presents . . .* series. Other big-screen credits include the 1966 film *Stop the World: I Want to Get Off*, while on television she worked with, among others, Charlie Chester and Matt Monro.

HORTON, MISS
Played by Lucy Griffiths
Seen in *Constable*, Miss Horton, of 33 Nathaniel Road, reports an intruder at number 35. PC Potter investigates and discovers that Sally Barry, the daughter of the house, has returned home unexpectedly from Cornwall.

HOSGOOD, STANLEY
Assistant Director on *Nurse*
During the 1950s and '60s, Stanley Hosgood was busy working on a host of films, including *To Paris With Love*, *The Woman for Joe*, *Simon and Laura*, *Hell Drivers*, *Doctor in Love* and his last credit, 1961's *No My Darling Daughter*.

HOSPITAL BOARD MEMBER
Played by Elspeth March
When Doctor Nookey in *Again Doctor* is called in front of the hospital board, after his escapade in Miss Armitage's room, it's this member who doesn't want him to continue working at the Long Hampton Hospital or any other.

HOSPITALITY GIRLS
Played by Valerie Leon, Carmen Dene, June Cooper, Josephine Blain, Vicki Murden, Karen Young, Angie Grant and Sue Vaughan
The girls, seen in *Up The Khyber*, are found in the Khasi's abode, entertaining Captain Keene, Sergeant MacNutt, Private Widdle and Brother Belcher who've arrived to retrieve the embarrassing photo revealing the Foot and Mouth regiment wearing underpants.

HOTCHKISS, MRS
Not seen in *Matron* but Mrs Hotchkiss gives birth to twin boys at the Finisham Maternity Hospital.

HOTEL GENTLEMAN
Played by Harold Kasket
In *Follow That Camel* he's seen at the Hotel Miramar, in the middle of the Sahara, wearing a fez, stating to his business associate that they built the hotel in the wrong location because everyone passes by believing they're seeing a mirage instead of a real hotel.

HOTEL MANAGER
Played by David Glover
In *Follow That Camel* the hotel manager arrives, donning a tarboosh, to welcome Lady Jane Ponsonby to the Kifa Hotel. She stays there during her journey to find Bertram West, who's run off and joined the Foreign Legion.

HOTEL MANAGER
Played by Peter Burton
Manager of the hotel in Brighton where the employees of W.C. Boggs and Son, on their annual jolly to the seaside, were planning to lunch. They head for the bar, though, when the manager breaks the bad news that the catering staff have gone on strike, which ironically infuriates Vic Spanner. Seen in *At Your Convenience*.

HOTEL MIRAMAR
A hotel in the middle of the Sahara offering dancing, a bar and restaurant; the trouble is, the few people who pass by believe they're seeing a mirage because no one in their right minds would build a hotel in such an isolated position. Seen in *Follow That Camel*.

HOUSEMAN
Played by Fraser Kerr
Busy writing when we first see him in *Regardless*, this doctor later gives the VIP treatment to Bert Handy, mistaking him for Sir Theodore, an important visitor expected at the hospital.

HOUSTON, DONALD
Role: 1st Officer Jonathan Howett in *Jack*
Donald Houston, who was born in Tonypandy, Wales in 1923, served in the RAF during World War Two as an air gunner and wireless operator, before being invalided out and going to work in the mines.

He made his acting debut, aged seventeen, with the Pilgrim Players in Penzance and then joined the Oxford Repertory Company. Fame came nine years later through *The Blue Lagoon* film, which he followed up with *A Run For Your Money*, before returning to the stage to act in *The Cocktail Party* in the West End. Much of his career was spent torn between the two media and his credits include the films *Dance Hall*, *Doctor in the House*, *Room at the Top*, *A Study in Terror* and *Where Eagles Dare* as well as stage credits such as *Under Milk Wood*.

He also appeared in a number of television series including *Now, Take My Wife* and *Moonbase 3*.

He died in 1991, aged sixty-seven.

HOUSTON, RENÉE
Roles: Molly in *Cabby*, Madame in *Spying* and Agatha Spanner in *At Your Convenience*. (Note: was also going to play Mrs Dukes in *Girls* but contract cancelled due to ill-health.)
Born in Johnstone, Scotland, in 1902, Renée Houston, the daughter of vaudeville performers James Gribbon and Elizabeth Houston, enjoyed an extensive career in stage, screen and radio.

She emerged on the scene during the 1920s, appearing in music halls as part of a double-act

---

MEMORIES

'Strangely, over the years, indeed throughout my entire acting career, I've had more enquiries about working on *Carry On Teacher* than any other job I've ever done. I can honestly say, too, that I've never enjoyed a job as much since – and I've had a lot of good times. It's a great shame, and also a bit disquieting, to find nearly all the cast – company and crew – have since died. As you can imagine, at the time of filming we – the kids – had no clue that we'd become part of a British institution!

'In the *Romeo and Juliet* school play scene we were prevented from leaving the stage and consequently were all given a thorough drenching. We had no idea we'd been "set up", but it was typical of the pranks played on everyone in the company.

'Kenneth Williams had been warned to behave himself and mind his language when he was around us – or so he said – but in all the time we were in his company I never ever heard him being vulgar or coarse. He was brilliantly funny, and told us long-drawn-out anecdotes, all of which he claimed to be true! Mr and Mrs Rotter and her peppermint creams, Mr Rotter having his dinner on the stairs . . . they were legion. I remember he told us only one joke, but kept it going for three days. It concerned Mr Buzzard, Mr Turtle and Mr Rabbit. It had a rhyming tag line regarding Mr Rabbit who'd been sent to fetch fertiliser for the garden: "Will you tell them Mr Rabbit is here with the manure" and that's as risqué as he ever got!

'Ted Ray was unbelievably funny, too; his ability to top every gag he told was phenomenal. He easily had us in tears of mirth to the point where we could laugh no longer for the pain.'

GEORGE HOWELL

with her sister, Billie. When her sister's ill-health forced the break-up of the act, she became a character actress of note over the coming decades on screen and stage. Her film credits included *2000 Women, Lady Godiva Rides Again, A Town Like Alice, Time Without Pity, Twice Round the Daffodils, Out of the Fog* and *Legend of the Werewolf.*

She also made occasional appearances on television in shows such as *The Saint, Doctor in the House, Dixon of Dock Green* and *Dr Finlay's Casebook.* On radio she's probably best remembered for BBC's *The Petticoat Line.*

She died in 1980, aged seventy-seven.

HOUSTON, SAM
Played by Sydney Bromley
The bearded Colonel Sam Houston owns a ranch near Stodge City. A friend of Judge Burke, he's seen in *Cowboy.*

HOWARD, KATHERINE
Played by Monica Dietrich
Queen Marie of Normandy's new lady-in-waiting replaces Bettina when she heads across the channel to become Queen of France in *Henry.* Just when it looks as if Henry will settle down to married life with Marie, he decides, yet again, that perhaps a divorce is the only answer with someone like Katherine now on the scene.

HOWELL, GEORGE
Role: Billy Haig in *Teacher*
Born in London in 1943, George Howell was eight when he enrolled at the Corona Academy. Before he left, aged sixteen, he'd worked on various radio and television programmes, as well as several films. His small-screen work during this period included roles in *The Adventures of Robin Hood, Ivanhoe, The Adventures of Sir Lancelot* and ABC's *Those Kids,* which saw him work with Peter Butterworth. On radio he played Bobby Huggett in *Meet the Huggetts.*

Upon leaving stage school he embarked on a three-year stint in rep, appearing in such destinations as Jersey, Barrow, Oldham and Watford, before moving to Scotland and joining the cast of *High Living,* one of many Scottish soaps Howell, who lived in Australia during 1986, has appeared in during his career.

Other screen credits include the Norman Hudis-scripted film, *Please Turn Over,* and television shows such as *Sutherland's Law, Crossroads, Sherlock Holmes* and *The Eagle of the Ninth.*

He retired from acting in 1996.

HOWERD, FRANKIE
Roles: Francis Bigger in *Doctor* and Professor Inigo Tinkle in *Up the Jungle*
TV: *Christmas* (69)
Frankie Howerd, who was one of the Queen Mother's favourite comedians, was born in York but moved to Eltham, Kent, where his father, a sergeant in the Royal Artillery, was posted.

His interest in showbusiness was ignited when he appeared in the local church's dramatic society production of *Tilly of Bloomsbury,* but began his working life as an office clerk until receiving his call-up papers in 1940. By the time he was demobbed, he was running a concert party touring northwest Germany.

In 1946, his name was seen low down on the billing at the Sheffield Empire, but it was the start of a career containing its fair share of highs and lows, that would see him become one of the country's most recognisable comics. He came to the fore in the highly successful radio show, *Variety Bandbox,* and was soon topping the bill at numerous variety theatres around the country.

His film credits included *The Runaway Bus, Jumping for Joy, The Ladykillers, A Touch of Sun, The Fast Lady* and *Up the Front.* His many successes on the small screen included his own series *Frankly Howerd, Frankie Howerd* and *Up Pompeii.*

Filled with self-doubt throughout his career, Howerd's popularity saw a resurgence in the 1990s when he became a cult icon among students. He died in 1992, aged seventy-five.

HOWETT, 1st OFFICER JONATHAN
Played by Donald Houston
Seen in *Jack,* he's first officer on the frigate Venus, who's initially seen roaming the Plymouth streets looking for two people to pressgang into joining the ship's crew for their journey to Spanish waters. A man who has no respect for his incompetent superior, Captain Fearless, believing he's the one who runs *Venus* and should be given the rank to acknowledge it. When he picks up on an idea floated by Mr Angel, the ship's bosun, he organises a plan to relieve Fearless of his post.

HOWITT, PETER
Set Dresser on *Loving, Henry* and *At Your Convenience*
Born in Wimbledon in 1928, Peter Howitt left school and studied at a college in Reigate and then the Royal College, London. A trained painter, he eventually found work in the theatre and, subsequently, ballet and opera venues, including Covent Garden.

He began working in films from the mid-1960s in various capacities as a set dresser/

Frankie Howerd poses for a publicity shot

decorator, production designer and art director. His early credits include *The Mikado*; *Anne of the Thousand Days*; *Mary, Queen of Scots*; *Follow Me!*; *A Touch of Class*; *The Great Gatsby* and *Royal Flash*. He's also worked on *Superman*, *James Bond* and *Indiana Jones* movies, while more recently he was set decorator on 1997's *Fierce Creatures* and 2002's *The Four Feathers*, his last film.

For a while he ran his own display business, designing scenery and displays for many leading retailers, such as Selfridges and Harrods. Now living in Malta full-time, he occasionally works at the Government Theatre in Valletta.

HUDIS, NORMAN

Wrote the screenplays for *Sergeant, Nurse, Teacher, Constable, Regardless* and *Cruising*

Writer of the opening six *Carry On*s, East Ender Norman Hudis was born in Stepney, in 1922. Part of his childhood was spent north of the border when his father's job took the family to Glasgow for a time.

Always wanting to be a writer, he was sixteen when he became a junior reporter in London. A year later, war broke out and upon reaching eighteen, he volunteered for the Royal Air Force. Rejected for flying on medical grounds (vision), he spent six years in the Air Force, the last two as entertainments columnist on *Air Force News*, stationed in Cairo.

A post-war dearth of opportunities in journalism saw him follow a friend into the Pictorial Publicity Department of the Rank Organisation. He was eventually offered a screenwriting contract at Pinewood Studios, a post he held for two years. He gained valuable experience, but nothing he wrote was filmed, so he quit, turned freelance, wrote about twenty produced B pictures, and most of the scripts for two seasons of

Norman Hudis' scripts always contained a degree of pathos

the one-hour television comedy series, *Our House*, which he created. His film credits during this period included *Passport to Treason, Breakaway, High Terrace* and his breakthrough success, *The Tommy Steele Story*.

He went on to write, under a six-year contract with Peter Rogers, the trend-setting first six *Carry On*s, as well as such titles as *Please Turn Over, Twice Round the Daffodils* and *Nurse On Wheels*. The surprise success of *Nurse* in America saw him being invited to Hollywood where he has worked and lived ever since. His first significant US credits were two *Man From Uncle* movies, and he subsequently wrote for such television series as *The F.B.I.*; *Hawaii Five-O*; *Marcus Welby, M.D.*; *McCloud*; *Cannon, It Takes A Thief* and *Beretta*. He has won several American awards, notably three for the television biblical epic, *The Story of Esther*.

Hudis occasionally returns to the UK to work. One European project, the animated feature movie, *A Monkey's Tale*, has also collected several awards. In Germany he was employed as story editor and wrote several scripts on the animated television series, *Waldo*.

He is currently working on his autobiography, entitled *Running Late*.

HUGHES, GEOFFREY

Role: Willie in *At Your Convenience*

Liverpudlian Geoffrey Hughes, who was born in 1944, began acting at Newcastle University and gained early stage experience at a rep company in Stoke-on-Trent. Although he's best known for his roles as Eddie Yeats in *Coronation* Street, Onslow in *Keeping Up Appearances* and Vernon Scripps in *Heartbeat*, he's enjoyed a varied career to date.

His many TV credits include *The Likely Lads, Shadows of Fear, Randall and Hopkirk (Deceased), Don't Drink the Water, Doctor Who, Spender, Boon* and *The Upper Hand*. Among his film credits are appearances in *Till Death Us Do Part* and providing the voice of Paul McCartney in *Yellow Submarine*.

HULKE, BERNIE

Played by Bernard Bresslaw

A friend of Vic Spanner in *At Your Convenience*, Bernie certainly lives up to his name. A lumbering giant of a man, he's not the brightest star in the universe and is easily led astray by the militant Vic.

HUME, ALAN

Camera operator on *Sergeant, Nurse, Teacher* and *Constable*. Director of Photography on *Regardless, Cruising, Cabby, Jack, Spying, Cleo, Cowboy, Screaming!, Don't Lose Your Head, Follow That Camel, Doctor, Henry, Abroad, Girls, Emmannuelle* and *Columbus*

Alan Hume was born in Putney, London, in 1924. His father worked on the London

Underground and found him a job working in the stores. He disliked the job, so when he met a man while travelling to work who suggested joining him at the Olympic Film Laboratories, Hume jumped at the chance.

He later secured a job as a clapper boy in the early 1940s at Denham Studios working, initially, on *The First of the Few* with Leslie Howard and David Niven. Before being called up into the Fleet Air Arm, where he worked as a photographer, Hume progressed to focus puller.

After returning to civvy street it wasn't long before he was back at Denham, working as a camera assistant until given his break as a camera operator, later becoming a director of photography. His long and eventful career has seen him work on over a hundred films, including three James Bond movies, a *Star Wars* picture and, among others, *Portrait of Alison, The Green Man, The Silent Enemy, Watch Your Stern, Raising the Wind, The Iron Maiden, Nurse On Wheels, The Big Job, Zeppelin* and *A Fish Called Wanda*. For television, he worked on *The Avengers, Father Dear Father* and *For the Love of Ada*.

Hume has now retired from the industry.

HUME, A.

The unseen Junior Fourth Officer on the *Happy Wanderer* in *Cruising*. His name is seen on the crew list and it's obviously a reference to the film's director of photography.

HUME, FIELD MARSHAL

Played by uncredited actor

Seen in *Emmannuelle*, the Field Marshal is a dinner guest of Emile Prevert's.

HUMP, HAROLD

Played by Henry McGee

The television presenter hosts *The Hump Report* and is seen during *Emmannuelle* interviewing the French Ambassador's sex-mad wife, Emmannuelle Prevert, about her numerous affairs. To his surprise, and the viewers', she doesn't deny the rumours that abound concerning her liaisons, including one with the Prime Minister.

HUMP REPORT, THE

The television show hosted by Harold Hump in *Emmannuelle*. It's broadcast by the PTV channel.

HUMPHRYS, LARAINE

Roles: Eileen Denby in *Girls* and one of the 'Birds of Paradise' in *Dick*

TV: *Christmas* (73)

Model Laraine Humphrys was cast in small roles in several productions during the '70s, including television shows *Barlow at Large, Space: 1999, The Benny Hill Show* and as a secretary in *Rough With The Smooth*. She was also

'The *Carry On* films could be quite challenging at times because the schedules were short. Six weeks to shoot a ninety-minute film means you've got to go some. One thing I learnt early on was that I had to get on with it and not mess about. I got a reputation for being not only quite good, but very quick, which used to get me a lot of work.

'I remember in *Sergeant* the actors had a rough time. We were shooting at barracks in Guildford with the real army and a real sergeant major putting them through their paces. He tried to make them look like genuine soldiers, a very difficult job. They were learning to be soldiers and being drilled, trying to get them to march and about turn – you can imagine what a shambles it was. It was a lot of fun working on that film, but they were always fun – I used to look forward to going to work. By the time Sunday came I was looking forward to Monday morning.

'I'll always remember *Cabby*. It was a good film to work on – quite difficult. There were a lot of close-ups in taxi cabs. When they were travelling along I was often hanging outside the cab with the camera, or fixing cameras on the bonnet or inside looking forward. It was difficult lining the shot up and getting the actors to look as if they were driving the taxi.

'While driving one of the cabs, Charlie Hawtrey banged into my car in the car park and made a dent. Not only did he do that, but he knocked my scooter down as well, making a few dents in that, too. They were side by side in the car park, although I don't know why I had them both there.

'They built the taxi office in the studio's car park. In fact, we never went very far. We used Windsor a lot for locations, usually down the side streets not the main drags. They were nearby and it was easy to park our equipment in the roads. We always had great cooperation from the police who'd occasionally close off roads so we had total control of proceedings.

'*Cruising*, the first colour film, was rather challenging. The ship was built on the studio stage at Pinewood but it was difficult to shoot, partly because we had backing that was supposed to look like seascapes and were supposed to be moving along. We got up to all sorts of little tricks like blowing smoke in front of the camera, just to give a sense of moving; and we'd have lights on jibs and move them up and down so that the balcony shadows underneath were moving, to create a sense of movement. It never went to sea, although we did go to Southampton to film the exterior of a ship with passengers getting on board, but that was about it.

'*Follow That Camel* was a challenge, too. We shot it at Camber Sands and erected artificial palm trees but the day we started the wind blew like hell and most of them came down. So we had to shoot away from where the palm trees would be while they were put up again. The camel we used was funny. It came from Chessington Zoo and when it was led out of the truck, everything looked fine. It walked across the concrete road without any problems but as soon as it touched the sand it wouldn't walk any further. It had been so used to concrete in the zoo, it wouldn't walk on sand. We had to put some big sheets of board down and persuade it gently, but it didn't like it at all. Such happy days!'

ALAN HUME

seen in *Say Hello to Yesterday* and 1979's *The Great Riviera Bank Robbery*. She continues to work as a model.

HUNTER, BERNARD
Role: Wine Waiter in *Regardless*
A busy character actor during the 1950s and '60s, Bernard Hunter is best known for his portrayal of Captain Pilsworthy in the comedy, *The Army Game*. Other small-screen credits include *Frankly Howerd* and *O. S. S.*

On the big screen, he was seen in such films as *The Tommy Steele Story*, *The Hellfire Club*, *Invasion Quartet*, *Raising the Wind* and *Operation Snatch*.

HUNTER, ROBIN
Role: Mr Darling in *Matron*
Born in London in 1929, Robin Hunter was raised in Hollywood where his father, actor Ian Hunter, worked for most of the year.

He trained at London's Webber Douglas Drama School and upon graduating was employed in the theatre for some years before screen work during the 1960s became a prominent part of his career. His big-screen credits included *Three Spare Wives*, *Doctor in Clover* and *Vampire Circus*. On television, his more notable credits were *Richard the Lionheart*, *The Troubleshooters*, *Up Pompeii* and *Poirot*.

He died in 2004, aged seventy-four.

HURNDELL, WILLIAM
Role: Riff in *Follow That Camel*
During the 1960s and '70s, William Hurndell chalked up several credits, mainly on television in shows like *Catch Hand*, *Danger Man*, *Doctor Who*, *Adam Adamant Lives!* and *The Borderers*.

His occasional film credits included 1965's *The City Under the Sea*.

HUSBAND
Played by Lauri Lupino Lane
In *Loving* he attends the Bliss's wedding reception at the Marie Antoinette Room. He joins in the fun when the cakes start flying by depositing a blancmange down his wife's cleavage, but he soon regrets his actions.

HUTCHINSON, BILL
Role: 1st Reporter in *Emmannuelle*
Bill Hutchinson's screen credits include the films *Battle Beneath the Earth*, *The Adding Machine*, *Diamonds Are Forever*, *Riders of the Storm* and, in 1992, *Bullseye!*. On television he appeared in *The Troubleshooters*, *Doctor Who*, *Doctor Caraibes*, *Lace* and *To Be the Best*.

HYDE-WHITE, WILFRID
Role: The Colonel in *Nurse*
Son of a vicar, Wilfrid Hyde-White, who established his name playing the quintessential Englishman, was born in the Gloucestershire town of Bourton-on-the-Water in 1903.

He decided he wanted to become an actor from an early age, against his parents' wishes, and trained at RADA. His first professional appearance was in 1922, aged nineteen, in *Tons of Money* on the Isle of Wight. His London debut, in *Beggar on Horseback*, came three years later, before countless stage appearances.

His film career, meanwhile, began in the 1930s and he was seen in plenty of cameos and more substantial parts throughout the rest of his life, which was latterly lived out in America. Arguably the zenith of his film career was playing Colonel Pickering in the 1964 movie, *My Fair Lady*. Other screen credits included *Two Way Stretch*, *Night Boat to Dublin*, *The Ghosts of Berkeley Square*, *My Brother's Keeper*, *Adam and Evelyne*, *Mr Denning Drives North* and *King Solomon's Treasure*. He was also seen occasionally on the small screen.

Hyde-White, who was declared bankrupt in 1979, died in Los Angeles in 1991, aged eighty-seven.

HYDES, JIM
Make-up artist on *Cabby* and *Jack*
Jim Hydes entered the film industry in the 1940s, with early credits including *Pastor Hall*, *London Belongs to Me* and *Once a Jolly Swagman*. Other credits ranged from *Appointment in London* and *Passport to Shame* to *Trouble With Eve* and *On the Beat*. Hydes also worked on numerous episodes of *The Avengers*.

IDEAL HOUSE EXHIBITION

At this major event in *Regardless* the staff of Helping Hands are hired to demonstrate some of the exhibits – with disastrous results.

IMI, TONY
Director of Photography on *That's Carry On*

Born in London in 1937, Tony Imi began working as a cinematographer in the 1960s; his early credits include several instalments for the long-running television series, *The Wednesday Play*, including the classic *Cathy Come Home*.

He began concentrating on films and worked on, among others, *The Raging Moon, Universal Soldier, The Firefighters, Robin Hood Junior, International Velvet* and *Enemy Mine*. Most recently he's been busy on *Three* and *Victims*.

Other television assignments include, during the 1980s, *The Life and Adventures of Nicholas Nickleby* and *The Return of Sherlock Holmes*, while in 1994 he worked on the mini-series, *Scarlett*.

IMMIGRATION OFFICER
Played by Dino Shafeek

The unfortunate airport official who questions Emmannuelle Prevert when she arrives in England on Concorde. Seen in *Emmannuelle*.

IMPERIAL ORDER OF THE BATH

Awarded to Hengist Pod in *Cleo* for bravery after he slays several enemies of Julius Caesar.

INFIELD-HOPPING, MONTGOMERY
Played by Terence Longdon

In *Regardless*, Mr Infield-Hopping arrives at the local labour exchange in a chauffeur-driven car, which he claims is a friend's. This upper-class character notices an advert for Helping Hands Limited and is first out of the labour exchange door en route to Mr Handy's office. Becomes one of Handy's team of helpers who's allocated a series of menial tasks.

INGRAM, JOAN
Role: Bald-headed Dowager in *Don't Lose Your Head*

After spending her early career in the theatre, character actress Joan Ingram entered the film industry in the 1940s, appearing in such films as *2000 Women* and *Miranda*. She was later cast in two Norman Wisdom comedies, playing Miss Denby in *Trouble in Store* and the theatre sister in *Just My Luck*.

During the 1960s and '70s she mainly divided her time between television and the stage. Her film credits were sporadic throughout this period, although she was seen as a woman in an art gallery in Dick Emery's *Ooh, You Are Awful* and, a year later in 1973, playing a lady in a butcher's shop in the film *Steptoe and Son Ride Again*.

INJURED FOOTBALLER
Played by Philip Clifton

Seen in Emmannuelle Prevert's flashback sequence in which she describes her most amorous experience. Appears in *Emmannuelle*.

INJURED RECRUIT
Played by Bernard Kay

A one-line role in *Sergeant*. The Injured Recruit, who's nursing a damaged arm, is seen waiting beside Horace to see Captain Clark in the sick quarters.

IRELAND, JILL
Role: Jill Thompson in *Nurse*

Born in Hounslow, Middlesex, in 1936, she initially trained as a ballet dancer, making her debut, aged twelve, at the Chiswick Empire; she later performed at the Palladium. Her ballet skills saw her cast in Powell and Pressburger's version of *Die Fledermaus, Oh, Rosalinda* in 1955, before she began concentrating on acting. Early film credits included *Simon and Laura, Three Men in a Boat, Hell Drivers* and *Raising the Wind*.

Ireland died in 1990, aged fifty-four, after a courageous fight against cancer. But she hadn't let the disease stop her working and, in 1986, appeared alongside her husband, Charles Bronson, in *Assassination*.

She'd moved to Hollywood with her first husband, actor David McCallum, in 1962 and was soon appearing in numerous television shows. Later film credits included *Breakheart Pass, From Noon Till Three, Love and Bullets* and *Caught*.

IRENE
Played by Jane White

In *Teacher*, Irene is one of the schoolkids who set out to cause havoc when a school inspector and child psychiatrist visit Maudlin Street Secondary Modern School.

IRVING, PENNY
Role: A 'Bird of Paradise' in *Dick*

Former model Penny Irving was born in Hitchin, Hertfordshire, in 1955. She regularly popped up on the screen, most notably as Miss Bakewell, Young Mr Grace's longest-serving secretary, in the BBC sitcom *Are You Being Served?*. Other appearances include playing Mary in several episodes of *Hi-De-Hi!*, and Pam in the first episode of *The Professionals*. On the big screen, she was seen as Chiquita in *Percy's Progress*, Sandy in the film version of *The Likely Lads*, a serving wench in *The Bawdy Adventures of Tom Jones* and in *Vampira* with David Niven. She's no longer in the profession.

ISAAK THE TAILOR
Played by John Clive

The Tailor is seen in *Dick*.

ITV NEWSCASTER
Played by Corbet Woodall

During *Emmannuelle* he's seen on the box reporting on the numerous affairs of Emmannuelle, the French Ambassador's sex-mad wife.

IVES, DOUGLAS
Role: Fanatic Patient in *Regardless*

Born in Sheffield in 1909, Douglas Ives appeared in small film and television roles during the 1950s and early '60s, mainly in comedies. His earlier film credits included *Innocents in Paris, Doctor in the House, Room in the House, Miracle in Soho, Left Right and Centre* and, later on, *A Home of Your Own* and *Be My Guest*.

On the small screen he was seen portraying numerous characters in *Dixon of Dock Green* and as Potter in the successful medical series, *Emergency – Ward 10*, a role he later reprised for the big-screen version, *Life in Emergency Ward 10*.

Ives died in 1969, aged fifty-eight.

J

JACK, CARRY ON
See feature box on pages 140–1.

JACKSI
An Afghanistan town high in the Himalayas, Jacksi is the base for Bunghit Din and his Burpas; seen in *Up The Khyber* when the Khasi of Kalabar visits to talk to the townsfolk about supporting his plans for an uprising against the British.

JACKSON
Played by Patrick Durkin
Seen in *Nurse*, Mr Jackson is a patient at Haven Hospital. When he leaves the ward, his bed is allocated to an emergency admission.

JACKSON, BRIAN
Role: Recruit in *Sergeant*
Born in Bolton in 1931, Brian Jackson began his working life in the Royal Navy, serving five years as an aircrew cameraman in the Fleet Air Arm. Always a keen amateur actor, he returned to civvy street and worked as a commercial photographer for a while before turning to acting professionally.

Jackson, who appeared as 'the man from Del Monte' in the successful run of commercials from the mid-1980s to early 90s, has diversified over the years. As well as acting – his screen credits include *Danger Man, The Avengers, The Persuaders!, Secret Army* and *The Tomorrow People*, and for the big screen *Taste of Fear, The Heroes of Telemark, Revenge of the Pink Panther* and, in 1992, *Shadowchaser* – he has produced on Broadway and in the West End, directed and has his own studio where soundtracks for, among others, *Chariots of Fire* and *Bladerunner* were recorded.

JACKSON, RON
Unit Manager on *Cowboy* and *Screaming!*
Working as a production manager since the 1970s, Ron Jackson has worked primarily on films, including *That's Your Funeral, Dracula A.D. 1972, Legend of the Werewolf, The Ghoul* and several big-screen spin-offs from successful sitcoms, such as *Nearest and Dearest, Love Thy Neighbour, Holiday on the Buses* and *George and Mildred*. One of the last productions he worked on was *A Ghost in Monte Carlo*, a project for television.

JACOBSON, HELLI LOUISE
Role: Nudist in *Behind*
Born in Copenhagen, Denmark, in 1949, Helli Louise Jacobson left school and worked as a translator for a time before joining a singing outfit touring various European countries, including Greece, Germany and Sweden. She eventually returned to her homeland and began her film career, primarily in sex comedies, before moving to the UK in 1970.

Here, her work involved modelling and a continuation of her acting career. She toured in the musical *Hair* in 1975, appeared in television shows such as Kenny Everett's *Up Sunday* in 1972, *The Benny Hill Show* and three episodes of *The Goodies*. Her Big Screen credits include *The Ups and Downs of a Handyman, The Confessions of a Pop Performer* and, her last film, *The World Is Full Of Married Men* in 1979.

Since quitting acting, she's run a musical agency and managed bands and various box offices for companies and venues, including London's Prince Edward Theatre. She's now a project controller for a medical market research company in London.

JACQUELINE
Played by Dany Robin
A young French girl who meets Sir Rodney Ffing in *Don't Lose Your Head*. When she finds herself imprisoned, Ffing – better known as the Black Fingernail – returns to France to free her.

JACQUES, HATTIE
Roles: Captain Clark in *Sergeant*, Matron in *Nurse*, Grace Short in *Teacher*, Sergeant Laura Moon in *Constable*, Sister in *Regardless*, Peggy Hawkins in *Cabby*, Matron in *Doctor*, Miss Haggerd in *Camping*, Matron in *Again Doctor*, Sophie Bliss in *Loving*, Beattie Plummer in *At Your Convenience*, Matron in *Matron*, Floella in *Abroad* and Martha Hoggett in *Dick*
TV: *Christmas* ('69), *Christmas* ('72) and *Orgy and Bess*

Hattie Jacques's large physique may have restricted the variety of roles she was asked to play, thereby preventing her from fully exploiting the tremendous talent she undoubtedly possessed, but she still forged a successful career for herself on stage and screen. A comely, attentive woman, she was equally adept portraying stern, uncompromising characters, such as Matron in *Nurse* and Sister in *Regardless*, and those revealing a vulnerability or lack of confidence.

Born in Sandgate, Kent, in 1924, Jacques was educated at the Godolphin and Latymer Schools. She trained as a hairdresser and served in the Second World War in the Red Cross and, later, at a factory in north London.

Her entry into the world of showbusiness happened at the Players' Theatre in London. Her debut at the venue in 1944 marked the beginning of a long association with the theatre: she returned on numerous occasions to appear in revues, plays, pantomimes and to direct the Players' Minstrels.

She became involved in various stage shows, including touring with the Young Vic's production of *The King Stag* during 1947-48;

Hattie Jacques was cast as a matron four times

CARRY ON JACK

An Anglo Amalgamated film
A Peter Rogers production
Distributed through Warner-Pathe
Distribution Ltd
Released as an A certificate in 1963
in Colour
Running time: 91 mins

CAST

Kenneth Williams . . . . Captain Fearless
Bernard Cribbins . . . . . . Midshipman Albert
Poop-Decker
Juliet Mills . . . . Sally
Charles Hawtrey . . . . Walter Sweetley
Percy Herbert . . . . Mr Angel, the Bosun
Donald Houston   1st Officer Jonathan
Howett
Jim Dale . . . . Carrier
Cecil Parker . . . . 1st Sealord
Patrick Cargill . . . . Spanish Governor
Ed Devereaux . . . . Hook
Peter Gilmore . . . . Patch
George Woodbridge . . . . Ned
Ian Wilson . . . . Ancient Carrier

Jimmy Thompson . . . . Nelson
Anton Rodgers . . . . Hardy
Michael Nightingale . . . . Town Crier
Frank Forsyth . . . . 2nd Sealord
John Brooking . . . . 3rd Sealord

Barrie Gosney . . . . Coach Driver
Jan Muzurus . . . . Spanish Captain
Vivian Ventura . . . . Spanish Secretary
Marianne Stone
Sally Douglas
Dorinda Stevens
Jennifer Hill
Rosemary Manley
Dominique Don
Marian Collins
Jean Hamilton . . . . Girls at 'Dirty Dick's'

PRODUCTION TEAM

Screenplay by Talbot Rothwell
Music composed and conducted by Eric
Rogers
Art Director: Jack Shampan
Director of Photography: Alan Hume
Editor: Archie Ludski
Associate Producer: Frank Bevis
Assistant Director: Anthony Waye
Camera Operator: Godfrey Godar
Sound Editor: Christopher Lancaster
Sound Recordist: Bill Daniels
Unit Manager: Donald Toms
Make-up Artists: Geoffrey Rodway and Jim
Hydes
Continuity: Penny Daniels
Hairdressing: Olga Angelinetta
Costume Designer: Joan Ellacott
Technical Advisor: Ian Cox
Producer: Peter Rogers
Director: Gerald Thomas

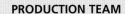

Captain Fearless (Kenneth Williams) never lived up to his name

From left to right: Albert Poop-Decker, Sally, Walter Sweetley and Captain Fearless on enemy territory

With Britain at war with Spain, Nelson's final words on his deathbed are that a bigger navy is required. To help boost the numbers, new recruits are sent off to sea even before they've passed through the naval academy; things are so desperate that even Albert Poop-Decker, who still hasn't graduated after eight and a half years, is given the rank of midshipman on the frigate *Venus*.

Upon arriving at Plymouth, where the ship is moored, a callow Mr Poop-Decker visits a local hostelry, which is full of plenty of dubious characters and local prostitutes. Whilst there he meets Sally, a friendly barmaid desperate to reach Spain to try and find her long-lost childhood sweetheart. When she hears Poop-Decker is heading south, she invites him upstairs, knocks him unconscious and steals his clothes and identity. She masquerades as Midshipman Poop-Decker, fooling everyone on board the frigate. When she later explains to Poop-Decker why she took such drastic actions, he feels sorry for the blonde – even though he's been pressganged into sailing as a lowly rating – and agrees not to blow the whistle on her until they reach Spain.

Meanwhile, Captain Fearless certainly isn't living up to his name: when a Spanish vessel is spotted, he avoids confrontation by sailing in the opposite direction, angering his battle-starved crew. Mr Angel and Mr Howett, the ship's bosun and first officer, have had enough of their captain's cowardice and hatch a plan to take over the ship's command. Desperate to avoid being convicted of mutiny, they pretend that the crew are being murdered by an unknown enemy and entrust the captain's safety to the hands of Mr Poop-Decker; as Captain Fearless flees with Sally, Poop-Decker and Walter Sweetley in a rowing boat, the first officer's plan pays dividends and he takes charge of the boat.

The group in the rowing boat, close to death, finally end up drifting onto the Spanish mainland where, to their surprise, they suddenly see *Venus* anchored in a port. Before long, they're on board and heading back to England, but before reaching home they encounter pirates, Sally comes face-to-face with her long-lost childhood sweetheart and they wipe out the Spanish Armada single-handedly.

Funny Scene!

The press-gang arrive at Dirty Dick's on the hunt for more sailors for the frigate *Venus*. Everyone rushes off except an inebriated Walter Sweetley, who's standing by the bar.

FIRST OFFICER HOWETT: (Seeing the pub is almost deserted.) Somebody must have warned them. (He spots Sweetley wavering at the bar and walks over.) Evening, friend.

SWEETLEY: Hello. (Giggles.)

HOWETT: You a sailor?

SWEETLEY: Who me? No, I'm a cesspit cleaner.

HOWETT: I wondered why there wasn't anybody else about. Wouldn't you like to go to sea, friend?

SWEETLEY: Like to go to see what?

HOWETT: Never mind. (Looks at Mr Angel, the bosun.) Sign the gentleman on, Mr Angel. (Mr Angel proceeds to whack him across the head.)

she also appeared in *Bells of St Martin's*, *Twenty Minutes South*, *Albertine By Moonlight* and *Large as Life*.

Her big break, however, was on radio. While learning her trade at the Players', she was spotted by Ted Kavanagh and invited to join the cast of the exceptionally popular series, *ITMA*. She settled quickly into the team and made a success, in particular, of the character Sophie Tuckshop, the greedy schoolgirl. Her adroitness across the airwaves led to work on other successful radio shows, including *Hancock's Half Hour*, playing Miss Pugh, and *Educating Archie*, as Agatha Danglebody; it was here that she met Eric Sykes, who was supplying scripts to the series, with whom she struck up a lasting relationship which saw them work together in various television series.

Other small-screen credits include *Catweazle*, *Doctor at Large*, *Our House*, *Miss Adventure*, *Knock Three Times*, *Howerd's Hour* and *The World of Beachcomber*. Her film work, meanwhile, covered serious roles in films such as *Green for Danger*, *Nicholas Nickleby*, *Oliver Twist*, *Trottie True*, *Chance of a Lifetime*, *Scrooge* and *The Pickwick Papers*, but eventually comedy became her forte and she was cast in such films as *The Love Lottery*, *The Square Peg*, *The Navy Lark*, *Follow a Star*, *School for Scoundrels* and *Watch Your Stern*.

Hattie Jacques, who was married to actor John Le Mesurier for several years, died suddenly in 1980, aged fifty-six.

JAGO, JUNE
Roles: Sister in *Regardless* and Sister Hoggett in *Doctor*

Australian-born actress June Jago had gained acting experience down-under by the time she came to England with the original company of *Summer of the Seventeenth Doll* in 1959.

She stayed this side of the world and worked on stage and screen: in the theatre she has enjoyed spells with the Royal Court and Royal Shakespeare companies, while on screen she has numerous credits to her name, including *Journey to the Unknown*, *Catweazle*, *Budgie* and *The Good Life*, as well as films such as *The Captain's Table*, *No Kidding*, *Journey Into Darkness*, *The Man From Snowy River* and, in 1986, *Departure*. Her most memorable role is, arguably, Gladys Worth in *Please Turn Over*.

She's now based in Australia.

JAILER
Played by Hugh Futcher

Seen in *Abroad* at the jail where the Brits are detained overnight after causing a disturbance at Madame Fifi's bawdyhouse.

JAKE
One of Sam Houston's men in *Cowboy*.

JAKE'S JEWELLERY/DRUGS
A shop seen in Stodge City in *Cowboy*.

JAMES, FRANCES
Played by Susan Beaumont

In *Nurse* the attractive nurse is at Ted York's bedside when he comes around after his operation. She doesn't get much sense out of him because all he can talk about is Ethel, the local barmaid, and enquiring about who stabbed him before pulling the nurse on to his bed.

JAMES, SIDNEY
Roles: Sergeant Frank Wilkins in *Constable*, Bert Handy in *Regardless*, Captain Wellington Crowther in *Cruising*, Charlie Hawkins in *Cabby*, Mark Antony in *Cleo*, Johnny Finger (The Rumpo Kid) in *Cowboy*, Sir Rodney Ffing (the Black Fingernail) in *Don't Lose Your Head*, Charlie Roper in *Doctor*, Sir Sidney Ruff-Diamond in *Up The Khyber*, Sid Boggle in *Camping*, Gladstone Screwer in *Again Doctor*, Bill Boosey in *Up the Jungle*, Sidney Bliss in *Loving*, King Henry VIII in *Henry*, Sid Plummer in *At Your Convenience*, Sid Carter in *Matron*, Vic Flange in *Abroad*, Sidney Fiddler in *Girls* and Dick Turpin (The Rev. Flasher) in *Dick*
TV: *Christmas* ('69), *Christmas* ('70), *What a Carry On!*, *Christmas* ('73), *Prisoner of Spenda*, *The Baron Outlook*, *The Sobbing Cavalier* and *Orgy and Bess*
STAGE: *London!*

First seen donning a policeman's uniform in *Constable*, Sid James became the linchpin for many of the films that followed, the anchor around which the stories revolved. With his crumpled face, dirty laugh and perfect timing, he was a stalwart of the film industry by the time he first appeared in the *Carry On*s and the confidence he exuded showed in an array of adroitly crafted characterisations.

James, son of vaudeville artists, was born in Johannesburg, South Africa, in 1913. He first arrived on British soil in 1946, determined to become a full-time actor; back home in Johannesburg he'd trained as a hairdresser and had run his own salon. But he'd set his heart on

The jovial Sid James

'Sid just loved doing the *Carry Ons*, partly because he knew it was a guarantee that he'd do two a year. He was the rock and everyone else bounced off him. He played it straight, which was his way of working really. He was a comedy actor up to a point, I suppose, but primarily an actor.

'He thoroughly enjoyed making them all, particularly *Cowboy* – that was his favourite. Oh, he loved *Cowboy* and even had lessons in how to ride a horse, attending lessons at the riding stable they had at Pinewood. He had a basic idea but was quite nervous about getting on a horse. Certainly for Sid, *Carry On Cowboy* was one of the best and I think shows just how much he enjoyed playing the part.

'My daughter also appears in a *Carry On*. She was about two when she played a little girl in *Constable*. Gerald wanted a little girl and we suggested her; she was in a scene with Sid.'

VALERIE JAMES – Sid James's widow

becoming an actor and had gained vital experience turning out for the Johannesburg Repertory Players, an amateur company, before enlisting for the South African Defence Force.

During the war he served in the Middle East with an anti-tank regiment and furthered his experience by working with an entertainments unit. After the cessation of hostilities, he headed for England and within a short period of arriving had secured an agent and a small part in a film.

Not cut out for the romantic leads, James made a decent living with his craggy appearance seeing him specialise in tough roles, often working-class guys, shifty individuals, army sergeants – the whole range of character studies. Through his work, particularly on the big screen, he quickly became a recognised character actor with credits such as *Night Beat*, *It Always Rains on Sunday*, *Once a Jolly Swagman*, *The Small Back Room*, *I Believe in You* and *The Gift Horse*. He was also seen in rep and worked at the Old Vic, often playing straight roles, but it wasn't long before his predilection for comedic roles came to the fore in films such as *The Lavender Hill Mob*, *Lady Godiva Rides Again*, *The Big Job*, *What a Carve Up*, *Raising the Wind*, *Double Bunk* and *The Pure Hell of St Trinian's*.

In his early forties, James joined the cast of the radio show, *Hancock's Half Hour*, and remained with the series when it transferred to the small screen. Although less experienced in radio, he quickly adapted to the medium and became a firm favourite with listeners. James enthused about the show and regarded it as one of the highlights of his career, but even he was eventually dropped when Tony Hancock decided to ring the changes and go it alone for the final series, simply titled *Hancock*.

James was devastated but his services were retained by the BBC when scriptwriters Galton and Simpson, who'd penned *Hancock's Half Hour*, provided him with his own show, *Citizen James*, which ran for three series between 1960-62.

More television roles followed in *East End, West End*; *Taxi*; *George and the Dragon*; *Two in Clover* and the popular sitcom, *Bless This House*, as well as continual parts in films.

A hardworking actor throughout his career, even a heart attack in 1967 failed to deter him from acting. Although it inevitably forced him to slow down during his period of recovery, he was still seen in *Doctor*, despite his ill-health restricting him to scenes sitting up in bed.

After touring Australia in *The Mating Season* to critical acclaim, he returned to the UK with the play. During the opening night at the Sunderland Empire in 1976, James suffered a further heart attack. He later died, aged sixty-two.

JANE
Played by Audrey Wilson
A saloon girl seen at Rumpo's Place in *Cowboy*.

JANE
Played by Elizabeth Knight
This petite blonde is seen in *Camping*. One of the girls from Chayste Place, a finishing school run by Dr Soaper and Miss Haggerd, she spends a few nights under canvas at the Paradise Camp Site in Devon, and a few hours with Peter Potter while the rest of the girls are out visiting a nearby abbey!

JANE
One of Henry VIII's former wives. He mentions her in *Henry* while talking to Queen Marie of Normandy; it appears he used to spend much time playing noughts and crosses with her in bed.

JELHI, PRINCESS
Played by Angela Douglas
The Khasi of Kalabar's kind-hearted daughter appears in *Up The Khyber*. She falls in love with Captain Keene, which explains why she warns him that her father is planning an uprising against the British. Also helps Lady Joan and the soldiers held captive escape the clutches of the Khasi when they face certain death.

JENKINS
Played by Vincent Ball
The PT instructor employed on the *Happy Wanderer*. Seen in *Cruising*, he catches the eye of not just Flo Castle, but Glad Trimble as well, even though she was supposed to be avoiding men on the trip.

JENKINS, MRS
Played by Amelia Bayntun
Dr Prodd is examining Mrs Jenkins at the Finisham Maternity Hospital when Nurse Ball brings a sample in for the doctor to assess. Deaf as a post, the aged Mrs Jenkins is, surprisingly, pregnant again. Seen in *Matron*.

JENNY
Played by Donna White
A saloon girl who frequents Rumpo's Place in *Cowboy*.

JEPSON, DR
An unseen character mentioned in *Cruising* by Captain Crowther. He was the previous ship's doctor until joining Consolidated Marmalade, with the company's former medical officer moving in the opposite direction.

JEREMY (Also known as the 'Expectant Father'.)
Played by Jim Dale
Seen in *Cabby*, a flustered Jeremy flags down Charlie Hawkins in his taxi when his pregnant wife goes into labour – or so he thinks. Hawkins is desperate to get home so he can take his wife out for an anniversary meal, so the last thing he wants is to make countless trips back and forth to the hospital thanks to a series of false alarms.

JESSON, PETER
Roles: Car Salesman in *Cabby*, Companion in *Cleo* and Lawrence in *Follow That Camel* (Note: the scene was cut from the film.)
A busy screen actor during the 1960s and early '70s, Peter Jesson appeared in television shows such as *Dixon of Dock Green*, *Suspense*, *Sherlock Holmes* and *Menace*. His film credits include *Twice Round the Daffodils*, *The Iron Maiden* and *The Big Job*.

JOE
Played by an uncredited actor
One of Sam Houston's men in *Cowboy*, Joe, a cowhand, is sitting beside a camp fire watching the cattle when he's attacked by Rumpo's men.

JOEY
Sid and Beattie Plummer's pet budgie in *At Your Convenience* hasn't made a sound until he suddenly starts picking winners at the horse racing, earning his owners a fortune in the process. When Sid started reading out the runners in the previous day's races, he noticed that the bird tweeted when he heard the name of the horse who – as Sid confirmed – won the race.

JOHNS, MALCOLM
Role: Sentry in *Emmannuelle*

During the 1960s and '70s, Malcolm Johns made occasional appearances on the screen. He played a soldier in *The Troubleshooters*, a workman in *Bless This House* and a Swiss boyfriend in the 1970 film, *Perfect Friday*.

JOHNSON, GLORIA
Role: Vestal Virgin in *Cleo*

Gloria Johnson made occasional screen appearances during the period she played a Vestal Virgin in *Cleo*. In the 1963 film, *What a Crazy World*, she was cast as a dancer.

JOHNSON, JUDI
Roles: Funhouse Girl in *Spying* and Gloria's Bridesmaid in *Cleo*

JOHNSON, SIDNEY
Role: Man in Glasses in *Behind*

Born in London in 1904, Sidney Johnson worked in the civil service, based at Somerset House, upon leaving school, before, at nineteen, heading for Australia and finding a job on a sheep farm.

He returned to England, trained as a commercial artist and ran his own publicity firm until he was sixty, when he fulfilled a lifetime ambition to work on the stage. From the 1930s he'd been involved in amateur dramatics (he'd also helped with ENSA concerts in Hertfordshire during the Second World War), but he secured an agent and was soon working professionally.

As well as plenty of stage roles, including several in the West End working with the likes of Donald Sinden, John Mills and Judi Dench, he began appearing on the screen. His television credits included one-off roles in *The Troubleshooters*, *Doctor Who*, *Arthur of the Britons* and *The Venturers*, while he had a short running part in *Crossroads*, playing Mr Mouri. His film credits included *A Nice Girl Like Me*, *Runners*, *Chitty Chitty Bang Bang* and his last picture, 1983's *Fords on Water*.

He was due to begin location filming on a BBC production the day he died of a heart attack in 1990, aged eighty-six.

JOHNSON, VIVIENNE
Role: Freda in *England*
TV: *The Case of the Coughing Parrot*, *And in My Lady's Chamber* and *Who Needs Kitchener?*

Sheffield-born Vivienne Johnson, normally cast as mistresses and femmes fatales, trained as a secondary teacher before working as an acting assistant stage manager in rep. She performed with various companies around the country, including Sheffield, Leicester and Manchester, before making her West End debut.

Film work soon followed, including *Yesterday's Hero* in 1979, and appearances in various television shows, such as *Odd Man Out*, *The Sweeney*, *Potter* and *Open All Hours*. After taking a break from the business to bring up her son, Johnson resumed her acting career and has made occasional screen appearances in programmes such as *Comedy of Errors*. Also works as a supply teacher.

JONAH, WILLIE
Role: A Nosha in *Up the Jungle*

Working on television from the 1960s, Willie Jonah has been cast in the likes of *Mogul*, *Jason King*, *Quiller*, *Angels*, *The Enigma Files*, *Terry and June* and, most recently, *Doctors*. His film credits include *The Bushbaby*, *Shaft in Africa*, *Being Human* and *Boesman and Lena*.

JONES, DOCTOR
Unseen in *Emmannuelle* but constantly referred to by Mrs Valentine during her conversations with her mollycoddled son, Theodore. He told Mrs Valentine that her son was very delicate when six months old and she's always had total confidence in the man of medicine.

JONES, HELGA
Role: Harem Girl in *Follow That Camel*

JONES, MISS
Played by Margaret Nolan

The commissioner's girlfriend in *Cowboy*. Seen kissing and cuddling the official until they're interrupted by Perkins, the commissioner's assistant.

JONES, MR
Played by Frank Thornton

Manager of Bourne and Jones, a milliner's shop in *Screaming!*.

JONES, PETER
Roles: Chaplain in *Doctor* and Brigadier in *England*

Peter Jones was born in Wem, Shropshire, in 1920; his career, which spanned more than six decades, often saw him portraying spivs with a cockney accent as he established himself as a regular in the British comedies of the 1950s and '60s.

He was completing his education at Ellesmere College when he contracted tuberculosis and spent a year recuperating. His medical history later prevented him joining the forces during the Second World War.

At the sanatorium he developed an interest in acting and soon after played an old man in *The Composite Man* at Wolverhampton. While performing in a production at Shrewsbury, Jones was spotted by a radio producer and offered a part in the Arnold Bennett radio play, *The Card*, marking the beginning of a busy radio career that would include becoming a stalwart on the panel game, *Just A Minute*.

He made his West End debut, aged twenty-two, in *The Doctor's Dilemma*, and his first film appearance in a bit part in *Fanny by Gaslight*. Other credits in this medium included *Dead of Night*, *I See A Dark Stranger*, *School for Scoundrels*, *Vice-Versa*, *Chance of a Lifetime*, *The Franchise Affair*, *The Magic Box* and *The Yellow Balloon*.

When film parts dried up, offers for television work came his way, including roles in *Beggar My Neighbour* and, most notably, Mr Fenner in *The Rag Trade*.

He died in 2000, aged seventy-nine.

JONES, ROBERT
Art Director on *Girls*

JOSH THE UNDERTAKER
Played by Davy Kaye

The busiest man in Stodge City, the cigar-puffing Josh Moses, who's seen in *Cowboy*, runs the city's undertaker's and walks around with a smile on his face because business hasn't been as brisk as when the Rumpo Kid – who sprays bullets like there's no tomorrow – rides into town.

JOY
Played by Georgina Moon

One of the girls who arrives at the Paradise Camp in *Camping*.

JUDD, EDWARD
Role: 5th Storeman in *Sergeant*

Born to British parents in Shanghai, China, in 1932, leading actor Edward Judd began his acting career as a teenager on stage in China before travelling to England, aged fifteen, to make his film debut in 1948's *The Small Voice*.

During a career encompassing stage and screen, he was seen in films such as *The Good Die Young*, *The Man Upstairs*, *The Shakedown*, *Sink the Bismarck!*, *The Day the Earth Caught Fire*, *Mystery Submarine*, *Invasion*, *Living Free*, *Night Train to Murder* and *The Kitchen Toto*.

He was also busy on television, popping up in shows such as *Ghost Squad*, *Hunter's Walk*, *Angels*, *The Sweeney*, *Casualty*, *Intrigue* and *Flambards*.

JULIAN, CHARLES
Role: Old Man in Ruby Room in *Regardless*

Other screen appearances include four episodes of *Hancock's Half Hour*.

JUNE
Played by Jacki Piper

Lady Bagley's maid in *Up the Jungle*, June is meek and mild until she meets Cecil, the Jungle Boy, at a lake and ends up falling in love. When the expedition finally arrives home, after escaping from the Noshas and the Lubidubies, June marries Cecil; the trouble is, unable to rid himself of all his jungle habits, they end up living, with their baby, in a treehouse in London.

KAREN, ANNA

Roles: Hefty Girl in *Camping* and Wife in *Loving*

Born in Durban, South Africa, in 1936, Anna Karen left her homeland in 1952 to attend LAMDA. After graduating she worked in Variety for years, but small parts in films and on television soon followed: on the big screen she was seen in *Nudist Memories*, *The Sandwich Man* and *Poor Cow* while on the box she was spotted in *Dixon of Dock Green*.

Her biggest role to date is playing Olive in the popular sitcom *On the Buses*, which ran to seventy-six episodes over four years. Other series she's appeared in include *The Rag Trade*, *Trouble and Strife* and *Revolver*. Most recently she's been seen in the David Jason-directed drama *The Second Quest* for ITV. Throughout her career, Anna Karen has frequently appeared in the theatre.

KASKET, HAROLD

Role: Hotel Gentleman in *Follow That Camel*

Born in London in 1926, Harold Kasket began his career as an impressionist before breaking into films with 1948's *No Orchids for Miss Blandish*. Over the next four decades he appeared in over fifty pictures and many television shows, often playing foreigners.

His big-screen credits included *The House of the Arrow*, *Beau Brummell*, *Out of the Clouds*, *Man of the Moment*, *The Scapegoat*, *The Navy Lark*, *Carlton-Browne of the F.O.*, *Arabesque* and *Trail of the Pink Panther*. On television he was seen in such shows as *Zero One*, *Hancock's Half Hour*, *Special Branch* and several episodes of *The Tomorrow People* playing Lord Dunning.

He died in 2002, aged seventy-five.

KATIE

Played by an uncredited actress

She's seen in the arms of the parish constable in *Dick*, giggling and having a bit of fun inside one of the police cells. Young enough to be the constable's granddaughter, the policeman's excuse is that her husband beats her and so he's trying to cheer her up; what he doesn't admit is that he's simply a dirty old man. She's a resident in

the parish of Upper Dencher who obviously likes a bit of extra-marital fun because she's also having an affair with Bodkin, landlord of the Old Cock Inn. Her husband eventually finds out when Bodkin, realising he's left his hat at her place, returns to collect it.

KAVANN, DARRYL

Role: Punchy in *Cabby*

Darryl Kavann played small parts during the 1960s and '70s, appearing in television shows such as *Man in a Suitcase*, *Out of the Unknown* and, in 1979, *Crime and Punishment*. He also appeared in occasional films.

KAY, BERNARD

Role: Injured Recruit in *Sergeant*

Bernard Kay, born in Bolton, Lancashire, in 1928, graduated from the Old Vic School and began a busy stage and screen career with his appearance in *Sergeant*. Other film credits include *Doctor Zhivago*, *They Came From Beyond Space*, *Interlude*, *The Hunting Party*, *The Great Riviera Bank Robbery*, *Steal This Movie* and 2004's *Puritan*.

On television he's appeared in such programmes as *The Baron*, *The Champions*, *Barlow at Large*, *Hannay*, *Doctors* and has had running parts in, among others, *Compact*, *Crossroads* and *Century Falls*.

KAYE, DAVY

Roles: Josh the Undertaker in *Cowboy* and Benny in *At Your Convenience*

Born in London in 1916, the diminutive Davy Kaye won a talent competition at Mile End Hippodrome and subsequently joined a double-act, Kaye and Vale, performing at Variety venues in the early 1930s. When the act split two years later, he continued in Variety before breaking into the theatre, initially in a West End production of *Guys and Dolls*.

During the 1950s he became resident host at the Embassy Club in London's Bond Street and stayed twelve years, by which time he'd started appearing on the screen in films such as *Fun at St Fanny's*, *The Pot Carriers* and *The World Ten Times Over*. Other credits in this medium

included *Crooks in Cloisters*, *Those Magnificent Men in Their Flying Machines*, *Chitty Chitty Bang Bang*, *Top of the Bill* and *A Nightingale Sang in Berkeley Square*.

His occasional television credits ranged from *It Takes A Thief* to *You Rang, M'Lord?*, and in 1981 he played Lord Mullrine in several episodes of *Sapphire and Steel*.

He died while holidaying in the Bahamas in 1998, aged eighty-one.

KEEN, PENNY

Role: Girl in *Don't Lose Your Head*

KEENE, CAPTAIN

Played by Roy Castle

The commander of the Devils in Skirts, alias the 3rd Foot and Mouth company, is seen in *Up The Khyber*. He's first to learn of the Khasi of Kalabar's plans for an uprising and leads an operation across the border into Afghanistan to try and recover a photo, showing the British soldiers wearing pants under their kilts, which has jeopardised the safety of the entire British force.

KEITH, PENELOPE

Role: Nurse in *Doctor* (Note: the scene was cut.)

For many she'll always be associated with playing Margo Leadbetter, the kind-hearted snob in *The Good Life*, but she's played a host of roles on screen and stage during a long career.

Born in Sutton, Surrey, in 1940, she always wanted to become an actress but received a temporary setback when she was rejected by the Central School of Dramatic Art for being too tall. Eventually accepted by the Webber Douglas Academy, she spent two years training before launching her professional career in rep around the country, beginning at Chesterfield.

Her first big break arrived in 1963 when she joined the Royal Shakespeare Company at Stratford and the Aldwych Theatre, London.

At this point her television appearances had been few and were limited to minor roles in shows such as *The Army Game*, *Emergency – Ward 10* and *Hadleigh*. But in 1965 she was cast in her first lead role, playing Lady Pandora Brewster in *There Is A Happy Land*, an hour-long play for Granada's *Six Shades of Black* series.

Although theatre has always remained her primary source of employment, she's made frequent appearances on television, including key roles in *The Pallisers*, *Kate*, *Two's Company* and, of course, leading roles in *To the Manor Born*, *Executive Stress* and *Next of Kin*.

KELLY, SAM
Roles: Sir Roger's Coachman in *Dick* and Projectionist in *Behind*
Mancunian actor Sam Kelly, born in 1943, trained at LAMDA after working for three years in the civil service in Liverpool. He graduated from drama school in 1967 and was soon spotted uttering one line as a newspaper reporter in an episode of *Emergency – Ward 10*.

Four years of rep work around the UK followed, including spells at Liverpool, Sheffield and Lincoln.

On the small screen, Kelly's credits include a series of *The Dave Allen Show*, *The Dick Emery Show*, playing Bob Challis in *Coronation Street*, Mr Snagsby in *Bleak House*, Norman in two series of *Now and Then*, Captain Geering in three series of *'Allo,'Allo!*, Grunge in two series of *Haggard*, Sam in three series of *On the Up* and Warren in *Porridge*.

Kelly, who's also appeared in a handful of films, including the *Porridge* movie, continues to act. More recently, he appeared in a ten-part series, *Barbara*, for Carlton, and *Beauty*.

KEMP, FRANCES
Played by Gwendolyn Watts
Seen in *Matron* working on the reception desk at Finisham Maternity Hospital.

KEMP, SALLY
Role: Girl with Cow in *Camping*
Born in 1939, Sally Kemp, daughter of Frank Kemp of the Essoldo cinema circuit, started her acting career in rep, appearing at various places around the British Isles, including Huddersfield, Southport and Bradford, as well as summer seasons at Filey, and Pwllheli. She also spent a year at the Palace Theatre, Watford.

Her film credits include *Behemoth*, *The Monster*, *The Nightcallers* and *The Pale-Faced Girl*, while on television she appeared in the likes of *Z Cars*, *Emergency – Ward 10* and *Silas Marner*.

KENNEDY, KEN
Role: Wall-eyed Man in *Constable*

KENT, FAITH
Role: Berkeley Nursing Home Matron in *Again Doctor*
Born in New York, USA; Faith Kent's father was a journalist employed by one of the country's

national papers while her mother was an actress. After leaving school she undertook several jobs before turning to acting. With her mother against drama schools, she pursued an alternative route into the profession, eventually being employed as an understudy in a production of *Vanity Fair*, where she met her husband, Anthony Nicholls.

She stopped work to raise a family but returned to the profession and, before long, made her film debut in 1964's *The Pumpkin Eater*, with her late husband playing the psychiatrist and their daughters playing her screen children. By this time, she'd already begun working on the small screen, with early credits including *Z Cars* and *Emergency – Ward 10*. Other television credits include *Dr Finlay's Casebook*, *Family Way*, *Emmerdale Farm*, *Blind Justice*, *Casualty* and fourteen months playing Olive King in *Eldorado*.

On the big screen she's been seen in films such as *Our Mother's House*, *Half-Moon Street*, *Home At Midnight* and *Beyond Bedlam*.

Over the years, she's regularly performed on stage, particularly in fringe theatre, while at the Edinburgh Festival she appeared in *Celestial Blue* and her own successful one-woman show, which she devised, directed and co-wrote.

Most recently, she's popped up in two episodes of *Little Britain*, the BBC children's serial *Looking for Tracy Beaker*, performed in fringe theatre and made a commercial.

KENWRIGHT, BILL
Role: Reporter in *Matron*
Now chairman of Everton Football Club, Bill Kenwright was born on Merseyside in 1945. During the 1960s he began appearing on the screen in films and television shows such as *King of the River*, *Dixon of Dock Green*, *The Liver Birds* and *The Zoo Gang*. But he's probably best remembered as Gordon Clegg in *Coronation Street*.

Now runs his own company, Bill Kenwright Limited, the UK's largest independent theatre and film production company. One of his most recent productions is the musical *Brighton Rock*, which opened in London in 2004.

KERNAN, DAVID
Role: Nicholas Phipps in *Abroad*
Born in London in 1938, David Kernan entered films and television in the late 1950s, beginning with the series, *On the Bright Side*. Other small-screen credits include *Dixon of Dock Green*; *The Avengers*; *Brett* and *Upstairs, Downstairs*. On the big screen he was seen in films such as *Mix Me A Person*, *Jailbreak*, *Farewell Performance*, *Zulu*, *Otley*, *The Chastity Belt*, *The Day of the Jackal* and *The Education of Sonny Carson*.

A busy stage actor, he's appeared in many productions, including *A Little Night Music* and *1776*, and is now a producer/director.

KERR, FRASER
Role: Houseman in *Regardless*
Born in Glasgow in 1932, Fraser Kerr began studying medicine at Glasgow University after leaving school but was soon enticed into the acting world, beginning as assistant stage manager at the Park Theatre, Glasgow.

Other than a break to complete National Service in the army, Kerr spent his entire working life as an actor. Back in civvies, he worked at Edinburgh Rep and managed a company at Retford, Nottingham.

On screen from the early 1960s, his television work included appearances in *Dixon of Dock Green*; *On the Buses*; *Doctor in the House*; *Mind Your Language*; *Yes, Minister*; *Kidnapped* and *Howard's Way*, playing Robert McIntyre. He appeared occasionally in films but was busiest on radio, making over 600 broadcasts for the BBC Drama Repertory Company.

He died in 2000, aged sixty-nine.

KEYS, BASIL
Associate Producer on *Regardless*
In films since the late 1940s, Basil Keys credits as assistant director, production manager and associate producer include *Don't Ever Leave Me*, *Operation Disaster*, *Tony Draws A Horse*, *The Sea Shall Not Have Them*, *Circus Friends*, *Zulu*, *Gumshoe* and his last film, *The Greek Tycoon*.

KEYS, ROD
Editor on *Cowboy*, *Screaming!* and *Don't Lose Your Head*
Other film credits Rod Keys has worked on as editor include *The Big Job* and *Island of the Burning Dead*.

KHASI OF KALABAR, THE
Played by Kenneth Williams
One of the richest, most powerful men in the northwest province of India, the Khasi, who's called Randy, was educated at Oxford before returning to his own country. Seen in *Up The Khyber*, he takes every possible opportunity to try and rid his country of British occupancy, which explains his eagerness at getting hold of a photo, secretly taken by Lady Joan Ruff-Diamond, of British soldiers from the 3rd Foot and Mouth, wearing underpants under their kilts. A man of many wives, the Khasi has a daughter, Princess Jelhi.

KHASI'S WIVES
Played by Wanda Ventham, Liz Gold, Vicki Woolf, Anne Scott, Barbara Evans, Lisa Noble, Eve Eden, Tamsin MacDonald and Katherina Holden
The wives of the Khasi of Kalabar appear in *Up The Khyber*. Some of them 'entertain' Sir Sidney Ruff-Diamond while his wife tries winning the heart of the Khasi.

KIFA HOTEL

A hotel in Algiers frequented by Lady Jane Ponsonby on her journey to find Bertram West, who's joined the Foreign Legion in *Follow That Camel*.

KILMORE, DR JIM

Played by Jim Dale

Chirpy Dr Kilmore works at the Borough County Hospital. Seen in *Doctor*, he's like a breath of fresh air around the wards; cracking jokes and sporting a perpetual smile, he's popular among patients and nurses alike, but his unorthodox style of doctoring isn't everyone's cup of tea and he's particularly disliked by Matron and Dr Tinkle.

When he's subsequently accused of being a sex maniac after a misconstrued incident on the roof of the nurses' home, he sees no alternative but to tender his resignation, only to be reinstated after the patients make a stand and decide drastic action is required.

KINDLY SEAMAN

Played by Alan Casley

In *Cruising* the Kindly Seaman helps Bridget Madderley through the crowds to the railings of the *Happy Wanderer*, enabling her to wave goodbye as the ship leaves port.

KING, DELIA

Played by Liz Fraser

Joins Helping Hands Limited in *Regardless* because she's frustrated at not being able to secure an interesting job. One of her first assignments at Bert Handy's company is modelling a new wardrobe of clothes a man intends buying his wife as a surprise anniversary present. When his beloved returns home unexpectedly, though, Delia has no choice but to hide in the cupboard.

KING GEORGE V WARD

One of the wards at the Haven Hospital in *Nurse*.

KITKATA

Played by Sally Douglas

Big Heap's new squaw in *Cowboy* whom he bought for two buffalo skins.

KLAUBER, GERTAN

Roles: Code Clerk in *Spying*, Marcus in *Cleo*, Spiv in *Follow That Camel* **(Note: scene cut from film although Klauber can still be seen.)**, Wash Orderly in *Doctor*, Bidet in *Henry*, Postcard Seller in *Abroad* and German Soldier in *Emmannuelle*

Born in Germany in 1932, character actor Gertan Klauber has been working in British films and television since the late '50s. His big-screen credits include *Don't Panic Chaps!*, *Three On A Spree*, *The Breaking Point*, *The Big Job*, *Up the Front*, *Operation Daybreak*, *Octopussy*, *Backbeat* and, in 2001, the TV movie, *Fugee Girl*.

He's appeared many times on television in shows such as *Crane*, *Doctor Who*, *Secret Agent*, *The Saint*, *The Prisoner*, *Hadleigh*, *Paul Temple*, *The Protectors*, *Whatever Happened to the Likley Lads?*, *Inspector Morse*, *The Famous Five* and, in 2003, *Red Cap*.

KNIGHT, ELIZABETH

Roles: Jane in *Camping* and Nurse Willing in *Again Doctor*

Elizabeth Knight first appeared on screen in the 1960s, with television credits including *Cluff*; *Within These Walls*; *Sorry, I'm Single*; *It's Awfully Bad For Your Eyes, Darling* and BBC's 1980 series, *Pride and Prejudice*. Her film work covers such pictures as *Oliver!*, *Villain*, *McCabe and Mrs Miller* and *Doing Time*.

KNIGHT, ROSALIND

Roles: Nurse Nightingale in *Nurse* and Felicity Wheeler in *Teacher*

Born in London in 1933, Rosalind Knight left secondary education and enrolled at London's

School inspector Felicity Wheeler (Rosalind Knight, right) prepares for fisticuffs with Sarah Allcock (Joan Sims) (*Teacher*)

Old Vic Theatre School. After graduating in 1952, she made her acting debut at Coventry, in a Midland Theatre Company's production of *Hobson's Choice*, playing Ada Figgins, before moving on to other rep companies, such as Ipswich, West of England Theatre Company (based in Exmouth), Amersham and Hornchurch.

Her television debut was in a 1955 production of *Nicholas Nickleby*, while her favourite roles in the medium include Great Aunt Effie in 1997's series, *Berkeley Square*, and Beryl Merit in BBC's *Gimme, Gimme, Gimme*.

Other films she's appeared in include *Blue Murder at St Trinian's*, *The Wildcats of St Trinian's*, *Prick Up Your Ears*, *Tom Jones* and *It Could Happen To You*.

Knight, who was classically trained and has worked extensively for the Royal Shakespeare Company, remains busy in all strands of the profession with recent appearances including *Jack and the Beanstalk* for the Henson Organisation.

KNOWLES, JOSEPHINE
Continuity on *Up the Jungle* and *Loving*
Other films Josephine Knowles worked on include *Those Fantastic Flying Fools*, *Here We Go Round the Mulberry Bush*, *Alfred the Great*, *When Dinosaurs Ruled the Earth*, *Fragment of Fear*, *Quest for Love*, *Flash Gordon* and *Loophole*.

KNUTT, MARSHALL P.
Played by Jim Dale
Poor old Marshall Knutt is an unassuming kind of guy who happens to find himself being sent to one of the most dangerous places in the Wild

West. A drainage, sanitation and garbage disposal engineer, Marshall is a graduate of the Chipping Sodbury Technical College who's job-hunting. He happens to visit the Bureau of Internal Affairs with his certificate and reference from a Lady Pushing when a frantic search is on for a marshal to try and clean up Stodge City. The commissioner picks up on Knutt's Christian name, thinks he's actually a marshal and offers him the job.

Worryingly, Knutt, who's seen in *Cowboy*, doesn't know one end of a gun from the other and has Annie Oakley, whom he finally marries, to thank for saving his life when the stage coach they're travelling in is attacked by Indians. Oakley is a crackshot who's travelling to Stodge to hunt down the man who killed her father, the previous marshal.

Knutt manages to stay alive, thanks largely to Annie, and uses his knowledge of drains to finally outwit the Rumpo Kid and his gang,

returning Stodge City back to the tranquillity it once knew.

KONYILS, CHRIS
Role: A Nosha in *Up the Jungle*
Other credits include three appearances in *Doctor Who* between 1965 and '68, as well as playing a policeman in the 1969 film, *The Bed-Sitting Room*.

KOUMANI, MAYA
Role: Amazon Guard in *Spying*
On screen since the 1950s, primarily in films, Maya Koumani has been seen in *Fire Maidens of Outer Space*, *It's A Wonderful World*, *The Fighting Wildcats*, *Assignment Redhead*, *The Diplomatic Corpse* and *The Price of Silence*.

KUKU ISLANDS
When Lewis Boggs takes Myrtle Plummer to the pictures in *At Your Convenience*, the first feature is set on the islands.

L

L. & H. NATHAN LIMITED
A costumier which supplied the costumes on *Henry*.

L'AUBERGE DE CALAIS
A public house in *Don't Lose Your Head* which Citizens Camembert and Bidet visit while searching for the Black Fingernail, who was last seen disguised as a woman.

LADY
The police dog in *Constable* is an Alsatian and a real handful, as PC Benson discovers when he's given the unenviable job of exercising her.

LADY
Played by Joy Harrington
In the opening scenes of *Dick*, depicting the Bow Street Runners' success in combating lawlessness, the Lady is seen walking along the road. Concealed under her hooped skirt is a member of the Runners, who's able to spring into action by apprehending a criminal who stops her at gunpoint.

LADY, 1st, 2nd and 3rd
Played by Jennifer Clulow, Valerie Van Ost and Jacqueline Pearce
The ladies attend Sir Rodney Ffing's charity ball in *Don't Lose Your Head* and are seen talking to the Duc de Pommfrit.

LADY IN LOW-CUT DRESS
Played by Alexandra Dane
A member of the audience at Professor Crump's lecture and film show in *Behind*.

LADY WITH HAT
Played by Lucy Griffiths
She attends Professor Crump's archaeological lecture and film show in *Behind*.

LAKE, JANETTA
Role: Girl with Dog in *Constable*

LAMONT, PETER
Assistant Art Director on *Matron*
Born in London in 1929, Peter Lamont, who's now a regular on the James Bond crew, started his career as a draughtsman on such 1950s films as *The Importance of Being Earnest* and *Miracle of Soho*; by the '60s he was plying his trade as a set dresser on films like *Watch Your Stern*, *Night of the Eagle* and *This Sporting Life*.

After working as assistant art director on 1968's *Chitty Chitty Bang Bang* he began securing jobs as art director and, in 1973, was engaged on *Live and Let Die*, the first of eleven Bond movies he's worked on. He's currently assigned to the next Bond picture, which is in pre-production.

Other film credits include *Aliens*, *Consuming Passions* and, in 1997, *Titanic*.

LANCASTER, ANN
Role: Miss Armitage in *Again Doctor*
Ann Lancaster, born in London in 1920, began her career in rep before branching out into films and television during the 1950s.

Her television credits include episodes of *The Vise*; *Hancock's Half Hour*; *Out of the Unknown*; *The Spies*; *Please, Sir!* and various roles in *The World of Beachcomber*. She was also cast, usually in small parts, in films such as *The Magic Box*, *Angels One Five*, *The Durant Affair*, *Bunny Lake Is Missing*, *A Nice Girl Like Me* and her last picture, *The Railway Children*.

She died in 1970, aged fifty.

LANCASTER, CHRISTOPHER
Sound Editor on *Jack*, *Spying* and *Cleo*.
Dubbing Editor on *That's Carry On*
Born in Fulham in 1930, Christopher Lancaster left school at fourteen and worked at Riverside Studios as a runner. The war years meant film technicians were scarce and he grabbed the opportunity to move into the cutting room, initially as an assistant editor. He transferred to Lime Grove and worked for Sydney Box Productions on a host of films, including 1948's *Good Time Girl* with Jean Kent and Dennis Price.

After completing National Service in the RAF, he returned to the film world at Pinewood Studios. After ten years as assistant editor he was promoted to editor and later offered the chance to move into sound editing, his early assignments being *A Town Like Alice* and *Reach For The Sky*.

He turned freelance at the end of the 1960s and retired, after more than five decades in the business, in 1992.

LANDLADY
Played by Marianne Stone
The landlady of the L'Auberge de Calais in *Don't Lose Your Head*. While searching for the Black Fingernail, Citizens Camembert and Bidet enter the public house; so desperate are they to find their man, who was last seen disguised as a woman, that they even try examining the landlady to check she's female.

LANDLORD, THE
Played by Stanley Unwin
Owns the building in Denver Street which houses Helping Hands Limited in *Regardless*. Talks gobbledygook, which means nobody, except language expert Francis Courtenay, can understand a word he's saying.

LANDLORD, THE
Played by David Lodge
Owns the pub near the Riverside Caravan Site in *Behind*. A loud, guffawing guy who annoys Fred Ramsden and Ernie Bragg. He tells them that he sold the field on which the caravan site is situated to Major Leep for £2000 because Roman mining left gaping holes just under the surface.

LANGDON, DONALD
Executive Producer for Cleves Investment Limited on *Emmannuelle*

LANGTON, DIANE
Role: Private Alice Easy in *England*
TV: *The Prisoner of Spenda*, *The Baron Outlook* and *One in the Eye for Harold*
Diane Langton trained at the Corona Academy in London and started her professional career as a dancer. Nowadays she's often seen on television: one of her notable roles in recent years was playing Ruby Rowan, Nick's mother, in *Heartbeat*. She's also appeared in shows such as *The Rag Trade*, *The Bill*, *Joking Apart*, *How To Be A Little Sod*, *EastEnders*, *Chicago* and *Holby City*.

Her stage credits include playing Miss Lucy and Pearl Lamonte in *Sweet Bird of Youth* and *Johnny On A Spot* respectively, at the Royal National Theatre, Vi in *Steaming* and Viv Nicholson in *Spend, Spend, Spend* at the Piccadilly Theatre.

She's also appeared in a handful of films, such as *Don't Just Lie There, Say Something*; *Percy's Progress*; *Eskimo Nell*; *Confessions of a Pop Performer* and *Trial By Combat*.

LARRY
Title sketches for *Doctor*, *Up The Khyber*, *Camping* and *Girls*
Real name Terence Parkes, this well-known cartoonist was born in Birmingham in 1927. He enrolled at the Birmingham School of Art but his studies were interrupted by two years' national service, spent in the army.

In 1948 he returned to art school, specialising in book illustration, and began selling the occasional piece to the local rag. After graduating he drifted into teaching children of the workers at Perkins Diesel in Peterborough, but realising it wasn't the career for him, returned to Birmingham and was employed in the Lucas Turbines factory. Drawing cartoons in his spare time, he sold his first piece to *Punch* magazine in 1954.

Two years later he was a cartoonist on the *Daily Express*, but the job never worked out and he left after three months. Within a year he was selling sufficient quantities of cartoons to newspapers that he became a freelance cartoonist. As well as selling work to papers, he was frequently commissioned by businesses.

He died in 2003, aged seventy-five.

LARRY
Played by Robin Askwith
Son of Augusta Prodworthy, Larry is an up-and-coming photographer who works for the local rag in *Girls*. He also completes freelance assignments but nothing prepares him for the job Dawn Brakes, the busty beauty contestant, has in mind when she asks him to venture on to the beach to take some nude shots; he's not experienced in taking full-frontal for dirty magazines, but seems to be adept at catching the mayor with his trousers down!

LAVINIA
Played by Hattie Jacques
For 'Lavinia' in *Doctor*, see 'Matron'.

LAVATORY ATTENDANT
Played by Harry Shacklock
In *Loving* the ageing attendant notices James Bedsop acting suspiciously in the toilets; when he sees him getting down on his hands and knees to peep under the cubicle doors, he gives him a sharp poke up the backside with a broom before chasing him out the door.

LAVELLY, MARJORIE
Continuity on *Girls*, *Behind*, *England* and *Emmannuelle*
Entered films in the late 1950s and before the decade was out had worked on several pictures, such as *Kill Me Tomorrow*, *Rag Doll*, *The Shakedown* and *Watch Your Stern*.

Particularly busy during the 60s, her credits include *Tarzan Goes to India*, *The Hi-Jackers*, *The Three Lives of Thomasina*, *The Night Caller*, *One Million Years BC*, and *Five Golden Dragons*. During the decade she was also seen in *The Saint*.

Films she worked on during the 1970s include *The Little Prince*; *Stand Up, Virgin Soldiers* and, her last film, *The Girl in a Swing*.

LAVENDER, IAN
Role: Joe Baxter in *Behind*
Son of a policeman, Ian Lavender, who's best known for playing Private Pike in *Dad's Army*, was born in Birmingham in 1946. He briefly considered becoming a detective before opting for the acting profession.

After finishing his schooling at Bourneville Technical College in 1965, he headed for drama school at Bristol's Old Vic. He graduated in 1967 and spent a season playing juvenile leads at the Marlowe Theatre, Canterbury.

In 1968 he made his TV debut in an ATV play, *Flowers At My Feet*, before being recruited to the ranks of Jimmy Perry and David Croft's classic sitcom, *Dad's Army*. Between series of the wartime show set in the fictitious town of Walmington, Lavender remained busy, appearing in television shows like *Z Cars*, *Smokescreen* and *The Canterbury Tales*. He also made his West End debut as Teddy Widgett in the musical *Ann Veronica*, enjoyed a successful run in the Mermaid Theatre production of *The Apple Cart* and toured in numerous other shows.

Lavender has also been heard on the radio and seen in various small-screen comedies, including *Yes, Minister*; *Rising Damp* and *Goodnight Sweetheart*. More recently he joined the cast of *EastEnders*, playing Derek Harkinson.

LAW, MARY
Role: 1st Shop Assistant in *Constable*
Mary Law made a handful of screen appearances in the 1950s and '60s. On television she played Janet Campbell in the 1954 series, *The Lost Planet*, and Peggy Simpson in 1960's *Deadline Midnight*. On the big screen she was seen in the occasional small role, such as an office girl in 1954's *For Better, For Worse*.

LAWRENCE
Played by Peter Jesson
In *Follow That Camel*, Lawrence passes the relief party as they plod along in the desert, increasingly weary and thirsty. He stops and asks the way to Arabia. **(Note: the scene was cut from the film.)**

WHAT MIGHT HAVE BEEN

When the relief party is marching through the desert they pass a character called Lawrence.

EXT. THE OPEN DESERT – DAY

The relief party is plodding along even more slowly. Their heads are right down and so they don't see the figure walking in sprightly fashion towards them until they are passing. Burger, in the lead, comes to a stop, and looks.

M.C.S. of the stranger, as he comes to a stop and smiles politely. It looks remarkably like O'Toole in full Lawrence kit.

LAWRENCE: Excuse me, but I was looking for Arabia.

BURGER: **(Points back.)** Straight on. Far as you can go.

LAWRENCE: Thanks a lot. Lovely weather!

(NOCKER and BURGER, looking after him, exchange an enquiring look, then NOCKER shakes his head.)

NOCKER: No, couldn't have been.

(And they move on, after the others.)

LAWRENCE, ALEC
Played by Ed Devereaux
A patient at the Haven Hospital in *Nurse*.

Lila (Dilys Laye, left) in the HQ of S.T.E.N.C.H. (*Spying*)

LAWRENCE, MARJIE
Role: Serving Maid in *Henry*
Born in Smethwick, West Midlands, in 1932, Marjie Lawrence trained at Birmingham School of Dramatic Art for three years before making her way to London and an audition for the legendary Joan Littlewood's theatre company.

From 200 people attending her first auditions in 1954, Lawrence was one of two chosen to join the Theatre Workshop Company. During the following two seasons she played leading roles in all the classics, including the acclaimed *Arden of Faversham* at the Paris International Festival.

On the first day of commercial television in the UK, she played the lead in the first soap on ITV, having been spotted at Theatre Royal Stratford. *Round at the Redways* ran for seven months and the exposure led to plenty of work in the medium. She also became busy on the stage and for the following forty years was regularly in demand; during this period she played seven leads in West End theatre productions.

Her film career kicked off with a leading role, opposite Ray Barrett, in Merton Park's *Moment of Decision* which was released in cinemas around the UK with *Summer Holiday*. Other film credits include *Hands of the Ripper*, *I Monster, Stranger in the House, Only Two Can Play, On the Beat, The Early Bird, Bless This House, Shiner* and, in 2001, playing Granny in *Large*.

On the stage, her favourite roles were playing Natasha opposite George Cole in *The Three Sisters* at the Royal Court and working with Peter Brook in the ensemble production of *US*, at the RSC (Aldwych).

On television her numerous credits include *Dixon of Dock Green, Z Cars, Gideon C. I. D., Nearest and Dearest, Catweazle, Angels, Hunter's Walk, Coronation Street, George and Mildred, Return of the Saint, Danger UXB, Driveway* and Anglia's soap *Weavers Green*, in which she played a leading role.

LAYE, DILYS
Roles: Flo Castle in *Cruising*, Lila in *Spying*, Mavis in *Doctor* and Anthea Meeks in *Camping*
Born in London in 1934, Dilys Laye, who had appeared in panto from the age of twelve, enrolled at the Aida Foster School. Soon after, she was cast as young Trottie in the 1949 comedy, *Trottie True*. Plenty of revue work followed before, aged eighteen, she spent eighteen months on Broadway, appearing with Julie Andrews in *The Boyfriend*.

Having trained as a dancer, she was in demand for plenty of musicals before straight roles came her way. Throughout her career, she's worked extensively in the theatre with recent productions including *My Fair Lady, An Ideal Husband, Les Liaisons Dangereus* and *Blonde Bombshells*. She's also performed with the Royal Shakespeare Company.

Her television work includes appearances in *Ghost Squad, Fraud Squad, The Gentle Touch, The Jimmy Tarbuck Show, Campion, Holby City, Midsomer Murders, Coronation Street, EastEnders* and *Doctors*. Among the many films she's appeared in are *Doctor at Large, Blue Murder at St Trinian's, Please Turn Over, On the Beat* and *Dog Eat Dog*.

LAYTON, GEORGE
Role: Doctor in *Behind*
Born in Bradford in 1943, George Layton, who's also a writer and director, is still a familiar face on television from his days spent playing Paul Collier in the long-running *Doctor* series, his favourite role. Other television credits include *Sunburn; United!; Minder; It Ain't Half Hot, Mum; Robin's Nest* and *My Brother's Keeper*. He was also a presenter on the first series of *That's Life!*

During the 1980s, Layton's writing career occupied much of his time (he wrote several novels and television scripts) and he became an infrequent visitor to the small screen. He hit a rich vein when he began writing *Don't Wait Up*, which ran for six series between 1983-90. This success story was followed by three series of *Executive Stress* with Penelope Keith and Geoffrey Palmer/Peter Bowles.

A RADA graduate, where he won the Emile Littler Award, Layton wanted to be an actor from the age of seven, but upon leaving school worked in a hospital for a few months until joining drama school. Afterwards he went straight to Coventry and one of the leading reps of the day; he stayed eighteen months before appearing on Broadway in *Chips With Everything*.

MEMORIES

'I've never seen *Behind* but must have been there all of a morning. I was a doctor attending to Kenneth Williams, and in one of the scenes I had to use a scalpel on his foot to remove a splinter but he moved on the shot and I accidentally cut him. He was furious and talking of spitting blood, it was flowing everywhere, although I'd only nicked him. I just apologised but he wasn't pleased. Afterwards I wrote to Kenneth and sent him an Elastoplast as a little peace offering – I never got a reply.

'Jonathan Lynn and I were later commissioned to write a script for *Carry On Again Nurse*, sometime during the 1970s. I was really pleased with it and thought it hilarious but it wasn't ever made. I'm not sure but I don't think it was saucy enough, which I think was what they were looking for.'

GEORGE LAYTON

Nowadays, Layton, who's just written a film script, is making a concerted effort to return to acting. He's been appearing on stage and has recently completed episodes of *Holby City* and *Casualty*.

LE PICE, CAPTAIN
Played by Charles Hawtrey

Captain Le Pice is seen in *Follow That Camel*. Reporting to Commandant Burger, he's one of the incompetent members of the Foreign Legion.

LEDA
Played by Valerie Leon

Despite King Tonka's lofty position amongst the Lubidubies, it's Leda that's really in charge of the all-female tribe in *Up the Jungle*. This tall, majestic woman flexes her leadership muscles when she usurps Walter Bagley when he becomes surplus to requirements after his wife, Lady Bagley, arrives on the scene.

LEE, PENNY
Played by Diana Beevers

Seen in *Teacher*, Penelope is one of the ringleaders at Maudlin Street Secondary Modern School who set out to wreak havoc when an inspector and celebrated child psychiatrist pay a visit. Given one of the leading parts (Juliet) in the school play, she takes the opportunity to cause more mayhem.

LEEP, MAJOR
Played by Kenneth Connor

An ex-military man, or that's what he likes people to believe, Major Leep owns the Riverside Caravan Site in *Behind*. He paid a local publican £2000 for the field unaware that the land is riddled with holes, thanks to the Romans who mined the area centuries ago. He only realises there's a problem when the caravans start disappearing down huge chasms.

LEFTY
Played by Freddie Mills

For 'Lefty' in *Regardless*, see 'Vincent, Lefty'.

LEMARE, PAUL
Sound Recordist on *Girls*

LEN
Played by Milo O'Shea

Seen in *Cabby*, Len drives cabs for Charlie Hawkins's firm, Speedee Taxis.

LEON, VALERIE
Roles: Hospitality Girl in *Up The Khyber*, Store Assistant in *Camping*, Deirdre in *Again Doctor*, Leda in *Up the Jungle*, Jane Darling in *Matron* and Paula Perkins in *Girls*
TV: *Christmas* ('72)

London-born Valerie Leon, who became a familiar face on television screens during the 1970s thanks to Hai Karate aftershave adverts, was educated at public school until the age of fifteen when she enrolled on a one-year college course in retail distribution.

After gaining retail experience she headed for France, working as an au pair while learning the language, before returning home to a job as a trainee fashion buyer with Harrods. She subsequently took singing lessons and entered the showbiz world after seeing an advert for chorus singers in *The Belle of New York*. The production folded after six weeks but it marked the start of a busy career which has included appearing on stage in *Funny Girl* with Barbra Streisand in 1966, and numerous screen roles in films such as *The Italian Job*, *Smashing Time*, *All the Way Up*, *The Wild Geese* and two Bond movies, *The Spy Who Loved Me* and *Never Say Never Again*. She was also seen in the Hammer Horror film, *Blood from the Mummy's Tomb*.

Her television credits started with an appearance in the 1960s detective series, *The Baron*, followed quickly by parts in *The Saint*, *Randall and Hopkirk (Deceased)*, *The Avengers*, *Rings On Their Fingers*, *The Persuaders!*, *Bowler* and *Misleading Cases*.

After retiring from showbusiness to raise her family, Leon, who was married to the late BBC producer Michael Mills, made a comeback and occasionally acts. She also runs her own public relations company.

LEWIN, MARGARET
Wardrobe Mistress on *Matron*, *Emmannuelle* and *Dick*. (**Note: although only credited on these three films, Lewin worked on several in the series.**)

Born in London in 1937, Margaret Lewin studied embroidery at Southwark College; she graduated in 1954 and worked in a factory making clothes before moving to Ladybird, the clothing firm.

She later joined Pinewood Studios as a wardrobe assistant and thus began a long career, beginning with the 1957 film, *The Secret Place*. She turned freelance in the 1960s and remained in the industry until 1989 when ill-health forced her retirement. Among the countless films she worked on are *Dangerous Exile*, *Just My Luck*, *Life for Ruth*, *Raising the Wind*, *Victim*, *Operation Amsterdam* and, latterly, *A Bridge Too Far*.

LEWIS, JACQUELINE
Role: Pat Gordon in *Teacher*

LEWIS, MRS
A non-speaking character in *Cruising*, Leonard Marjoribanks introduces Mr Jenkins, the PT instructor, to her at the captain's cocktail party on the *Happy Wanderer*, which takes place on the evening of 17 April.

LEYLAND
Played by Kenneth Connor

Emile Prevert's chauffeur is seen in *Emmannuelle*,

Valerie Leon (third left) playing Leda, one of her six roles in the *Carry Ons* (*Up the Jungle*)

'There were several of us playing hospitality girls in *Up The Khyber*. I think they had one of these big auditions and I was chosen, which was great. We were just floating around and if you look at the film, there is just one nice shot of me. But it was an enjoyable part and from that I graduated to a few lines in *Camping*. I enjoyed my scene in *Again Doctor* with Jim Dale, whom I'd worked with before in pantomime, because my character was totally over the top.

'I had a big part in *Jungle*. In retrospect, I think I should have been wilder and not so prim. I played her quite stilted, I think. I was supposed to be intimidated by inadequate men and enjoyed the role a lot. Then there was *Matron* and, of course, *Girls*. The spectacles I wore at the start of the film are very old ones I used to wear in real life when I was training to be a fashion buyer at Harrods. They were sold recently for charity at one of the British Heritage events, together with a framed picture of me wearing them in the film. They fetched quite a lot of money.

'Of course all the films are on DVD now and I'm still receiving fan mail from around the world. In fact, I'm getting more now than when I was in the public eye. It comes from everywhere – India, Hong Kong, Australia, America and Canada: they even want to start a fan club for me in Croatia!'

VALERIE LEON

driving the French Ambassador and his sex-mad wife, Emmannuelle, around the streets of London.

LIDDELL, DETECTIVE SERGEANT
Played by Victor Maddern
For Detective Sergeant Liddell in *Constable*, see 'Criminal Type'.

LIEBER & COMPANY
The company's boxes, containing carnival novelties, are seen in a Viennese warehouse during *Spying*.

LIGHTNING
Sheriff Earp's horse in *Cowboy*.

LIL, AUNT
Captain Fearless refers to his aunt from Littlehampton in *Jack*, although we learn nothing about this unseen character.

LILA
Played by Dilys Laye
A singer at the Café Mozart in Vienna, Lila is seen in *Spying*. She appears to be a member of S.T.E.N.C.H., a subversive organisation run by Dr Crow, but turns out to be working for S.N.O.G., the Society for the Neutralisation of Germs.

LILY
Played by Sally Geeson
Lily travels to Elsbels, the Mediterranean resort, with her friend, Marge, on the Wundatours trip in *Abroad*. She's keen on finding a fella and her wish comes true when she meets Nicholas.

LITTLE HEAP
Played by Bernard Bresslaw
Son of Big Heap, the chief of a tribe of Indians based near Stodge City, Little Heap is seen in *Cowboy*.

LITTLE MAN
Played by Ronnie Brody
Seen dancing with Desiree Dubarry at Sir Rodney Ffing's charity ball in *Don't Lose Your Head*. Desiree is wearing a locket which is intended to attract the attention of the Black Fingernail, a master of disguise who's desperately wanted by Citizen Camembert; the Little Man, who's obviously not the wanted man, asks her to remove it because it's bashing him in the face.

LIVINGS, HENRY
Role: Recruit in *Sergeant*
Born in the Lancashire town of Prestwich in 1929, Henry Livings began his career as an actor before gaining success as a television, film and theatre writer. He wrote nearly thirty plays and contributed to a handful of popular television shows, including *Juliet Bravo* – a series in which he also appeared as an actor – and *Bulman*.

After leaving grammar school, Livings began reading French and Spanish at Liverpool University but never finished the course. He completed National Service in the RAF and moved between jobs before starting his acting career at Joan Littlewood's Theatre Workshop at Stratford East.

Among the many plays he wrote are *Nil Carborundum*; *Jack's Horrible Luck*; *Stop It; Whoever You Are*; *Big Soft Nellie* and *Eh?*.

He died in 1998, aged sixty-eight.

LIZZIE
Played by Penny Irving
Lizzie is one of the Birds of Paradise seen performing at the Old Cock Inn in *Dick*.

LLOYD, HELEN
Played by Ann Firbank
An attractive staff nurse on night duty in *Nurse*. Based in Haven Hospital, she's seen carrying out her duties on the wards, including saving Nurse Frances James from the clutches of Ted York when he regains consciousness after his op.

LLOYD, VIVIEN
Role: Verna in *Camping*
Vivien Lloyd's other screen credits include appearing with Ronnie Corbett in a 1987 episode of *Sorry!*, although her earliest job on television was in 1959, in the series *Sea Hunt*. As well as *Camping*, she's appeared in the big-screen version of *Steptoe and Son*.

LOCATIONS
See feature box on pages 154–6.

LOCKE, HARRY
Roles: Mick in *Nurse*, Sam in *Doctor* and Porter in *Again Doctor*
Born in London in 1912, Harry Locke was regularly cast in small character parts but his finely-tuned portrayals won him much respect from contemporaries and audiences alike.

On stage from the early 1930s, his busy career, which was interrupted by six years in the Intelligence Corps during the Second World War, covered all media, including spells as a stand-up comedian.

He was in films from the early 1940s, building a lengthy list of credits, including *Piccadilly Incident*, *No Room at the Inn*, *Passport to Pimlico*, *Tread Softly*, *Angels One Five*, *Doctor in the House*, *The Teckman Mystery*, *Reach for the Sky*, *Sink the Bismarck!*, *Kill or Cure*, *The Family Way* and *The Creeping Flesh*. His television work covered such shows as *Dick and the Duchess* and *Dial 999* to *Mogul* and *Just William*. He died in 1987, aged seventy-four.

LOCKS, GOLDIE
Played by Barbara Windsor
Actress-cum-model Goldie Locks, real name Maude Boggins, arrives at the Long Hampton Hospital in *Again Doctor* with severe bruising sustained whilst filming a commercial for Bristol's Bouncing Baby Food at the Advertising Film Studios. She had to stand on an enormous mock-up packet and slipped. A former pin-up girl, Goldie is examined by Dr Nookey, who can't believe his luck when she arrives wearing an extremely skimpy outfit. Nookey proceeds to fall in love with Goldie, formerly of Flat 3, Howard Court, London SW3, but when she thinks he's only after her body, she accepts a job offer in Italy. By the time she re-enters Dr Nookey's life, when he's made it big courtesy of Gladstone Screwer's weight-losing serum, she's a well-known film actress working under the stage name of Melody Madder. This time Nookey is determined not to lose his girl.

LOCATIONS

There were no exotic locations for the *Carry On* team. When June Whitfield signed up to play Evelyn Blunt in *Abroad*, she had visions of jetting off to a sunny destination so was rather shocked when a corner of the car park at Pinewood was converted, thanks to a few deckchairs and a pile of sand, into the sunny Med, even though the weather was appallingly cold and damp. The nearest the team were going to get to heading off to warmer climes was Gatwick Airport where interior and exterior scenes were going to be shot using a BEA Comet, but the sequence was cancelled when the scene was deleted from the script.

The closely-monitored budgets never extended to such luxuries as filming abroad, and whenever a local location, or perhaps a convenient spot within the grounds of Pinewood would suffice, Peter Rogers and Gerald Thomas saved the pennies. In doing so, they were

helping establish the style and manner everyone came to expect of a *Carry On* production. There is a certain charm about watching the incongruously assembled holidaymakers trying to sun themselves in the Pinewood car park-cum-Elsbels Palace Hotel grounds rather than seeing them lazing around on a real Mediterranean beach.

The furthest afield the team travelled was to far-flung places like Camber Sands in Sussex to film *Follow That Camel*, Snowdonia for *Up The Khyber* and Brighton for *At Your Convenience* and *Girls*, while the rest of the time was mostly spent in and around the streets of Buckinghamshire.

If you ever wondered where certain scenes were filmed, the list below – detailing locations outside the grounds of Pinewood – will hopefully provide the answer. Divided into films, here are the various locations used for the majority of the filming sequences.

SERGEANT

Beaconsfield Church, Bucks, used for wedding scene. The production files also show a church in Harefield as being considered during the making of the film.

Queen's Barracks, Stoughton, Guildford (home of the Queen's Regiment) were used for parade-ground scenes.

The rear entrance at Pinewood was used for the closing scene showing the lorryload of soldiers leaving Heathercrest.

NURSE

Local streets around Iver Heath, including the Billet Roundabout, were used for the sequence involving the ambulance in the opening scene. The gates used are found at the south entrance of Pinewood Studios.

The rear of the Mansion House at Pinewood became Haven Hospital.

TEACHER

Drayton Secondary School, Drayton Gardens, West Ealing was used as the Maudlin Street school in all exterior shots.

CONSTABLE

Lothair Road, Ealing, for the scooter sequence.

Hanwell Parish Church for the church scene.

The Avenue, Ealing, for main street scenes.

F. H. Rowse, a store in Ealing, was used for the department store scene.

Manor Road, Ealing, for sequences involving Charlie and Gloria, the stolen braces and where Williams's character stops Victor Maddern whom he thinks is about to commit a crime.

St Stephen's Road, Ealing, for the neglected house.

Pinewood Green Estates for the police marching.

Hanwell, London, for the opening shots of the police station.

REGARDLESS

11 Clarence Crescent, Windsor, is where Williams visits to pick up Yoki.

12 Park Street, Windsor, used for the Helping Hands office.

Windsor and Eton Railway Station for the platform sequence.

Thames Street and Windsor Park seen when Williams walks away from the taxi.

CRUISING

Southampton docks for the opening shots of the liner.

CABBY

Maidenhead Autos Ltd., Bath Road, Taplow, Bucks, was where Peggy Hawkins ordered her fleet of spanking new Ford Cortinas.

Arthur Road, Windsor, was seen in the final chase sequence.

Black Park Road, Fulmer, Bucks, for the scene involving Sid and Jim Dale.

Windsor railway station and several streets around the town were used, including Victoria Street, Sheet Street and High Street, for opening scenes of Sid driving.

Pinewood Green Estate for taxi driving scenes.

Speedee Cabs' yard and head office was Pinewood's car park.

Pinewood Green Estate was utilised in *Camping*

The scene where Hawtrey has a near miss with an ambulance was filmed on Stovell Road, Windsor.

The newly-weds are picked up from a house on the Pinewood Green housing estate.

The heath in the closing scenes is found in Gerrards Cross.

JACK

Frensham Pond, Surrey, was used to represent the Spanish coastline and the beach with the path through the scrub.

SPYING

Although Denham Film Studios was considered for sequences in the long corridor, the Hall of Fame in Pinewood was chosen for the opening scenes involving Victor Maddern.

The rear entrance of Pinewood was chosen for the scene involving the milk float at the beginning of the film.

CLEO

Various locations in Iver Heath, Bucks, were used to film various scenes set in the countryside.

COWBOY
Chobham Common, Surrey, and Black Park, Fulmer, Bucks, were utilised for the Cowboy and Indian sequences and Wild West countryside scenes.

SCREAMING!
Fulmer Grange, now the home of the Teikyo School, Bucks was chosen to represent Olando and Virula Watt's house, the Bide-A-Wee Rest Home, while the police station and exterior of Bung's house were located in Windsor and the setting for Dan Dann's toilet block was the south lodge and south gates at Pinewood.

The police station is now Windsor Arts Centre, situated on St Mark's Road, while Inspector Bung's house can be found in Queen's Road, Windsor.

DON'T LOSE YOUR HEAD
Clandon Park House, Clandon Park, Surrey, was used extensively. The main hall at the house was used for a ballroom sequence, a room off the hall was seen as an ante-room and the exterior of the main entrance and the drive were used in scenes involving the arrival and departure of various characters.

The main entrance and drive at Cliveden, Bucks, were used in sequences involving the arrival of aristocrats for a ball.

Waddesdon Manor, near Aylesbury, Bucks, was used to replicate a French mansion.

The gardens at Pinewood were the scene of the duel and Black Park, Fulmer, was used for various scenes in the countryside.

FOLLOW THAT CAMEL
Camber Sands, Rye, was chosen for scenes in the dunes.

Manor Farm, Icklesham, Sussex, was the location for the square tent scene.

Swakeleys was used for the cricket ground exteriors.

Interior and exterior shots of the Ponsonby family mansion were filmed at Osterley Park House in London.

DOCTOR
Maidenhead Town Hall, St Ives Road, Berks, was used for exterior shots of Borough County Hospital.

The Royal Lancaster Hotel, London, was used for exterior scenes involving the nurses' home.

UP THE KHYBER
Snowdonia was used to represent the Himalayas. Parts of the mountain near Beddgelert were chosen.

CAMPING
The Orchard at Pinewood represented the camp site while the clubhouse doubled as Chayste Place School.

Sauls Farm and Dromenagh Farms in Iver Heath, Bucks, were used for location shooting, as was Glebe Farm, Northolt, for the scene where Derek Francis, playing an irate farmer, peppers an unsuspecting Terry Scott with gunshot.

Courts Shop, St Ives High Street, Maidenhead, Berks was used for the scenes in the camping shop. It closed its doors in 2000.

Scenes involving the girls travelling by coach to the hostel were filmed on the A412 between Slough and Iver Heath.

Pinewood Green Estate was used for scenes involving the Fusseys' and Potters' houses.

Ethorpe Place, Gerrards Cross, Bucks, was used for the opening cinema scene.

It's believed that Juniper Cottages, Burnham Beeches, Bucks was used as the entrance to Josh Fiddler's camp site, although in the absence of indisputable evidence, other people believe it was in Black Park Road, Iver Heath.

AGAIN DOCTOR
Maidenhead Town Hall, St Ives Road, Berks was used for external shots of Long Hampton Hospital.

The nursing home was located in Iver Heath, Bucks, while the street where Doctor Nookey has his consulting rooms is Park Street, Windsor.

The exterior shots of the Moore-Nookey Clinic were taken at Pinewood's Mansion House.

Top left: Terry Scott reveals his tummy on location (*Up The Khyber*)
Top right: Getting ready for action in Snowdonia (*Up The Khyber*)
Bottom right: The Royal Court Hotel, where the cast stayed while filming (*Up The Khyber*)

Maidenhead Town Hall doubled as the Long Hampton Hospital (*Again Doctor*)

UP THE JUNGLE
The exterior shots of the lecture hall used by Professor Tinkle were taken at the old Maidenhead library.

The treehouse outside the residential address was filmed in Windsor.

LOVING
The Wedded Bliss Agency was filmed at 12 Park Street, Windsor, Berks.

The ballroom at Pinewood was used for the closing scene showing the wedding party.

Windsor and Eton railway station is where Sid Bliss calls a cab.

The Co-op roundabout, Slough, Berks was used for the opening sequence involving the doubledecker bus.

The shop-window scene involving Richard O'Callaghan was in Thames Street, Windsor, next to the Theatre Royal.

45 Gloucester Square, Windsor, was used as Mr Snooper's house.

Rogerham Mansions was, in fact, Atherton Court, Meadow Lane, Eton.

HENRY
Black Park, Fulmer, was used for scenes in the country, while Southlea Farm in Datchet, Berkshire was the location for the scene where King Henry chases the Buxom Lass. The grounds of Windsor Castle and the gardens at Pinewood were also utilised.

AT YOUR CONVENIENCE
The Palace Hotel, Brighton, was seen in the film.

The now-demolished Odeon Cinema, High Street, Uxbridge, Middlesex, was used for two scenes: where Vic Spanner loses his trousers and where Myrtle Plummer waits for Spanner.

The Plummers' and Moores' houses were filmed in Pinewood Green Estate.

The factory scenes were shot in the grounds of Pinewood.

The pier scenes were filmed on Brighton's Palace Pier, while the A412 between Iver Heath and Slough was used again for the coach scenes.

The hotel where the employees stop for a drink was Clarges on Brighton's Marine Parade, the former boarding house owned by Dora Bryan.

The Whippit Inn, where Cope and Bresslaw spy on Richard O'Callaghan and Jacki Piper, is actually Pinewood Mansion.

MATRON
Heatherwood Hospital, Ascot, Berks represented the Finisham Maternity Hospital.

A church in Denham was used for the closing wedding sequence.

The High Street in Ascot, Berks, was used for a driving scene involving Sid Carter and his gang.

ABROAD
The Bargain Centre, 65 High Street, Slough, was used as the Wundatours office.

A road in Bagshot, Surrey, was chosen to represent the muddy track the holidaymakers travel along en route to their hotel.

The exterior shots of the Elsbels Palace Hotel were shot in the car park at Pinewood.

GIRLS
The Town Hall in Slough represented Fircombe's Council Hall.

Various locations were used in Brighton, including Madeira Drive where Larry takes photos of Dawn Brakes, the West Pier for all the pier scenes and the Clarges Hotel as Connie Philpotts' Palace Hotel.

The B410 between Slough and Datchet was used for filming Sid James and Barbara Windsor on the moped.

Marylebone railway station was picked to film the scenes where Peter Potter gets on the train.

The fire station was found in St Mark's Road, Windsor.

The exterior of 38 Lansdowne Avenue, Slough, was used as the mayor's house.

DICK
St Mary's Church, Hitcham, Bucks was used as the Rev. Flasher's church.

Black Park, Fulmer, was used for various scenes, while Stoke Manor, Stoke Poges, Bucks, became the Rev. Flasher's home.

Langley Park, Berks, was the location for the horse-chasing scenes.

The Jolly Woodman, Littleworth Common, Bucks, doubled as the Old Cock Inn.

BEHIND
The Orchard at Pinewood was used as the caravan park.

Fred Ramsden's butcher's shop was located at Robin Parade, Farnham Common, Farnham, Surrey, while Maidenhead Town Hall was used for some exterior shots for other scenes.

Properties in Pinewood Green, Iver Heath, were used for filming the houses of the Upmores and the Baxters.

ENGLAND
The Orchard at Pinewood was used for the army barracks while the rear of Pinewood Mansion became the army's HQ.

EMMANNUELLE
The airport scenes were filmed at Pinewood.

Pinewood Green was again used, this time for exterior shots of the Valentines' house.

The zoological gardens in London's Regent's Park were utilised for one of the fantasy sequences.

The launderette scenes involving Victor Maddern and Joan Sims were filmed at York House, The Parade, Bourne End, Bucks.

St Mary's Parish Church, Harefield, Middlesex was used for background.

There's a nip in the air while filming (*Behind*)

Lucy Griffiths, Terence Longdon and Liz Fraser (*Regardless*)

LODGE, DAVID

Roles: Connoisseur in *Regardless*, Police Inspector in *Girls*, Bullock in *Dick*, the Landlord in *Behind* and Captain Bull in *England*

TV: *The Prisoner of Spenda, The Baron Outlook, The Sobbing Cavalier, One in the Eye for Harold, The Nine Old Cobblers, The Case of the Screaming Winkles* and *The Case of the Coughing Parrot*

Despite winning no starring roles in a career spanning nearly fifty years, David Lodge, who was born in Strood, Kent, in 1921, made a decent living playing character parts from all walks of life. In the 1950s and '60s he was rarely off the screen, equally comfortable in comedies and dramas.

Son of a sailor, he worked as a post-office messenger for two years before serving with the RAF during the war, where he entertained the troops as part of the Ralph Reader Gang Shows. After demob, he worked in reps and holiday camps, becoming entertainments manager at a camp in Ireland and touring as half of a double-act before entering the film business, beginning with 1954's *Orders Are Orders*. His big break was in 1955's *Cockleshell Heroes*, but his long list of credits included *No Time To Die, Ice Cold in Alex, On The Beat* and *The Return of the Pink Panther.*

He was seen in many television shows, such as *The Avengers, The Sweeney, Nanny, Bless This House* and *Crossroads*. He died in 2003, aged eighty-two.

LOGAN, JIMMY

Roles: Bert Conway in *Abroad* and Cecil Gaybody in *Girls*

Born in Glasgow in 1928, Jimmy Logan left school at fourteen and went to work on the stage in a variety of roles including accordionist and juvenile lead. By the age of nineteen he had become the principal comedian at the Old Metropole Theatre in Glasgow and went on to star in Howard and Wyndham's *Five Past Eight* summer revues and to act in pantomimes, including a production at the London Palladium.

He later worked on BBC Scotland's radio show, *It's All Yours*, before breaking into television, aged twenty-eight, with a series for ATV. This led, one year later, to *The Jimmy Logan Show*, which ran between 1957-61, only finishing because Logan decided to return to the theatre, performing a one-man show and acting in productions such as *The Entertainer, Uncle Vanya* and *Death of a Salesman*.

He also appeared in several films, including *Throw A Saddle On A Star, The Wild Affair, Lucia* and *My Life So Far*.

He died in 2001, aged seventy-three.

LOGIE, SEYMOUR

Sound editor on *Sergeant*

Working as a sound editor from the mid-1950s, among the many productions Seymour Logie worked on are the films *Woman Eater, Small Hotel* and *The Young and the Guilty*, as well as the television series *The Scarlet Pimpernel* and *The Big Pull*.

LONGDON, TERENCE

Roles: Miles Heywood in *Sergeant*, Ted York in *Nurse*, Herbert Hall in *Constable* and Montgomery Infield-Hopping in *Regardless*

Terence Longdon's was a frequently-seen face during the 1950s and '60s, particularly in the medium of film. Before comedy roles began dominating his CV, he was often seen in dramas, particularly war films, playing brave-hearted airmen and carefree soldiers.

Born in Newark on Trent, Nottinghamshire, in 1922, the son of a businessman, he left grammar school in 1939, aged seventeen, intent on a career in the civil service. His plans were thwarted by the war, and after a series of short-lived jobs, he was conscripted into the forces in 1940.

Returning to civvy street he decided upon an acting career and studied at RADA. After a short spell as assistant stage manager at a Sheffield repertory company he began a contract with H. M. Tennent, then the leading theatrical producers in London.

By the early 1950s he'd launched his film career, beginning with *Angels One Five*, followed quickly by a plethora of titles, such as *Appointment in London, Jumping for Joy, Simon and Laura, The Man Who Never Was, Helen of Troy* and *Ben-Hur*.

Although Longdon frequently worked in the film industry, he spent most of his career in theatre. For two years he worked with the Royal Shakespeare Company in Stratford, as well as on tour in Australia and New Zealand. As the film roles decreased – minor roles in *The Wild Geese* and *The Sea Wolves* have been among his most recent – he's spent more time working in the theatre and television. His biggest small-screen jobs to date have been four years in *Garry Halliday* and playing Wilf Stockwell, a business associate of Mike Baldwin, in *Coronation Street*.

LONG HAMPTON ADVERTISER

The newspaper carries the story of Dr Carver's lucky escape while returning from the Beatific Islands. When the schooner *Bella Vista* foundered off the islands, he was fortunate to escape with his life. Dr Nookey is seen reading the front-page story in *Again Doctor*.

LONG HAMPTON HOSPITAL

The hospital featured in *Again Doctor*.

LORD CHIEF JUSTICE

Played by Llewellyn Rees

The Lord Chief Justice of the Appeals Court is seen dining at the French Ambassador's residence in *Emmannuelle*.

LOUISE

An unseen Glamcab driver in *Cabby*, whose name is mentioned by Flo over the radio when she asks the driver to pick up a fare at 20 Chester

CARRY ON LOVING

Alternative titles . . . *It's Not What You Feel, It's The Way That You Feel It; Two's Company But Three's Quite Good Fun Too; Love Is A Four-Letter Word* and *It's Just One Thing On Top Of Another*

A Peter Rogers production
Distributed through Rank Organisation
Released as an A certificate in 1970 in colour
Running time: 88 mins

CAST

Sidney James	Sidney Bliss
Kenneth Williams	Percival Snooper
Charles Hawtrey	James Bedsop
Hattie Jacques	Sophie Bliss
Joan Sims	Esme Crowfoot
Bernard Bresslaw	Gripper Burke
Terry Scott	Terence Philpot
Jacki Piper	Sally Martin
Richard O'Callaghan	Bertrum Muffet
Imogen Hassall	Jenny Grub
Patsy Rowlands	Miss Dempsey
Peter Butterworth	Sinister Client
Joan Hickson	Mrs Grubb
Julian Holloway	Adrian
Janet Mahoney	Gay
Ann Way	Aunt Victoria Grubb
Bill Maynard	Mr Dreery
Amelia Bayntun	Corset Lady
Gordon Richardson	Uncle Ernest Grubb
Tom Clegg	Trainer
Lucy Griffiths	Woman
Valerie Shute	Girl Lover
Mike Grady	Boy Lover
Anthony Sagar	Man in Hospital
Harry Shacklock	Lavatory Attendant
Derek Francis	Bishop
Alexandra Dane	Emily
Philip Stone	Robinson
Sonny Farrar	Violinist
Patricia Franklin	Mrs Dreery
Hilda Barry	Grandma Grubb
Josie Bradley	Pianist
Bart Allison	Grandpa Grubb
Anna Karen	Wife
Dorothea Phillips	Aunt Beatrice Grubb
Lauri Lupino Lane	Husband
Bill Pertwee	Barman
Colin Vancao	Wilberforce Grubb
Gavin Reed	Window Dresser
Joe Cornelius	Second
Len Lowe	Maître d'Hotel
Fred Griffiths	Taxi Driver
Ronnie Brody	Henry
Kenny Lynch	Bus Conductor
Robert Russell	Policeman

PRODUCTION TEAM

Screenplay by Talbot Rothwell
Music composed and conducted by Eric Rogers
Production Manager: Jack Swinburne
Art Director: Lionel Couch
Editor: Alfred Roome
Director of Photography: Ernest Steward
Assistant Editor: Jack Gardner
Make-up: Geoffrey Rodway
Continuity: Josephine Knowles
Camera Operator: James Bawden
Assistant Director: David Bracknell
Hairdresser: Stella Rivers
Sound Recordists: J.W.N. Daniel and Ken Barker
Costume Designer: Courtenay Elliott
Assistant Art Director: William Alexander
Set Dresser: Peter Howitt
Dubbing Editor: Marcel Durham
Titles and Opticals: G.S.E. Ltd
Processed by Rank Film Laboratories
Producer: Peter Rogers
Director: Gerald Thomas

The flans begin to fly at the Bliss' wedding reception

Bertie Muffet, an undertaker's assistant, is looking for love so decides to try his luck at the Wedded Bliss Agency; not that the company's proprietors, Sidney and Sophie Bliss, are good examples for their business because they fight like cat and dog, and Sophie suspects Sidney of having affairs with virtually all their female clients, particularly Esme Crowfoot whom he's constantly vetting!

For the sake of their company, Sidney and Sophie claim to have been married ten years, but as Sophie later divulges to Mr Snooper, a bachelor who works as a marriage guidance counsellor and is threatened with the sack unless he finds a wife, they've never tied the knot.

But Bertie Muffet doesn't know about that, and probably doesn't care, when he registers with the agency. During his interview he admits his hobbies include constructing model aeroplanes out of milk-bottle tops, making Sidney realise it's going to be tough finding him a suitable partner; but then he has the hi-tech computer to sort all that out, which impresses the clients, even though behind the scenes it's none other than Sophie doing the matchmaking with the help of card indexes.

When Esme Crowfoot's name is spewed out by the computer, Sidney realises it's Sophie playing games and isn't amused. But rather than admitting to Sophie he's having a fling with Miss Crowfoot, he rings her number and sets up a date for Bertie; before he can complete the call she puts the phone down, unbeknown to Mr Muffet or Sophie.

Bertie heads to the cocktail bar at the Parkway Hotel, expecting to meet Esme Crowfoot, but instead mistakes a model, Sally Martin, who happens to be waiting for a photographer, for her. Confusion ensues and Bertie ends up going back to Sally's flat, but when she starts stripping off and asking if he wants her in the bath, he suspects something is up. By the time he eventually meets an unsuspecting Esme Crowfoot, he ends up being hospitalised by Gripper Burke, a man-mountain of a wrestler with an awful temper who has returned home from America and hopes to resume his relationship with Esme, his old girlfriend; when Muffet comes calling he suspects him of fancying his girl and tries out a few of his wrestling moves on the poor, feeble undertaker's assistant. But some good comes from his hospitalisation when he's visited by Sally Martin and a romance blossoms.

Other clients of the Wedded Bliss Agency include Percival Snooper and Terence Philpot, whose first two dates, with Jenny Grubb and a Miss Adams, are a complete nightmare. When he's had enough, Mr Philpot demands his money back but soon changes his mind when a beautiful brunette, wearing a low-cut dress, walks into the Wedded Bliss office. Terence Philpot can't believe his eyes when he learns she's none other than Jenny Grubb, the unsexy, dowdily-dressed girl he'd once visited. When she announces she's now a model and shares a flat, Mr Philpot is keen to try his luck again.

Mr Snooper, meanwhile, is a bachelor who works as a marriage guidance counsellor; he has a habit of rubbing people up the wrong way. After a series of bust-ups at work, his boss tells him he must find a wife or he'll be dismissed. He furtively makes his way to the Wedded Bliss office and after considering his requirements, Sophie Bliss tells him she's not really married to Sidney and she's the perfect match for him.

Funny Scene!

Mr Snooper, a marriage guidance counsellor who works at the Citizens' Advice Bureau, is trying to help Mr and Mrs Dreery who are experiencing marital problems.

MRS DREERY: We just seem to have rows all the time.

MR SNOOPER: Ah, rows, yes. About what precisely?

MRS DREERY: Oh, everything. Like the way he went on about that fireside chair I got him.

MR DREERY: Bloody think so an' all. I mean, look at it? Must have been made for a bloody midget. I couldn't get half my ass on it.

MR SNOOPER: Hardly the cause for a row, Mr Dreery, you must learn to turn the other cheek (starts laughing.) in a manner of speaking! (Continues to laugh at his own joke.)

MR DREERY: (Angry.) I didn't come here for a laugh you know, mate, I can stay at home and look at her for that.

Miss Dempsey, who's Mr Snooper's long-serving housekeeper, has other ideas, though, and starts acting very strangely when Sophie visits his home, making plenty of improper suggestions about her life with Percival. Meanwhile, believing he's in danger of losing Sophie, Mr Bliss hatches a plan, which involves Esme Crowfoot, to win her back.

Gripper Burke (Bernard Bresslaw) gets hot under the collar

Road, which turns out to be a derelict address. It's a deliberate ploy to confuse rival firm, Speedee Taxis, who are intercepting the Glamcab messages and attempting to steal their business.

LOVEGROVE, ARTHUR
Role: Old Cowhand in *Cowboy*
Born in London in 1913, Arthur Lovegrove – who was also a playwright – appeared in films from the 1940s, and his credits included *Passport to Pimlico, Meet Simon Cherry, Genevieve, The Runaway Bus, Passage Home, Safari, The Night We Dropped A Clanger, Clash by Night* and *Eye of the Needle*. On television he was seen in the likes of *Dixon of Dock Green; Glencannon; The Avengers; On the Buses; Please, Sir!; Bootsie and Snudge; Bless This House* and *Shoestring*.

Despite appearing in almost a hundred films and television shows, his greatest achievement was arguably writing the play, *Goodnight Mrs Puffin*, which has been staged worldwide.

He died in 1981, aged sixty-eight.

LOVELL, DUDLEY
Camera Operator on *Regardless* and *Cruising*
In films as a camera operator since the 1940s working on titles such as *Dear Murderer, Miranda, Don't Ever Leave Me, Cockleshell Heroes, Up in the World, The Captain's Table, Twice Round the Daffodils, The Fast Lady* and *The Wild Geese*. His television credits include *The Champions* and *Rumpole of the Bailey*.

LOVELL, D.
The unseen 4th Officer on the *Happy Wanderer* in *Cruising*. His name is seen on the crew list and it's obviously a reference to the film's camera operator. He was the captain's steward until a broken leg prevents him resuming his duties on an April cruise around the Med. His place is taken by Tom Tree.

LOVERS' WALK
Mentioned by Peter Potter in *Girls* while talking to the mayor of Fircombe, Frederick Bumble. Potter sees it as a suitable location for a possible publicity campaign that will help put the mayor's name in a good light.

LOVING, CARRY ON
See feature box on pages 158–9.

LOW, MICHAEL
Role: Lusty Youth in *Camping*

LOWE, LEN
Role: Maître d'Hotel in *Loving*
One half of a popular pre-war variety act with his brother Bill, which saw them appear in the films *A Date With A Dream* and *Melody Club*, Len Lowe was born in London in 1916. He worked as a singer and guitarist with Jack Hylton's band and, when his brother moved to America, he formed another duo, Lowe and Ladd, until he began concentrating on acting,

mainly on television. His credits in this medium included *Benny Hill, Bless This House, It's A Square World, One Foot in the Grave* and *Keeping Up Appearances*.

He died in 1999, aged eighty-three.

LOWE, OLGA
Role: Madame Fifi in *Abroad*
Olga Lowe, who was appearing with Sid James in *The Mating Game* at Sunderland when he died of a heart attack, was born in Durban, South Africa, in 1919. She began training as a dancer from the age of five and as a teenager started performing in shows, including being a member of Carmen Miranda's troupe. She met James in one of the productions and he subsequently taught her to tap dance before they performed together in a charity do.

She came to England in 1946, found an agent and started appearing on stage, primarily in musicals, and in films such as *Trottie True, The Great Manhunt, Hotel Sahara, Where Eagles Dare, Steptoe and Son Ride Again* and, more recently, *Cous-cous*. On television, she's been seen in, among others, *The Avengers, The Persuaders!, Return of the Saint, EastEnders* and *Poirot*.

She retired from the business in 1997 after completing a year at the Old Vic as a member of Peter Hall's company.

LOWER DENCHER
A parish mentioned in *Dick*. Between Lower and Upper Dencher is the Old Cock Inn, a hostelry regularly frequented by criminals.

LUBIDUBIES
An all-female tribe from the region of Aphrodisia, a valley beyond the mountains in the depths of the African jungle. For the last hundred years only girls have been born in the tribe so drastic action is taken to try and encourage the birth of boys; when the last man in the tribe dies, a desperate search begins for a man who can become the King of the tribe, mating with the hundred or so women of child-bearing age; so acute is their problem that they're prepared to settle for Walter Bagley, who adopts the title King Tonka, but they're always on the look-out for more men, hence their excitement upon finding members of the expedition led by Bill Boosey in *Up the Jungle*.

LUBI LIEUTENANTS
Played by Valerie Moore and Cathi March
Seen in *Up the Jungle* with Leda, captain of the Lubidubies, when they invade the Nosha camp with the intention of taking Boosey and his party away with them.

LUCAS, MIKE
Role: Lusty Youth in *Camping*
Born in Coventry in 1941, Mike Lucas studied law for three years at the London School of

Economics but became so interested in running the school's drama society that upon graduating he enrolled at the Webber Douglas School of Singing and Dramatic Art.

His first professional engagement after leaving drama school was a month of weekly rep at the Palace Pier, Brighton, followed by a year as acting assistant stage manager at the Manchester Library Theatre. Soon after he got his initial taste of television, playing the first of three roles in *Crossroads*. Other jobs on television saw him pop up in *Doctor Who, The First Lady, Thicker Than Water* and the first series of *The Liver Birds*. He's only appeared in two films other than *Camping*, including *Assassin*.

Since 1972, Lucas has been running the Mikron Theatre, a theatre company which travels by canal during the summer months performing at pubs, village halls and similar venues. Since 1985 he no longer performs but continues to write, direct and deal with the admin involved in running the company.

LUDSKI, ARCHIE
Sound Editor on *Cruising*; Editor on *Cabby, Jack, Spying* and *Cleo*
Born in London in 1929, Archie Ludski began his fifty-year career straight from school. He worked for all the top British studios, including Denham, Ealing, Shepperton and Pinewood. His job also occasionally took him abroad: during the mid-1980s he spent five months in Australia working on a television series.

By the time he retired in 1994, at the age of sixty-five, his extensive list of film credits included *Passage to India, Gandhi, The Iron Maiden, Above Us the Waves, The Quiller Memorandum, Gorgo* and, more recently, *The Run of the Country, A Month By The Lake* and *Hamlet*.

LUGG, BERNIE
Played by Bernard Bresslaw
Seen in *Camping*, Bernie Lugg is one half of Boggle and Lugg, plumbing and sanitation engineers. As well as workmates, Bernie and Sid Boggle are chums; they date Anthea Meeks and Joan Fussey respectively but are frustrated at the progress they're making towards the bedroom, so Sid suggests visiting a nudist camp they saw in a film at the local cinema. Unfortunately, they pick the wrong site and end up in a mudpit in Devon. A kind-hearted but rather dimwitted guy, Bernie is easily led by his older mate.

LUIS, DON
Played by Patrick Cargill
For Don Luis in *Jack*, see 'Spanish Governor'.

LUMB, JANE
Roles: Amazon Guard in *Spying* and Vestal Virgin in *Cleo*
No longer acting, Jane Lumb made a few appearances during the 1960s, including a role

in the 1965 film for television, *The Debussy Film*, the same year as she appeared in *Doctor Who and the Daleks*.

LUPINO LANE, LAURI
Role: Husband in *Loving*
Born in London into a theatrical family stretching back centuries, Lauri Lupino Lane first appeared on stage at the age of eight. He became a regular panto performer and made his name in Variety, teaming up with George Truzzi from a famous circus family.

In 1970, Lupino Lane was appearing at the Palladium, the stage of his career when he began making occasional appearances in films such as *A King in New York*, *The Great Waltz*, *Side by Side* and *Confessions from a Holiday Camp*.

He died in 1986, aged sixty-four.

LUSTY YOUTHS
Played by Michael Low and Mike Lucas
Seen in *Camping*, the youths appear at an open window at Chayste Place, a finishing school for girls. After they whistle to the girls, Babs tells them to wait at the normal place; it looks like their wait was worth it because they're later seen kissing two of the girls passionately on the garden benches.

LYNCH, KENNY
Role: Bus Conductor in *Loving*. Also wrote the theme song, '*Love Crazy*', which was sung by Masterplan in *Emmannuelle*
Born in London in 1939, Kenny Lynch began singing with his sister, Maxine, in 1950, before enjoying minor hits during the early '60s. He charted again in 1983. An all-round entertainer, he's also worked as a stand-up comedian and acted in television shows such as *Till Death Us Do Part*, *Dawson's Weekly*, *The Sweeney* and *Room at the Bottom*. His film credits include *The Plank*, *The Playbirds* and *Confessions from the David Galaxy Affair*.

Lynch is now heavily involved in management and promotion, encouraging and helping new acts into the business.

LYNN, JACK
Role: Admiral of the Fleet in *Emmannuelle*
Born in London in 1923, Jack Lynn entered films in the early 1940s and his credits include *A Yank At Eton*, *Something of Value*, *Never Take Sweets From A Stranger* and *Yentl*. His television work ranges from *Champion House* and *The Befrienders* to *The Professionals* and *Shoestring*.

LYONS
Played by Jack Douglas
Emile Prevert's butler in *Emmannuelle* looks after the French Ambassador's every need, and doesn't do too badly with his wife, Emmannuelle, either, helping to satisfy her relentless sexual desires.

M

MacDONALD, TAMSIN
Role: Khasi's Wife in *Up The Khyber*

MacKENZIE, VERNA LUCILLE
Role: Gong Lubi in *Up the Jungle*

MacNAMARA, DIANA
Role: Princess Stephanie in *Don't Lose Your Head*. She also doubled for Angela Douglas in riding scenes on *Cowboy*
Diana MacNamara, who worked at a riding school in Sussex when she was appearing in the *Carry On* films, also doubled and appeared as an extra in other films, particularly those involving horse-riding sequences. In *Khartoum* she played a Sudanese soldier on horseback, complete with false moustache.

As well as working in repertory theatre, she's held various other jobs, including driving instructress, model, saleswoman and nanny.

MacNUTT, SERGEANT MAJOR
Played by Terry Scott
In *Up The Khyber* the constantly bellowing, foot-stamping Sergeant Major MacNutt is a hard taskmaster in charge of the soldiers from the 3rd Foot and Mouth regiment guarding the Khyber Pass.

MacNUTT'S LURE
Played by Dominique Don
This attractive girl is asked by Sergeant Major MacNutt to lure Brother Belcher, a missionary seen preaching in a Himalayan town, into a compromising position where he's susceptible to blackmail; when the girl kisses him passionately and Captain Keene and MacNutt catch them together, they force him to act as a guide on a military operation across the border to Afghanistan during *Up The Khyber*.

MacPHEE, ROBERT T.
Sound recordist on *Sergeant, Nurse, Teacher, Constable, Regardless, Cruising, Cowboy, Up The Khyber* and *Up the Jungle*
He worked as a sound recordist from the late 1950s, with credits including the films *True as a Turtle, Campbell's Kingdom, Watch Your Stern, Raising the Wind, A Pair of Briefs, The Mind*

Benders and, in 1969, *The Spy Killer*, made for ABC in America.

MADAME
Played by Renée Houston
In *Spying*, Madame is in charge of a harem based in Hakim's Fun House in the city of Algiers.

MADAME DESIREE ET SES OISEAUX DES PARADIS
For Madame Desiree et ses Oiseaux des Paradis in *Dick*, see either 'Desiree, Madame' or 'Birds of Paradise'.

MADDER, MELODY
The stage name used by Goldie Locks when she begins working in the film industry. Seen in *Again Doctor*. Refer to 'Locks, Goldie' for more details.

MADDERLEY, BRIDGET
Played by Esma Cannon
An eccentric, nervy passenger who likes a drink. She boards the *Happy Wanderer* for a Mediterranean cruise in *Cruising*.

MADDERN, VICTOR
Roles: Criminal Type (Detective Sergeant Liddell) in *Constable*, 1st Sinister Passenger in *Regardless*, Milchmann in *Spying*, Sergeant Major in *Cleo* and Man in Laundrette in *Emmannuelle*
TV: *Orgy and Bess, The Nine Old Cobblers* and *Under the Round Table*
Victor Maddern, born in Seven Kings, Essex, in 1928, was hardly ever out of work during the 1950s and '60s. Never the officer, always the sergeant, he was regularly seen playing tough, working-class characters in an array of British movies.

His working life began as a general dogsbody for a shipping firm during the war, before spending three years serving in one of the company's ships. Back on home soil after the cessation of hostilities, he trained at RADA and upon graduating taught drama at a college of further education alongside appearances at repertory theatres.

His rugged features were soon in demand on the screen, with early film credits including *Morning Departure, Seven Days to Noon, The Franchise Affair* and *Pool of London*. More notable appearances saw him playing Sergeant Craig in *Cockleshell Heroes*, Private Blake in *Private's Progress* and Private Lindop in *A Hill in Korea*. When the film parts tailed off during the 1970s, he concentrated on television, appearing in shows such as *Crossroads* and *The Dick Emery Show*.

His interests outside the profession saw him set up a company printing film scripts and running a school for public speaking. He died in 1993, aged sixty-five.

MADGE
Unseen in *Matron* but Madge, a nurse, is heard in the nurses' home acknowledging her friend's request for help with her hair.

MADISON, LEIGH
Roles: Sheila in *Sergeant* and Miss Winn in *Nurse*
Born in Aldershot, Hampshire, in 1940, Leigh Madison initially trained as a dancer at the Cone Ripman School in London. She left at seventeen and completed a summer season at Bournemouth, followed by several musicals.

Realising she needed to diversify to further her career, she wrote to casting director Betty White for guidance and soon found herself cast in *Ivanhoe*, alongside Roger Moore. Although she returned to dancing from time to time, including appearances in a Harry Secombe television series and the film version of *Six-Five Special*, she concentrated on acting. Her television credits included *The Flying Doctor* and *The Invisible Man*, while among the handful of films she appeared in are *High Jump, Serious Charge, Please Turn Over* and *Naked Fury*.

Her biggest screen role was in the Norman Hudis series, *Our House*, playing Marcia Hatton. Two series were produced for ABC Television by Ernest Maxin, whom Madison later married.

She left the profession during the 1960s to

Madame Desiree (Joan Sims) and her entertaining Birds of Paradise (*Dick*)

raise her son, returning briefly in the late 1970s; she appeared in the 1979 mini-series, *A Family Affair*. She had just been recommended by Rod Steiger for a Broadway play when she decided to retire from the business in the early 1980s.

MAGGIE
Played by Marianne Stone
The old lady is seen in the Old Cock Inn during *Dick*. Despite having one foot in the grave she's actually the midwife in the parish of Upper Dencher and tells Captain Fancey and Sergeant Strapp of the Bow Street Runners, who are searching for Dick Turpin, that she'd recognise the highwayman anywhere because he's got a distinctive birthmark on his 'diddler'.

MAHONEY, JANET
Role: Gay in *Loving*
Janet Mahoney made occasional appearances on the screen during the 1970s, appearing in films such as *Doctor in Trouble* and *Mutiny On the Buses*, as well as television programmes including *Up Pompeii* and *Dad's Army*.

MAID
Played by Valerie Shute
In *Henry* the maid was busily tidying Wolsey's desk. When the Cardinal enters the room, he's tempted to pinch her bottom before a flunkey

stops him in his tracks to announce the arrival of the Conte di Pisa. (**Note: the scene was cut.**)

MAÎTRE D'HOTEL
Played by Len Lowe
During Sid and Sophie's wedding reception in *Loving* he's seen running in to put a stop to the custard pie fight before slipping on a jelly and sliding across the room into a table.

MAJOR-DOMO
Played by Derek Sydney
In *Up The Khyber* the Major-domo announces the arrival of the Governor of Kalabar, Sir Sidney Ruff-Diamond, who's accompanied to the Khasi's palace by Captain Keene and Sergeant Major MacNutt.

MAJOR-DOMO
Played by David Davenport
In *Henry* the Major-domo advises Francis, the King of France, that Henry will be with him shortly.

MALABONCE
Played by Leon Greene
Dressed appropriately in black in *Don't Lose Your Head*, Malabonce is in charge of the guillotine in the Place de la Tête Pruner, where executions provide popular entertainment for the residents of Paris.

MAN FROM COX & CARTER
Played by Brian Wilde
In *Doctor* the man from Cox & Carter arrives at the Borough County Hospital to take measurements for the new rubber sheets the hospital is buying. He's told to use one of the private rooms for his measurements but picks the one occupied by Mr Bigger; already believing, incorrectly, that he has only days to live, Mr Bigger thinks the man is an over-eager undertaker measuring him for his coffin.

MAN IN CINEMA
Played by Michael Nightingale
A man at the Picture Playhouse in *Camping* who becomes irritated at Sid Boggle and Joan Fussey's constant chatting during the screening of *Nudist Paradise*. He eventually tells them to refrain from talking.

MAN IN GLASSES
Played by Sidney Johnson
Seen in the audience, sitting next to the Short-sighted Man at Professor Crump's lecture and film show in *Behind*.

MAN IN HOSPITAL
Played by Anthony Sagar
Occupies the bed next to Bertie Muffet's when

Bertie is hospitalised in *Loving* after being attacked by the ape-like wrestler, Gripper Burke.

MAN IN LAUNDRETTE
Played by Victor Maddern
The man appears in Mrs Dangle's flashback sequence during *Emmannuelle*, in which she recalls her most amorous experience.

MAN IN TWEEDS
Played by Michael Ward
In *Cabby* the smartly-dressed man alights from a taxi and begins walking down the road when Ted Watson, spotting a lost earring in his cab, asks if it's his, to which he replies: 'What, with tweeds?'

MAN MOUNTAIN MARTIN
Gripper Burke's last wrestling opponent in America before he returned to the UK is mentioned by Burke in *Loving*.

MAN WITH SALAD
Played by Billy Cornelius
The man is sitting peacefully at the side of his caravan, just about to tuck into some crispy salad, when a beach ball lands in his plate. He's staying at the Riverside Caravan Site with his wife in *Behind*.

MAN WITH WATER
Played by Ray Edwards
The man is washing up his dishes at the side of his caravan when Fred Ramsden, who's trying to impress two girls, wildly kicks a beach ball which lands in the man's water. He's staying at the Riverside Caravan Site in *Behind*.

MANGER, MELITA
Role: Woman with Salad in *Behind*
Born in Neath, Melita Manger always wanted to be a dancer and after leaving school studied at Brighton School of Music and Drama. Pantos, summer seasons and her first professional play, a production of Arnold Ridley's *The Ghost Train*, soon came her way. Before long, she was also being offered small parts in television shows, such as *Are You Being Served?*, *Doctor on the Go* and *The Basil Brush Show*.

Throughout the 1970s, Manger was also busy in commercials, but after getting married took a break from acting to raise a family. Today, she helps run the family business in Wales but still acts if asked: her last appearance was as a Welsh woman in *Waiting for God*.

MANLEY, PETER
Assistant Director on *Constable*
He worked on a host of films during his career, including *The Life and Death of Colonel Blimp*, *Hotel Sahara*, *The Colditz Story*, *Passage Home*, *The One That Got Away*, *The Spanish Gardener*, *Circus of Fear* and *The Red Baron*.

MANLEY, ROSEMARY
Role: Girl at Dirty Dick's in *Jack*

MANN, DORIS
Played by Angela Douglas
Seen in *Screaming!*, Doris, who's in her twenties, goes missing while out in Hocombe Woods with her boyfriend, Albert Potter. She's whisked away by a monster, Odbodd, who takes her to the Bide-a-Wee Rest Home, whose mysterious owners turn her into a shop-window dummy. Fortunately, the process is reversible and when a determined Potter finally tracks her down, the sound of wedding bells is soon heard.

MANOR DINING ROOM, THE
The Manor Dining Room is just down the road from where PC Benson questions a man he suspects of contemplating a crime in *Constable*.

MANOR ROAD
In *Constable*, Constable Constable is walking along Manor Road when he finally reveals his true feelings for WPC Passworthy. The trouble is, she doesn't hear him.

MARCH, CATHI
Role: Lubi Lieutenant in *Up the Jungle*

MARCH, ELSPETH
Roles: Lady Binder in *Don't Lose Your Head* and Hospital Board Member in *Again Doctor*
Born in 1911, the daughter of a colonel in the Indian medical service, Elspeth March completed her education in England before, aged twenty-one, landing small roles in the West End and later joining the Birmingham Repertory Theatre.

During World War Two, she worked as a driver with the American Red Cross for four years before returning to the West End with roles in *Peace in Our Time*, *Medea*, *The Turn of the Screw* and Shaw's *Caesar and Cleopatra*. She also played prominent parts in many of Shaw's other plays including *Saint Joan*, *The Millionairess*, *The Apple Cart* and *Arms and the Man*.

March moved to America in 1955 where she acted in Synge plays in New York, returning to England in the early '60s where, despite having trouble re-establishing her career, she appeared in films like *Goodbye Mr Chips*, on stage in shows including *On the Town* and *The Madras House* and in various repertory theatres.

Her television work included roles in *The Saint*, *Tales of the Unexpected*, *Sir Francis Drake* and, in 1982, Thames's comedy series, *Let There Be Love*, playing a mother.

She died in 1999, aged eighty-eight.

MARCH, LINDSAY
Role: Shapely Nurse in *Matron* (**Note: she was also cast as an air hostess in *Abroad* but the scene was cut.**)
Other screen credits during the late 1960s and early '70s include *Never Mind the Quality, Feel the Width*, an episode of the *Armchair Theatre*

series, as well as small roles in the films *Burke and Hare*, *Bless This House* and *Can You Keep It Up for a Week?*.

MARCUS
Played by Gertan Klauber
Seen in *Cleo* as one half of the partnership Marcus and Spencius, a business trading in slaves which he runs with his brother, Spencius.

MARDEN, RICHARD
Editor on *England*
Born in Wembley, Greater London, Richard Marden knew from his childhood years that he wanted his future to be in films. He secured his first job as a sound trainee at Carlton Hill Studios in London aged eighteen, subsequently becoming assistant editor on the 1948 film, *The Monkey's Paw*.

He later worked freelance until forming a partnership with three colleagues to make sponsored films, several in 3D, including a photographic record of Queen Mary's funeral. When 3D films were no longer in vogue, he returned to sound editing. From the 1960s he was working as an editor and among his many credits are *Othello*, *Hot Millions*, *Sleuth*, *Hellraiser* and, in 1996, *Hearts and Minds*. He was also employed in Singapore for two years, working for the Shell Film Unit editing their films and training local technicians.

MARGE
Played by Carol Hawkins
Marge travels to Elsbels, the Mediterranean resort, with her friend, Lily, on the Wundatours trip. Seen in *Abroad*, she's keen on finding a fella while away and sees her wish come true when she meets Brother Bernard, who gives up his missionary work to be with her.

MARIE ANTOINETTE ROOM, THE
The room hired by Sidney and Sophie Bliss to celebrate their wedding in *Loving*.

MARIE OF NORMANDY, QUEEN
Played by Joan Sims
The garlic-loving wife of King Henry VIII appears in *Henry*; her love for the strong-smelling plant repulses the King who seeks an annulment of the wedding moments after getting spliced. Marie, who was chased all over France by admirers before coming to England, is imprisoned at the Tower of London, but when she sneaks a message out to her cousin, Frances, the King of France, he sends a messenger before coming over himself to investigate her predicament. When she becomes pregnant, suspicions fall on Sir Roger de Lodgerley. The King's dislike of the smell of garlic meant he hadn't managed to get near enough to his Queen to consummate the marriage, and with Sir Roger being the King's equerry and claiming his job is to taste and test everything before His Majesty, he's

suspected of being the father. As a result he's also marched off to the Tower where he's subjected to a little stretching on the rack!

MARIO
Played by Peter Butterworth
For Mario in *Abroad*, see 'Pepe'.

MARION-CRAWFORD, HOWARD
Role: Wine Organiser in *Regardless*
Character actor Howard Marion-Crawford, born in London in 1914, worked on stage and screen from the mid-1930s and remained busy throughout his career. By the time the 1930s had ended, he'd already appeared in five films, including *Brown on Resolution*, *Music Hath Charms* and *Secret Agent*. Other films included *Night Train to Munich*, *Freedom Radio*, *The Hasty Heart*, *Reach for the Sky*, *The Longest Day* and, his last film, *Avalanche*.

On television he was seen in *Wire Service*, *Interpol Calling*, *Danger Man*, *The Saint*, *Detective*, *Man in a Suitcase* and *The Avengers*.

He died in 1969, aged fifty-five.

MARJORIBANKS, LEONARD
Played by Kenneth Williams
The new First Officer on the *Happy Wanderer* in *Cruising*. His first trip sees him sailing the Mediterranean in April.

MARQUIS DE SADE
The title of the book read by Duc de Pommfrit whilst awaiting his turn at the guillotine in *Don't Lose Your Head*.

MARSDEN, BETTY
Roles: Mata Hari in *Regardless* and Harriet Potter in *Camping*
Liverpudlian Betty Marsden, who was born in 1919, had one of the most recognisable voices in the industry thanks to the array of characters she created on the 1960s radio series, *Beyond Our Ken* and *Round the Horne*.

Soon after her music teacher spotted Marsden's potential as an entertainer, she made her stage debut in Bath, aged eleven, as a supporting fairy in *A Midsummer Night's Dream*. By the time she won a scholarship to the Italia Conti Stage School a year later, she'd already experienced the London stage, appearing in *The Windmill Man*.

After graduating from Italia Conti, she worked regularly on the stage before entertaining the troops with ENSA. Her radio work became the mainstay of her career, although she remained busy in the theatre. She made occasional appearances on television and in films, including *The Young Lovers*, *The Big Day*, *Eyewitness* and *Britannia Hospital*.

She died in 1998, aged seventy-nine.

MARTIN, BILL
Co-wrote the song, 'Don't Lose Your Head', heard in the film of the same name

MARTIN, BROTHER
Played by Derek Francis
In charge of the group of missionaries, including Brother Bernard, which travels to Elsbels, the Mediterranean resort, on the Wundatours trip. Seen in *Abroad*, the old, crusty leader shows he's still retained his sense of humour, though, when the punch starts flowing at the farewell party.

MARTIN, REUBEN
Role: Gorilla in *Up the Jungle*. Also an uncredited role as a gorilla in *Emmannuelle*
TV: *Lamp Posts of the Empire*
Reuben Martin, who died in 1994, was a stunt man and bit-part player who made several appearances as a gorilla during his career. Other credits include playing a henchman in the 1968 film, *Great Catherine*.

MARTIN, SALLY
Played by Jacki Piper
A model in *Loving* who regards herself as an unknown star of stage, screen and television. She accepts a modelling job and awaits the photographer at the cocktail bar of the Parkway Hotel. He doesn't turn up but Bertie Muffet does, waiting for a date; they both think they've found the person they're waiting for and head off back to Sally's flat. It only dawns on them that something is wrong when Sally starts stripping off and Bertie gets his model aeroplanes out; however, theirs is a fortuitous meeting because it's the start of a long-lasting relationship.

MARTINUS, DEREK
Role: Recruit in *Sergeant*
Born in 1931, Derek Martinus began his screen career as an actor before moving behind the camera in the early 1960s to write and direct. His credits as a director, primarily on television, include *Doctor Who*, *United!*, *Angels*, *The Paper Lads*, *Penmarric* and an episode of *Blake's 7*.

MARTYN, LARRY
Roles: Rifle-Range Owner in *At Your Convenience* and Electrician in *Behind*
Born in London in 1934, Larry Martyn entered the industry in the 1950s, working in Variety as a singer and comedian until the age of twenty-two. His early small-screen career was dominated by drama until the 1970s, when he was employed more frequently in light entertainment.

His television appearances included *Dad's Army*, *Rising Damp*, *Spring and Autumn*, *The Dick Emery Show*, *Up Pompeii!*, *Mike Yarwood in Persons*, *Never Mind the Twain* and *The Bill*. He also made several films, such as *Up the Junction*, *The Great St Trinian's Train Robbery*, *Breath of Life* and *The Troublesome Double*.

Martyn served with the Parachute Regiment

during the war and continued the activity as a hobby. He died in 1994.

MARY'S MUM
Played by Helen Goss
Mary's mother pops up in the opening scenes of *Sergeant*, attending her daughter's wedding to Charlie Sage.

MASKELL, MARIANNE
Role: Nurse in Hospital in *Emmannuelle*

MASTER OF CEREMONIES
Played by Jack Taylor
In *Regardless* the Master of Ceremonies disappoints the crowd at a boxing match by announcing the bout between Dynamite Dan and Massive Micky has been cancelled because Dan has hurt his little finger.

MASTERPLAN
Sang Kenny Lynch's title song, 'Love Crazy', in *Emmannuelle*.

MATA HARI
Played by Betty Marsden
With her elongated cigarette holder, expensive clothes and curious wink, this female rail passenger in *Regardless* intrigues Sam Twist on his fruitless trip to the Forth Bridge – that is until she slaps him around the face for pestering her.

MATHEWS, SERGEANT
Played by John Mathews
In *Sergeant*, Mathews is in charge of Baker Platoon at Heathercrest National Service Depot.

MATHEWS, JOHN
Roles: Sergeant Mathews in *Sergeant* and Tom Mayhew in *Nurse*
Also seen in a small role during the 1960 film, *Watch Your Stern*.

MATRON
Played by Joan Hickson
In *Regardless* the Matron mistakes Bert Handy for Sir Theodore, an important visitor who's arriving to inspect the hospital.

MATRON
Played by Hattie Jacques
In *Nurse* the Matron is a strict disciplinarian who marches around the wards of Haven Hospital leaving staff quaking with fear. She has plenty of pet hates, such as seeing men lying around on top of their beds: she feels it makes the ward look untidy, a point which doesn't go down well with Oliver Reckitt, one of the patients.

MATRON
Played by Hattie Jacques
In *Doctor* the Matron, who's called Lavinia, is madly in love with Dr Tinkle; when she finds him in the clutches of Nurse May, she assumes incorrectly that he's entertaining a nurse in his

room and threatens to tell the hospital authorities unless he's a little more receptive to her own advances.

MATRON
Played by Hattie Jacques

Matron, who's called Miss Soper, is seen in *Again Doctor*. She initially works at the Long Hampton Hospital but quits her job when offered employment by Dr Nookey at his new luxurious clinic, helping the obese lose weight almost instantaneously thanks to a miracle cure.

MATRON
Played by Hattie Jacques

The Matron of Finisham Maternity Hospital in *Matron* runs the establishment in an orderly, efficient manner. She lives in room 18 in the living quarters and is single, though she eventually realises a dream by getting hitched to Sir Bernard Cutting, whom she's admired for almost the entire fifteen years she's worked at the maternity hospital.

MATRON
Played by Brenda Cowling

The matron in *Girls* works at the maternity hospital in Fircombe and shows the mayor and councillors around when the Frederick Bumble Nursery is opened.

MATRON, CARRY ON
See feature box on pages 168–9.

MATT
Played by Michael Balfour

One of three thieves involved in the wages snatch in *Constable*. They hide in an empty house until they're finally caught by the young rookie policemen.

MAUD
Played by Marianne Stone

With a laugh like a hyena, Maud works at Boggs and Son and is seen in *At Your Convenience*. She's best friends with Chloe Moore, also an employee of the company.

MAUDLIN STREET SECONDARY MODERN SCHOOL
The setting for *Teacher*, this tough secondary modern is every teacher's nightmare. Unruly kids charging around corridors, showing little respect for their elders, it seems the cane is the only way of keeping this rabble under control. But they show a more sensitive side to their nature when they do whatever they can to prevent their acting head, Mr Wakefield, from heading off to pastures new. The trouble is, the way they go about achieving their goal leaves much to be desired.

MAUREEN
Played by Diana Darvey

A local girl who attends the cabaret evening at the Riverside Caravan Site in *Behind*. She's accompanied by her friend, Sally, and ends up chatting away to Fred and Ernie.

MAVIS
Played by Dilys Laye

Brunette Mavis Winkle is a patient in the Caffin Ward at the Borough County Hospital. Seen in *Doctor*, she strikes up a hospital romance with Ken Biddle; she's also responsible for summoning up the support from the women's ward when the patients decide to take action against Matron and Dr Tinkle, who were instrumental in Dr Kilmore tendering his resignation.

MAXINE, MARGOT
Role: Harem Girl in *Follow That Camel*

MAY, MRS
Played by Joan Hickson

Seen in *Constable*, Mrs May is a regular in the police cells. Usually inebriated, she's a menace around the local streets and on this occasion is arrested by the keen young WPC Passworthy. Once again drunk, May hit a barman at the Coach and Horses over the head when he asked her to leave. Claims to be friends with numerous figures of authority, including various politicians.

MAY, NURSE SANDRA
Played by Barbara Windsor

In *Doctor*, Nurse May arrives at the Borough County Hospital as a student nurse desperate to meet Dr Tinkle, whom she classes as her saviour even though he only operated on her for tonsillitis, once again. She's infatuated with him and thought that the fact he spent a lot of time delivering after-care, visiting her room for months and remarking on her lovely enlarged glands, must mean he feels for her; Tinkle is embarrassed she's arrived at the hospital and is keen to get rid of her, something which happens when she feels Dr Kilmore has invaded her privacy while she sunbathed on the roof of the nurses' home, although he was only trying to help, believing she was planning to jump.

MAYHEW, TOM
Played by John Mathews

Seen in *Nurse*, Mr Mayhew is a patient at Haven Hospital.

MAYNARD, BILL
Roles: Mr Dreery in *Loving*, Guy Fawkes in *Henry*, Fred Moore in *At Your Convenience*, Fred in *Matron* and Bodkin in *Dick* **(Note: also cast as Mr Fiddler in *Abroad* but scene cut.)**
Born in Farnham, Surrey, in 1928, Bill Maynard, who'll always be remembered as Claude Greengrass in Yorkshire's police drama, *Heartbeat*, began his career as a children's entertainer in the Midlands, before working as a singer at Butlin's; by the early '50s, Maynard

was earning £100 a week at the Windmill Theatre.

His television break came with *Great Scott – It's Maynard*, a series with Terry Scott, while other small-screen credits include *The Life of Riley*, *The Gaffer*, his own sitcom, *Oh No, It's Selwyn Froggit* and *Worzel Gummidge*, as well as appearances in films such as *It All Goes to Show*, *One More Time*, *A Hole Lot of Trouble*, *Bless This House* and *Confessions of a Window Cleaner*.

He was forced to take a break from acting in 2000 when he suffered a series of strokes but has since returned to the profession. Recent credits include an episode of *Dalziel and Pascoe*, as well as reprising Greengrass in the *Heartbeat* off-shoot, *The Royal*.

McCALLUM, GORDON K.
Sound recordist on *Sergeant*, *Teacher*, *Regardless*, *Cabby*, *Cleo* and *England*
Born in Chicago in 1919, Gordon K. McCallum enjoyed a long career which saw him work in various capacities within the sound departments at Elstree, Denham and Pinewood.

He chalked up over 300 credits, beginning in the mid-1940s with such productions as *A Canterbury Tale*, *I Know Where I'm Going*, *Carnival*, *Great Expectations*, *Blanche Fury* and *The Red Shoes*. Later films he worked on include *Funeral in Berlin*, *Billion Dollar Brain*, *Battle of Britain*, *Ryan's Daughter*, *Superman* and several Bond movies.

He died in 1989.

McCALLUM TAIT, KENNETH
Set Dresser on *Girls*

First credited as a set decorator on the 1950 film, *Shadow of the Eagle*, McCallum Tait proceeded to work on numerous episodes of cult television series *The Avengers*, as well as films such as *State Secret*, *Innocents in Paris*, *One Million Years BC*, *The Best Pair of Legs in the Business* and, in 1974, *Kronos*.

McCORD, CAL
Role: Mex in *Cowboy*

From the late 1950s, Cal McCord appeared in such television shows as *International Detective* and films *Kill Me Tomorrow*, *Too Young to Love*, *The V.I.P.s* and *The Adding Machine*.

McCORKINDALE, DON
Roles: Recruit in *Sergeant* and Tubby in *Cabby*
Born in London in 1939, Don McCorkindale attended the Italia Conti Academy on Saturday mornings from the age of eleven, turning full-time upon leaving school. His early work saw him appear in the 1955 film, *The Blue Peter*, and the BBC's children's programme, *Space School*, playing Tubby Thompson.

After appearing in *Sergeant* he completed his National Service in the army, based in Germany, before turning to the theatre; his work on stage has included a four-week tour of Canada in Bernard Miles's production of *Treasure Island*; he was later directed by Miles's daughter, Sally, in *The Wakefield Mystery Cycle* at London's Mermaid Theatre. He also enjoyed a long stint at the Players' Theatre.

His screen work covers shows such as *The Adventures of Sherlock Holmes, Call Me Mister, Bad Girls, Heartbeat* and *Grange Hill* (playing Mr Forbes) on television, as well as films like *Killer Force* and *Doctor Sleep*.

Between 1968-76 he lived and worked in South Africa before returning to England and continuing his career. Other than a few years spent working as a theatrical agent in the late 1990s, he's remained in the business with recent television credits including *EastEnders* and *D-Day to Berlin*.

McGEAGH, STANLEY
Roles: Short-sighted Man in *Behind* and Fleet Street Journalist in *Emmannuelle*
Stanley McGeagh, who now lives in Australia, appeared regularly on the screen during the 1960s and '70s. On television he played the hero in 'An Author in Search of Two Characters', an episode of *Jason King*, a police sergeant in a 1969 episode of *Doctor in the House* and several appearances in *Doctor Who*. His film credits include playing a prison guard in 1982's *Gandhi* and Hiller in the 1975 picture, *The Land That Time Forgot*.

McGEE, HENRY
Role: Harold Hump in *Emmannuelle*
Born in London in 1929, Henry McGee turned to acting after completing National Service. After two years training at the Italia Conti Stage School as a mature student, he worked at numerous reps, including three years at Northampton, before spending two years down-under playing the lead in a stage production of *For Better, For Worse*. Upon his return more rep work was followed by his television debut in Associated Rediffusion's *Uncle Harry*.

His big break on the small screen came in 1965, playing Mr Pugh, a Labour Exchange clerk, alongside Charlie Drake in *The Worker*. He went on to work with Max Wall, Frankie Howerd, Dick Emery, Reg Varney and Benny Hill, an association lasting twenty-three years. McGee has worked little on television for some years and for the last decade has concentrated on stage work, particularly Ray Cooney farces.

He's also made occasional appearances in films, including *Sailor Beware* in 1956, *The Italian Job, Digby, Holiday on the Buses* and *Revenge of the Pink Panther*.

McGEE, MASSIVE MICKY
Played by Tom Clegg
A hulk of a man, Massive Micky is a boxer in *Regardless*. Not someone to mess with, he's billed to fight the new boy on the scene,

Dynamite Dan, until an injury causes the bout's cancellation. Before he can leave the ring, though, the puny Gabriel Dimple steps in; in advance of Dimple being flattened by the oversized fists of Micky, an accidental headbutt knocks the heavyweight out cold.

McGUIRK, WILLIAM
Role: Flunkey in *Henry*
Born in Preston, Lancashire, in 1930, William McGuirk intended to become a priest but eventually dropped out and completed his National Service. Afterwards, McGuirk worked in various offices during the day, while his evenings were occupied with amateur dramatics in Wigan, where his family had moved years earlier.

His professional acting career started when an American friend offered a job with On Target, an instructional drama group touring US Air Force bases in Europe and Africa. He remained with the company for four years before securing employment in repertory theatres; he also worked with the Royal Shakespeare Company. On television, his credits included *Doctor Who, Coronation Street, Angels, Juliet Bravo* and *Call Me Mister*.

He died in 2001, aged seventy.

MEDICAL CORPORAL
Played by Ian Whittaker
Seen in *Sergeant* the corporal helps run the medical centre at Heathercrest National Service Depot, and happens to be on duty when Horace Strong, a member of the twenty-ninth intake who believes he's suffering from

the entire world's ailments, makes the first of many visits.

MEDWIN, MICHAEL
Role: Ginger in *Nurse*
Since making his professional acting debut in 1941, Michael Medwin has been frequently cast as Cockney crooks or jovial types.

Born in London in 1923, he began his education at public school in Dorset before finishing his schooling at the Fischer Institute in Montreux, Switzerland. Wanting to be an actor, he returned to England at sixteen and enrolled at the Italia Conti drama school. His professional debut was in Priestley's *They Came to a City* in Newcastle upon Tyne, but the highlight of his stage work was playing the lead role in West End hit *Alfie*.

His first film role was in 1946's *Route of All Evil*, playing a grocer's boy, followed quickly by a string of film credits, including *Piccadilly Incident, The Courtneys of Curzon Street, Trottie True, The Long Dark Hall, Above Us the Waves* and *A Hill in Korea*. The film offers continued to pour in, and in 1952 he headed for Dorset to film *The Oracle*, with Virginia McKenna, in a Group 3 production. Although it never excited the critics, it was Medwin's favourite picture.

By the age of thirty he'd notched up over forty film appearances, but soon became a favourite on the small screen as the uncouth, anti-establishment hero, Corporal Springer, in the popular series *The Army Game*. Medwin remained with the show two years, and its success led to his own show, *The Love of Mike*.

Ginger (Michael Medwin) visits Bernie Bishop (Kenneth Connor) (*Nurse*)

CARRY ON MATRON

Alternative titles . . . *From Here To Maternity*, *Familiarity Breeds*, *Womb At The Top* and *The Preggers Opera*

A Peter Rogers production
Distributed through Rank Organisation
Released as an A certificate in 1972 in colour
Running time: 87 mins

CAST

Sidney James	Sid Carter
Kenneth Williams	Sir Bernard Cutting
Charles Hawtrey	Dr Francis A. Goode
Hattie Jacques	Matron
Joan Sims	Mrs Tidey
Bernard Bresslaw	Ernie Bragg
Barbara Windsor	Nurse Susan Ball
Kenneth Connor	Mr Tidey
Terry Scott	Dr Prodd
Kenneth Cope	Cyril Carter
Jacki Piper	Sister
Bill Maynard	Freddy
Patsy Rowlands	Evelyn Banks
Derek Francis	Arthur
Amelia Bayntun	Mrs Jenkins
Valerie Leon	Jane Darling
Brian Osborne	Ambulance Driver
Gwendolyn Watts	Frances Kemp
Valerie Shute	Miss Smethurst
Margaret Nolan	Mrs Tucker
Michael Nightingale	Pearson
Wendy Richard	Miss Willing
Zena Clifton	Au pair Girl
Bill Kenwright	Reporter
Robin Hunter	Mr Darling
Jack Douglas	Twitching Father
Madeline Smith	Mrs Pullitt
Juliet Harmer	Mrs Bentley
Gilly Grant	Nurse in Bath
Lindsay March	Shapely Nurse
Laura Collins	Nurse

PRODUCTION TEAM

Screenplay by Talbot Rothwell
Music composed and conducted by Eric Rogers
Production Manager: Jack Swinburne
Art Director: Lionel Couch
Editor: Alfred Roome
Director of Photography: Ernest Steward
Camera Operator: James Bawden
Continuity: Joy Mercer
Assistant Director: Bert Batt
Sound Recordists: Danny Daniel and Ken Barker
Make-up: Geoffrey Rodway
Hairdresser: Stella Rivers
Costume Designer: Courtenay Elliott
Assistant Art Director: William Alexander
Set Dresser: Peter Lamont
Dubbing Editor: Peter Best
Titles: G.S.E. Ltd
Processed by Rank Film Laboratories
Assistant Editor: Jack Gardner
Wardrobe Mistresses: Vi Murray and Maggie Lewin
Producer: Peter Rogers
Director: Gerald Thomas

Gerald Thomas consults the script with Hattie Jacques and Terry Scott

Small-time crook Sid Carter and his gang are preparing for their next job: Finisham Maternity Hospital holds huge stocks of the contraceptive pill and Sid has plans to steal a consignment and sell them abroad.

Meanwhile, the daily routines of hospital life continue like clockwork with the arrival of Sir Bernard Cutting, chief surgeon, who suffers from an acute case of hypochondria; Matron only has to mention the bout of Asian flu affecting the local area and Cutting spots the symptoms within himself. His latest worries stem from a visit to a colleague, Mr Pearson, who examines X-rays of his stomach and confirms Cutting has nothing to worry about. An innocent aside concerning how his pelvic cavity resembles a women's has Cutting racing up to his office, consulting various tomes concerning sex change and meeting another of his colleagues, Dr Goode, a psychiatrist, to discuss the matter, claiming he's finding out for a friend to save himself embarrassment. Goode lifts a considerable weight from Cutting's shoulders when he explains that all this person is suffering from is a desire to prove his masculinity. Goode suggests finding a partner as soon as possible, so Cutting sets his sights on Matron, who's always had a soft spot for him, but when he finds Dr Goode hiding in her cupboard one evening, he suspects them of having an affair, and won't believe the truth that the two good friends were just watching television together.

Sid Carter pretends to be an expectant father in an attempt to find out where the pills are kept but when he doesn't succeed, he decides there is only one option: to send his son, Cyril, into the hospital disguised as a nurse. Cyril, who's been offered a career in insurance, doesn't want to follow a life of crime like his father, but Sid and the rest of the gang, Ernie and Fred, try making him feel guilty by referring to the time he promised his dying mother that he'd follow in his father's footsteps, even though he was only six at the time. Reluctantly, he feels obliged to go along with the plan and joins a group of student nurses arriving at Finisham Maternity Hospital. When the elastic snaps in his black knickers, though, he heads to the loo with a safety pin but inadvertently goes into the men's toilet, where Cyril encounters the randy Dr Prodd, whose sole reason for becoming a doctor was to chase the nurses.

When they cross each other's paths later, Cyril discovers Prodd has a

plan of the hospital in his room and is amenable to the idea of meeting up, but when Cyril arrives at Prodd's room, he soon discovers that the doctor has other things on his mind than the hospital plan; he manages to escape the doctor's clutches with his clothes intact, but just when he thinks his nursing responsibilities are over, he gets dragged into the back of an ambulance when a nurse is required urgently to attend an emergency call, alongside none other than Dr Prodd. Film star Jane Darling's baby has decided to enter the world prematurely, but when a mishap finds Prodd knocked unconscious, it's down to Cyril to help deliver Mrs Darling's triplets. Making the front page of the national newspapers isn't the kind of low-key role Sid Carter had planned for his son; worse still, his roommate realises she's sharing a room with a man masquerading as a nurse but agrees to bite her tongue when she falls for Cyril.

Thanks to all the attention Cyril has brought to the hospital, Sid Carter knows the job has to be completed quickly and plans to raid the place that evening. Dressed up as a doctor, with Ernie donning a dress and an unrealistic lump, Sid pretends to be Dr Zhivago arriving at the hospital with a pregnant woman, but their attempt to steal the pills fails and they're prevented from escaping; fortunately Sid Carter persuades Sir Bernard Cutting against calling the police by pointing out that it would reflect badly on the hospital if news ever got out that Nurse Carter was actually a man.

Wedding bells ring for Bernard Cutting and Matron

However, it's for his role as Don Satchley, head of Radio West in BBC's detective series *Shoestring*, that he's more recently remembered.

Through the 1970s and '80s, Medwin's stage and screen appearances were infrequent as he dedicated more time to producing. During the 1990s, Medwin continued to make the occasional appearance as an actor, including roles in *The Endless Game*, *Staggered*, *Alice Through the Looking Glass* and *Fanny and Elvis*.

MEEKS, ANTHEA
Played by Dilys Laye
In *Camping*, Anthea Meeks is the girlfriend of Bernie Lugg, who goes on a camping holiday with him and their friends, Sid Boggle and Joan Fussey. Suffers from travel sickness which explains why the party is constantly stopping en route to their camp site in Devon.

MEG
Played by June Whitfield
In *Nurse*, Meg is Jack Bell's girlfriend who visits him at Haven Hospital. They had been planning a little trip along the coast, staying at secluded hotels en route, until Bell's bunion played up.

MELLINGER, MICHAEL
Role: Chindi in *Up The Khyber*
Born in Kochel, Germany, in 1929, Mellinger was working on the British screen from the 1950s. His film credits include *South of Algiers*, *Radio Cab Murder*, *The Password Is Courage*, *Goldfinger* and, in 2001, *Charlotte Gray*. His television work ranged from appearances in *Assignment Foreign Legion*, *Corrigan Blake* and *Crossroads* to *Bergerac*, *Jonathan Creek* and *Strange*.

He died in 2004, aged seventy-four.

MELLY, CAPTAIN S.
Played by Kenneth Connor
Takes charge of the experimental anti-aircraft 1313 battery in *England*, replacing Captain Bull who's been driven to the bottle by the antics of the rabble he tried in vain to command. Melly arrives full of good intentions, primarily to turn the unit into an efficient fighting force, with the Sergeant Major giving them hell in the meantime. It's not long, though, before he realises the enormity of the task he faces.

MELLY'S DRIVER
Played by Johnny Briggs
The corporal is tasked with driving Captain S. Melly around in *England*.

MEN'S WARD NURSE
Played by Georgina Simpson
The blonde nurse appears in *Again Doctor* trying to intercept an inebriated Doctor Nookey as he runs through the ward.

MERCER, JOY
Continuity on *Follow That Camel*, *Doctor* and *Matron*
In continuity from the 1960s, she worked on television series like *The Saint* and films such as *The Fast Lady*, *The Long Duel*, *Night of the Big Heat*, *Hot Millions* and *Bless This House*.

MERCHANDISE
See 'Merchandise' on page 277.

MEREDITH, JILL MAI
Roles: Shapely Miss in *Cruising* and Cigarette Girl in *Spying*
Jill Mai Meredith, who trained at the Aida Foster School of Dance and Drama, was occasionally seen on the screen during the 1960s, in films such as *The Cool Mikado*, *The Leather Boys*, *You Must Be Joking!* and, in 1967, *Billion Dollar Brain*. She also worked on television and was a successful model.

MERRY, SUSANNA
Continuity on *Again Doctor*
Other films Merry has worked on include *When Dinosaurs Ruled the Earth*, *The Wicker Man*, *Swallows and Amazons* and *The Rocky Horror Picture Show*.

MERVYN, WILLIAM
Roles: Sir Cyril Ponsonby in *Follow That Camel*, Lord Paragon in *Again Doctor* and Physician in *Henry*
Born in Nairobi, Kenya, in 1912, William Mervyn spent the first five years of his career in repertory theatres at Hull and Liverpool before making his London debut, after the war, in *The Guinea Pig*.

He had a long list of theatre credits to his name by the time he started appearing on the screen. His film credits included *Conflict of Wings*, *The Long Arm*, *Carve Her Name With Pride*, *Invasion Quartet*, *Murder Ahoy* and *The Railway Children*. On television, he appeared in such shows as *Follyfoot*, *Doctor Who* and *Raffles*, but is probably best remembered for playing Justice Cambell in *Crown Court* for four years and the Bishop of St. Ogg's in the series, *All Gas and Gaiters*.

He died in 1976, aged sixty-four.

MESSENGER
Played by Ian Wilson
Seen in *Cleo*, the Messenger arrives all the way from Rome with a note from Seneca, Caesar's father-in-law.

MESSENGER
Played by Nikki Van Der Zyl
The messenger brings an urgent message for Duc de Pommfrit in *Don't Lose Your Head*. The trouble is, he's just about to be decapitated by guillotine, so asks her to drop the letter in the basket which collects the severed head and he'll read it later.

MESSENGER
Played by Anthony Bailey
Seen in *Dick* delivering an urgent message from the Parish Constable in Upper Dencher to Sir Roger Daley concerning the supposed capture of Dick Turpin, which turns out to be untrue. The captive is none other than Captain Fancey.

MESSENGER, DUDLEY
Sound Recordist on *Don't Lose Your Head*, *Follow That Camel* and *Doctor*
During a long career, Dudley Messenger was first credited as a sound recordist on the 1948 film, *It's Hard to Be Good*. He built up a healthy list of credits, including films such as *The Purple Plain*, *A Stitch in Time*, *Goldfinger*, *Nobody Runs Forever* and his last film, *The Private Life of Sherlock Holmes*, in 1970.

METAMORPHOSIS: A STUDY OF THE SEX CHANGE IN MAN
The title of a book Sir Bernard Cutting consults when he thinks he's turning into a woman. He reads it during *Matron*.

MEX
Played by Cal McCord
Seen in *Cowboy*, Mex helps to bring a blindfolded Judge Burke to Rumpo's hideout. Rumpo wants to bribe the judge to help rid Stodge City of the newly-arrived marshal.

MEXICAN GIRL
Played by Carmen Dene
In *Cowboy* the Mexican Girl is seen with Sam Houston exiting a barn as Rumpo arrives to inform him someone has stolen his cattle.

MICHAEL SAMMES SINGERS, THE
Sang the song, 'Don't Lose Your Head', in the film of the same name
Born in Reigate, Surrey, Michael Sammes, who studied the cello, singing and arranging, began his working life at a music publisher before, in the 1950s, forming the Mike Sammes Singers.

They completed session work, were hired by the BBC and sang in Variety shows up and down the country, including many staged at the London Palladium. They also performed as backing singers on recordings, such as Cliff Richard and The Shadows' 'Schoolboy Crush', which was the B-side of their first single in 1958. The Singers remained busy throughout the 1970s and '80s.

MICHELE
A beauty salon in *Regardless* which stages a demonstration of the salon's latest beautification routine. The trouble is, they asked Helping Hands for a woman to help in the demonstrations but confusion results in Montgomery Infield-Hopping turning up instead.

MICK
Played by Harry Locke
Mick is the amiable ward orderly in *Nurse*. He

spends most of his day running errands for the Colonel – a patient who has his own private room in the Haven Hospital – which usually entail placing bets on the afternoon's horse racing.

MILCHMANN
Played by Victor Maddern
Disguised as a milkman in *Spying*, Milchmann arrives at Bilkington Research Establishment and delivers milk to Professor Stark's laboratory before planting a bomb and stealing a secret formula. He eventually meets his maker in a warehouse in Vienna.

MILL LANE
A road mentioned in *Cabby* during the scene where Peggy and Sally are driving while held at gunpoint by crooks.

MILLER, COLIN
Dubbing Editor on *Up The Khyber*, *Camping*, *Again Doctor* and *Up the Jungle*
Born in London in 1940, Colin Miller left school and began working for a production company, based at Shepperton, making commercials. He was eventually offered the chance to assist on the John Mills 1961 World War II film, *The Valiant*. He spent six years in the position before being promoted to sound editor; his first picture in this capacity was *Up The Khyber*.

Other film credits include *The Best Pair of Legs in the Business*; *Soft Beds, Hard Battles*; *The Wild Geese*; *The Sea Wolves*; *The Return of the Musketeers*; *Fierce Creatures* and *The Remains of the Day*. He's also worked on six Bond movies. His occasional television includes Alan Bleasdale's 1991 series, *G.B.H.*

After four decades in the business he remains busy and has recently completed work on the film, *Nouvelle France*.

MILLS, FREDDIE
Roles: Crook in *Constable* and Lefty in *Regardless*
Born in Parkstone, Dorset, in 1919, Freddie Mills was a professional boxer who fought his first bout in 1936, aged sixteen. Six years later, he was crowned British light-heavyweight champion and went on to challenge for the world title twice, eventually winning in 1948. But his reign was shortlived and he lost making his first defence.

After quitting boxing in 1950, he became a screen personality and appeared in a handful of films, including *Emergency Call*, *One Jump Ahead*, *Breakaway*, *Chain of Events* and *Joey Boy*. He also hosted the music show, *Six-Five Special*, and his own keep-fit programme, *Keep Fit with Freddie Mills*.

He died in 1965, aged forty-six, outside his nightclub, The Freddie Mills Nite Spot.

MILLS, INSPECTOR
Played by Eric Barker
The inefficient, ineffectual Inspector Mills runs the police station in *Constable* – well on paper,

anyway. The real driving force behind day-to-day duties is his long-suffering sergeant, who's always being unfairly threatened with transfer if he doesn't pull his socks up. It's Mills – who started his career at Sidcup North – who needs to improve; approaching retirement from the force he's more interested in the well-being of his tropical fish than his staff. A man who's continually passing the buck, he's always apportioning blame wherever possible for the station's lack of discipline instead of accepting responsibility himself. He's quick enough, though, to take the credit when some of his raw recruits happen to catch robbers; as a result, the chief constable transfers him to the area college, in charge of, ironically, morale and discipline.

MILLS, JULIET
Role: Sally in *Jack*
Born in Great Missenden, Buckinghamshire, in 1941, the daughter of Sir John Mills, she completed her education at the Elmhurst Ballet School in Camberley, Surrey.

Her first experience of the screen was as a baby when she appeared with her father in *In Which We Serve*. As a girl, she was also seen in three of his other films: *So Well Remembered*, *The October Man* and *The History of Mr Polly*.

She returned to the big screen in her twenties – by which time she'd also found success in the West End and on Broadway in *Five Finger Exercise* aged just fifteen – appearing in a string of titles such as *No, My Darling Daughter*; *Twice Round the Daffodils*; *Nurse on Wheels* and *The Rare Breed*.

In the 1960s she moved to America and worked on a host of films and television programmes, including *The Man from U.N.C.L.E.*, *Ben Casey*, *Alias Smith and Jones*, *Medical Story*, *Hawaii Five-O*, *The Love Boat*, *Fantasy Island* and *Hart to Hart*. She continued to work throughout the 1990s, with one of her most recent shows being *Passions*.

MILTON, EDWIN
Played by Kenneth Williams
The English teacher at Maudlin Street Secondary Modern School, Milton is seen in *Teacher*. One of his main tasks is to produce the school play, an interpretation of *Romeo and Juliet*.

MINNIE
Played by Andrea Allen
A saloon girl seen at Rumpo's Place in *Cowboy*.

MITCHELL, BILLY J.
Role: Gunner Childs in *England*
Born in 1942, Billy J. Mitchell began working on the British screen in the 1970s; his television credits include *Space: 1999*, *Shoestring*, *Bergerac*, *Kavanagh QC* and *Coronation Street*, while the list of films he's appeared in includes such titles as *Superman*, *The Lonely Lady*, *Indiana Jones*

and the Last Crusade and two Bond movies – *Never Say Never Again* and *GoldenEye*.

MITCHELL, NORMAN
Roles: Bespectacled Business Man in *Cabby*, Native Policeman in *Spying*, Heckler in *Cleo*, Cabby in *Screaming!* and Drunken Husband in *Emmannuelle*
Veteran actor and scriptwriter Norman Mitchell, born in Sheffield in 1919, built a career out of small parts in film, television and theatre. After studying medicine at Sheffield University for three years, he changed direction and began acting at a local rep.

Other than a six-year spell in the Royal Army Medical Corps during World War Two, he had a busy career, clocking up over 2000 television credits alone since his screen debut in the 1950s. Among the many programmes he appeared in were *Crossroads*; *All Creatures Great and Small*; *Are You Being Served?*; *Yes, Minister*; *Beryl's Lot*; *One by One*; *You Rang, M'Lord?*; *Whatever Happened To The Likely Lads?* and *Worzel Gummidge*. He's also appeared in over a hundred films, such as *Barry Lyndon*, *Revenge of the Pink Panther*, *A Night to Remember*, *Invasion*, *Oliver!*, *Mess Mates*, *Legend of the Werewolf*, *Goodbye Mr Chips* and *The Price of Silence*.

His numerous stage appearances included Anthony Quayle's production of *The Clandestine Marriage* in the West End, *A View from the Bridge*, *The Visit* and *Shadow of Heroes*. He was also a member of the RSC for three years, touring Australia. One of Mitchell's last jobs was the film, *The Lighthouse*, playing Brownlow, the lighthouse keeper.

He died in 2001, aged eighty-one.

MITCHELL, WARREN
Role: Spencius in *Cleo*
Born in London in 1926, Warren Mitchell studied at Oxford and RADA before gaining valuable experience in repertory theatre. His television and film career began in the '50s, appearing in the likes of *Hancock's Half Hour*, *William Tell* and *Interpol Calling* on television and films such as *Passing Stranger*, *Manuela*, *Barnacle Bill* and *The Trollenberg Terror*.

Despite hundreds of screen appearances over the decades, he'll forever be remembered as bigoted Alf Garnett in the hugely successful sitcom, *Till Death Us Do Part*. He still occasionally appears on the screen, but is busiest on stage these days, being the recipient of several awards, including the 2004 Laurence Olivier Theatre Award for best performance in a supporting role for *The Prince* at London's Apollo Theatre.

MOIRA
Played by Gail Grainger
For Moira in *Abroad*, see 'Plunkett, Moira'.

MOLINEAUX, CHERYL
Role: Women's Ward Nurse in *Doctor*
Other screen credits include the films *Eight O'Clock Walk* and *Cuckoo Patrol* as well as television shows such as *Dixon of Dock Green* and *Doctor Who*.

MOLLY
Played by Renée Houston
Seen in *Cabby* this cigarette-puffing blonde serves at the cab drivers' café.

MONICA
Played by an uncredited actress
Seen in *Teacher*, Monica attends Maudlin Street Secondary Modern School and can't stop itching and fidgeting during one of Miss Allcock's PE lessons.

MONKHOUSE, BOB
Role: Charlie Sage in *Sergeant*
Born in Beckenham, Kent, in 1928, Bob Monkhouse began his career, aged fifteen, by selling jokes to comedians and providing cartoon strips to comics. Two years later, he was performing as a stand-up comedian and training as a cartoon film animator for Gaumont British before later acting on the radio and in RAF productions.

He formed a successful scriptwriting partnership with Denis Goodwin and went on to appear in television, films and on stage. His many credits include the films *The Secret People*, *Beat Up the Town*, *Dentist in the Chair* and *She'll Have to Go*, as well as television series *Jonathan Creek*, *The Golden Shot*, *Celebrity Squares*, *Family Fortunes* and *Bob's Full House*.

He died in 2003, aged seventy-five.

MONTEZ, RICHARD
Role: Riff at Abdul's Tent in *Follow That Camel*
Appearing on screen from the 1960s, his film credits include *The Girl Hunters*, *633 Squadron*, *Maroc 7* and *Incognito*, while his television work has seen him appear in, among others, *The Saint*, *Man in a Suitcase*, *UFO*, *Barlow at Large*, *Mind Your Language*, *Duty Free* and, in 2004, *Auf Wiedersehen, Pet*.

MONTGOMERY, BRUCE
Composed and directed the music for *Sergeant*, *Nurse*, *Teacher*, *Constable*, *Regardless* and *Cruising*
A talented composer and successful writer of detective stories, using the pseudonym Edmund Crispin, Bruce Montgomery was born at Chesham Bois, Buckinghamshire, in 1921.

Educated at Oxford University, where his interest in detective fiction started, Montgomery began writing a series of novels set in Oxford. After a brief spell teaching at Shrewsbury, he moved to Devon and spent his time writing books and music, initially background music. In addition to the six Carry On

films he wrote music for, his credits include *Heart of a Child*, *Home Is The Hero*, *Watch Your Stern* and *Twice Round the Daffodils*.

He died in 1978, aged fifty-six.

MOON, GEORGE
Roles: Scrawny Man in *Camping* and Mr Giles in *Dick*
Born in London in 1909, George Moon – whose daughter, Georgina, appeared in two *Carry On*s – forged a successful screen career for himself, beginning in films in the 1930s and, three decades later, on television. His big-screen credits included *Diggers*, *Time Flies*, *Carry On Admiral*, *Breath of Life*, *Half a Sixpence*, *Eskimo Nell* and *Yesterday's Hero*.

His work on the small screen saw him appear in such programmes as *The Hidden Truth*, *Doctor in the House*, *The Dustbinmen*, *Special Branch*, *The Fosters*, *Shadow Squad*, *Skyport* and, in 1977, *Lord Tramp*.

He died in 1981, aged seventy-two.

MOON, GEORGINA
Roles: Joy in *Camping* and Sally in *Behind*
Daughter of actor George Moon, she turned to acting and appeared in films and on television from the 1960s through until the '80s. Her big-screen credits include *The Mind Benders*, *Fragment of Fear* and the film version of the successful television sitcom, in which she also appeared, *Bless This House*. On the small screen she was seen in *Up Pompeii*, *UFO*, *How's Your Father?*, *You're Only Young Twice*, *Dawson's Weekly* and *That's My Boy*.

MOON, SERGEANT LAURA
Played by Hattie Jacques
Seen in *Constable*, Sergeant Moon is in charge of the WPCs. She works alongside Sergeant Wilkins, whom she's very fond of. An efficient policewoman whose experience is valuable to the station.

MOORE, CHLOE
Played by Joan Sims
Seen in *At Your Convenience*, Chloe Moore works at W.C. Boggs and Son. One of the biggest flirts around, especially where Sid Plummer, the works foreman, is concerned. But theirs is a platonic relationship, although it wouldn't be given half the chance. They work together and live next-door to each other, but that's as close as they get to sharing their lives.

Chloe has been married to her husband, Fred, a sales rep at Boggs and Son, for years and, at times, she'd be the first to admit that it feels like it.

MOORE, FRED
Played by Bill Maynard
Husband of Chloe, sales rep Fred works for Boggs and Son, the toiletware manufacturer. He drives his red Ford Capri (registration

RON 759G) but finds his job hampered by the constant striking at the factory; a man who lost out when a sense of humour was dished out, he's conscious that Sid Plummer fancies his wife.

He might lack charisma but makes up for it with hard work, earning a feather in his cap by landing a lucrative contract from the Middle East for 1000 bidets worth £90,000.

MOORE MEDICAL MISSION
This wooden shack is seen in *Again Doctor* standing precariously in the middle of a rainforest in the inhospitable Beatific Islands. The mission was established by the wealthy Ellen Moore as a way of saying thank you to the islanders for taking care of her late husband during his final days. The reality is that the mission is rarely used because locals prefer the witch doctor; a succession of doctors has been employed at the mission, where the only element of stability is the orderly, Gladstone Screwer.

MOORE-NOOKEY CLINIC, THE
The clinic established by Ellen Moore and Dr James Nookey in *Again Doctor*. The clinic's motto is 'Come Unto Us All You Who Are Heavy Laden', which supports their field of work in providing a serum to help clients reduce weight almost instantaneously.

MOORE-NOOKEY-GLADSTONE-CARVER CLINIC, THE
Offering sex changes and immediate weight loss, the clinic is formed out of the Moore-Nookey Clinic. Seen in *Again Doctor*.

MOORE, MRS ELLEN
Played by Joan Sims
A wealthy widow in *Again Doctor*. When her husband died on the far-flung Beatific Islands she established the Moore Medical Mission as a way of showing her gratitude to the islanders who cared for him. Her affluence attracts Dr Carver, an eminent surgeon at the Long Hampton Hospital, who's keen to launch a private clinic and thinks he might finance the project if he plays his cards right. A lonely forty-year-old, who has only Slap and Tickle, her Siamese cats, for company, she's desperate to find love again and eventually enters into a partnership with Dr Nookey, much to Carver's chagrin, when he claims to have discovered a revolutionary weight-loss serum.

MOORE, MAUREEN
Role: Pretty Probationer in *Regardless*

MOORE, VALERIE
Role: Lubi Lieutenant in *Up the Jungle*

MORGAN, TERENCE
Set dresser on *Teacher*
Credited as a set dresser from the 1960s, his many credits include the films *The Trials of*

Oscar Wilde, Sebastian, Loot, The 39 Steps, Alfie, Casino Royale and *Something to Hide.*

MORRISON, MISS
Played by Lucy Griffiths

For 'Miss Morrison' in *Doctor*, see 'Patient'.

MOSES, ALBERT
Role: Doctor in *Emmannuelle*

Born in Sri Lanka in 1937, Albert Moses, the son of teachers, had appeared in films in India and made documentaries in Africa by the time he arrived in the UK in the early 1970s. He's since built up an extensive list of stage and screen credits beginning with a stint at the National Theatre alongside Diana Rigg.

On television he's been seen in *Budgie, On the Buses, Shoestring, The Loser, Warship, Robin's Nest, The Chinese Detective, Boon* and *Holby City*, but he's probably recognised most for his time on the ITV sitcom, *Mind Your Language.* His film credits, meanwhile, include *White Cargo, What's Up Nurse!, An American Werewolf in London, Foreign Body* and *East Is East.*

No longer working in the theatre, Moses concentrates on screen work and writing, directing and producing.

MOSES, JOSH
Played by Davy Kaye

For Josh Moses, the undertaker in *Cowboy*, see 'Josh the Undertaker'.

MOSSMAN, GEORGE
Role: Stagecoach Driver in *Dick*. Also supplied the coach and horses in *Dick*

His skills in horsemanship have been utilised on such films as *Dr Terror's House of Horrors, Barry Lyndon* and *Jabberwocky.*

MOTHERSILL, DON
Wardrobe on *England*

Other productions he's worked on include the films *The Legacy, Lifeforce, Henry V, A Ghost in Monte Carlo* and the Bond movie, *The Living Daylights.*

MOWER, PATRICK
Role: Sergeant Len Able in *England*

Born in Pontypridd in 1940, Patrick Mower was an apprentice engineering draughtsman before swapping careers and training at RADA. He began acting on the West End stage before landing a leading role in the popular television series *Callan*, which led to a string of major characters in shows such as *Special Branch* and *The Avengers.* He was also seen in *UFO, Paul Temple, Bergerac, Target* and is currently playing Rodney Blackstock in the soap, *Emmerdale.*

He's appeared in several films, such as *Black Beauty, Cry of the Banshee, The Devil Rides Out, To Catch a Spy* and *The Asylum.*

MUCH-SNOGGING-ON-THE-GREEN
The town where *Loving* begins. At the station we see Terence Philpot jumping on a train, waving goodbye to a friend, with whom he's been staying, then shouting out of the compartment window that his wife makes loves fantastically.

MUFFET, BERTRUM
Played by Richard O'Callaghan

Bertrum Muffet, an undertaker's assistant, turns to the Wedded Bliss Agency when he wants a partner in *Loving.* A weak-willed, ineffectual twenty-seven-year-old whose main hobbies are making aeroplanes out of milk bottle tops and collecting book matches.

A fortuitous meeting with a young model, Sally Martin, in the cocktail bar at the Parkway Hotel, leads to a lasting relationship; he was expecting to meet Esme Crowfoot, but Sidney Bliss hadn't actually told her about the appointment, not that Bertie minded in the end. Confusion leads to him thinking Sally was his date and he goes back to her flat only to be embarrassed when she procedes to undress; what he later found out was that Sally Martin was expecting to meet a photographer she'd hired to take some saucy snaps of her.

MUGGINS, CHARLIE
Played by Charles Hawtrey

In *Camping*, Charlie Muggins heads for the Paradise Camp Site and en route is inclined to irritate those he meets, beginning with an agitated farmer who ends up thinking he was responsible for impregnating his daughter. When, later, he is drenched in the rain, fellow camper Harriet Potter takes pity and invites him into the tent she shares with her husband, Peter, but once in they find it difficult to rid themselves of him.

MUM
Played by Marianne Stone

Seen in *Doctor* arriving at the Borough County Hospital with her son who's got his grandad's chamber pot stuck on his head.

MUNT, PETER
Role: Henry's Courtier in *Henry*

Dividing his time between acting and stunt work, Peter Munt was seen in small roles on films such as *Hands of the Ripper* and *A Room With A View*, as well as offering his expertise in stunt work on, among others, *Goldfinger, Moonraker, Superman* and *Superman II.*

MURDEN, VICKI
Role: Hospitality Girl in *Up The Khyber*

MURDOCH, JANE
Role: Nurse in *Doctor* (Note: scene cut.)

Other screen credits include appearing in an episode of Frankie Howerd's series, *Whoops Baghdad!.*

MURRAY, PRIVATE
Played by Tricia Newby

Based at the experimental 1313 anti-aircraft battery featured in *England*, she's one of the shirkers who suffers a severe shock to the system when the tough-speaking Captain Melly is placed in charge of the unit.

MURRAY, VI
Wardrobe Mistress on *Matron, Dick* and *England*

Working as a wardrobe mistress since the 1950s, Vi Murray's other credits include *The Battle of the Sexes, Very Important Person, Cat Girl, The Vicious Circle, Tiger Bay, Every Day's A Holiday* and *Anne of the Thousand Days.*

MURTON, LIONEL
Role: Clerk in *Cowboy*

Born in London in 1915, Lionel Murton grew up in Montreal, Canada. He'd been working on the Canadian naval show, *Meet the Navy,* and had appeared in the 1946 film version when he returned to the UK and became a busy stage and screen actor.

His film credits include *Dangerous Assignment, The Long Dark Hall, The Pickwick Papers, The Runaway Bus, The Battle of the River Plate, Up the Creek, Summer Holiday* and *Seven Nights in Japan.* Meanwhile on television he's worked on *Dial 999, The Invisible Man, Danger Man, Compact* and *George and Mildred.*

MURTON, PETER
Set dresser on *Sergeant*

His other credits include *The Ruling Class, The Eagle Has Landed, Dracula, King Kong Lives* and *The Black Windmill.*

MUZURUS, JAN
Role: Spanish Captain in *Jack*

N

NARRATOR
Voice of E.V.H. Emmett
Heard in *Cleo*.

NARRATOR
Voice of Patrick Allen
Heard in *Don't Lose Your Head*, *Doctor* and *Up The Khyber*.

NATIVE POLICEMAN
Played by Norman Mitchell
In *Spying* the Native Policeman is stopped on a street corner in Algiers by Simkins who tells him he's looking for a woman. The copper gets the wrong end of the stick and says he'll take him to his sister, but Simkins is actually looking for Daphne Honeybutt, a fellow agent presumed lost in the city.

NED
Played by George Woodbridge
Seen at Dirty Dick's in *Jack*, this lecherous old man is a crew member of *Venus*, a frigate due to sail to Spain. When Sally, the barmaid, who's desperate to reach Spain, hears about his impending journey, she asks if he'll smuggle her aboard for five sovereigns. He's happy to smuggle her aboard but wants her body instead of money, prompting her to pour beer over his head.

NELSON
Played by Jimmy Thompson
Seen on his deathbed in the opening scene of *Jack*.

NELSON, HOWARD
Role: Harry Hernia in *Emmannuelle*
Other film credits for this former champion bodybuilder include *Pattern of Evil*, *The Nine Ages of Nakedness*, *The Swordsman* and *The Playbirds*.

NELSON, WALLY
Sound Editor on *Don't Lose Your Head* and Dubbing Editor on *Follow That Camel*
Born on the Isle of Man in 1928, Wally Nelson began an engineering apprenticeship until the war interrupted his training. Invalided out of the army, he was unable to continue with plans to become an engineer and studied photography at college instead.

After graduating, he moved to London and secured a job with Rembrandt Studios; he ended up running the Chiswick studios. In the early 1950s he joined Republic Films, based at Shepperton, working in the repair and despatch unit, but it wasn't long before he was given a break at Walton Studios, working as an assistant film editor. Early films he worked on include *Portrait in Smoke* and *Soho Incident*.

As a freelancer, Nelson worked with many of the top companies, including ABPC and Disney for three years. Other film credits include *The Square Peg*, *Fiddler on the Roof*, *Some May Live*, *Every Day's A Holiday* and the Bond movie, *Never Say Never Again*.

By the time ill-health forced Nelson's retirement in 1989, he'd spent four decades in the industry. He now lives back on the Isle of Man.

NEPTUNE BAR
The bar is in the Pier Theatre. Augusta Prodworthy, the women's libber, stands by a sign pointing to it in *Girls* when she's ready to launch Operation Nobble, part of a campaign to cause mayhem at the Miss Fircombe beauty contest.

NERDA
Played by Edwina Carroll
Seen in *Up the Jungle* being leered at by Bill Boosey, the expedition leader. She's later chosen as King Tonka's mate for the night, although he dismisses her in front of his wife Evelyn.

NEW CANTEEN GIRL
Played by Anouska Hempel
The leggy new canteen girl sets Vic Spanner's pulse racing when she approaches the gates of Boggs and Son and asks where she has to go because it's her first day. The stubborn union representative was prepared to make a stand for workers' rights, despite the rest of his colleagues having returned to work – that is until the new girl arrives on the scene. Seen in *At Your Convenience*.

NEW MATRON
Played by Pat Coombs
By the time Dr Carver returns to Long Hampton Hospital from his harrowing trip to the stormy Beatific Islands, where he nearly drowned after the schooner he was travelling in sank, some faces have changed at the hospital, including that of matron. Miss Soper has moved to pastures new and been replaced by the New Matron, who doesn't recognise the eminent surgeon, telling him to move on because there is no place for vagrants at the hospital. Appears in *Again Doctor*.

NEW NURSE
Played by Stephanie Schiller
A member of staff at the Haven Hospital in *Nurse*.

NEWBY, TRICIA
Roles: Private Murray in *England* and Nurse in Surgery in *Emmannuelle*
Londoner Tricia Newby completed her education at Chalfont St Giles, Buckinghamshire and enrolled at the Guildhall Drama School where she won the women's Shakespeare prize.

Upon graduating she toured with a theatre company, Theatre Centre, appearing in various productions including *The Tempest* and *Macbeth*. After completing the tour she began concentrating on screen work – credits include playing a French girl in 1976's *Aces High* and a small part in *The Amorous Adventures of Tom Jones*.

NEWTS
During an argument between Sir Bernard Cutting and Dr Goode in *Matron* we learn that they're both Newts, although we never discover more about this unusual organisation. While Goode has been Master of the Grand Order of Newts for five years, before which he was a Tadpole for three years, Cutting explains he's a Grand Salamander Newt of the Watford Pond.

NICHOLAS
Played by David Kernan
For Nicholas in *Abroad*, see 'Phipps, Nicholas'.

NICHOLS, DANDY
Role: Mrs Roper in *Doctor*

Born in London in 1907, Dandy Nichols worked as a secretary for twelve years before being spotted in a charity show and offered a job with the Cambridge Repertory Theatre.

World War Two drew her back to office work for two years, however she went on to carve out a successful career, appearing in numerous films including *The Deep Blue Sea*, *Georgy Girl*, *The Knack* and *Doctor Dolittle*, as well as featuring regularly in television and theatre productions.

The height of her fame came after she'd been acting for thirty years and was offered the role of Else, Alf Garnett's wife, in the television comedy *Till Death Us Do Part*. The series, which began in 1964, exploited Nichols's flair for comedy and propelled her to national celebrity status, also leading to other prominent parts, such as the landlady in the film *The Birthday Girl*, and in theatre productions *The Clandestine Marriage* and *Plunder* and *Home*, with Ralph Richardson and John Gielgud.

She died in 1985, aged seventy-eight.

NIGHT NURSE
Played by Jenny Counsell

In *Again Doctor* this young nurse helps settle Miss Armitage into a new room. She's been scared out of her wits by Doctor Nookey, who mistakenly entered her room while looking for his girlfriend, Goldie Locks.

NIGHT PORTER
Played by Gordon Rollings

The Night Porter is on duty in *Doctor* when the patients, angry that Dr Kilmore was left with no alternative but to resign after a series of mishaps at the hospital, revolt and head off to find Matron and Dr Tinkle. Mr Biddle shuts the Night Porter up by trapping his head in the pull-down window of his office.

NIGHT SISTER
Played by Gwendolyn Watts

Helps the Night Nurse settle Miss Armitage into her new room in *Again Doctor*.

NIGHTINGALE, MICHAEL
Roles: Wine Bystander in *Regardless*, Business Man in *Cabby*, Town Crier in *Jack*, Caveman in *Cleo*, Bank Manager in *Cowboy*, 'What Locket?' Man in *Don't Lose Your Head*, Nightingale the Butler in *Follow That Camel*, Man in Cinema in *Camping*, Pearson in *Matron*, City Gent on Tube in *Girls*, Squire Trelawney in *Dick*, Officer in *England* and Police Commissioner in *Emmannuelle*
TV: *The Case of the Screaming Winkles* and *Lamp Posts of the Empire*

Michael Nightingale was born into a theatrical family in Brighton in 1922. He left school and served in the Royal Navy during the war before following previous generations of his family onto the stage, appearing in various repertory companies.

He soon progressed to films and television, but when his first wife contracted multiple sclerosis he restricted his work to small parts to enable him to care for her.

His film credits included *The Man Who Watched The Trains Go By*, *Man in the Shadow*, *Ice Cold in Alex*, *Watch Your Stern*, *Sky West and Crooked*, *The Raging Moon* and *Dominique*. His small-screen work covers such titles as *Danger Man*, *The Prisoner*, *UFO*, *Raffles* and, in 1994, his last television role in an episode of *Cadfael*, filmed in Hungary.

He died in 1999, aged seventy-six.

NIGHTINGALE, NURSE
Played by Rosalind Knight

A bespectacled young nurse who's recently started on the night shift in *Nurse*. When given the job of keeping an eye on Mr Mayhew, who's lost a lot of blood, she takes the task literally, never glancing away from her subject for a moment.

NIGHTINGALE THE BUTLER
Played by Michael Nightingale

A butler employed at Sir Cyril Ponsonby's mansion in *Follow That Camel*, he's seen delivering a letter to Lady Jane, and cutting Humphrey Bagshaw down when he tries hanging himself in the house.

NOBLE, LISA
Role: Khasi's Wife in *Up The Khyber*

NOBLE, TRISHA
Role: Sally in *Camping*

Trisha Noble, born in Sydney, Australia, in 1944, began acting as a child, performing on a Saturday radio programme, *Anthony Horden's Children's Party*, and appearing in her parents' stage productions and variety shows.

Her small-screen debut, aged sixteen, led to a regular role in *Bandstand* on Australian television. Also a singer, she released her first song in 1960, followed by a string of singles and albums.

She arrived in England with her mother in the early 1960s and found herself appearing on her first BBC radio show with The Beatles. She continued her singing career until, in 1965, she started concentrating on acting. Early screen credits include *Danger Man*, *Out of the Unknown*, *Up Pompeii* and *The Benny Hill Show* on television, and *Death Is A Woman* in the cinema.

She later moved to Los Angeles and was seen in numerous series, ranging from *The Rockford Files* and *Columbo* to *Fantasy Island* and *Hart to Hart*. In the early 1980s, she returned to Australia to be with her family after her father suffered a heart attack.

She has since returned to acting.

NOCKER, SERGEANT ERNIE
Played by Phil Silvers

In *Follow That Camel*, Colour Sergeant Ernie Nocker is responsible for knocking into shape the soldiers of the Foreign Legion. With an eye for the girls, he has a close relationship with Zig-Zig, a local café owner, but when he's eventually promoted to commandant, it's Corktip, a former belly dancer, who he hires as his batman and personal – in every sense of the word – assistant.

NOLAN, MARGARET
Roles: Miss Jones in *Cowboy*, Buxom Lass in *Henry*, Popsy in *At Your Convenience*, Mrs

Dawn Brakes (Margaret Nolan) won plenty of admirers (*Girls*)

CARRY ON NURSE

Nat Cohen and Stuart Levy present a Peter Rogers production
Distributed by Anglo Amalgamated Film Distributors Ltd
Based on an idea by Patrick Cargill and Jack Beale
Released as a U certificate in 1959 in black & white
Running time: 86 mins

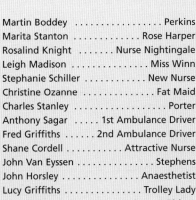

CAST

Shirley Eaton ...... Nurse Dorothy Denton	Cyril Chamberlain .... Bert Able	Martin Boddey .... Perkins
Kenneth Connor .... Bernie Bishop	Michael Medwin .... Ginger	Marita Stanton .... Rose Harper
Charles Hawtrey .... Humphrey Hinton	Norman Rossington .... Norm	Rosalind Knight .... Nurse Nightingale
Kenneth Williams .... Oliver Reckitt	Jill Ireland .... Jill Thompson	Leigh Madison .... Miss Winn
Hattie Jacques .... Matron	Ed Devereaux .... Alec Lawrence	Stephanie Schiller .... New Nurse
Leslie Phillips .... Jack Bell	Ann Firbank .... Helen Lloyd	Christine Ozanne .... Fat Maid
Terence Longdon .... Ted York	Frank Forsyth .... John Gray	Charles Stanley .... Porter
Wilfrid Hyde-White .... The Colonel	John Mathews .... Tom Mayhew	Anthony Sagar ..... 1st Ambulance Driver
Joan Sims .... Nurse Stella Dawson	Graham Stewart .... George Field	Fred Griffiths ...... 2nd Ambulance Driver
Harry Locke .... Mick	Patrick Durkin .... Jackson	Shane Cordell .... Attractive Nurse
Susan Shaw .... Jane Bishop	David Williams .... Andrew Newman	John Van Eyssen .... Stephens
Joan Hickson .... Sister	June Whitfield .... Meg	John Horsley .... Anaesthetist
Bill Owen .... Percy Hickson	Marianne Stone .... Alice Able	Lucy Griffiths .... Trolley Lady
Irene Handl .... Madge Hickson	Hilda Fenemore .... Rhoda Bray	Jeremy Connor .... Jeremy Bishop
Susan Beaumont .... Frances James		
Brian Oulton .... Henry Bray		
Susan Stephen ..... Nurse Georgie Axwell		

PRODUCTION TEAM

Screenplay by Norman Hudis
Music composed and directed by Bruce Montgomery
Director of Photography: Reginald Wyer
Art Director: Alex Vetchinsky
Production Manager: Frank Bevis
Editor: John Shirley
Camera Operator: Alan Hume
Assistant Director: Stanley Hosgood
Sound Editor: Roger Cherrill
Sound Recordists: Robert T. MacPhee and Bill Daniels
Continuity: Penny Daniels
Make-up: George Blackler
Hairdressing: Pearl Orton
Dress Designer: Joan Ellacott
Casting Director: Betty White
Set Dresser: Arthur Taksen
Nurses uniforms by Courtaulds
Produced by Peter Rogers
Directed by Gerald Thomas

It's off to the operating theatre for a little fun

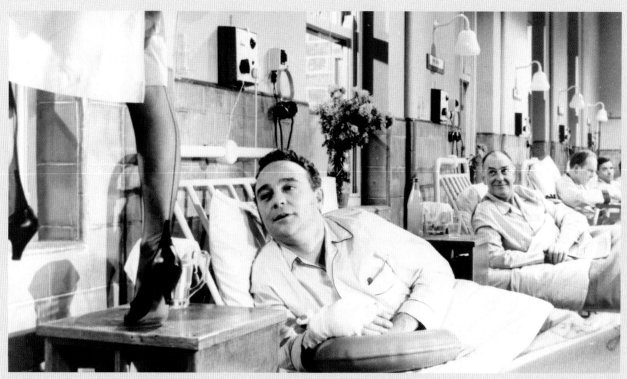

Bernie Bishop (Kenneth Connor) catches an eyeful

While covering a local baby show for his newspaper, journalist Ted York is taken ill with appendicitis and rushed to nearby Haven Hospital. Before he's even had the chance to warm up his bed, his editor, Mr Perkins, visits and gives York an undercover job: to write a series of articles about hospital life from the patient's point of view.

York doesn't need to look beyond his own ward when it comes to source material for his copy. The day-to-day business is full of incidents and memorable characters, including the Colonel whose private room resembles a betting office more than a hospital. The avid gambler who'll bet on anything, including how long it takes Matron to complete her rounds, drives the nurses mad and keeps Mick, a ward orderly, busy by asking him to place a myriad of bets for him.

The reporter takes a shine to Nurse Denton but attempts to strike up a relationship are fruitless at first because she only has eyes for Mr Stephens, a doctor at the hospital. The film spotlights the relationship between staff and patients, and patients and visitors. Boxer Bernie Bishop is hospitalised with a broken hand, while the studious Oliver Reckitt seems more interested in his reading matter than the pretty Jill Thompson who replaces her brother at visiting time. Humphrey Hinton spends his entire day listening to the radio and Henry Bray takes great pleasure purporting to be a well-to-do citizen from the west side of the common.

A late arrival in the ward is the affable Jack Bell. When his bunion operation is delayed, he's annoyed because it scuppers his plans for a holiday with his girlfriend, who smuggles in some champagne for her loved one. Bell decides to drown his sorrows in alcohol with some of the other patients. When Oliver Reckitt happens to mention a book he's reading on practical surgery, a tipsy Mr Bell asks Reckitt to operate on his bunion. A plan is hatched whereby the night nurse is ambushed, Humphrey Hinton dons her uniform to keep things looking normal and the gang head for the operating theatre to perform the operation. But before the first cut can be administered, the bed-bound Percy Hickson, who's desperate for the toilet, is left with no alternative but to ring the bell for attention; in summoning the nurse, he gives the game away.

Spared the knife, Jack Bell returns to the ward with the rest of the patients, but it's not long before we start waving goodbye to them as they leave Haven Hospital.

Funny Scene!

Inexperienced Nurse Dawson walks over to Ted York's bed with a suppository. Mr York is putting on his dressing-gown.

```
DAWSON:          Just a minute, Mr York.
YORK:            (Looking in Nurse Dawson's bowl.)
                 Hello, what's that?
DAWSON:          For your bowels; sit down please.
YORK:            (Looking nervous.) You, um, given
                 one of these before?
DAWSON:          Oh, good gracious, hundreds. Get it
                 down now. (Hands him the suppository
                 and a glass of water.)
NURSE DENTON:    (Walking by and noticing what's
                 going on.) Other end, Nurse!
YORK:            (Noticing Dawson is embarrassed.)
                 Never mind, with a face like mine
                 it's a mistake anyone might make.
```

Tucker in *Matron*, Dawn Brakes in *Girls* and Lady Daley in *Dick*

Margaret Nolan, who now divides her time between the UK and Spain, was born in London in 1943. She worked as a glamour model for some years and trained to be an English teacher before ditching the profession to become an actress in the early 1960s.

Her small screen credits include *The Saint, Danger Man, Nearest and Dearest, The Adventures of Don Quick, The Newcomers, Whatever Happened to the Likely Lads?, Crossroads*, the Q series, *Last of the Summer Wine* and *I Didn't Know You Cared*. In films, she appeared in, among others, *Saturday Night Out, A Hard Day's Night, Ferry Cross the Mersey, The Great St Trinian's Train Robbery, No Sex Please: We're British* and the Bond movie, *Goldfinger*.

'NON CRAPITO SUUM JANUUM'

The long-standing motto of King Henry VIII's family which translates to 'Never Spit On Your Own Doorstep'. Seen in *Henry*.

NOOKEY, DR JAMES

Played by Jim Dale

In *Again Doctor* the accident-prone Dr Nookey courts trouble and his carefree manner isn't liked by everyone at the Long Hampton Hospital. When the latest in a series of incidents means he's likely to be sacked, Dr Carver, with an ulterior motive, pretends to campaign on his behalf at the disciplinary meeting. Trying to impress the rich widow, Ellen Moore, he identifies in Nookey someone who's fool enough to fill the vacancy at Mrs Moore's medical mission in the undesirable Beatific Islands.

With little option but to accept the job, Nookey heads off to the distant isles and endures a torrid time until discovering that his medical orderly, Gladstone Screwer, has a serum which induces weight loss. Identifying a golden opportunity to make his fortune, Nookey pays Screwer in cigarettes and returns to Britain with the serum. Before long, he's driving around in a Rolls-Royce and working at a private clinic he's launched with the help of Mrs Moore.

NORAH

Played by Dora Bryan

The slightly eccentric cook works in the NAAFI at Heathercrest National Service Depot in *Sergeant*. She's so overworked when we first meet her that she's relieved to see Mary Sage walk through the door claiming to be the new girl. Her suspicions are roused, though, when she notices Mary, donning stockings and high heels, is hardly dressed for work as a skivvy. When she discovers Mary's circumstances, she takes her under her wing; but it isn't long before she's falling in love with her own man in uniform, in the unlikely shape of Horace Strong.

NORM

Played by Norman Rossington

Boxer Bernie Bishop's former sparring partner. Seen in *Nurse*, this punch-drunk numbskull arrives with Ginger to visit Bishop at Haven Hospital.

NORMA

Played by Lesley Duff

In *Camping* Norma is a student at the Chayste Place finishing school, just one member of the gang when the girls enjoyed a spell under canvas at the Paradise Camp Site.

NORMAN, JANE

Role: 3rd Reporter in *Emmannuelle*

Other screen credits include 1977's *The Magic Pony Ride*.

NORRINGTON, MR

An unseen character in *Cruising*, Norrington was the long-standing chef on the *Happy Wanderer*. He's mentioned by the captain when he realises Wilfred Haines is replacing him on the latest Mediterranean cruise.

NOSHA CHIEF

Played by Danny Daniels

The chief of the Nosha tribe in *Up the Jungle*.

NOSHA WITH GIRL

Played by Lincoln Webb

In Walter Bagley's flashback sequence in *Up the Jungle*, the Nosha is seen behind a tree kissing and cuddling his lover. Bagley disturbs them when he spots a butterfly resting on the bark and goes over for a peep. It was an unwise move because Bagley is captured by the Nosha tribe and faces almost certain death until rescued by the Lubidubies.

NOSHAS

Played by Roy Stewart, John Hamilton, Willie Jonah and Chris Konyils

Seen in *Up the Jungle* the Noshas are a feared tribe of cannibals living in the jungles bordering the Limpopo river.

NUCIE

This acronym in *At Your Convenience* stands for the National Union of Chinaware Industrial Employees, the trade union which represents the workers at Boggs.

NUDIST

Played by Helli Louise Jacobson

In *Behind* she's caught naked in the showers when Henry Barnes, the odd-job man at the Riverside Caravan Site, is frog-marched into the women's shower block by Carol who thinks a man is hanging around, although it turns out to be a loose myna bird. But Barnes can't believe his eyes when he's inside the shower block, and we're not talking about the naked girl. Instead, he comes face-to-face with his wife, from whom he's been separated for years,

taking a shower: he nearly collapses in shock and in doing so pulls open a cubicle door, revealing a rather buxom lady.

NUDIST PARADISE

The film shown in the Picture Playhouse in *Camping*. Watched by Sid Boggle, Bernie Lugg and their girlfriends, Joan Fussey and Anthea Meeks, it spotlights nudists enjoying a holiday at the Paradise Camp. One of the film's main characters is the busty blonde, Sally, whose convent-based education means she's a little shy about exposing herself to fellow campers.

NURSE

Played by Penelope Keith

Henry is waiting for a nurse by the ambulance in *Doctor*. When Nurse Sandra May walks by he's disappointed the nurse he's waiting for isn't up to Sandra's standard in the vital statistics department. Instead of all curves, she's plain and rather flat-chested. (**Note: scene was cut.**)

WHAT MIGHT HAVE BEEN

Following on from the scene in *Doctor* where Henry, standing by an ambulance, shares a joke over the line, 'Oh, what a lovely looking pear!', another nurse comes running up to Henry. She's in mufti, plain and flat-chested.

NURSE: Here I am, Henry.

HENRY: (**Looks at her, sighs.**) From the sublime to the ridiculous! All right, let's go.

(**And he takes her arm and walks towards gates.**)

NURSE

Played by Jenny White

Seen in the nurses' home in *Doctor*, rushing downstairs as Nurse Clarke arrives.

NURSE

Played by Valerie Shute

Works at the Long Hampton Hospital and seen in *Again Doctor* frantically trying to gather together enough bed pans to meet the unexpected demand when all the patients' buzzers start sounding; what she doesn't realise is that Dr Nookey's escapades in the X-ray room have caused horrendous problems with the electrics.

NURSE

Played by Laura Collins

A black nurse seen checking in at reception in front of the disguised Cyril Carter in *Matron*. (**Note: scene was cut.**)

WHAT MIGHT HAVE BEEN

The Receptionist gets to the nurse just ahead of Cyril – a rather pretty black girl.

RECEP: Name?

NURSE: (**Sweetly.**) Knightley.

RECEP: (**Writing it down.**) First name?

NURSE: Rose.

RECEP: (Writing it.) Rose Knightley.

NURSE: (Very sweetly.) I was the first in my family.

RECEP: Interesting. Next, please?

(It is CYRIL's turn.)

RECEP: Surname?

CYRIL: Oh er . . . Carter.

RECEP: First name?

(CYRIL, intent on keeping his knickers up and still aware of the PORTER answers absent-mindedly.)

CYRIL: Cyril

RECEP: Cyril?

CYRIL: Oh sorry, I was thinking of something else. Er . . . Magna.

RECEP: (Starting to write.) Magna . . . Magna Carter?

CYRIL: I was the biggest in my family.

RECEP: Oh. (To them all.) All right, if you'll all just take a seat.

NURSE
Played by Linda Hooks
Helps the doctor examine Professor Crump at the hospital in *Behind*.

NURSE
Played by Linda Hooks
Works at the experimental 1313 anti-aircraft battery and seen in *England* assisting Major Butcher, who's in charge of sick bay.

NURSE, CARRY ON
See feature box on pages 176–7.

NURSE IN BATH
Played by Jenny White
Just as she's relaxing amongst the soap suds in *Doctor*, Dr Kilmore, who's been trying to rescue Nurse May, comes crashing into her room and lands in the bath.

NURSE IN BATH
Played by Gilly Grant
The nurse, who's quietly enjoying a bath at the Finisham Maternity Hospital in *Matron*, has her pleasure rudely interrupted by Cyril Carter and others.

NURSE IN HOSPITAL
Played by Marianne Maskell
During *Emmannuelle* she's seen entering the doctor's surgery, undoing her overalls and revealing her nakedness, all part of her duties because she's checking to see if the French Ambassador, who's consulting the doctor because he's unable to make love to his wife, reacts to the sight of the naked female body.

NURSE IN SURGERY
Played by Tricia Newby
In *Emmannuelle* the 'Nurse in Surgery' is seen holding two of Emmannuelle's babies at her bedside in hospital, smiling and commenting on how they look like their father – the trouble is, no one knows who that is!

O

OAKLEY, ANNIE
Played by Angela Douglas
The pretty blonde travels to Stodge City in a stagecoach. Accompanying her is another passenger, Marshall P. Knutt, a drainage, sanitation and garbage disposal engineer, who's been mistaken for a marshal and sent to Stodge to tidy up the place; he couldn't fire a gun to save his life, which is what Annie has to do when their coach is attacked by Indians en route.

An expert shot, Annie, who's seen in *Cowboy*, is on her way to Stodge to track down the man who murdered her father, the late Albert Earp, the town's former sheriff. She seeks revenge and upon arrival soon discovers it was none other than Johnny Finger, the Rumpo Kid, who pulled the trigger. She fails to get her man, killing his sidekick, Charlie, instead, but is satisfied when she eventually sees the Kid run out of town by Marshall Knutt, with whom she's struck up a relationship.

OASIS EL NOOKI
Located in the Sahara Desert, the oasis is seen in *Follow That Camel*.

OATES, JULIE
Played by Barbara Wise
Julie is introduced by Peter Potter in *Girls* as she parades on the catwalk during the beauty contest.

O'BRIEN, RICHARD
Role: Rider in *Cowboy*
Born in Cheltenham, Gloucestershire, in 1942, Richard O'Brien emigrated with his parents to New Zealand after his father quit his job with the local council to try his hand at sheep-farming down-under.

After completing his education he moved to Hamilton, on the North Island, but jobs as a barber and trainee glazier didn't last and he returned to the UK in the late 1960s. He flitted between jobs before persuading a stunt agency to utilise his horse-riding skills, something they

did in not just *Cowboy* but also *Casino Royale*.

The multi-talented O'Brien, who's also a singer and composer, enjoyed his big break when he penned the highly successful *The Rocky Horror Show*, but more recently he's been seen as an actor. While on television he's appeared in the likes of *Robin of Sherwood*, *The Detectives*, *The Racing Game* and, of course, presenting *The Crystal Maze*; his film work includes *The Odd Job*, *Flash Gordon*, *Dungeons and Dragons* and *Elvira's Haunted Hills*.

O'BRIEN, SERGEANT PADDY
Played by Terry Scott
In *Sergeant*, O'Brien takes charge of Charlie Platoon at Heathercrest National Service Depot, and bets Sergeant Grimshaw, who's retiring from the army, fifty quid that his final platoon won't march out as champions. O'Brien wishes he'd kept his mouth shut, though, when Grimshaw's platoon – against all odds – wins the coveted prize, forcing O'Brien to dig deep into his pockets.

O'CALLAGHAN, RICHARD
Roles: Bertrum Muffet in *Loving* and Lewis Boggs in *At Your Convenience*
Born in London in 1940, Richard O'Callaghan, son of the late actress Patricia Hayes, left school and tried his hardest not to become an actor. He moved swiftly between jobs, including being a car salesman in Wandsworth, a farmer in Tonbridge and a sales assistant in Selfridge's, before eventually enrolling at LAMDA in 1962. He left two days before the end of the three-year course to join the cast of *Spring Awakening*, at the Royal Court, and stayed throughout its three-week run.

It wasn't long before he secured screen work, with early television credits including *Out of the Unknown*, *The Ronnie Barker Playhouse*, *Public Eye* and a running part in the serial, *The Flower of Gloster*. Recent small-screen work includes *Boon*, *Born and Bred*, *Mr Pye* and *McCallum*.

On the big screen he'd only appeared in a couple of films before joining the *Carry On* team. Other credits during his career include *Galileo*, *Butley* (he also played Joey Keyston in

The Rumpo Kid fancies his chances with Annie Oakley (*Cowboy*)

the original stage version) and, more recently, *Dangerous Beauty*.

In addition to his screen work (he's just recorded an episode of *Midsomer Murders*) he's remained busy on the stage, where one of his favourite parts saw him appearing alongside Diana Dors in *Three Months Gone*.

ODBODD
Played by Tom Clegg
The monster in *Screaming!* kidnaps Doris Mann in Hocombe Woods and brings her back to the Watts' house, Bide-a-Wee Rest Home. Unfortunately he loses a finger in the process, a vital clue in the kidnapping investigation headed by the incompetent Sidney Bung.

ODBODD JUNIOR
Played by Billy Cornelius (Voice supplied by Gerald Thomas.)
Seen in *Screaming!*, Odbodd Junior is born when Dr Fettle, the police doctor, sends an electric current through the severed finger found in Hocombe Woods and a monster forms before his very eyes. Odbodd Junior isn't very grateful, though, because he kills the doctor before heading out into the cold night air.

O'FENEY, PADDY
Unseen in *Cowboy* but his nameplate hangs above a barn in Stodge City, although it's unclear what type of business he runs.

OFFICER
Played by John Carlin
Seen in *England* discussing plans regarding the future command of 1313 battery, an experimental anti-aircraft battery stationed in the countryside. The brigadier decides to post Captain Melly to the base.

OFFICER
Played by Michael Nightingale
Also spotted in *England* discussing plans regarding the future command of 1313 battery, the experimental anti-aircraft battery. The brigadier eventually decides to post Captain Melly to the base.

OFFORD NEW TOWN
This new town in Sussex is the location for a new secondary modern school. Expected to accommodate 540 boys, its setting amidst glorious countryside is just one reason William Wakefield, acting head at Maudlin Street

Secondary Modern School, wants to apply. The primary reason, though, is the chance to gain a permanent headship. Mentioned in *Teacher*.

OLD BEN
Unseen in *Cowboy*, Old Ben, who was a friend of Judge Burke's, was killed by Jesse James, a female version, before she was eventually run out of Stodge City by Burke. Against everyone's warnings, the ninety-two-year-old married Jesse and it's assumed he met his death trying to satisfy his new bride's sexual needs.

OLD COCK INN, THE
The Old Cock Inn, in the parish of Upper Dencher, is set in the countryside and frequented by all the local criminals. Captain Fancey and Sergeant Strapp of the Bow Street Runners visit during *Dick* in the hope they can unearth clues concerning the whereabouts of the legendary highwayman, Dick Turpin. The pub landlord is Bodkin.

OLD COWHAND
Played by Arthur Lovegrove
The inebriated old codger is seen in *Cowboy*, guzzling beer at Rumpo's Place. He propositions Belle, who's angry that Johnny Finger – whom she's taken a shine to – is paying more attention to the new arrival at Stodge City: Annie Oakley. The Old Cowhand gets more than he bargained for when a jealous Belle throws his drink in his face when he enquires as to whether she can do something for him.

OLD LADY
Played by Nancy Roberts
In *Regardless* the Old Lady asks a railway porter where she can find the platform for the Ely train.

OLD LADY IN HEADPHONES
Played by Lucy Griffiths
Seen in *Again Doctor* the Old Lady is a patient at the Long Hampton Hospital; she's happily passing the time with a little knitting while listening to some music when her headphones explode as a result of Dr Nookey's escapades with the hospital's electric system.

OLD LOU
An unseen character mentioned in *Regardless* by the receptionist at the Philosophers' Club. Sam Twist takes over his duties when Lou is off work sick.

OLD MAN IN RUBY ROOM
Played by Charles Julian
In *Regardless* a drunk Lily Duveen, an employee of Helping Hands, accidentally bumps into the old man at the wine-tasting session held at the Ruby Room.

OLLEY, RICHARD
Role: Gunner Parker in *England*
Richard Olley's other credits include episodes

MEMORIES

'Bertie Muffet and Sally Martin, played by Jacki Piper, were the young love interests in *Loving*. I was appearing in *Three Months Gone*, a play in Town at the Duchess Theatre, which was making quite a splash. I was playing a northern Bertrum Muffet-like character so perhaps one of the *Carry On* team saw me. Anyway, my agent phoned and said Peter Rogers and Gerald Thomas would like to see me. I told him I was doing a matinée that day so it was arranged that they'd pick me up from the theatre during the break. I'll always remember it because this white Rolls-Royce turned up and I was taken to the Dorchester to meet them. We had tea, chatted and I was then bundled back into the Rolls and returned to the theatre. I was terribly impressed being driven to the Dorchester for tea.

'I've never been a huge *Carry On* fan. I find them amusing but I wouldn't say I ranked among their greatest fans, but at least they looked fun and I admired many of the actors in them. In fact, I'd known Charles Hawtrey since I was a small boy because my mother [Patricia Hayes] did a radio series with him for years; it was called *Norman and Henry Bones, the Boy Detectives* for Children's Hour.

'Bertrum Muffet was the kind of part I was getting at that point in my career. I'd just reached thirty but probably looked a good deal younger than that and was very naïve. I used to play characters like that so it wasn't difficult bringing Bertrum to life.

'There was a wonderful props man on the production who said to me, "There's your briefcase over there." When I opened it and saw it was full of aeroplanes made out of milk bottle tops I fell about laughing and couldn't believe they'd gone to the trouble of making them – it must have taken someone hours, unless they got plastic kits and placed the tops all over them.

'I wasn't in *Henry* but returned for *At Your Convenience*. I loved appearing with Jacki and I guess Peter and Gerald thought we worked well together. The character wasn't as naïve as Bertrum and I didn't enjoy playing him as much. *At Your Convenience* seemed so right-wing, and although it was only jokey, it was very much poking fun at trade unions.

'Filming down at Brighton was enormous fun, though. I didn't get to drive the sports car much but I've always loved driving and being behind the wheel of a sports car for the first time was very enjoyable.

'I wasn't asked to do any more *Carry On*s after *At Your Convenience*. Although I had had a great time I felt that perhaps I wasn't quite the sort of person they wanted.'

RICHARD O'CALLAGHAN

Odbodd Jnr. (centre) began life as a severed finger (*Screaming!*)

of BBC's successful sci-fi series, *Blake's 7*, and *Doctor Who*. In the former he played a guard in an episode from 1981, while he was cast as a mutant in a 1983 episode of *Doctor Who*.

OLLIE

This enormous grey dog, owned by Norma Baxter, causes havoc at the Riverside Caravan Site in *Behind*.

OOZULUM BIRD

The bird is understood to be extinct until Professor Tinkle's assistant, Claude Chumley, finds what he believes is the tail feather of the bird while climbing a tree in *Up the Jungle*.

OPERATION NOBBLE

Just one of the stages of Operation Spoilsport, a campaign organised by Fircombe's Women's Lib Movement intended to cause mayhem at the Miss Fircombe beauty contest in *Girls*.

OPERATION SCARPER

Put into practice in *England* when Captain Melly approaches the Nissen huts where the men are entertaining female members of the experimental anti-aircraft battery.

OPERATION SPOILSPORT

Operation Spoilsport is executed by members of the Fircombe Women's Lib Movement, led by Augusta Prodworthy, in order to ruin the Miss Fircombe beauty contest in *Girls*, a competition Prodworthy opposed strongly before the decision to hold the event was taken behind her back.

OPERATION WAR OF NERVES

In *Teacher* the children carry out a myriad of stunts in an attempt to blacken the school's reputation in the eyes of Felicity Wheeler, a school inspector, and Alistair Grigg, a child psychiatrist. Operation War of Nerves is the codename given to one stage of the children's war of attrition, where they try and give the impression that they are making a bomb.

ORCHARD, JULIAN

Roles: Rake in *Don't Lose Your Head*, Doctor in *Follow That Camel*, Fred in *Doctor* and Duc de Poncenay in *Henry*

Although Julian Orchard, who was born in Wheatley, Oxfordshire, in 1930, appeared in many television shows, including *Culture for the Masses*, *Whack-O!*, *Odd Man Out* and an episode of *The Goodies*, he's best known for his busy film career. His long, lugubrious face and expressive features were seen in, among others, *The Great Van Robbery*, *The London Connection*, *Crooks Anonymous*, *Father Came Too*, *Bless This House*, *Man About the House*, *The Slipper and the Rose* and *The Revenge of the Pink Panther*.

He died in 1979, aged forty-nine.

ORTON, PEARL

Hairdresser on *Nurse*

The late Pearl Orton began working as a hair stylist in the film industry from the early 1950s, with such films as *The Kidnappers*, *Reach for the Sky*, *True as a Turtle* and *Operation Amsterdam*. Among the films she worked on during the 1960s are *Doctor in Love*, *Man in the Moon* and the Miss Marple pictures, *Murder She Said* and *Murder at the Gallop*.

Orton occasionally worked on television productions, most notably numerous episodes of *The Avengers*.

O'SHEA, MILO

Role: Len in *Cabby*

Milo O'Shea, born in Dublin in 1926, started acting at the age of twelve in *Oliver Twist*, a series for Radio Eire. By fourteen he was appearing on stage in Dublin and three years later turned professional, joining a small acting company touring Ireland.

He entered films in the 1940s and television the following decade thus beginning a long screen career. His big-screen credits include *Contraband*, *Mrs Gibbons' Boys*, *Barbarella*, *The Adding Machine*, *Loot*, *The Verdict*, *Steptoe and Son Ride Again*, *Moonglow* and, in 2002, *Mystics*. On the small screen, meanwhile, he's appeared in a host of shows, such as *Out of this*

World, The Protectors, St Elsewhere, Cheers, Frasier, Spin City and, in 2004, an episode of *The West Wing*. Alongside his film and television work, O'Shea has remained busy on stage, ever since making his first West End appearance in 1949.

Work frequently took O'Shea to America and, in 1976, he moved to New York, where he still resides.

O'SULLIVAN, MR

Unseen in *Behind* but he's the theatrical agent Major Leep turns to when he wants to book a singer. Confusion sees Mr O'Sullivan sending a stripper to the Riverside Caravan Site by mistake.

O'SULLIVAN, RICHARD

Role: Robin Stevens in *Teacher*

Born in London in 1944, Richard O'Sullivan – who's best known for playing Robin Tripp in the '70s sitcom *Man About the House* and the sequel, *Robin's Nest* – was a busy child actor, appearing in film and on television from a young age.

On the big screen his early credits include *The Stranger's Hand, The Secret, The Green Scarf, The Dark Avenger, It's Great To Be Young* and *No Time for Tears*. On television, meanwhile, he's been seen in shows such as *The Adventures of Robin Hood, The Four Just Men* and *Sword of Freedom*.

O'Sullivan accomplished the transition into adult roles and was seen in running roles in *Father Dear Father* and *Doctor at Large* before being cast as Robin in *Man About the House*. He was seen in television roles up until the mid-1990s.

OSBORNE, BRIAN

Roles: Ambulance Driver in *Matron*, Stall-Holder in *Abroad*, 'Half a quid' Citizen in *Girls*, Browning in *Dick*, Bob in *Behind* and Gunner Owen in *England*

TV: *The Baron Outlook; The Sobbing Cavalier; Orgy and Bess; One in the Eye for Harold; The Case of the Coughing Parrot; Under the Round Table, Short Knight;, Long Daze* and *Who Needs Kitchener?*

Born in Bath in 1940, Brian Osborne trained as an engineer upon leaving school. At the age of nineteen, he paid for elocution lessons and weeks after completing his apprenticeship received an offer to join a children's theatre company, The Theatre for Youth, based at Birkenhead's Theatre Royal.

For six months, he toured schools in England and Scotland before accepting jobs at Manchester and then Bromley Repertory Theatre. After playing a policeman in his one and only radio play, *Saturday Night Theatre*, his first television role came along in the BBC production, *Six Men of Dorset*, about the Tolpuddle Martyrs. His extensive list of small-screen credits ranges from *All Creatures Great and Small, Secret Army* and *Minder* to *New Scotland Yard, Sorry!* and *Upstairs, Downstairs,* while his film appearances include playing a miner in 1969's *Women in Love*.

More recently, he's played the lead in the stage play, *The Farm*, and continued appearing on the screen. He's also set up a decorating business which he runs when not acting.

OSBORNE, ZORENAH

Role: Harem Girl in *Follow That Camel*

Zorenah Osborne's other credits from the 1960s include episodes of *White Hunter, The Avengers* and *Danger Man* as well as appearing in an uncredited role, as the High Priestess, in The Beatles' film, *Help!*.

OULTON, BRIAN

Roles: Henry Bray in *Nurse*, Store Manager in Constable, Brutus in *Cleo* and Store Manager in *Camping*

TV: *Christmas* ('72)

Born in Liverpool in 1908, Brian Oulton trained at RADA. At the age of twenty, he joined the Liverpool Playhouse before going on to roles in the West End.

His acting career was punctuated by service in the army during World War Two; however, it was quickly resumed with leads at the Birmingham Repertory and a two-year stint on the radio in the *Just William* series. He went on to become a familiar face in British films with credits including *The Huggetts Abroad, Private's Progress, I'm All Right Jack* and *The Young Sherlock Holmes*. However, Oulton never forgot his love of the stage and returned to star in many plays, including several by Pinero for which he held a long-standing passion.

MEMORIES

'When I first became an actor I joined a children's theatre and travelled around schools performing *The Pied Piper of Hamlyn*. We were in Rochester when I noticed that Kenneth Williams was appearing in a review in the town. I wrote to him and told him I'd been trained in elocution by John Vere, an actor who'd also taught Kenneth at RADA before going on to work with him on a few of the *Hancock's Half Hour* episodes. Kenneth wrote back and told me to come and see him afterwards, which I did. To cut a long story short, he introduced me to his agent who agreed to represent me.

'It was through the agent that I was introduced to Peter Rogers and Gerald Thomas. He arranged an interview for me and I met them in the foyer of the Dorchester Hotel in London.

'My first appearance was as an ambulance driver in *Matron*. The one amazing thing I remember about my first day of filming was that after spending all day at a building that was supposedly a maternity hospital, I got home and my wife told me she was pregnant. I remember joking with Gerald Thomas about it. I said: "If you ask me into any of your future films, I'll have to be very careful what the subject is in case of ongoing events!"

'Playing the seller at a market in *Abroad* was interesting because I added a few words to my lines which threw Sid James initially. I thought my dialogue sounded boring so I added the words "drinky, drinky", trying to get Sid's character to taste this love potion I was selling. It all stemmed from a holiday we had in Spain. Every morning we'd go down to the beach and this guy could be heard from miles away selling ice lollies and drinks. He'd say: "Lully, lully, licky, licky, drinky, drinky!" So I wacked my line in and from that moment I was always regarded as "drinky, drinky" by the crew. It became my nickname. Sid James laughed about it and so did Gerald. He said: "Christ, where did that come from? Keep it in!" We did another take and it worked fine.

'I remember when we filmed *Behind* we had enormous amounts of rain, sleet and even snow, although it was supposed to be mid-summer. They actually sprayed the mud green. I remember thinking: "Crikey, what the hell is this going to look like?" But when you see it, it looks unbelievable.

'One shot I was in, we had a perfect blue sky, then it would cloud over and we'd get some snow. We did the shot and Gerald said: "Everybody OK?" The cameraman replied: "Well, we had a few flecks of snow." Gerald said: "Don't worry, they'll think it's apple blossom." When we did *Abroad* it seemed just as cold – in fact, it was freezing. Everybody sat in the coach with the engine running, heater on and wrapped in coats. We'd go out to rehearse and Gerald would tell us we could keep our coats on. He'd then say: "Right, camera running, coats off." You would rush in, take your coat off and rush out to film the scene. I enjoyed being in those *Carry On* films.'

BRIAN OSBORNE

Before his death in 1992, at the age of eighty-four, he'd also moved into directing, management and writing.

OUTPATIENT'S SISTER
Played by Valerie Van Ost
In *Again Doctor* the sister ushers Mrs Beasley through to see Dr Nookey.

OVEN WARD
One of the wards in Finisham Maternity Hospital in *Matron*.

OWEN, BILL
Roles: Corporal Bill Copping in *Sergeant*, Percy Hickson in *Nurse*, Mike Weston in *Regardless* and Smiley in *Cabby*
Born in London in 1914, Bill Owen will forever be remembered as Compo, the dishevelled OAP in *Last of the Summer Wine*, but his career spanning more than seven decades encompassed all facets of the profession.

Owen, who wrote and directed for the theatre, received no academic training before entering rep as a teenager. He worked as a holiday camp entertainer for a time, but after World War Two concentrated his efforts on films. Frequently in cockney roles, his credits in this medium include *Perfect Strangers*, *The Way to the Stars*, *Daybreak*, *Easy Money*, *Trottie True*, *The Square Ring*, *The Ship That Died of Shame*, *The Comeback* and *Davy*.

On television he appeared in, among others, *Three Piece Suite*, *The Challengers*, *Coppers End*, *Treasure Island*, *Brideshead Revisited* and *Tales of the Unexpected*.

He died in 1999, aged eighty-five.

OWEN, GUNNER
Played by Brian Osborne
Based at the experimental 1313 anti-aircraft battery featured in *England*, he's one of the shirkers who suffers a severe shock to the system when the tough-speaking Captain Melly is placed in charge of the unit.

'I did four days on *Carry On Nurse* and because it was set on a ward I met virtually all the regulars every day; of course, it was only the second *Carry On* film so no one knew it was going to take off and become a legend – as far as everyone was concerned they were just doing a quick film.

'I didn't have to see anybody and was just given a contract; my agent secured the job for me and all I had to do was turn up on the first day. I did my one famous line, which was three words long, on that day. The rest of the time was spent in background shots.

'I'd never been in a film studio in my life, having just left RADA, and it was all very exciting. My character was called the "Fat Maid". I was fatter in those days but am much slimmer now – two stone lighter! It was such a small part it didn't have any great significance. She was a cleaner who came around the wards polishing the floors with a machine; the point of having her there, I think, was this one moment when Joan Hickson, as the Sister, had to tell Harry Locke, the ward orderly, to go and clean the verandah. In a hurry, he bumps into me, knocks me over and, if I remember right, his broom handle hits me on the backside and I turn around, saying: "Do you mind!" That was my one line.

'But it's wonderful to have on my CV and, funnily enough, it's the one part that gets more attention than almost anything else I've done. I still get fan mail – I can't believe it!'

CHRISTINE OZANNE

OWEN, JOHN
Casting Director on *Dick* and *England*
Other productions John Owen has appeared in include the popular '60s ITC show, *The Champions*.

OZANNE, CHRISTINE
Role: Fat Maid in *Nurse*
Born in Leicester in 1936, Christine Ozanne worked as a clerk for the Automobile Association for five years before turning to acting. Always keen on amateur dramatics, she spent many evenings with the Leicester Drama Society so it came as no surprise when she eventually quit the AA and enrolled at RADA in 1956.

Graduating in 1958 with three comedy prizes, she quickly secured work in repertory theatre, beginning in Sidmouth; within six months of leaving RADA she'd also made her only appearance in the *Carry On*s.

During her career she's worked on television, film and theatre, as well as making over fifty commercials. While her film credits include *Fuel* and the recently released *In the Dark*, her small-screen work, which began with a small role in 1959's *Tell It To The Marines*, covers such shows as *Nearest and Dearest*; *The Two Ronnies*; *Six Dates With Barker*; *The Dustbinmen*; *Within These Walls*; *The Two of Us*; *Take A Letter, Mr Jones* and *Casualty*. She also played two parts in *Angels*, including Sister Muncey.

Ozanne, who remains active in the profession, founded her own touring company, The Original Shakespeare Company. She's also just completed a book, entitled *The Actor's Survival Handbook*, and recently appeared in the theatre.

PAINTER
Played by Hugh Futcher

The disgruntled painter is trying to decorate the Riverside Club in *Behind* but Major Leep, the owner, keeps changing his mind regarding what colour he wants the chairs painted.

PALACE HOTEL, THE
Owned by Connie Philpotts, the £7-a-night Palace Hotel in Fircombe hosts the beauty contestants during the Miss Fircombe competition, much to the disgust of its owner who's been railroaded into letting the dollybirds stay by her long-standing boyfriend, Sidney Fiddler. Occupying a favoured spot on the seafront, the hotel provided accommodation for many elderly residents before they left in droves when the shapely beauties took over in *Girls*.

PALMER, EDWARD
Role: Elderly Resident in *Girls*

In films from the mid-1940s, his credits included *The Small Voice, Room at the Top, Design for Loving* and *The Mind Benders* while his television work, dating back to the '60s, saw him appear in programmes such as *Dixon of Dock Green*; *The Rat Catchers*; *Adam Adamant Lives!*; *Upstairs, Downstairs* and *Smuggler*.

PANTING, MR
Played by Ed Devereaux

Penny Panting's husband in *Regardless* returns home to find his wife in the arms of Sam Twist. It's all a cunning plan of Penny's to try and make her hubby jealous; feeling neglected, she hires Twist from Helping Hands on the pretence that she needs a babysitter, but she's intent on making her beloved think she's seeing another man. Mr Panting doesn't take too kindly to Twist hanging around his wife and delivers a knockout punch.

PANTING, PENNY
Played by Fenella Fielding

Penny Panting, with her seductive voice, is seen in *Regardless*. She hires Sam Twist from Helping Hands, explaining she needs a babysitter. Twist soon discovers her ulterior motive: with no baby, she's using him to help make her husband jealous. Feeling neglected by her hubby, she decides it might help if Mr Panting finds her in the arms of another man, but Twist doesn't want anything to do with her cunning plan. Before he can escape, though, her husband returns and ends up punching him in the face.

PARADISE CAMP
A nudist camp seen in the film, *Nudist Paradise*. In *Camping*, Sid and Bernie want to take their unsuspecting girlfriends to the camp but get their Paradise Camp Sites confused and end up in a mudpit, owned by Josh Fiddler, in Devon, much to their chagrin. But the site has its compensations in the shape of the young nubiles from Chayste Place, a finishing school for girls, who turn up for a stint under canvas.

PARADISE CAMP SITE
This unattractive mudpit of a camp site is situated in Devon. Seen in *Camping*, its owner is Josh Fiddler, who certainly lives up to his name.

PARAGON, LORD
Played by William Mervyn

Presides over the board meeting in *Again Doctor* to decide Doctor Nookey's fate. Accidentally venturing into Miss Armitage's room whilst looking for his girlfriend Goldie Locks, causing the nervous patient much distress, is just the first in a long list of mishaps befalling the unfortunate medic.

Sam Twist (Kenneth Connor) gets more than he bargained for when he visits Penny Panting (*Regardless*)

PARKER, CECIL
Role: 1st Sealord in *Jack*

Born in Hastings, East Sussex, in 1897, Cecil Parker served in World War One before making his first stage appearance in 1922 at the age of twenty-five.

He worked at various repertory theatres and toured South Africa with *The Matriarch* and other plays before embarking on a film career, in 1933. Often seen playing bumptious officials, his numerous film credits include *Caesar and Cleopatra*, *Captain Boycott*, *Hungry Hill*, *Ships With Wings*, *The First Gentleman*, *Quartet*, *The Chiltern Hundreds*, *The Ladykillers* and *The Man in the White Suit*.

Always a busy stage actor, his many credits included productions such as *Lady Windermere's Fan*, *The Rats of Norway*, *The Constant Wife*, *Bonnet over the Windmill*, *Blithe Spirit*, *The Skin of our Teeth*, *Daphne Laureola* and *The Private Life of Helen*.

Never a busy television actor, but was seen in shows of the 1950s and '60s, such as *Studio One*, *The Aquanauts*, *I Spy*, *The Saint* and *The Avengers*.

He died in 1971, aged seventy-three.

PARKER, GUNNER
Played by Richard Olley

Based at the experimental 1313 anti-aircraft battery featured in *England*, he's one of the shirkers who suffers a severe shock to the system when the tough-speaking Captain Melly is put in charge of the unit.

PARKER, MRS
Played by Marianne Stone

A friend of Emily Bung in *Screaming!*. When Emily suspects her husband, Detective Sergeant Sidney Bung, of having an affair, Mrs Parker accompanies her in a taxi as they set out to follow him.

PARKER, MARY
Played by Caroline Whitaker

One of the beauty contestants rushed on stage during the itching powder fiasco in *Girls*.

PARKIN, NURSE
Played by Valerie Van Ost

Nurse seen in *Doctor* tidying Charlie Roper's bed and from the look on his face he's certainly enjoying it. (**Note: in an early version of the script, Nurse Parkin was going to be an attractive West Indian nurse.**)

PARKWAY HOTEL, THE
In *Loving* the cocktail bar at the Parkway Hotel is where, at 7.30, Bertie Muffet expects to meeting Esme Crowfoot; the trouble is, Miss Crowfoot doesn't know anything about the date and fails to turn up. Confusion ensues when Muffet notices a girl hanging around the bar, presumes it's Miss Crowfoot, introduces himself and ends up heading back to her flat.

PARSONS, NICHOLAS
Role: Wolf in *Regardless*

Born in Grantham, Lincolnshire, in 1928, Nicholas Parsons will, for many, always be remembered as chairman of the long-running Radio 4 show, *Just A Minute*, and for posing the questions on the television quiz, *Sale of the Century*.

After reading engineering at Glasgow University, he completed his apprenticeship on Clydebank while gaining acting experience with local repertory companies. He eventually turned professional and worked in reps all around the country. During the 1950s he was resident comedian at the Windmill Theatre and, later, began a partnership with Arthur Haynes lasting over a decade.

On stage he's appeared in the West End, while his film credits, dating back to the late 1940s, include *Master of Bankdam*, *To Dorothy a Son*, *Simon and Laura*, *Eyewitness*, *Brothers in Law*, *Doctor in Love* and *The Wrong Box*. On television, he's worked on, among others, *Here and Now*, *The Benny Hill Show*, *Call My Bluff* and *Cluedo*.

PARTLETON, W. T.
Make-up designer on *Spying*

Worked on over a hundred films as a makeup artist from the early 1940s, including *The Man in Grey*, *Love Story*, *Caravan*, *Snowbound*, *Helter Skelter*, *The Malta Story*, *Value for Money*, *Sapphire*, *The Iron Maiden*, *Kidnapped* and his last picture, *A Warm December*, in 1973. Television credits include *The Avengers* and *David Copperfield*.

PASSER-BY
Played by Terence Holland

In *Cruising* Flo and Glad see an advert for a beauty contest. As Glad tries to persuade Flo to enter a handsome man passes by. (**Note: this scene was cut from the film.**)

WHAT MIGHT HAVE BEEN

Arrangements are underway for the ship's beauty contest. Several characters mentioned never made it onto the screen.

INT. CAPTAIN'S OFFICE – DAY

CROWTHER: (**Doubtfully.**) Bathing-beauty

Wolf (Nicholas Parsons) gets drenched (*Regardless*)

MEMORIES

'I only did one *Carry On* film although I'd liked to have done more. Problem was, I was very busy on television with Arthur Haynes at the time so wasn't available when they asked me to do one before *Regardless*.

'There was very much a family atmosphere on the set – Peter Rogers and Gerald Thomas were very clever that way. Those who became regulars knew that when the next film came along they would probably be thought of and a part allocated to them. You don't get much loyalty among actors in our profession, so if you find people who *are* loyal you normally give much more in return. They all felt part of a team so always worked well together, having a good laugh while they were making other people laugh.

'When I did *Regardless* I'd been working for the Boulting Brothers and if they weren't happy with a particular scene and felt they could get a better take, they'd try again. In a *Carry On* film, once they had a take that was good, they didn't say: "I think we can do better." There wasn't the time, it was a case of, "We have a good take – keep it."

'Gerald Thomas, who was a charming man, once asked after a long and complicated scene involving Joan Sims, how I felt. Being honest, I said the run-through of the scene in rehearsal had been better. He agreed, but said that he was satisfied. I should have been happy with that, but when he asked if I'd like to go again, being that it was my big moment in the film, which finished with Joan pouring a bottle of wine over me, I replied that I felt I could make the part funnier. We did another take and both agreed it was better. The following day, however, I heard through my agent that I'd been reported as being fussy. I never worked on another *Carry On*.

'I hadn't the faintest idea; it was just that I hadn't done a *Carry On* before and hadn't got to grips with the style in which they worked. Another thing I remember from that film was the suit they produced for me. It was absolutely ghastly and didn't really fit me properly. I knew it was going to be ruined so it didn't really matter, but I was supposed to be terribly smart, so mistakenly said, "Don't worry, I can wear my own clothes and get them cleaned afterwards." Because the clothes had been bought for me, I was misunderstood and was, I think, taken as being a bit fussy.

'But overall I thoroughly enjoyed working on the film and the whole atmosphere of the *Carry On* scene.'

NICHOLAS PARSONS

contest . . . I don't know . . . I usually go for knobbly knees.

M'BANKS: Each to his taste, of course, sir – but *please* allow me, this trip, to handle the bathing-beauties.

CROWTHER: Over my dead body.

M'BANKS: (**False laugh.**) Oh you're so *quick*, sir! I meant, of course . . .

CROWTHER: I know what you meant. Well – (**Grudgingly.**) I suppose so . . . What can go wrong at a bathing-beauty contest?

M'BANKS: In my hands, sir – *nothing*. (**Crowther doesn't look so sure.**) You'll judge of course?

CROWTHER: Not by myself. Let's have . . .

M'BANKS: (**Before Crowther can suggest anybody.**) Leave it to me, sir. I'll pick a panel properly to pro-and-con the pulchritude, with probity and precision.

CROWTHER: You do that. (**Delayed.**) Eh?

M'BANKS: (**Going to door.**) Vivid eh? And alliterative. Rather good I must say . . .

INT. BACK OF SHIP'S BAR – DAY

M'BANKS: (**Hisses.**) Fixed! You're a judge! Tomorrow!

TURNER: (**Delighted.**) Now we'll show him, sir!

M'BANKS: That's the spirit. Tree'll take your place in charge of refreshments at the contest. (**Vision.**) All the new boys – co-operating in a splendidly-organised entertainment!

TURNER: You'll have Dr Binn as a judge as well then?

M'BANKS: (**Nod.**) Just going to tell him. Any idea where he is?

EXT. BATHING POOL – DAY

(BINN is flat on his back. Astride him, MISS MADDERLEY performs artificial respiration.)

NOTICE

QUEEN OF THE *HAPPY WANDERER*!

GRAND BATHING-BEAUTY CONTEST

TOMORROW

3PM – AT THE POOL

(The notice is displayed in a nebulous corridor allegedly en route to dining saloon. The JOHNSON-BARCLAYS pass it, led by ramrod-backed AUNTIE G. The girls dawdle by the notice.)

AUNTIE G: Come-come girls – we'll be late for dinner.

(They scuttle past her. She yawns, delicately covering her mouth of course.)

AUNTIE G: Dear, dear – the sea air – makes me so drowsy . . .

(She follows the girls as if convinced they might be raped round the corner if she's not with them. Her place is immediately taken by FLO and GLAD, the latter spotting the notice and reacting extravagantly, hauling FLO back for:)

GLAD: Look!

FLO: (**Practical.**) Says nothing about prizes.

GLAD: Oh *Flo* – who cares about *prizes*? The thing *is* – if you *win* . . .

FLO: (**Squeak.**) Win? I'm not even going *in* for it.

GLAD: Oh yes you are, my girl. (**Rapid now.**)

FLO: (**Squeakier.**) Me? Parade about in front of all those men?! (**Suddenly begins, albeit quavering, to get the point.**) I *say* – d'you think I *could*?

GLAD: Of *course*!

FLO: (**Wriggling.**) I'd *die*!

GLAD: You'd *live* – *really* live! Why – (**Delirious.**) any girl who wins a thing like this *must* be the centre of attraction for the rest of the voyage! You'll be able to take your *pick*! You could be *engaged* before we get back home – (**Going mad.**) – maybe even *married* – the Captain can do you, you know!

FLO: (**Prim.**) Really, Glad!

GLAD: (**Injured.**) What did I *say*?

FLO: (**Resuming quivering excitement.**) You said – I'd have my pick!

GLAD: (**Resuming quivering excitement.**) Queen of the *Happy Wanderer*!

FLO: Belle of the Ball!

GLAD: Cock of the North!

FLO: (**Deflated, shaking.**) I'd *never* win . . .

GLAD: Why *not*? You've got what it takes!

FLO: How come I've never *took*, then?

GLAD: This could be the turning point!

FLO: Yeh – it could prove I'm *really* on the turn. Now if *you* went in for it . . .

GLAD: I'm not looking for romance: you are.

HANDSOME-PASSERBY: (**Courteous, unexcited.**) Cabin 149. (**And he's gone.**)

FLO: *Sauce!!*

GLAD: (**Grasping her.**) Flo – will you?

FLO: 'Course I won't! I don't even know his *name*.

GLAD: Will you *enter*?

FLO: I'll – think it over during dinner.

GLAD: *DINNER?* This is no time for *food*! (**Hauls her away.**)

FLO: But I'm hungry!

GLAD: We've got work to do.

They disappear. MISS MADDERLEY passes the notice. Turns. Looks at it. And sighs. Just that. But perks up and marches off towards dinner.

EXT. DECK – NIGHT

BINN leaning on the rail, lost in thought. Clutching papers, M'BANKS bustlingly appears.

M'BANKS: Ah Binn, my dear fellow – been searching for you. Want you to look at my modus operandi.

PASSWORTHY, WPC GLORIA
Played by Joan Sims
A newly-qualified constable who's on temporary attachment to the station in *Constable* where a flu epidemic has caused a shortage of manpower. An industrious, career-minded individual who finally lets her guard down for a little romance with Charlie Constable, a fellow police officer.

PAT
Played by Valerie Shute
In *Camping* Pat is one of the girls from Chayste Place Finishing School for Girls.

PATCH
Played by Peter Gilmore
Real name Roger, this pirate turns out to be none other than Sally's long-lost childhood sweetheart. In *Jack,* Sally sets sail for Spain on the frigate *Venus* in an attempt to locate the man she thinks she loves only to come face-to-face with him in unexpected circumstances, when he ambushes the frigate. Originally pressganged into sailing to Spain many years ago, he deserted in Morocco, adopted the name Patch and turned to piracy. Although he's keen to make up for lost time, Sally realises he isn't the man for her.

PATIENT
Played by Lucy Griffiths
A patient in the Borough County Hospital's Caffin Ward in *Doctor.* Miss Morrison occupies the bed recently vacated by Mavis Tinkle, which causes problems for Ken Biddle, who has a crush on Mavis, when he asks his friend Fred to pass on a letter. Instead of it reaching its intended recipient, Miss Morrison has a surprise.

PATIENT
Played by Pat Coombs
A patient in the Borough County Hospital's Caffin Ward in *Doctor.* When she needs to spend a penny, she stops Mr Biddle, a male patient, who's a sight for sore eyes when he dons a nurse's uniform in order to talk to Mavis Winkle, with whom he is trying to strike up a relationship.

PATIENT
Played by Donald Bisset
For 'Patient' in *Again Doctor,* see 'Bean, Mr'.

PATIENT IN PLASTER
Played by Billy Cornelius
A patient at Long Hampton Hospital whose legs are in plaster. He struggles to pull himself up when Matron instructs everyone to sit up because Dr Carver is carrying out his rounds. Later on in *Again Doctor* he gets in a terrible mess and finds himself hanging upside-down while writhing in agony.

PAUL, MARTIN
Played by Jerry Desmonde
Seen in *Regardless,* Mr Paul is a well-known thespian and womaniser. He's recently been divorced from his fifth wife and is ready for number six when Lily Duveen arrives on his doorstep. He'd asked Helping Hands to send someone to help with his rehearsals but a mix-up sees Miss Duveen arrive instead.

PAVLOVIC, DRINA
Role: Courting Girl in *Behind*
Occasionally appeared on screen during the 1970s and '80s, usually in one-off episodes. She appeared in instalments of *Victorian Scandals* and *Play for Today,* playing Arabella in *Hell's Angel,* while in *Sorry!* she was cast as a nurse. Her biggest role was Celia for two years in *Please, Sir!.* On the big screen she's appeared in a handful of productions, including 1972's *Vampire Circus.*

PAYNE, GERALDINE
One of the beauty contestants eager to win the coveted Miss Fircombe crown in *Girls.* In the mayhem at the Pier Theatre she ends up sneezing incessantly after pepper is sprinkled on the contestants by members of the local women's lib movement who vehemently oppose the competition.

PEACOCKS OF BALHAM
In *Cabby* Peggy Hawkins buys her fleet of fifteen Ford Cortinas from Peacocks.

PEARCE, JACQUELINE
Role: 3rd Lady in *Don't Lose Your Head*
Born in Byfleet, Surrey, in 1943, Jacqueline Pearce trained at RADA. Her screen work began in the mid-1960s in television shows such as *Danger Man, The Avengers, Public Eye* and *Man in a Suitcase.* Before the decade was out, she crossed the Atlantic to study at the Actors' Studio, resuming her career in the UK in the '70s.

Other television credits include *Callan, Hadleigh, Special Branch, Doctor Who, Churchill's People, Moondial* and BBC's 2002 production of *Daniel Deronda,* but it's probably as Supreme Commander Servalan in *Blake's 7* that she's best remembered.

Her film work includes roles in *The Plague of the Zombies, The Reptile, White Mischief* and *Guru in Seven.*

PEARSON
Played by Michael Nightingale
A doctor at the Finisham Maternity Hospital who checks Sir Bernard Cutting's stomach and allays his fears that he has something wrong with that part of his anatomy. Appearing in *Matron,* he then jokingly remarks on Cutting's interestingly shaped pelvic cavity, commenting that it will be useful for child-bearing, causing Cutting, who's a hypochondriac, to start worrying that he's changing sex.

PEART, PAULINE
Role: Gloria Winch in *Girls*
Born in Jamaica in 1952, Pauline Peart left home in the early '60s and began appearing occasionally in films from the 1970s, including playing a vampire girl in Hammer's 1974 film, *The Satanic Rites of Dracula,* a secretary in the big-screen version of *Man About the House* the same year and Dolores in 1979's *Cuba.* She also appeared in the film *The Doomsday Bomb,* and toured in the play *Birds of Paradise,* both just before her appearance in *Girls.*

PEG 1
Seen in *Cabby,* this antiquated taxi is the first vehicle Charlie Hawkins owned. Its registration is a clear indication of the affection he has for his wife, Peggy – if only he'd show it more overtly occasionally.

PEGGE, EDMUND
Role: Bowler in *Follow That Camel*
A graduate of Sydney's National Institute of Dramatic Art and the Elizabethan Players, Edmund Pegge, who divides his time between Australia and the UK, has led a busy stage and screen career. More recently he's performed poetry around the world in schools, on stage and television.

In the UK, his television career began in the 1970s and has included roles in shows such as *Crossroads, The Troubleshooters, Paul Temple, Division 4, Secret Army, Sorry!, Home Sweet Home, One By One* and, more recently, an episode of *Doctors* in 2003 and, a year later, an instalment of *Jessica.*

On the big screen from the late '60s, his credits include *Scream . . . and Die!, Nightmares* and *Sweet Talker.*

PENTAGON FILM TITLES LTD
The company designed and created the titles for *Sergeant.*

PEPE
Played by Peter Butterworth
Pepe owns the Elsbels Palace Hotel in the Mediterranean resort of Elsbels. His blood pressure rockets in *Abroad* when the construc-

tion of his hotel falls behind schedule because the builders are constantly striking. Although he should have delayed the opening date, Pepe tries accommodating the party of tourists arriving on the Wundatours trip, assisted by Floella, the cook, and Georgio, his son, who runs the bar.

PERCIVAL, LANCE
Role: Wilfred Haines in *Cruising*
Born in Sevenoaks, Kent, in 1933, Lance Percival's talents range from satire and revue to comedy and singing, perfectly exploited on shows such as *That Was The Week That Was* and *Impromptu* in the early 1960s.

After completing National Service in the army, he lived in Canada for four years. While holding a series of jobs, including selling encyclopaedias, he spent his spare time performing at hospitals and other institutions with his own calypso group. He subsequently toured Canada and America before returning to the UK. Initially he entertained at nightclubs before joining a satirical revue touring the country, entitled *Here Is The News,* followed by *One Over the Eight* with Kenneth Williams.

His television work, meanwhile, includes appearances in such shows as *Jason King, Target, Lance at Large, Up the Workers, Shoestring* and *Happy Families,* while on the big screen his many credits include *What a Whopper!, Raising the Wind, In the Doghouse, Twice Round the Daffodils* and *Up the Chastity Belt.*

Now an award-winning after-dinner speaker, he also prepares scripts for company executives.

PERKINS
Played by Martin Boddey
In *Nurse,* Perkins is Ted York's newspaper editor. He visits the journalist at Haven Hospital and gives him an assignment while he's lying in his sick bed. York's task is to write a series of articles about hospital life from the patient's point of view.

PERKINS
Played by Larry Cross
Seen in *Cowboy,* Perkins bursts in on the Commissioner of the Bureau of Internal Affairs in Washington, just when he's getting fresh with Miss Jones. He breaks the news that Stodge City is experiencing problems of lawlessness and is in desperate need of a peace marshal.

PERKINS, PAULA
Played by Valerie Leon
Paula, who's seen in *Girls,* is engaged to Peter Potter and helps run his publicity firm, Potter Publicity Bureau. She takes the call from Sidney Fiddler, not her favourite person, when he calls to offer Peter the contract for publicising the Miss Fircombe beauty contest. Paula's jealous streak means Peter is afraid to tell his fiancée what the job entails; when she eventually finds out, she decides it's time she gave Peter a taste of his own medicine and becomes a late entrant in the Miss Fircombe competition.

PERTWEE, BILL
Roles: Barman in *Loving* and Fire Chief in *Girls*
Born in Amersham, Buckinghamshire, in 1926, Bill Pertwee has enjoyed a varied career in entertainment which began in earnest when Beryl Reid accepted some of his comedy material for a London revue. As a result, he was later invited to join the company, turning professional some months later. But before entering the world of showbiz, Pertwee held down a number of jobs, including making parts for Spitfires, window-cleaning and assistant baggage boy to the Indian cricket team in 1946.

He experienced a precarious early education and was unable to write even his own name accurately before the age of twelve, but after moving to a small private school where learning was fun, Pertwee's education was back on track. Upon finishing his schooling at sixteen, he searched for work, but until breaking into

Jon Pertwee plays the crazy old Soothsayer (*Cleo*)

the entertainment business in 1954, some twelve years later, experienced a chequered career encompassing numerous jobs.

In the 1950s he began spending time with various acting groups, and when the offer to help his cousin, the late Jon Pertwee, on a variety tour came along, he jumped at the chance, even though it involved no actual acting.

When the tour finished, he found employment at a school outfitters in London, until he received a phone call from producer Ronnie Hill that changed his life. The producer's call led to Pertwee joining Beryl Reid's revue at the Watergate Theatre. For eight weeks, he continued working at the outfitters during the day while appearing in the revue every evening. But by 1955 he knew he wanted to act professionally and settled down to concentrate on his future career.

His first professional summer season saw him spend two weeks with a small acting company at Bognor Regis before the eight performers making up the company moved to Gorleston on Sea, near Great Yarmouth, for the main season.

As the years passed, Pertwee kept busy with radio, small television parts and plenty of Variety seasons. The 1950s closed in style with an offer to join the second series of radio's popular weekly comedy show, *Beyond Our Ken*, with Kenneth Williams and Kenneth Horne among the cast. Soon after the show finished in 1964, Bill was recruited for the equally funny *Round the Horne*.

In 1967 he was offered a couple of lines in an episode of *Hugh and I*, a BBC sitcom produced by David Croft. Working for Croft in this one-off episode led to a few lines as the air raid warden in *Dad's Army*, a character who became a regular in the long-running series.

Other TV appearances include *Lollipop Loves Mr Mole*, *Jackanory*, *The Dick Emery Show*, *Frost Weekly*, *Billy Liar*, *The Larry Grayson Show* and *You Rang, M'Lord?*. He's continued with occasional theatre work – he toured as Sergeant Beetroot, the Crowman's assistant in *Worzel Gummidge* – and pantomimes. He has also written several books, including his autobiography, *A Funny Way To Make A Living!*, published in 1996.

PERTWEE, JON
Roles: Soothsayer in *Cleo*, Sheriff Albert Earp in *Cowboy*, Dr Fettle in *Screaming!* and the Duke of Costa Brava in *Columbus*
Jon Pertwee, born in London in 1919, trained at RADA before spending much of the 1930s acting in repertory theatre and performing on radio before beginning his film career in the latter part of the decade.

During World War Two he served as an officer for the RNVR, sailing on HMS *Hood* just before it was sunk by the *Bismarck*, before undertaking broadcasting work within the navy.

After the war, he continued working in radio, but by the 1950s was juggling radio work with roles on television, in summer shows and in more films, including *Trouble in the Air*, *Helter Skelter*, *Nearly a Nasty Accident* and *A Funny Thing Happened on the Way to the Forum*.

A major break for Pertwee came in 1969 when he became the new Doctor in the long-running television series *Doctor Who*; another popular role saw him, in 1979, playing a scarecrow in another children's television series, *Worzel Gummidge*.

During the 1990s he notched up further roles in films such as *The Boys in Blue*, *Cloud Cuckoo*, *Adventures of a Private Eye* and *Discworld*, as well as touring with his one-man show, *Who Is Jon Pertwee?*

He died in 1996, aged seventy-six.

PETERS, LANCE
Wrote the original screenplay for *Emmannuelle*
Author, producer and screenwriter Lance Peters was born in Auckland, New Zealand, in 1934. His mother died when he was only three and he was raised by an aunt in Sydney, Australia.

Upon leaving school, he worked at Sydney's Tivoli Theatre before becoming a singer and then a disc jockey for a radio station in the city. His talents extended to comedy and he began securing work as a stand-up comedian in clubs. He wrote his own material which led to the offer of a writing job on a local television station; one of his first projects was to script *Memoirs*, a series about famous Australians. So successful was he that he decided to quit his job as an entertainer to focus on writing, primarily for stage and screen.

He arrived in England in 1972 when Bill Kenwright was interested in buying the rights of a stage play he'd written, titled *Mother's Little Murderer*. He's since written numerous plays for stage and a myriad of scripts for the big and small screen.

He returned to Australia in 1981 and has since formed his own production company, Underworld Productions. Among the many productions he's currently developing is *The Red Collar Gang*, a thriller based on one of his novels, which will star John Travolta and Mel Gibson.

PHILIP
An unseen polo player whose name is uttered by Sir Sidney Ruff-Diamond in *Up The Khyber*, who's impressed with his performance. He compliments him before telling his wife that Philip has prospects.

PHILLIPS, DOROTHEA
Role: Aunt Beatrice Grubb in *Loving*
Born in Penygraig, Wales, in 1928, Dorothea Phillips, whose father was a vicar and mother an opera singer, studied English and law at Aberystwyth University before launching her acting career in rep at Hunstanton, Norfolk. Years of repertory theatre followed before she made her West End debut in the 1955 production of *Under Milk Wood*.

She entered films in the late 1960s and has appeared in, among others, *Santa Claus*, *Duet for One*, *The Little Match Girl*, *102 Dalmatians* and, in 2001, *Chopsticks*. She has, however, spent the lion's share of her career in television. Her credits, dating back to the late 1950s, include *Dixon of Dock Green*, *Jason King*, *Within These Walls*, *Sexton Blake*, *Angels*, *Mind Your Language*, *The House of Eliott*, *Grange Hill*, *Lovejoy* and *Goodnight Sweetheart*.

She remains in the business.

PHILLIPS, LESLIE
Roles: Jack Bell in *Nurse*, Alistair Grigg in *Teacher*, PC Tom Potter in *Constable* and the King of Spain in *Columbus*
Born in London in 1924, Leslie Phillips studied at the Italia Conti stage school, making his stage debut, aged five, in a production of *Peter Pan*. He made further stage and screen appearances as a child.

After serving four years in the army during the Second World War, he returned to showbusiness. Phillips, who played Lt. Pouter in the hit radio series *The Navy Lark*, has appeared in over a hundred films and a myriad of television shows. On the small screen he's been seen in productions such as *The Vise*, *The Adventures of Robin Hood*, *The Invisible Man*, *Father Dear Father*, *Lovejoy*, *Monarch of the Glen* and *Where The Heart Is*, while his film work includes appearances in *Train of Events*, *Pool of London*, *Value for Money*, *Brothers in Law* and *I Was Monty's Double*. During the 1960s he took over from Dirk Bogarde in the *Doctor* films.

He's remained busy through the decades on stage and screen, with recent film credits including *Lara Croft: Tomb Raider*, *Collusion* and *Churchill: The Hollywood Years*.

PHILLIPS, MRS
An unseen character in *At Your Convenience* who's mentioned by Beattie Plummer. It seems that Mrs Phillips's budgie was speaking sentences after just three months, although the bird's limited vocabulary was restricted to a handful of expletives, hence the reason its cage was always covered up when the vicar called.

PHILLPOTTS, AMBROSINE
Roles: Yoki's Owner in *Regardless* and Aristocratic Lady in *Cabby*
Born in London in 1912, Ambrosine Phillpotts,

niece of playwright Eden Phillpotts, studied music in Paris before attending RADA.

She made her stage debut in 1930's *The Ringer*, before spending three years at Hull Rep and forging a successful theatre career which has included entertaining the troops in Western Europe in a production of *Blithe Spirit*.

Film and television roles soon began dominating her work schedule. Her big-screen credits included *The Chiltern Hundreds, The Franchise Affair, Up in the World, Doctor in Love, Life at the Top, Diamonds on Wheels* and *The Wildcats of St Trinian's*. On the small screen she's best remembered as Lady Helen Hadleigh in *Hadleigh*.

She died in 1980, aged sixty-eight.

PHILOSOPHERS' CLUB, THE

A stuffy, old-fashioned gentlemen's club in *Regardless*. Sam Twist, from Helping Hands, replaces Lou, who's ill, but his squeaky shoes and inability to stop laughing at some of the sights he encounters sees him thrown out by the Club Receptionist.

PHILPOT, TERENCE
Played by Terry Scott
The bow-tie-wearing Mr Philpot is a client of the Wedded Bliss Agency in *Loving*. He signs on at Sidney and Sophie Bliss's agency but his first two dates are a failure. Arriving in his lemon MG sportscar at the home of Jenny Grubb, he soon realises she's not the girl for him, partly because she lives in an eerie building with her extended family, including her overbearing mother. His next date, with Miss Adams, is equally unsatisfactory considering she's five months pregnant.

Philpot storms over to confront Mr Bliss and requests a refund, that is until a transformed Jenny Grubb, now all lowcut dress and big hairdo, arrives at the office. Philpot, who has a private income of £3000 per annum, decides that perhaps he's being hasty and heads off with Miss Grubb. Before long, they're married.

PHILPOTTS, CONNIE
Played by Joan Sims
A widow who owns the Palace Hotel on Fircombe's seafront. Seen in *Girls*, she becomes frustrated when her boyfriend, Sidney Fiddler, lets all the spare rooms, free of charge, to girls entering the Miss Fircombe beauty contest. As a result of half-naked girls strolling around the place, Connie loses seven of her elderly residents within two days because they can't take the strain. She gets her own back on Sid by agreeing to help at the contest by collecting entrance fees before running off with the takings.

The bubbly Jacki Piper was a valuable addition to the *Carry On* team

PHIPPS, NICHOLAS
Played by David Kernan
He travels to the Mediterranean resort of Elsbels with Wundatours in *Abroad*. Nicholas takes the trip with his partner, the camp and grumpy Robin Tweet, but tells him to 'push off' when he becomes interested in Lily, a girl who also takes the trip.

PHOTOGRAPHER
Played by Michael Ward
Seen in *Regardless*, the effeminate photographer takes pictures of Francis Courtenay modelling a beekeeper's hat.

PHYSICIAN
Played by William Mervyn
In *Henry* the court physician, Dr Finlay, uses leeches on Queen Marie of Normandy when she faints, before breaking the news to the King that she's expecting.

PIANIST
Played by Eric Rogers
Seen in *Cowboy* entertaining at Rumpo's Place.

PIANIST
Played by Josie Bradley
Seen in *Loving* entertaining in the Marie

Antoinette Room at Mr and Mrs Bliss's wedding reception.

PICTON, DONALD
Set Dresser on *England*
Other films Donald Picton worked on are the 1956 war movie, *The Battle of the River Plate*, and, in 1965, *Three Hats for Lisa*.

PICTURE PLAYHOUSE
The cinema in *Camping* where Sid Boggle takes his girlfriend, Joan Fussey, and friends, Bernie Lugg and Anthea Meeks, to see a film; the trouble is, he didn't tell them it was entitled *Nudist Paradise*.

PIER THEATRE
The venue for the Miss Fircombe beauty contest in *Girls*.

PIPER, JACKI
Roles: June in *Up the Jungle*, Sally Martin in *Loving*, Myrtle Plummer in *At Your Convenience* and Sister in *Matron*
Born in Birmingham in 1946, Jacki Piper completed her education at King Edward's Grammar School in the city and enrolled at the Birmingham Theatre School.

After graduating she was accepted as a

MEMORIES

'I remember going along to be interviewed at Pinewood. They were doing *Carry On Up The Jungle* and I read for Peter Rogers and Gerald Thomas. I had only done one small film part up to then, playing the secretary in *The Man Who Haunted Himself* with Roger Moore, and I said: "You can't possibly employ me, I haven't done much film work because I've come from the theatre." Peter roared with laughter.

'Before the film ended, Peter Rogers rang up my agent and asked if I could come back again, which was very lucky for me. At that time, I didn't have a lot of money but knew what I would be earning for the next few years.

'Most of my memories come from *Jungle*. Before they started shooting one day, Gerald Thomas said to me: "I'm afraid I've got something unpleasant to tell you." I thought I was going to be fired. He explained: "You have to have a bucket of water thrown over your face this afternoon." I had this hairpiece on and they threw this bucket of water so forcefully that everything was struck off – the hair, my eyelashes, everything. They had to dry me down and throw the water again, this time gently.

'I also remember Terry Scott and I had to wear these trusses for when we were swinging on the ropes. We got terribly cut between our legs and had to go and see the nurse; we could barely walk properly with them on. I think we should have practised a bit more, though, because occasionally we'd go flying and land on mats.

'For *At Your Convenience* we spent a few days in Brighton, filming on the pier. When we were on the ghost train, Bernard Bresslaw's and Maggie Nolan's car, which was behind mine, never emerged from the tunnel; it had derailed and they were on the floor in the dark. Apparently they'd both lunged to the side as it went around a corner and tipped the car over. It was quite funny, really.

'I was very young when I was working on the films, whereas all the others were established. I couldn't believe my luck, so I'd just sit around and listen to all their stories. It absolutely delighted me. When I look back they were so lovely to me. Very friendly, looking out for me.'

JACKI PIPER

student ASM at Rhyl for a ten-week season. She moved on to play the juvenile at Colwyn Bay, earning £2 per week, and, at the age of nineteen, the juvenile lead at York for a year. When her contract was up, she toured in the play, *Boeing, Boeing*, before taking over a role in *Dear Charles*, playing Cicely Courtneidge's daughter at the Savoy Theatre.

Soon she was working on television, beginning with *Softly, Softly*. Other small-screen credits include *The Two Ronnies*, *The Generation Game*, *Dick Emery*, *Call My Bluff*, *Dangerfield*, *The Bill*, *Barbara* and, most recently, *Wire in the Blood*. On the big screen, meanwhile, she appeared in, among others, *Doctor in Trouble* and *The Love Ban*.

After taking a career break for six years when her second child was born, Piper returned to the industry and spent a year at the Garrick Theatre in *No Sex Please We're British*, but she never retrieved the heights of success experienced in her early career. She still continues to act.

PLACE DE LA TÊTE PRUNER

The Parisian square where the guillotine provides regular entertainment to the residents of the city in *Don't Lose Your Head*.

PLASTERER

Played by Johnny Briggs
Seen in *Behind* putting up plaster sheets in the clubhouse. An early version of the scene had the Major claiming the sheets were on crooked.

WHAT MIGHT HAVE BEEN

INT. CLUBHOUSE – DAY

The building is prefabricated and almost finished. The inner walls are lined with plaster sheets held to the studding with adhesive. Two plasterers are engaged in putting up the slabs. Two painters are painting a number of second-hand stacking chairs bright green. THE MAJOR enters with DAPHNE and looks around. He reacts and goes up to the painters in annoyance.

MAJOR: Dammit man, that's not the colour I ordered.

PAINTER: It's what we were given.

MAJOR: I ordered *leaf* green. That's not leaf green. You'll have to change it.

(The MAJOR walks away accompanied by an admiring DAPHNE. He stops to look at a slab being put in place.)

MAJOR: And that's on crooked.

PLASTERER: Not from here it ain't.

MAJOR: Well it is from here.

(The MAJOR puts two hands on the slab and moves it. If it wasn't on crooked before, it is now.)

MAJOR: That's better.

DAPHNE: Oh much.

(He stalks away with DAPHNE.)

PLASTERER: He's broken the bond now.

(They look at the slab with misgivings.)

PLOTTER, 1st and 2nd

Played by Norman Chappell and Douglas Ridley
Friends of Lord Hampton of Wick involved in the plot to overthrow King Henry VIII in *Henry*.

PLUMMER, BEATTIE

Played by Hattie Jacques
Sid's lazy wife of twenty-five years in *At Your Convenience* spends her entire day trying to get her pet budgie, Joey, to talk. It seems she has little to offer her husband, who has been smitten with Chloe Moore, his next-door neighbour and work colleague, for years.

PLUMMER, MYRTLE

Played by Jacki Piper
Myrtle works at William Boggs and Son, the toilet ware manufacturer, in the canteen. Sid's and Beattie's attractive daughter is pursued by union rep, Vic Spanner, and the boss's son, Lewis Boggs, who finally wins her hand in marriage courtesy of a special licence he presents to her while on the firm's annual jolly to Brighton. Seen in *At Your Convenience*.

PLUMMER, SID

Played by Sidney James
Works foreman at William Boggs and Son, the toilet ware company, Sid has been married to Beattie for twenty-five years, and they have one daughter, Myrtle, who works in the company's canteen. A vital link between management and shop-floor workers, Sid has a friendly working relationship with the employees, especially Chloe Moore, whom he's fancied for years. Unfortunately it's a relationship he knows he'll never have the chance of pursuing.

Sid comes up trumps when the family's pet budgie, Joey, who hasn't tweeted a word all his life, suddenly reveals a gift for predicting winners in the horse racing. Over the following months, Sid wins a fortune at his local bookmaker's office and is even able to bail out Boggs and Son when the financial future looks bleak after the bank refuses to provide a bridging loan. When the firm recovers from the financial blip, Sid is offered a directorship as a way of thanking him, but he's not interested because he regards himself as a worker.

PLUMP NATIVE GIRL

Played by Heather Emmanuel
One of Gladstone's nurses at the mission in *Again Doctor*. She's seen brewing coffee on a workbench but runs off giggling when

Gladstone gives her a quick squeeze and a pat on the bottom.

PLUNKETT, MOIRA
Played by Gail Grainger

Miss Moira Plunkett works for Wundatours Limited and assists the courier, Stuart Farquhar, on the long weekend trip to the Mediterranean resort of Elsbels. Seen in *Abroad*, Moira, who's a confident, outspoken girl, falls for Farquhar by the end of the break in the Med.

PLYTAS, STEVE
Role: Arabian Official in *Emmannuelle*

Born in Istanbul, Turkey, in 1913, Steve Plytas was often seen playing Greek or Turkish officials in films and television shows from the late 1950s. His big-screen debut was an uncredited role in *A Night to Remember* and he went on to appear in such productions as *Very Important Person, Theatre of Death, Revenge of the Pink Panther, Batman* and *Dilemma*.

His television credits included *Interpol Calling, The Cheaters, Ghost Squad, Crane, Danger Man, The Champions* and *Tales of the Unexpected*, but for some people he's best remembered as Kurt, the chef, in *Fawlty Towers*.

He died in 1997, aged eighty-three.

POD, HENGIST
Played by Kenneth Connor

A simple wheelmaker, whose unhappy marriage to the nagging Senna has lasted ten years, he appears in *Cleo*. Hengist's claim to fame is making a square wheel which means if you stop your cart on a hill, it doesn't roll backwards. A feeble, unassuming man, a major misunderstanding after being captured by the Romans finds him promoted to centurion and commander of the Praetorian Guard; the most feared and admired man in Rome, he stands alongside Caesar as his bodyguard.

POD, SENNA
Played by Sheila Hancock

The nagging wife of Hengist the wheelmaker in *Cleo*. Her henpecking might have worsened since the death of her mother, who was eaten by a brontosaurus a few days previous; she couldn't have tasted very good, though, because the dinosaur was dead within the hour. Still, one postive about Senna is that she keeps a tidy cave.

POHLMANN, ERIC
Roles: Sinister Man in *Regardless* and The Fat Man in *Spying*

Born in Vienna in 1913, Eric Pohlmann spent his early years entertaining at the Reiss Bar in the city before coming to England in 1939.

He began appearing on stage and, from the late '40s, in films. He clocked up over a hundred credits in this medium, including *Portrait for Life, The Third Man, Travellers' Joy,*

The Clouded Yellow, Venetian Bird, A Prize of Gold, No Kidding, Shadow of Fear and *The Return of the Pink Panther*. He also provided the voice for Blofeld in the Bond movies, *From Russia With Love* and *Thunderball*.

His small-screen work, meanwhile, included appearances in *Colonel March of Scotland Yard, The Four Just Men, The Baron, Hadleigh* and much work on German television.

He died in 1979, aged sixty-eight, in Germany while rehearsing for the Salzburg Festival.

POLICE CHIEF
Played by Alan Curtis

In charge of the local police force at the village visited by the Brits staying at the Elsbels Palace Hotel in *Abroad*. As the brother of Madame Fifi, who runs the bawdyhouse in the village, he has little sympathy for the party when they're arrested for brawling and causing criminal damage to his sister's establishment.

POLICE COMMISSIONER
Played by Michael Nightingale

Seen dining at the French Ambassador's residence in *Emmannuelle*.

POLICE INSPECTOR
Played by David Lodge

Called to Fircombe's Palace Hotel in *Girls* by Augusta Prodworthy who's tipped him off that one of the beauty contestants is, in fact, a man. With Prodworthy against the contest, she looks for any excuse to discredit the event.

POLICEMAN
Played by uncredited actor

In *Cabby* the policeman receives a message on his radio asking him to intercept the crooks driving out of town with Peggy and Sally held at gunpoint.

POLICEMAN
Played by Anthony Sagar

In *Screaming!* the policeman accompanies Detective Constable Slobotham to Bourne and Jones, a milliner's shop, where a window has been broken.

POLICEMAN
Played by Robert Russell

In *Loving* the policeman arrests James Bedsop for acting suspiciously in the men's lavatories. He first spots Bedsop putting on a false beard as a disguise before entering the toilets. When he's chased out by the attendant and admits he's looking for a man, the policeman decides it's time to take him down to the station.

POLICEMEN
Played by Jack Taylor and Cyril Chamberlain

They arrest Francis Courtenay at a railway station in *Regardless,* for making a nuisance of himself.

POLLY
Played by Vicki Smith

One of the saloon girls at Rumpo's Place in *Cowboy,*

PONSONBY, LADY JANE
Played by Angela Douglas

Blue-blooded Lady Jane Ponsonby appears in *Follow That Camel*. Liked by all the men, she had a fling with Maximillion Burger – her fencing tutor – while attending her Viennese finishing school. She stumbles across him again in the Sahara, where he's a commandant in the Foreign Legion whose newest recruit, Bertram West, happens to be her latest flame. Eventually marries West, although their first child bears a striking resemblance to Mr Burger.

PONSONBY, SIR CYRIL
Played by William Mervyn

Lady Ponsonby's father, Sir Cyril, is seen at the family mansion in *Follow That Camel*, hosting a cricket match. He thinks it's terribly bad form when Bo West is accused of cheating and banishes him from the house.

POOLE, JACKIE
Role: Betty in *Camping*

Jackie Poole trained at the Aida Foster drama school during the early 1960s. Other film credits include the 1968 film, *For Men Only,* and, three years later, *Dr Jekyll and Sister Hyde*.

POOP-DECKER, MIDSHIPMAN ALBERT
Played by Bernard Cribbins

The gullible, inadequate midshipman joins the frigate *Venus* in *Jack*. Son of a farmer, he's hardly cut out for a life on the ocean wave, considering he spent eight and a half years trying to graduate from the naval academy instead of the normal twelve months. He's called into service, however, with the navy short of men to fight the Spanish, and is presented with his midshipman's sword by the First Sealord. He travels to Plymouth to join the boat but is caught up in a terrible mess which finds him losing his identity and being pressganged into joining the crew of *Venus* as a rating.

POPSY
Played by Margaret Nolan

An employee of W.C. Boggs and Son who's seen in *At Your Convenience* on the firm's annual jolly to Brighton. Only taken on the day of the latest strike, she accompanies Bernie Hulke around the seaside town.

PORTER
Played by Charles Stanley

When Stella and Georgie in *Nurse* return home late to the nurses' home, Stella ends up in the mortuary, in an attempt to hide from the Home Sister, and nearly frightens the porter to death when she rushes into him from the darkness. (**Note: this scene was cut from the film.**)

The hospital porter suffers the fright of his life when Stella and Georgie, two nurses, arrive back late in *Nurse*.

EXT. NURSES' HOME – NIGHT

This is fully-seen. A fair-sized pleasant building, in the hospital grounds. Main buildings are nearby.

EXT. HOSPITAL GROUNDS – NIGHT

Guard placidly patrolling with Alsatian. Georgie and Stella in civilian clothes, hurrying along. Georgie checks her watch.

GEORGIE: I *told* you we shouldn't've had supper after the film.

STELLA: Oh it'll be all right. I *felt* like some supper, after seeing all that fish.

GEORGIE: Suppose you're caught? *I'll* get the blame for encouraging a student nurse to stay out late.

STELLA: Stop *worrying* . . .

(They reach:)

EXT. PORCH, NURSES' HOME – NIGHT

(As they mount the steps:)

GEORGIE: Quietly now . . .

STELLA: OK . . .

GEORGIE: Shhh! Wait. I'll check. Maybe Home Sister's on the prowl.

(STELLA nods. GEORGIE enters.)

INT. HALL, NURSES' HOME – NIGHT

(GEORGIE looks around. All clear. She turns to door to motion STELLA in.)

HOME SISTER: (O.S.) Good evening, Nurse.

(GEORGIE starts, transforms the action into slamming the door.)

EXT. PORCH, NURSES' HOME – NIGHT

(The slamming door nearly takes STELLA'S nose off. She blinks, blenches, takes what cover she can, listens closely.)

INT. HALL, NURSES' HOME – NIGHT

(HOME SISTER – quite a nice woman – now visible. GEORGIE tries to pull herself together, producing a ghastly smile, but naturally there's a quivering edge of nerves in everything she now says and does.)

GEORGIE: G-good evening – (For STELLA's benefit.) *SISTER!*

EXT. PORCH, NURSES' HOME – NIGHT

STELLA: (GULP!)

INT. HALL, NURSES' HOME – NIGHT

HOME SISTER: Beautiful evening . . .

GEORGIE: Gorgeous, Sister. The sort one never wants to let – (For STELLA) *GET AWAY!*

HOME SISTER: I beg your pardon, Nurse?

GEORGIE: I – I mean – one always hopes that

weather like this will – (For STELLA) *COME BACK LATER!*

EXT. PORCH, NURSES' HOME – NIGHT

(STELLA, recovered from immediate shock, takes GEORGIE'S advice. She backs slowly.)

INT. HALL, NURSES' HOME – NIGHT

HOME SISTER: I quite agree. We don't have nearly enough evenings like this, do we?

GEORGIE: (Quite enough for her.) Oh – (Gaily.) we mustn't grumble, must we . . . ?

(STELLA's careful footsteps are heard O.S.)

HOME SISTER: Do you hear something outside, Nurse?

GEORGIE: Er – no . . . Oh no . . .

HOME SISTER: (Approaching door.) Are you sure?

GEORGIE: It must be the guard and his dog.

EXT. PORCH, NURSES' HOME – NIGHT

(STELLA frozen. She looks determined.)

STELLA: (Falsetto.) Arrrrrowww! Wuff-wuff-wuff!

INT. HALL, NURSES' HOME – NIGHT

GEORGIE: (Offhand.) There . . . Just a little doggy . . .

HOME SISTER: Quite. But the guard's dog is a big Alsatian.

GEORGIE: (Faintly.) Maybe he's been doctored . . .

EXT. PORCH, NURSES' HOME – NIGHT

STELLA: Oh crikey . . .

(She composes her features quickly into a big-dog look, and, in deep asthmatic tones–)

STELLA: WOOF – WOOF – WOOF – WOOF!

(She turns – and falls down the steps.)

INT. HALL, NURSES' HOME – NIGHT

GEORGIE: (Gaunt.) There, Sister. I'm sure he'll – (For STELLA.) *GO AWAY!!!*

HOME SISTER: I'll just take a look.

(She goes for door.)

EXT. PORCH, NURSES' HOME – NIGHT

(STELLA picking herself up – and *running* – *anywhere* – so long as it's out of view of the porch.)

INT. HALL, NURSES' HOME – NIGHT

(GEORGIE praying silently behind HOME SISTER'S back as Home Sister opens door. Over her shoulder, HOME SISTER'S eyeline is achieved. All's clear. She shuts the door.)

HOME SISTER: Most curious . . .

GEORGIE: Goodnight, Sister.

HOME SISTER: Goodnight, nurse . . .

(GEORGIE thankfully turns away.)

EXT. HOSPITAL GROUNDS – NIGHT

(STELLA belting breathlessly away. She reaches

the shelter of a long, low building, dives gratefully for its shadows. Puffing, she leans against the door – which opens – and she falls into the darkness. Door swings shut. On it:)

MORTUARY

EXT. HOSPITAL GROUNDS – NIGHT

(GEORGIE running, looking for STELLA. She reaches the mortuary door, doesn't give it a second glance. Turns her back on it, looking this way and that. She's in the shadows.)

EXT. HOSPITAL GROUNDS – NIGHT

(GUARD and Alsatian patrolling, skirting the mortuary. An owl hoots. GUARD glances at mortuary, shudders a little.)

(GUARD'S eyeline –)

(GEORGIE emerges slowly from the shadows of the mortuary. Her intention is *not* to shock him.)

GEORGIE: (Sweetly.) Excuse me . . . I'm looking for . . .

(Medium shot GUARD, eyes wide.)

GUARD: *Yaaaaaah!*

(He drops dog-lead, runs for his life. Barking, dog pursues. Close shot GEORGIE.)

GEORGIE: (Puzzled.) Idiot . . .

(She realises what building is behind her. Can't help smiling, in a superior indulgent way. Looks this way and that again, for signs of STELLA.)

INT. MORTUARY – NIGHT

(STELLA in the dark, the refrigerated 'filing-cabinets' vaguely seen. She stumbles towards the other door. She doesn't like it in here a bit.)

STELLA: Oo-er . . .

INT. MORTUARY CORRIDOR – NIGHT

(PORTER approaching, mumbling to himself, carrying keys.)

PORTER: Fancy me leaving the back door unlocked . . . dear oh dear . . .

(He reaches corridor-door to mortuary (lettered), unlocks it. Before he can enter, STELLA rushes on him from the darkness within.)

STELLA: Oh – am I glad to see *you!*

(PORTER's eyes turn up to heaven and he slumps to the floor in a dead faint.)

STELLA: Oh *crikey!*

(She hears other footsteps O.S. Looks this way and that for a moment, nerves herself, plunges back into:)

INT. MORTUARY – NIGHT

(. . . stumbles through, opens back door on to grounds . . .)

EXT. MORTUARY – NIGHT

(. . . fetching up against GEORGIE'S back, tapping her on the shoulder.)

STELLA: Georgie – I want you!

(GEORGIE spins around, eyes wide.)

GEORGIE: (Screaming.)

STELLA: Come quick! The porter – First-Aid!

GEORGIE: (Hand on heart.) P-porter? What about *me*? Ooh – the *shock* . . . !

STELLA: Quick – he may be *dead*!

GEORGIE: (Going in.) If he is – he won't have far to walk . . .

(Gingerly, both girls enter mortuary.)

Fade out.

PORTER
Played by Harry Locke
A porter at the Long Hampton Hospital in *Again Doctor*.

PORTER
Played by Frank Singuineau
A porter in *Again Doctor*.

POSTA, ADRIENNE
Role: Norma Baxter in *Behind*
Born in London in 1948, Adrienne Posta attended afternoon classes at the Corona Academy from the age of six. Although she harboured dreams of becoming a ballerina, she began acting in juvenile roles on the London stage at the age of twelve.

When her dreams of becoming a professional dancer were dashed, she opted for a career in the music industry, forming a band which supported, among others, The Beatles on tour. But by the mid-1960s she'd changed direction and was projected into a successful film career. Although she'd already made her screen debut in the 1957 picture, *No Time for Tears*, playing Moira Jackson in '67's *To Sir, With Love* provided her big break in the medium. Other roles quickly followed in films such as *Up the Junction*, *Some Girls Do*, *Spring and Port Wine* and *Up Pompeii*.

On television, which eventually began dominating her career, she was seen in shows such as *Top Secret*, *Journey to the Unknown*, *Budgie*, *Don't Ask Us*, *We're New Here*, *Moody and Pegg*, *Till Death Us Do Part*, *Minder* and *Red Dwarf*.

POSTCARD SELLER
Played by Gertan Klauber
Tries selling dirty postcards to Stuart Farquhar during an excursion to a local village in *Abroad*.

POTTER, ALBERT
Played by Jim Dale
In *Screaming!*, Albert contacts the police when his girlfriend, Doris, whom he's been dating for a year, goes missing in Hocombe Woods. A window cleaner by trade, he lives at 33 Hogsmere Road and is distraught when he believes he spotted Doris standing in the shop window at Bourne and Jones, a milliner's.

Understandably the police don't believe him, especially as he's claiming she's one of the dummies on display. Unperturbed, he's relentless in his attempts to find his girl and is finally rewarded by discovering her alive and well.

POTTER, HARRIET
Played by Betty Marsden
Seen in *Camping*, the hyena-laughing Harriet Potter is married to Peter. A keen camper, she's oblivious to the fact her husband is fed up to the back teeth with spending his holidays under canvas. Instead of some sun-baked Mediterranean resort, their annual break is spent cycling their tandem to the Paradise Camp Site in Devon.

POTTER, PATRICIA
Played by Bernard Bresslaw
The name Peter Potter adopted when he masqueraded as an entrant for the Miss Fircombe beauty contest in *Girls*.

POTTER, PC TOM
Played by Leslie Phillips
In *Constable*, Potter arrives with Constable and Benson, three naïve policemen fresh from training college. They're thrown into the deep end when a flu epidemic causes havoc with police personnel. An upper-class twit, Hertfordshire-born Tom Potter doesn't start his new career well when he taps a jewel thief on the shoulder and asks for directions to the police station.

POTTER, PETER
Played by Terry Scott
Seen in *Camping*, Peter, who works in the City, is married to the hyena-laughing Harriet Potter. While his wife is an ardent fan of camping, he longs for a holiday abroad but his subtle hints get him nowhere. When yet another holiday is spent cycling their tandem to the Paradise Camp Site in Devon, and sharing their tent with the annoying Charlie Muggins, Peter decides it's time he took a stance.

POTTER, PETER
Played by Bernard Bresslaw
Runs his own publicity business, Potter Publicity Bureau, and is given the job of promoting the Miss Fircombe beauty contest, thanks to his friend, Sidney Fiddler, who happens to be organising the event. Peter is engaged to Paula and is seen in *Girls*.

POTTER PUBLICITY BUREAU
Peter Potter's publicity business in *Girls* is given the task of publicising the Miss Fircombe beauty contest. It helps, of course, that Sid Fiddler, who organises the contest, is a friend.

POTTS, CAPTAIN
Played by Eric Barker
Known as 'Potts the Perfect', the pedantic Captain

Potts is in charge of training at Heathercrest National Service Depot in *Sergeant*. He lives and breathes army life despite coming from a family of porcelain manufacturers.

POWELL, IVOR
Assistant Director on *Again Doctor*. Also worked as Second Assistant Director on *Up The Khyber* although not credited
Born in London in 1943, Ivor Powell completed his education at St Paul's School intent on entering the business, either as an actor or director. His aunt, the renowned critic Dilys Powell, helped introduce him to various individuals in the industry, but he began his career in the theatre, joining, in 1959, H.M. Tennent's theatrical productions in London's West End as a trainee assistant stage manager on *West Side Story*.

After completing his stage management training he joined the Terence Rattigan/H.M. Tennent production of *Ross* with Alec Guinness playing Lawrence of Arabia. During the production he was promoted to stage manager and deputy company manager.

He joined Augusta Productions in 1962 before, in 1963, moving to the BBC as an assistant floor manager during the recruitment drive in preparation for the launch of BBC2. He remained with the Corporation until he met Roger Caras, an American novelist working as exploitation and publicity agent for Stanley Kubrick. Within months, Powell had left the BBC and was working with Kubrick on *2001: A Space Odyssey*.

He later worked as a location manager on the Paramount/Lewis Gilbert production, *The Adventurers*, before joining Ridley Scott Associates as a freelance producer making commercials and developing feature-film projects. He was subsequently hired on Scott's *The Duellists*, *Alien* and *Blade Runner*.

After fourteen years (1984-98) as producer/managing director for a commercials production company, he left to pursue a full-time writing career. His most recent work is the screenplay, *Patience*, which he co-wrote.

POWELL, NOSHER
Role: Footpad in *Dick*
TV: *One in the Eye for Harold*
Stunt artist and actor Nosher Powell, who was born in London in 1928, left school at fifteen and worked in Covent Garden market before becoming a professional heavyweight boxer, later winning several championships.

After being offered a small part as a boxer in a 1949 television show, he turned his attention to the entertainment business. He's been a stuntman for many years, working on numerous films, most recently *First Knight* and *Legionnaire* during the 1990s, and television shows such as *The Saint*, *The Avengers*, *The*

PRODUCTION TEAM

SCREENPLAY
Norman Hudis (*Sergeant* [Based on *The Bull Boys* by R.F. Delderfield], *Nurse* [Based on an idea by Patrick Cargill & Jack Beale], *Teacher*, *Constable* [Based on an idea by Brock Williams], *Regardless* and *Cruising* [From a story by Eric Barker])
Talbot Rothwell (*Cabby* [Based on an original idea by S.C. Green & R.M. Hills], *Jack*, *Cleo*, *Cowboy*, *Screaming*, *Don't Lose Your Head*, *Follow That Camel*, *Doctor*, *Up The Khyber*, *Camping*, *Again Doctor*, *Up The Jungle*, *Loving*, *Henry*, *At Your Convenience*, *Matron*, *Abroad*, *Girls* and *Dick* [Based on a treatment by Laurie Wyman & George Evans])
Talbot Rothwell & Sid Colin (*Spying*)
Dave Freeman (*Behind* and *Columbus*)
Sid Colin (*That's Carry On*)
David Pursall & Jack Seddon (*England*)
Tony Church (*That's Carry On*)
Lance Peters (*Emmannuelle*)

ADDITIONAL MATERIAL
John Antrobus (*Sergeant* and *Columbus*)

MUSIC COMPOSED & CONDUCTED BY
Bruce Montgomery (*Sergeant*, *Nurse*, *Teacher*, *Constable* and *Regardless*)
Bruce Montgomery & Douglas Gamley (*Cruising*)
Eric Rogers (*Cabby*, *Jack*, *Spying*, *Cleo*, *Cowboy*, *Screaming!*, *Don't Lose Your Head*, *Follow That Camel*, *Doctor*, *Up The Khyber*, *Camping*, *Again Doctor*, *Up The Jungle*, *Loving*, *Henry*, *At Your Convenience*, *Matron*, *Abroad*, *Girls*, *Dick*, *Behind*, *That's Carry On* and *Emmannuelle*)
Max Harris (*England*)
John Du Prez (*Columbus*)

PRODUCTION MANAGER
Jack Swinburne (*Don't Lose Your Head*, *Follow That Camel*, *Doctor*, *Up The Khyber*, *Camping*, *Again Doctor*, *Up The Jungle*, *Loving*, *Henry*, *At Your Convenience*, *Matron* and *Abroad*)
Roy Goddard (*Girls*, *Dick*, *Behind*, *England*, *That's Carry On* and *Emmannuelle*)

PRODUCTION EXECUTIVE FOR CLEVES INVESTMENT LTD
Donald Langdon (*Emmannuelle*)

PRODUCTION DESIGNER
Harry Pottle (*Columbus*)

PRODUCTION CO-ORDINATOR
Lorraine Fennell (*Columbus*)

PRODUCTION SUPERVISOR
Joyce Herlihy (*Columbus*)

PRODUCTION BUYER
Brian Winterborn (*Columbus*)

PRODUCTION RUNNER
Stuart Gladstone (*Columbus*)

FLOOR RUNNER
Natasha Goldstone (*Columbus*)

DIRECTOR OF PHOTOGRAPHY
Peter Hennessy (*Sergeant*)
Reginald Wyer (*Nurse* and *Teacher*)
Ted Scaife (*Constable*)
Alan Hume (*Regardless*, *Cruising*, *Cabby*, *Jack*, *Spying*, *Cleo*, *Cowboy*, *Screaming!*, *Don't Lose Your Head*, *Follow That Camel*, *Doctor*, *Henry*, *Abroad*, *Girls*, *Emmannuelle* and *Columbus*)
Ernest Steward (*Up The Khyber*, *Camping*, *Again Doctor*, *Up The Jungle*, *Loving*, *At Your Convenience*, *Matron*, *Dick*, *Behind* and *England*)
Tony Imi (*That's Carry On*)

DIRECTOR OF PHOTOGRAPHY (LOCATION)
H.A.R. Thompson (*Up The Khyber*)

ART DIRECTOR
Alex Vetchinsky (*Sergeant*, *Nurse*, *Spying*, *Follow That Camel*, *Up The Khyber* and *Up The Jungle*)
Lionel Couch (*Teacher*, *Regardless*, *Don't Lose Your Head*, *Camping*, *Loving*, *Henry*, *At Your Convenience*, *Matron*, *Abroad*, *Dick*, *Behind* and *England*)
Carmen Dillon (*Constable* and *Cruising*)
Jack Stephens (*Cabby*)
Jack Shampan (*Jack* and *Emmannuelle*)
Bert Davey (*Cleo*, *Cowboy* and *Screaming!*)
Cedric Dawe (*Doctor*)
John Blezard (*Again Doctor*)
Robert Jones (*Girls*)
Peter Childs (*Columbus*)

ART DEPARTMENT ASSISTANT
Peter Francis (*Columbus*)

ASSISTANT ART DIRECTOR
William Alexander (*Loving*, *Henry*, *At Your Convenience* and *Matron*)
Peter Lamont (*Matron*)
Bill Bennison (*Abroad*)
Edward Ambrose (*Columbus*)

EDITOR
Peter Boita (*Sergeant* and *Emmannuelle*)
John Shirley (*Nurse*, *Teacher*, *Constable*, *Regardless* and *Cruising*)
Archie Ludski (*Cabby*, *Jack*, *Spying* and *Cleo*)
Rod Keys (*Cowboy*, *Screaming!* and *Don't Lose Your Head*)
Alfred Roome (*Follow That Camel*, *Doctor*, *Up The Khyber*, *Camping*, *Again Doctor*, *Up The Jungle*, *Loving*, *Henry*, *At Your Convenience*, *Matron*, *Abroad*, *Girls*, *Dick* and *Behind*)
Richard Marden (*England*)
Jack Gardner (*That's Carry On*)
Chris Blunden (*Columbus*)

ASSISTANT EDITORS
Jack Gardner (*Cowboy*, *Follow That Camel*, *Doctor*, *Up The Khyber*, *Camping*, *Again Doctor*, *Up The Jungle*, *Loving*, *Henry*, *At Your Convenience*, *Matron*, *Abroad*, *Dick*, *Behind*, *England* and *Emmannuelle*)
Jack Gardner & Ken Behrens (*Girls*)
Steve Maguire (*Columbus*)

SECOND ASSISTANT EDITOR
Natalie Baker (*Columbus*)

DIALOGUE EDITOR
Alan Paley (*Columbus*)

ASSISTANT DIALOGUE EDITOR
Andrew Melhuish (*Columbus*)

FOOTSTEPS EDITOR
Richard Hiscott (*Columbus*)

ASSOCIATE PRODUCER
Basil Keys (*Regardless*)
Frank Bevis (*Cabby*, *Jack*, *Spying*, *Cleo*, *Cowboy* and *Screaming!*)

PRODUCTION MANAGER
Frank Bevis (*Sergeant*, *Nurse*, *Teacher* and *Constable*)
Bill Hill (*Cruising*)

CAMERA OPERATOR
Alan Hume (*Sergeant*, *Nurse*, *Teacher* and *Constable*)
Dudley Lovell (*Regardless* and *Cruising*)
Godfrey Godar (*Cabby*, *Jack*, *Spying*, *Cleo*, *Cowboy*, *Screaming!*, *England* and *Emmannuelle*)
Jimmy Devis (*Don't Lose Your Head*, *Abroad*, *Girls* and *Dick*)
Alan Hall (*Follow That Camel*)

PRODUCTION TEAM

James Bawden (*Doctor, Up The Khyber, Camping, Again Doctor, Up The Jungle, Loving, At Your Convenience* and *Matron*)
Derek Browne (*Henry*)
Neil Binney (*Behind*)
Martin Hume (*Columbus*)

CAMERA FOCUS
Simon Hume (*Columbus*)

CLAPPER LOADER
Sean Connor (*Columbus*)

CAMERA GRIP
Colin Manning (*Columbus*)

GAFFER ELECTRICIAN
Denis Brock (*Columbus*)

BEST BOY
Billy Poccetty (*Columbus*)

UNIT PUBLICIST
Ann Tasker (*Columbus*)

ASSISTANT DIRECTOR
Geoffrey Haine (*Sergeant*)
Stanley Hosgood (*Nurse*)
Bert Batt (*Teacher* and *Matron*)
Peter Manley (*Constable*)
Jack Causey (*Regardless, Cruising, Don't Lose Your Head, Camping, Up The Jungle, Girls* and *England*)
Peter Bolton (*Cabby, Spying, Cleo, Cowboy* and *Screaming!*)
Anthony Waye (*Jack*)
David Bracknell (*Follow That Camel, Loving, Henry, At Your Convenience, Abroad* and *Dick*)
Terry Clegg (*Doctor*)
Peter Weingreen (*Up The Khyber*)
Ivor Powell (*Again Doctor*)
Gregory Dark & Mike Higgins (*Emmannuelle*)
Gareth Tandy, Terry Bamber & Becky Harris (*Columbus*)

ASSISTANT TO JOHN GOLDSTONE
Lisa Bonnichon (*Columbus*)

ASSISTANT TO ROGERS & THOMAS
Audrey Skinner (*Columbus*)

SCRIPT SUPERVISOR
Maggie Unsworth (*Columbus*)

SOUND EDITORS
Seymour Logie (*Sergeant*)
Roger Cherrill (*Nurse*)
Leslie Wiggins (*Teacher* and *Constable*)

Arthur Ridout (*Regardless, Cabby* and *Screaming!*)
Arthur Ridout & Archie Ludski (*Cruising*)
Christopher Lancaster (*Jack, Spying* and *Cleo*)
Jim Groom (*Cowboy*)
Wally Nelson (*Don't Lose Your Head* and *Follow That Camel*)

SOUND RECORDISTS
Robert T. MacPhee & Gordon K. McCallum (*Sergeant, Teacher* and *Regardless*)
Robert T. MacPhee & Bill Daniels (*Nurse, Constable* and *Cruising*)
Bill Daniels & Gordon K. McCallum (*Cabby* and *Cleo*)
Bill Daniels (*Jack*)
C.C. Stevens & Bill Daniels (*Spying*)
Robert T. MacPhee & Ken Barker (*Cowboy* and *Up The Jungle*)
C.C. Stevens & Ken Barker (*Screaming!*)
Dudley Messenger & Ken Barker (*Don't Lose Your Head, Follow That Camel, Doctor* and *Up The Khyber*)
Bill Daniels & Ken Barker (*Camping* and *Again Doctor*)
J.W.N. Daniel & Ken Barker (*Loving*)
Danny Daniel & Ken Barker (*Henry, At Your Convenience, Matron, Dick, Behind* and *That's Carry On*)
Taffy Haines & Ken Barker (*Abroad*)
Paul Lemare & Ken Barker (*Girls*)
Danny Daniel & Gordon McCallum (*England*)
Danny Daniel & Otto Snel (*Emmannuelle*)
Chris Munro (*Columbus*)

SOUND MAINTENANCE
Graham Nieder (*Columbus*)

CHIEF DUBBING EDITOR
Otto Snel (*Columbus*)

DUBBING EDITOR
David Campling (*Doctor*)
Colin Miller (*Up The Khyber, Camping, Again Doctor* and *Up The Jungle*)
Marcel Durham (*Loving*)
Brian Holland (*Henry* and *At Your Convenience*)
Peter Best (*Matron, Dick* and *Emmannuelle*)
Patrick Foster (*Girls, Behind* and *England*)
Christopher Lancaster (*That's Carry On*)
Peter Horrocks (*Columbus*)

ASSISTANT DUBBING EDITOR
Christine Newell (*Columbus*)

DUBBING MIXERS
Kevin Taylor & Michael Carter (*Columbus*)

LOCATION MANAGER
Terry Clegg (*Follow That Camel*)

UNIT MANAGER
Claude Watson (*Regardless*)
Donald Toms (*Cabby, Jack, Spying* and *Cleo*)
Ron Jackson (*Cowboy* and *Screaming!*)

CONTINUITY
Joan Davis (*Sergeant* and *Constable*)
Penny Daniels (*Nurse, Cruising, Cabby, Jack, Spying* and *Screaming!*)
Tilly Day (*Teacher*)
Gladys Goldsmith (*Regardless* and *Cowboy*)
Olga Brook (*Cleo*)
Rita Davison (*Don't Lose Your Head, Henry* and *At Your Convenience*)
Joy Mercer (*Follow That Camel, Doctor, Matron* and *Abroad*)
Yvonne Richards (*Up The Khyber*)
Doreen Dernley (*Camping*)
Susanne Merry (*Again Doctor*)
Josephine Knowles (*Up The Jungle* and *Loving*)
Marjorie Lavelly (*Girls, Behind, England* and *Emmannuelle*)
Jane Buck (*Dick*)

MAKE-UP
Geoffrey Rodway (*Sergeant, Cleo, Cowboy, Screaming!, Don't Lose Your Head, Follow That Camel, Doctor, Up The Khyber, Camping, Again Doctor, Up The Jungle, Loving, Henry, At Your Convenience, Matron, Abroad, Girls, Dick, Behind* and *England*)
George Blackler (*Nurse, Teacher, Constable* and *Regardless*)
George Blackler & Geoffrey Rodway (*Cruising*)
Geoffrey Rodway & Jim Hydes (*Cabby* and *Jack*)
W.T. Partleton (*Spying*)
Robin Grantham (*Emmannuelle*)
Sarah Monzani & Amanda Knight (*Columbus*)

HAIRDRESSING
Stella Rivers (*Sergeant, Constable, Cowboy, Screaming!, Don't Lose Your Head, Follow*

PRODUCTION TEAM

That Camel, Doctor, Up The Khyber, Camping, Again Doctor, Up The Jungle, Loving, Henry, At Your Convenience, Matron, Abroad, Girls, Dick, Behind and *England)*
Pearl Orton *(Nurse)*
Olga Angelinetta *(Teacher* and *Jack)*
Biddy Chrystal *(Regardless, Cruising, Cabby* and *Spying)*
Ann Fordyce *(Cleo)*
Betty Sheriff *(Emmannuelle)*
Sue Love & Sarah Love *(Columbus)*

DRESS DESIGNER
Joan Ellacott *(Sergeant* and *Nurse)*
Yvonne Caffin *(Constable)*

COSTUME DESIGNER
Joan Ellacott *(Regardless, Cruising, Cabby* and *Jack)*
Yvonne Caffin *(Spying, Doctor* and *Camping)*
Julie Harris *(Cleo)*
Cynthia Tingey *(Cowboy)*
Emma Selby-Walker *(Screaming!, Don't Lose Your Head, Follow That Camel* and *Up The Khyber)*
Anna Duse *(Again Doctor)*
Courtenay Elliott *(Up The Jungle, Loving, Henry, At Your Convenience, Matron, Abroad, Girls, Dick, Behind, England* and *Emmannuelle)*
Phoebe De Gaye *(Columbus)*

SET DECORATOR
Denise Exshaw *(Columbus)*

SCENIC ARTIST
Ted Michell *(Columbus)*

BOAT CONSULTANT
David Raine *(Columbus)*

STUNT ARRANGER
Jason White *(Columbus)*

TECHNICAL ADVISOR
Ian Cox *(Jack)*

UNIT NURSE
Nicky Gregory *(Columbus)*

PROPERTY MASTER
Charles Torbett *(Columbus)*

CASTING DIRECTOR
Betty White *(Sergeant, Nurse, Teacher, Constable, Regardless* and *Cruising)*
John Owen *(Dick* and *England)*

CASTING
Jane Arnell *(Columbus)*

CASTING ASSISTANT
Gina Jay *(Columbus)*

DANCE STAGING
Peter Gordeno *(Columbus)*

STILLS CAMERAMAN
Tom Cadman *(Dick)*
Ken Bray *(England* and *Emmannuelle)*
Keith Hamshere *(Columbus)*

SPECIAL EFFECTS
Effects Associates *(Columbus)*

TITLE DESIGN
Gillie Potter *(Columbus)*

CONSTRUCTION MANAGER
Ken Pattenden *(Columbus)*

CHARGEHAND CARPENTER
Bill Hearn *(Columbus)*

CHARGEHAND RIGGER
Les Beaver *(Columbus)*

CHARGEHAND PAINTER
Michael Gunner *(Columbus)*

CHARGEHAND PLASTERER
Ken Barley *(Columbus)*

STAND-BY PROPS
Philip McDonald *(Columbus)*

STAND-BY CARPENTER
David Williams *(Columbus)*

STAND-BY PAINTER
Peter Mounsey *(Columbus)*

STAND-BY RIGGER
Gordon Humphrey *(Columbus)*

STAND-BY STAGEHAND
Leonard Serpant *(Columbus)*

UNIT DRIVERS
Keith Horsley & Brian Baverstock *(Columbus)*

WARDROBE
Laurel Staffell *(Teacher)*
Vi Murray & Don Mothersill *(England)*
Margaret Lewin *(Emmannuelle)*
Ken Crouch, Sue Honeyborne, Jane Lewis & Jo Korer *(Columbus)*

WARDROBE MISTRESSES
Vi Murray & Margaret Lewin *(Matron* and *Dick)*

SET DRESSING
Peter Murton *(Sergeant)*
Arthur Taksen *(Nurse)*
Terence Morgan *(Teacher)*
Vernon Dixon *(Constable)*
Peter Howitt *(Loving, Henry* and *At Your Convenience)*
Kenneth McCallum Tait *(Girls)*
Charles Bishop *(Dick* and *Behind)*
Donald Picton *(England)*
John Hoesli *(Emmannuelle)*

TITLES & OPTICALS
Pentagon Films Titles Ltd *(Sergeant)*
General Screen Enterprises (G.S.E) Ltd. *(Up The Jungle, Loving, Henry, At Your Convenience, Matron, Abroad, Girls, Dick, Behind, England, That's Carry On, Emmannuelle* and *Columbus)*

MASTER OF HORSE
Jeremy Taylor *(Cowboy* and *Don't Lose Your Head)*

EXECUTIVE PRODUCER
Peter Rogers *(Columbus)*

PRODUCER
Peter Rogers *(Sergeant, Nurse, Teacher, Constable, Regardless, Cruising, Cabby, Jack, Spying, Cleo, Cowboy, Screaming!, Don't Lose Your Head, Follow That Camel, Doctor, Up The Khyber, Camping, Again Doctor, Up The Jungle, Loving, Henry, At Your Convenience, Matron, Abroad, Girls, Dick, Behind, England, That's Carry On* and *Emmannuelle)*
John Goldstone *(Columbus)*

DIRECTOR
Gerald Thomas *(Sergeant, Nurse, Teacher, Constable, Regardless, Cruising, Cabby, Jack, Spying, Cleo, Cowboy, Screaming!, Don't Lose Your Head, Follow That Camel, Doctor, Up The Khyber, Camping, Again Doctor, Up The Jungle, Loving, Henry, At Your Convenience, Matron, Abroad, Girls, Dick, Behind, England, That's Carry On, Emmannuelle* and *Columbus)*

Prisoner, Morecambe and Wise, Monty Python's Flying Circus, Sykes and *The Comic Strip Presents*. He also appears in small screen parts.

PRATT, ALDERMAN
Played by Arnold Ridley

The decrepit Alderman Pratt is supposed to be a member of Fircombe Town Council but ends up sleeping through most of the meetings. His sole contribution to the meeting in *Girls* is to wake for a moment and suggest a bowls competition to help bring visitors to the seaside resort.

PREGNANT LUBI
Played by Heather Emmanuel

When Walter Bagley, alias King Tonka, talks to a Lubi tending a flowerbed in *Jungle*, he asks if they've met before and agrees they must have when she shows her very pregnant stomach.

PRETTY BIDDER
Played by Wanda Ventham

Seen in *Cleo* bidding for Horsa. Unfortunately for him, the Pretty Bidder loses out to the rotund Willa Claudia.

PRETTY PROBATIONER
Played by Maureen Moore

When Bert Handy, who's mistaken for Sir Theodore, an important visitor due at the hospital in *Regardless*, is given a tour of the building, he notices the pretty probationer carrying too many blankets. Handy stops her and asks the rather put-out Sister to help carry some of the bed linen; the same nurse later takes the phone call confirming Bert Handy isn't Sir Theodore.

PREVERT, EMILE
Played by Kenneth Williams

The French Ambassador based in London appears in *Emmannuelle*. He's married to the world's worst flirt, Emmannuelle, a nymphomaniac whose sole aim in life is to sleep with every man in the world. From the confines of a toilet on Concorde to the dressing room at a football stadium, there isn't a place where she doesn't enjoy a steamy sex session, and by the end of the film is cradling a myriad of babies in her hospital bed.

PREVERT, EMMANNUELLE
Played by Suzanne Danielle
See 'Prevert, Emile'.

PRIME MINISTER
Played by Robert Dorning

Seen dining at the French Ambassador's residence in *Emmannuelle*.

PRINCESS BEATRICE SUITE
A new-style toilet suite in *At Your Convenience*. Poor old Miss Withering is tasked with testing the durability of the prototype designed by Charles Coote.

PRODD, DR
Played by Terry Scott

The randy Dr Prodd works at Finisham Maternity Hospital and enjoys chasing after the pretty young nurses in the profession. He has his sights set on Nurse Carter from the moment he encounters her pinning up her – or I should say his – knickers in the gents' toilet. What Prodd doesn't realise is that it's Cyril Carter pretending to be a nurse. Carter is a reluctant small-time crook who has been forced by his father, who's the leader of the gang, to find a plan of the hospital.

A former boxing champ from his days at Guy's Hospital, he resides in room number 15 on the fifth floor of the hospital, with plaques showing his numerous conquests adorning the walls of the apartment. Seen in *Matron*.

PRODUCTION TEAM
See feature box on pages 196–8.

PRODWORTHY, AUGUSTA
Played by June Whitfield

Augusta Prodworthy is an opinionated, vocal member of the Fircombe Town Council who's also leader of the Fircombe Women's Lib Movement. She vehemently protests when Sidney Fiddler, a fellow councillor, suggests a beauty contest in the tatty seaside resort as a way of attracting more visitors to the town. When the contest is approved behind her back, she determines to cause havoc, which she succeeds in doing. Seen in *Girls*.

PRODWORTHY, LAWRENCE
Played by Robin Askwith

For Lawrence the photographer in *Girls*, see 'Larry'.

PROJECTIONIST
Played by Sam Kelly

The bespectacled projectionist is in control of the film projector while Professor Crump presents his lecture and film show, 'Getting to the Bottom of Things', in *Behind*.

PROWSE, DAVE
Role: Torturer in *Henry*

Born in Bristol in 1935, Dave Prowse, a former weightlifting champion, is remembered by many as the Green Cross Code Man who appeared in public information films during the '70s, but he's equally famous for playing Darth Vader in *Star Wars*, although the voice was that of James Earl Jones.

He's appeared in a host of films, such as *Casino Royale*, *A Clockwork Orange*, *Vampire Circus* and *Gulliver's Travels*, and on television in, among others, *The Champions*, *The Benny Hill Show*, *Ace of Wands*, *The Tomorrow People* and *Crossbow*.

He also trained Christopher Reeve for his role in the 1978 *Superman* film.

PRYOR, CHRISTINE
Role: Girl in *Don't Lose Your Head*

During the 1960s and '70s she appeared occasionally on screen in films such as *Curse of the Crimson Altar*, *All Neat in Black Stockings* and *The Adding Machine*, while on television she was seen in episodes of *Department S* and *The Befrienders*.

PSYCHOLOGY OF JEALOUSY, THE
Written by Ernest Steward (an in-joke aimed at the film's director of photography), Sir Bernard Cutting refers to the book in *Matron* and surmises that he's in love with Matron.

Emile (Kenneth Williams) can't cope with his sexually demanding wife, Emmannuelle (Suzanne Danielle) (*Emmannuelle*)

PUDDLETON, LADY
Played by Charles Hawtrey

Disguised as Lady Puddleton, Dr Stoppidge hopes to discover the constituents of the miracle weight-losing serum administered by Dr Nookey at his new clinic. Unfortunately having to share a bedroom with Mrs Moore, and being pursued by the randy Gladstone Screwer, is a recipe for disaster as Stoppidge soon finds out. Appears in *Again Doctor*.

PULLEN, MR
Played by Wilfrid Brambell

Visits the outpatients department of the Long Hampton Hospital in *Again Doctor*. He sees Dr Nookey for his regular hormone injection, but the lecherous old man can't keep his hands off Nurse Willing.

PULLITT, MRS
Played by Madeline Smith

Seen in bed at the Finisham Maternity Hospital, Mrs Pullitt is worried about the state of a particular part of her baby boy's anatomy. She doesn't disclose which particular part but the fact that she's worried about it being bent to one side cuts the possibilities down somewhat! Seen in *Matron*.

PUMP PATIENT
Played by Bob Todd

When accident-prone Dr Nookey wreaks havoc with the electrics at the Long Hampton Hospital in *Again Doctor*, this patient's ventilator goes haywire, inflating his stomach to near bursting point.

PUNCHY
Played by Darryl Kavann

One of the crooks in *Cabby*. They jump into a Glamcab and hold Peggy and Sally at gunpoint while they try to escape from the scene of their crime.

PURSALL, DAVID
Co-wrote the screenplay for *England*

Born in Kirkintilloch, Scotland, David Pursall served in the Fleet Air Arm during the war, leaving with the rank of commander. When veteran filmmaker George Archibald introduced him to producers Frank Launder and Sidney Gilliat, he was recruited as their publicity director at Pinewood on, among others, *Green for Danger* and *Captain Boycott*.

He later joined the Rank Organisation as publicity news editor before moving back to Pinewood as the company's production publicity controller. During this time he met Jack Seddon and they subsequently became full-time scriptwriters. Writing credits, which date back to the 1950s, include the films *The Longest Day*, *The Alphabet Murders*, *Tomorrow Never Comes* and *Black Arrow*, while for the small screen he co-wrote (with Jack Seddon) six episodes of *The Liver Birds* and instalments of *Arthur and the Britons* and *Oil Strike North*.

PUSHING, LADY
Not seen in *Cowboy* but Marshall P. Knutt carries a reference from her to help in his search for a job.

PUTZOVA, MRS
Played by Marianne Stone

In *Matron*, a pregnant Mrs Putzova visits Dr Goode to discuss her condition. (**Note:** scene was cut.).

WHAT MIGHT HAVE BEEN

INT. GOODE'S OFFICE – DAY

A PREGNANT WOMAN of about thirty-four is stretched out on the treatment couch. GOODE is seated beside it.

GOODE: . . . so it's most important that you have no mental problems at this time, Mrs Pushover.

WOMAN: It's not Pushover. It's Putzova, Russian, you know.

GOODE: Oh, I do beg your pardon. Anyway, Mrs Putzover, I want you to talk to me absolutely frankly. In Russian, if it will make it easier.

WOMAN: Do you speak Russian then, Doctor?

GOODE: Oh no, but as long as one understands what's going on it'll be all right.

(He gives her a bland smile. His telephone rings.)

GOODE: Oh, excuse me.

(He crosses to his desk and picks up the phone.)

GOODE: Doctor Goode, psychiatry, can I help you? . . . Oh hullo, Miss Banks . . . Oh, does he? Oh, well I'll come as soon as I've finished my consultation, Miss Banks.

(He replaces telephone, looking a bit worried.)

GOODE: Now then . . . er . . . where were we?

WOMAN: About this problem, Doctor.

GOODE: Oh yes. Well you see, I have this wife who thinks she's a Great Dane, and she won't let me watch television, so I . . .

(He comes to a stop, seeing her surprised expression, and giggles.)

GOODE: Oh, I am sorry. It's your problem we're worried about, isn't it? Do tell!

WOMAN: Well, it's my husband. He's very jealous and he don't believe the baby is *his*. He keeps accusing one of his friends of being the father!

GOODE: Oh, dear, dear. Well, the only advice I can give you is to tell him straight out – stop worrying, it's nobody *you* know.

WOMAN: (Doubtfully.) I don't think that would satisfy him, Doctor. It's not myself I worry for. But all this rowing we do about it might affect the baby.

GOODE: Oh, not a chance. There's really no such thing as pre-natal influence, you know.

WOMAN: No?

GOODE: Oh, no. Take me for instance. When my mother was carrying me she cracked her favourite gramophone record but it's had no effect on me whatever – me whatever – me whatever –

(And as he continues, stuck in the groove, we see her bewildered reaction . . .)

PYLE, JENNIFER
Role: Hilda in *Camping*

QUEEN
Played by Patsy Rowlands

Henry VIII's Queen of six months doesn't last long in *Henry* because she's sent to her death in the opening scene.

QUINCE, PETER
Role: Gunner Sharpe in *England*

Peter Quince, born in Nottingham in 1944, left school at fifteen and began the first two years of his working life at an air and shipping company in London. A series of jobs followed, including working at a tailor's and at his father's shoe repair business, before he turned to acting.

A keen amateur thespian – he'd spent time at the Tower Theatre, one of London's top amateur companies – he was persuaded to turn professional and soon secured his first job as assistant stage manager at The Peggy Ashcroft Theatre, London.

After spending several years in repertory theatre and a summer season at Butlin's in Clacton, he was offered his first television role as a young doctor in London Weekend's *Doctor at Sea*. His initial year in the film world, meanwhile, saw him play two soldiers in *England* and *A Bridge Too Far*.

Once he'd married and started a family, Quince began concentrating on the screen and has gone on to appear in over sixty commercials and shows such as *Van der Valk, Minder, George and Mildred, Secret Army, Target, Robin's Nest, Bergerac, The Bill* and his most recent credit, *My Family*. He's also made occasional appearances in films such as *Rogue Trader* and *Fever Pitch*.

Nowadays, when he's not acting, he runs a painting and decorating business with his brother.

RAFFETY

This estate agent is responsible for selling the twenty-room mansion Dr Carver has set his heart on to house the private clinic he's hoping wealthy widow Mrs Moore will finance. The 'For Sale' board is spotted in *Again Doctor*.

RAFFISH CUSTOMER
Played by Patrick Cargill

In *Regardless* the Raffish Customer attends the Ideal House Exhibition, where the staff of Helping Hands are demonstrating exhibits. He sidles up to Montgomery Infield-Hopping, who's showing off a bachelor pad, and claims there should be a P.C. – a Popsy Cupboard. He's more than satisfied when Delia King, who's working on an exhibit next-door, comes crashing through the partition.

RAKE
Played by Julian Orchard

Seen at Sir Rodney Ffing's charity ball in *Don't Lose Your Head* ogling Desiree Dubarry's ample bosom.

RAMSDEN, FRED
Played by Windsor Davies

A butcher who holidays with his friend, Ernie Bragg, in *Behind*. When their respective wives decide on a break in a health farm, Fred persuades Ernie to accompany him to the Riverside Caravan Site under the guise of a fishing trip. What he's hoping they catch is a couple of birds – and not the feathery kind! They're out of luck, though not through lack of trying, which is just as well because their wives eventually turn up at the camp site. Although they'd sent a telegram to inform their husbands of their arrival, the message never reached Fred and Ernie.

RAMSDEN, SYLVIA
Played by Liz Fraser

Fred's wife who helps in the butcher's shop. When her husband heads with his mate, Ernie Bragg, to the Riverside Caravan Site, Sylvia opts for a health farm with her friend, Vera. The women later surprise their husbands by turning up at Riverside unannounced. They had tried to inform their spouses of their impending visit via a telegram but their message never reached Fred and Ernie. Seen in *Behind*.

RATTLESNAKE BILL

Bill Boosey's nickname in *Up the Jungle*.

RAWLINGS, WIDOW

Unseen in *Cowboy*, Widow Rawlings's affairs have been looked after by Judge Burke since her husband's death, although it's uncertain how far his favours extend.

RAWLINSON, BRIAN
Roles: Steward in *Cruising*, Hessian Driver in *Cleo* and Stagecoach Guard in *Cowboy*

Born in Stockport, Cheshire, in 1931, Brian Rawlinson was a busy character actor, always in demand for theatre and screen productions. He began his stage career at the Old Vic, while his work in the screen world, which started in the mid-1950s, was split between television and films.

His small-screen work included appearances in *The Count of Monte Cristo*, *William Tell*, *Danger Man*, *Last of the Summer Wine*, *Heartbeat* and *Goodnight Sweetheart*. In the '60s he enjoyed a spell in *Coronation Street*, playing Joe Makinson, and during the '70s was seen as Robert Onedin in *The Onedin Line*.His film credits include *Life in Danger*, *Ladies Who Do*, *Blind Terror* and *Sunday Pursuit*.

He died in 2000, aged sixty-nine.

RAY, ROBIN
Role: Assistant Manager in *Constable*

Born in London in 1935, Robin Ray studied at RADA before completing National Service in the Royal Army Service Corps. After returning to civvies, he was soon offered acting roles on stage and television, appearing in ITV's *The Guv'nor* in 1956, and making his stage debut with *The Changeling* in 1961, followed by a period understudying Dudley Moore in *Beyond The Fringe*.

William Wakefield (Ted Ray, left) blackmails science teacher Gregory Adams (*Teacher*)

In the early '60s, Ray also took up a teaching position as Chief Technical Instructor at RADA where he remained for four years whilst trying to break into broadcasting.

He became the first presenter of television's *Call My Bluff* in the 1960s and subsequently hosted shows such as *The Movie Quiz, Cabbages and Kings* and the popular television quiz of the 1970s, *Face The Music*. He appeared in a handful of films, such as *I'm All Right, Jack; Watch Your Stern* and *A Hard Day's Night*.

On radio he had a successful Saturday show on Radio Four, reviewed records for Capital Radio and, in the early 1990s, worked as a consultant for Classic FM. But he remained involved in the theatre, appearing in the musical *Side by Side, Tomfoolery, Café Puccini* and *Let's Do It*.

He died in 1998, aged sixty-three.

RAY, TED
Role: William Wakefield in *Teacher*
The son of a comedian, Ted Ray was born in Wigan in 1905 and had several jobs, including ship's steward, before making his stage debut in Lancashire in 1927. Three years later, he was working in London and his career blossomed, including a tour of South Africa and three Royal Variety performances.

He established his name on radio and was given his own show, *Ray's A Laugh*, and recruited as resident master of ceremonies for the radio show, *Calling All Forces*.

By the mid-1950s he was appearing on television in *The Ted Ray Show*; other small-screen credits included *Spot the Tune, Joker's Wild* and *It's Saturday Night*. His foray into the film world saw him cast in, among others, *Meet Me Tonight, Escape By Night, My Wife's Family* and *Please Turn Over*.

He died in 1977, aged seventy-two.

RAYMOND, CYRIL
Role: Army Officer in *Regardless*
Born in Rowley Regis, West Midlands, in 1897, Cyril Raymond had graduated from RADA and launched his stage and screen career by 1915. Other than six years in the RAF during the Second World War, he spent his entire working life in showbusiness, often playing policemen and military types, although his most memorable screen role was as Celia Johnson's understanding husband in the classic tearjerker, *Brief Encounter*.

Only occasionally on television, he made up for this absence by notching up a myriad of film credits, including *The Frightened Lady, Keep It Quiet, Night Alone, Quartet, Angels One Five, The Baby and the Battleship, Dunkirk* and *Night Train to Paris*.

He died in 1973, aged seventy-five.

READY, BOMBARDIER
Played by Jack Douglas
Based at the experimental 1313 anti-aircraft battery featured in *England*, he's one of the shirkers who suffers a severe shock to the system when the tough-speaking Captain Melly is put in charge of the unit.

RECKITT, OLIVER
Played by Kenneth Williams
A bookworm who's studying nuclear physics. A patient at Haven Hospital in *Nurse*, he doesn't let his hospitalisation stop his studies and has his books to thank for an unexpected introduction to the attractive Jill Thompson. When her brother, Harry, is unable to visit Oliver in hospital, he sends Jill in his place to deliver fresh reading matter, marking the beginning of their relationship. Oliver doesn't suffer fools gladly, which he beautifully demonstrates on numerous occasions, like the time he has to spruce himself up just to please Matron on her rounds, something he's quick to raise with her.

RECRUITS
Played by Jack Smethurst, Brian Jackson, Don McCorkindale, Leon Eagles, Malcolm Webster, Patrick Durkin, James Villiers, Haydn Ward, Graydon Gould, Jeremy Dempster, Terry Dickenson, Henry Livings, Bernard Kay and Michael Hunt
The recruits – all part of Able Platoon – are seen in various scenes at Heathercrest National Service Depot in *Sergeant*.

REED, GAVIN
Role: Window Dresser in *Loving*
Liverpudlian Gavin Reed, born in 1935, made a handful of screen appearances during the '70s and '80s, including roles in the films *The Body Beneath, Tattoo, Tootsie* and Walt Disney's film for television, *The Return of the Shaggy Dog*.

He died in 1990, aged fifty-five.

REES, LLEWELLYN
Role: Lord Chief Justice in *Emmannuelle*
Llewellyn Rees was born in Dorset in 1901 and worked as a private tutor before later training at RADA and going on to tour and act in repertory theatre. During the mid-1930s he landed roles in a number of West End productions and also moved into directing, working with the Scottish National Players and on *George and Margaret* in New York.

In 1940, Rees abandoned acting and began an administrative career, becoming General Secretary of British Actors' Equity, joint Secretary of the London Theatre Council and Governor of the Old Vic, amongst other positions.

Before the decade was out he'd become Drama Director of the Arts Council and Chairman of the Executive Committee of the International Theatre Institute until, in 1956, Rees decided to return to the stage. He went on to act in productions such as *Lock Up Your Daughters* and *The Right Honourable Gentleman*, making his final West End appearance in *Whose Life Is It Anyway?* in 1978.

His television credits included *Detective, Strange Report, Budgie, Crossroads, The Professionals, Boon* and *Inspector Morse*, while on the big screen he appeared in films such as *You Can't Escape, Brothers in Law, Cromwell, The Dresser* and *A Fish Called Wanda*.

He died in 1994, aged ninety-three.

REEVES, KYNASTON
Role: Testy Old Man in *Regardless*
Frequently cast as magistrates or waspish officials, Kynaston Reeves, born in London in 1893, spent more than five decades entertaining audiences on stage and screen.

After serving in the First World War, he studied at RADA and made his professional stage debut in 1920, touring in *Betty at Bay*, before travelling to America with Sir Ben Greet's company. Among his numerous theatre credits were various roles in Shakespeare's plays, including *Twelfth Night* in 1937.

His film debut was in 1919 after which he clocked up nearly a hundred credits in such films as *Sons of the Sea, The Stars Look Down, The Flying Squad, The Night Invader, The Winslow Boy, The Guinea Pig, Tony Draws a Horse* and, his last film, 1970's *The Private Life of Sherlock Holmes*.

On the small screen his work included playing Uncle Nicholas in *The Forsyte Saga*, Eustace Evepitt in *United!* and Mr Quelch in the 1950s series *Billy Bunter*.

He died in 1971, aged seventy-eight.

REFEREE
Played by Norman Rossington
He is just about to referee a boxing match in *Regardless* between Dynamite Don and Massive Micky when Don falls off his stool and damages his little finger, halting proceedings, much to the crowd's disgust.

REGAN, LINDA
Role: Private Taylor in *England*
TV: *Again Christmas*
Born into a theatrical family in 1959, Londoner Linda Regan began her screen career as a child, appearing in various television shows, including *Z Cars, Dixon of Dock Green* and playing an island girl in 1970's *Carry On Again Christmas*.

Upon leaving school, she worked in clubs as a comedienne before joining Worcester Rep; she continued to tread the boards until the 1980s when she enjoyed her last foray into repertory theatre with an appearance at Chelmsford.

She appeared occasionally in films, including roles in *Adolf Hitler – My Part in His Downfall, Confessions of a Pop Performer* and *Adventures of a Private Eye*, but was seen frequently on television. Her small-screen credits include *Special Branch, Bergerac, Dempsey and Makepeace, Birds of a Feather, Over the Rainbow* and *The Bill,* as well as playing April in several series of holiday camp sitcom, *Hi-de-Hi!,* and Dennis Waterman's girlfriend in the opening episode of *Minder.* Still busy, she recently recorded an episode of *Doctors* and played a mum for four years in Channel 5's series for teenagers, *Harry and Cosh,* as well as completing her first novel.

REGARDLESS, CARRY ON

See feature box on pages 206–7.

REID, BERYL

Role: Mrs Valentine in *Emmannuelle*

Born in Manchester in 1920, Beryl Reid left home at sixteen and worked in a shop but soon realised it wasn't the job for her and left within weeks. She turned her attention to acting and secured a job in a revue during a summer season at Bridlington. She later worked at the National Theatre as a comedy actress, but it was for her role in the radio show, *Educating Archie,* that brought her to the public's attention.

Her extensive stage career included a starring role in 1965's *The Killing of Sister George* in the West End and on Broadway, winning her a Tony Award in the process; she subsequently appeared in the Hollywood version of the play.

A variety of films and television credits included *Tinker, Tailor, Soldier, Spy; Smiley's People; The Beiderbecke Tapes; The Goodies; Cracker; Bold as Brass; Father, Dear Father* and her own show, *Beryl Reid Says Good Evening* for television. Films include *The Belles of St Trinian's, The Extra Day, Two Way Stretch* and *Entertaining Mr Sloane.*

She also published several books and was awarded the Comedy Award for a lifetime's achievement at 1991's British Comedy Awards, to complement her appointment as OBE, five years earlier.

She died in 1996, aged seventy-six.

RELPH, S.

The unseen Junior 2nd Officer on the *Happy Wanderer* in *Cruising.* His name is seen on the crew list.

REPORTER

Played by Bill Kenwright

In *Matron* the reporter arrives at the Finisham Maternity Hospital – together with a photographer, Dick – to cover the story of film actress Jane Darling giving birth.

REPORTER, 1st , 2nd and 3rd

Played by Bill Hutchinson, Neville Ware and Jane Norman respectively

In *Emmannuelle* they're seen trying to elicit a response from Emmannuelle Prevert, the French Ambassador's wife, after news breaks that she's had affairs with many high-profile names, including the Prime Minister.

REUBER-STAIER, EVA

Role: A 'Bird of Paradise' in *Dick*

Crowned Miss World in 1969, Austrian-born Eva Reuber-Staier exploited her newly-found status and appeared in a handful of acting roles during the '70s and '80s. She was seen in episodes of television series like *Doctor at Sea* and *Space: 1999,* as well as playing small roles in three Bond movies: *The Spy Who Loved Me, For Your Eyes Only* and *Octopussy.*

REVEREND FLASHER, THE

Played by Sidney James

For the Reverend Flasher in *Dick,* see 'Turpin, Dick'.

RICHARD, WENDY

Roles: Miss Willing in *Matron* and Ida Downe in *Girls*
TV: *Christmas* (70)

Born in Middlesbrough in 1946, Wendy Richard moved to London as a baby when her parents took over a pub in Mayfair. As a girl she harboured dreams of becoming an archaeologist, but never pursued her ambitions upon finishing her education. Instead, she completed a course in shorthand and typing before working briefly as a sales assistant at Fortnum and Mason's.

She eventually joined the Italia Conti Stage School. While studying, she earned money as a photographic model, working for magazines and retailers.

Her small-screen debut was in the 1960s, playing a runaway teenager in *Dixon of Dock Green,* followed quickly by an appearance with Sammy Davis Jnr in ATV's *Sammy Davis Meets the Girl.* Other credits in a busy career include playing Miss Brahms in *Are You Being Served?* and *Grace and Favour;* Doreen, the clippie, in *On the Buses; Please, Sir!; The Fenn Street Gang;* a barmaid in ITV's *Not On Your Nellie; Up Pompeii!; Harpers West One* and *Danger Man.* In the late 1960s, she also spent three years as Joyce Harker in the popular BBC series, *The Newcomers.* Most recently she's been playing Pauline in *EastEnders.*

On the big screen, she made her debut with two lines in *Doctor in Clover,* but has appeared in a handful of other movies, including *Bless this House* and *No Blade of Grass.*

RICHARDS, YVONNE

Continuity on *Up The Khyber*

In continuity from the 1950s, Yvonne Richard's credits include *Assignment Redhead, Stormy Crossing, Danger Within, Faces in the Dark* and, her last picture in 1970, *Connecting Rooms.*

RICHARDSON, GORDON

Role: Uncle Ernest Grubb in *Loving*

Gordon Richardson, who died in 1995, appeared in television shows such as *Doctor Who* and *The Borderers,* as well as films *A High*

Wind in Jamaica, The Go-Between, Tess, Kill or Be Killed and *Kill and Kill Again.*

RICHMOND

Played by Peter Butterworth

An employee of the French Ambassador, Emile Prevert, Richmond is hard of hearing and seen in *Emmannuelle.*

RIDER

Played by Richard O'Brien

Appearing in *Cowboy,* the Rider is involved in the attack on the stagecoach transporting Marshall Knutt and Annie Oakley to Stodge City.

RIDLEY, ARNOLD

Role: Alderman Pratt in *Girls*

Born in Bath in 1896, Arnold Ridley was educated at Clarendon School in his home town before studying at Bristol University, where he began his acting career. For a time he harboured doubts regarding where his future lay: he'd trained as a schoolteacher and taught for a short spell, but quickly turned to acting, making his first professional stage appearance in *Prunella* at Bristol's Theatre Royal, in 1913.

During the First World War he served in the army, but was invalided out in 1917 after being severely wounded at the Somme. Injuries to an arm left it virtually useless, while being hit on the head with a rifle butt led to blackouts affecting him for the remainder of his life.

Ridley resumed his acting career in 1918 at Birmingham Rep. During three years at the company he appeared in over forty productions. He moved to Plymouth but his stage career was brought to an abrupt end when forced to give up acting because of his war injuries. With his life in turmoil, he returned to Bath and worked in his father's boot shop while contemplating a bleak future, but success was soon bestowed upon Ridley. He began writing plays and, although his first attempt was unsuccessful, the second struck gold.

In 1923 he penned *The Ghost Train,* which was produced two years later and eventually became a worldwide success, being adapted for both big and small screen. His career as a playwright produced more than thirty plays, including *Easy Money* and *Beggar My Neighbour.*

In the mid-1930s he established his own film company with a partner. The first release, *Royal Eagle,* was favourably received by critics, but the company's life was brief. During the making of their second film, the bank acting as financial backers went bankrupt, leaving the film company seriously in debt – it took nearly twenty years to clear the deficit.

When the Second World War began, Ridley worked with ENSA, and one of the plays he went on to direct was his own, *The Ghost Train.*

Afterwards, he resumed his acting career and, in 1940, returned to the stage as director of productions with the Malvern Company for two years. He then appeared in the West End in several productions, such as *Twelve Angry Men*, and toured with shows like *Rain* and *Roar Like a Dove*.

Although he'll forever be remembered for playing Private Godfrey in *Dad's Army* and writing *The Ghost Train*, Ridley made a handful of films, notably *The Interrupted Journey* and *The Man Who Knew Too Much*. On radio he spent over two decades as Doughy Hood in *The Archers*, and on television was seen playing the vicar in *Crossroads* and two characters in *Coronation Street*.

He died in 1984, aged eighty-eight.

RIDLEY, DOUGLAS

Role: 2nd Plotter in *Henry*

Other screen credits in the early 1970s include an episode of *Up Pompeii!* and the films *Loot* and *Cool It Carol!*.

RIDOUT, ARTHUR

Sound Editor on *Regardless*, *Cruising*, *Cabby* and *Screaming!*

A sound editor from the early 1950s, the late Arthur Ridout worked on such films as *Reach for the Sky*, *Checkpoint*, *Miracle in Soho*, *Sapphire*, *The Wild and the Willing*, *Catch Us If You Can*, *Doctor in Clover* and the Rogers/Thomas productions *Raising the Wind* and *Twice Round the Daffodils*.

RIFFS

Played by Larry Taylor and William Hurndell

Two of Abdul's fierce-looking warriors seen during various scenes of *Follow That Camel*.

RIFFS AT ABDUL'S TENT

Played by Richard Montez, Frank Singuineau and Simon Cain

As Sheikh Abdul Abulbul prepares to consummate his marriage to wife number thirteen, who happens to be Lady Jane Ponsonby, Riffs follow tradition and deliver money and gifts to his tent in *Follow That Camel*.

RIGBY ROAD

A road mentioned in *Cabby* during the scene where Peggy and Sally are held at gunpoint by crooks while driving along.

RIGBY, PETER

Role: Henry's Courtier in *Henry*

RIVERS, STELLA

Hairdresser on *Sergeant*, *Constable*, *Cowboy*, *Screaming!*, *Don't Lose Your Head*, *Follow That Camel*, *Doctor*, *Up The Khyber*, *Camping*, *Again Doctor*, *Up the Jungle*, *Loving*, *Henry*, *At Your Convenience*, *Matron*, *Abroad*, *Girls*, *Dick*, *Behind* and *England*

Born in North Shields in 1920, Stella Rivers served her hairdressing apprenticeship in her home town before her family moved to Iver Heath, Buckinghamshire, and she joined the forces – serving as a hairdresser in the ATS – in the early 1940s.

When she left the services, she was successful in acquiring a job at Denham Studios, with one of her early assignments seeing her responsible for the extras in crowd scenes during *Cleopatra*. Other films she worked on at this point included *A Matter of Life and Death* with David Niven.

She soon graduated to chief hairdresser and became responsible for performers' hair on hundreds of productions, including *The Thirty-Nine Steps*, *Robbery Under Arms*, *Venetian Bird*, *Whistle Down the Wind*, *Doctor In Distress*, *Island of Terror*, *Legend of the Werewolf* and *Superman*.

Stella retired from the industry circa 1980, when her husband became ill.

RIVERSIDE CARAVAN SITE, THE

The Riverside Caravan Site is the setting for *Behind*. Owned by Major Leep, who acquired the land from the local landlord for £2000; what the landlord conveniently forgot to tell the Major was that the field is riddled with holes, dating back to Roman times when mining was prevalent. The holes open up later like giant chasms, nearly swallowing the caravans on the site.

RIVERSIDE CLUB

In *Behind* the clubhouse at the Riverside Caravan Site is where Major Leep receives a surprise when he hosts his first cabaret evening and his supposed singer turns out to be a stripper.

ROBERTS, NANCY

Role: Old Lady in *Regardless*

Born in St Asaph, Wales, in 1892, Nancy Roberts began working on screen during the Silent days and subsequently appeared in films such as *Prison Without Bars*, *Warning to Wantons*, *Black Narcissus* and *Cosh Boy*.

On television she appeared in, among others, *Hancock's Half Hour*, *The Avengers* and the '50's series, *The Secret Garden*, as Mrs Medlock, but she's probably best remembered as Gran in the ever-popular *The Grove Family*. She later played the role in the feature film, *It's A Great Day*.

She died in 1962, aged seventy.

ROBERTS, TREVOR

Role: Henry's Courtier in *Henry*

ROBESPIERRE, CITIZEN

Played by Peter Gilmore

In *Don't Lose Your Head*, Citizen Camembert, who's chief of the secret police, reports to Robespierre, a demanding man who plays an important role in the French Revolution.

ROBIN

Played by John Clive

For Robin in *Abroad*, see 'Tweet, Robin'.

ROBIN, DANY

Role: Jacqueline in *Don't Lose Your Head*

Blonde beauty Dany Robin was born in Chamart, France, in 1927. She trained in ballet and performed at the Opéra de Paris before turning to a career in films. After studying at the Paris Conservatoire, she made her big screen debut in 1946's *Lunegarde* before completing a string of French pictures.

Although the lion's share of her career was spent working in France, she did make the occasional appearance outside her homeland, including roles in *Waltz of the Toreadors*, *Follow the Boys* and *The Best House in London*, directed by Philip Saville.

She tragically died in 1995, aged sixty-eight, when a fire engulfed her Paris apartment.

ROBINSON, CARDEW

Role: The Fakir in *Up The Khyber*

Born in Goodmayes, Essex, in 1917, Cardew Robinson found fame on the radio and in Variety during the 1940s for his schoolboy creation, Cardew the Cad, spawning a strip cartoon and film, *Fun at St Fanny's*.

He worked in all media. A busy stage actor, he was frequently seen in the West End, making 650 performances as King Pellinore in *Camelot* in Drury Lane. He also appeared on the screen, with television credits including *Hancock's Half Hour*, *Dixon of Dock Green*, *The Avengers*, *Call My Bluff* and *Celebrity Squares*. On the big screen, meanwhile, he popped up in such films as *Happy Is The Bride*, *Light Up the Sky!*, *Smashing Time* and, during the 1980s, *Pirates* and *Shirley Valentine*.

He died in 1992, aged seventy-five.

ROBINSON, JOE

Role: Dynamite Dan in *Regardless*

Born in Newcastle upon Tyne in 1929, actor and stuntman Joe Robinson followed in his father's footsteps and fought professionally as a wrestler during his early twenties, before, in the 1950s, he started being offered small parts in films such as *A Kid for Two Farthings* after being noticed in the stage musical, *Wish You Were Here*, by the writer whose novel was being adapted for the big screen. Other film credits include *The Flesh is Weak*, *Fighting Mad*, *Strange Awakening* and *Sea Fury*.

During the '60s he was also seen in occasional episodes of television shows, including *Hancock's Half Hour*, *The Avengers* and *The Saint* while continuing to appear in films. RADA-trained Robinson has also owned a martial-arts centre in Brighton and a gym in London, and together with his brother taught Honor Blackman some self-defence techniques

CARRY ON REGARDLESS

An Anglo Amalgamated release
A Peter Rogers production
Released as a U certificate in 1961 in black & white
Running time: 90 mins

CAST

Sidney James	Bert Handy
Kenneth Connor	Sam Twist
Charles Hawtrey	Gabriel Dimple
Kenneth Williams	Francis Courtenay
Joan Sims	Lily Duveen
Liz Fraser	Delia King
Terence Longdon	Montgomery Infield-Hopping
Bill Owen	Mike Weston
Esma Cannon	Miss Cooling
Fenella Fielding	Penny Panting
Hattie Jacques	Sister
Stanley Unwin	Landlord
Ed Devereaux	Mr Panting
Cyril Chamberlain	Policeman
Ambrosine Phillpotts	Yoki's Owner
Joan Hickson	Matron
Molly Weir	Bird Owner
Sydney Tafler	Strip Club Manager
Eric Pohlmann	Sinister Man
June Jago	Sister
Norman Rossington	Referee
Terence Alexander	Trevor Trelawney
Jerry Desmond	Martin Paul
Eric Boon	Young Man
Jimmy Thompson	Mr Delling
Anthony Sagar	Bus Conductor
Howard Marion-Crawford	Wine Organiser
Fred Griffiths	Taxi Driver
Bernard Hunter	Wine Waiter
David Lodge	Connoisseur
Nicholas Parsons	Wolf
Michael Nightingale	Wine Bystander
Patrick Cargill	Raffish Customer
Kynaston Reeves	Testy Old Man
Fraser Kerr	Houseman
Douglas Ives	Fanatic Patient
Maureen Moore	Pretty Probationer
Victor Maddern	1st Sinister Passenger
Denis Shaw	2nd Sinister Passenger
Betty Marsden	'Mata Hari'
Freddie Mills	Lefty
Tom Clegg	Massive Micky McGee
Joe Robinson	Dynamite Dan
Lucy Griffiths	Auntie
Ian Whittaker	Shop Assistant
Julia Arnall	Trudy Trelawney
Jack Taylor	MC/Policeman
George Street	Club Receptionist
Cyril Raymond	Army Officer
Nancy Roberts	Old Lady
Michael Ward	Photographer
Ian Wilson	Advertising Man
Madame Yang	Chinese Lady
Judith Furse	Formidable Lady
David Stoll	Distraught Manager
Carole Shelley	Helen Delling
Charles Julian	Old man in Ruby Room
Ian Curry	Leonard Beamish

PRODUCTION TEAM

Screenplay by Norman Hudis
Music composed and directed by Bruce Montgomery
Art Director: Lionel Couch
Director of Photography: Alan Hume
Editor: John Shirley
Associate Producer: Basil Keys
Assistant Director: Jack Causey
Camera Operator: Dudley Lovell
Sound Editor: Arthur Ridout
Sound Recordists: Robert T. MacPhee and Gordon McCallum
Unit Manager: Claude Watson
Hairdressing: Biddy Chrystal
Continuity: Gladys Goldsmith
Make-up: George Blackler
Costume Designer: Joan Ellacott
Casting Director: Betty White
Producer: Peter Rogers
Director: Gerald Thomas

Even Sam Twist (Kenneth Connor, right) hankers after a fresh challenge

Francis Courtenay tucks in at the chimps' tea party

Bert Handy has formed Helping Hands Limited, an organisation that's 'always ready to lend a hand'. The trouble is he can't get any staff, so places another advert in the paper. When the regulars at the local labour exchange notice the ad they rush to Handy's basement office in Denver Street hoping to be the successful candidate. Fortunately, Mr Handy signs them all up.

Business starts off slow, but eventually the phone starts ringing. One of the first jobs goes to Delia King, modelling a woman's wardrobe for Mr Delling. Wanting to surprise his wife with a completely new set of clothes for her anniversary, King tries everything on for size, but when Mrs Delling returns home unexpectedly, Delia's forced to hide in the cupboard.

Sam Twist, meanwhile, is lured to Penny Panting's flat. Thinking he's being hired to babysit, he soon discovers she wants his help in making her husband jealous. Feeling neglected by her hubby, she decides it might help if Mr Panting finds her in the arms of another man, but Twist doesn't want anything to do with her cunning plan. Before he can escape, though, her husband returns and ends up punching Twist in the face.

Other jobs find Francis Courtenay walking a pet monkey and modelling a beekeeper's mask, Lily Duveen collecting invitation cards at a wine-tasting session and getting tipsy in the process, and Mr Handy keeping someone's place at the outpatients and being mistaken for an important process. Gabriel Dimple ends up in the boxing ring with a heavyweight brute while Sam Twist finds himself soaking wet on the Forth Bridge instead of being a fourth at bridge as originally requested before Miss Cooling, the easily confused secretary at Helping Hands, messed up the request.

A frequent visitor to the Helping Hands office returns. Until now no one has been able to understand his peculiar vernacular, but this time language expert Francis Courtenay is present. To the man's relief, Courtenay identifies his language as Gobbledygook and translates the bad news that he's the landlord and is giving Helping Hands notice to leave the premises. He later has second thoughts and agrees they can stay so long as they help clean a derelict house he's bought, but when they end up demolishing the home instead of cleaning it, it looks as if they've signed their own eviction order. Fortunately, their luck is in when the landlord comes calling for a progress report.

Funny Scene!

Sam Twist arrives at Mrs Panting's apartment thinking he's been hired for a spot of babysitting. Penny Panting answers the door in her negligée.

TWIST: Good evening. (Notices how she's dressed.)
           I'm from . . . (Gulps.) . . . Helping Hands.

PANTING: Hello. Come in — do.

TWIST: Is this the right place? I mean,
           have I . . .

PANTING: Yes, this is the right place.

TWIST: (Pulls a note from his pocket and looks
           at it.) Um. P-p-p-panting?

PANTING: No, that's the way I always breathe.

ready for the Bond movie, *Goldfinger*. Robinson himself later appeared in *Diamonds Are Forever*.

ROBINSON, MR
Played by Philip Stone
Mr Snooper's boss at the Citizens' Advice Bureau in *Loving*. When Snooper seems to do nothing but irritate people who have come seeking advice, Mr Robinson warns him that he has to find a wife, and experience married life if he wants to retain his job.

RODERICK, GEORGE
Role: Waiter in *Again Doctor*
George Roderick, who died in 1976, appeared on screen from the 1950s. On television he was seen in such productions as *Man from Interpol*, *International Detective*, *The Spies*, *Codename* and *Boy Meets Girl*.

His film credits, which saw him play plenty of policemen, included *The Quatermass Experiment*, *Women Without Men*, *The Crooked Sky*, *Rattle of a Simple Man*, *Operation Third Form*, *The Ski Wheelers* and the big-screen version of sitcom *Love Thy Neighbour*.

RODGERS, ANTON
Roles: Young Man in *Cruising* and Hardy in *Jack*
Born in Wisbech, Cambridgeshire, in 1933, Anton Rodgers trained at the Italia Conti Stage Academy and acted as a child on stage before subsequently enrolling at LAMDA; he was treading the boards in the West End soon after, and it wasn't long before he began working in television and appearing in films, such as *Crash Drive*, *Petticoat Pirates*, *To Chase a Million*, *Scrooge* and, in 2004, *Secret Passage*.

On television he's appeared in the likes of *Maigret*, *Gideon's Way*, *The Duchess of Duke Street*, *Midsomer Murders* and *May to December*, but is probably best remembered for playing William Fields in the comedy *Fresh Fields* and the sequel, *French Fields*.

RODGERS, CHRISTINE
Roles: Amazon Guard in *Spying* and Hand Maiden in *Cleo*
During the late 1960s and early '70s, Christine Rodgers made the odd appearance on television, appearing in shows such as *Suspense*, *At Last the 1948 Show* and *The Benny Hill Show*.

RODWAY, GEOFFREY
Make-up designer on *Sergeant*, *Cruising*, *Cabby*, *Jack*, *Cleo*, *Cowboy*, *Screaming!*, *Don't Lose Your Head*, *Follow That Camel*, *Doctor*, *Up The Khyber*, *Camping*, *Again Doctor*, *Up the Jungle*, *Loving*, *Henry*, *At Your Convenience*, *Matron*, *Abroad*, *Girls*, *Dick*, *Behind* and *England*
Born in Johannesburg in 1911, Geoffrey Rodway moved to England with his parents at the age of eighteen months. After completing his education he studied art in Sheffield before, aged nineteen, moving to Nairobi to work for his father's company. He returned two years later and began a long career in the film business.

Responding to an advert in *The Stage* newspaper for trainee make-up artists, he was offered a job with Gaumont British Film Studios in London, splitting his week between Hammersmith Art School and the studio.

His career was interrupted in 1941 when called up in to the army, but after five years in uniform he returned to the film world and found employment at, initially, Denham Studios and, finally, Pinewood. His extensive list of credits include not just twenty-three *Carry On*s but a raft of pictures ranging from *Vice Versa*, *A Day To Remember*, *Forbidden Cargo*, *Twice Round the Daffodils* and *The Purple Plain* to *Doctor at Sea*, *Man of the Moment*, *The Night of the Big Heat* and *Whistle Down the Wind*.

He died in 1999, aged eighty-eight, having retired from the business in 1981.

RODWAY, NORA
Assistant make-up designer (Assisted her husband, Geoffrey, on all his films from *Don't Lose Your Head*. For full list, see 'Rodway, Geoffrey'.)
Nora Rodway, who was born in Sheffield in 1912, met her husband, Geoffrey, at the city's College of Art while studying fine art. After graduating she never pursued a career in art and, instead, found herself working in the drawing office at the English Steel Company, based in Sheffield, until marrying at the age of twenty-two.

She followed Geoffrey to London and raised a family, but when her children had grown-up, she embarked on a new career. Aged forty-seven, she began working as a make-up assistant on occasional projects. Geoffrey persuaded her to train and before long she was freelancing and assisting her husband, beginning with the 1958 Dirk Bogarde film, *A Tale of Two Cities*. Other film credits included *The Private Life of Sherlock Holmes*.

She retired from the industry in 1981 and died in 2005.

ROGER
For 'Roger' in *Jack*, see 'Patch'.

ROGER
Played by Julian Holloway
A friend of Lewis Boggs seen in *At Your Convenience*. They bump into each other on the dance-floor at the Whippit Inn and Roger tells Lewis that he's sorry he hadn't managed to return his call but it's OK for him to use the flat for the night. The trouble is, Myrtle's within earshot and thinks Lewis has ulterior motives behind taking her out on a date.

ROGER DE LODGERLEY, SIR
Played by Charles Hawtrey
The King's equerry is seen in *Henry*. His brief is to test and taste everything before his employer, Henry VIII, which he uses as his excuse for jumping into bed with Queen Marie. When she becomes pregnant, Sir Roger is thrown into prison and subjected to the rack until he signs a confession admitting to the fling; but it's the start of several requests from Henry for retractions and confessions to suit his own needs as he tries desperately to free himself of his wife, Marie.

ROGERS, ALAN
Wrote the lyrics for 'Carry On Cowboy' and 'This is the Night for Love' heard in *Cowboy*.

ROGERS, ERIC
Composed and conducted the music for *Cabby*, *Jack*, *Spying*, *Cleo*, *Cowboy*, *Screaming!*, *Don't Lose Your Head*, *Follow That Camel*, *Doctor*, *Up The Khyber*, *Camping*, *Again Doctor*, *Up the Jungle*, *Loving*, *Henry*, *At Your Convenience*, *Matron*, *Abroad*, *Girls*, *Dick*, *Behind*, *That's Carry On* and *Emmannuelle*. Also the pianist on *Cowboy* and bandleader on *Again Doctor*
TV: Provided the music for *Laughing's Christmas Classics*
Born in Halifax, Yorkshire, in 1921, Eric Rogers' musical education began at the age of thirteen when he received tuition from the local church organist. During the Second World War he served in the RAF. By the time of his demob he was flying Spitfires but had utilised his piano-playing skills at NAAFIs and pubs, much to the enjoyment of his fellow airmen.

Upon returning to civvy street, Rogers used his gratuity to raise a small orchestra to play at various London venues. He was soon noticed and worked as an accompanist/arranger for such artists as Fred Emney and Julie Wilson, before becoming a musical director and, eventually, composer of background music for films and television. He also orchestrated the West End musical, *Oliver!*, for Lionel Bart, a production which took him to Broadway.

He wrote film scores for, among others, *Highly Dangerous*, *Genevieve*, *The Iron Maiden*, *The Three Lives of Thomasina*, *Nurse On Wheels*, *The Big Job* and the 1975 television series, *Return to the Planet of the Apes*.

He died in 1978.

ROGERS, PETER
Producer of all *Carry On* films except *Columbus*, where he was executive producer
TV: *Christmas* ('69 and '70) by arrangement with Peter Rogers. Executive Producer on *Christmas* ('72 and '73); the entire *Laughing*

R

Peter Rogers on location with his portable office

series. Co-creator of *Laughing's Christmas Classics*

Peter Rogers, who was born in Gillingham, Kent, in 1914, had been a keen scriptwriter ever since he began writing plays at school; his interest continued after he joined his father's business, when most evenings he'd be huddled over his typewriter. But burning the candle at both ends finally took its toll. Ineffective at work, his father decided to pay his son an allowance for staying at home and attempting to sell his plays but constant rejections led Rogers' father to secure him a job as a cub reporter on the *Kentish Express*.

Upon reading that American theatre producer Auriol Lee was arriving in London to produce a play, Rogers sent her one of his efforts, and although she rejected the play, she offered him the chance to work as an assistant on her production of J. B. Priestley's *People at Sea*.

By twenty-one, Rogers had seen two of his own plays, *Human Straws* and *Mr Mercury*, staged, but both were short-lived, and were followed by a barren spell artistically, before his call-up papers arrived in 1941. Before he could don a uniform, though, a severe bout of cerebral spinal meningitis confined him to a hospital bed for twelve months and put paid to any military service.

During the war years, Rogers achieved further success when the BBC broadcast several

of his radio productions, including *The Man Who Bounced, Mr South Starts A War, Cross Questions* and *Cards On the Table*, leading to an offer to join J. Arthur Rank's religious film company as a scriptwriter. The film unit's subsequent closure saw Rogers return to journalism with the trade paper, *World Press News*. In charge of the publication's film section, he

interviewed British writer-producer Sydney Box and was invited to submit ideas for a forthcoming comedy drama, *Holiday Camp;* on the strength of his material he was offered a full-time contract at Gainsborough Studios. It was during this period that he met Sydney's sister, film producer Betty Box, whom he married in 1948.

Gerald Thomas and Peter Rogers inspect the Riverside Caravan Site, alias The Orchard at Pinewood in *Behind*

MEMORIES OF MAKING-UP THE CARRY ON STARS

Months before her death in 2005, Nora Rodway shared her memories of working on the *Carry On* films

'My years working on the *Carry On* films, assisting my husband, Geoff, have provided me with plenty of memories, of both particular films and just some of the people who appeared in them, like Angela Douglas, who was in four films. She was a very beautiful young woman and, although I never made her up, so didn't know her as well as Geoff did, I remember her as a very sweet-natured, kind and friendly girl – and a very good actress, too.

'I have one very vivid memory of her, during the making of *Up The Khyber*, when she, Bernard Bresslaw and, I think, Kenneth Williams were sitting waiting for a shot of the three of them. Everything was ready for the shot when Bernard suddenly said, "Nora, I think my beard's coming unstuck." Geoff was upstairs in the make-up department I think, making up Joan Sims, so I was alone and in control of any make-up required. I was quite experienced by then but still felt uneasy when Geoff wasn't on the set and I never, in all my years in the business, managed to get over my shyness. It is quite nerve-wracking to be the only one working with every eye fixed on you, and the knowledge that every second is costing money so you must hurry. Anyway, I went forward with my little bottle of spirit gum held in my left hand, while with my right hand I lifted the edge of his beard and started to apply the spirit gum when there was an alarmed cry from Bernard of, "Look out, Nora, you're spilling the spirit gum", and so I was – one really needs three hands for a job like this.

'The really terrible thing was that it had spilled onto his beautiful, white, flowing robe which I knew had been hired at great expense, and was made of very expensive material called Nun's Veiling, and they only had one! I had no idea what to do and foolishly started to dab the awful dark brown stain with tissues which, of course, stuck to the spirit gum. I was scarlet with embarrassment and anxiety and afraid I might burst into tears when a little hand was gently placed on mine, and the soft, sympathetic voice of Angela Douglas said, "It's all right, Nora darling, Geoff isn't going to beat you when you get home tonight." Then I heard Gerald's voice, saying, "No, but I shall!" I knew he was joking, of course. Gerald was the kindest director Geoff and I ever worked with. He was a lovely man.

'At that moment, an old make-up man, whom none of us knew – in fact, none of us had ever seen him before as he'd just been called in for the day to help make up the hundreds of extras called in for the film – came over. He was holding a piece of white chalk which he handed to me and said, "Try this." So I did, just chalking over the stain. It worked marvellously. Sighs of relief all round! Of course, I was in great trouble later with the wardrobe ladies who had to wash the robe, so it wasn't a good day for me. I shall never forget dear Angela, though, for her kind and gentle attempt to ease my discomfort.

'Jacki Piper was a great favourite with Geoff and me and we became friends, visiting each other's homes. She was very pretty and a bright little actress, always good-humoured, amusing and kind. I knew her better than Geoff because I made her up, but we both found her very good fun to know and absolutely no trouble to make up. One incident we both remember was during the making of *Up The Jungle* when Terry Scott was playing the part of the world's worst Tarzan-like character, who'd never mastered the swinging from trees bit and kept smashing through them and falling at people's feet.

'There was a scene, on the set, of a pool of water where Jacki was about to have a dip when he suddenly crashed at her feet. He was wearing nothing but a leopard skin nappy fastened with an enormous safety pin. The shot went well and he did his usual crash and Gerry should have then called "cut" and Terry could have got up and the shot would have been complete, but Gerry didn't call "cut" so everyone remained still and waited, trying very hard not to laugh. Terry was the only one who didn't know that in the fall, his loincloth had slipped sideways and he was lying there on the artificial grass exposing his private parts for all to see. I didn't actually see it happen because I was over by the make-up table and the first I knew of it was when I heard Gerald's voice call, "Nora, you're needed over here to powder something off!" So off I trotted with my powder puff and then the laughter exploded and Terry himself joined in which was very noble of him, I thought. It really was a funny sight – mostly his puzzled face trying to work out why he was left lying in, I'm sure, a very uncomfortable position.

'Of all the people I worked with on the *Carry On*s, Kenneth Williams was my favourite. He was completely different in real life from all the over-acting and false voices that, of course, made him so funny. Frequently his wit could be cruel and he was aware of this and bitterly regretted it – but he was always extremely funny. When I first joined the *Carry On* crew, I tried to keep a low profile. I was so afraid of doing something idiotic, I didn't want anyone to know I was Geoff's wife. Of

Various snaps from the Rodways' own photo album show the husband and wife team at work on *Follow That Camel*

course, they quickly found out on the first film I did, which was *Don't Lose Your Head*. On the film I found I had to make Kenneth up and felt very nervous.

'About the second day he was late returning to the set after lunch. All the actors in the next shot are supposed to go to the make-up department to have their make-up checked after lunch, and on this day he didn't come at all, so after all the others had been I went down on the set hoping to "do" him there but he wasn't around.

'When he did arrive the second assistant said, "Mr Williams, you are holding us all up and I don't believe you have been to have your make-up checked." Kenneth replied, "Well I did go up to the make-up room but both their doors were locked because they were having it off as they do every lunch time." Now, you may not believe this but at forty-seven I was still learning the facts of life – well, the slang version. I didn't know what "having it off" meant so I turned to Geoff and asked, "What does he mean, having it off?" Lots of people heard me and I could hear stifled laughter. Geoff said very quietly, "Well, what do you think it means? If Kenneth says anything it's bound to mean only one thing." I made it all much worse and more amusing for everyone by going bright red and saying to them all, "We weren't doing anything of the kind, I swear we weren't."

'Gerald was the only one not laughing apart from Geoff and he came across and patted my hand and apologised on behalf of Kenneth before giving him a few sharp words. Just before Kenneth left that evening, he came to the make-up room and after shutting the door behind him said, in his real voice, "I'm deeply sorry, I can't imagine what made me say it – well, I can because I'm afraid I'll do anything for the sake of getting a laugh. It's all I know how to do." We became friends from that minute.

'Bernard Bresslaw was one of the nicest of the *Carry On* gang. Truly, a gentle giant – the very opposite of the parts he always played. He was an erudite, well-educated, decent, respectable, loving family man and nearly drove Geoff mad by doing *The Times* (I think it was that newspaper) crossword by lunch-time every day, while Geoff was floundering.

'If he [Bernard] was the giant on the set, I was the dwarf and although it was quite easy making him up when he was sitting in a chair in the make-up room, it was quite impossible for me to reach him on the set unless he bent down, which he always did until one day he decided to tease me and refused. He said, "No, you jump up." That, of course, was ridiculous. After some time of my pleading and his refusing with an amused group standing round, I said, "All right, well you won't get your make-up checked then." And at that moment I felt his two huge hands round my waist and I was lifted off my feet till I was level with his face, so I did what was necessary on his face with my feet dangling in mid-air. The stills cameraman took several shots of this.

'Then there was the time Sid James asked me to help him with his crossword puzzle. He came over to me on the set one day and said, "Can you help me, Nora, I've only got one more word to do and I just can't get it? It's actually two words, five and two, and means to continue." I replied, "Well, you of all people should have been able to get that – it's 'carry on'." If you can imagine his crumpled face becoming even more crumpled with laughter, his eyes streaming – he was really helpless with laughter and went off to tell Gerald.

'We really had so much fun and [there was] laughter making those films. It may sound as though it was all fun and games but it wasn't; it was extremely hard work and very long hours. Also, it was difficult dealing with volatile actors and actresses, especially first thing in the morning. But, overall, it was a joy to work on the films and, for me, they were happy days.'

NORA RODWAY

Between 1947-57 he wrote various screenplays and contributed towards many film scripts, including *When the Bough Breaks, Dear Murderer, Here Come the Huggetts, To Dorothy a Son, Circus Friends* and *Time Lock*, but by the mid-1950s, he was running Beaconsfield Film Studios, and busy producing films, during which period his forty-year working partnership with Gerald Thomas began. In addition to the *Carry On* films, his long list of credits in this capacity includes *Marry Me, Don't Ever Leave Me, A Passionate Stranger, The Vicious Circle, Chain of Events, The Solitary Child, Please Turn Over, Watch Your Stern, Raising the Wind, Twice Round the Daffodils, The Iron Maiden, Nurse on Wheels, The Big Job* and *Bless This House*.

Most recently involved as executive producer on *Carry On London*, which at time of writing is currently in pre-production. Rogers has also penned several novels.

ROLLINGS, GORDON
Role: Night Porter in *Doctor*

Gordon Rollings, born in Batley, Yorkshire, in 1926, began his career in radio in Israel before training as a clown with a Paris-based circus.

He started appearing on British screens in the 1960s with television credits including *The Avengers, Dawson's Weekly, Sykes, Danger UXB, Play School* and *Coronation Street*. In films he appeared in, among others, *The Valiant, Rhubarb, The Pink Panther Strikes Again* and *Superman III*.

In later years, Rollings achieved cult status in the popular advertisements for John Smith's Yorkshire bitter.

He died in 1985, aged fifty-eight.

RONAY, EDINA
Role: Dolores in *Cowboy*

Born in 1945, Edina Ronay – daughter of famous culinary expert, Egon Ronay – first appeared on screen in the early 1960s. She was seen in television shows such as *Crane, Riviera Police, Department S* and *Jason King*, as well as films like *The Pure Hell of St Trinian's, The Big Job, A Study in Terror, Night Train to Paris, To Grab the Ring* and her last film, in 1974, *The Swordsman*.

Since leaving the acting profession she's become one of Britain's leading fashion designers.

ROOME, ALFRED
Editor on *Follow That Camel, Doctor, Up The Khyber, Camping, Again Doctor, Up the Jungle, Loving, Henry, At Your Convenience, Matron, Abroad, Girls, Dick* and *Behind*

Many in Alfred Roome's family expected him to follow his father, a general manager at the *Daily Mirror*, into the newspaper industry but he had his sights set on the film world and secured his first post in 1927, working in the property department at Elstree during the days of silent films.

Born in London in 1908, Roome later moved into the cutting room and edited his first title – *Thark, Turkey Time* – in 1933 for Gaumont British. He edited for Herbert Wilcox and Alfred Hitchcock during the 1930s and was resident editor for Gainsborough during the '40s before moving to Pinewood in the '50s.

His countless credits included *My Brother's Keeper, It's Not Cricket, Helter Skelter, Don't Ever Leave Me, Broken Journey, Trio, Holiday Camp, A Tale of Two Cities* and *A Pair of Briefs*.

Soon after editing *Behind*, his final *Carry On*, he retired from the industry. He died in 1997, aged eighty-nine.

ROPER, CHARLIE
Played by Sidney James

Regarded as a layout by his wife, Charlie Roper hasn't done a stroke of work for three years. Seen in *Doctor*, he's a patient in the Fosdick Ward at the Borough County Hospital.

ROPER, MRS
Played by Dandy Nichols

Seen in *Doctor* visiting her husband, Charlie, in the Borough County Hospital. A real moaner who thinks her husband is a loafer because he's been sponging off the state for three years.

ROSEMARY
Played by Patricia Franklin

Augusta Prodworthy's second-in-command at the Fircombe Women's Lib Movement. Her masculine tendencies, including style of dress, often lead to her being mistaken for a man in *Girls*.

ROSENBLAT, BARBARA
Role: ATS Girl in *England*

Born in London, Barbara Rosenblat moved to America as a baby and was brought up in New York. She trained as a teacher-actress at the City College of New York, then toured in various musicals including *Kismet*.

When, in later years, she returned to England to attend a wedding, she decided to stay. After working as a secretary in an electronics factory for a while, she joined the cast for the second national tour of musical *Godspell*, which helped secure her Equity card. Work in radio and on stage and screen soon followed, such as the films *Turtle Diary, Haunted Honeymoon* and *Little Shop of Horrors*, while on television she was seen in, among others, *Tales of the Unexpected*.

She moved back to New York, where she currently resides, in 1987, and continues to act, recently appearing on Broadway; she is also a prolific, award-winning narrator for audio books.

ROSSINGTON, NORMAN
Roles: Herbert Brown in *Sergeant*, Norm in *Nurse* and Referee in *Regardless*
TV: *Christmas* ('72)

Son of a publican, Norman Rossington was born in Liverpool in 1928. He left school at fourteen and held a series of jobs, ranging from messenger to carpenter's apprentice before his interest in acting with a local theatre group led him to the Bristol Old Vic where he completed his training.

He began his career in theatre before encompassing both film and television, most notably as Private Cupcake in the long-running comedy show, *The Army Game*. His film credits included *The League of Gentlemen, Saturday Night and Sunday Morning, The Longest Day, Crooks Anonymous, Go to Blazes, Nurse On Wheels* and *Young Winston*. His television credits ranged from *Hunter's Walk* and *Heartbeat* to *Last of the Summer Wine* and *Spooner's Patch*.

In later years, Rossington was busiest on the West End stage. He died in 1999, aged seventy.

ROSSINI, JAN
Role: Hoopla Girl in *At Your Convenience*
(Note: the scene was cut.)

ROTHWELL, TALBOT
Wrote the screenplay for *Cabby, Jack, Spying* (co-written with Sid Colin), *Cleo, Cowboy, Screaming!, Don't Lose Your Head, Follow That Camel, Doctor, Up The Khyber, Camping, Again Doctor, Up the Jungle, Loving, Henry, At Your Convenience, Matron, Abroad, Girls, Dick*
TV: Wrote *Christmas* ('69), *Christmas* ('72), *Christmas* ('73) and his material was used in *Laughing's Christmas Classics*
STAGE: Co-writer of *London!*

Talbot Rothwell, who scripted the lion's share of the *Carry On* films, was born in Bromley, Kent, in 1916. Upon leaving school he attended art school at Brighton for a year, but began his working life as a clerk at Brighton's town hall. The job lasted three months at which point he joined, in 1936, the Palestine Police, a job he kept for eighteen months before returning home.

During the Second World War he was commissioned as a pilot in the RAF. While based at 224 Coastal Command Squadron in Leuchars, Scotland, he was shot down over Norway and spent the next five years as a prisoner of war in Stalag Luft 3 Air Force Prisoners' Camp.

During his time at the POW camp, he met Peter Butterworth, with whom he would later work on the *Carry On*s, and began writing comedy sketches for camp concerts. At the end of the war, and back on home territory, the Air Ministry, in conjunction with Jack Hylton, staged a show for members of the RAF imprisoned during the war in aid of the Benevolent Fund. Using the cast and material from the camp shows, the concert took place at London's Stoll Theatre in 1945, with Rothwell acting as compère and comedian. Such was the success of the show that it ran for a year before

Talbot Rothwell introduced the *Carry On* films to the world of double-entendres

Rothwell, wishing to pursue a career as a writer, resigned from the Forces.

He began writing for the Crazy Gang and Arthur Askey and, in 1948, saw his first play, *Queen Elizabeth Slept Here*, staged, followed quickly by another, *Once Upon a Crime*. Simultaneously, he was penning material for Michael Howard and Terry-Thomas's radio shows. He later worked for Thomas again, this time writing for his television show, *How Do You View?*, as well as programmes such as Arthur Askey's *Before Your Very Eyes*, *The Ted Ray Show*, *Friends and Neighbours* and *Dear Dotty*.

His early film work included contributing to the Norman Wisdom movie, *One Good Turn*, and *Make Mine A Million*, as well as penning titles including *The Crowded Day*. His great success, however, came when he teamed up with Peter Rogers and Gerald Thomas and scripted twenty *Carry On* films, beginning with *Cabby*. His scripts became increasingly double-

entendre laden which appealed to the millions who flocked to cinemas around the British Isles and abroad to watch his scripts being brought to life by the *Carry On* gang. On the small screen, meanwhile, his greatest success was working with Frankie Howerd on the popular series *Up Pompeii*.

He died in 1981, aged sixty-four.

ROWAN, MRS
Played by Marianne Stone
Elsie Rowan is a customer of Fred Ramsden, the butcher, in *Behind*.

ROWLANDS, PATSY
Roles: Miss Fosdick in *Again Doctor*, Miss Dempsey in *Loving*, Queen in *Henry*, Hortence Withering in *At Your Convenience*, Evelyn Banks in *Matron*, Miss Dobbs in *Abroad*, Mildred Bumble in *Girls*, Mrs Giles in *Dick* and Linda Upmore in *Behind*
TV: *The Nine Old Cobblers*

Such was her screen presence that one could easily have been mistaken for thinking red-haired Patsy Rowlands appeared in all of the *Carry On*s. Surprisingly, she appeared in just nine but what memorable characters she created. Whether it was cameo roles like the waspish travel clerk, Miss Dobbs, in *Abroad* or more substantial characterisations such as the slovenly, cigarette-puffing Mildred Bumble in *Girls*, she quickly became a fans' favourite.

She was born in London in 1934; her parents believed they would further their daughter's chances of employment upon leaving school if she attended elocution lessons. She excelled at the classes and was encouraged by her tutor to apply for a Guildhall School of Speech and Drama scholarship; she sat the exam and came out top in the whole of England, securing her a place at the drama school.

She graduated after three years and went straight into the chorus of a nationwide tour of *Annie Get Your Gun* followed by a summer season at Torquay and her first spell at the Players' Theatre in London, where she met Hattie Jacques. Her association with the Players' was to last for over eight years.

During the early 1960s she appeared in, among other stage shows, the musical *Valmouth* before her big break arrived playing Laurence Olivier's daughter in *Semi-Detached* in London. By now she was also appearing on the screen, with early credits including films such as *Over the Odds*, *On the Fiddle*, *In the Doghouse*, *A Kind of Loving*, *Tom Jones* and *A Stitch in Time*, as well as television programmes *Danger Man*, *Out of the Unknown* and *The Avengers*.

Later credits on the big screen include *Please, Sir!*, *Sammy's Super T-Shirt* and *Tess* while on the small screen she was seen in *Doctor at Large*, *Not On Your Nellie*, *Dawson's Weekly*, *George and Mildred*, *Robin's Nest*, *Peak Practice*, *Tottering Towers* and *Vanity Fair*. But she's best remembered as Betty, the neighbour in *Bless This House*, which saw her cast alongside Sid James.

Throughout her career she continued to work in the theatre, where recent assignments included *Oliver!* at the Palladium, *Into the Woods* at London's Phoenix Theatre and *My Fair Lady* at Drury Lane. She died of cancer in 2005.

ROXBY, MR AND MRS
Played by James Beck and Yutte Stensgaard
The married couple appeared in a scene in *Loving* talking to Mr Snooper at the Citizens' Advice Bureau about their marital problems. **(Note: the scene was cut although the back of Mr Roxby can still be seen as Snooper opens his office door and Sophie Bliss walks in.)**

EXT. MARRIAGE GUIDANCE BUREAU – DAY

SOPHIE, dressed to conquer, approaches and enters the building.

INT. SNOOPER'S OFFICE – DAY.

(SNOOPER, grinning complacently, is at the door, inviting someone to come in.)

SNOOPER: It's all right, you can come in now, Mr Roxby.

(A worried-looking man of about fifty comes in.)

SNOOPER: Do sit down.

(He leads him to a chair beside another in which sits MRS ROXBY, a very pert lush–looking little blonde of about twenty-two. As SNOOPER goes round to his own chair . . .)

SNOOPER: You'll be pleased to hear that I've had a jolly good session with your wife here.

MR ROXBY: You and others.

SNOOPER: I knew if I could get her alone for long enough that I'd get something out of her. In a manner of speaking, of course.

MR ROXBY: Well, it'll have to be good, I can promise you.

MRS ROXBY: See what I mean? He doesn't trust me.

SNOOPER: All right, leave this to me, Mrs Roxby. (Referring to notes.)

Now then, Mr Roxby, it seems that you started to have suspicions about your wife last month when you came home unexpectedly and found her in bed with another man.

MR ROXBY: Well, wouldn't you think it a bit funny?

SNOOPER: Not in the circumstances, no.

MR ROXBY: Eh? What circumstances?

SNOOPER: Well, to re-cap. You went away on a business trip, got through earlier than you expected, and sent your wife a telegram to say you were coming home.

MR ROXBY: Yes, yes.

SNOOPER: But – when you arrived home and went upstairs – there they were.

MR ROXBY: Yes, yes, yes. Well?

SNOOPER: Well, as I told you, I was convinced that if I could talk to her alone, Mrs Roxby would have a satisfactory explanation.

MR ROXBY: Well, what?

SNOOPER: Simple. She didn't get your telegram!

(And sits back, beaming, well satisfied with himself.)

MRS ROXBY: (To MR ROXBY.) You see? It was all your fault.

(MR ROXBY sits there, astounded, hardly able to believe his ears, and unable to find his tongue.)

SNOOPER: Well, I'm glad we got that sorted out. (Getting up.) I expect you'd like to go out for a celebratory lunch or something, eh?

(MRS ROXBY gets up.)

MRS ROXBY: He can if he wants. I've already got a date with someone.

SNOOPER: Come along, Mr Roxby. And next time, take a tip from me, and use a telephone!

(He gets the bewildered MR ROXBY to his feet and steers him towards the door. MR ROXBY suddenly finds his voice.)

MR ROXBY: ust a minute! Whether she'd got my telegram or not has nothing to do with it! She was still with this fellow, wasn't she?

SNOOPER: Ah well, that's another little problem altogether. You'll have to sort that one out for yourself. I can't do everything.

MR ROXBY: I'm afraid this has been a complete waste of time.

SNOOPER: Not at all, Mr Roxby. That's what I'm here for – to waste time. Goodbye, goodbye. (They go out.) And good luck!

ROYAL BIRDWATCHING SOCIETY, THE
Prominent ornithologist Professor Inigo Tinkle gives a lantern slide lecture to the Society in *Up the Jungle*.

ROYAL DOULTON SANITARY POTTERIES
The company provided the toilets seen in *At Your Convenience*.

ROYAL OAK, THE
In *Cabby* the pub is seen in the background when Ted Watson drops off the Man in Tweeds.

ROYAL TAILOR
Played by John Bluthal
In *Henry* the Royal Tailor makes a goat's hair tunic for Henry VIII and is seen at a fitting with the King.

RUBBATITI
Played by Denis Blake
In *Screaming!* Rubbatiti is the mummy Dr Watt has been trying to rejuvenate to no avail; his sister thinks he's been wasting his time because the mummy has been gone too long, but it seems there is still life left in it yet when it chases Olando around the Bide-a-Wee Rest Home.

RUBY ROOM, THE
A wine-tasting session for the Connoisseurs de Londres is held in the Ruby Room. Seen in *Regardless*.

RUFF-DIAMOND, LADY JOAN
Played by Joan Sims
The wife of Sir Sidney, the governor of the northwest province in India, Lady Joan is a little coarse at times, with her manner often being remarked upon by her husband. In *Up The Khyber* she takes a liking to the Khasi of Kalabar and tries winning a place in his heart by giving him a secretly-taken photo showing the British soldiers wearing underpants – affording the Khasi the chance to undermine the British soldiers' authority. Unfortunately her plan fails and she heads back to Sir Sidney, narrowly escaping death; fortunately, he's happy to take her back, perhaps because he's feeling equally guilty after accepting the Khasi's offer of being entertained by his many wives in compensation for losing, temporarily, his own wife.

RUFF-DIAMOND, SIR SIDNEY
Played by Sidney James
The British governor of the northwest province in India, Sir Sidney is seen in *Up The Khyber*; a benevolent ruler, he's married to the coarse Lady Joan and protected by the men of the 3rd Foot and Mouth, known as Devils in Skirts, guarding the Khyber Pass.

RUMPO KID, THE
Played by Sid James
For 'The Rumpo Kid' in *Cowboy* see 'Finger, Johnny'.

RUSSELL, ROBERT
Role: Policeman in *Loving*

RUSSELL, SERGEANT
Played by Ed Devereaux
In *Sergeant*, Russell is in charge of a platoon at Heathercrest National Service Depot.

S

SAGAR, ANTHONY
Roles: Stores Sergeant in *Sergeant*, 1st Ambulance Driver in *Nurse*, Citizen in *Constable*, Bus Conductor in *Regardless*, Cook in *Cruising*, Policeman in *Screaming!*, Man in Hospital in *Loving* (Note: played a heckler in *Henry* but scene cut.)

Anthony Sagar, who was born in Burnley in 1920, enjoyed a busy career. As well as working on the stage, he appeared in television shows such as *Spyder's Web, Doomwatch, Swallows and Amazons, The Avengers, The Plane Makers, Special Branch, Randall and Hopkirk (Deceased)* and *Dad's Army*.

On the big screen he appeared in many films, including playing a coxswain in 1957's *Barnacle Bill,* a Customs official in 1958's *Law and Disorder,* the Sergeant of the Guards in *I Was Monty's Double,* an instructor's assistant in *The Bulldog Breed* and a drunk in *The Loneliness of the Long Distance Runner*.

He died in 1973.

SAGE, CHARLIE
Played by Bob Monkhouse
Poor old Charlie Sage gets called up for National Service on his wedding day in *Sergeant*. A mix-up between father and son, both of whom thought the other was applying for a twenty-eight-day deferment, leaves him no choice but to rush from the reception to Heathercrest National Service Depot. Distraught by her misfortune, his new bride, Mary, joins him unexpectedly at the camp by securing a job at the NAAFI. A confident, popular guy in the billet, we discover that he worked at a factory making Bren guns, which explains his adroitness at reassembling the gun during a training lecture. Completes his ten-week initial training and receives special recommendation to go on and train as an armourer.

SAGE, MARY
Played by Shirley Eaton
In *Sergeant* blonde-haired Mary Sage is dismayed when her wedding day is ruined by news that her husband, Charlie, has been called up for National Service. A mix-up means a deferment application was never made, leaving Charlie no option but to report to Heathercrest National Service Depot. Desperate not to be separated from her hubby, even before they've had the chance to consummate the wedding, Mary steals herself into the camp in the back of a laundry truck and pretends to be a new girl employed to help out in the NAAFI. She later makes the appointment official and works at Heathercrest for the ten weeks of her husband's training.

SAGE, MR
Played by Martin Wyldeck
Seen in the opening scenes of *Sergeant* reading out the telegrams at his son's wedding. Amid all the hectic arrangements, both Mr Sage and his son forgot to apply for a National Service deferment and consequently Charlie is summoned to Heathercrest National Service Depot asap.

SALLY
Played by Liz Fraser
In *Cabby,* Sally works in the canteen at Speedee Taxis Limited. Her whole life revolves around the cab firm because she dates Ted Watson, the company's manager, and is best friends with Peggy Hawkins, the boss's wife.

SALLY
Played by Juliet Mills
Sally is seen in *Jack,* initially working at Dirty Dick's as a barmaid. But she's desperate to reach Spain to try and trace her long-lost childhood sweetheart, Roger, who was pressganged into joining the crew of a ship later taken over by the Spanish. To achieve her objective, when she hears Albert Poop-Decker is joining the ship, she knocks him out, steals his clothes and masquerades as the midshipman. She joins the crew of the frigate *Venus,* leaving Poop-Decker, who's also pressganged into joining the crew as a rating, to spend most of the voyage trying to convince Captain Fearless that he's the real Albert Poop-Decker. She eventually discovers Roger has turned to piracy and is no longer the man she thought she knew, even though he was only thirteen at the time. She ends up falling in love with none other than Albert.

SALLY
Played by Lisa Thomas
One of the saloon girls seen at Rumpo's Place in *Cowboy*.

SALLY
Played by Trisha Noble
The attractive Sally is seen in *Camping*. She's one of the girls from Chayste Place, a finishing school run by Dr Soaper and Miss Haggerd, and spends a few nights under canvas at the Paradise Camp Site in Devon.

SALLY
Played by Georgina Moon
A local girl who attends the cabaret evening at the Riverside Caravan Site in *Behind*. She's accompanied by her friend, Maureen, and ends up chatting to Fred and Ernie.

SALLY G-STRING
Played by Gilly Grant
Appears in the film, *Nudist Paradise,* which is showing at the Picture Playhouse in *Camping*. A busty blonde, Sally is one of the film's main characters who finds her convent-based education has left her rather shy about exposing herself to fellow campers.

SALOME BATH BUBBLES
In *Regardless,* Lily Duveen demonstrates Salome Bath Bubbles at the Ideal House Exhibition.

SAM
Played by Harry Locke
An ambulance man in *Doctor*. He's employed by the Borough County Hospital and works alongside his colleague, Henry, whose erratic driving is to blame for Francis Bigger's abrupt arrival at the hospital, crashing through the entrance doors after flying out of the back of the ambulance.

CARRY ON SCREAMING!

An Anglo Amalgamated film
A Peter Rogers production
Distributed through Warner-Pathe Distribution Ltd
Song: 'Carry On Screaming' by Myles Rudge and Ted Dick
Sung by Anon
Released as an A certificate in 1966 in colour
Running time: 97 mins

CAST

Harry H. Corbett	Detective Sergeant Sidney Bung
Kenneth Williams	Doctor Olando Watt
Jim Dale	Albert Potter
Charles Hawtrey	Dan Dann
Joan Sims	Emily Bung
Fenella Fielding	Virula Watt
Peter Butterworth	Detective Constable Slobotham
Bernard Bresslaw	Sockett
Angela Douglas	Doris Mann
Jon Pertwee	Dr Fettle
Tom Clegg	Odbodd
Billy Cornelius	Odbodd Junior
Norman Mitchell	Cabby
Michael Ward	Vivian (Window Dresser)
Frank Thornton	Mr Jones (Shop Manager)
Frank Forsyth	Desk Sergeant
Anthony Sagar	Policeman
Sally Douglas	Girl
Marianne Stone	Mrs Parker
Denis Blake	Rubbatiti

PRODUCTION TEAM

Screenplay by Talbot Rothwell
Music composed and conducted by Eric Rogers
Associate Producer: Frank Bevis
Art Director: Bert Davey
Director of Photography: Alan Hume
Editor: Rod Keys
Camera Operator: Godfrey Godar
Assistant Director: Peter Bolton
Sound Editor: Arthur Ridout
Sound Recordists: C.C. Stevens and Ken Barker
Make-up: Geoffrey Rodway
Unit Manager: Ron Jackson
Hairdresser: Stella Rivers
Costume Designer: Emma Selby-Walker
Continuity: Penny Daniels
Producer: Peter Rogers
Director: Gerald Thomas

Doctor Watt (Kenneth Williams) gets an unexpected charge

The Watts (Fenella Fielding and Kenneth Williams) aren't too pleased with their latest catch

With the investigation getting nowhere, Bung decides the only way to catch the criminal is to provide some bait in the shape of a woman, or to be precise, DC Slobotham disguised as a woman. When Bung and Slotbotham, dressed in women's clothes, are spotted together by Mrs Bung, who has suspected her husband of having an affair for some time, she decides to follow them into Hocombe Woods, where she's abducted, too.

When the monster's prints lead them, once again, to Bide-a-Wee Rest Home, Sidney Bung insists they stay the night to protect Virula; little do they know that it's just the beginning of many strange goings-on, including Mrs Bung being turned into a dummy and Rubbatiti coming alive and chasing Doctor Watt into the vats.

By the end of the adventure, though, Albert and a revived Doris are married but Sidney Bung has opted for a new model. Deciding he much prefers his old, nagging wife as a dummy, he opts for a life with Virula Watt instead.

While Albert Potter and Doris Mann, a courting couple, are canoodling in Hocombe Woods, Doris hears a noise. When Albert goes off to look around, a monster whisks Doris away, but loses one of his fingers in the process. Albert rushes to the police and discovers Doris is the sixth person to disappear from the same spot that year.

Detective Sergeant Sidney Bung, his subordinate, Detective Constable Slobotham, and Albert head to the scene of the crime to investigate. They stumble across a house, deep in the woods, called Bide-a-Wee Rest Home and decide to knock on the door. Their call is answered by Sockett, a butler looking like death warmed up, who claims the owner of the house has been dead fifteen years before suggesting he might be available to meet the visitors. In the bowels of the house, Doctor Olando Watt is receiving some extra electrical charge and is annoyed at being interrupted by his sister, Virula Watt; insufficiently charged, he has to break off his conversation with the policemen and Albert to ask them to plug him in because he needs further regeneration, causing the visitors to flee, scared out of their wits.

At the police laboratory, meanwhile, Dr Fettle is examining the severed finger found in the woods; when he sends some electric current through the digit he ends up making another monster who repays his creator by killing him before escaping into the night. Someone else undergoing a metamorphosis is Doris, who's turned into a mannequin by the Watts and taken to Bourne and Jones, a milliner's shop.

As the newly-formed monster returns home, much to the delight of the Watts, Detective Sergeant Bung arrives on the scene, too, and soon finds himself smitten by the mysterious charms of Virula.

Albert, increasingly frustrated with the lack of progress in the hunt for Doris, notices the shop-window dummy, but the police find it hard to believe that his beloved is one of the mannequins. Sidney Bung, by now besotted with Virula, returns to the Watts's house and notices a 'Made in England' sticker similar to that found on the dummy Albert insisted was actually Doris; suitably worried, Virula drugs the policeman's drink and he turns into a monster, and is sent off to the milliner's shop to retrieve the dummy. By the time he recovers from his ordeal, Bung can't remember anything of the incident.

Funny Scene!

Detective Sergeant Sidney Bung is getting dressed because he has to go to the police station. He rolls his wife, Emily, over in the bed because she's lying on his trousers.

```
SIDNEY:  I'll say this for you, you make a very good
         trouser press.
EMILY:   You're not going out?
SIDNEY:  No, I'm putting these on to take a bath.
EMILY:   And where do you think you're going at
         this time of night?
SIDNEY:  To find another woman.
EMILY:   Don't lie to me, you're going to that
         wretched police station of yours, I know.
SIDNEY:  Uh, you've caught me out.
EMILY:   You haven't any time for me, let alone any
         other woman.
SIDNEY:  I wouldn't bet on that.
EMILY:   Police, police, police, that's all you ever
         think about; never mind about me, oh dear
         no, do you realise you haven't taken me out
         for years?
SIDNEY:  Don't exaggerate, we went out a couple of
         months ago — had a lovely time.
EMILY:   Do you call that lovely, to my poor, dear
         mother's funeral?
SIDNEY:  Well I enjoyed it.
```

SANDRA

Played by Carol Hawkins

In *Behind* she arrives at the Riverside Caravan Site by bike with her friend, Carol. They hoped to camp at the site but are disappointed to find it only allows caravans, that is until she shows a bit of leg to the owner, Major Leep, and suggests she might need a massage later to aid her aching thigh; the sight of flesh leaves the Major drooling and he bends the rules to accommodate the girls; others who take a fancy to Sandra and her mate include Fred and Ernie, two middle-aged men enjoying a short break away from their wives, and students from the University of Kidburn helping Professor Crump with his archaeological dig.

SANTA CECILIA'S ELIXIR

In *Abroad* the tourists head off on an excursion to a local village where a trader is selling a love potion, 'liquera por l'amoura'. It's powerful stuff, so when several members of the group buy a bottle and pour it into the punch at the following day's farewell party at the Elsbels Palace Hotel, it certainly gets the party going.

SARGE

Played by Cyril Chamberlain

Sarge is seen in *Cabby* working as the radio operator at Speedee Taxis Limited.

SCAIFE, TED

Director of Photography on *Constable*

Born in London in 1912, Ted Scaife began working at Gainsborough's sound department in the 1930s, followed by several years with Technicolor Limited. As a cinematographer, he worked on many pictures, including *Outcast of the Islands*, *The Ringer*, *An Inspector Calls*, *The Constant Husband*, *Please Turn Over*, *633 Squadron* and *The Water Babies*.

He died in 1994, aged eighty-two.

SCHILLER, STEPHANIE

Role: New Nurse in *Nurse*

SCHWINDLEHOFFER, PROFESSOR

An unseen character mentioned by Professor Crump during his lecture, 'Getting to the Bottom of Things', in *Behind*. He trained Amelia Fosdyke who was supposed to have appeared in a film Crump was showing. Unfortunately the film he intended to show was accidentally switched with another, not that the audience seem to mind because it shows a woman stripping!

SCOTT, ANNE

Roles: Harem Girl in *Follow That Camel* and Khasi's Wife in *Up The Khyber*

Anne Scott's other credits during the 1960s include playing Beatrice in *Sons and Lovers* and, a year later in 1961, Margo in *Jungle Street*.

SCOTT, STEVEN

Role: Burpa Guard in *Up The Khyber*

Steven Scott's other film credits include *Make Mine Mink*, *Sammy Going South* and *That Riviera Touch*, while on television he was seen in isolated episodes of shows such as *Ivanhoe*, *The Avengers*, *Doctor Who* and *The Jazz Age*.

SCOTT, TERRY

Roles: Sergeant Paddy O'Brien in *Sergeant*, Sergeant Major MacNutt in *Up The Khyber*, Peter Potter in *Camping*, Cecil the Jungle Boy in *Up the Jungle*, Terence Philpot in *Loving*, Cardinal Wolsey in *Henry* and Dr Prodd in *Matron*. (Note: also cast as Mr Allcock, general secretary of the union in *At Your Convenience*, but scene cut.)
TV: *Christmas* ('69 and '70)

One of Britain's best-loved comedians, Terry Scott, who was born in 1927, enjoyed five decades in the industry, entertaining on stage, screen and radio, but for most people he's best remembered for the years spent in the BBC sitcom, *Terry and June*.

He grew up in Watford and wanted to act from an early age, but after persuasion by his parents delayed entering his chosen profession to spend two years in an accountancy office, before serving in the Royal Navy during the war. After demob, he determined to make acting his living and worked, initially, as a stage manager before turning to acting in rep at Grange-over-Sands in Cumbria.

Eventually offers to appear on television and radio came his way and, in 1955, he starred alongside Bill Maynard in *Great Scott – It's Maynard!*, which ran to three series. The early 1960s were dominated by *Hugh and I*, a successful BBC sitcom which saw Scott partnering Hugh Lloyd for seven series. By the 1970s he was fronting his own show, *Scott On . . .* where he was joined regularly by June Whitfield, who played his argumentative wife in many sketches. Soon after they were reunited in *Happy After Ever*, the precursor to the long-running *Terry and June*.

In the medium of film his credits included *Too Many Crooks*, *The Bridal Path*, *Mary Had A Little*, *A Pair of Briefs*, *Doctor in Clover*, *Ghost of a Chance* and *Bless This House*.

He died of cancer in 1994, aged sixty-seven.

SCRAWNY MAN

Played by George Moon

Works for Josh Fiddler at the Paradise Camp Site. He's seen in *Camping* nailing a letter 'p' to a board at the site's entrance. Enters into a brief conversation with Sid Boggle.

Peter Potter (Terry Scott) spending yet another holiday under canvas (*Camping*)

SCREAMING!, CARRY ON
See feature box on pages 216–7.

SCREWER, GLADSTONE
Played by Sidney James

The orderly at the Moore Medical Mission, Gladstone Screwer appears in *Again Doctor*. His father was a missionary who travelled to the Beatific Islands, where Gladstone was born. He has five wives, appropriately named Monday through to Friday, giving him two days off a week from his marital duties – that is until Miss Fosdick, Mr Carver's secretary, becomes Saturday after visiting and staying on after Carver heads for home.

His greatest claim to fame is inventing a serum which reduces fat at an incredible speed; when Dr Nookey, who was employed for a time as the mission's doctor, spots the potential back home, Gladstone is happy to accept payment in cigarettes, the normal form of currency on the islands. When he realises, however, that Nookey is making a fortune out of his serum, he returns to Britain to claim his rightful share of the proceeds, eventually becoming a partner in the Moore-Nookey-Gladstone-Carver Clinic.

SCRUB, MISTRESS
Played by Marjie Lawrence

For 'Mistress Scrub' in *Henry*, see 'Serving Maid'.

SCRUBBA
Played by Shakira Baksh

First seen in *Again Doctor* as an overweight native of the Beatific Islands; on the islands a woman's attractiveness is judged by her size, so the bigger the better as far as the men of these far-flung specks of land are concerned. Gladstone Screwer introduces her to Dr Nookey, who's arrived to take up the post of doctor at the Moore Medical Mission, as a way of cheering him up; when it has little effect and Nookey shows Screwer a photo of Goldie Locks, Gladstone prescribes her some of his magic serum which has the weight dropping off in days.

SEALORD, 1st
Played by Cecil Parker

In *Jack* it's a reluctant First Sealord who interviews Albert Poop-Decker and tells him he's being given the role of midshipman on the frigate *Venus*, although he still hasn't passed out at the naval academy, after eight and a half years.

SEALORDS 2nd and 3rd
Played by Frank Forsyth and John Brooking respectively

Seen in *Jack* at the meeting where Captain Fearless is promoted to the rank of admiral and given a desk job, which pleases him because he suffers from seasickness. Poop-Decker and Sweetley, meanwhile, rise to the post of honorary captain.

SECOND
Played by Eric Boon

Sometimes credited as 'Young Man', the Second attends the boxing match between Dynamite Dan and Massive Micky McGee in *Regardless*.

SECOND
Played by Joe Cornelius

Seen in the ring with Gripper Burke during a training fight in *Loving*. Looks like he's a relieved man when Gripper has to break to take a phone call.

SEDDON, JACK
Co-wrote the screenplay for *England*

Born in Farnworth, Lancashire, in 1924, Jack Seddon completed his education in Manchester and began his career as a regional journalist during the late 1940s before moving on to the nationals.

Noticing an advert for a job in Rank's publicity department, based in London, he was successful in securing the job. He subsequently met David Pursall and began working with him controlling production publicity at Pinewood Studios.

Eventually deciding to form a writing partnership, Seddon and Pursall ditched their jobs in publicity to write many popular films and television shows. Among the productions they worked on are *The Secret Partner*, *The Longest Day*, *Kill or Cure*, *Village of Daughters*, *Murder Ahoy*, *Murder Most Foul* and *Tomorrow Never Comes*, while on television, *Arthur of the Britons* and *Oil Strike North*.

He died in 2001, aged seventy-seven.

SELBY-WALKER, EMMA
Costume Designer on *Screaming!*, *Don't Lose Your Head*, *Follow That Camel* and *Up The Khyber*

Other films she's worked on as costume designer include 1962's *Corridors of Blood* and Norman Wisdom's 1965 comedy, *The Early Bird*.

SENECA
Played by Charles Hawtrey

Seneca, the father of Caesar's wife, Calpurnia, appears in *Cleo*. He's prone to the occasional premonition, which are always dismissed by Caesar who regards him as a fool. Perhaps Caesar should have taken him seriously, though, because one of the visions showed Caesar's life in danger.

SENECA'S SERVANT
Played by Thelma Taylor

Seen in *Cleo*, Seneca's Servant is an attractive blonde.

SENNA
Hengist Pod's square-wheeled vehicle named after his wife. Seen in *Cleo* the fragile contraption crumples when he crashes into a milestone en route to Carlisle.

SENT-OFF FOOTBALLER
Played by Nick White

Seen in Emmannuelle Prevert's flashback sequence in which she describes her most amorous experience. Appears in *Emmannuelle*.

SENTRY
Played by Malcolm Johns

The soldier is standing guard and doesn't even bat an eyelid when the sexy Emmannuelle begins stripping in front of him during *Emmannuelle*. She eventually gives up and returns to her chauffeur-driven car only to see the sentry wink when a gay man wanders by.

SERGEANT
Played by David Davenport

In *Don't Lose Your Head* the Sergeant climbs into a carriage with Jacqueline, who's been taken prisoner, to be whisked away to a secret place of detention – just as Sir Rodney, Lord Darcy and Duc de Pommfrit arrive in Paris to attempt a rescue.

SERGEANT, CARRY ON
See feature box on pages 220–1.

SERGEANT MAJOR
Played by Victor Maddern

Mark Antony's number two in *Cleo*, the Sergeant Major is a key member of the Roman army which attempts to conquer the world.

SERVING MAID
Played by Marjie Lawrence

The serving maid, who's called Mistress Scrub, is seen in *Henry* serving Thomas Cromwell and Cardinal Wolsey when they toast the King and his new wife. The randy Cardinal can't keep his eyes off the voluptuous blonde – nor his hands, for that matter, and ends up pinching her bottom.

SEX TECHNIQUES
A book Sir Bernard Cutting consults during *Matron* when in his pursuit to find a woman to help release his pent-up frustration and prove to himself that he's a man.

SHACKLOCK, HARRY
Role: Lavatory Attendant in *Loving*

During the 1960s and '70s, Harry Shacklock was seen in various television shows, including *The Avengers*, *Z Cars*, *Callan* and *Cluff*, but he's best remembered as Mr Wimberley in several episodes of the *Doctor* series.

SHAFEEK, DINO
Role: Immigration Officer in *Emmannuelle*

Born in Dhaka, Bangladesh, in 1930, Dino Shafeek studied at the city's university before arriving in the UK on the SS *Ranchro* and training at the Guildhall School of Music and Drama.

On screen since the 1960s, Shafeek, who possessed a trained singing voice and who

CARRY ON SERGEANT

Nat Cohen and Stuart Levy present a Peter Rogers production
Distributed by Anglo Amalgamated Film Distributors Ltd
Based on a story, The Bull Boys, by R. F. Delderfield
Released as a U certificate in 1958 in black & white
Running time: 83 mins

CAST

William Hartnell	Sergeant Grimshaw
Bob Monkhouse	Charlie Sage
Shirley Eaton	Mary Sage
Eric Barker	Captain Potts
Dora Bryan	Norah
Bill Owen	Corporal Bill Copping
Charles Hawtrey	Peter Golightly
Kenneth Connor	Horace Strong
Kenneth Williams	James Bailey
Terence Longdon	Miles Heywood
Norman Rossington	Herbert Brown
Gerald Campion	Andy Galloway
Hattie Jacques	Captain Clark
Cyril Chamberlain	Gun Sergeant
Ian Whittaker	Medical Corporal
Gordon Tanner	1st Specialist
Frank Forsyth	2nd Specialist
Basil Dignam	3rd Specialist
John Gatrell	4th Specialist
Arnold Diamond	5th Specialist
Martin Boddey	6th Specialist
Anthony Sagar	Stores Sergeant
Alec Bregonzi	1st Storeman
Graham Stewart	2nd Storeman
Alexander Harris	3rd Storeman
Pat Feeney	4th Storeman
Edward Judd	5th Storeman
Ronald Clarke	6th Storeman
David Williams	7th Storeman
Terry Scott	Sergeant Paddy O'Brien
John Mathews	Sergeant Mathews
Edward Devereaux	Sergeant Russell
Leigh Madison	Sheila
Bernard Kay	Injured Recruit

The following actors appeared as Recruits:

Jack Smethurst
Haydn Ward
Brian Jackson
Graydon Gould
Don McCorkindale
Jeremy Dempster
Leon Eagles
Terry Dickenson
Malcolm Webster
Henry Livings
Patrick Durkin
Derek Martinus
James Villiers
Michael Hunt

PRODUCTION TEAM

Screenplay by Norman Hudis
Additional material by John Antrobus
Music composed and directed by Bruce
    Montgomery
Played by the Band of the Coldstream
    Guards
Director of Photography: Peter Hennessy
Art Director: Alex Vetchinsky
Production Manager: Frank Bevis
Editor: Peter Boita
Camera Operator: Alan Hume
Assistant Director: Geoffrey Haine
Sound Editor: Seymour Logie
Sound Recordists: Robert T. MacPhee and
    Gordon K. McCallum
Continuity: Joan Davis
Make-up: Geoffrey Rodway
Hairdressing: Stella Rivers
Dress Designer: Joan Ellacott
Casting Director: Betty White
Set Dresser: Peter Murton
Titles by Pentagon Film Titles Ltd
Produced by Peter Rogers
Directed by Gerald Thomas

Horace Strong (Kenneth Connor) tries to cheer up a glum-looking Charlie Sage (Bob Monkhouse)

Captain Potts (Eric Barker) is unimpressed with Able Platoon

that prized accolade. He agrees to a £50 bet with other training sergeants but is soon regretting the decision when he sets eyes on the rag-bag collection of men he's responsible for during the coming weeks. With this being his last attempt at success, Grimshaw tells his corporal, Bill Copping, that he's going to try a different tack: to curb his temper and treat them with kid gloves.

On the matrimonial front, Mary Sage manages to steal herself into the camp via a laundry van and pretends to be a new employee at the NAAFI. Needing to make arrangements official, when Sage is finally given some compassionate leave in order to enjoy a honeymoon, they visit the local labour exchange and arrange an official post for Mary, assisting the eccentric Norah at the canteen.

The training goes from bad to worse: while Horace Strong is a regular at the sick bay, the others see their platoon's results slip to rock bottom, with Captain Potts classing them as the worst he's ever seen at Heathercrest. But the tide is about to turn: when dimwit Herbert Brown overhears Grimshaw and Copping conversing about the sergeant's imminent retirement and his wish to have waved goodbye to his military career with the champion platoon, he tells the rest of the men; believing that Grimshaw's experimental approach deserves reward, they decide that they'll pull out all the stops to be crowned top platoon – but they had forgotten about Horace, who's bound to let the side down. But when he walks into the barracks a changed man, no one can believe their eyes. After he had reported sick virtually every day, Captain Clark, running the sick bay, had reached the end of her tether when she decided to refer Horace to a team of experts. During a word-association test, his deep-rooted love for Norah is revealed.

At the following day's exercises, Able Platoon score top marks and pass out as the champions, much to the delight of their retiring sergeant.

The dampers are put on Charlie Sage's wedding reception when one of the telegrams his father reads out is none other than his call-up papers. A mix-up between father and son means no one applied for a twenty-eight-day deferment and there is no alternative but for Charlie to catch the next train to Heathercrest National Service Depot.

Joining him for the ten-week introductory course is a bunch of oddballs, including the world's leading hypochondriac, Horace Strong, the effete Peter Golightly and the educated snob, James Bailey – all part of Able Platoon. Assigned the unenviable task of trying to lick them into shape is Sergeant Grimshaw, a veteran soldier who's never enjoyed a champion platoon during his six years at the depot. With this being his final intake before retirement, he'd love to walk back into civvy street with the memory that his final stint at Heathercrest saw him win

Funny Scene!

Charlie Sage shares a train compartment with the world's worst hypochondriac, Horace Strong. Feeling hot, Sage loosens his tie and walks over to open a window.

STRONG: (Jumping up in shock, shouting.) Please, please, the draught.

SAGE: But it's stifling in here.

STRONG: Please, my eardrums are very thin, very weak. The least suspicion of a draught and I'm finished.
(Sage shuts the window and sits down.)

STRONG: (Rubbing his ear.) Cor! Thanks, mate.
(Sage prepares to light a cigarette.)

STRONG: (Spotting Sage, he leaps from his seat.) Ah, don't!

SAGE: Now what?

STRONG: Please, do you mind not smoking? It affects me — I've got a weak stomach.

SAGE: (Smiling.) Now, look here . . .

STRONG: (Offering him an alternative.) Have a catarrh pastel.

SAGE: I haven't got catarrh.

STRONG: (Swallowing a few.) You don't know you're living, mate.

SAGE: You going to hospital?

STRONG: Into the army.

SAGE: The army?

STRONG: Yeah.

SAGE: Huh. (Looks shocked.) So am I. How did you pass the medical — influence?

STRONG: Medical? Huh. A farce, a criminal farce. A1 — me! A flaming 1. Army doctors, huh. I'll tell you, mate. Two of everything you should have two of and you're in.

worked as an electrician with various drama groups during the early part of his career, clocked up plenty of small-screen credits in shows such as *The Troubleshooters*, *The Jazz Age*, *Softly Softly*, *Hazell*, *Minder* and, arguably his most famous roles, playing Char Wallah Muhammed in Perry and Croft's sitcom, *It Ain't Half Hot, Mum*, and Ali Nadim in three series of *Mind Your Language*.

On the big screen, his credits include *The Long Duel*; *The Charge of the Light Brigade*; *Stand Up, Virgin Soldiers* and, in 1983, *High Road to China*.

He died of a heart attack in 1984.

SHAMPAN, JACK
Role: Art Director on *Jack* and *Emmannuelle*
London-born Jack Shampan, who was born in 1913, trained at St Martin's School of Art and worked as an architect for Parson's Paint in London before the outbreak of the Second World War. He served as an officer in the fire service during the war, nearly losing his life in the East End of London during the Blitz.

Returning to civvy street he worked as an architect before securing an opportunity to enter the film industry in the mid-1940s. By the 1960s he was working as an art director on films such as *Circus of Horrors*, *Payroll*, *Live It Up*, *Cuckoo Patrol*, *White Cargo*, *The Ghoul* and, latterly, *Yellowbeard* in 1983. His television work includes the 1960s series, *The Prisoner*. Subsequently worked on commercials.

He retired from the film industry in the mid-1980s and died in 1989, aged seventy-six.

SHAPELY MISS
Played by Jill Mai Meredith
Seen briefly in *Cruising* the curvaceous beauty strolls by the table-tennis table while Leonard Marjoribanks, who accidentally whacks her bottom with his bat, is playing a game with Bridget Madderley.

SHAPELY NURSE
Played by Lindsay March
This shapely blonde is a nurse at the Finisham Maternity Hospital. In *Matron* she's seen in her underwear in the nurses' quarters shouting down the stairs to her friend, Madge, about helping with her hair.

SHARPE, GUNNER
Played by Peter Quince
Based at the experimental 1313 anti-aircraft battery featured in *England*, he's one of the shirkers who suffers a severe shock to the system when the tough-speaking Captain Melly is put in charge of the unit.

SHAW, DENIS
Role: 2nd Sinister Passenger in *Regardless*
A busy character actor, Denis Shaw was born in London in 1921. He became a screen regular from the 1950s, although he'd made his debut earlier. His film credits include *The Long Memory*, *The Colditz Story*, *Passport to Shame*, *The Night We Dropped A Clanger*, *Trouble with Eve*, *The Runaway* and his last film, *The File of the Golden Goose*.

His television work includes appearances in *The Vise*, *Stryker of the Yard*, *International Detective*, *Outbreak of Murder* and *The Prisoner*.

He died in 1971, aged forty-nine.

SHAW, GUNNER
Played by Larry Dann
Based at the experimental 1313 anti-aircraft battery featured in *England*, he's one of the shirkers who suffers a severe shock to the system when the tough-speaking Captain Melly is put in charge of the unit.

SHAW, RICHARD
Role: Captain of Soldiers in *Don't Lose Your Head*
Born in London in 1918, Richard Shaw began his career as a dancer, forming his own act and performing on cruise ships and in cabaret before the Second World War. After serving in the army during hostilities, he resumed his career in the entertainment world, deciding to focus on acting instead of dance.

He worked as an assistant stage manager at Altrincham Rep for a year before turning his attention to stunt work. Before long he was being offered acting parts, including his first, Lieutenant Bowman Hall in 1945's *The Caribbean Mystery*, while working in America. He went on to appear in over fifty more pictures, including *Hidden Homicide*, *West of Suez*, *Man From Tangier*, *The Safecracker*, *First Man Into Space*, *Partners in Crime* and *633 Squadron*.

His television work includes shows such as *Quatermass and the Pit*, *Crossroads*, *The Sandbaggers*, *Steptoe and Son*, *Robin's Nest*, *Matlock*, *Coronation Street* and various roles in *Dixon of Dock Green*.

During the mid-1980s he formed a production company, Bright Rose Productions, with director Paul Bernard and was just about to film their major picture, *Tragic Victory*, in Bulgaria when Bernard died.

He retired from the acting profession in 1988.

SHAW, SUSAN
Role: Jane Bishop in *Nurse*
Born in West Norwood, London, in 1929, Susan Shaw, graduated from the Rank 'Charm School' of the 1940s and was working on stage from her teenage years. First seen on screen as an extra in 1946's *London Town*, her other credits include *Jassy*, *My Brother's Keeper*, *London Belongs to Me*, *Quartet*, *Pool of London*, *The Diplomatic Corpse*, as well as *Here Come the Huggetts* and *The Huggetts Abroad*, playing Susan Huggett. Her last film was *Stranglehold* in 1962.

In later years she fell on hard times and died penniless in 1978, aged forty-nine.

SHEILA
Played by Leigh Madison
In *Sergeant*, Miles Haywood's girlfriend drops him off at Heathercrest National Service Depot in her sports car.

SHELLEY, CAROL
Roles: Helen Delling in *Regardless* and Dumb Driver in *Cabby*
Despite being born in London in 1939, Carol Shelley has spent almost her entire career in America. A prominent performer in many Broadway productions, she made her debut playing Gwendolyn Pigeon in *The Odd Couple*, a role she reprised in the 1968 film version and, later, in the television series.

In addition to an incredibly busy stage career – which in the UK included shows such as *The Art of Living*, *New Cranks* and *Boeing, Boeing* – RADA-trained Carol Shelley has appeared in television and films. Her small-screen credits range from *The Avengers* to *Frasier*, while her big-screen credits include *It's Great To Be Young*, *The Cool Mikado*, *The Boston Strangler* and *Quiz Show*.

SHERRIFF, BETTY
Hairdresser on *Emmannuelle*
Working in films as a hair stylist since the 1950s, her many credits include *The Late Edwina Black*, *Street of Shadows*, *Passport to Treason*, *Blue Murder at St Trinian's*, *Strongroom*, *The Three Lives of Thomasina*, *Man About the House* and, in 1985, *Murder Elite*.

SHIP'S OFFICER
Played by Vincent Ball
Seen in *Follow That Camel* popping in to Lady Jane Ponsonby's cabin to check her porthole while she's crossing the channel; he ends up drawing the curtains and having his wicked way with her.

SHIRLEY, JOHN
Editor on *Nurse*, *Teacher*, *Constable*, *Regardless* and *Cruising*
Born in Shepherd's Bush, London, in 1922, John Shirley spent a year in an architect's office before being offered a job by Gainsborough as assistant editor at Lime Grove. He moved on to Denham Studios before the war interrupted his career. After serving in the Royal Air Force as a pilot, he returned to civvy street and straight back into the film industry with the Lewis Gilbert-directed picture, *Little Ballerina*, in 1948.

Shirley worked for many major studios and his list of film credits include *Up in the World*, *Chitty Chitty Bang Bang*, *Live and Let Die*,

Superman IV, *Please Turn Over* and *Raising the Wind*, both produced and directed by Peter Rogers and Gerald Thomas respectively. His last assignments before retiring in the early 1990s were *Jekyll and Hyde*, *Voice of the Heat* and *To Be the Best*.

SHOP ASSISTANT
Played by Ian Whittaker (**Note: the line was cut.**)

When Sam Twist in *Regardless* is desperate for a cigarette, just hours after taking the pledge, he runs maniacally to the local shop and buys a packet without waiting for his change. The Shop Assistant ambles out, clutching a ten-shilling note, saying: 'Sir, sir, your change.'

SHOP ASSISTANT, 1ST
Played by Mary Law

An employee of F.H. Rowse, a department store seen in *Constable*, the Shop Assistant asks PC Benson and PC Gorse, who are disguised as women in an attempt to catch shoplifters, if they need any help. She then becomes suspicious and contacts management.

SHORT
Played by Simon Cain

One of the Rumpo Kid's men in *Cowboy* who run Stodge City to their own game plan.

SHORT, MISS GRACE
Played by Hattie Jacques

The maths teacher at Maudlin Street Secondary Modern School, she's seen in *Teacher*. A tough disciplinarian, she believes the only answer in dealing with disruptive schoolchildren is to reach for the cane, something she doesn't think Mr Wakefield, the acting head, does enough.

SHORTHOUSE, GUNNER
Played by Melvyn Hayes

Based at the experimental 1313 anti-aircraft battery featured in *England*, he's one of the shirkers who suffers a severe shock to the system when the tough-speaking Captain Melly is placed in charge of the unit.

SHORTHOUSE, MAJOR
Played by Julian Holloway

Seen in *Up The Khyber*, Major Shorthouse reports directly to Sir Sidney Ruff-Diamond, the British governor in the northwest province of India. A member of the 3rd Foot and Mouth Regiment.

SHORT-SIGHTED MAN
Played by Stanley McGeagh

Seen in the audience at Professor Crump's lecture and film show in *Behind*. He's quick to put his glasses on for a better view when the film Crump was supposed to have shown has been swapped and instead features not an archaeological dig but a female stripper!

SHORTY
Played by Eric Boon

In *Constable* he's one of the thieves involved in the wages snatch.

SHUFFLING PATIENT
Played by Peter Butterworth

A patient at Long Hampton Hospital who becomes the focus of Dr Nookey and his medical colleague Henry's game of diagnosis in *Again Doctor*. Both diagnose incorrectly and are embarrassed when the patient tells them that the reason he was walking so oddly was because he expected to break wind.

SHUTE, VALERIE
Roles: Pat in *Camping*, Nurse in *Again Doctor*, Girl Lover in *Loving*, Maid in *Henry* (**Note: scene cut from film.**) and Miss Smethurst in *Matron*

Born in London in 1945, Valerie Shute left grammar school at fifteen and enrolled at the Aida Foster drama school. After graduating in the mid-1960s, she made her professional stage debut in a production of *Salad Days* at Clacton, followed by various stints in rep.

In between acting jobs she subsidised her income by working in various capacities, including clerical work at a hospital. Most of her acting assignments were in the theatre, but other screen credits include appearances in the 1971 film *Assault* and television shows such as *The Fenn Street Gang*, *Secret Army* and *Emmerdale Farm*, playing teacher Sarah James.

Disillusioned with the acting profession by the 1980s, Shute – whose father worked in film advertising for Warner Brothers – retired from the industry and concentrated on writing. She's since written for children's comics and annuals, and has seen one of her children's musicals performed in her local theatre.

SIDI-BEL-ABBES
A Saharan town in *Follow That Camel* where Captain Le Pice heads with wounded Foreign Legion soldiers to secure reinforcements. It's also where the Foreign Legion's headquarters are found – eventually – by Bo West.

SILHOUETTE
The company who supplied the beachwear for Liz Fraser and Dilys Laye in *Cruising*.

SILVERS, PHIL
Role: Sergeant Ernie Nocker in *Follow That Camel*

Forever remembered for playing Sergeant Bilko, the fast-talking army sergeant on American television during the 1950s, Phil Silvers' career suffered, somewhat, by the inevitable typecasting that followed the worldwide success of his comic creation.

Born in New York in 1912, Silvers was appearing in vaudeville by the age of thirteen before becoming a nightclub comedian and

touring with the renowned Minsky's burlesque troupe. He enjoyed several successes on Broadway, such as *High Button Shoes* in 1948, *Top Banana* in 1951 and *Do-Re-Mi* in 1961.

He appeared in many films, including *Tom, Dick and Harry*, *The Penalty* and *The Wild Man of Borneo* during the 1940s, and *Summer Stock* and *Lucky Me* in the '50s. He was making occasional screen appearances through until the early 1980s.

He died in 1985, aged seventy-three.

SIMKINS, DESMOND
Played by Kenneth Williams

In charge of the trainee agents despatched to Vienna, then Algiers, to retrieve a stolen formula. Seen in *Spying*, the incompetent Simkins, whose code name is Red Admiral, surprises everyone, particularly his bosses, when he brings the members of S.T.E.N.C.H. to book, but it's not long before his actions see everything go up with a bang.

SIMMONS
Played by Julian Holloway

In charge of X-rays at the Borough County Hospital, this former portrait photographer is on duty when Francis Bigger arrives for X-rays of his bruised back, only to be shaken up when the machine explodes. Seen in *Doctor*.

SIMPSON
Played by Peter Butterworth

Bertram West's loyal butler in *Follow That Camel*. He's so dedicated to his employer that he even follows him into the ranks of the Foreign Legion and stands in for Lady Jane, who nearly becomes Sheikh Abdul Abulbul's thirteenth wife.

SIMPSON, GEORGINA
Role: Men's Ward Nurse in *Again Doctor*

On television, Georgina Simpson's other credits include *Dixon of Dock Green*, *The Persuaders!* and *Jason King*, while her film work saw her appear in such titles as *Otley*, *Perfect Friday* and *A Hole Lot of Trouble*.

SIMS, FLO
Played by Esma Cannon

Smiley's wife, Flo, arrives at Speedee Taxis with the intention of taking over her hubby's duties while he's in hospital. However, Mr Allbright, the shop steward, is having none of it leaving Charlie with no option but to refuse her work. She's then offered employment at Glamcabs by Peggy Hawkins, who secretly launches her own taxi firm as a form of revenge for the way she feels she's being treated by her husband. Seen in *Cabby*.

SIMS, JOAN
Roles: Nurse Stella Dawson in *Nurse*, Sarah Allcock in *Teacher*, WPC Gloria Passworthy in *Constable*, Lily Duveen in *Regardless*,

Joan Sims dressed for action

Calpurnia in *Cleo*, Belle in *Cowboy*, Emily Bung in *Screaming!*, Desiree Dubarry in *Don't Lose Your Head*, Zig-Zig in *Follow That Camel*, Chloe Gibson in *Doctor*, Lady Joan Ruff-Diamond in *Up The Khyber*, Joan Fussey in *Camping*, Mrs Ellen Moore in *Again Doctor*, Lady Evelyn Bagley in *Up the Jungle*, Esme Crowfoot in *Loving*, Queen Marie of Normandy in *Henry*, Chloe Moore in *At Your Convenience*, Mrs Tidey in *Matron*, Cora Flange in *Abroad*, Connie Philpotts in *Girls*, Madame Desiree in *Dick*, Daphne Barnes in *Behind*, Private Jennifer Ffoukes-Sharpe in *England* and Mrs Dangle in *Emmannuelle*
TV: *Christmas* ('72); *Christmas* ('73); *The Prisoner of Spenda*; *The Baron Outlook*; *The Sobbing Cavalier*; *One in the Eye for Harold*; *The Nine Old Cobblers*; *The Case of the Screaming Winkles*; *The Case of the Coughing Parrot*; *Under the Round Table*, *Short Knight, Long Daze*; *And in My Lady's Chamber* and *Who Needs Kitchener?*
A stalwart of the *Carry On* team, Joan Sims was employed on more titles than any other actress. Such was her adaptability, she was equally successful playing the green, rip-roaringly funny, accident-prone Nurse Dawson in *Nurse* to the nagging, unsmiling Daphne Barnes in *Behind*.

Frequently cast as the neglected partner whose other 'arf – usually Sid James – is eyeing up younger models, characterisations she so adeptly portrayed in, among others, *Screaming!*, *Camping*, *Loving*, *Abroad* and *Girls*, she was occasionally given the chance to play vamps such as Zig-Zig in *Follow That Camel* and Belle in *Cowboy*.

Born at Laindon, Essex, in 1930, Joan Sims, daughter of the local stationmaster, completed her education at Brentwood County High School for Girls. By then she'd already begun developing an interest in acting by performing with the Langdon Players, the local amateur dramatic society.

Keen to pursue an acting career, she applied for RADA but failed her audition; however, she accepted the Academy's advice and enrolled at the preparatory academy, PARADA, in 1947. It wasn't until the fourth attempt, however, that she was finally accepted into RADA.

After graduating she learnt her trade at various repertory theatres around the country, including Chorlton-cum-Hardy, Luton and Salisbury, and appeared as principal girl in *The Happy Ha'penny*, a new pantomime at Glasgow's Citizens' Theatre, before making her West End debut at the Irving Theatre in the revue, *Intimacy at Eight*.

She began in films during the early 1950s and established a long list of credits, mainly in comedies, over the decades, including *The Square Ring*, *Trouble in Store*, *To Dorothy a Son*, *The Belles of St Trinian's*, *Doctor in the House*, *The Sea Shall Not Have Them*, *Lost*, *Passport to Shame*, *Please Turn Over*, *Nurse On Wheels*, *Twice Round the Daffodils*, *One of Our Dinosaurs is Missing* and *The Fool*.

On the small screen, where her debut was providing voices for the children's show, *Vegetable Village*, she was seen in *Colonel March of Scotland Yard*, *The Buccaneers*, *Our House*, *Father Dear Father*, *The Howerd Confessions*, *Till Death Us Do Part*, *Sykes*, *In Loving Memory*, *Pie in the Sky*, *Martin Chuzzlewit*, *As Time Goes By* and *My Good Friend*.

She died in 2001, aged seventy-one.

SINGUINEAU, FRANK
Roles: Riff at Abdul's Tent in *Follow That Camel* and Porter in *Again Doctor*

SINISTER CLIENT
Played by Peter Butterworth
In *Loving* this creepy individual goes to the Wedded Bliss Agency looking for a woman, but Sidney Bliss quickly declines to help when he learns that the client's first wife died after eating mushrooms and the second of a fractured skull because she refused to eat the mushrooms.

SINISTER MAN
Played by Eric Pohlmann
With his sinister voice, the man phones Helping Hands when he wants a fourth player for his bridge match. Miss Cooling, the secretary, gets confused and thinks he's requesting someone to travel to the Forth Bridge. Seen in *Regardless*.

SINISTER PASSENGERS, 1st and 2nd
Played by Victor Maddern and Denis Shaw respectively
Both men enter the train compartment occupied by Sam Twist on his fruitless trip to the Forth Bridge in *Regardless*. Initially, Twist views the men suspiciously, that is until they get out a pack of cards to help pass some time.

SIR ROGER'S COACHMAN
Played by Sam Kelly
The unfortunate driver of Sir Roger Daley's coach is forced to hand over his possessions, including his clothes, when they're stopped by highwayman Dick Turpin en route to York. Seen in *Dick*.

SISTER
Played by Joan Hickson
The Sister works at the Haven Hospital in *Nurse*. Has the unenviable task of reporting to the dreaded Matron.

SISTER

Played by June Jago

Seen in *Regardless* the hospital Matron tells the Sister that as soon as she spots Sir Theodore, an important visitor who's inspecting the hospital, she's to phone her immediately.

SISTER

Played by Hattie Jacques

Seen in *Regardless* the Sister helps show Bert Handy around the hospital, believing he's Sir Theodore, an important visitor.

SISTER

Played by Jacki Piper

The Sister at the Finisham Maternity Hospital is seen in *Matron*.

SLAP

One of Ellen Moore's Siamese cats mentioned in *Again Doctor*.

SLIM

Played by Garry Colleano

One of the Rumpo Kid's men who helps run Stodge City through fear. Shot in the closing scenes of *Cowboy* by Marshall P. Knutt.

SLOAN, CAROL

Harem Girl in *Follow That Camel*

SLOBOTHAM, DETECTIVE CONSTABLE

Played by Peter Butterworth

Reports to Detective Sergeant Sidney Bung in *Screaming!*. This incompetent copper tries his best to help Bung resolve the case involving the disappearance of Doris Mann in Hocombe Woods.

SMALL BOY

Played by Stephen Garlick

Seen in *Doctor* the small boy arrives at Borough County Hospital with his grandad's chamber pot stuck on his head.

SMETHURST, JACK

Role: Recruit in *Sergeant*

Born in Manchester in 1932, Jack Smethurst, who remains busy on screen and stage, is probably best known for playing Leslie Pollitt in the '70s comedy *For the Love of Ada* and bigot Eddie Booth in *Love Thy Neighbour*. Other television credits include *Z Cars*, *Cluff*, *Boy Meets Girl*, *Budgie*, *Coronation Street* and, more recently, *Heartbeat*, *Dinnerladies* and *City Central*.

His film credits include *Watch Your Stern*, *A Kind of Loving*, *King Ralph* and *La Passione*.

SMETHURST, MISS

Played by Valerie Shute

In *Matron* she bursts into tears and runs out of Dr Prodd's consulting room when he breaks the news that she's pregnant.

SMILEY

Played by Bill Owen

Employed by Charlie Hawkins as a driver at Speedee Taxis Limited in *Cabby*. When he ends up going into hospital, his wife – Flo – turns up to drive his cab because they need the money. However, Mr Allbright, the shop steward, puts paid to any chance of a woman taking a man's job, which leads to her joining Mrs Hawkins when she launches Glamcabs.

SMITH, MADELINE

Role: Mrs Pullitt in *Matron*

Born in Hartfield, East Sussex, in 1949, Madeline Smith worked at Biba's fashion store in London for a few weeks upon leaving school in 1967. Although she'd never envisaged becoming an actress, she was persuaded to answer an advert in *The Stage* newspaper and ended up playing a small part in the 1967 film, *The Mini-Affair*.

Other film roles soon came her way in the shape of *The Vampire Lovers*, *Up Pompeii*, *Galileo* and *The Passionate Pilgrim*, but arguably her most memorable role was playing Miss Caruso in the Bond movie, *Live and Let Die*. It's reputed that Roger Moore, whom she'd worked with in an episode of *The Persuaders!*, suggested her for the part.

For a while, she combined acting with modelling, as well as studying full-time for an English degree during the late 1970s.

Her television work includes appearances in shows such as *Doctor At Large*, *His and Hers*, *Steptoe and Son*, *The Bagthorpe Saga* and *All Creatures Great and Small*, although she regards her work on the first series of *The Two Ronnies* as her big break on the small screen.

Shortly after her husband, actor David Buck, died in 1989, Smith – whose theatre career has included three year-long runs in the West End – retired from the business to look after her daughter. She's currently writing her autobiography.

SMITH, MR

Played by Peter Butterworth

A patient in Fosdick Ward at the Borough County Hospital. Seen in *Doctor*, we learn little about his condition other than it's a unsightly lump that was beginning to show through his clothes!

SMITH, MRS

Played by Jean St Clair

Seen in *Doctor* visiting her hubby at the Borough County Hospital, she ends up eating all his grapes.

SMITH, V.

The unseen Male Purser's Clerk on the *Happy Wanderer* in *Cruising*. His name is seen on the crew list.

SMITH, VICKI

(See 'Smith, Vicky')

SMITH, VICKY

Roles: Amazon Guard in *Spying*, Vestal Virgin in *Cleo*, Polly in *Cowboy*

SNEL, OTTO

Sound Recordist on *Emmannuelle*

Born in the industrial city of Tilburg, Holland, in 1937, Otto began his working life in South Africa after his family emigrated in 1952. By the time he moved to England in 1962, he'd already gained experience in the film industry.

He joined Pinewood Studios in 1963 and his first job was *55 Days at Peking*. Other films he worked on include *On Her Majesty's Secret Service*, *Superman*, *The Water Babies* and *The Human Factor*. He subsequently became an assistant dubbing mixer, remaining at Pinewood until retiring in 1999. Later credits range from *The Saint* and *True Blue* to *The Pillow Book* and *Something To Believe In*.

SNELL, PATSY

Role: Harem Girl in *Follow That Camel*

Patsy Snell's other screen credits include appearances in the films *The Wrong Box*, *Cuckoo Patrol*, *Baby Love* and *Up Pompeii*.

SNOG

Mentioned by Lila in *Spying*, who works for the organisation, the acronymn stands for the Society for the Neutralisation of Germs.

SNOOPER, PERCIVAL

Played by Kenneth Williams

Mr Snooper is a bachelor who works as a marriage guidance counsellor at the local Citizens' Advice Bureau seen in *Loving*. A man of habit and order, his life follows a familiar pattern: once a week he plays squash, once a week plays bridge and once a week dines at his club.

He has a habit of rubbing people up the wrong way, forcing his boss, Mr Robinson, to warn him that unless he finds himself a wife he'll be dismissed. He furtively makes his way to the Wedded Bliss office in the hope of finding a partner. His particulars are recorded by Sophie Bliss, who announces that he doesn't have to look any further because she's what he's been looking for. Depressed and angry that her partner, Sidney, hasn't proposed after ten years together, she's reached the end of her tether and decides it's time to move on, with Mr Spooner perhaps an ideal candidate. His long-serving housekeeper, Miss Dempsey, has other ideas, though, and starts acting peculiarly, making plenty of improper suggestions about her life with Percival when he entertains Sophie Bliss. Her efforts are rewarded when she eventually captures her man and becomes Mrs Snooper.

SNOW HILL

A road mentioned in *Cabby* during the scene when Peggy and Sally are forced to drive along by crooks holding them at gunpoint.

SOAPER, DR KENNETH

Played by Kenneth Williams

In *Camping*, Dr Soaper is the principal of Chayste Place Finishing School for Girls. It's his idea – although he probably lives to regret it – to take the unruly girls off on an educational trip to the Paradise Camp Site where he struggles to fight off the advances of Miss Haggerd.

SOCIETY OF TOTAL EXTINCTION OF NON-CONFORMING HUMANS, THE
For this organisation in *Spying*, see 'S.T.E.N.C.H.'

SOCKETT
Played by Bernard Bresslaw
Looks like death warmed up in *Screaming!*; the lanky butler is employed by the Watts at Bide-a-Wee Rest Home.

SOLDIER
Played by Billy Cornelius
Seen in *Don't Lose Your Head* the soldier stands alongside a woman, who happens to be the Black Fingernail in disguise, while she's being interviewed by Citizens Camembert and Bidet.

SOMMER, ELKE
Role: Professor Anna Vooshka in *Behind*
Born in Berlin in 1940, Elke Sommer, who'd previously worked as a model before turning to acting, had originally considered a career as an interpreter and translator. To brush up on her English, she travelled to England and worked as an au pair for a year before returning to her homeland.

While travelling in Italy with her mother, she took part in and won a beauty contest in a town near Pisa. Her photograph appeared in the local rag and was spotted by a film producer who offered her a part in his next production. Before long she established herself as an actress across Europe, including Germany, before arriving in the UK for her debut alongside Richard Todd in 1961's *Don't Bother to Knock*.

She's since worked both sides of the Atlantic and now lives in Los Angeles. Her film credits include *Café Oriental*, *A Shot in the Dark*, *The Money Trap*, *The Venetian Affair*, *Zeppelin* and *The Prisoner of Zenda*. Her television credits include American shows such as *The Six Million Dollar Man*, *The Love Boat* and *Fantasy Island*. Most recent acting work has been back in Germany.

Sommer is also a highly-rated stage director and respected artist: her work has been exhibited in Munich and Los Angeles.

SOOTHSAYER
Played by Jon Pertwee
In *Cleo* the long-haired Soothsayer can see into the future and is brought to Caesar by Seneca. He predicts Caesar's demise when he travels to see Cleopatra.

SOPER, MISS
Played by Hattie Jacques
For Miss Soper in *Again Doctor*, see 'Matron'.

SOSAGES
Played by Tom Clegg
Cleopatra's personal bodyguard, who's seen in *Cleo*, is a mute who rarely leaves her side.

SPANISH CAPTAIN
Played by Jan Muzurus
Seen in *Jack* the Spanish Captain is in charge of one of the country's vessels.

SPANISH GOVERNOR
Played by Patrick Cargill
Don Luis appears in *Jack* kissing a girl when Mr Angel and other members of the *Venus*'s crew storm into his residency.

SPANISH SECRETARY
Played by Vivianne Ventura

In *Jack* the secretary is seen canoodling with the Spanish Governor.

SPANNER, AGATHA
Played by Renée Houston
The loud-mouthed mother of Vic, Boggs and Son's union representative, appears in *At Your Convenience*. She runs a lodging house but it seems her only lodger is Charles Coote, chief designer at the toilet ware company. Agatha, a widow, doesn't suffer fools gladly and is the driving force behind getting the workers at the factory, which suffers endless strikes, back to work. When her marriage to Charles is threatened due to yet another strike, one which might force the company to be sold off, she finally loses her patience and, gathering the rest of the women together, marches to the factory, crosses the picket line and offers their services to keep the production line running.

SPANNER, VIC
Played by Kenneth Cope
Trade union representative at William Boggs and Son, Vic is seen in *At Your Convenience* causing mayhem at the factory by constantly calling the workers out on strike; a pernickety individual who lives by the union's rule book, Vic still lives at home with his mother, Agatha, who is equally fed up with her son's militant attitudes. Other than football and trade unions, Vic's other interest is girls, especially Myrtle Plummer, who works in the factory canteen; he loses out to Lewis Boggs in this instance, though. He eventually turns over a new leaf at work, dropping his aggressive tendencies to the benefit of all at Boggs and Son.

SPECIALIST (1st)
Played by Gordon Tanner **(Note: John Stuart was originally cast in role but contract cancelled.)**
A medical specialist in *Sergeant* who examines Horace Strong's heart and lungs.

SPECIALIST (2nd)
Played by Frank Forsyth
A specialist from the medical profession who checks Horace Strong's stomach and pulse in *Sergeant*.

SPECIALIST (3rd)
Played by Basil Dignam
In *Sergeant* the doctor tests Horace Strong's blood pressure.

SPECIALIST (4th)
Played by Jack Gatrell
A medical specialist who checks Horace Strong's blood in *Sergeant*.

SPECIALIST (5th)
Played by Arnold Diamond
The specialist checks Horace Strong's rib cage and general bone structure in *Sergeant* and is so

Elke Sommer makes her only *Carry On* appearance (*Behind*)

impressed he invites his colleagues into the cubicle to take a peek.

SPECIALIST (6th)
Played by Martin Boddey
A specialist in the field of psychiatry who, during an association test in *Sergeant*, gets Horace Strong to reveal his love for Norah from the NAAFI at Heathercrest National Service Depot, which becomes a turning point in Strong's life.

SPEEDEE TAXIS LIMITED
The taxi company owned by Charlie Hawkins in *Cabby*. Speedee Taxis, which operates forty-four vehicles after taking on a few more new recruits, was the first firm to operate in the district. But for a while the company's future looks bleak when, unbeknown to Hawkins, his neglected wife launches a rival taxi firm.

SPENCIUS
Played by Warren Mitchell
Spencius is in business with his brother, Marcus, trading as Marcus and Spencius. They specialise in buying and selling slaves and are seen in *Cleo*.

SPENSER, DAVID
Role: Bunghit's Servant in *Up The Khyber*
Born in Colombo, Ceylon, in 1934, David Spenser has appeared on screen since the 1950s. His film credits include *Conflict of Wings*, *The Earth Dies Screaming* and *Battle Beneath the Earth* while his television work covers such shows as *Studio Four*, *The Spies*, *Adam Adamant Lives!* and *Doctor Who*.

During the 1990s he co-ran a television production company and now lives in Spain.

SPIV
Played by Gertan Klauber (Note: scene was cut from the film although the Spiv can still be seen in the background.)
In *Follow That Camel* the Spiv is enjoying forty winks outside Café Zigazig until he's woken by Simpson who wants to find directions to the Foreign Legion's headquarters. Spotting Simpson and West are British, he attempts to sell them dirty postcards.

WHAT MIGHT HAVE BEEN

When Bo and Simpson are looking for the Foreign Legion HQ they seek the help of a spivvy-looking character. L.S. as they walk across to the 'café'. We see that there is a rather spivvy little character in a fez sleeping against the wall outside. They stop as they spot him and Simpson nudges him awake with a finger.

SIMPSON: You! My good man . . . !

(The SPIV wakes up and is immediately alert seeing what he thinks are tourists.)

SPIV: Ah, Englishmen! (**Jumps up.**) Welcome, dear sirs. You like to buy postcards?

SIMPSON: No thank you. We . . .

BO: Oh yes, get some, Simpson. I'd like to send one to Mother.

SIMPSON: Very good, sir.

SPIV: Oh, yes, you like these, dear sirs. Very good! Very artistic!

SIMPSON: (**Taking them in.**) Really?

(He takes the cards, looks at the top one, reacts in horror. Then goes through the rest, his expression changing from curiosity to interest and finally leering appreciation.)

BO: Well? Are they any good?

SIMPSON: Not 'alf! (**And remembering himself.**) But not quite good enough for our mother, I fear, sir.

BO: Let's see.

SIMPSON: I wouldn't bother, sir . . .

BO: Let me see!

(SIMPSON hands them across reluctantly. BO looks at them wide-eyed, then turns a cold look on the SPIV.)

BO: You filthy beast!

(And to SIMPSON, who hangs his head in shame . . .)

BO: Simpson! I had no idea you could sink to such depths of depravity!

(He throws the postcards down and stalks into the café.)

(As the SPIV, muttering angrily in Arabic, stoops to pick them up, SIMPSON looks craftily round, then quickly gives the SPIV a banknote and pockets the cards.)

SPORRAN SOLDIER
Played by Johnny Briggs
In *Up The Khyber* the Sporran Soldier is a member of the 3rd Foot and Mouth Regiment who's shot in the sporran during the final battle scene.

SPRAGG, MRS
Played by Amelia Bayntun
A neighbour of Mrs Spanner in *At Your Convenience*, Mrs Spragg pokes her head out of her living-room window and congratulates Mrs Spanner for telling Bernie Hulke to stop revving his noisy motorbike; Agatha Spanner, though, doesn't like Mrs Spragg interfering and tells her so.

SPRINGS, HOPE
Played by Barbara Windsor
Hope Springs, real name Muriel Bloggs, is seen in *Girls* arriving at the Palace Hotel on a moped in time for the Miss Fircombe beauty contest. After recently beating fourteen girls for the title of Miss Easy Rider, Hope is in confident spirits

and soon strikes up a relationship with Sidney Fiddler, the event organiser, much to the disgust of Sid's regular girl, hotelier Connie Philpotts.

SPYING, CARRY ON
See feature box on following spread.

ST CLAIR, JEAN
Role: Mrs Smith in *Doctor*
Among Jean St Clair's other film credits are appearances in *Doctor at Large*, *Dentist in the Chair*, *The Great St Trinian's Train Robbery*, *Impulse* and *John and Julie*. Her television work includes roles in *Dad's Army*, *Crown Court*, *The Saint*, *Dick and the Duchess* and *All the Year Round*.

ST MICHAEL'S
A church in the parish of Upper Dencher where the Reverend Flasher is vicar. What no one realises is that Flasher is the dastardly criminal, Dick Turpin. The church is seen in *Dick*.

STAFFELL, LAURELL
Dress Designer on *Teacher*
Laurell Staffell began working in costumes in the 1950s, with film credits including *Whistle Down the Wind*, *The Mouse on the Moon*, *The Looking Glass War*, *Live and Let Die* and, in 1982, *Better Late Than Never*.

STAGECOACH DRIVER
Played by George Mossman
Burt drives the Wells Fargo and Company stagecoach carrying Marshall P. Knutt and Annie Oakley to Stodge City. Appears in *Cowboy*.

STAGECOACH GUARD
Played by Brian Rawlinson
While en route to Stodge City, ferrying Marshall P. Knutt and Annie Oakley, he spots smoke signals in the distance. When the coach comes under attack by Indians, he grabs a shotgun but before he can pick off any of the enemy, he's knocked out when Knutt pulls a heavy case off the top of the stagecoach. Seen in *Cowboy*.

STAGESHOWS
See feature box on pages 230–1.

STALL-HOLDER
Played by Brian Osborne
Seen in *Abroad* the Stall-Holder sells a secret love potion, Elixir, at a village market. When the holidaymakers, who are staying at the Elsbels Palace Hotel, come visiting, trade soon picks up when several members of the party buy samples. Back at the hotel, everyone secretly pours their potion into the punch and it's not long before the farewell party is in full swing!

STANFAST ABBEY
A local monastery visited by the girls of Chayste Place Finishing School in *Camping*. It's famous for the mineral drink the monks

CARRY ON SPYING

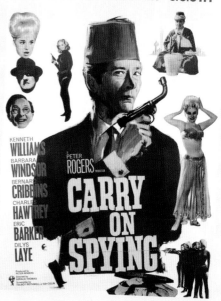

An Anglo Amalgamated film
A Peter Rogers production
Distributed through Warner-Pathe Distribution Ltd
Songs: 'Too Late' by Alex Alstone and Geoffrey Parsons
'The Magic of Love' by Eric Rogers
Released as an A certificate in 1964 in black & white
Running time: 92 mins

CAST

Kenneth Williams	Desmond Simkins
Barbara Windsor	Daphne Honeybutt
Charles Hawtrey	Charlie Bind
Bernard Cribbins	Harold Crump
Jim Dale	Carstairs
Eric Barker	The Chief
Richard Wattis	Cobley
Dilys Laye	Lila
Eric Pohlmann	The Fat Man
Victor Maddern	Milchmann
Judith Furse	Dr Crow
John Bluthal	The Headwaiter
Renée Houston	Madame
Tom Clegg	Doorman
Gertan Klauber	Code Clerk
Norman Mitchell	Native Policeman
Frank Forsyth	Professor Stark
Derek Sydney	Algerian Gent
Jill Mai Meredith	Cigarette Girl
Angela Ellison	Cloakroom Girl
Hugh Futcher	Bed of Nails Native
Norah Gordon	Elderly Woman
Jack Taylor	
Bill Cummings	Thugs
Anthony Baird	
Patrick Durkin	Guards

Virginia Tyler
Judi Johnson
Gloria Best . . . . Funhouse Girls
Audrey Wilson
Vicky Smith
Jane Lumb
Marian Collins
Sally Douglas
Christine Rodgers
Maya Koumani . . . . Amazon Guards

PRODUCTION TEAM

Screenplay by Talbot Rothwell and
  Sid Colin
Music composed and conducted by Eric
  Rogers
Associate Producer: Frank Bevis
Art Director: A. Vetchinsky
Director of Photography: Alan Hume
Editor: Archie Ludski
Camera Operator: Godfrey Godar
Assistant Director: Peter Bolton
Unit Manager: Donald Toms
Continuity: Penny Daniels
Hairdressing: Biddy Chrystal
Sound Editor: Christopher Lancaster
Sound Recordists: C.C. Stevens and Bill
  Daniels
Costume Designer: Yvonne Caffin
Make-up: W.T. Partleton
Producer: Peter Rogers
Director: Gerald Thomas

Simkins and his team of agents are watched by Milchmann (Victor Maddern, centre)

A top-secret formula is stolen from a research unit at Bilkington by none other than the infamous Milchmann, and it soon becomes clear that Dr Crow and her subversive organisation, S.T.E.N.C.H., are behind the crime. When the Director of Security Operations, known as The Chief, receives a message from Carstairs, one of his agents, informing him that Milchmann has arrived in Vienna, it's imperative a team of agents is despatched immediately. A shortage of personnel leaves him no alternative but to send the incompetent Simkins and three new trainees with the stark instructions that they must retrieve the formula at all costs.

In Austria, the team gather at the Café Mozart, their rendezvous point, where Milchmann and another criminal involved in the crime, The Fat Man, are dining. Carstairs has followed the crooks but his attempts at securing the formula are thwarted by the bumbling new recruits, something they do with increasing regularity.

The Fat Man is given a message by Dr Crow to meet with Milchmann, secure the formula and then dispose of him. A note suggesting a meeting is hidden away inside a cigarette and given to a cigarette girl to deliver to Milchmann, but a mix-up finds Simkins ending up with it instead. Believing it to be a message from Carstairs, the agents head for the suggested meeting point, but the only person they meet is a dying Milchmann, whose final words inform the agents that they must travel to Algiers and meet the Fat Man in a café on the 'Street of a Thousand . . .'. But before he can convey the complete address he dies.

Eventually the gang track down the Fat Man and follow him to the disreputable Hakim's Fun House, where he takes a keen interest in Daphne, the British agent with a photographic memory, who's disguised as one of the girls in the harem. His interests don't extend as far as her mate, who's none other than Harold, another agent, disguised as a woman. Between them they retrieve the formula and are soon homeward bound on a train, but the Fat Man and other employees of Dr Crow are hot on their heels. When they spot their enemies, the agents know they have to take drastic measures, so Daphne lodges the formula inside her photographic memory and they rip up the document and eat it with their soup.

Before reaching home, the agents have to endure being captured and taken to S.T.E.N.C.H.'s headquarters, but when they escape Simkins presses a self-destruct button inside the building in an attempt to rid the world of the organisation once and for all. What he didn't expect, though, is to establish, when it's too late, that their HQ is directly below his employer's.

Simkins (Kenneth Williams) tries his best to blend into the scenery by donning a fez

Funny Scene!

The Chief hears a knocking coming from a secret cupboard. He takes out his pistol and carefully opens the door. Out pops Simkins.

SIMKINS: (Relieved.) Oh, thank goodness for that, I thought I'd be filed for life.

THE CHIEF: What the hell are you doing in there, Simkins?

SIMKINS: You'll never believe it, chief, but last night I came in here to put some files away and some stupid, interfering, over-efficient nit went and slammed the door on me.

CHIEF: (Agitated.) I was the one who locked up in here last night, Simkins.

SIMKINS: (Embarrassed.) Oh, yes, well, a very good job you made of it, sir, I must say. If everyone was as conscientious as you were, we wouldn't need a secret service, would we?

CHIEF: Haven't you got anything to do?

SIMKINS: Not 'arf, after being in there all night.

CHIEF: (Shouting.) Work, man! Have you got any work to do?

SIMKINS: Oh, yes Chief, rather I've got security drill with the trainee agents; you know, showing them how to go out on their passes.

CHIEF: Well get on with it or you'll go out on yours.

SIMKINS: Now, don't be like that, Chief.

CHIEF: (Screaming.) Get out!

STAGE SHOWS

By September 1973, when several of the main *Carry On* players were donning greasepaint for the preview of *Carry On London!* at Birmingham's Hippodrome theatre, twenty-four films had been completed and another – *Girls* – was in the can. Meanwhile their familiar faces had also entertained millions who'd tuned in to their television sets during the Christmases of 1969, '70 and '72 to watch the festive offerings from the team.

Transferring the *Carry On* gang to the stage was something Peter Rogers had dreamt about for some time so when he was approached by Louis Benjamin – then head of Moss Empires, which owned various venues including the London Palladium and Victoria Palace – who wanted to turn the dream into reality, he was keen to pursue the idea. After discussing the project, it was agreed that a *Carry On*-style revue would ultimately enter the famous Victoria Palace after a preview at another theatre (which turned out to the Birmingham Hippodrome). By this stage, leading agent Michael Sullivan, who represented many of the *Carry On* team, was involved in the project and everyone agreed that the Palace, home of the popular Crazy Gang who'd had audiences laughing there between 1947 and '62, was the ideal location.

As well as Sid James, Barbara Windsor, Kenneth Connor, Peter Butterworth, Bernard Bresslaw and Jack Douglas, other artists were required to complete the cast, culminating in members of the production team flying around the world to find the right talent. Trips to America, France, Spain and other parts of the globe were made in search of new acts, such as Aussie singer Lynn Rogers who'd been wowing audiences in Miami. All-rounder Trudi Van Doorn, who'd impressed Louis Benjamin while appearing in pantomime, was recruited along with acts such as Les Silhouettes from Paris and Les Quatre Rosetti from Italy.

The final pieces of the jigsaw saw Albert J. Knight, a top-level producer of pantomimes at the London Palladium, given responsibility for staging the show, respected dance arranger Tommy Shaw hired to choreograph the production and Bill Roberton – brother of actor Jack Douglas – employed as stage comedy director.

With material written by Talbot Rothwell, Dave Freeman, Eric Merriman and Ian Grant, the show kicked off at Birmingham on 14 September 1973. By 29 September it was ready to make its London entrance, which happened five days later on 4 October. The show ran for eighteen months and became one of British theatre's most profitable revue shows in history.

Just over a year later, Jack Douglas, Kenneth Connor and Peter Butterworth were treading the boards again, but this time in Scarborough. The death of Sid James, a mainstay of the *Carry Ons*, two months earlier, had rocked the team and public alike, but in line with the old showbiz adage, 'The show must go on', *Carry On Laughing* opened at the Royal Opera House on 16 June as planned.

The final stage production, titled *Wot A Carry On In Blackpool*, was staged on the seaside resort's North Pier between 22 May and 27 June 1992. Bernard Bresslaw and Barbara Windsor were the only familiar faces from the world of *Carry On* in this Barry Cryer and Dick Vosburgh-scripted revue, spotlighting a 1940s repertory company. The show was a success with the audiences, many of whom delighted in seeing two of the *Carry Ons* biggest names reviving some of the corny gags and double entendres which had made the run of films so successful.

Louis Benjamin Presents the Peter Rogers Production

CARRY ON LONDON!

Performed at the Victoria Palace, London, 4 October 1973–March 1975.

1 Night 7pm, then 6:15pm / 8:45pm.

Previewed at the Birmingham Hippodrome 14 September 1973–29 September 1973; Fri. 14 Sept. 8pm, Sat 15 Sept. 6:15pm / 8:45pm; w/c 17 Sept. Mon, Tues, Thurs, Fri. 8pm; w/c 24 Sept. Wed and Sat 6:15pm / 8:45pm. Seats 75p–£6

CAST
Sidney James
Barbara Windsor
Kenneth Connor
Peter Butterworth
Bernard Bresslaw
Jack Douglas

ACT 1
Overture!
Orchestra under the direction of Richard Holmes
Round-About Victoria!
The Dancing Girls & Boys (Sidney James, Barbara Windsor, Kenneth Connor, Peter Butterworth, Bernard Bresslaw, Jack Douglas)

What A Carry On!
Sidney James, Barbara Windsor, Kenneth Connor, Jack Douglas, Peter Butterworth, Bernard Bresslaw, George Truzzi and Billy Tasker
Carry On Girls
Trudi Van Doorn
The Carry On Showgirls, The Dancing Girls & Boys
Introducing Les Quatre Rosetti
Emergency Ward 99 and a bit
Peter Butterworth . . . . Dr Hacker
Kenneth Connor . . . . Dr Ram
Barbara Windsor. . . . . Nurse Booby
Bernard Bresslaw . . . . Matron
Sidney James . . . . Dr McAndrew
Jack Douglas . . . . The Patient
Deauville 1900
The Showgirls, The Dancing Girls & Boys, Les Silhouettes
Elizabethan Madrigals
Sidney James, Barbara Windsor, Kenneth Connor, Peter Butterworth, Bernard Bresslaw, Jack Douglas
London Night Out
The Showgirls & Boys
Curtain Time At The Royal Standard Music Hall
Trudi Van Doorn . . . . . . Miss Lottie Collins
Jack Douglas . . . . Our Worthy Manager
Miss Barbara Windsor

The Glamazons
Our Patriotic Tableaux to The British Empire: A Tribute To Our Gallant Soldiers

ACT 2
Carry On London
Trudi Van Doorn, The Dancing Girls & Boys, The Showgirls
Hello Dollies
Introducing The New Dollies
Be Prepared
Sidney James . . . . The Scoutmaster
Bernard Bresslaw . . . . Scout Badcock
Jack Douglas . . . . Scout Muggeridge
Kenneth Connor . . . . Scout Pennimore
Barbara Windsor . . . . Barbara
Peter Butterworth . . . . Ethel
The Girls & Boys introduce singing star Lynn Rogers
. . . and now 'The Maestro' Sidney James
Cleopatra's Palace on the Nile
The Dancing Girls & Boys, The Carry On Showgirls
Cleopatra's Boudoir
Barbara Windsor   Cleopatra (Queen of the Nile)
Bernard Bresslaw . . . Abdul (a Hefty, Dusky Eunuch)
Peter Butterworth . . Grabatiti (High Priest)
Kenneth Connor . . Mark Antony (Lend me your ears)

Sidney James . . Caesar (Rome's Godfather)
Jack Douglas . . . . . . Titus Atticus (Captain of the Guard)

Smile

Sidney James, Barbara Windsor, Kenneth Connor, Peter Butterworth, Bernard Bresslaw, Jack Douglas and the Full Company

PRODUCTION TEAM

Written by Talbot Rothwell, Dave Freeman and Eric Merriman
Additional Material by Ian Grant
Orchestra Directed by Richard Holmes
Based on the *Carry On* films as directed by Gerald Thomas
Choreography: Tommy Shaw
Designer: Tod Kingman
Painted by Tod Kingman Ltd
Costumes designed and made by R. St. John Roper Ltd
Special Period Costumes by Bermans Ltd
Film Sequences by World Background Ltd
Electrical Equipment by Rank Strand Electric Ltd
Special Properties by Peter Pullen
Wigs by Simon Wigs Studios
Shoes by Anello & Davide Ltd
Manager and Stage Director: Alan West
Wardrobe Mistress: Eve Barnes
Assistant Choreographer and Ballet Mistress: Lynette Leisham
Executive Producer: Albert J Knight
Comedy Director: Bill Roberton

Don Robinson in association with Peter Rogers and Gerald Thomas presents . . .

CARRY ON LAUGHING

With 'The Slimming Factory'

Performed at the Royal Opera House, Scarborough 16 June–September 1976

First Night: 8pm, then 6:10pm / 8:45pm

CAST (in order of appearance)

Liz Fraser . . . . Milly
Kenneth Connor . . . . Major Chambers
Beau Daniells . . . . Mrs Babbington
Peter Butterworth . . . . Willie Strokes
Jack Douglas . . . . Alf Hardy
Linda Hooks . . . . Hilde
Barbara Sumner . . . . Alice Pringle
Anne Aston . . . . Candy Maple
Danny O'Dea . . . . Albert Waterman

The action takes place in The Get-U-Fit Health Farm

Act 1 Sc. 1 – Monday morning
Sc. 2 – Wednesday morning
Act 2 Sc. 1 – Thursday afternoon
Sc. 2 – Thursday night

PRODUCTION TEAM

Written by Sam Cree
Designer: Saxon Lucas
Theatre & General Manager: John Palmer
Company & Stage Manager: Tommy Layton
Deputy Stage Manager: Sue Smith
Assistant Stage Manager & Sound Control: Alan Bone
Wardrobe Mistress: Judi Tillotson
Telephone kindly loaned by GPO
Sporting equipment supplied by B. & J.M. Jungeling Ltd
Scenery Constructed and Painted by Northern Scenery Services Ltd
Hair Styles by Mr Paul, Marshall House, Scarborough
Director: Bill Roberton

Mike Hughes for Liver Promotions Ltd. presents . . .

WOT A CARRY ON IN BLACKPOOL

Performed on the North Pier, Blackpool, 22 May 1992–27 June 1992 6pm / 8:30pm; 26 July 1992–25 October 1992 Sundays only 5pm / 7:30pm.

From an original idea by Associate Producer/ Production Manager, Martin Witts

STARRING

Bernard Bresslaw . . . . Leading Man
Barbara Windsor . . . . Leading Lady
Andrew Grainger . . . . Juvenile Lead
Richard Gauntlett . . . . Light Comedy Relief
Jacqueline Dunnley & Natalie Holtom . . . . . The Merry Maids
Jonathan Blazer & Julian Essex Spurrier . . . The Jolly Juveniles

ACT 1

Arrival – 'You've Got To Carry On'
Barbara Windsor, Bernard Bresslaw and Full Company
'Phone Home'
Barbara Windsor
'At The Digs'
Bernard Bresslaw, Andrew Grainger and Richard Gauntlett
Rehearsals – 'T'aint Nobody's Business If I Do'
Barbara Windsor and The Jolly Juveniles
'Speciality'
Richard Gauntlett
'Tricky Business'
Bernard Bresslaw and Barbara Windsor
Out of Town – 'Old Fashioned Girl'
The Merry Maids and The Jolly Juveniles
'Slippin' Around The Corner'
Andrew Grainger and Rachel Woolrich
'Blackpool's Own Darby and Joan'
Bernard Bresslaw and Barbara Windsor
'Slippin' Around The Corner to The Rose & Crown'
Full Company

ACT 2

It's Show Time – 'Get Happy'
Barbara Windsor and Company

'Out Of Their Minds'
Barbara Windsor and Bernard Bresslaw
London Medley – 'Vultures For Culture'
The Company
'Chelsea Party'
Barbara Windsor, Bernard Bresslaw, Andrew Grainger, Rachel Woolrich and Richard Gauntlett
'Convent Garden'
Barbara Windsor and Andrew Grainger
'Speciality'
Richard Gauntlett
Just Go To The Movies – 'Charlie Chaplin'
Barbara Windsor
'Nelson Eddy'
Richard Gauntlett
'Frankenstein's Monster'
Bernard Bresslaw
'Betty Grable'
Barbara Windsor
'Wot A Carry On'
Full Company
'Mum Interrupts'
Barbara Windsor
Finale – 'One Step'
Full Company

PRODUCTION TEAM

Written by Barry Cryer and Dick Vosburgh
The Orchestra under the direction of Tim Parkin
Synthesisers: Peter Lingwood
Bass Guitar: John Saunders
Drums: Dave Tyas
Directed and Devised by Tudor Davies
Choreography: Paul Robinson
Set Design: Gareth Bowen
Costume Designer: Kathryn Waters
Sound Design: Clement Rawling
Music Associate: Phil Phillips
Company Stage Manager: James Skeggs
Stage Manager: Sharon Curtis
Wardrobe Mistress: Heidi Wynter
Lighting Design: Graham McLusky
Additional Orchestrations: Phil Phillips and Colin Fretcher
Assistant Stage Manager: Fiona Cheese-Hayward
Production Electrician: James Long
Production Sound Operator: Adrian Watts
Production Carpenters: Drew Taylor and Phil Lawson
Orchestral Management: London Music Associates
Sound System: Mac
Electrical Equipment: White Light North
Computer and Synthesiser Programming: Tim Parkin
Press Representative: Clifford Elson for *First Leisure*
General Manager: Peter Walters
Deputy General Manager: Eileeen Rawcliffe
Stage Staff: Keith Faulkner, Ian Sayle and Glen Ewen

produce. (**Note: recorded in the script as Mucklast Abbey.**)

STANLEY, CHARLES
Roles: Porter in *Nurse* and Geoff in *Cabby*

Stanley's other screen credits include *Ivanhoe* on television and films such as *23 Paces to Baker Street*, *Shadow of the Cat*, *Raising the Wind*, *Basket Case* and *Stuck On You!*.

STANLEY, NORMAN
Role: Drunk in *Cowboy*

London-born Norman Stanley, who died during the 1970s, began his career as a stand-up comic, entertaining audiences in Variety venues; he was also sidekick to comedian Clarkson Rose during his summer seasons.

Gradually began receiving offers to play small parts on screen, such as in the 1954 film, *Girl Gang*, and playing a telephone mechanic in a 1971 episode of *Doctor Who*.

STANTON, MARITA
Role: Rose Harper in *Nurse*

STARK, PROFESSOR
Played by Frank Forsyth

A respected figure working at the top-secret research centre, Bilkington Research Establishment. He's blown up in the early scenes of *Spying* by Milchmann, who enters the establishment disguised as a milkman before stealing a secret formula Stark was working on.

STATION HOTEL
The destination at which the 'Business Man' asks Anthea, a Glamcab driver, to drop him. Mentioned in *Cabby*.

STELFOX, SHIRLEY
Role: Bunny Waitress in *At Your Convenience*

Born in Dukinfield, Cheshire, in 1941, Shirley Stelfox knew she wanted to act from childhood and took every opportunity to appear in amateur plays. She made her first film as a child in David Lean's classic *Hobson's Choice*, but is best known for her television work.

Although currently playing Edna Birch in *Emmerdale*, she's appeared in most of the soaps. During the 1980s she was seen as Madge Richmond in *Brookside* while during the 1990s she appeared as Shirley Henderson in *Coronation Street* and as Jane Healy in *EastEnders*. Other television credits include *Bergerac*, *Juliet Bravo*, *Keeping Up Appearances* and *Making Out*.

S.T.E.N.C.H.
The Society of Total Extinction of Non-Conforming Humans is a subversive organisation run by Dr Crow. A threat to mankind, S.T.E.N.C.H. is seen in *Spying*, responsible for stealing a secret formula and murdering to achieve their aim. Eventually the organisation's HQ is blown to pieces, thanks to Simkins,

although what he didn't realise until it was too late is that the accommodation was directly below his own organisation's HQ.

STENSGAARD, YUTTE
Role: Trolley Nurse in *Again Doctor* (**Note: also played Mrs Roxby in *Loving* but scene cut.**)

Born in Thisted, Denmark, in 1946, this former au-pair and model arrived in Britain during the early '60s to develop a film career, but it was an Italian production, *La Ragazza Con La Pistola*, in which she made her debut. She went on to appear in films such as *Some Girls Do*, *Scream and Scream Again*, *The Buttercup Chain*, *Doctor in Trouble* and *Burke and Hare*, as well as television shows like *On the Buses*, *Special Branch*, *Jason King*, *Doctor in the House* and *The Golden Shot*, in which she was a hostess alongside Bob Monkhouse.

She emigrated to America in the 1970s and initially worked for a radio station.

STEPHANIE, PRINCESS
Played by Diana MacNamara

A busty young woman who steps up to the guillotine in *Don't Lose Your Head* only to find the blade is missing. Whilst the officials try to sort it out she's rescued by the Black Fingernail.

STEPHEN, SUSAN
Role: Nurse Georgie Axwell in *Nurse*

Born in London in 1931, Susan Stephen was being offered leading roles just months after graduating from RADA. She made the occasional television appearance in shows such as *Little Women*, *Stryker of the Yard* and *The Adventures of Robin Hood*, but most of her work was on the big screen, with credits ranging from *A Stolen Face*, *Father's Doing Fine* and *The Red Beret* to *Dangerous Cargo*, *Golden Ivory* and *Return of a Stranger*.

She died in 2000, aged sixty-eight.

STEPHENS, JACK
Art Director on *Cabby*

In films as an art director from the 1950s, Jack Stephen's credits include *The Clue of the Missing Ape*, *French Dressing*, *The Homecoming* and *Tess*, and as a set dresser on *The Slipper and the Rose*, *The Medusa Touch* and *The Mission*.

STEPHENS, MR
Played by John Van Eyssen

In *Nurse*, Mr Stephens is the doctor responsible for many of the patients at Haven Hospital. With an eye for pretty young nurses, as well as female doctors, he tries chatting up Dr Winn on her arrival at the hospital.

STEVENS & SON
In *Cabby*, Charlie Hawkins, who runs Speedee Taxis, is planning a reduction in fares in a drive to win back the trade lost to the newly-formed Glamcabs. Wanting some leaflets printed, he visits the office of Stevens & Son but decides

against it when he realises that Glamcabs are also having leaflets printed, offering even better reductions.

STEVENS, C. C.
Sound Recordist on *Spying* and *Screaming!*

Born in Andover, Hampshire, in 1907, Charles Cyril Stevens began working in films in Paris in 1930, where his duties involved the post-synchronising of foreign versions of American films. He returned to England in the early 1930s and worked at Pinewood and Denham studios.

His film credits this side of the English Channel include *A Yank at Oxford*; *The Citadel*; *Goodbye, Mr Chips*; *Contraband*; *In Which We Serve*; *This Happy Breed*; *A Canterbury Tale*; *A Matter of Life and Death*; *Passage Home*; *Passionate Summer*; *The Big Job* and *Pretty Polly*.

He died in 1974.

STEVENS, DORINDA
Roles: Young Woman in *Constable* and Girl at Dirty Dick's in *Jack*

Born in Southampton in 1932, Dorinda Stevens played a host of roles on screen during the 1950s and '60s. On television she was seen in *Dial 999*, *African Patrol*, *The Pursuers* and *Danger Man*, while her film credits include *Scotland Yard Inspector*, *It Started in Paradise*, *Jack the Ripper*, *The Gentle Trap*, *Night Train to Munich* and, her last film in 1964, *The Verdict*.

STEVENS, JULIE
Role: Gloria in *Cleo*

Born in Prestwich, Greater Manchester, in 1936, Julie Stevens has worked frequently in children's television, including presenting *The Sunday Break*, a religious show for teenagers for ABC in the '60s. Later switched channels and was a regular presenter on *Play School* and, subsequently, *Play Away*. Other small-screen credits include *The Avengers*, *Girls About Town* and *Cabbages and Kings*.

STEVENS, ROBIN
Played by Richard O'Sullivan

In *Teacher*, Stevens is the schoolkid responsible for the war of attrition against the teachers of Maudlin Street Secondary Modern School. He's seen in the film's opening scenes reporting to the acting head after larking about in maths. His motives for the array of pranks carried out during the visit of an eminent child psychiatrist and school inspector are honourable, though. He, along with the rest of his friends, wants Mr Wakefield, the acting head, to remain at the school and not apply for a new post in Sussex.

STEVENS, RONNIE
Role: Drunk in *Cruising*

Born in London in 1925, Ronnie Stevens began his theatrical career crooning at the age of twelve at the Peckham Co-Op and East

Dulwich Public Baths for his older brothers' Saturday night dance band whilst working variously for Dunn & Co. and as a fitter in an optical glass manufacturers.

Prior to the Second World War he was a student at Camberwell School of Art before serving in the Air Force during the latter stages of the war. Upon demob he trained at RADA and quickly established himself as a star of intimate revue alongside Joan Sims, Millicent Martin, Ron Moody, Ian Carmichael and others of that era before turning to straight theatre with the Prospect Theatre Company in the late '60s.

His career spanned all media and he achieved critical acclaim as an actor in comedic and straight roles from Shakespeare to musicals and children's theatre. His film credits include *I'm All Right, Jack*; *Top Secret*; *Value for Money*; *No Smoking*; *I Was Monty's Double*; *Doctor in Love*; *On the Beat*; *Dentist in the Chair*; *Dentist on the Job*; *Those Magnificent Men In Their Flying Machines*; *Smashing Time* and *Brassed Off*.

On television he's appeared in shows such as *The Goodies*, *Only When I Laugh*, *The Bounder*, *Ever Decreasing Circles*, *Roll Over Beethoven*, *Terry and June* and *Goodnight Sweetheart*. His last professional screen role was playing the grandfather in the Disney film, *The Parent Trap*, in 1998. A founding member of the Actors Centre (he served on the Board of Directors for nearly twenty years), the last few years of his career have seen him working for Robbie Swales's STEPS. Ill-health has now forced his retirement from the industry.

STEWARD
Played by Brian Rawlinson
New to his job aboard the *Happy Wanderer* in *Cruising*, the Steward is afraid of making mistakes. He's spotted by the captain preparing himself before entering cabin 309 to present newlyweds with a tea tray. He's later seen delivering tea to Bridget Madderley and thinks she's gone potty when he hears her reading aloud sentences from a phrase book.

STEWARD, ERNEST
Director of Photography on *Up The Khyber*, *Camping*, *Again Doctor*, *Up the Jungle*, *Loving*, *At Your Convenience*, *Matron*, *Dick*, *Behind* and *England*
Ernest Steward, who was born in London in 1914, began working on films such as *Take My Life*, *London Belongs to Me*, *The Clouded Yellow* and *Appointment with Venus*, before becoming prolific during the latter part of the 1950s until the early 1970s. His credits included such films as *The Wrong Arm of the Law*, *Hot Enough for June* and instalments in the *Doctor* series. One of his last films was *The Wildcats of St Trinian's* in 1980.

Occasionally worked on television, most notably on *The Avengers* during the 1960s. He died in 1990, aged eighty-two.

STEWART, GRAHAM
Roles: 2nd Storeman in *Sergeant* and George Field in *Nurse*
Scottish actor Graham Stewart, born in 1927, worked as an actor before moving behind the camera to produce television shows.

After growing up in Australia and Scotland, he was given the chance to broadcast on the Forces radio network in Germany and Italy while serving in the army at the end of the war. He enjoyed the experience and after returning to home shores, spent time at Dundee Rep before joining RADA.

As well as theatre work, he made occasional film appearances, most notably in *Cockleshell Heroes*, *Stormy Crossing*, *The Man Upstairs* and *The Unstoppable Man*. On television he was spotted in such shows as *Danger Man*, *The Adventures of Robin Hood* and *Ivanhoe*.

He eventually switched careers and established Commodity Appointments, a recruitment agency, with offices in London and New York. He ran the company until ill-health forced his retirement in 2001.

He died in 2003, aged seventy-five.

STEWART, ROY
Role: Nosha in *Up the Jungle*
Roy Stewart's other film credits include *The Curse of the Mummy's Tomb*, *Leo the Last*, *Twins of Evil* and *Arabian Adventure*, and on television *Out of the Unknown*, *Detective*, *Sherlock Holmes*, *Quiller*, *Sykes* and *I, Claudius*.

STINGHI
Played by Leon Thau
Appearing at the famous dinner-party scene in *Up The Khyber*, Stinghi works for Sir Sidney Ruff-Diamond, the British governor in the northwest province of India.

STOATS HOLLOW
In *Camping* it's where the all-nite rave takes place on Saturday 10 August at 8pm, until it's abandoned prematurely when the campers staying at the Paradise Camp Site in the adjacent field drive the revellers out.

STODGE CITY
A small, quiet Western town, or it was until the Rumpo Kid rode into town and took over. Belle's Place is renamed Rumpo's Place and all the rules relating to impropriety set by Judge Burke, the town's mayor, are scrapped. Originally the residents weren't allowed to shoot one another, fight, drink, gamble or, as Burke put it himself, 'no nothing'. Under Rumpo's reign, the town becomes noisy, dirty, rowdy and downright dangerous. It's so dangerous, the population count keeps changing by the second. But thanks to Marshall Knutt and Annie Oakley the town's sanity is restored. The setting for *Cowboy*.

STOLL, DAVID
Role: Distraught Manager in *Regardless*
David Stoll's other screen credits include the films *Death of an Angel*, *The Night We Dropped a Clanger*, *King Ralph* and *The Secret Garden*, while on television he's appeared in *Randall and Hopkirk (Deceased)*, *Tottering Towers*, *Mr Bean* and *Casualty*.

STONE, MARIANNE
Roles: Alice Able in *Nurse*, Girl at Dirty Dick's in *Jack*, Mrs Parker in *Screaming!*, Landlady in *Don't Lose Your Head*, Mum in *Doctor*, Maud in *At Your Convenience*, Miss Drew in *Girls*, Maggie in *Dick* and Mrs Rowan in *Behind* (Note: cast as Mrs Putzova in *Matron* but scene cut.)
TV: *The Case of the Screaming Winkles*
During more than fifty years in the profession, Marianne Stone notched up hundreds of stage and screen appearances. Although rarely offered more than pint-sized roles, with few lines to match, she always made an impact and became a popular face within the industry.

Usually seen portraying waitresses, barmaids, shop assistants and other working-class roles, Stone was born in King's Cross, London, in 1923 into a musical household. Her grandmother ran her own music school, with over a hundred pupils; it wasn't a surprise when Stone won a music scholarship to the Camden School for Girls, followed by a place at the Royal College of Music.

But she harboured dreams of becoming an

MEMORIES

'On *Nurse* I met Kenneth Williams for the first time. I'll always remember my first day on the set because I was a new girl and a bit withdrawn, keeping myself to myself. Kenneth was at the other end of the set, and it was a hospital ward so a very big set. He shouted: "Marianne, why are you ignoring me? You don't want to know me, I suppose." I'd never met him before in my life. I don't think he wanted to embarrass me, perhaps just to bring me in on it all and include me. I told him he didn't know me, to which he replied: "You? I know you." Then he started telling me all the films he'd seen me in.'

MARIANNE STONE

actress, yet before achieving her goal studied shorthand and typing and worked as a bank clerk, until she won a London County Council scholarship for RADA in 1940. After graduating, Stone gained vital experience as assistant stage manager at the Intimate Theatre, Palmers Green, London, and, in 1945, made her West End debut in *The King Maker*.

Two years later, she'd made her first screen appearance, playing a shop assistant in *When the Bough Breaks*. Film offers were soon rolling in and she was seen in, among others, *Brighton Rock, Escape Dangerous, Angels One Five, Private's Progress, Quatermass II, Hell Drivers* and *Just My Luck*.

Stone remained in demand until the 1980s, after which offers of work began drying up; she made the occasional television appearance in shows such as *Bless This House, Secret Army, Return of the Saint* and *The Nineteenth Hole*.

STONE, PHILIP
Roles: Robinson in *Loving* and Mr Bulstrode in *At Your Convenience* (Note: this scene was cut.)
Philip Stone, son of a headmaster, was born in Kirkstall, Leeds, in 1924, and enjoyed a long career in the industry but is probably best remembered for his roles in three Stanley Kubrick films and for playing Brigadier Davidson in television's *The Rat Catchers*.

While working as a clerk for an engineering company, Stone attended Leeds College of Music and Drama as a part-time student. After serving in the RAF during the Second World War, Stone happened upon a career in entertainment, working in various repertory theatres before making his West End debut in 1947's *A Sleeping Clergyman*.

Upon contracting tuberculosis he had an enforced break from acting for a while, returning to the engineering company where he'd started his working life. But eventually, in 1958, he was strong enough to resume life as an actor. Screen work soon followed, including appearances in the first two episodes of *The Avengers*. Other small-screen credits included *Champion House, Jason King, Budgie, Home to Roost, Heartbeat* and *A Touch of Frost*. His many films include *A Clockwork Orange, The Medusa Touch* and *Flash Gordon*.

He died in 2003, aged seventy-nine.

STOPPIDGE, DR ERNEST
Played by Charles Hawtrey
In *Again Doctor*, Doctor Stoppidge is employed at the Long Hampton Hospital. Possessing a nasty streak, he's desperate to see the fun-loving, accident-prone Doctor Nookey sacked from the hospital. Although he doesn't get his wish, he's satisfied when Nookey is eventually shipped off to the remote Beatific Islands. However, it's not the last he sees of Nookey, because later Dr Carver forces Stoppidge to

dress up as a woman in an attempt to discover the secret ingredients in the weight-losing serum which has made Dr Nookey a wealthy man, much to the envy of Carver and Stoppidge.

STORE ASSISTANT
Played by Valerie Leon
In *Camping* the leggy store assistant, Miss Dobbin, works at Courts. She serves Sid Boggle and Bernie Lugg as well as Charlie Muggins, who wants her to show him one of the display tents while he, in return, demonstrates his liking for straying hands!

STOREMAN (1st, 2nd, 3rd and 4th)
Played by Alec Bregonzi, Graham Stewart, Alexander Harris and Pat Feeney respectively
Seen in *Sergeant*, the storemen issue kit to members of Able Platoon.

STOREMAN (5th)
Played by Edward Judd
In *Sergeant* the storeman dishes out kit to Able Platoon and is involved in a small scene with Miles Heywood.

STOREMAN (6th)
Played by Ronald Clarke
In *Sergeant* the storeman is involved in kitting out Able Platoon and makes Peter Golightly's day by issuing him with a penknife.

STOREMAN (7th)
Played by David Williams
While helping to kit out Able Platoon in *Sergeant*, the storeman is seen issuing James Bailey with his oversized hat.

STORE MANAGER
Played by Brian Oulton
In *Constable* the store manager of F.H. Rowse, a department store, is worried because shoplifting is rife. He decides to take action but goes off sick before having chance to inform his assistant manager of plans to use PC Benson and PC Gorse on undercover duty, resulting in both of them being accused of shoplifting.

STORE MANAGER
Played by Brian Oulton
The Store Manager, Mr Short, is in charge at Courts. He's seen in *Camping* rescuing his assistant, Miss Dobbin, from the irritating Charlie Muggins.

STORES SERGEANT
Played by Anthony Sagar
In charge of the stores at Heathercrest National Service Depot, the Stores Sergeant is responsible for kitting out all the platoons. Seen in *Sergeant*.

STOUT WOMAN
Played by Alexandra Dane
Seen in *Again Doctor* on an exercise machine that spins out of control after Dr Nookey

causes chaos with Long Hampton Hospital's electrics.

STRAPP, SERGEANT JOCK
Played by Jack Douglas
The sergeant in the Bow Street Runners is seen in *Dick*. He reports to Captain Fancey but both are as ineffective and empty-headed as each other, particularly when it comes to catching the legendary Dick Turpin.

STREET, GEORGE
Role: Club Receptionist in *Regardless*
George Street's other screen credits include *Night Journey, Dreaming, Chance of a Lifetime, Please Turn Over, The Hellfire Club* and, on television, 1962's *The Big Pull*.

STREET OF MANY FOOLS, THE
In *Follow That Camel*, the tenth house in the Street of Many Fools is where Corktip, the belly dancer who's colluding with Sheikh Abdul Abulbul, asks Sergeant Nocker to meet her, even though it's a plot to kill him.

STREET OF A THOUSAND ARTISANS, THE
Seen in *Spying* this street in Algiers is where the British agents spot the Fat Man while searching for the stolen formula.

STREET OF A THOUSAND MOUSE-HOLES, THE
A nickname given to a road in *Constable*. PC Gorse mentions it because he's familiar with the road where criminals involved in a wages snatch are hiding.

STRIP CLUB MANAGER
Played by Sydney Tafler
In *Regardless* the manager runs a strip club and calls Helping Hands when he needs a bouncer. A mix-up sees Gabriel Dimple turn up, expecting to protect birds of the feathery kind!

STRONG, CARLOTTA
Played by an uncredited actress
The principal of the Fircombe School of Dancing, who was was crowned Miss Charleston in 1932, is one of the judges at the Miss Fircombe beauty contest. Seen but not heard in *Girls*.

STRONG, HORACE
Played by Kenneth Connor
In *Sergeant*, Horace is a hypochondriac who can't believe he's been classed as A1 condition and fit for National Service. His long list of ailments extends to, among others, thin eardrums and a weak stomach, and he doesn't travel anywhere without his medicine cabinet of concoctions. A liability in an already liability-ridden Able Platoon, Horace is a regular visitor to the camp's medical centre, that is until, with the help of a psychiatrist, he discovers he's in love with Norah, from the NAAFI; this revelation

turns him into a new man and marks the turning point for the platoon which is soon crowned champion platoon.

STUDENT
Played by Caroline Whitaker
One of the students helping Professor Crump on his archaeological dig in *Behind*.

STUDENT WITH ICE-CREAM
Played by Jeremy Connor
Seen in the audience at Professor Crump's lecture and film show in *Behind*.

STUNT DOUBLE
Nick Hobbs
Seen riding the moped instead of Barbara Windsor's character, Hope Springs, in *Girls*.

STUNT ORDERLY
Played by Rupert Evans
When Dr Nookey causes havoc with the electrics at the Long Hampton Hospital in *Again Doctor*, the poor orderly, who was polishing a floor in a ward, gets dragged underneath the beds by the mechanical polisher.

SUBSTITUTE FOOTBALL PLAYER
Played by John Hallett
Seen in Emmannuelle Prevert's flashback sequence in which she describes her most amorous experience. Appears in *Emmannuelle*.

SURGEONS, THE
The title of the television series which keeps Matron and Dr Goode glued to the box each week in *Matron*. With Dr Goode's wife not a fan of the show, he opts to watch it in Matron's room instead, although it has to be done furtively to ensure no one gets the wrong idea and starts spreading rumours.

SUSPECT
Played by Joan Young
While PC Benson and PC Gorse are working undercover trying to catch shoplifters at the department store, F.H. Rowse, they see an old lady stuff a garment into her shopping bag. Suspecting her of shoplifting, they tackle her outside the store, just as she's about to climb into her chauffeur-driven car. To their horror, they find out she's none other than the lady mayoress of the district who has an account with the store. Seen in *Constable*.

SWEET GLORY OF LOVE, THE
The title of the film Lewis Boggs takes Myrtle Plummer to see in *At Your Convenience*. Its sexual content does little for the ambience of the evening and a disgusted Myrtle storms out of the cinema.

SWEETLEY, WALTER
Played by Charles Hawtrey
First seen as a drunk in Dirty Dick's in *Jack*, Walter is a cesspit worker who finds himself pressganged into joining the frigate *Venus* on her trip to Spanish waters. He becomes a friend of Albert Poop-Decker on the voyage.

SWINBURNE, JACK
Production Manager on *Don't Lose Your Head*, *Follow That Camel*, *Doctor*, *Up The Khyber*, *Camping*, *Again Doctor*, *Up the Jungle*, *Loving*, *Henry*, *At Your Convenience*, *Matron* and *Abroad*
Working as a production manager from the early 1940s, Jack Swinburne's long list of credits besides the *Carry On*s includes *Millions Like Us*, *Mr Denning Drives North*, *Folly To Be Wise*, *Jumping for Joy*, *Rooney* and *Man in the Moon*.

SYDNEY, DEREK
Roles: Algerian Gent in *Spying* and Major-domo in *Up The Khyber*
Born in London in 1920, Derek Sydney was awarded an Alexander Korda Scholarship to RADA and proceeded to establish a healthy catalogue of stage and screen credits, including the films *The Constant Husband*, *Passport to Treason*, *Man in the Shadow* and *Hand in Hand* as well as television shows such as *The Invisible Man*, *Crane*, *The Champions* and *Timeslip*.

He retired in 1990 and divided his time between London and California, where he died in 2000, aged eighty.

TAFLER, SYDNEY

Role: Strip Club Manager in *Regardless*

Born in London in 1916; Sydney Tafler's was a familiar face to cinemagoers during the heydays of the British Cinema. He began his stage career at the age of twenty and early experiences saw him performing with the BBC Repertory Company and at the Old Vic, understudying Laurence Olivier just after the war.

Throughout the 1940s and '50s he was regularly spotted in pictures such as *London Belongs to Me, Passport to Pimlico, Mystery Junction, The Lavender Hill Mob, The Galloping Major, Venetian Bird, Operation Diplomat, The Crowded Day, Cockleshell Heroes, The Long Arm* and *Sink the Bismarck!*. He also appeared occasionally on television, most notably alongside Sid James in the sitcom, *Citizen James*.

He died in 1979, aged sixty-three.

TAKSEN, DR

Not seen in *Nurse* but the name appears outside the Colonel's private room in Haven Hospital, indicating he's the doctor responsible for the Colonel's well-being while in hospital. It also happens to be the name of the set dresser, Arthur Taksen.

TAKSEN, ARTHUR

Set dresser on *Nurse*

A set dresser who joined the profession in the mid-1940s, Arthur Taksen's credits included *It's Hard to Be Good, The Importance of Being Earnest, Hell Drivers, Operation Amsterdam, The League of Gentlemen, A Stitch in Time, Where Eagles Dare, In the Doghouse, Tiara Tahiti* and *Kidnapped*.

TANKARD, TERRY 'PINTPOT'

Played by Charles Hawtrey

Accident-prone Terry Tankard is a walking disaster from the moment he arrives at the yard of Speedee Taxis in *Cabby* looking for a job. Charlie Hawkins takes him on, purely because he looks after ex-army personnel and, believe it or not, Tankard wore khaki and drove bulldozers. Despite his shortcomings, he's a keen individual who doesn't mind working nights

providing he has one evening off a week – he's a keen rambler and fancies a girl who attends the local club.

TANNER, GORDON

Role: 1st Specialist in *Sergeant*

Born in Toronto, Canada, in 1918, Gordon Tanner debuted in British films in the late 1940s and appeared sporadically during the next three decades in such pictures as *Golden Arrow, Talk of a Million, Time Lock, On the Run, The Return of Mr Moto, The Vulture* and *Eskimo Nell*.

His television credits included *The Four Just Men, International Detective, The Saint, Zero One, The Prisoner* and *The Zoo Gang*. He was also frequently seen in the '50's detective series, *The Vise*. He died in 1983, aged sixty-five.

TANNER, JIM

Played by Julian Holloway

The coach driver in *Camping* who drives the girls from Chayste Place Finishing School to the Devonshire camp site, a job of a lifetime as far as Jim is concerned, who spends most of the time ogling the girls.

TARR, RON

Role: Bearded Man in Audience in *Girls*

A former market stall-holder, Ron Tarr, who was born in London in 1937, turned to acting in the 1970s when a friend suggested his distinctive features might secure him work. Usually playing small parts, he popped up on television in shows like *Are You Being Served?, Hale and Pace, Cannon and Ball* and as Big Ron, a market stall-holder, in *EastEnders*.

He died of cancer in 1997, aged sixty.

TAXI DRIVER

Played by Fred Griffiths

The taxi driver is seen in *Regardless* sitting in his cab (registration TUW 793). He refuses to allow Francis Courtenay in the taxi when he wants to bring Yoki, a pet monkey he's been asked to exercise, with him.

TAXI DRIVER

Played by Fred Griffiths

The cab driver in *Loving* is asked by Sidney

Bliss to go to Rogerham Mansions, where Esme Crowfoot lives; the trouble is he tears off before Sidney has a chance to jump in.

TAYLOR, JACK

Roles: Cliff in *Constable*, MC/Policeman in *Regardless* and Thug in *Spying*

For a decade between the mid-1950s and mid-'60s, Jack Taylor was frequently seen on the screen. His television credits include *White Hunter, Man From Interpol, The Pursuers, Ghost Squad* and *The Saint*, while his film work ranges from *The Sea Shall Not Have Them, The Hideout* and *The Crooked Sky* to *My Bare Lady, Saturday Night Out* and *The Black Torment*.

TAYLOR, JEREMY

Master of Horse on *Cowboy* and *Don't Lose Your Head*

His expertise in horsemanship was called upon for several films, such as *Richard III, Lawrence of Arabia, Anne of the Thousand Days* and, in 1971, *The Tragedy of Macbeth*. He was also hired for stunt work involving horses, such as in the 1952 series, *Ivanhoe*.

TAYLOR, LARRY

Roles: Riff in *Follow That Camel*, Burpa at Door-Grid in *Up The Khyber* and Tough Man in *Dick*

Born in Peterborough in 1918, Larry Taylor, who appeared as Captain Birdseye in a string of successful television adverts, was working in films from the early 1940s, with early credits including *The Hasty Heart, Wings of Danger, Sea Devils* and *Johnny On the Spot*. His early television work, meanwhile, included episodes of *Sword of Freedom, The Invisible Man, The Saint* and *Danger Man*.

Other film credits included *Too Hot To Handle, Zulu, Skeleton Coast, Lethal Woman* and, in 1995, his last film, *The Mangler*. On television in later years he was spotted in *UFO* and, in 1992, an episode of *Sweating Bullets*.

He died in 2003, aged eighty-four.

TAYLOR, PRIVATE

Played by Linda Regan

Based at the experimental 1313 anti-aircraft

battery featured in *England*, she's one of the shirkers who suffers a severe shock to the system when the tough-speaking Captain Melly is put in charge of the unit.

TAYLOR, THELMA
Role: Seneca's Servant in *Cleo*
During the 1960s she was seen playing various roles in *The Benny Hill Show* and *The World of Beachcomber*.

TEA ORDERLY
Played by Simon Cain
Works at the Borough County Hospital and seen in *Doctor* bringing the tea trolley around to Fosdick Ward at six in the morning.

TEACHER, CARRY ON
See feature box on pages 238–9.

TELEVISION EPISODES
See feature box on pages 242–5.

TEMPLE OF VESTAL VIRGINS
Also known as the Temple of Vesta, it's where the vestal virgins are found in *Cleo*.

TEMPLETON
Templeton in the Devon countryside is where the archaeological dig takes place in *Behind*.

TESTY OLD MAN
Played by Kynaston Reeves
A grumpy old millionaire in *Regardless* who storms into the Helping Hands office requesting the services of the top man. He wants Bert Handy to keep his place at the local outpatients while he attends various board meetings and completes a company takeover. He's a busy man who owns Amalgamated Scrap Iron and can't waste a second of his day sitting around waiting to be seen at the hospital.

TEX HART
An unspecified business in Stodge City. The establishment is seen in *Cowboy*.

THAT'S CARRY ON
A Peter Rogers production
Compiled by Gerald Thomas
A 1977 Rank / EMI film released through the Rank Organisation
Released as an A certificate in 1978 in colour and black & white
Running time: 95 mins

PRODUCTION TEAM
Original Screenplay by Tony Church
Archive Material by Talbot Rothwell, Norman Hudis, Sid Colin and Dave Freeman
Music arranged by Eric Rogers
Director of Photography: Tony Imi
Editor: Jack Gardner
Production Manager: Roy Goddard
Dubbing Editor: Christopher Lancaster
Sound Recordists: Danny Daniel and Ken Barker
Titles: G.S.E. Ltd

Producer: Peter Rogers
Director: Gerald Thomas

Kenneth Williams and Barbara Windsor are back at Pinewood trawling through the *Carry On* archives to present a cavalcade of memorable scenes from the long-running series of films.

THAU, LEON
Role: Stinghi in *Up The Khyber*
Born in 1926, Leon Thau began his career as an actor – appearing in such television shows as *Z Cars*, *Up Pompeii* and *All Square*, as well as the films *The Great St Trinian's Train Robbery* and *The Magic Christian* – before turning his attention to directing and producing, primarily on the small screen.

His credits in these capacities include *Potty Time*; *It's Awfully Bad For Your Eyes, Darling*; *Shadows*; *Prisoner*; *Save the Lady* and the various *T-Bag* shows during the late 1980s.

THEODORE, SIR
An unseen character mentioned in *Regardless*. He's a high-ranking man of medicine who's expected at the hospital where he'll be inspecting the building. The staff get mixed up and believe Mr Handy, who's standing in for someone at the outpatients, is Sir Theodore and proceed to give him a tour of the building.

'THERE'S FIDDLER' CITIZEN
Played by Hugh Futcher
This guy leads the chase to get Sidney Fiddler after the Miss Fircombe beauty contest turns into a fiasco at The Pier in *Girls*.

THEY DO IT FOR FUN
A book Fred Ramsden is seen reading in *Behind*. From the look of the cover, and the expression on his face, it can be surmised that the content is rather explicit.

THIEF
Played by Peter Bennett
Seen walking along the High Street in *Constable*, the quick-thinking Thief – whom PC Benson regards as 'honest as the day is long' – passes by Benson and without him knowing snatches the copper's braces. It's only when Benson feels chilly that he realises something is up – or down in the case of his trousers.

3rd FOOT AND MOUTH
The name of the British army's contingent guarding the Khyber Pass in the mountainous northwest province of India. The company's motto is 'Always Ready for Action' and they're well known for not wearing underwear under their kilts unless on church parade or giving a gymnastics display with ladies present. Their reputation, however, is soured when rumours spread amongst the Khasi of Kalabar's people, arch-enemies of the British, that they do, in fact, wear underwear. Seen in *Up The Khyber*.

32 DAWSON STREET
In *Cabby*, Anthea is sent to the address by Flo to pick up a customer.

33 HOGSMERE ROAD
Albert Potter's address in *Screaming!*.

THOMAS, GERALD
Director on all *Carry On* films. Comedy Consultant on television episodes *Christmas* ('69) and *Again Christmas* ('70). Producer on television episodes *Christmas* ('72 and '73) and the *Laughing* series. Co-creator and producer on *Laughing's Christmas Classics*. Also provided the voice for Odbodd Junior in *Screaming!* and the mynah bird in *Behind*
Gerald Thomas, born in Hull in 1920, completed his education in Bristol and decided to train as a doctor. His studies were suspended by the outbreak of World War Two, in which he served in Europe and the Middle East as part of The Royal Sussex Regiment.

After returning to civvy street, Thomas decided to swap a life in medicine for the film industry. Starting in the cutting rooms at Denham Studios with Two Cities Films, he soon progressed to assistant editor on films such as *Hamlet* with Laurence Olivier, and *October Man*. His first fully-fledged editorial assignment was on 1948's *Madness of the Heart* after which he left Denham to edit *The Twenty Questions* and *Murder Mystery*. Following this the talented young cutter was appointed associate editor on Carol Reed's acclaimed *The Third Man* and *Pandora and the Flying Dutchman* before rejoining Pinewood and editing, among others, *Tony Draws a Horse*, *Appointment with Venus*, *Venetian Bird*, *Day to Remember* and *Doctor in the House*, as well as *Mad About Men* and naval epic, *Above Us the Waves*, on which he also directed the second unit.

In 1955 he travelled to Hollywood to edit Walt Disney's *The Sword and The Rose* but upon returning to England left the Rank Organisation to join Peter Rogers at Beaconsfield; he was appointed associate producer on *After The Ball* after which he made his directing debut with the Children's Film Foundation drama *Circus Friends* in 1956.

The successful partnership of Gerald Thomas and producer Peter Rogers flourished with Thomas directing numerous films, including *Time Lock*, *The Vicious Circle*, *The Duke Wore Jeans* and *Twice Around The Daffodils*. However, his career was sealed with the success of the first *Carry On* film, *Sergeant*, in 1958. From then until 1992, he directed all the *Carry On* movies and, in 1990, won a Lifetime Achievement Award for Film Comedy. He died in 1995.

THOMAS, GUNNER
Played by Peter Banks
Based at the experimental 1313 anti-aircraft

CARRY ON TEACHER

Anglo Amalgamated present a Peter Rogers production
Distributed by Anglo Amalgamated Film Distributors Ltd
Released as a U certificate in 1959 in black & white
Running time: 86 mins

CAST

Ted Ray	William Wakefield
Kenneth Connor	Gregory Adams
Charles Hawtrey	Michael Bean
Leslie Phillips	Alistair Grigg
Kenneth Williams	Edwin Milton
Hattie Jacques	Grace Short
Joan Sims	Sarah Allcock
Rosalind Knight	Felicity Wheeler
Cyril Chamberlain	Alf
Richard O'Sullivan	Robin Stevens
George Howell	Billy Haig
Roy Hines	Harry Bird
Diana Beevers	Penny Lee
Jacqueline Lewis	Pat Gordon
Carol White	Sheila Dale
Paul Cole	Atkins
Jane White	Irene
Larry Dann	Boy

PRODUCTION TEAM

Screenplay by Norman Hudis
Music composed and directed by Bruce
   Montgomery
Director of Photography: Reginald
   Wyer
Art Director: Lionel Couch
Production Manager: Frank Bevis
Editor: John Shirley
Camera Operator: Alan Hume
Assistant Director: Bert Batt
Sound Editor: Leslie Wiggins
Sound Recordists: Robert T. MacPhee and
   Gordon K. McCallum
Continuity: Tilly Day
Make-up: George Blackler
Hairdressing: Olga Angelinetta
Dress Designer: Laurell Staffell
Casting Director: Betty White

Set Dresser: Terence Morgan
Produced by Peter Rogers
Directed by Gerald Thomas

William Wakefield, who's been acting head at the troublesome Maudlin Street Secondary Modern School for one term in the absence of Mr Carson, has spotted his dream job: the head of a newly-built secondary modern at Offord New Town in Sussex. He intends to apply but knows his chances of success hinge on his current school receiving a satisfactory report from Alistair Grigg, a reputable child psychiatrist, and Felicity Wheeler, a school inspector, who happen to be visiting

Maudlin Street. Wakefield realises that the school's poor disciplinary record means obtaining a glowing report will be difficult, so calls an extraordinary staff meeting to discuss the matter.

While every member of staff wishes Wakefield the best of luck in his pursuit of a new position, not all are so confident that the pupils will be on best behaviour for the impending visit, particularly with caning banned to fall in line with Griggs's views on the subject. Eavesdropping on the teachers' discussions is Robin Stevens, a pupil, who decides to organise a plan of action to ensure as much mayhem as possible is caused.

Soon after their arrival, the visitors are given a tour of the school, encountering as they do numerous pranks organised by the kids, including Mr Bean's piano collapsing on the floor after one of the legs is sawn in two, and Miss Allcock's shorts – which have been swapped for a smaller pair – tearing while she bends over in a PE lesson. The staff seem helpless to stop the children causing havoc.

Mr Wakefield's chances of securing the new headship in Sussex seem grim, but then a glimmer of hope appears on the horizon. As well as noticing Alistair Grigg has taken a shine to Miss Allcock, he sees that Felicity Wheeler, the inspector, only has eyes for the bumbling Mr Adams, the science teacher. Knowing his only chance is to encourage their relationship, he bribes Adams with the prospect of a better job at the new school if he tries

Idealist Alistair Grigg (Leslie Phillips) addresses the staff of Maudlin Street Secondary

Science teacher Gregory Adams (Kenneth Connor) experiments in the lab

wooing Miss Wheeler. Reluctantly, Adams agrees, but makes a hash of his early attempts.

The pranks continue with itching powder in the staffroom, frightening the teachers by pretending they're making a bomb and a series of disasters during the school play. While preparing for another round of surprises for the end of term prize-giving, Mr Wakefield catches the children red-handed. Calling them to his office, he reluctantly picks up the cane; as he prepares to administer the punishment, Miss Short, the maths teacher, rushes into his office. Upon hearing that Wakefield was contemplating a move to a new school, the children, not wanting him to leave, decided to wreak havoc to ensure he was unsuccessful. After thinking long and hard about his future, he casts aside any thoughts of applying for the new job and marks the end of the school year by informing the children that he'll see them next term.

Funny Scene!

Science teacher Mr Adams has been cajoled by Mr Wakefield into chatting up Miss Wheeler, the school inspector. Knowing Wheeler has a soft spot for Adams, the headmaster thought that it might stop her being too critical in her report and, thus, killing any chance he had of securing the headship at a new school. Bribed with the promise of a dream job at the new school, Adams scans the bookshelves in the library and turns to *Sonnets of Shakespeare* for inspiration. Miss Wheeler enters.

WHEELER: (Seeing Mr Adams.) Oh, don't let me distract you, Mr Adams, I'm just doing a bit of research.

ADAMS: Oh, so am I.

WHEELER: I always inspect a school library thoroughly.

ADAMS: Oh, very revealing, I'm sure. (He tentatively approaches Miss Wheeler, flipping through the pages of his book for the right lines.) Um!

WHEELER: Yes?

ADAMS: Ah, nothing, nothing. (Walks back to the table. Miss Wheeler joins him. He finds an appropriate sonnet and prepares for action.) Miss Wheeler, I have something to say to you.

WHEELER: Yes?

ADAMS: The light makes your hair look like burnished gold. (Getting tongue-tied.) Your eyes twinkle like the sties in your eyes — the skies, scars . . .

WHEELER: What suddenly makes you say that?

ADAMS: (Hesitates.) I'm a scientist you see, I . . . I . . . observe these things and . . . I hope you don't mind?

WHEELER: Why should I?

ADAMS: I didn't want you to think that I was being personal.

WHEELER: Aren't you?

ADAMS: No . . . just scientific.

WHEELER: (Disappointed.) In that case I don't mind at all.

ADAMS: Good. (Realising he's getting nowhere fast, he gets up from the table and puts the book back on the shelf. He summons up courage and turns towards Miss Wheeler.) (Shouting.) Miss Wheeler! Miss Wheeler. There is something I must say to you. Miss Wheeler . . . (Sits down and falls through the chair.)

WHEELER: Oh! (Stands up.) You've fallen.

ADAMS: Yes, Miss Wheeler, that's it, I have. Miss Wheeler, I've fallen in . . . (Still can't bring himself to say the magic words.) . . . fallen in through the hole in the chair.

Gerald Thomas and Kenneth Williams discuss the finer points

battery featured in *England,* he's one of the shirkers who suffers a severe shock to the system when the tough-speaking Captain Melly is put in charge of the unit.

THOMAS, LISA
Role: Sally in *Cowboy*
Other roles for Lisa Thomas during the 1960s included playing several characters in ITC's detective series *The Baron,* and Sura in Hammer's 1966 film, *One Million Years BC.*

THOMAS, SIR
Played by Julian Holloway
In *Henry,* Sir Thomas is one of King Henry VIII's riding pals.

THOMPSON
An unseen pupil of Maudlin Street Secondary Modern School. Mr Adams shouts his name in *Teacher* when he wants him to turn off the sprinkler that is spraying water everywhere during the school's production of *Romeo and Juliet.*

THOMPSON, HARRY
Not seen in *Nurse,* but Harry should have been visiting his friend, Oliver Reckitt, at Haven

Hospital. When he can't make it, he sends his sister, Jill, instead, sparking off an unexpected relationship.

THOMPSON, JILL
Played by Jill Ireland
In *Nurse,* donning a beret, Jill Thompson deputises for her brother and visits bookworm Oliver Reckitt at Haven Hospital. She takes a shine to Oliver, and before long the feeling is reciprocated. By the time Reckitt is discharged, they walk off hand in hand.

THOMPSON, JIMMY
Roles: Mr Delling in *Regardless*, Sam Turner in *Cruising* and Nelson in *Jack*
Born in Halifax, Yorkshire, in 1924, Jimmy Thompson began working on the screen from the mid-1950s, appearing in television shows such as *Here and Now* and the children's favourite, *Pinky and Perky.* Other credits in this medium included *Six More Faces of Jim, The Benny Hill Show, George and Mildred* and *The Very Merry Widow.*

His film work included roles in *The Whole Truth, The Man Who Liked Funerals, Band of*

Thieves, Those Magnificent Men in Their Flying Machines and, in 1970, *Doctor in Trouble.*

THOMSON, H.A.R.
Director of Photography for Khyber location work on *Up The Khyber*
Known as Bob to his colleagues and friends, Harold Thomson was born in London in 1910. He began his film career, aged fifteen, in the negative development department at Gaumont British's lab in London.

In 1930 he transferred to Beaconsfield and by 1935 was working as a camera operator before the war interrupted his career. He initially served with the Fleet Air Arm as an aerial photographer before transferring to the Naval Film Unit.

After being demobbed he joined Denham Studios and worked on films such as *Odd Man Out.* When the studio closed he moved to Pinewood. Among the numerous films he worked on are such classics as *Sleeping Car To Trieste, Doctor in the House, Above Us The Waves, Checkpoint, What A Crazy World* and *Where Eagles Dare.*

He died in 2003, aged ninety-two.

THORNTON, FRANK
Role: Mr Jones in *Screaming!*

Born in London in 1921, Frank Thornton always wanted to be an actor, but upon leaving school spent two years in an insurance office. When a colleague left the company to pursue an acting career, Thornton enrolled at drama classes in the evenings. Invited to become a day student for the second year, he persuaded his reluctant father to finance his studies.

Shortly after, the Second World War saw him evacuated with the drama school until he secured his first job, touring four plays in Ireland. Three years later he joined the RAF, but as soon as he was demobbed in 1947, he was being offered jobs in rep and occasional small parts in films, such as *Radio Cab Murder*.

His busy career has included over fifty films, ranging from *Portrait of Alison*, *A Flea in Her Ear* and *The Big Job* to *The Early Bird*, *Crooks and Coronets* and *The Three Musketeers*. On television he's best remembered for playing Captain Peacock in *Are You Being Served?* and more recently Truly in *Last of the Summer Wine*. He's also appeared in *Grace and Favour*, *Love Thy Neighbour*, *The Upper Hand*, *The Tommy Cooper Show* and *Steptoe and Son*.

THRUSH, MR
Played by Norman Chappell **(Note: this scene was cut.)**

Mr Thrush would have been seen in *Loving* if the editor's knife hadn't cut him from the final print. He was written into a scene in James Bedsop's office, hearing the sordid details of what his wife has been up to when he's away. Bedsop, a private investigator, has Mr Thrush worried when he informs him that the milkman, paperman and dustmen all paid a visit one morning!

THUGS
Played by Jack Taylor and Bill Cummings

In *Spying* the thugs are seen with the Fat Man on the train as they try to snatch the secret formula from Simkins, the British agent who's attempting to return it to Britain where it rightfully belongs.

THURSTON
Played by Cyril Chamberlain

Seen in *Constable*, Thurston is a long-serving policeman reporting to Sergeant Wilkins.

TICKET COLLECTOR
Played by Julian Holloway

Is seen punching tickets on the train Lady Jane Ponsonby catches in *Follow That Camel*. When he enters her carriage, he closes the blind and has his wicked way with her.

TICKLE
One of Ellen Moore's Siamese cats. Mentioned in *Again Doctor*.

Julian Holloway in a cut scene (*Camping*)

TIDEY, MR
Played by Kenneth Connor

A railway guard in *Matron* who spends virtually every hour at Finisham Maternity Hospital waiting for his wife – who's eating like a pig and whose baby is three weeks overdue – to give birth. Finally, after an agonising wait, and with the help of the sound of an explosion in the hospital, she gives birth to a baby boy, much to the relief of Mr Tidey.

TIDEY, MRS
Played by Joan Sims

In *Matron*, Mrs Tidey is more concerned with her input than output. A patient at Finisham Maternity Hospital, her baby is three weeks overdue but she seems more interested in stuffing her face with food than producing her baby – so much so that her husband comments that her liking for fish cakes will result in their baby popping out smothered in breadcrumbs. The wait is agony for her poor old husband, but Mrs Tidey isn't prepared to rush matters, stating it's taken seven years to get pregnant so she's taking her time. Eventually when an explosion goes off in the hospital, the bang jolts Mrs Tidey into action and she produces a baby boy.

TINGEY, CYNTHIA
Costume Designer on *Cowboy*

A costume designer whose early credits date back to the 1950s, she worked on a host of films

during a thirty-year period, including *The Scamp*, *Double Bunk*, *Finders Keepers*, *Salt and Pepper* and *Sinbad and the Eye of the Tiger*. She also worked on the 1980 mini-series, *The Martian Chronicles*, for the BBC.

TINKLE, DR KENNETH
Played by Kenneth Williams

The registrar at Borough County Hospital is seen in *Doctor*. His prowess in the world of medicine is indubitable but he's not a well-liked man around the wards of Borough County Hospital, except by Matron, whose heart burns passionately for Tinkle, and a student nurse, Sandra May, who regards him as her saviour, even though he only treated her for tonsillitis. When he discovers May is nursing at the Borough County Hospital he's horrified, perhaps because he thinks his career will be jeopardised if news gets out that he spent more than enough time providing after-care service!

TINKLE, PROFESSOR INIGO
Played by Frankie Howerd

A renowned ornithologist who gives a lantern slide lecture for the Royal Birdwatching Society in *Up the Jungle*. A well-travelled man, whose recent expeditions have seen him visit the Virgin Islands and the jungles of Africa – the subject of his lecture – in his attempts to spot exotic and rare birds. He was accompanied on his African trip by his assistant, Claude Chumley, and couldn't believe his luck when

TELEVISION EPISODES

The *Carry On*s were riding high when the gang's first festive offering emerged in 1969. *Camping* had been released earlier that year, becoming one of the box office's highest grossing films in '69, and television executives were beginning to wake up to the fact that perhaps the successful *Carry On* formula could be transferred to the small screen.

Peter Eton, an experienced television producer whose list of credits included *The Army Game, Bootsie and Snudge, Mr Aitch* and the television adaptation of *The Goon Show*, approached Peter Rogers with the idea, and after receiving his backing, discussed the matter with Philip Jones, Head of Light Entertainment at Thames Television, who'd subsequently commissioned Peter Eton Productions Limited to produce *Carry On Christmas.* Suggesting the storyline could be based on *Scrooge*, Eton contracted scriptwriter Talbot Rothwell to pen the screenplay.

By the end of July 1969 contractual matters had been finalised and, a month later, Eton met with Rothwell to discuss the basis of the script in detail. Before September was out, the first draft had been delivered and on Monday 1 December rehearsals began at the Teddington Yacht Club, just a few hundred yards from Thames Studios at Teddington Lock. The strong line-up included most of the *Carry On* heavyweights, including Sid James as Scrooge, Charles Hawtrey as the Spirit of Christmas Past, among other roles, and Bernard Bresslaw as Bob Cratchit and four other characters.

Screened on Christmas Eve, the show was a great success and led to three other Yuletide servings of *Carry On* mania: *Carry On Again Christmas*, broadcast on Christmas Eve 1970, *Carry On Christmas* on the 20 December 1972 and another fifty-minute show of the same name on Christmas Eve 1973. All were shown on Thames Television.

Other productions specially made for the small screen were *What A Carry On!*, an ATV production fronted by Shaw Taylor which in its fifty-minute slot crammed in highlights from the popular *Carry On London!* stage show's first night at London's Victoria Palace. A decade later we saw Kenneth Williams and Barbara Windsor introducing Thames Television's *Carry On Laughing's Christmas Classics*, a compilation of favourite moments from the film series.

As 1974 dawned, plans were afoot to make a series for ATV, which would kill off any schemes Philip Jones at Thames Television might have had to screen another *Christmas* show. Upon hearing news of the forthcoming series, Philip Jones wrote to Gerald Thomas agreeing that it made sense not to have considered a festive helping of *Carry On* fun because he had a commitment to repeat the last two his channel had made.

The first six episodes of *Carry On Laughing* were recorded later in 1974 and screened between the 4 January '75 – 8 February '75, with a further batch of half-hour shows beginning on 9 November '75 and running through until early December. Sadly, there were no scripts from Talbot Rothwell; writing duties were divided between Dave Freeman, Barry Cryer, Dick Vosburgh and Lew Schwarz, all accomplished writers, but no one could recapture that Rothwell magic, the successful blend of double entendres and farce which had been such a success for so long.

Carry On Christmas
Made at Thames Television
Broadcast: 24 December 1969, 9:15pm
Colour
Duration: 50 mins

CAST
Sidney James . . . . Ebenezer Scrooge
Terry Scott . . . . Dr Frank N. Stein /
Convent Girl / Mr Barrett and Baggie the
Ugly Sister
Charles Hawtrey . . . Spirit of Christmas Past /
Angel / Convent Girl and Buttons
Hattie Jacques . . . . Elizabeth Barrett /
Nun and Bemused Passer-by
Barbara Windsor . . . . Cinderella /
Fanny and Spirit of Christmas Present
Bernard Bresslaw . . . . Bob Cratchit /
Frankenstein's Monster / Spirit of
Christmas Future / Convent Girl / Town
Crier and Policeman
Peter Butterworth . . . . Dracula /
Street Beggar / Convent Girl and Haggie
the other Ugly Sister
Frankie Howerd . . . . . . Robert Browning and
Fairy Godmother

PRODUCTION TEAM
Written by Talbot Rothwell
Comedy Consultant: Gerald Thomas
Choir routine staged by Ralph Tobert
Designer: Roger Allan
Director: Ronnie Baxter
Producer: Peter Eton
By arrangement with Peter Rogers – Creator
and Producer of the Carry On series.

PLOT
This is the *Carry On* team's interpretation of Dickens's festive novel, *A Christmas Carol*, with Sid James cast as Scrooge and Bernard Bresslaw playing poor old Bob Cratchit. A loose translation of the story with some surprise appearances from Cinderella and Dr Frank N. Stein.

Carry On Again Christmas
Made at Thames Television
Broadcast: 24 December 1970, 9:10pm
Black and White
Duration: 50 mins

CAST
Sidney James . . . . Long John Silver
Terry Scott . . . . Squire Treyhornay
Charles Hawtrey . . . . Old Blind Pew /
Nightwatchman and Nipper the Flipper
Kenneth Connor . . . . Dr Livershake
Bernard Bresslaw . . . . Rollicky Bill
Bob Todd . . . . Ben Gunn and Shipmate
Wendy Richard . . . . Kate
Barbara Windsor . . . . Jim Hawkins

PRODUCTION TEAM
Written by Sid Colin and Dave Freeman
Comedy Consultant: Gerald Thomas
Designer: Roger Allan
Executive Producer: Peter Eton
Producer/Director: Alan Tarrant
By arrangement with Peter Rogers – Creator
and Producer of the Carry On series.

PLOT
A spoof on Robert Louis Stevenson's *Treasure Island*, Sid James, with a stuffed parrot perched on his shoulder, dons a wooden leg to become Long John Silver. He sets sail with the likes of busty Jim Hawkins, Rollicky Bill and others to find the hidden treasure of notorious pirate, Captain Flint.

Carry On Christmas
Thames Television Production
Broadcast: 20 December 1972, 8:00pm
Colour
Duration: 50 mins

CAST
Hattie Jacques . . . . . Fiona Clodhopper / Miss
Harriet / Miss Molly Coddles and the Fairy
Godmother
Joan Sims . . . . . Lady Rhoda Cockhorse / Miss
Esmerelda / Princess Yo-Yo and
Clodhopper's Mother-in-Law

Barbara Windsor .... Milk Maiden / Eve / Maid / Miss Clodhopper and Aladdin
Kenneth Connor .... Club Chairman / Lt Bangham / Inspector Knicker / General Clodhopper and Hanky Poo
Peter Butterworth ....Captain Alistair Dripping / Sir Francis Fiddler / Admiral Rene and Widow Holinone
Norman Rossington .... Valet / Tardy Dinner Guest and Genie of the Lamp
Jack Douglas .... Mr Firkin / Adam / Ringworm the Butler / Charles Burke and The Demon King
Brian Oulton .... Oriental Orator
Billy Cornelius .... Waiter
Valerie Leon .... Serving Wench
Valerie Stanton .... Demon King's Vision

PRODUCTION TEAM
Written by Talbot Rothwell and Dave Freeman
Costumes: Frank Van Raay
Designer: Tony Borer
Director: Ronald Fouracre
Producer: Gerald Thomas
Executive Producer: Peter Rogers
By arrangement with Peter Rogers – Creator and Producer of the *Carry On* series.

PLOT
Members of the Pudding Club meet on this festive occasion to enjoy good food and frivolity, regaling each other with stories and verses including *The Last Outpost*, *The Sailor's Story*, *Adam and Eve* and *Aladdin*.

Carry On Christmas
Thames Television Production
Broadcast: 24 December 1973, 9pm
Colour
Duration: 50 mins

CAST
Sidney James .... Mr Belcher the Store Santa Claus / Seed Pod / Sir Henry / Sgt. Ball and Robin Hood
Joan Sims .... Bishop's Wife / Adele / Virginia's Mum / Salvation Army Lady / Traffic Warden / Maid Marian / Ballet Dancer and Senna Pod
Barbara Windsor ....Virginia / Crompet the Pit Cavegirl / Fifi / Lady Fanny / Ballet Dancer and Lady Frances of Bristol
Kenneth Connor .... Mr Sibley, the Store Manager / Bishop / Anthro Pod / Pte Parkin / Will Scarlet and Ballet Dancer
Peter Butterworth ....Caveman Carol Singer / Ancient Gent / Darts Player / German Soldier / Friar Tuck and Ballet Dancer
Bernard Bresslaw ....Bean Podkin the Cave Teenager / Captain Ffing-Burgh / Dart Player / Merry Man / Police Officer and Ballet Dancer

Julian Holloway .... Captain Rhodes
Laraine Humphrys .... Bed Customer

PRODUCTION TEAM
Written by Talbot Rothwell
Choreographer: Terry Gilbert
Music Associate: Norman Stevens
Designer: Allan Cameron
Director: Ronald Fouracre
Producer: Gerald Thomas
Executive Producer: Peter Rogers

PLOT
Sid James as Mr Belcher, the store Santa, feels the spirit of Christmas has vanished from today's society and reflects on Christmases past, from the cavemen in 2001 BC to the trenches and battlefields of the Great War in 1917, when the true meaning of Christmas was respected and honoured.

What A Carry On!
ATV Network Production
Broadcast: 4 October 1973, 9pm
Colour
Duration: 50 mins
Introduced by Shaw Taylor

CAST
Sidney James
Barbara Windsor
Kenneth Connor
Peter Butterworth
Bernard Bresslaw
Jack Douglas

PRODUCTION TEAM
Programme Associate: Tony Hawes
Director / Producer: Alan Tarrant

SYNOPSIS
Fronted by *Police 5* presenter, Shaw Taylor, this fifty-minute offering was a compilation of the best bits from the highly successful *Carry On London!* stage extravaganza, interspersed with clips from the films and interviews with cast members.

CARRY ON LAUGHING
1: The Prisoner of Spenda
ATV Network Production
Broadcast: 4 January 1975, 8:45pm
Colour
Duration: 21 mins

CAST
Sid James .... Prince Rupert / Arnold Basket
Barbara Windsor .... Vera Basket
Peter Butterworth .... Count Yerackers
Joan Sims .... Madame Olga
Kenneth Connor .... Nickoff
Jack Douglas .... Colonel Yackoff
David Lodge .... Duke Boris
Diane Langton .... Tzana

Rupert Evans .... Major
Ronnie Brody .... Waiter

The Crown Prince, Rupert, has been kidnapped just before his coronation but attempts to save him are confused by a case of mistaken identity.

2: The Baron Outlook
ATV Network Production
Broadcast: 11 January 1975, 8:45pm
Colour
Duration: 24 mins

CAST
Sid James .... Baron Hubert
Joan Sims .... Lady Isobel
Barbara Windsor .... Marie
Kenneth Connor .... Sir William
Peter Butterworth .... Friar Roger
Linda Hooks .... Rosie
Diane Langton .... Griselda
David Lodge .... Sir Simon de Montfort
John Carlin .... Ethelbert
John Levene .... Soldier
Brian Osborne .... Gaston
Anthony Trent .... Herald

France has been invaded by the English but one nobleman escapes capture by swapping clothes with a woman. But what happens when his captors discover his secret?

3: The Sobbing Cavalier
ATV Network Production
Broadcast: 18 January 1975, 8:45pm
Colour
Duration: 23 mins

CAST
Sid James .... Lovelace
Jack Douglas ..... Sir Jethro Houndsbotham
Barbara Windsor .... Sarah
Joan Sims .... Lady Kate Houndsbotham
Peter Butterworth .... Oliver Cromwell
David Lodge .... Colonel
Brian Osborne .... Cavalier
Bernard Holley .... Captain

It's nearing the end of the war and Cromwell's on the lookout for any Royalists, leaving Sir Jethro – who's desperate to be on the winning side – in a bit of a quandary.

4: Orgy and Bess
ATV Network Production
Broadcast: 25 January 1975, 8:45pm
Colour
Duration: 24 mins

CAST
Sid James .... Sir Francis Drake
Hattie Jacques .... Queen Elizabeth I
Kenneth Connor .... King Philip
Barbara Windsor .... Lady Miranda

Jack Douglas .... Master of the Rolls
and Lord Essex
Victor Maddern .... Todd
McDonald Hobley .... Quaker Reporter
Simon Callow .... 1st Crew Member
Brian Osborne .... 2nd Crew Member
John Carlin .... Sir Walter Raleigh
Norman Chappell .... Lord Burleigh

With war between England and Spain looking increasingly likely, Queen Elizabeth sets out to ward off hostilities by calling upon the services of Sir Francis Drake.

5: One In The Eye For Harold
ATV Network Production
Broadcast: 1 February 1975, 8:45pm
Colour
Duration: 24 mins

CAST
Jack Douglas .... Ethelred
Kenneth Connor .... Athelstan
Joan Sims .... Else
Diane Langton .... solde
David Lodge .... William the Conqueror
Linda Hooks .... Nellie
Norman Chappell .... King Harold
Patsy Smart .... Old Hag
John Carlin .... Egbert
Brian Osborne .... Herald
Paul Jesson .... Messenger
Jerold Wells .... Black Cowl
Billy Cornelius
Nosher Powell .... Pikemen

It's 1066 and the French are gearing up to storm British shores. The fate of the Brits seems sealed with territorial waters full of enemy ships, but King Harold has a secret weapon up his sleeve.

6: The Nine Old Cobblers
ATV Network Production
Broadcast: 8 February 1975, 8:45pm
Colour
Duration: 24 mins

MEMORIES

'*Orgy and Bess* was one of my first small-screen *non*-appearances. As it happens. I was cut. All I remember was the very sketchy rehearsal period and the consequent panic during taping, where no one could remember their lines, except for Kenneth Connor, who was razor-sharp. Hattie was sweet, otherwise none of us who weren't part of the team seemed to exist. Not their finest hour, probably – though the script, by Barry Cryer, was a work of genius.'

SIMON CALLOW

CAST
Jack Douglas .... Lord Peter Flimsy
Kenneth Connor .... Punter
Barbara Windsor .... Maisie
Joan Sims .... Amelia Forbush
David Lodge .... Inspector Bungler
Victor Maddern .... Charlie
Patsy Rowlands .... Miss Dawkins
John Carlin .... Vicar

It's murder mystery for real at the village show when the vicar finds a dead body behind the curtain. It seems like another case for that respected detective, Lord Peter Flimsy, but how will he discover the murderer when all the chief suspects are wearing the same outfit?

7: The Case Of The Screaming Winkles
ATV Network Production
Broadcast: 2 November 1975, 7:25pm
Colour
Duration: 24 mins

CAST
Jack Douglas .... Lord Peter Flimsy
Kenneth Connor .... Punter
Joan Sims .... Mrs MacFlute
Peter Butterworth .... Admiral Clanger
David Lodge .... Inspector Bungler
Sherrie Hewson .... Nurse Millie Teazel
Norman Chappell .... Potter
Marianne Stone .... Madame Petra
John Carlin .... Major Merridick
Melvyn Hayes .... Charwallah Charlie
Michael Nightingale .... Colonel Postwick

There's a mysterious death at a country hotel after one of the guests eats Admiral Clanger's dinner. The question is whether it's murder or suicide, something Lord Peter Flimsy has to resolve.

8: The Case Of The Coughing Parrot
ATV Network Production
Broadcast: 23 November 1975, 7:25pm
Colour
Duration: 24 mins

CAST
Jack Douglas .... Lord Peter Flimsy
Kenneth Connor .... Punter
Joan Sims .... Dr Janis Crunbitt
David Lodge .... Inspector Bungler
Sherrie Hewson .... Irma Klein
Peter Butterworth ... Lost Property Attendant
Norman Chappell .... Ambulance Driver
Brian Osborne .... Harry
Johnny Briggs .... Norman
Vivienne Johnson .... Freda Filey

What seemed like a simple bequest in a will leads to a chain of murders, a king's missing ruby and a parrot with a cough! And it's left to Lord Peter Flimsy, with the aid of his butler, Punter, to solve the mystery.

9: Under The Round Table
ATV Network Production
Broadcast: 26 October 1975, 7:25pm
Colour
Duration: 25 mins

CAST
Kenneth Connor .... King Arthur
Joan Sims .... Lady Guinevere
Peter Butterworth .... Merlin
Bernard Bresslaw .... Sir Pureheart
Jack Douglas .... Sir Gay
Oscar James .... Black Knight
Victor Maddern .... Sir Osis
Norman Chappell .... Sir William
Valerie Walsh .... Lady Ermintrude
Billy Cornelius .... Man-at-Arms
Desmond McNamara .... Minstrel
Ronnie Brody .... Shortest Knight
Brian Capron .... Trumpeter
Brian Osborne .... Knight

After Sir Pureheart saves King Arthur from the Black Knight, and becomes head of the Knights of the Round Table, he forces a life of chastity on the other knights. There's soon unrest, but an attempt to trick Pureheart into a night of passion with a woman fails when King Arthur's wife gets mistaken for the bait.

10: Short Knight, Long Daze
ATV Network Production
Broadcast: 16 November 1975, 7:25pm
Colour
Duration: 25 mins

CAST
Kenneth Connor .... King Arthur
Joan Sims .... Lady Guinevere
Peter Butterworth .... Merlin
Bernard Bresslaw .... Sir Lancelot
Jack Douglas .... Sir Gay
Susan Skipper .... Mabel
Norman Chappell .... Sir William
Brian Osborne .... Herald-Knight
Desmond McNamara .... Minstrel
Billy Cornelius .... Man-at-Arms
Brian Capron .... Trumpeter

King Arthur's got many worries, but as foreseen by Merlin a man comes to solve his problems. The King is so grateful he knights him, Sir Lancelot, but his title is shortlived when he starts revealing his true colours.

11: And In My Lady's Chamber
ATV Network Production
Broadcast: 9 November 1975, 7:25pm
Colour
Duration: 25 mins

CAST
Kenneth Connor ... Sir Harry Bulger-Plunger
Barbara Windsor .... Baroness Lottie Von
Titsenhausen

Jack Douglas . . . . Clodson
Joan Sims . . . . Mrs Breeches
Peter Butterworth . . . . Silas
Bernard Bresslaw . . . . Starkers
Sherrie Hewson . . . . Virginia
Andrew Ray . . . . Willie
Carol Hawkins . . . . Lilly
Vivienne Johnson . . . . Teeny

PLOT

Sir Harry's son, Willie, is back from the Amazon and a celebratory meal is planned, but Willie has a few surprises for his father.

12: Who Needs Kitchener?

ATV Network Production
Broadcast: 30 November 1975, 7:25pm
Colour
Duration: 25 mins

CAST

Kenneth Connor . . . Sir Harry Bulger-Plunger
Barbara Windsor . . . . Baroness Lottie Von Titsenhausen
Jack Douglas . . . . Clodson
Joan Sims . . . . Mrs Breeches
Bernard Bresslaw . . . . Klanger
Andrew Ray . . . . Willie
Sherrie Hewson . . . . Lilly
Vivienne Johnson . . . . Teeny
Brian Osborne . . . . Newsboy

War is imminent and Sir Harry is looking for recruits from his household to help with the effort. But he's got to handle a son who's reluctant to fight and another recruit who sounds suspiciously German, with pigeons in his room and notes ready to attach.

13: Lamp Posts Of The Empire

ATV Network Production
Broadcast: 7 December 1975, 7:25pm
Colour
Duration: 24 mins

CAST

Barbara Windsor . . . . Lady Mary Airey-Fairey
Kenneth Connor . . . . Stanley
Jack Douglas . . . . Dick Darcy
Bernard Bresslaw . . . . Dr Pavingstone
Peter Butterworth . . . . Lord Gropefinger
Oscar James . . . . Witchdoctor
Reuben Martin . . . . Mabel the Gorilla
Wayne Browne . . . . Native
Norman Chappell . . . . Businessman
John Carlin . . . . Old Man
Michael Nightingale . . . . Neighbour

At the B.U.G.S.'s (Bermondsey University Geographical Society) AGM, the disappearance of one of the members, Dr Pavingstone, is top of the agenda. It's decided that a search party, led by Stanley, should be mounted, but if his task wasn't hard enough, he's lumbered with Lady Mary and Dick Darcy.

PRODUCTION TEAM FOR LAUGHING

Writers:
Dave Freeman (episodes 1-3, 6-8); Barry Cryer and Dick Vosburgh (4); Lew Schwarz (5, 9-13)
Music:
John Marshall and Richie Tattersall, except 9-11 by John Marshall, Richie Tattersall and Max Harris

Graphics:
George Wallder
Animator:
Len Lewis
Designer:
Stanley Mills (1); Ray White (2 and 5); Richard Lake (3, 4 and 6); Lewis Logan (7 and 8); Brian Holgate (9 and 10); Anthony Waller (11 and 12); Michael Bailey (13)
Cameras:
Jack Atchelor (6); Mike Whitcutt (7-13)
Sound:
Len Penfold (7-13)
Wardrobe:
James Dark (7-13)
Make-up:
Sheila Mann (7-13)
Lighting:
Pete Dyson (7-13)
Vision Control:
Gerry Taylor (7, 8); Jim Reeves (9-12); John Crane (13)
Vision Mixer:
Felicity Maton (7 and 8); Carole Legg (9 and 10); Mary Forrest (11-13)
VTR Editor:
Peter Charles (7-12); John Hawkins (13)
Executive Producer:
Peter Rogers
Producer:
Gerald Thomas
Director:
Alan Tarrant

Carry On Laughing's Christmas Classics

Introduced by Kenneth Williams and Barbara Windsor
Thames Television Production
Broadcast: 22 December 1983, 7:30pm
Colour
Duration: 24mins

PRODUCTION TEAM

Created by Peter Rogers and Gerald Thomas
Original Material by Talbot Rothwell and Dave Freeman
Music by Eric Rogers
Designer: Bill Laslett
Production Assistant: Caroline Hahn
Editor: Jack Gardner
Director: David Clark
Producer: Gerald Thomas
Synopsis:
Introduced by Kenneth Williams and Barbara Windsor, this half-hour compilation presents the best and most popular moments from the successful *Carry On* film series.

MEMORIES

'It was a mangled mess because I hated the laughter track – there's no way you could ever believe you were listening to real people laughing at the material. The laughter never stopped. In order to be able to laugh at the tag of the joke you have to hear the build-up. These machine-type people were too busy laughing non-stop.

'I was away when it was transmitted but when I came back I phoned Barry Cryer to ask if I could come over and watch it. He said "no", so when I asked why he said: "Because you'll throw my television set out of the window or kick it in!" Years later, I had a musical called *A Day in Hollywood, A Night in the Ukraine* playing in Baltimore and I was having an all-night writing session. I turned the television to sound about 3.50 in the morning and there was *Orgy and Bess*. I saw and heard what Barry had meant. I didn't trash the hotel room or even throw the set out of the window, but it was infuriating because we thought we'd written a funny script.

'It wasn't an easy script to write and we probably stole too much for our plot! If you ever watch it you'll notice that it's basically the plot of *Duck Soup* and *A Day At The Races* – in other words, Margaret Dumont. I've always been a Marx Brothers nit, and I said to Barry: "Why don't we imagine that Sir Francis Drake is Sidney James as Groucho and that Queen Elizabeth I is Hattie Jacques as Margaret Dumont, in a Marx Brothers movie."

'Barry and I were commissioned to write two. We were very proud of the other one, *The Count of Monte Cristo*, but they chose not to do it. It's one of the only things Barry and I ever wrote that we didn't find a home for eventually.'

DICK VOSBURGH – wrote *Orgy and Bess* with Barry Cryer

Chumley found the tail feather of a bird thought to be extinct. When Tinkle was captured, along with other members of the expedition, by the Lubidubies, a female tribe in the the jungle, he noticed they had the oozulum bird caged in their camp. When they managed to escape he ensured he took the bird with him, although when he unveils it at his lantern slide presentation, he's horrified to find it's flown the nest!

TIPSON, ROGER

The borough sanitary engineer is one of the judges at the Miss Fircombe beauty contest. Seen but not heard in *Girls*.

TIT AND SPARROW

This pub in Camden Passage is seen in *Emmannuelle* during a flashback sequence. It's Leyland's favourite haunt and where he met the unforgettable blonde.

TODD, BOB

Role: Pump Patient in *Again Doctor*
TV: *Christmas* ('70)
Born in Kent in 1921, Bob Todd trained as a dentist until joining the Royal Air Force, serving as a bomber navigator during World War Two.

After the cessation of hostilities, Todd changed direction and went into cattle breeding but lack of success drove him, aged forty-two, into acting. His first professional appearances were in films and the television comedy series, *Citizen James*, in 1963. He subsequently established himself as a successful supporting comedy actor with parts in many films like *Postman's Knock* and *Digby the Biggest Dog in the World*, both with Spike Milligan, *The Intelligence Men* with Morecambe and Wise, *The Private Lives of Sherlock Holmes* and *Raising the Wind* with Leslie Phillips.

He also regularly featured on the radio show, *Listen to this Space*, impersonating Harold Wilson, had his own television series, *In for a Penny*, and performed alongside numerous successful comedians, particularly Benny Hill.

He died in 1991, aged seventy.

TOGETHERNESS MARRIAGE AGENCY

Mentioned by Leonard Beamish in *Regardless*. He phones the agency when he wants a wife in time for a party he's throwing for his aunt in two weeks.

TOM

Played by Peter Butterworth
One of Dick Turpin's sidekicks in *Dick*, Tom also assists Turpin with his day job as the softly-spoken Reverend Flasher.

TOMB OF ST CECILIA, THE

St Cecilia was the founder of the Order which Brother Bernard, Brother Martin and the others belong to in *Abroad*. Her tomb lies in the middle of a Mediterranean island, five miles north of the port of Elsbels. The party of brothers, all of whom are staying at the Elsbels Palace Hotel, head off to try and find it without much success.

TOMKINS, MISS SADIE

Played by Barbara Windsor
The diminutive blonde, who loves showing off her assets, is travelling to Elsbels for a secret break with Vic Flange, the local landlord, in *Abroad*. But when his wife, Cora, finds out they're booked on the same trip, she puts aside her aversion to flying in order to keep an eye on her hubby. Miss Tomkins – a widow after losing two husbands, both firemen who died on the job – strikes up a relationship with the loud-mouthed Scot, Bert Conway, instead, while Vic is left to dream of what might have been.

TOMS, DONALD

Unit Manager on *Cabby*, *Jack*, *Spying* and *Cleo*
Born in London in 1929, Donald Toms always wanted to be a motor mechanic but on the advice of a family friend applied to Denham Studios and was recruited, in 1945, as a messenger boy. He progressed through the ranks before retiring, in 1992, as a production supervisor.

A lengthy list of credits includes *Play It Cool*, *The Iron Maiden*, *Three Hats for Lisa*, *Stranger in the House*, *International Velvet*, *The World is Full of Married Men*, *Young Sherlock Holmes* and *Bellman and True*. He also worked on television, most notably three years spent on London Weekend's *Poirot* series, just before his retirement.

TONKA, KING

Played by Charles Hawtrey
For King Tonka in *Up the Jungle*, see 'Bagley, Walter'.

TOOTHILL, PAUL

Role: Gunner Gale in *England*
Bradford-born actor Paul Toothill trained at the Rose Bruford College before embarking on an acting career.

TORTURERS

Played by Leon Greene and Dave Prowse
In *Henry* the torturers are tasked with forcing Sir Roger de Lodgerley to sign the confession admitting he's the father of the Queen's baby; initially reluctant to sign on the dotted line, he changes his mind after some stretching exercises on the rack!

TOUGH MEN

Played by Larry Taylor and Billy Cornelius
At the Old Cock Inn in *Dick* the tough men throw Sergeant Strapp, of the Bow Street Runners, into a dirty horse trough outside the hostelry. They become agitated after Strapp follows them into the toilet to check whether they have birthmarks on their private parts, something the legendary villain, Dick Turpin, reputedly possesses.

TOWB, HARRY

Role: Doctor in Film in *At Your Convenience*
Irish actor Harry Towb was born in Larne, Country Antrim, in 1925. Upon leaving school he held several jobs, including working as a shipping clerk, in a sawmill and as an apprentice accountant. Aged eighteen, he established his own photographic business before the chance to appear in *Flashing Stream* in Belfast came along in 1945.

Broadcasts for the BBC in Belfast followed before he joined a touring company travelling around Ireland. He arrived in England in 1947 and worked in repertory theatres up and down the country. By 1951 he'd made his film debut, playing Jim Cranshaw in *The Quiet Woman*. Other film credits include *Gift Horse*, *Above Us the Waves*, *Eyewitness*, *Crossroads to Crime*, *Barry Lyndon* and *Cheeky*.

On stage he established a busy career, including spells in the West End (seventeen productions at the National Theatre) and Broadway, while on television (he made his debut in 1949's *The Courts of Justice* at Alexandra Palace) he's been seen in, among others, *Z Cars*, *Suspense*, *Thorndyke*, *The Spies*, *The Army Game*, *The Champions*, *Callan*, *Home James!*, *The Bill* and *Doctors*. He also provided the commentary and appeared as ringmaster in the BBC's coverage of Billy Smart's Circus for four years.

TOWN CRIER

Played by Michael Nightingale
Seen near the end of the film in *Jack* announcing that the Spanish invasion fleet has been destroyed off Cornwall by a single frigate.

TRAINER

Played by Tom Clegg
Gripper's trainer is seen in the gym during *Loving*. He takes the phone call from Sidney Bliss warning Gripper that Mr Snooper is trying to seduce his fiancée, Esme Crowfoot. It's all a devious plan, of course, instigated by Mr Bliss.

TRAPPER

Played by Brian Coburn
Seen in *Cowboy* trying to sell furs to Belle. Spotting an opportunity to impress Belle, the Rumpo Kid offers to buy the furs for her, but he needs some cash first so heads to the bank, resulting in yet another bank clerk biting the dust.

TREE, TOM

Played by Cyril Chamberlain
Captain Crowther's new steward in *Cruising* replaces Mr Lovell, who's broken his leg. One of

many new faces on an April cruise around the Mediterranean. Adapting to change isn't the captain's greatest strengths, but this time his nervousness may be justified considering Tree has only made three trips on water, and they were between Tower Bridge and Margate, so he's hardly a seasoned sailor.

TRELAWNEY, SQUIRE
Played by Michael Nightingale

The Squire in *Dick* admires the goods that have been collected for the grand jumble sale in aid of church funds and organ reconstruction. He looks perplexed, though, when Miss Hoggett says he's one of their chief benefactors: Reverend Flasher – alias Dick Turpin – had told Miss Hoggett that he'd collected goods from him, so when the Squire states he hasn't donated a thing, she begins to worry about what else the Reverend might be lying about.

TRELAWNEY, TREVOR
Played by Terence Alexander

Mr Trelawney hires language expert Francis Courtenay in *Regardless* to translate during a family argument. Trelawney's foreign wife is irate because she feels neglected and suspects him of having an affair with his secretary. When she reverts to her native tongue, Trevor can't understand a word so calls Helping Hands.

TRELAWNEY, TRUDY
Played by Julia Arnall

The foreign wife of Trevor in *Regardless*. She reaches the end of her tether when her hubby doesn't compliment her on her new hat and hairstyle; it just reinforces her view that her beloved is having an affair with his secretary. She becomes so distraught she argues in her native tongue, leaving Trevor no alternative but to hire an interpreter from Helping Hands.

TRIMBLE, GLAD
Played by Liz Fraser

A passenger on the *Happy Wanderer* in *Cruising*. She's on the cruise with her friend, Flo Castle, supposedly helping her find a husband. Glad is fed up with men, that is until she spots the PT instructor, Mr Jenkins.

TROLLEY LADY
Played by Lucy Griffiths

Seen in *Nurse* the trolley lady tours Haven Hospital selling cakes and other assorted goodies.

TROLLEY NURSE
Played by Yutte Stensgaard

As Doctor Nookey in *Again Doctor* attempts to escape from the hospital staff, after accidentally entering Miss Armitage's room whilst looking for Goldie Locks, he runs down the corridor and straight into a trolley being pushed by a nurse.

TRUMPER, NURSE

An unseen nurse mentioned in *Again Doctor* by Matron. She works at Dr Nookey's private clinic and Matron moves into her room for the night after being forced to give up her own bed to accommodate Gladstone Screwer, who's suddenly arrived from the Beatific Islands.

TUBBY
Played by Don McCorkindale

One of the new drivers hired by Charlie Hawkins for his Speedee Taxis business. Seen in *Cabby*.

TUCKER, MRS
Played by Margaret Nolan

The busty Mrs Tucker is seen in *Matron* talking to Dr Prodd. It appears she spoke to Prodd three months previous about the likelihood of her husband, who's eighty-eight, being able to

father a child; Prodd's off-the-record advice was to get a lodger, which they did; the trouble is, the lodger is pregnant now as well.

TUM-TUM

The God worshipped by the Noshas, mentioned in *Up the Jungle*.

TURNER, SAM
Played by Jimmy Thompson

Seen in *Cruising*, Sam is the new head barman on the *Happy Wanderer*. He scores a few brownie points with Captain Crowther when he finally learns how to make an Aberdeen Angus, the captain's favourite tipple.

TURPIN, DICK
Played by Sidney James

The nation's most wanted highwayman terrorises the roads of Britain in *Dick*. By day he's disguised as the Reverend Flasher, doing his good deeds in the community, but by night he dons his mask, packs his pistols and heads off into the darkness to rob unsuspecting members of the public. With a reward of one hundred guineas to anyone providing information leading to his arrest, he's largely to blame for the increase in crime and the need to form the Bow Street Runners, a special police unit whose job is to try and stem the increase in violence. Turpin is helped in his job by the trusty Tom and Harriett.

TUTTLE, EUSTACE
Played by Charles Hawtrey

Tuttle appears to be a mollycoddled mummy's boy when he's shown on to the coach by his fussing mother in *Abroad*. The bowler-hatted Eustace is off to Elsbels with Wundatours on their long weekend trip, but as soon as he's away from the influence of his mother, he turns into a different man, someone who can't get enough booze and loves playing leapfrog, which gets him, and the rest of the party, into trouble when he asks the prostitutes at Madame Fifi's, a bawdyhouse he accidentally stumbles upon, to play the game.

TUTTLE, MRS
Played by Amelia Bayntun

Eustace's mother in *Abroad* helps her mollycoddled son on to the coach ready for his Wundatours trip to the Mediterranean resort of Elsbels.

TWEET, ROBIN
Played by John Clive

A member of the party travelling to the Mediterranean resort of Elsbels with Wundatours in *Abroad*. The camp and huffy Robin is partnered on the trip by his boyfriend, Nicholas, but finishes the weekend break alone when Nicholas runs off with Lily, who's also splashed out £17 to join the group.

MEMORIES

'The *Carry On*s were fun to work on. You knew you weren't going to earn a fortune, but that you'd enjoy life and wouldn't have to work long hours. At 5.30pm you could normally phone your wife and say you were on your way home and wouldn't suddenly be asked to work another hour like most productions. You always finished on time and under budget and I thoroughly enjoyed being with everyone.

'I remember during *Cleo* I was walking down a corridor at Pinewood with Frank Bevis when Kenneth Williams, who was a bit of a character to say the least, was coming towards us dressed in a toga. He lifted the toga up, had nothing on underneath, and showed what he hadn't got, saying: "What about that fellas, don't you wish you had one like that?" Frank said: "No, if I had one like that I'd cover it up." The office girls around couldn't believe what they were seeing. He was such a character.

'I also remember when Charles Hawtrey was in a scene involving a pulley but accidentally got hooked up the wrong way. The rope was pulled and almost throttled him. He started going a funny colour and Gerry [Thomas] just said: "Oh let's do another take." They did it again, got the shot and then lowered him down. While they carried on, Charles Hawtrey was lying there as if he'd died. It was so funny.'

DONALD TOMS

20 CHESTER ROAD

In *Cabby*, Flo asks Louise, one of the Glamcab drivers, to go to the address and pick up a fare; unbeknown to Charlie and Sarge, who intercept the message, it's a false address, and when Allbright turns up all he finds is a derelict house.

TWIST, SAM

Played by Kenneth Connor

A nervous individual seen in *Regardless*. He's a clerk at the labour exchange when we first meet him but admits to being bored with his job; when the regulars at the exchange race off after hearing that a new company, Helping Hands, needs staff, he's quick to join them. An ex-corporal of the Pioneer Corps, one of his most memorable assignments finds him catching a train to the Forth Bridge, before jumping off and landing in a puddle. While he nearly freezes to death, it's clear there has been a mistake – he should have helped a man who wanted a fourth at bridge!

TWITCHING FATHER

Played by Jack Douglas

With his nerves all a quiver, he's ushered into the waiting room at the Finisham Maternity Hospital in *Matron* where he's straight on the phone calling the Guinness Book of Records because his wife has just given birth – again!

TYLER, VIRGINIA

Roles: Funhouse Girl in *Spying* and Hand Maiden in *Cleo*

Virginia Tyler's other credits include playing Thal in 1965's *Dr Who and the Daleks*.

UBANGI TRIBE

Mentioned by Upsidasi in *Up the Jungle*, who tells Bill Boosey a useless piece of information concerning the women of the Ubangi tribe stuffing buffalo bones up their noses.

UNIVERSITY OF KIDBURN

One of the university's lecturers, Professor Crump, from the archaeological department, travels to Templeton when a Roman encampment is unearthed. He's accompanied on his trip by some enthusiastic students and Professor Vooshka, acting as his assistant. The party stay at the nearby Riverside Caravan Site after arriving in the university's blue Commer van, registration VHY 488G. The university's exterior is seen in *Behind*.

UNWIN, STANLEY

Role: Landlord in *Regardless*

Born in Pretoria, South Africa, in 1911, Stanley Unwin had several manual jobs before moving to England and joining the BBC in 1940, where his various duties saw him helping maintain transmitters, working within the war reporting department and employed as a mobile engineer.

In 1948 he appeared on radio performing a monologue which led to work on several radio shows including *Midday Music Hall*, *Variety Bandbox* and *Beyond Our Ken*. Screen work soon came his way, including appearances in films such as *Fun At St Fanny's*, *Press For Time* and *Chitty Chitty Bang Bang*. On the small screen he became a regular face, his credits including *Early to Braden*, *The David Nixon Show*, *The Dickie Henderson Show* as well as his own show, *Unwin Time*.

He narrated an album for the pop group Small Faces, where he employed his comical language Unwinese; he also wrote several books and became a regular guest on BBC Radio 2's *The Arthur Smith Lectures*.

He died in 2002, aged ninety.

UPMORE, ARTHUR

Played by Bernard Bresslaw

In *Behind* the henpecked Arthur Upmore is looking forward to a caravan holiday with his wife, Linda, until he learns that her mother is coming, too. They don't see eye-to-eye which leads to an uncomfortable break for everyone, that is until Daphne Barnes bumps into someone she hasn't seen for ten years – her ex-hubby – and turns over a new leaf.

UPMORE, LINDA

Played by Patsy Rowlands

Still a mummy's girl despite her age, she can't do anything without her mother, Daphne Barnes, tagging along. She appears in *Behind* and is married to Arthur.

UPPER DENCHER

The parish where Dick Turpin resides, disguised as the Reverend Flasher, in *Dick*.

UP THE JUNGLE, CARRY ON

See feature box on pages 250–1.

UP THE KHYBER, CARRY ON

See feature box on pages 252–3.

UPSIDASI

Played by Bernard Bresslaw

In charge of the natives carrying supplies on the jungle expedition in *Up the Jungle*.

US AMBASSADOR

Played by Bruce Boa

Seen dining at the French Ambassador's residence in *Emmannuelle*.

CARRY ON UP THE JUNGLE

Alternative Titles . . . *The African Queens, Stop Beating About the Bush, Show Me Your Water Hole And I'll Show You Mine*

A Peter Rogers production
Distributed through Rank Organisation
Released as an A certificate in 1970 in colour
Running time: 89 mins

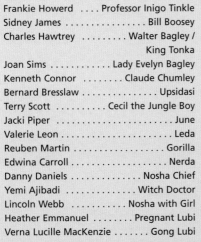

CAST

Frankie Howerd . . . . Professor Inigo Tinkle
Sidney James . . . . Bill Boosey
Charles Hawtrey . . . . Walter Bagley / King Tonka
Joan Sims . . . . Lady Evelyn Bagley
Kenneth Connor . . . . Claude Chumley
Bernard Bresslaw . . . . Upsidasi
Terry Scott . . . . Cecil the Jungle Boy
Jacki Piper . . . . June
Valerie Leon . . . . Leda
Reuben Martin . . . . Gorilla
Edwina Carroll . . . . Nerda
Danny Daniels . . . . Nosha Chief
Yemi Ajibadi . . . . Witch Doctor
Lincoln Webb . . . . Nosha with Girl
Heather Emmanuel . . . . Pregnant Lubi
Verna Lucille MacKenzie . . . . Gong Lubi

Valerie Moore
Cathi March . . . . Lubi Lieutenants
Nina Baden-Semper . . . . Girl Nosha
Roy Stewart
John Hamilton
Willie Jonah
Chris Konyils . . . . Noshas

PRODUCTION TEAM

Screenplay by Talbot Rothwell
Music composed and conducted by Eric Rogers
Production Manager: Jack Swinburne
Director of Photography: Ernest Steward
Editor: Alfred Roome

Art Director: Alex Vetchinsky
Assistant Editor: Jack Gardner
Camera Operator: James Bawden
Assistant Director: Jack Causey
Continuity: Josephine Knowles
Make-up: Geoffrey Rodway
Sound Recordists: R.T. MacPhee and Ken Barker
Hairdresser: Stella Rivers
Costume Designer: Courtenay Elliott
Dubbing Editor: Colin Miller
Titles: G.S.E. Ltd
Producer: Peter Rogers
Director: Gerald Thomas

During a lantern slide lecture for the Royal Birdwatching Society, Professor Inigo Tinkle, an esteemed ornithologist, discusses one of his latest expeditions, to the depths of the African jungle in his continued search for rare and exotic birds.

Other members of the expedition led by 'Rattlesnake Bill' Boosey, included Tinkle's assistant, Claude Chumley, Lady Bagley and her maid, June. It was an emotional time for Lady Bagley because she was returning to the location where, many years ago, she lost both her husband and baby boy, Cecil. Soon after her son was born, her husband brought her to the African jungle on a belated honeymoon. Tragedy struck when he took his son for an early morning walk along the banks of the Limpopo River and neither were seen again. When her husband's fob watch was discovered inside a crocodile's stomach, and her son's nappy found abandoned on the riverbank, she feared the worst. She returned to try and find her little boy's nappy pin, just something she could cling on to as a memory of her son.

Whilst trekking through the jungle, the party was watched by a group of natives belonging to the feared Nosha tribe, who still practise cannibalism. When their drums sounded through the trees, the natives helping to carry the party's supplies were scared and refused to go any further. With little option but to camp for the night, everyone settled down to an evening under canvas;

Lady Bagley's maid, June, decided to go for a walk and happened upon an inviting lake; deciding on a dip, she was soon joined on the shoreline by a Tarzan-like character wearing nothing but a loincloth, and whose vocabulary extended to just a few grunts and groans. Before long, they were kissing and arranging to meet later.

Unfortunately, when June was unable to meet Jungle Boy, he decided to try and find her. Meanwhile, a gorilla had strayed into the

Bill Boosey (Sid James) and his party are captured by the Lubidubies

U

Upsidasi (Bernard Bresslaw, left) is in charge of the natives carrying the expedition's supplies

camp and when he entered June's tent she mistook him for Jungle Boy, until he became overly rough and she discovered she was sharing a bed with a gorilla. In the next tent, Lady Bagley had an uninvited guest, not that she minded when she turned on the oil lamp and found Jungle Boy beside her; she later discovered he was wearing the nappy pin her little Cecil used all those years ago, so began to realise that he was her long-lost son.

When the drum sounds of the Nosha tribe reverberated around the jungle once more, Bill Boosey wanted to head back but Lady Bagley, desperate to find her boy, and Professor Tinkle, who believed he was on the trail of a bird that was previously thought extinct, were desperate to continue. First they had to deal with the Noshas and frantically dug a deep hole in the ground, intending to use it to trap the tribesmen. But when they realised they had dug so deep they couldn't get out, they were soon captured by the cannibalistic Noshas and heading for the cooking pot.

Just as they were about to be thrown in the boiling water, the captives were saved by the Lubidubies, an all-female tribe; Claude Chumley and Bill Boosey could hardly believe their luck, particularly when they learnt the Lubidubies were desperate for men. With just one man in their camp – King Tonka – Chumley, Boosey and Tinkle were required for mating purposes.

Arriving at the camp, Lady Bagley was shocked to discover King Tonka was none other than her long-lost hubby, Walter, who she thought was dead. The mating arrangements weren't what the men were expecting either, especially when they saw their first customers; after three months performing their duties, the men were worn out and desperate to escape their heavy workloads. Their prayers were answered by Upsidasi, the chief native in the expedition, who had returned to help, as

well as Jungle Boy and June, who had been living together in the jungle since splitting from the rest of the party earlier in the trip.

It wasn't long before everyone was heading home, Lady Bagley having found both her husband and son; June and Cecil, alias Jungle Boy, having discovered true love; and Professor Tinkle and Claude Chumley proud to be able to show the ornithological world the rare oozulum bird, or so they had hoped!

Funny Scene!

Professor Tinkle, Bill Boosey, Lady Bagley and Claude Chumley have been captured by the Noshas, a tribe of cannibals; tied to stakes, they're just about to be thrown in the cooking pot.

TINKLE:	Oh, the indignity of it all. I, Professor Tinkle, ornithologist, trussed like a chicken.
BOOSEY:	Just keep hoping they don't like stuffing.
LADY BAGLEY:	Do they just . . . drop us into boiling water?
BOOSEY:	Oh no, nothing as barbaric as that; they just drain all the blood out of us first.
TINKLE:	That's all we need — kosher noshas.

CARRY ON UP THE KHYBER

Alternative title . . . *The British Position in India*

A Peter Rogers production
Distributed through Rank Organisation
Released as an A certificate in 1968 in colour
Running time: 88 mins

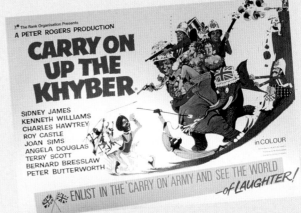

CAST

Sidney James . . . . Sir Sidney Ruff-Diamond
Kenneth Williams . . . . The Khasi of Kalabar
Charles Hawtrey . . . . Private James Widdle
Roy Castle . . . . Captain Keene
Joan Sims . . . . Lady Ruff-Diamond
Bernard Bresslaw . . . . Bunghit Din
Peter Butterworth . . . . Brother Belcher
Terry Scott . . . . Sgt Major MacNutt
Angela Douglas . . . . Princess Jelhi
Cardew Robinson . . . . The Fakir
Peter Gilmore . . . . Pte Ginger Hale
Julian Holloway . . . . Major Shorthouse
Leon Thau . . . . Stinghi
Michael Mellinger . . . . Chindi
Alexandra Dane . . . . Busti
Dominique Don . . . . MacNutt's Lure
Derek Sydney . . . . Major-domo
David Spenser . . . . Bunghit's Servant
Johnny Briggs . . . . Sporran Soldier
Simon Cain . . . . Bagpipe Soldier
Steven Scott . . . . Burpa Guard
Larry Taylor . . . . Burpa at Door-grid
Patrick Westwood . . . . Burpa in Crowd
John Hallam . . . . Burpa on Rooftop

Wanda Ventham
Liz Gold
Vicki Woolf
Anne Scott
Barbara Evans
Lisa Noble
Eve Eden
Tamsin MacDonald
Katherina Holden . . . . . . The Khasi's Wives
Valerie Leon
Carmen Dene
June Cooper
Josephine Blain
Vicki Murden
Karen Young
Angie Grant
Sue Vaughan . . . . Hospitality Girls
Patrick Allen . . . . Narrator

PRODUCTION TEAM

Screenplay by Talbot Rothwell
Music composed and conducted by Eric
  Rogers
Art Director: Alex Vetchinsky

Production Manager: Jack Swinburne
Editor: Alfred Roome
Director of Photography: Ernest Steward
Assistant Editor: Jack Gardner
Continuity: Yvonne Richards
Camera Operator: James Bawden
Assistant Director: Peter Weingreen
Sound Recordists: Robert T. MacPhee and
  Ken Barker
Make-up: Geoffrey Rodway
Hairdressing: Stella Rivers
Costume Designer: Emma Selby-Walker
Title Sketches by 'Larry'
Dubbing Editor: Colin Miller
Khyber location Director of Photography:
  H.A.R. Thomson
Camera Operator: Neil Binney
Producer: Peter Rogers
Director: Gerald Thomas

It's 1895 and the British rulers in India are living the life of Riley, particularly Sir Sidney Ruff-Diamond, the governor, and his wife, Lady Joan; but their luxurious lifestyle is threatened by Private Jimmy Widdle and his underpants!

Widdle, a member of the 3rd Foot and Mouth, who guard the Khyber Pass high in the mountains, feels the cold draughts blowing up his kilt so much that he risks the army's reputation as the 'Devils in Skirts' by slipping on his underwear. Once feared by the indigenous people, who believed they wore nothing under their kilts, their secret is out when Widdle is confronted by Bunghit Din and collapses in a heap on the ground, revealing his underwear in the process; this single act jeopardises the reputation of the British force and drastic action is taken to try and dispel the rumour. Sir Sidney Ruff-Diamond visits the Khasi of Kalabar to persuade him to pass on the word to his people that the rumour is untrue; Kalabar, who will grasp any opportunity to ridicule the British, won't help unless it can be proven that other soldiers don't wear underpants; Sir Sidney faces further embarrassment when the two soldiers accompanying him are wearing them, too.

Private Widdle et al wanted a bit of fun with the Khasi's wives

A break in filming

A plan is hatched to recover the photo and Lady Joan at the same time, although Sir Sidney isn't too sure retrieving his wife is such a good idea. Knowing they have to cross the border, Captain Keene, who's in charge of the operation, blackmails a missionary, Brother Belcher, to act as a guide. Soon after entering Afghanistan they see the Khasi addressing the Burpas, but when they're too scared to help defeat the British, he informs them of the photo he's acquired. Captain Keene and his men's attempts to recover the photo fail and they face execution along with Lady Joan, who's become reluctant to hand the picture over to the Khasi in time for him to show it to representatives of the Burpas.

Just in the nick of time, Princess Jelhi helps them escape but upon returning to the Pass they discover dead soldiers everywhere. Soon the Burpas reach the fort and an almighty battle ensues, but as bullets and shells explode around them, Sir Sidney and Lady Joan won't let anything disturb their dinner. Meanwhile, on the battle front, the British soldiers claim victory when they form a line, raise their kilts and frighten the Burpas away!

Worse is to come for the governor when, during a parade, he discovers all his men have donned undies to protect themselves from the cold mountain air. Just when he didn't think things could get any worse, Lady Ruff-Diamond, who has a soft spot for the Khasi, secretly takes a photo of the spectacle and offers it to the Khasi in return for his affections. He tells Lady Joan that he's planning an uprising and will use the photo to incite the Burpas. Overhearing her father's plans, Princess Jelhi rushes off to Captain Keene, whom she loves, to warn him of the Khasi's plans.

The Khasi of Kalabar (Kenneth Williams) surrounded by a bevy of beauties

Funny Scene!

Sir Sidney Ruff-Diamond is meeting the Khasi of Kalabar. They hate each other but enter into polite chat, albeit sarcastically at times, for appearances sake.

KHASI: And how is her most gracious majesty, Queen Waterloo?

SIR SIDNEY: Victoria!

KHASI: Oh, yes, of course, silly me, I never can remember.

SIR SIDNEY: She's well. I had a postcard from her the other day: she sends you all her love.

KHASI: Oh, she is most generous; I must make her another gift — some more elephants perhaps?

SIR SIDNEY: Oh, I wouldn't do that your honour, no more elephants. I mean Buckingham Palace isn't all that big — and they do need a lot of clearing up after.

KHASI: If you say so, but in India the more elephants a man has, the higher his standing.

SIR SIDNEY: Yes, and the higher his rhubarb.

V

VAGUE WOMAN
Played by Noel Dyson

Seen in *Constable* the Vague Woman loses her cat Fluff on the way back from the vet's. She notices the black moggy running into a church, but when it climbs into the belfry she asks the police for help. PC Gorse goes to the cat's rescue but ends up in trouble himself, hanging precariously from one of the ropes. Fortunately Sergeant Wilkins is on hand to assist.

VALENTINE, MRS
Played by Beryl Reid

The overprotective mother of Theodore Valentine appears in *Emmannuelle*, tucking her son into bed at night and trying her hardest to prevent him dwelling on his infatuation for Emmannuelle Prevert, the French Ambassador's nymphomaniacal wife. Mrs Valentine is, unsurprisingly, separated from her husband, who ran off with 'a slip of a girl'.

VALENTINE, THEODORE
Played by Larry Dann

A bespectacled mummy's boy who can't believe his luck when the bored nymphomaniac, Emmannuelle Prevert, decides to seduce him inside the claustrophobic toilet on Concorde while flying to London. The thirty-four-year-old, who drives an orange Triumph, registration KRT 144P, is soon besotted with Emmannuelle and tries his utmost, in vain, to form a relationship, not realising that she uses men like there is no tomorrow. Seen in *Emmannuelle*.

VAN DER ZYL, NIKKI
Role: Messenger in *Don't Lose Your Head*

Born in Berlin in 1935, Nikki Van Der Zyl came to England at the beginning of the war in 1939 and was raised in Surrey. She left school and enrolled at the Central School of Speech and Drama in the early 1950s, already experienced in the medium of film thanks to an opportunity with Elstree Studios to provide the voices for a German film.

Upon graduating from drama school, she went straight into the West End, understudying Amanda Barrie in *The Pet Shop*. She subsequently joined the cast of the Brian Rix farces at the Whitehall Theatre, before touring with the company for several years.

She started being offered small parts in films and on television, but it was her voice-over abilities that earned her most work, often uncredited, in a host of television shows and films, such as *Funeral in Berlin*, *The Ipcress File*, *Battle of Britain* and many Bond movies, including *Dr No* for which she provided nearly every female voice.

She changed career and after six years training qualified as a barrister in 1973. Later worked as David Mellor's PA, became a correspondent for TVS and monitored television coverage for the Tory Party during the 1992 General Election, before studying art. Nowadays, she works as a painter.

VAN EYSSEN, JOHN
Role: Mr Stephens in *Nurse*

Born in Fauresmith, South Africa, in 1922, John Van Eyssen arrived in the UK after the Second World War and trained at the Central School of Speech and Drama. He found employment with the Royal Shakespeare Company, where he subsequently performed many classical leads.

Before long, he branched out into other divisions of the industry. His film credits included his debut in *The Angel with the Trumpet*; *Three Steps in the Dark*; *Cockleshell Heroes*; *Brothers in Law*; *Account Rendered*; *I'm All Right, Jack*; *The Concrete Jungle* and *Partners in Crime*. On television he was seen in, among others, *Interpol Calling* and *The New Adventures of Charlie Chan*.

He left acting in the early 1960s to work as an agent, before, in 1965, joining the UK division of Columbia Pictures. As managing director, he was a driving force behind some classic British films, including *To Sir, With Love* and *Born Free*. By the 1970s he was working in America but, in 1974, left to become an independent producer.

He died in 1995, aged seventy-three.

VAN OST, VALERIE
Roles: Glamcab Driver in *Cabby*, 2nd Lady in *Don't Lose Your Head*, Nurse Parkin in *Doctor* and Outpatients Sister in *Again Doctor*

Nurse Parkin (Valerie Van Ost) gets a cuddle from Charlie Roper (Sid James) (*Doctor*)

'My darling mama, who was a singer in the Ivor Novello shows at Drury Lane, said to me once: "Never say that you can't do something, darling, learn to do it afterwards." So I went along to the audition for *Cabby* and when they asked if I could drive, I said "yes" and got the job. Then I had to learn, so had one lesson a day for a fortnight before being set loose on the back lot. Because we were filming at the studio rather than on the main road, a provisional licence would do. I wasn't nervous because I had all the confidence of someone who'd never had an accident, but I think the cameraman was more nervous than me.

'After *Don't Lose Your Head*, I appeared as Nurse Parkin in *Doctor*. That was good fun and one of the most famous doctor-patient pictures was taken of me tucking up Sidney James in bed and telling him off because he's smoking. They blew this up to about ten feet by twenty feet and stuck it outside the Odeon in Leicester Square; it was very exciting having a large blow-up picture of me and Sid. It became an amazingly famous picture and has been used to advertise all manner of things. I've actually got a colour print of it hanging in my loo. When the filming was taking place there was this terrific din when the nurses and cleaners marched through the ward first thing in the morning. I thought it was rather theatrical and over-the-top. Since then, having visited people in hospital, I've been appalled at the noise and realise it wasn't over-the-top at all.

'Everything went to plan and ran very smoothly. In those days we had to have absolutely immaculate hairdos so we had Carmen hair rollers put in our hair first thing in the morning right through to the end of the day. It was a glamorous look. I was then upgraded to Sister for my last role in *Again Doctor* and had a more conservative hairdo, not requiring quite so many hair rollers. Appearing in the *Carry On*s was a great experience.'

VALERIE VAN OST

Born in Berkhamsted, Hertfordshire, in 1944, Valerie Van Ost attended the Arts Educational School in London before becoming, at the age of sixteen, the youngest dancer to perform at the Palladium. She danced at the venue for a year, followed by two months in Paris, dancing with Johnny Halliday at the Olympia.

Returning to England, she turned her attention to acting, always her preferred career, and joined a repertory company in Eastbourne, then Bexhill and before long venues up and down the country. During the late 1960s she toured with David Jason in *Partners*. Her theatre career has included many West End performances, such as two productions with Spike Milligan at the Comedy and Mermaid theatres.

It wasn't long before she began appearing in television and films. Her small-screen debut was in an episode of comedy series *Pardon the Expression* in the mid-1960s followed by the likes of *The Avengers* (playing Patrick Macnee's co-driver), *Dixon of Dock Green*, *Strange Report*, *Ace of Wands*, *Arthur of the Britons*, *The Venturers*, *Crossroads*, *Bless This House* and *Mrs Thursday*. Her first film credit was *Cabby*, the first of four appearances in the *Carry On* films, but she was also seen in *Corruption*, *School for Unclaimed Girls*, *It All Goes to Show*, *The Insomniac*, *Incense for the Damned*, *The Satanic Rites of Dracula* and her last film, the TV movie *Alien Attack*, based on two episodes of *Space: 1999*.

In 1976, Valerie Van Ost retired from acting and together with husband, Andrew Millington, launched a casting company, Van Ost and Millington Casting, involved, primarily, in commercials. During the 1960s, Van Ost was in a long-running commercial herself, making approximately a dozen adverts advertising Cadbury's Bournville chocolate.

VANCAO, COLIN
Role: Wilberforce Grubb in *Loving*
Character actor Colin Vancao was seen on the small screen from the 1950s, appearing in such programmes as *Dixon of Dock Green*, *Adam Adamant Lives!*, *The Persuaders!* and *Jason King*. His film work included *The Charge of the Light Brigade*.

He moved to Australia during the 1970s and remained busy until his death in 1992. His film credits down-under included *Starting Out* and *A Thousand Skies*, while he was cast many times in the cult prison drama, *Prisoner: Cell Block H*.

VAUGHAN, SUE
Role: Hospitality Girl in *Up The Khyber*
During the 1960s, Sue Vaughan also appeared in an episode of *Randall and Hopkirk (Deceased)*.

VENTHAM, WANDA
Roles: Pretty Bidder in *Cleo* and Khasi's Wife in *Up The Khyber*
Born in Brighton in 1939, Wanda Ventham studied stage design at art school before enrolling at the Central School of Drama in London. She made her professional debut in 1959, and repertory theatre dominated the early years of her career, at venues including Bath and Cardiff. On stage she's been seen in shows such as *Watch It Sailor* at London's Apollo Theatre, and *Two Into One* at the capital's Shaftesbury Theatre.

Her film work includes productions like *The Knock*, *Mister Ten Per Cent*, *Doctor Kronos* and *Mrs Caldicot's Cabbage War*, while her host of television roles extend from two series as Sylvia in *Executive Stress*, Alexandra in *Out of the Shadows* and Mrs Ridge in *All Creatures Great and Small* to Marion Kershaw in *Boon*, three series as Rosie in *Next of Kin* and Fiona in *Heartbeat*. Her favourite television role was Ann Shepherd in the BBC's *The Lotus Eaters*.

Recent jobs have seen her appear in *Coupling* for television and the films *Affair of the Necklace* and *Asylum*.

VENTURA, VIVIANNE
Role: Spanish Secretary in *Jack*
Born in London in 1947, Vivienne Ventura's screen career includes appearances in series such as *The Saint*, *The Loner*, *The Man From U.N.C.L.E.*, *I Spy*, *The Persuaders!* and *Doomwatch*.

On the big screen she was first seen in an uncredited role in 1963's *Summer Holiday*, before going on to appear in, among others, *Lord Jim*, *A High Wind in Jamaica*, *Promise Her Anything* and *Battle Beneath the Sea*.

VENUS
The name of the frigate which sets sail from Plymouth in *Jack*.

VERNA
Played by Vivien Lloyd
One of the girls from Chayste Place Finishing School who's seen in *Camping*.

VERONICA
Played by Jenny Cox
A stripper who's sent to perform at the Riverside Caravan Site's cabaret evening. She arrives in her MG, registration XPP 226J, and certainly entertains the male element of the crowd! Pleases the punters in *Behind*.

VERY FAT MAN
Played by Willoughby Goddard
In *Cruising* this portly passenger on the *Happy Wanderer* is seen sidling up to Glad Trimble at the captain's cocktail party when all she wants to do is find the opportune moment to talk to Mr Jenkins, the PT instructor. He's later seen relaxing in a deckchair until an over-excited Dr Binn falls on him.

VESTAL VIRGINS
Played by Gloria Johnson, Joanna Ford, Donna White, Jane Lumb and Vicki Smith
In *Cleo* the Vestal Virgins are the priestesses of Vesta in charge of maintaining the sacred fire within the Temple of Vesta. Caesar consults them at the temple when he's uncertain about his future.

Horsa (Jim Dale) is pampered on set (*Cleo*)

VETCHINSKY, ALEX

Art director on *Sergeant, Nurse, Spying, Follow That Camel, Up The Khyber* and *Up the Jungle*
Born in London in 1904, Alex Vetchinsky qualified as an architect in London before hearing about a vacancy at Gainsborough Studios for an assistant art director. He was offered a position and began working on early films from the 1930s, beginning with *Michael and Mary*, as well as *Love On Wheels* and *The Phantom Light*.

He later transferred to Pinewood Studios where he remained for the rest of his career, which latterly saw him loaned out to an American film company. Other big-screen credits during his long career included *The Tawny Pipit, The October Man, The Weaker Sex, Trouble in Store, A Town Like Alice, A Night to Remember, Life For Ruth* and *Night of the Big Heat*.

Vetchinsky retired in 1976 but still accepted the occasional job in an advisory capacity. He died in 1980, aged seventy-six.

VIDEO

See 'Video' p.283.

VILLIERS, JAMES

Role: Recruit in *Sergeant*
Born in London in 1933, James Villiers was a firm favourite when casting directors were looking for an actor to play anything from bumptious military officials to mordant barristers.

After completing his education at Wellington College he joined RADA. Upon graduating he made his professional debut in 1953, appearing in *The Ten Little Niggers* at Frinton Rep. He went on to work with the Old Vic company, at the Royal Court and in various West End productions, beginning with 1960's *Tomorrow With Pictures*.

He was busiest in films during the 1960s, appearing in, among others, *Petticoat Pirates, Operation Snatch, Murder At the Gallop, Girl in the Headlines, The Nanny* and *Some Girls Do*. Other credits include *For Your Eyes Only* and *Under the Volcano*. On television he was seen in the likes of *Two's Company, The Famous Five, The First Churchills, Pygmalion* and *Hemingway*.

He died in 1998, aged sixty-four.

VINCENT, 'LEFTY'

Played by Freddie Mills
Seen in *Regardless*, 'Lefty' is an old friend of Bert Handy who visits the Helping Hands office when he wants to hire some people to help at a boxing bout between Dynamite Dan and Massive Micky. He knows Bert from their days together as boxers, but now he's turned to management and has a new figher, Dynamite Dan Grimsby, whose first fight is being staged in the fairground booth.

VIOLINIST

Played by Sonny Farrar
In *Loving* the violinist entertains in the Marie Antoinette Room at Mr and Mrs Bliss's wedding reception.

VIRGINIA

Played by Tanya Binning
In *Cleo*, Virginia is head of the Vestal Virgins whom Caesar consults whenever he's in need of inspiration or guidance.

VIVIAN, MR

Played by Michael Ward
The window-dresser is employed by Bourne and Jones and seen in *Screaming!* He's injured when a window collapses on him.

VOOSHKA, PROFESSOR ANNA

Played by Elke Sommer
An expert in Roman remains, Russian archaeologist Professor Vooshka – whose numerous expeditions included a trip to the Gobi Desert – helps Professor Crump in *Behind* when he travels to Templeton for an archaeological dig. A confident, chatty woman, who takes a shine to the Professor, but has one weakness: her careless use of the English language could land her in hot water, especially if she goes around too often asking people, 'How are your doings?'.

W

WADES CERAMICS

In *At Your Convenience*, William Boggs writes to the directors of the company, a competitor in the toilet ware industry, regarding their earlier interest in taking over Boggs and Son. After two weeks of strikes, Boggs's company is struggling to survive. Fortunately, selling off the firm isn't necessary when Sid Plummer, courtesy of his winnings at the bookie's, bails the company out in its hour of need.

WAGE BILL

See feature box on pages 258–9.

WAIN, GERRY

Master of Horse on *Dick*

Other credits for Gerry Wain during the 1960s and '70s include *Doctor Who*, *Arthur of the Britons*, *Z Cars* and *The Benny Hill Show*.

WAITER

Played by George Roderick

Serves Dr Carver and Mrs Moore with wine during the Long Hampton Hospital's grand buffet and dance in *Again Doctor*. Starts pouring just as Carver launches into one of his chat-up lines, courtesy of Dr Nookey, to which the waiter suggests he tries the wine before extolling its virtues!

WAKEFIELD, WILLIAM

Played by Ted Ray

In *Teacher*, William Wakefield is acting head at Maudlin Street Secondary Modern School in the absence of Mr Carson. He joined Maudlin Street straight from training college, twenty years ago. His career has seen him spend seven years as assistant headmaster and one term as acting head. He's striving for his own headship and sees the perfect answer in an advert for a new school at Offord New Town in Sussex. What he didn't expect, though, was for the Maudlin Street children to set up a campaign to keep him at their school. A modernist in terms of child behaviour, he resents the use of the cane, believing – much to some of his teachers' chagrin – that there are more constructive ways of disciplining a child.

WALLER, KENNETH

Role: Barman in *Behind*

Best known for playing Grandad in the popular sitcom, *Bread*, Kenneth Waller was born in Huddersfield in 1927. He made his stage debut at the age of six, performing in a concert party organised by his mother. While carrying out National Service on the Isle of Man, he formed a dramatic society with a friend, presenting shows around the island.

Back in civvy street he worked for an auctioneer and estate agent while appearing in amateur dramatics, but when invited to join the local theatre, Waller turned professional. After eighteen months of rep, he moved into the West End in 1960.

On the big screen he appeared in a handful of films, beginning with *Room At the Top* in 1958. He was later seen as a dotty professor in *Chitty Chitty Bang Bang* and in, among others, *Fiddler On the Roof* and *Scrooge* with Albert Finney. His television credits, meanwhile, included *Are You Being Served?*, *All Creatures Great and Small*, *Coronation Street*, *Doctor Who*, *Juliet Bravo* and *Big Deal*.

He died in 2000, aged seventy-two.

WALL-EYED MAN, THE

Played by Ken Kennedy

A non-speaking character seen in *Constable*, the Wall-eyed Man bumps into the superstitious Constable Constable while walking down the High Street.

WARD CLEANER

Played by Helen Ford

Appears in *Doctor* hoovering the men's ward, waking Mr Bigger in the process, who's not a happy bunny.

WARD, GUY

Role: Dandy in *Emmannuelle*

Guy Ward's other screen credits during the 1960s and '70s include an episode of *Please, Sir!* and the role of Dennis Harper in *Crossroads*. His film work includes an appearance in *The Beast in the Cellar* in 1971.

Francis Courtenay (Kenneth Williams) always fancied himself as a model (*Regardless*)

WAGE BILLS

It's now become public knowledge that the wage bill for the *Carry Ons* was modest. It seems the actors who have committed their memoirs to paper make a point of highlighting this matter: in her autobiography, *High Spirits*, Joan Sims said that 'pay was a constant bugbear for all the actors'. At least the films, which became a series in their own right, provided regular work with, at times, two films being made in the same year. The wages may have been regarded as low by some people, but the upside was that those establishing themselves as regulars could almost guarantee work each year. So just how much did the principal actors earn?

SERGEANT
Eric Barker £525
Gerald Campion £500
Kenneth Connor £1250
Shirley Eaton £1000
William Hartnell £2000
Charles Hawtrey £1000
Hattie Jacques £150
Terence Longdon £750
Bob Monkhouse £1500
Bill Owen £1000
Norman Rossington £360
Terry Scott £50
Kenneth Williams £900

NURSE
Cyril Chamberlain £425
Kenneth Connor £1250
Shirley Eaton £1250
Wilfred Hyde White £2000
Hattie Jacques £250
Terence Longdon £900
Bill Owen £800
Leslie Phillips £720
Joan Sims £750
Kenneth Williams £450

TEACHER
Cyril Chamberlain £60
Kenneth Connor £1750
Charles Hawtrey £900
Hattie Jacques £700
Richard O'Sullivan £250
Leslie Phillips £1000
Ted Ray £2500
Joan Sims £1500
Kenneth Williams £1500

CONSTABLE
Eric Barker £700
Cyril Chamberlain £400
Kenneth Connor £2250
Charles Hawtrey £1100
Hattie Jacques £375
Sid James £2500
Leslie Phillips £1200
Joan Sims £2000
Kenneth Williams £2000

REGARDLESS
Kenneth Connor £4000
Liz Fraser £1100
Charles Hawtrey £2500
Hattie Jacques £100
Sid James £2000
Terence Longdon £500
Bill Owen £1200
Joan Sims £2500
Kenneth Williams £3000

CRUISING
Vincent Ball £400
Kenneth Connor £4500
Liz Fraser £1650
Sid James £4000
Dily Laye £900
Lance Percival £600
Kenneth Williams £5000

CABBY
Kenneth Connor £5000
Jim Dale £160
Liz Fraser £1800
Charles Hawtrey £3000
Hattie Jacques £4500
Sid James £5000
Bill Owen £325

JACK
Bernard Cribbins £5000
Jim Dale £150
Charles Hawtrey £3000
Donald Houston £3250
Juliet Mills £4500
Cecil Parker £500
Kenneth Williams £5000

SPYING
Eric Barker £400
Bernard Cribbins £5000
Jim Dale £450
Charles Hawtrey £3000
Richard Wattis £450
Kenneth Williams £5000
Barbara Windsor £4000

CLEO
Amanda Barrie £550
Kenneth Connor £4500
Jim Dale £1000
Charles Hawtrey £4000
Sid James £5000
Warren Mitchell £120
Jon Pertwee £150
Joan Sims £750
Kenneth Williams £5000

COWBOY
Bernard Bresslaw £750
Peter Butterworth £750
Jim Dale £1600
Angela Douglas £200
Charles Hawtrey £3000
Sid James £5000
Jon Pertwee £375
Joan Sims £1750
Kenneth Williams £5000

SCREAMING!
Bernard Bresslaw £900
Peter Butterworth £1400
Harry H. Corbett £12,000
Jim Dale . . . . £200 per week
Angela Douglas £600
Fenella Fielding . . . . £300 per week
Charles Hawtrey £400
Jon Pertwee £150
Joan Sims £175
Kenneth Williams £5000

DON'T LOSE YOUR HEAD
Jim Dale £2100
Charles Hawtrey £3500
Sid James £5000
Dany Robin £3500
Joan Sims £2500
Kenneth Williams £5000

FOLLOW THAT CAMEL
Bernard Bresslaw £2000
Peter Butterworth £2000
Jim Dale £3000
Angela Douglas £1200
Anita Harris £2000
Charles Hawtrey £4000
Phil Silvers £30,000
Joan Sims £150
Kenneth Williams £6000

DOCTOR

Bernard Bresslaw	£2000
Peter Butterworth	£250
Jim Dale	£3000
Anita Harris	£2000
Charles Hawtrey	£1500
Kenneth Williams	£5000
Barbara Windsor	£1500

UP THE KHYBER

Peter Butterworth	£1500
Roy Castle	£3500
Charles Hawtrey	£3500
Sid James	£4500
Terry Scott	£2500
Joan Sims	£2500
Kenneth Williams	£5000

CAMPING

Bernard Bresslaw	£2500
Peter Butterworth	£200 pw
Charles Hawtrey	£3500
Hattie Jacques	£3000
Sid James	£5000
Terry Scott	£2500
Joan Sims	£2500
Kenneth Williams	£5000
Barbara Windsor	£3000

AGAIN DOCTOR

Jim Dale	£3250
Charles Hawtrey	£3500
Hattie Jacques	£3000
Sid James	£4000
Patsy Rowlands	£720
Joan Sims	£2500
Kenneth Williams	£5000
Barbara Windsor	£2000

UP THE JUNGLE

Bernard Bresslaw	£2000
Kenneth Connor	£2000
Charles Hawtrey	£3000
Frankie Howerd	£9000
Sid James	£4000
Valerie Leon	£600
Jacki Piper	£600
Terry Scott	£2500
Joan Sims	£3000

LOVING

Bernard Bresslaw	£200
Imogen Hassall	£750
Charles Hawtrey	£3000
Hattie Jacques	£3000
Sid James	£5000
Richard O'Callaghan	£1200
Jacki Piper	£750
Patsy Rowlands	£250
Terry Scott	£2500
Joan Sims	£2250
Kenneth Williams	£5000

HENRY

Sid James	£5000
Kenneth Williams	£5000
Charles Hawtrey	£3000
Barbara Windsor	£2000
Peter Butterworth	£625
Kenneth Connor	£2000
Joan Sims	£3000
Terry Scott	£3000
Patsy Rowlands	£75

AT YOUR CONVENIENCE

Bernard Bresslaw	£3000
Kenneth Cope	£2000
Charles Hawtrey	£3000
Renée Houston	£600
Hattie Jacques	£2000
Sid James	£5000
Richard O'Callaghan	£1500
Jacki Piper	£1750
Patsy Rowlands	£660
Joan Sims	£2500
Kenneth Williams	£5000

MATRON

Bernard Bresslaw	£1800
Kenneth Connor	£1000
Kenneth Cope	£2000
Jack Douglas	£25
Derek Francis	£250
Charles Hawtrey	£2500
Hattie Jacques	£2500
Sid James	£5000
Bill Maynard	£800
Patsy Rowlands	£120
Terry Scott	£200
Kenneth Williams	£5000
Barbara Windsor	£2400

ABROAD

Bernard Bresslaw	£2500
Peter Butterworth	£750
John Clive	£500
Kenneth Connor	£2250
Derek Francis	£750
Sally Geeson	£500
Gail Grainger	£500
Carol Hawkins	£500
Charles Hawtrey	£3000
Hattie Jacques	£500
Sid James	£3500
Jimmy Logan	£1000
Patsy Rowlands	£60
Joan Sims	£2500
June Whitfield	£1000
Kenneth Williams	£5000
Barbara Windsor	£2500

GIRLS

Robin Askwith	£350
Bernard Bresslaw	£2500
Peter Butterworth	£1000
Kenneth Connor	£3000
Joan Hickson	£300
Sid James	£5000
Valerie Leon	£1000
Jimmy Logan	£300
Margaret Nolan	£600
Wendy Richard	£500
Patsy Rowlands	£360
Joan Sims	£2500
June Whitfield	£1000
Barbara Windsor	£3000

DICK

Bernard Bresslaw	£2500
Peter Butterworth	£1800
Kenneth Connor	£3000
Jack Douglas	£1800
Hattie Jacques	£2000
Sid James	£5000
Joan Sims	£2000
Kenneth Williams	£5000
Barbara Windsor	£3000

BEHIND

Bernard Bresslaw	£2500
Peter Butterworth	£1800
Kenneth Connor	£3000
Windsor Davies	£2500
Jack Douglas	£1600
Liz Fraser	£750
Ian Lavender	£1000
Patsy Rowlands	£800
Joan Sims	£2000
Kenneth Williams	£5000

ENGLAND

Peter Butterworth	£800
Kenneth Connor	£3000
Windsor Davies	£2500
Jack Douglas	£2000
Judy Geeson	£2000
Melvyn Hayes	£1500
Julian Holloway	£300
Peter Jones	£2000
Diane Langton	£1625
Patrick Mower	£2500
Joan Sims	£2000

EMMANNUELLE

Peter Butterworth	£2000
Kenneth Connor	£3500
Suzanne Danielle	£2750
Larry Dann	£1000
Jack Douglas	£2500
Beryl Reid	£750
Joan Sims	£2500
Kenneth Williams	£5750

The bespectacled Richard Wattis turns up in as Cobley (*Spying*)

WARD, HAYDN

Role: Recruit in *Sergeant*

Other screen credits include playing a painter in a 1962 episode of *The Avengers*.

WARD, MICHAEL

Roles: Photographer in *Regardless*, Man in Tweeds in *Cabby*, Archimedes in *Cleo*, Vivian in *Screaming!* and Henri in *Don't Lose Your Head*

Born in the tiny Cornish village of Carnmenellis in 1909, Michael Ward belonged to that clutch of character actors whose services were in such demand during the heyday of the British film industry that they seemed to appear in every post-war movie. He made his name playing small parts throughout the 1950s and '60s, in films such as *Tom Brown's Schooldays*, *The Love Lottery* and *Doctor in Love*, while his more substantial contributions included appearances as Maurice in Norman Wisdom's *Up in the World*, and as Elvin, an ornithologist, in *Sleeping Car to Trieste*.

Ward, whose father was a parish vicar, trained at the Central School of Speech and Drama, after a brief stint as a teacher. By the outbreak of the Second World War he'd already made several stage appearances, and returned to the theatre when the war ended. His film debut in the 1947 picture, *The First Gentleman*, marked the beginning of a busy career, which included appearances in five Norman Wisdom movies. His last

film was *Revenge of the Pink Panther*, playing a real estate agent. On television he appeared in shows such as *Morecambe and Wise*, *Crossroads*, *Hancock's Half Hour*, *The Two Ronnies*, *Steptoe and Son* and *The New Avengers*.

Ill-health forced his retirement from acting in 1980. He died in 1997, aged eighty-eight.

WARDER

Played by Brian Wilde **(Note: this scene was cut.)**

In *Henry*, the warder was involved in a scene with Cromwell and Sir Roger de Lodgerley, who was strung out on the rack ready to receive more torture. The trouble is, he's been stretched so much he's outgrown the rack.

> **WHAT MIGHT HAVE BEEN**

INT. THE TORTURE CHAMBER – DAY

Cromwell and two warders are by the rack, obviously at loggerheads. Roger stands dispassionately listening.

CROMWELL: What do you mean – he won't fit it any more?

WARDER 1: The rack won't go any further! He's outgrown it!

CROMWELL: But that's ridiculous! There must be some way . . . !

ROGER: (**Matter-of-factly.**) Make a bigger one.

CROMWELL: Would you please mind your own business!

ROGER: I should have thought it *was* my business. I've got to go on it.

CROMWELL: Well, I'm sorry we've neither the time nor the funds to make a bigger one for you!

ROGER: Oh dear. Couldn't you try stretching me sideways?

CROMWELL: Look, will you please stop butting . . . (**To WARDER.**) That's not a bad idea. How about sideways?

WARDER 1: Not very nice for a man.

CROMWELL: Why?

(**The WARDER gets close to whisper in his ear, making splitting movements with his hands.**)

CROMWELL: Ooh! Yes, I see what you mean.

ROGER: What?

(**CROMWELL gets close and whispers in *his* ear.**)

ROGER: Oh, perhaps you're right.

CROMWELL: Depends whether you want to use it again, I suppose.

ROGER: Well, I'd like to.

CROMWELL: Look, couldn't you sign the confession without being tortured?

ROGER: No!

CROMWELL: Oh dear, sometimes I think this torture business does more harm than good.

ROGER: What about the Iron Maiden? I've never tried that.

(He indicates the Iron Maiden standing against the wall close by.)

WARDER 1: No good. He'll be too big for it now.

ROGER: Nonsense, I'm sure I could squeeze in somehow.

CROMWELL: Well, we can try it, I suppose.

(He goes to the Iron Maiden and knocks on the outside gently.)

CROMWELL: Anybody in there?

(Listens for a moment, then laughs and points to the slide bolt opening in front.)

CROMWELL: Oh no, it says 'vacant', look.

(And, indeed, in the usual lavatory style, it does.)

ROGER: Well, that's a bit of luck.

(CROMWELL opens the door and we now see all the spikes inside, on back and inside of front. Also a notice on the inside of the front, saying 'PLEASE CLOSE THE DOOR AFTER YOU'.) (ROGER starts to squeeze himself in.)

ROGER: There . . . I think I can manage it all right.

CROMWELL: Mind you don't prick yourself!

ROGER: I'm all right. There! I'm in!

CROMWELL: Quite comfortable?

ROGER: Fine.

CROMWELL: Right. I'll close the door then.

ROGER: Oh, could I have something to read first?

CROMWELL: Certainly.

(He produces a book from his pocket and gives it to ROGER. And as he closes the door on him . . .)

CROMWELL: But don't stay in there *too* long now. Others may want to use it.

(And to the WARDERS . . .)

CROMWELL: Move the spikes in one inch daily!

WARE, NEVILLE

Role: 2nd Reporter in *Emmannuelle*

Born in New Malden, Surrey, in 1952, Neville Ware studied for two years at the Guildford School of Acting; possessing a musical bent, he also trained at the Trinity College of Music, but his early work was based in the theatre, most notably appearing in the West End in Alan Bennett's first stage play, *Forty Years On*, in 1968.

Ware, who made just a handful of television appearances, including an episode of *Z Cars*, gave up acting in 1978, the same year he

appeared in *Emmannuelle*, his only film. He moved into stage management and spent three years working with the National Theatre (1980-83) and a small-scale touring company, London Opera Players (1989-97).

Nowadays, Ware, who also worked for a theatre consultancy for a time, does voiceover work for Sky and teaches speech and drama.

WARWICK, GINA

Role: Harem Girl in *Follow That Camel*

Other screen credits during the 1960s and '70s include television shows *Department S, On the Buses* and *We Have Ways of Making You Laugh*, while on the big screen she was seen in such films as *Mister Ten Per Cent* and *The Haunted House of Horror*.

WASH ORDERLY

Played by Gertan Klauber

Seen in Fosdick Ward at the Borough County Hospital in *Doctor*. He arrives at Mr Bigger's bed ready to give him a morning wash.

WATSON, CLAUDE

Unit Manager on *Regardless*

Working from the 1960s as a production manager and second unit assistant director, his film credits include *The Innocents, The Caretaker, The Fanatics, Modesty Blaise, Our Mother's House, Isadora* and *Oh! What a Lovely War.*

WATSON, TED

Played by Kenneth Connor

Manager of Speedee Taxis Limited, Ted is employed by Charlie Hawkins, his best mate. His loyalty is unquestionable and he'll do anything for his boss, even if that results in a row with his girlfriend, Sally, who works in the firm's canteen. Seen in *Cabby.*

WATT, DOCTOR OLANDO

Played by Kenneth Williams

A former chemist who made liver pills, Olando Watt is the brother of Virula and lives at Bide-a-Wee Rest Home. He's been dead fifteen years but brings himself back to life with an electric charge every now and again. Seen in *Screaming!*. (Note: in an early version of the script, Olando was to be Virula's father, not brother.)

WATT, VIRULA

Played by Fenella Fielding

Seen in *Screaming!* the mysterious Virula is the sister of Doctor Olando Watt who lives at Bide-a-Wee Rest Home with her brother. Detective Sergeant Sidney Bung takes quite a shine to Virula when he visits while investigating the disappearance of Doris Mann in Hocombe Woods. He likes her so much they end up living together. (Note: in an early version of the script, Virula was to be called Verbena.)

WATTIS, RICHARD

Role: Cobley in *Spying*

Born in Wednesbury, Staffordshire, in 1912,

Richard Wattis's trademark was the old-fashioned specs he wore while portraying a host of bland and irksome ministerial men, frequently engulfed in red tape, such as the harassed education official, Manton Bassett, in the *St Trinian's* films. They became such a trademark that often film contracts stipulated their use.

Often playing cameo roles, he popped up in nearly a hundred films during his thirty-seven years in the profession. As well as movies, he also worked in theatre, radio and television, a medium for which he'll always be remembered as Mr Brown, the nosey, meddling neighbour in *Sykes*.

Although he wanted to become an actor from an early age, he worked at his uncle's electrical switchgear manufacturing business for a short time. Attempts at market gardening and chartered accountancy followed before, in 1935, he joined J. Baxter Somerville's Repertory Company, Croydon, as a student.

He moved on to the Theatre Royal, Brighton, and by the time the Second World War saw him join the army, he'd established his name in the theatre and made his television and film debut, in 1937's *A Yank at Oxford*.

He resumed his career after the war and went on to appear in a myriad of films, including *Helter Skelter, Stop Press Girl, The Happiest Days of Your Life, Penny Princess, The Final Test, Doctor in The House, The Clouded Yellow, Hobson's Choice* and *The Prince and the Showgirl*. On television he was seen in *Call My Bluff, Hancock's Half Hour, Dick and the Duchess, Coppers End* and *Father, Dear Father.*

He died in 1975, aged sixty-two.

WATTS, GWENDOLYN

Roles: Mrs Barron in *Doctor*, Night Sister in *Again Doctor* and Frances Kemp in *Matron*

Born in 1937, Gwendolyn Watts worked in theatre before breaking into films and television during the early 1960s. On the big screen she was seen in such pictures as *Sons and Lovers, Billy Liar, My Fair Lady, The Wrong Box, All Neat in Black Stockings* and *The Games.*

Her television work included *The Avengers, Adam Adamant Lives!, The Ronnie Barker Playhouse* and playing Iris in *On the Buses*. Her last small-screen credit saw her playing a 'sturdy woman' in *The Final Cut.*

She died in 2000, aged sixty-two.

WAY, ANN

Role: Aunt Victoria Grubb in *Loving*

Born in Wiveliscombe, Somerset, in 1915, petite actress Ann Way was busy on stage and screen for over four decades, usually seen in small character parts. Among her many television credits are *Detective, The Jazz Age, The Goodies, Follyfoot, Crossroads, Castle Haven, Fawlty Towers, Within These Walls, Mind Your Language, Ripping Yarns* and *The Bill.*

In films, she was seen in *Twinky*, *Hands of the Ripper*, *Endless Night*, *Clockwise*, *Crystalstone* and *Anchoress*.

She died in 1993, aged seventy-seven.

WAYE, ANTHONY
Assistant Director on *Jack*

Anthony Waye has worked in the film industry for over four decades ever since joining Pinewood Studios as a trainee. He quickly climbed the promotion ladder to first assistant director, spending twenty years in this capacity on films such as *Star Wars*, *The Elephant Man*, *Clash of the Titans* and the Bond movies *For Your Eyes Only* and *Octopussy*.

Now working as an executive producer on the latest Bond picture, other films he's worked on during his career include *A Pair of Briefs*, *A Stitch in Time*, *Where Eagles Dare*, *Diamonds on Wheels* and *The Deadly Bees*.

WEBB, LINCOLN
Role: Nosha with Girl in *Up the Jungle*

Other screen credits during the 1960s and '70s include the television series *Doctor at Large* and *Doctor at Sea*, as well as films such as *Scream and Scream Again*, *Love Thy Neighbour* and, in 1974, *Barry McKenzie Holding His Own*.

WEBSTER, MALCOLM
Role: Recruit in *Sergeant*

After making his screen debut in *Sergeant*, Malcolm Webster went on to appear in films such as *The Gentle Terror* and the television plays, *For Tea On Sunday* and *Alice*.

WEDDED BLISS AGENCY, THE
The proprietors of the business, which is based in a fourth floor office, are Sidney and Sophie Bliss, who for the company's benefit claim to have been married ten years, although they haven't even walked down the aisle yet. They try to instil confidence into their clients by boasting about their state-of-the-art computer which within seconds will assess an individual's needs and select a suitable partner. Behind the scenes, though, sits Sophie, who collects the cards Sidney pushes through a little slot and proceeds with the laborious task of matchmaking. The company's fees are two guineas for registration, two guineas for the introduction and two guineas when they 'click', and if the person 'clicks' with his partner without getting married it's four guineas.

WEEKLY ECHO, THE
A newspaper in *Again Doctor* carrying the story of the mayhem Dr Nookey caused at the Long Hampton Hospital.

WEEKLY GAZETTE, THE
A newspaper, incorporating other papers including *The Advertiser* and the *Cherrywood Comet*, in *Again Doctor* covering the story of Dr Nookey's antics at the Long Hampton Hospital.

WEINGREEN, PETER
Assistant Director on *Up The Khyber*

WEIR, MOLLY
Bird Owner in *Regardless*

Born in Glasgow in 1910, Molly Weir left school and worked as a shorthand typist before turning to showbusiness. She came to prominence on radio during the Second World War, in the role of Tattie Macintosh in the BBC comedy, *ITMA*, and subsequently spent many years in the medium. Other work saw her contribute to *Woman's Hour* and write and perform on *Children's Hour*.

Busy on television from the '60s, her credits include *Suspense*, *The Troubleshooters*, *Doctor on the Go*, *All Creatures Great and Small*, *The High Life* and many series of *Rentaghost* playing Hazel the McWitch. Her film work, which began in the 1940s, includes roles in *Something in the City*, *Cheer the Brave*, *The Lyons in Paris*, *Value for Money*, *The Bridal Path*, *Scrooge* and, in 1999, *Captain Jack*.

She died in 2004, aged ninety-four.

WELLS, FARGO & COMPANY
The company runs the overnight stagecoaches travelling back and forth from Stodge City. One of their coaches is seen in *Cowboy* ferrying Marshall P. Knutt and Annie Oakley to Stodge.

WENTWORTH STREET
A road mentioned in *Cabby* during the scene where Peggy and Sally are held at gunpoint by crooks.

WEST, BERTRAM OLIPHANT
Played by Jim Dale

Better known as Bo West, the upper class, Eton-educated gentleman appears in *Follow That Camel*. When he's accused of cheating during a cricket match and banned from the home of Lady Jane Ponsonby, with whom he's smitten, he runs off and joins the Foreign Legion. It later transpires that he never cheated during the match organised by Sir Cyril Ponsonby, so Lady Jane sets off to find him. He eventually marries Lady Jane although their baby looks amazingly like Commandant Burger, who happens to be an old flame from her days in Vienna!

WESTERN ENGINEERING COMPANY
In *Constable* one of the company's vans (an A35, registration WLU 545) is involved in a wages snatch. The drivers are still tied up in the back when PC Potter and Sergeant Wilkins use the vehicle to chase the criminals.

WESTON, MIKE
Played by Bill Owen

Mike is employed by Helping Hands Limited in *Regardless*. A peaked-cap-wearing guy who's best suited to being a bouncer at a nightclub rather than looking after an old lady's pet birds,

something which happens when the job cards at Helping Hands get mixed up one day.

WESTWOOD, PATRICK
Role: Burpa in Crowd in *Up The Khyber*

In films since the late 1940s, Patrick Westwood's credits include *A Gunman Has Escaped*, *Happy Ever After*, *Passage Home*, *The Tommy Steele Story* and *Cash in Hand*. On television, he's been seen in, among others, *Space: 1999*, *Shoestring*, *The Quatermass Experiment*, *Poldark*, *Breakaway* and *The Last Detective*.

'WHAT LOCKET?' MAN
Played by Michael Nightingale

Seen in *Don't Lose Your Head*, the 'What Locket?' Man is seen dancing with Desiree Dubarry at Sir Rodney Ffing's charity ball. Desiree is wearing a locket which is intended to attract the attention of the Black Fingernail, a master of disguise who's desperately wanted by Citizen Camembert.

WHEELER, FELICITY
Played by Rosalind Knight

In *Teacher*, Miss Wheeler is a school inspector who accompanies Alistair Grigg, a well-known child psychiatrist, on his visit to Maudlin Street Secondary Modern School. Straitlaced at first, her views and feelings mellow when she sets eyes on Gregory Adams, the science teacher.

WHIPPIT INN, THE
An inn where Lewis Boggs takes Myrtle Plummer in *At Your Convenience* for a meal and a dance after the cinema.

WHITAKER, CAROLINE
Roles: Mary Parker in *Girls* and Student in *Behind*

Surrey-born Caroline Whitaker's other credits include playing Angela in BBC's 1974 drama, *The Carnforth Practice*.

WHITE, BETTY
Casting director on *Sergeant*, *Nurse*, *Teacher*, *Constable*, *Regardless* and *Cruising*

In casting since the 1950s, other films Betty White worked on include the Rogers and Thomas productions *Watch Your Stern*, *Raising the Wind* and *Twice Round the Daffodils*.

WHITE, CAROL
Role: Sheila Dale in *Teacher*

Born in London in 1941, Carol White, daughter of a scrap-metal dealer, began acting as a teenager after attending the Corona Stage School. She appeared in films such as *The Belles of St Trinian's*, *Blue Murder at St Trinian's*, *A Prize of Gold*, *An Alligator Named Daisy* and *Never Let Go*.

It was, however, her role in the television play, *Cathy Come Home*, which brought her to prominence and led to interest from Hollywood. She went on to appear alongside

Oliver Reed, Dean Martin and Rod Taylor. She continued making occasional film appearances in the 1970s and '80s and returned to the stage in *Steaming*, but personal problems meant the engagement was shortlived.

White, who many labelled the 'Battersea Bardot', died in 1991, aged fifty.

WHITE, DONNA
Roles: Vestal Virgin in *Cleo* and Jenny in *Cowboy*

Other film credits include playing a street-walker in the 1965 film, *A Study in Terror*.

WHITE, JANE
Role: Irene in *Teacher*

Sister of the late actress Carol White, who also appeared in *Teacher*, Jane White's other credits include the classic 1956 film, *A Town Like Alice*.

WHITE, JENNY
Role: Nurse in Bath and Nurse (descending staircase in nurses' home) in *Doctor*

Born in 1944, Jenny White's other credits during the 1960s include *Night Train to Paris* and *If It's Tuesday, This Must Be Belgium*.

WHITE, NICK
Role: Sent-off Footballer in *Emmannuelle*

WHITFIELD, JUNE
Roles: Meg in *Nurse*, Evelyn Blunt in *Abroad*, Augusta Prodworthy in *Girls* and Queen Isabella of Spain in *Columbus*

Born in London in 1925, June Whitfield graduated from RADA and has since worked in every area of the business, making her television debut in 1951's *The Passing Show*.

She supported in many sitcoms until, in 1966, she won a leading role in *Beggar My Neighbour*. But on the small screen it's her long-running association with Terry Scott in *Happy Ever After* and *Terry and June*, as well as her recent portrayal in *Absolutely Fabulous* for which she's best remembered.

Other small-screen credits include *Hancock's Half Hour*; *Steptoe and Son*; *Six More Faces of Jim*; *Father, Dear Father*; *Bless This House*; *The Pallisers*; *The Goodies*; *Minder*; *Days Like These* and *Common As Muck*. She's also appeared in films such as *Quiet Weekend*, *Friends and Neighbours*, *Romance With A Double Bass* and *Jude*.

WHITTAKER, IAN
Roles: Medical Corporal in *Sergeant* and Shop Assistant in *Regardless* (Note: the Shop Assistant's scene was cut.)

Born in London in 1928, Ian Whittaker's parents were in the business, so it was no surprise when he followed suit. He enrolled at RADA upon leaving school but was delayed in starting his career by two years National Service in the army.

Returning to civvy street, he began his career in earnest at the Reunion Theatre before touring in a production of *Cosh Boy*. He later reprised his role of Alfie Collins in the big-screen version, the first of many film credits, which include *Passage Home, Reach for the Sky, My Wife's Family, The Revenge of Frankenstein, The Silent Enemy, Sink the Bismarck!* and *Operation Snatch*.

On television he popped up in the likes of *The Vise, The Adventures of Robin Hood, The Adventures of Sir Lancelot* and *Tell It To The Marines*.

In between acting jobs, Whittaker earned money as an interior decorator. One of his clients worked in the film industry and offered him a job as a set decorator on the 1965 film, *Catch Us If You Can*, which led to a change of career.

Nowadays, Whittaker continues to work as a set decorator – recent credits include *Being Julia, Possession, Anna and the King* and *Dangerous Beauty* – but still makes the occasional film appearance.

WIDDLE, PRIVATE JIMMY
Played by Charles Hawtrey

A private in the 3rd Foot and Mouth, Widdle places the company's reputation for toughness, as well as the safety of his fellow soldiers, in jeopardy by wearing underpants under his kilt. Feeling the cold while guarding the Khyber Pass is no excuse for wearing such a garment; to make matters worse, Bunghit Din passes the underpants on to the Khasi of Kalabar, an enemy of the British, who has a field day.

WIFE
Played by Anna Karen

During the custard-pie scene at Sid and Sophie's wedding reception in *Loving*, she's seen feeling quite disgusted by the behaviour but soon joins in when her husband decides to slip a plate of blancmagne down the front of her dress. Ends up throwing a plate-load in his direction but it hits Jenny Grubb instead.

WIFE
Played by Brenda Cowling

Seen in the audience at Professor Crump's lecture and film show in *Behind*.

WIGAN MISSION SOCIETY
In *Up The Khyber*, Brother Belcher, a missionary, arrives in India's Himalayan region to preach, claiming, 'Sinners welcome with open arms'. When a guide is needed for a military operation across the border in Afghanistan, Belcher is blackmailed into taking the job.

WIGGINS, LESLIE
Sound Editor on *Teacher* and *Constable*

Leslie Wiggins, born in Harefield, Middlesex in 1931, joined Denham Studios in 1945, working as a messenger boy. He moved to the editing department in 1947 and remained with the studios until leaving to complete his National Service in the army between 1949-51.

He returned to Denham and worked on, initially, 1952's *Hunted* with Dirk Bogarde. Other film credits included *Just My Luck, Carve Her Name With Pride, The Square Peg, Victim, Chitty Chitty Bang Bang, Jesus Christ Superstar, A Bridge Too Far, The Last Emperor* and, in 1999, *The Cherry Orchard*.

He retired in 1999.

WILDE, BRIAN
Role: Man from Cox and Carter in *Doctor* (Note: also played a warder in *Henry* but scene cut.)

Born in Lancashire in 1921, Brian Wilde's career has been dominated by two long-running, highly successful characters: Barrowclough in *Porridge* and Foggy in *Last of the Summer Wine*. But as well as parts in two of Britain's most popular sitcoms, his television credits include a debut in 1951's *Black Limelight*, playing Sir Thomas Landers in 1954's *The Scarlet Pimpernel*, a cemetery attendant in 1961's *Jango*, Happy Dwyer in a 1964 episode of *The Protectors*, several roles in *The Man in Room 17*, a year later, and appearances in *The Avengers, The Dustbinmen, Out of the Unknown, The Sweeney, The Love of Mike* and *Elizabeth R*.

In *Wyatt's Watchdogs* he was cast in the lead role, but the 1988 sitcom, about a retired army major who formed a neighbourhood watch, failed to impress and was ditched after just one series.

He grew up in Hertfordshire before training at RADA. After graduating he spent six months unemployed until finally earning his first wage packet on stage at St Andrew's, Scotland, before joining Liverpool Rep. The swift turnaround of plays in repertory theatre afforded Wilde the chance to play different characters, a rich learning curve for any actor.

During the 1950s and '60s he worked extensively in the theatre, with credits including *The Power and the Glory, The Ring of Truth, The Visit* and the Peter Ustinov play, *The Moment of Truth*.

As well as working on the stage and television, Wilde has appeared in a handful of films, such as *Simon and Laura, Street Corner, Will Any Gentleman . . . ?, Tiger in the Smoke, Night of the Demon, Girls at Sea, On the Run, Rattle of a Simple Man, Darling, The Informers* and *The Jokers*.

Now semi-retired.

WILKINS, SERGEANT FRANK
Played by Sid James

The linchpin of the police station in *Constable*, Sergeant Wilkins is forever being threatened with a transfer by the inefficient Inspector Mills, unless there is an upturn in the station's efficiency. Undervalued, the station would fall apart if it wasn't for Wilkins, whose caring attitude towards the green young constables drafted in when a flu epidemic depletes the number of regular police officers on duty is admirable. Finally gets his rewards for years of loyal service when he's promoted to inspector, replacing Mills when he moves to the area college in charge of, surprisingly, morale and discipline.

WILLA CLAUDIA
Played by Peggy Ann Clifford
The portly woman is seen at the slave market in *Cleo* bidding for Horsa.

WILLIAM
Played by Jack Douglas
Works at the Palace Hotel as a porter-cum-doorman-cum-general dogsbody. A dullard who twitches his way through life, the kind-hearted William is seen in *Girls*.

WILLIAM
Played by Patrick Durkin
Seen at the Old Cock Inn in *Dick,* William is obviously a petty thief because he's stopped by the Reverend Flasher and asked if he'll return the collection from last Sunday's service.

WILLIAM BOGGS AND SON.
Makers of fine toilet ware, the company, which is the subject of *At Your Convenience,* was established in 1870 and is now run by William Boggs, the managing director, and his son, Lewis Boggs; while William is staid and traditional in his outlook, preferring to remain with the tried and tested products the company has sold for years, the more ambitious forward-thinking Lewis is keen the company keeps up with new trends, such as designing its own bidets, something his father resists for a considerable time. Despite its history, the company isn't without its financial problems and is nearly sold to a competitor before being bailed out by Sid Plummer and his magic budgie who can predict winners at horse racing.

WILLIAMS, BROCK
Carry On Constable was based on an idea originally supplied by the experienced writer, Brock Williams, who was born in Truro, Cornwall, in 1894. He worked on a myriad of films, including *Trouble With Eve, Ticket to Paradise, Date With Disaster, Tony Draws a Horse* and *His Brother's Keeper.* He also wrote for the 1950s police series, *Fabian of the Yard.*

He died in 1968, aged seventy-three.

WILLIAMS, DAVID
Roles: 7th Storeman in *Sergeant* and Andrew Newman in *Nurse*
Born in 1922, David Williams entered films and television in the late 1950s. His small-screen work included appearances in *The Flying Doctor, Riptide, Shannon's Mob, The Outsiders,*

Dear Ladies and, in 1983, ABC's series *Scales of Justice,* his last television role before dying in Australia in 1984.

His film roles, meanwhile, included *The Shiralee, Time Lock, Soapbox Derby,* and *Danger Within.*

WILLIAMS, KENNETH
Roles: James Bailey in *Sergeant,* Oliver Reckitt in *Nurse,* Edwin Milton in *Teacher,* PC Stanley Benson in *Constable,* Francis Courtenay in *Regardless,* Leonard Marjoribanks in *Cruising,* Captain Fearless in *Jack,* Desmond Simkins in *Spying,* Julius Caesar in *Cleo,* Judge Burke in *Cowboy,* Doctor Olando Watt in *Screaming!,* Citizen Camembert in *Don't Lose Your Head,* Commandant Burger in *Follow That Camel,* Dr Kenneth Tinkle in *Doctor,* The Khasi of Kalabar in *Up The Khyber,* Dr Kenneth Soaper in *Camping,* Dr Frederick Carver in *Again Doctor,* Percival Snooper in *Loving,* Thomas Cromwell in *Henry,* W. C. Boggs in *At Your Convenience,* Sir Bernard Cutting in *Matron,* Stuart Farquhar in *Abroad,* Captain Desmond Fancey in *Dick,* Professor Roland Crump in *Behind* and Emile Prevert in *Emmannuelle.* Also introduced *That's Carry On* with Barbara Windsor
TV: Introduced *Laughing's Christmas Classics* with Barbara Windsor
Nostril-flaring and highly expressive mannerisms mixed with a myriad of funny voices were qualities the outrageous Kenneth Williams exploited during his twenty-year association with the *Carry On* canon. In addition to the ill-fated *Columbus,* four films – *Cabby, Up the Jungle, Girls* and *England* – were denied the presence of this master of comedy acting whose

Kenneth Williams was a mainstay of the film series

characterisations were always sniffy, frequently arrogant but always guaranteed to generate uproarious bursts of laughter.

Born in London in 1926, Kenneth Williams completed his education at fourteen and was accepted for training as a litho draughtsman at Bolt Court, the School of Lithography in London's Fleet Street; he was apprenticed to a cartographer and after learning his trade during the day, he started spending his evenings performing in amateur dramatics with the Tavistock Repertory Theatre until he was conscripted into the army.

His initial duties saw him compiling maps for the Royal Engineers before transferring to Combined Services Entertainment. Within this unit he performed a double-act with Stanley Baxter, which they toured with in Malaysia, Burma and Singapore.

On returning to post-war England in 1947, he resumed his career in draughtsmanship until realising that his future lay not on the drawing board but on stage. He wrote to several repertory companies before being offered a job at Newquay, the start of a lengthy theatre career which saw him appear in a myriad of productions, including *Peter Pan*, *Saint Joan*, *Share My Lettuce* and Orson Welles's production of *Moby Dick*.

In 1958 he joined the *Carry On* series and became, for many people, the most memorable member of the team; despite the success and recognition this association brought, he always remained busy plying his trade in other media: on radio he became popular for *Beyond Our Ken*, *Hancock's Half Hour*, *Round The Horne* and *Just A Minute*, while on television he secured his own show and presented *International Cabaret*. He also established a niche for himself in children's television during the 1980s, appearing in *The Whizzkids' Guide* and supplying voices for *Galloping Galaxies* and *Willo the Wisp*. He also wrote several books, including his autobiography, *Just Williams*.

In addition to the *Carry On* films, his big-screen work, primarily during the 1950s and '60s, included appearances in such pictures as *Trent's Last Case*, *Innocents in Paris*, *The Beggar's Opera*, *The Seekers*, *Tommy the Toreador*, *Raising the Wind*, *Make Mine Mink*, *His and Hers* and *Twice Round the Daffodils*.

In latter years his workload reduced and he was limited to occasional television appearances, particularly on chat shows such as *Parkinson* and *Wogan*, which he hosted for a time. He died in 1988, aged sixty-two.

WILLIAMS, MRS

An unseen character mentioned in *Nurse*. She's a friend of Bernie and Jane Bishop and looks after their son, Jeremy, while Jane visits her husband at Haven Hospital.

WILLIE
Played by Geoffrey Hughes
Works at Boggs and Son and is seen in *At Your Convenience*.

WILLING, MISS
Played by Wendy Richard
Miss Willing, who appears in *Matron*, leaves Finisham Maternity Hospital with a new-born baby, but she's far from happy about the situation.

WILLING, NURSE
Played by Elizabeth Knight
In the outpatients department at the Long Hampton Hospital, Nurse Willing has the unenviable task of leading Mr Pullen through to Dr Nookey's consulting room. Pullen has a severe case of straying hands, as the pretty nurse soon finds out. Seen in *Again Doctor*.

WILLING, SERGEANT TILLY
Played by Judy Geeson
Along with her boyfriend, the lazy, conniving troublemaker, Leonard Able, Sergeant Willing tries to make her captain's life hell in *England*. Together with Able, the love of her life, she attempts anything to avoid working at the experimental 1313 anti-aircraft battery.

WILLOUGHBY, ANNA
Role: Girl in *Don't Lose Your Head*
Anna Willoughby's other credits include playing a boutique attendant in the 1967 film, *The Man Outside*, and an uncredited role as a dancer in the 1971 production, *The Tragedy of Macbeth*.

WILLY
Played by Jeremy Connor
Seen in *Constable* this little boy is presumed lost by his distraught mother. As soon as PC Gorse arrives on the scene to help, Willy returns home whizzing down the road on his toy scooter.

WILSON, AUDREY
Roles: Amazon Guard in *Spying* and Jane in *Cowboy*. Also an uncredited role as a Glamcab driver in *Cabby*
Born in Wembley, Middlesex, in 1939, Audrey Wilson worked as a magazine fashion model until breaking into the film world in 1962's *Stolen Hours*, the first of a string of film roles she was offered.

WILSON, IAN
Roles: Advertising Man in *Regardless*, Clerk in *Cabby*, Ancient Carrier in *Jack* and Messenger in *Cleo*
Born in London in 1902, the diminutive, oft-bespectacled actor Ian Wilson was appearing in films from as far back as the 1920s. His lengthy list of credits includes *Seven Days to Noon*, *The Last Page*, *Mother Riley Meets the Vampire*, *Hindle Wakes*, *Jumping for Joy*, *The Big Money*,

Hell Drivers, *Just My Luck*, *Two Way Stretch*, *The Iron Maiden*, *Rotten to the Core*, *Heavens Above!*, *The Plank* and, his last film, *The Wicker Man*. On television, he was seen in the likes of *The Vise*, *Studio Four* and *The Avengers*.

He died in 1987, aged eighty-five.

WINCH, GLORIA
Played by Pauline Peart
One of the beauty contestants eager to win the Miss Fircombe crown in *Girls*.

WINDOW DRESSER
Played by Gavin Reed
The effeminate window dresser is seen in *Loving* dressing a female mannequin in a wedding shop. He gets rather huffy when Bertie Muffet stares in the window.

WINDSOR, BARBARA
Roles: Daphne Honeybutt in *Spying*, Nurse Sandra May in *Doctor*, Babs in *Camping*, Goldie Locks in *Again Doctor*, Bettina in *Henry*, Nurse Susan Ball in *Matron*, Miss Sadie Tomkins in *Abroad*, Hope Springs in *Girls* and Harriett in *Dick*. Also introduced *That's Carry On* with Kenneth Williams
TV: *Christmas* ('69), *Christmas* ('70), *Christmas* ('72), *What a Carry On!*, *Christmas* ('73), *The Prisoner of Spenda*, *The Baron Outlook*, *The Sobbing Cavalier*, *Orgy and Bess*, *The Nine Old Cobblers*, *And in My Lady's Chamber*, *Who Needs Kitchener?* and *Lamp Posts of the Empire*. Also introduced *Laughing's Christmas Classics* with Kenneth Williams
STAGE: *London!* and *Wot a Carry On in Blackpool*

Bubbly Barbara Windsor, who was born in Shoreditch, East London, in 1937, breezed into the ninth *Carry On* (*Spying*) with an air of cheekiness and charm that quickly endeared her to audiences; although there was a four-year gap before she reappeared, this time donning a nurse's uniform in *Doctor*, she was to establish herself as a regular in the team.

Daughter of a bus conductor and dress-maker, she enjoyed singing and dancing from her early years and knew she wanted to make it her career from the moment she appeared in a school production. In 1950 she joined the Aida Foster stage school and earned her first stage role the same year. Two years later, aged just fifteen, she made her West End debut in the chorus of *Love from Judy*.

She was given her big break by theatre producer Joan Littlewood in the production, *Fings Ain't Wot They Used T'Be*, before appearing in Littlewood's version of *Oh! What a Lovely War*, a production with which she toured America. Her subsequent stage work has taken her all around the world.

Her film debut was as a schoolgirl in 1954's comedy, *The Belles of St Trinian's*, but it was her appearance in 1963's *Sparrows Can't Sing*

The bikini top sequence became one of *Carry Ons* most famous scenes (*Camping*)

which brought her to the attention of Peter Rogers and recruited for the *Carry On* series. Other film credits include *Lost, Make Mine a Million, On the Fiddle, Flame in the Streets, Crooks in Cloisters, San Ferry Ann, Chitty Chitty Bang Bang, Not Now Darling* and *Closed for Business*.

Although she's best known on television for her portrayal of Peggy Mitchell in *EastEnders*, other work has seen her appear in *The Rag Trade*; *Up Pompeii!*; *Dad's Army*; *Wild, Wild Women*; *You Rang, M'Lord?*; *One Foot in the Grave* and two series of *Worzel Gummidge*, playing Saucy Nancy. In 2000, she also made a cameo appearance in *Cor Blimey!*, Terry Johnson's small-screen film based on his well-received stage play, *Cleo, Camping, Emmannuelle and Dick*.

WINE BYSTANDER
Played by Michael Nightingale
At the wine-tasting session held at the Ruby Room for the Connoisseurs de Londres, the Wine Bystander is accused by a tipsy Lily Duveen, an employee of Helping Hands, of making advances towards her. Seen in *Regardless*.

WINE ORGANISER
Played by Howard Marion-Crawford
In *Regardless* the wine organiser is responsible for the wine-tasting session at the Ruby Room for the Connoisseurs de Londres. He employs Lily Duveen, from Helping Hands, to collect invitations from the guests, before asking her to hang around at the function as his guest; he soon regrets his decision when she gets sloshed and starts throwing her weight around.

WINE WAITER
Played by Bernard Hunter
First seen in *Regardless* offering Lily Duveen a glass of the 1952 vintage at the wine-tasting session held for the Connoisseurs de Londres. He's later sent crashing to the floor, thanks to the inebriated Helping Hands' employee.

WINGFIELD MATERNITY HOSPITAL
The maternity hospital in *Cabby* where Jeremy, the expectant father, and his wife are taken by Charlie Hawkins in his taxi.

WINKLE, MAVIS
Played by Dilys Laye
For 'Mavis Winkle' in *Doctor*, see 'Mavis'.

WINN, MISS
Played by Leigh Madison
In *Nurse* the attractive Miss Winn is a new doctor who sets the male pulses racing at Haven Hospital. Initially assigned less complicated cases, one of her first duties is to sort out Mr Bell's bunion.

WINSOR, ELSIE
Role: Cloakroom Attendant in *Girls*

WISE, BARBARA
Role: Julia Oates in *Girls*
A former beauty queen, one of the many crowns she held was Miss Variety Club of Great Britain. Had to change her name to Wise when applying to join Equity because there was already an actress registered in the same name. Seen in a few other productions during the 1970s, including *The Benny Hill Show, Whoops Baghdad* and *Space: 1999* on television, as well as the film, *Escort Girls*.

WIT TO WOO, THE
The booklet compiled by Sidney Bliss and handed out to new clients registering at the Wedded Bliss Agency. Bertie Muffet forks out sixteen shillings to buy one in *Loving*.

WITCH DOCTOR
Played by Yemi Ajibadi
Seen at the Nosha village in *Jungle* with a huge stew pot, shouting out the name of his god, Tum-Tum. Tinkle and Boosey also negotiate with him for the release of the party by pretending Tinkle is a magic man.

WITHERING, HORTENCE
Played by Patsy Rowlands
William Boggs's loyal and long-serving secretary is seen in *At Your Convenience*; as well as her secretarial duties, she's also the unofficial loo tester at the factory and is frequently bouncing up and down on prototype models testing their durability. When she learns that Mr Boggs has no option but to sell the company, which has been crippled by continuous strikes, she expresses her feelings for Mr Boggs, pouring her heart out to the man she's loved for so long.

WOLF
Played by Nicholas Parsons
Seen in *Regardless* attending the wine-tasting session at the Ruby Room.

WOMAN
Played by Lucy Griffiths (Note: the scene was cut.)
Elderly woman seen at a window in *Loving* as Sid, down to his undies, makes his escape from Rogerham Mansions, and the grasp of Gripper.

WHAT MIGHT HAVE BEEN

EXT. A LOWER PLATFORM OF THE FIRE ESCAPE – NIGHT

Sid rushes down to it, sees a lit curtained window with the top half open, and tries to open the other half, at which moment an elderly woman inside in underclothes pulls the curtains aside, and goes to close the top half of the window. For a moment they just gape at each other, then the woman suddenly finds her voice.

SID: (**Quickly.**) Don't scream!

WOMAN: I wasn't going to. Are you coming in?

SID: (**Horrified.**) No thanks!

WOMAN: Oh, I might as well then.

(She screams. SID tears down the escape.)

WOMAN WITH SALAD
Played by Melita Manger
The woman is sitting peacefully at the side of her caravan, just about to tuck into some crispy salad, when a beach ball lands in her plate. She's staying at the Riverside Caravan Site with her husband in *Behind*.

WOMEN'S WARD NURSE

Played by Cheryl Molineaux

In *Doctor* the nurse spots Ken Biddle trying to attract the attention of Mavis, a patient he's fond of at the Borough County Hospital. The nurse gets up and walks over to the window through which Biddle is staring, causing him to rush off down the corridor.

WOODALL, CORBET

Role: ITN Newscaster on *Emmannuelle*

Born in London in 1929, television newsreader Corbet Woodall completed his education at Eton and began training at Sandhurst for a military career. His time in uniform, however, was shortlived when he quit and travelled to New Zealand, where he began broadcasting.

Returning to the UK, he worked as a schoolteacher in Derbyshire until moving to London and securing a job with the BBC. He began his newscasting on radio before transferring to television. In later years, away from the Beeb, he made a living appearing in commercials and playing a newsreader in several television shows, most notably in over a dozen episodes of *The Goodies*. He was also seen in *A Fine Romance*, *Steptoe and Son*, *The Troubleshooters* and several films.

He died in 1982, aged fifty-three.

WOODBRIDGE, GEORGE

Role: Ned in *Jack*

Born in Exeter in 1907, after completing university studies in the late 1920s, George Woodbridge started his acting career at the Cambridge Festival Theatre. He went on to appear all over the country, including a spell during the 1930s with the Old Vic Company.

His innumerable film credits included *The Big Blockade*, *Green for Danger*, *The October Man*, *The Fallen Idol*, *Cloudburst*, *An Inspector Calls* and *What A Carve Up*. On television, meanwhile, he was seen in such shows as *Out of the Unknown*, *The Flying Doctor* and *The Persuaders!* His more substantial roles included playing Sergeant Hawker in *Stryker of the Yard*, Jacob Penrose in *The Newcomers* and Inigo Pipkin in *The Pipkins*.

He died in 1973, aged sixty-six.

WOOING TO WIN

The book that engrosses Dr Kilmore when he sharpens his chat-up techniques in *Doctor*. He practises his newly-acquired lines on a skeleton he keeps in his room.

WOOLF, VICKI

Role: Khasi's Wife in *Up The Khyber*

Born in Brighton, East Sussex, in 1945, Vicki Woolf followed her parents (her father was a comedian, her mother an actress) into the entertainment industry.

She began acting while still at school, performing at various repertory theatres, such as Brighton and Cromer during school holidays, before training at the Florence Moore Theatre Studios. She soon became busy in all media, appearing on screen from the early 1960s. Her television credits include *The Saint*, *Paul Temple*, *Are You Being Served?*, *Doctor at Sea*, *Crossroads*, *Minder* and *Three Up, Two Down*, playing Michael Elphick's girlfriend, Rhonda, in the fourth series.

Her film work includes roles in *The Hands of Orlac*, *The Vampire Lovers*, *Hands of the Ripper*, *The Great Waltz* and, her last film, *Confessions of a Pop Performer*.

Woolf, who has been running the Centre Stage School of Performing Arts in London, has written several books including a biography of Ida Rubinstein.

WOLSEY, CARDINAL

Played by Terry Scott

In *Henry* the Cardinal is first seen leading one of Henry VIII's wives to her death simply because the King no longer has any use for her; he's heavily involved in trying to arrange the annulment of his next wedding, too, when the King discovers Queen Marie has a liking for garlic.

WRIGLEY, MR

Covered in bandages, Mr Wrigley is a patient in Fosdick Ward at the Borough County Hospital. Seen, or rather his bandages are, in *Doctor*, although nothing is learnt about his medical condition.

WUNDATOURS LIMITED

The travel company organises the short break to Elsbels, the Mediterranean Resort in *Abroad*. Among its employees are Stuart Farquhar, courier Moira Plunkett, who works as his assistant, and Miss Dobbs, who's left behind to man the office.

WYER, REGINALD

Director of Photography on *Nurse* and *Teacher*

Born in London in 1901, Reginald Wyer began his career in cinematography in 1918 but didn't take charge of his first feature film until 1946's *The Seventh Veil*. During the Second World War he was making documentaries for the Ministry of Information, before moving on to Gainsborough and, then, in the mid-1950s, Pinewood.

His film credits include *Daybreak*, *Trio*, *Home to Danger*, *Spaceways*, *True As A Turtle*, *Operation Amsterdam*, *Island of Terror* and *Night of the Big Heat*.

He died in 1970, aged sixty-nine.

WYLDECK, MARTIN

Role: Mr Sage in *Sergeant*

Born in Birmingham in 1914, Martin Wyldeck, son of a Reuters correspondent, moved to Innsbruck with his family soon after he was born. Educated in Austria until the age of eleven, he returned to England to complete his education after his father's death.

He started training as an electrician but before long decided he wanted to act, joining Colchester Rep until war broke out. He served in Burma with the army for four years before returning to Colchester.

He was gradually offered work on television, including *Suez 1956* and his own series with Eleanor Summerfield, *My Wife's Sister*. A versatile actor, Wyldeck appeared in over thirty films from 1948, such as *Street Corner*, *The Frightened City* and *Tiffany Jones*.

He died in 1988, aged seventy-four.

WYLER, CAROL

Role: Maureen Darcy in *Girls*

WYLLIE, BRUCE

Role: Football Referee in *Emmannuelle*

Other screen credits include *Law and Order*, the 1978 mini-series for the BBC.

WYMAN, LAWRIE

Co-wrote the treatment with George Evans on which *Dick* was based.

Born in the 1920s, the late Lawrie Wyman worked in a bank before serving in the army. After returning to civvy street, he launched his career in writing. He began working with his long-term writing partner, George Evans, on *The Navy Lark*; together, they also contributed towards television productions such as *The Lighter Side*, in 1951, and the 70s sitcoms, *Bless This House* and *Love Thy Neighbour*.

X-RAY MAN
Played by Simon Cain
In *Again Doctor* the employee at Long Hampton Hospital arranges Goldie Locks's X-ray before informing Miss Locks and Dr Nookey, who are awaiting the results, that she doesn't have a fracture.

YANGE, MADAME
Role: Chinese Lady in *Regardless*

YE OLDE TEA SHOPPE
A tea house seen in the High Street in *Screaming!*.

YOKI
A monkey Francis Courtenay is hired to exercise in *Regardless*. Courtenay takes him to the zoo and ends up joining in a tea party with the other chimps.

YOKI'S OWNER
Played by Ambrosine Phillpotts
Seen in *Regardless* the owner of Yoki, a monkey, is suffering from a bad cold so asks Helping Hands to send someone around to exercise the monkey.

YORK, TED
Played by Terence Longdon
Journalist Edward York is a patient in *Nurse*. While covering a local baby show, he's taken ill with appendicitis and rushed to Haven Hospital. Aged thirty-five, he lives at 24 Paschendale Avenue, and not long after being admitted is given an assignment by his slave-driving editor, Mr Perkins, to write a series of articles about hospital life from a patient's point of view. During his hospitalisation, York falls in love with blonde nurse Dorothy Denton and they end up fixing a date prior to his discharge.

YOUNG, JOAN
Role: Suspect in *Constable*
Born into a theatrical family in Newcastle-upon-Tyne in 1903, Joan Young's parents were music-hall performers. Educated at convents in England and France, Young was on stage from 1918 and had a long spell in radio before film and, latterly, television roles came her way.

During the Second World War her voice became familiar to listeners as she regularly sang on *Navy Mixture*, a variety show aimed at those serving in the navy. She was also heard in *Workers' Playtime*, *Variety Bandbox* and other hit shows of the day.

Her film work included appearances in *School for Secrets*, *Good Time Girl*, *All for Mary*, *In the Doghouse*, *The Fallen Idol* and 1971's *Blood from the Mummy's Tomb*. She died in 1984, aged eighty-one.

YOUNG, KAREN
Roles: Girl in *Don't Lose Your Head*, Harem Girl in *Follow That Camel* and Hospitality Girl in *Up The Khyber*

Sgt Wilkins apologies to the Young Woman (Dorinda Stevens) (*Constable*)

As well as appearing in three *Carry On* films, Karen Young was cast in several television series, including an episode of *The Saint*, titled 'The Ex-King of Diamonds', in 1969.

YOUNG MAN
Played by Anton Rodgers

Seen in *Cruising* the Young Man sits next to Flo Castle and makes polite chat until Dr Binn arrives on the scene. Binn wants to propose to Flo and is desperate to get rid of the man, so tells him he looks ill and should report to the medical room.

YOUNG MAN
Played by David Essex (Note: the scene was cut. See 'Dandy' entry.)

In *Henry* a crowd at Speakers' Corner gather to debate the new Sex Enjoyment Tax being imposed by the King. The Young Man finds himself drawn into the discussion.

YOUNG OFFICER
Played by Ed Devereaux

An officer serving on the SS *Happy Wanderer* in *Cruising*.

YOUNG WIDOW

Mentioned in *Loving* by Sophie Bliss. She's a client of the Wedded Bliss Agency whom Sidney took a fancy to and decided to vet on numerous occasions, much to Sophie's disgust. The widow isn't seen in the film.

YOUNG WOMAN
Played by Dorinda Stevens

While out patrolling his beat in *Constable*, Charlie Constable hears screaming coming from a window. He races up to the flat and storms into the young woman's room, only to find her standing in her underwear, ironing while listening to the radio. Fortunately she's good-natured and doesn't make a formal com-plaint when Sergeant Wilkins happens to arrive on the scene to check on Constable.

ZHIVAGO, DR

When local criminal Sid Carter – who's out to steal some contraceptive pills to sell abroad – dons a false beard, spectacles and pretends to be a doctor in order to enter Finisham Maternity Hospital in *Matron,* he calls himself Dr Zhivago when confronted by Arthur, the security guard.

ZIG-ZIG
Played by Joan Sims

In *Follow That Camel* the dark-haired seductress, Zig-Zig, owns Café ZigaZig. She's in love with Sergeant Nocker and becomes jealous when he can't keep his eyes off Corktip, a belly dancer.

CARRY ON REVISITED

Over the years numerous ideas for potential *Carry On* storylines were discussed. While some were swiftly rejected and consigned to the wastepaper basket, others were deliberated over before learning their fate. Occasionally, though, an idea would be taken a stage further and a scriptwriter commissioned to prepare a script.

Carry On Smoking, about the fire brigade, went up in smoke even before pen was put to paper because it was deemed inappropriate to seek comedy out of a serious matter like fire, while a script entitled *Carry On Flying*, written by Norman Hudis, with Jim Dale in mind for the lead role, failed to get off the ground. *Carry On Spaceman*, meanwhile, was kicked into orbit when Peter Rogers decided that perhaps it wasn't the right subject to pursue, and *Carry On Yank* was put into cold storage. In the late 1980s, a script titled *Carry On Dallas*, a spoof on the successful '80s soap, was penned by Vince Powell. Focusing on the Screwing family, subsequently changed to Ramming family, the storyline followed the family's fortunes as they discover not oil, but fertiliser. Eventually crooks try to elbow their way in on the act and a battle ensues. Casting offers were made, and several of the intended cast were even interviewed on *TV-am*, but the film never materialised.

A year later, Powell met with director Gerald Thomas and was asked to write *Carry On Down Under*. When a businessman in Australia wanted to finance a new *Carry On* film, the production wheels were set in motion: Thomas travelled down-under to source suitable locations followed by Powell, who happened to be travelling to Australia on business with Thames Television. Whilst there, he met the film's financier on several occasions and began work on the script. He was nearing completion when he received news that the finance had fallen through and the project had been scrapped. Some time later, Peter Rogers, Gerald Thomas and Vince Powell tried to rescue the project by re-writing the script and setting it in the Yukon at the time of the Gold Rush but the project never progressed beyond the discussion stage.

Writers George Layton, who played the doctor in *Behind*, and Jonathan Lynn submitted a script entitled *Carry On Again Nurse* in the late 1970s, but it never saw the light of day; almost a decade later, in 1988, Norman Hudis completed a screenplay of the same name. Concerning a London hospital saved from the threat of closure, Hudis rekindled old times by flying over from his home in America to discuss the project; soon he was writing for many of the old favourites, including Kenneth Williams who'd be playing the surgeon, Joan Sims the matron, Charles Hawtrey a patient and Kenneth Connor a hospital porter. Alas, with a budget estimated at £1.5 million, the film was regarded as too expensive and dropped.

In 1992, some fourteen years since the last film, *Emmannuelle*, another entry joined the *Carry On* catalogue. The thirty-first in the series, *Carry On Columbus* was one of three films released to coincide with the five-hundredth anniversary of America's discovery, but the only comedy; many historians credit Columbus with being the man who actually discovered this new land, and what producer John Goldstone wanted was to take a lighthearted look at the traditional story, placing a different slant on that momentous occasion.

With Gerald Thomas appointed director, and Peter Rogers executive producer, a cast was assembled, headed by Jim Dale as Christopher Columbus, who by chance discovers America while en route to the Far East. Other occasional *Carry On* faces, including Jack Douglas, Bernard Cribbins, Leslie Phillips and Peter Gilmore, were joined by a new clutch of contemporary comedians and comedy actors, such as Julian Clary, Rik Mayall, Alexei Sayle, Richard Wilson and Nigel Planer: the mix of old and new style didn't, as far as many critics were concerned, knit together. With so many original faces missing from the line-up, there was little which rooted the production in the *Carry On* genre. As critic Derek Malcolm reported in the *Guardian*, the film was 'but a shadow of what it might have been'. Reflecting on the new faces joining the team, he added: '*Carry On Columbus* conclusively shows that the modern generation of comics are totally unable to compete, at least on these particular terms, with those we know from the past and once sadly underrated.'

Getting the new and old faces to jell was something that had worried director Gerald Thomas initially, as he explained in the original press pack, but when production began his fears disappeared. 'It was a problem I thought

we might have,' he said. 'The new generation tend to be stand-up comics and individual performers but they have worked in with us very well. The whole thing is a team from top to bottom and they have joined the team.'

Sadly, Thomas's views weren't shared by all. Hugo Davenport of the *Daily Telegraph* acknowledged that the new faces always faced an uphill struggle to blend with the stalwarts 'so deeply ingrained in British consciousness that they're now an institution'. But, just like Malcolm, he felt the bonding hadn't worked. 'It would be nice to say that they had carried off the new *Carry On* in the traditional style . . . but, well, they haven't. The new recruits look out of place or uncomfortable.'

Many other critics echoed the views Davenport and Malcolm expressed, giving the film a forceful thumbs-down, with Nigel Andrews, writing in the *Financial Times*

CARRY ON COLUMBUS

Island World presents a Comedy House Production
In association with Peter Rogers productions
A Gerald Thomas film
Distributed by Island World
Released as a PG certificate in 1992 in colour
Running time: 91 mins

CAST

Jim Dale . . . . Christopher Columbus
Bernard Cribbins . . . . . . Mordecai Mendoza
Maureen Lipman . . . . . .Countess Esmerelda
Alexei Sayle . . . . Achmed
Rik Mayall . . . . The Sultan
Sara Crowe . . . . Fatima
Julian Clary . . . . Don Juan Diego
Keith Allen . . . . Pepi the Poisoner
Leslie Phillips . . . . King Ferdinand
Richard Wilson . . . . Don Juan Felipe
Rebecca Lacey . . . . Chiquita
Jon Pertwee . . . . Duke of Costa Brava
June Whitfield . . . . Queen Isabella
Nigel Planer . . . . The Wazir
Larry Miller . . . . The Chief
Jack Douglas . . . . Marco the Cereal Killer
Andrew Bailey . . . . Genghis
Burt Kwouk . . . . Wang
Philip Herbert . . . . Ginger
Tony Slattery . . . . Baba the Messenger
Martin Clunes . . . . Martin
David Boyce . . . . Customer with Ear

Sara Stockbridge . . . . Nina the Model
Holly Aird . . . . Maria
James Faulkner . . . . Torquemada
Don Maclean . . . . Inquisitor with Ham
Sandwiches
Dave Freeman
Duncan Duff
Jonathan Tafler
James Pertwee
Toby Dale
Michael Hobbs . . . . Inquisitors
Peter Grant . . . . Cardinal
Su Douglas . . . . Countess Joanna
John Antrobus . . . . Manservant
Lynda Baron . . . . Meg
Allan Corduner . . . . Sam
Nejdet Salih . . . . Fayid
Mark Arden . . . . Mark
Silvestre Tobias . . . . Abdullah
Danny Peacock . . . . Tonto the Torch
Don Henderson . . . . The Bosun
Harold Berens . . . . Cecil the Torturer
Peter Gilmore . . . . Governor of the Canaries

Marc Sinden . . . . Captain Perez
Charles Fleischer . . . . Pontiac
Chris Langham . . . . Hubba
Reed Martin . . . . Poco Hontas
Prudence Solomon . . . . Ha
Peter Gordeno . . . . The Shaman

PRODUCTION TEAM

Screenplay by Dave Freeman
Additional material by John Antrobus
Music composed and directed by John Du Prez
Recorded at The Hit Factory
Mixer: Mike Ross Trevor
Song 'Carry On Columbus' written and produced by Malcolm McLaren and Lee Gorman
Performed by Jayne Collins and Debbie Holmes
Published by Chrysalis Music / Warner Chappell Music / Island World Music
Production Supervisor: Joyce Herlihy
Costume Designer: Phoebe De Gaye

stating: 'A few early puns raise a faint smile. But the film is soon bare of wit in the script . . . and barer still of that wild, honking energy in the acting that once . . . covered the naked bits in the dialogue.'

Scriptwriter Dave Freeman didn't rate the project as one of his happiest experiences. 'I felt I could have done a better job but I only had a few weeks to write the script. I didn't like the film and thought a lot of it was miscast. We missed all the regulars.'

But despite the negative reaction from, among others, the press and some of those involved, or who chose not to be involved, in the film, *Carry On Columbus* took more at the UK box office than the other two Columbus-related films released around the same time: the John Glen-directed *Christopher Columbus: The Discovery* and Ridley Scott's *1492: Conquest of Paradise*.

Inevitably, if you make a film under the *Carry On* banner you're always going to be judged against the magic the original pictures created: everyone appreciates that they're not technical masterpieces, and weren't meant to be. As Gerald Thomas once said: 'There is nothing in a *Carry On* to tax your intelligence, it is just there to make you laugh.' Their inimitable style and repertory company feel created a unrivalled charm in their own right; like any time a familiar, well-loved situation is revisited, whether on the big or small screen, there is always a significant risk that it won't, in people's eyes, fare well.

At the time of writing, discussions are still under way regarding yet another addition to the *Carry On* series. *London* is at pre-production stage but only time will tell whether it will earn the right, like most of its predecessors, to be regarded as another pearl in the canon.

Editor: Chris Blunden
Production Designer: Harry Pottle
Director of Photography: Alan Hume BSC
Casting: Jane Arnell
Dance Staging: Peter Gordeno
Production Co-ordinator: Lorraine Fennell
Art Director: Peter Childs
Script Supervisor: Maggie Unsworth
Assistant Directors: Gareth Tandy, Terry Bamber and Becky Harris
Assistant to John Goldstone: Lisa Bonnichon
Assistant to Rogers/Thomas: Audrey Skinner
Accounts: Bob Blues, Gordon Davis and Jacky Holding
Art Director: Peter Childs
Set Decorator: Denise Exshaw
Assistant Art Director: Edward Ambrose
Scenic Artist: Ted Michell
Production Buyer: Brian Winterborn
Boat Consultant: David Raine
Camera Operator: Martin Hume
Camera Focus: Simon Hume
Clapper Loader: Sean Connor
Camera Grip: Colin Manning
Art Department Assistant: Peter Francis
Gaffer Electrician: Denis Brock
Best Boy: Billy Poccetty
Sound Recordist: Chris Munro
Sound Maintenance: Graham Nieder
Chief Dubbing Editor: Otto Snel
Dubbing Mixers: Kevin Taylor and Michael Carter
Assistant Editor: Steve Maguire
Dialogue Editor: Alan Paley
Stunt Double: Paul Jennings

Assistant Dialogue Editor: Andrew Melhuish
Footsteps Editor: Richard Hiscott
Wardrobe: Ken Crouch, Sue Honeyborne, Jane Lewis and Jo Korer
Dubbing Editor: Peter Horrocks
2nd Assistant Editor: Natalie Baker
Stunt Arranger: Jason White
Assistant Dubbing Editor: Christine Newell
Make-up: Sarah Monzani and Amanda Knight
Hairdresser: Sue Love and Sarah Love
Unit Nurse: Nicky Gregory
Production Runner: Stuart Gladstone
Floor Runner: Natasha Goldstone
Unit Publicist: Ann Tasker
Casting Assistant: Gina Jay
Special Effects by Effects Associates
Title Design: Gillie Potter
Stillsman: Keith Hamshere
Property Master: Charles Torbett
Costumes supplied by Angels and Bermans
Construction Manager: Ken Pattenden
Chargehand Carpenter: Bill Hearn
Chargehand Rigger: Les Beaver
Chargehand Painter: Michael Gunner
Chargehand Plasterer: Ken Barley
Stand-by Props: Philip McDonald
Stand-by Carpenter: David Williams
Stand-by Painter: Peter Mounsey
Stand-by Rigger: Gordon Humphrey
Stand-by Stagehand: Leonard Serpant
Unit Drivers: Keith Horsley and Brian Baverstock
Colour by Rank Laboratories
Originated on Eastman Colour Film from Kodak

Lighting services by Michael Samuelson Lighting
Stills processing by Pinewood Studios
Camera supplied by Camera Associates
Titles and Opticals: General Screen Enterprises
Title Backgrounds: C & P Graphics Enterprises
Insurance Arranged by Rollins Burdick Hunter Limited
Production Legal Services: Marriott Harrison
Completion Guarantee furnished by The Completion Bond Company
Prosthetics (Ear): Aaron Sherman
Computer Services: Sargent-Disc Limited, London.
Glasses by Onspec
All Hair Products supplied by Paul Mitchell Systems
Thanks to: The Spanish Tourist Office
Executive Producer: Peter Rogers
Producer: John Goldstone
Director: Gerald Thomas

Spanish map-maker Christopher Columbus is determined to discover a new route from Europe to the Far East without having to pass through the Sultan of Turkey's territory and paying exorbitant taxes. The Sultan is far from pleased when he hears about Columbus's expedition, which is financed by the King and Queen of Spain, so sends his top spy, Fatima, to ruin the trip.

BOOKS

Carry On Emmannuelle
Lance Peters
- Paperback 192 pages (1977)
- Publisher: Arrow Books
- ISBN: 0099182203

The film was based on the novel.

The Carry On Book
Kenneth Eastaugh
- Paperback (1979)
- Publisher: David & Charles
- ISBN: 0715374036

What a Carry On: The Official Story of the Carry On films
Sally & Nina Hibbin
- Hardback 127 pages (1988)
- Publisher: Hamlyn
- ISBN: 0600558193

The Carry On Companion
Robert Ross
- Paperback (1996)
- Publisher: B.T. Batsford
- ISBN: 0713479671

A 40th Anniversary Edition was released by Batsford in 1998

Carry On Abroad / Doctor / Up The Khyber / Loving / England / Henry
Norman Giller
- Paperbacks (1996)
- Publisher: Chameleon
- ISBN: *Abroad* – 0233990313
  Doctor – 0233990275
  Up The Khyber – 0233990305
  Loving – 0233990291
  England – 0233990283
  Henry – 0233990321

Novelisations continuing the stories from where the films left off.

Carry On Laughing: A Celebration
Adrian Rigelsford
- Paperback 192 pages (1997)
- Publisher: Virgin Books
- ISBN: 075350006X

Carry On Uncensored
Morris Bright & Robert Ross
- Hardback (1999)
- Publisher: Boxtree
- ISBN: 0752217984

The Lost Carry Ons
Morris Bright & Robert Ross
- Hardback (2000)
- Publisher: Boxtree
- ISBN: 1852279907

Mr Carry On – The Life and Works of Peter Rogers
Morris Bright & Robert Ross
- Hardback (2000)
- Publisher: BBC
- ISBN: 0563551836

The Carry On Films (Pocket Essentials)
Mark Campbell
- Paperback (2002)
- Publisher: Pocket Essentials
- ISBN: 1904048303X

The Carry On Book of Statistics
Kevin Snelgrove
- Paperback (2003)
- Publisher: Kas Publications
- ISBN: 0954420004

The Carry On Story
Robert Ross
- Hardback (2005)
- Publisher: Reynolds and Hearn
- ISBN: 190311196X

Others . . .

Cleo, Camping, Emmannuelle & Dick – Scripts
Terry Johnson
- Paperback 1998
- Publisher: BFI

MERCHANDISE

Carry On T-shirts
Supplier: Charactershop
Contact: www.charactershop.co.uk

Carry On mugs
Supplier: Charactershop
Contact: www.charactershop.co.uk
Product Details: 5 Mugs: Sid/Babs/Carry On Loving/Carry On Camping/Carry On Girls – £5.99 each

Carry On character jugs
Supplier: Royal Doulton
Contact: www.royaldoulton.com
Product Details: Issued as a pair at £150 but now obsolete
  Hattie Jacques as Matron – D7172 – 11.9 cm height – 2001 limited edition of 1000: special commission for Doulton Direct – designer Davide Losi
  Kenneth Williams as Doctor Tinkle – D7173 – 2001 limited edition of 1000: special commission for Doulton Direct – designer Haili Sun
  Sid James as Sir Sidney Ruff Diamond – D7162 – 10.1 cm height – 2001 limited edition of 1500: special commission for Doulton Direct – designer Alexander Down
  Charles Hawtrey as Private James Widdle – D7163 – 10.1 cm height – 2001 limited edition of 1500: special commission for Doulton Direct – designer Davide Losi

Carry On bobblehead dolls
Supplier: Cards Inc.
Product Details: £14.99 each
This first series, taken from *Camping*, includes Sid James as the raunchy Sid Boggle, Kenneth Williams as the repressed Doctor Kenneth Soaper and Barbara Windsor as the bouncy Babs. Each doll is hand-painted and includes an individually numbered certificate of authenticity.
  The second series is based on *Up The Khyber* and includes Sid James as Sir Sidney Ruff-Diamond, Kenneth Williams as the scheming Khasi of Kalabar, Bernard Bresslaw as Bunghit Din and Charles Hawtrey as Private Jimmy Widdle of Her Majesty's 3rd Foot and Mouth regiment.

Carry On figures
Supplier: Product Enterprise Limited
Product Details: The range is still under development with an expected release date of 2005

Carry On die-cast models
Supplier: Lledo UK
Product Details: Released 1998

Carry On postcards
Supplier: London Postcard Company
Product Details: Released 1997, individual cards were available at 50p each

Carry On beer mats 'What a Carry On at the MOMI' exhibition
Supplier: Museum of the Moving Image (MOMI)
Product Details: Produced in 1998 for promotional purposes

Carry On yo-yo 'What a Carry On at the MOMI' exhibition
Supplier: Museum of the Moving Image (MOMI)
Product Details: Produced in 1998 for promotional purposes

Carry On phonecards
Product Details: Released 2001

Carry On birthday cards
Supplier: Carlton International Limited
Product Details: Released in 1998 at £1.95 each. A Father's Day card has since been deleted but two cards currently available are:
  i) *Carry On Camping* + audio card, published by DANILO (www.danilo.com), bar code 8992314184
  ii) Ooh Saucy! Babs, barcode: 8992314025

Carry On calendars
Supplier: Slow Dazzle
Product Details: First released in 1999, costing £9.99. The 2005 edition, which was published in August 2004, cost £7.99

Carry On first-day covers
Supplier: Benhams
Product Details: Produced by Inter-Governmental Philatelic Corporation of New York (www.igpc.net). It was officially released by Grenada with the full authorisation of *Carry On Laughing*

Carry On busts
Supplier: British Comedy Society
Product Details: Available from 1998. For the 40th anniversary of the British Comedy Society, busts of Sid James, Kenneth Williams, Charles Hawtrey and Hattie Jacques were produced. At the society's anniversary celebration, a celebrity auction was held, at which all four were sold for prices in excess of £300 each. Reproductions were offered for sale by the BCS at a cost of £64.95

Carry On fruit machine
Supplier: Maygay
Product Details: When produced in 1998, it cost £2695

Carry On clothing
Supplier: Burton's Menswear
Product Details: T-shirts, boxer shorts and socks were produced for the retailer in 1998

Carry On beer mats & posters
Supplier: KP Nuts
Product Details: In 1995, the company produced the items for promotional use only

MUSIC

The Carry On Album
Artist: Gavin Sutherland & The Prague
Philharmonic Orchestra
Newly performed renditions of the classic
Carry On themes
Label: ASV
Format: CD
Release Date: 1999

Oh! What A Carry On
Artist: Various artists from the *Carry On* films
Label: Music For Pleasure (EMI)
Format: LP

Carry On Screaming / The Baby Song
Artist: Boz
Label: Capitol
Format: 7" Single
Release Date: 1966
*Often incorrectly attributed to Jim Dale, the
singer is Raymond 'Boz' Burrell, better known
for his work with King Crimson and Bad
Company*

Love Crazy (Theme from Carry On Emmannuelle)
Artist: Masterplan
Format: 7" Single
Release Date: 1977

Carry On Columbus
Artist: Fantastic Planet (Malcolm McLaren)
Label: A&M
Format: 7" / 12" / CD Single
Release Date: 1992

Carry On CD
Music and dialogue from each of the films
Label: Silva Screen Records
(www.silvascreen.co.uk)
Format: Two-CD set (catalogue no:
SILCD1168), price £14.95
Release Date: 2005

AUDIO TAPES

Carrying On – Entertainment from the Carry On team
Artist: Various
Label: EMI
Format: Tape
Release Date: 1993

Carry On Camping / Doctor / Don't Lose Your Head / Follow That Camel / Up The Khyber / Up the Jungle
Artist: Original Cast (audio copy of the film
with additional linking narration)
Label: EMI
Format: Tape
Release Date: 1996

Also available as double packs:
Camping / Doctor
Don't Lose Your Head / Follow That Camel
Up The Khyber / Up the Jungle

DVD RELEASES

Carry On Collection DVD
CARLTON VISUAL ENTERTAINMENT LTD

The *Carry On Collection* DVD box set contains the following seventeen films in Special Edition versions, complete with a selection of commentaries, documentaries or other features on each disc, plus *That's Carry On*, a celebration of twenty years of the series hosted by Kenneth Williams and Barbara Windsor. The individual films are: *Don't Lose Your Head, Follow That Camel, Doctor, Up The Khyber, Camping, Again Doctor, Up the Jungle, Loving, Henry, At Your Convenience, Matron, Abroad, Girls, Dick, Behind, England, Emmannuelle* and *That's Carry On*

Release Date: 1 September, 2003
Edition Details:
- Region 2 encoding (Europe, Middle East & Japan only)
- PAL, Box set
- Number of discs: 18
- ASIN: B0000AGVR6
- Catalogue Number: 3711505413

Carry On Don't Lose Your Head
Release Date: 17 February, 2003
Edition Details:
- Region 2 encoding (Europe, Middle East & Japan only)
- PAL, Special Edition, Widescreen
- ASIN: B000085ROE
- Catalogue Number: 3711503393

Carry On Follow That Camel
Release Date: 17 February, 2003
Edition Details:
- Region 2 encoding (Europe, Middle East & Japan only)
- PAL, Special Edition
- ASIN: B000085ROH
- Catalogue Number: 3711503423

Carry On Doctor
Release Date: 17 February, 2003
Edition Details:

- Region 2 encoding (Europe, Middle East & Japan only)
- PAL, Special Edition
- ASIN: B000085ROC
- Catalogue Number: 3711503373

Carry On Up The Khyber
Release Date: 12 May, 2003
Edition Details:
- Region 2 encoding (Europe, Middle East & Japan only)
- PAL, Special Edition
- ASIN: B00008YNFU
- Catalogue Number: 3711503443

Carry On Camping
Release Date: 7 July, 2003
Edition Details:
- Region 2 encoding (Europe, Middle East & Japan only)
- PAL, Special Edition, Widescreen
- ASIN: B00009PAJS
- Catalogue Number: 3711504463

Carry On Again Doctor
Release Date: 17 February, 2003
Edition Details:
- Region 2 encoding (Europe, Middle East & Japan only)
- PAL, Special Edition, Widescreen
- ASIN: B000085ROD
- Catalogue Number: 3711503383

Carry On Up the Jungle
Release Date: 7 July, 2003
Edition Details:
- Region 2 encoding (Europe, Middle East & Japan only)
- PAL, Special Edition
- ASIN: B00009PAJN
- Catalogue Number: 3711503433

Carry On Loving
Release Date: 7 July, 2003
Edition Details:

- Region 2 encoding (Europe, Middle East & Japan only)
- PAL, Special Edition, Widescreen
- ASIN: B00009PAJO
- Catalogue Number: 3711503463

Carry On Henry
Release Date: 7 July, 2003
Edition Details:
- Region 2 encoding (Europe, Middle East & Japan only)
- PAL, Special Edition
- ASIN: B00009PAJM
- Catalogue Number: 3711503413

Carry On At Your Convenience
Release Date: 7 July, 2003
Edition Details:
- Region 2 encoding (Europe, Middle East & Japan only)
- PAL, Special Edition
- ASIN: B00009PAJQ
- Catalogue Number: 3711503453

Carry On Matron
Release Date: 7 July, 2003
Edition Details:
- Region 2 encoding (Europe, Middle East & Japan only)
- PAL, Special Edition, Widescreen
- ASIN: B00009PAJL
- Catalogue Number: 3711503353

Carry On Abroad
Release Date: 17 February, 2003
Edition Details:
- Region 2 encoding (Europe, Middle East & Japan only)
- PAL, Special Edition, Widescreen
- ASIN: B000085ROI
- Catalogue Number: 3711503363

Carry On Girls
Release Date: 12 May, 2003
Edition Details:
- Region 2 encoding (Europe, Middle East & Japan only)

- PAL, Special Edition, Widescreen
- ASIN: B00008YNFO
- Catalogue Number: 3711503813

Carry On Dick
Release Date: 12 May, 2003
Edition Details:
- Region 2 encoding (Europe, Middle East & Japan only)
- PAL, Special Edition, Widescreen
- ASIN: B00008YNFQ
- Catalogue Number: 3711503403

Carry On Behind
Release Date: 12 May, 2003
Edition Details:
- Region 2 encoding (Europe, Middle East & Japan only)
- PAL, Special Edition, Widescreen
- ASIN: B00008YNFS
- Catalogue Number: 3711503473

Carry On England
Release Date: 7 July, 2003
Edition Details:
- Region 2 encoding (Europe, Middle East & Japan only)
- PAL, Special Edition, Widescreen
- ASIN: B00009PAJP
- Catalogue Number: 3711503483

Carry On Emmannuelle
Release Date: 12 May, 2003
Edition Details:
- Region 2 encoding (Europe, Middle East & Japan only)
- PAL, Special Edition, Widescreen
- ASIN: B00008YNFT
- Catalogue Number: 3711503493

That's Carry On
Release Date: 7 July, 2003
Edition Details:
- Region 2 encoding (Europe, Middle East & Japan only)
- PAL
- ASIN: B00009PAJR
- Catalogue Number: 3711503833

All above DVDS are part of the DVD box set. Also available individually.

Carry On – The Ultimate Carry On
WARNER HOME VIDEO
Synopsis
> Twelve classic titles in one box set: *Cabby, Cleo, Constable, Cowboy, Cruising, Jack, Nurse, Regardless, Screaming, Sergeant, Spying* and *Teacher*.
Release Date: 8 October, 2001
Edition Details:
- Region 2 encoding (Europe, Middle East & Japan only)

- PAL, Box set
- ASIN: B00005Q59X
- Catalogue Number: D038464

Carry On Cabby
Release Date: 27 August, 2001
Edition Details:
- Region 2 encoding (Europe, Middle East & Japan only)
- PAL, Black & White, Widescreen
- ASIN: B00005MFJ6
- Catalogue Number: D038031

Carry On Cleo
Release Date: 27 August, 2001
Edition Details:
- Region 2 encoding (Europe, Middle East & Japan only)
- PAL, Widescreen
- ASIN: B00005MFJ7
- Catalogue Number: D038032

Carry On Constable
Release Date: 27 August, 2001
Edition Details:
- Region 2 encoding (Europe, Middle East & Japan only)
- PAL, Black & White, Widescreen
- ASIN: B00005MFJ8
- Catalogue Number: D038033

Carry On Cowboy
Release Date: 27 August, 2001
Edition Details:
- Region 2 encoding (Europe, Middle East & Japan only)
- PAL, Widescreen
- ASIN: B00005MFJ9
- Catalogue Number: D038034

Carry On Cruising
Release Date: 27 August, 2001
Edition Details:
- Region 2 encoding (Europe, Middle East & Japan only)
- PAL
- ASIN: B00005MFJA
- Catalogue Number: D038035

Carry On Jack
Release Date: 27 August, 2001
Edition Details:
- Region 2 encoding (Europe, Middle East & Japan only)
- PAL, Widescreen
- ASIN: B00005MFJB
- Catalogue Number: D038036

Carry On Nurse
Release Date: 27 August, 2001
Edition Details:
- Region 2 encoding (Europe, Middle East & Japan only)

- PAL, Black & White, Widescreen
- ASIN: B00005MFJC
- Catalogue Number: D038037

Carry On Regardless
Release Date: 27 August, 2001
Edition Details:
- Region 2 encoding (Europe, Middle East & Japan only)
- PAL, Black & White, Widescreen
- ASIN: B00005MFJD
- Catalogue Number: D038038

Carry On Screaming!
Release Date: 27 August, 2001
Edition Details:
- Region 2 encoding (Europe, Middle East & Japan only)
- PAL, Widescreen
- ASIN: B00005MFJE
- Catalogue Number: D038039

Carry On Sergeant
Release Date: 27 August, 2001
Edition Details:
- Region 2 encoding (Europe, Middle East & Japan only)
- PAL, Black & White, Widescreen
- ASIN: B00005MFJF
- Catalogue Number: D038040

Carry On Spying
Release Date: 27 August, 2001
Edition Details:
- Region 2 encoding (Europe, Middle East & Japan only)
- PAL, Black & White, Widescreen
- ASIN: B00005MFJG
- Catalogue Number: D038041

Carry On Teacher
Release Date: 27 August, 2001
Edition Details:
- Region 2 encoding (Europe, Middle East & Japan only)
- PAL, Black & White, Widescreen
- ASIN: B00005MFJI
- Catalogue Number: D038042

All above DVDS are part of the DVD box set. Also available individually

PREVIOUS DVD RELEASES

Carry On Loving
CINEMA CLUB
Release Date: 27 August, 2001
Edition Details:
- Region 2 encoding (Europe, Middle East & Japan only)
- PAL
- ASIN: B000051WBU
- Catalogue Number: CCD8327

Carry On Girls
CINEMA CLUB
Release Date: 27 August, 2001
Edition Details:
- Region 2 encoding (Europe, Middle East & Japan only)
- PAL
- ASIN: B00004S8IJ
- Catalogue Number: CCD8225

Carry On Emmannuelle
CINEMA CLUB
Release Date: 27 August, 2001
Edition Details:
- Region 2 encoding (Europe, Middle East & Japan only)
- PAL
- ASIN: B000051WC1
- Catalogue Number: CCD8321

Carry On England
CINEMA CLUB
Release Date: 27 August, 2001
Edition Details:
- Region 2 encoding (Europe, Middle East & Japan only)
- PAL
- ASIN: B000051WC1
- Catalogue Number: CC CCD8322

Carry On Matron
CINEMA CLUB
Release Date: 27 August, 2001
Edition Details:
- Region 2 encoding (Europe, Middle East & Japan only)
- PAL
- ASIN: B000051WBN
- Catalogue Number: CCD8328

Carry On Abroad
CINEMA CLUB
Release Date: 27 August, 2001
Edition Details:
- Region 2 encoding (Europe, Middle East & Japan only)
- PAL
- ASIN: B000051WBO
- Catalogue Number: CCD8317

Carry On Henry
CINEMA CLUB
Release Date: 27 August, 2001
Edition Details:
- Region 2 encoding (Europe, Middle East & Japan only)
- PAL, Widescreen
- ASIN: B000051WC2
- Catalogue Number: CCD8323

Carry On Dick
CINEMA CLUB
Release Date: 27 August, 2001

Edition Details:
- Region 2 encoding (Europe, Middle East & Japan only)
- PAL
- ASIN: B00004S8II
- Catalogue Number: CCD8224

Carry On Doctor
CINEMA CLUB
Release Date: 27 August, 2001
Edition Details:
- Region 2 encoding (Europe, Middle East & Japan only)
- PAL, Widescreen
- ASIN: B000051WBP
- Catalogue Number: CCD8320

Carry On Again Doctor
CINEMA CLUB
Release Date: 27 August, 2001
Edition Details:
- Region 2 encoding (Europe, Middle East & Japan only)
- PAL
- ASIN: B00004S8IH
- Catalogue Number: CCD8223

Carry On At Your Convenience
CINEMA CLUB
Release Date: 27 August, 2001
Edition Details:
- Region 2 encoding (Europe, Middle East & Japan only)
- PAL
- ASIN: B00004S8IF
- Catalogue Number: CCD8222

Carry On Up the Jungle
CINEMA CLUB
Release Date: 27 August, 2001
Edition Details:
- Region 2 encoding (Europe, Middle East & Japan only)
- PAL, Widescreen
- ASIN: B000051WBS
- Catalogue Number: CCD8325

Carry On Up The Khyber
CINEMA CLUB
Release Date: 27 August, 2001
Edition Details:
- Region 2 encoding (Europe, Middle East & Japan only)
- PAL, Widescreen
- ASIN: B000051WBT
- Catalogue Number: CCD8326

Carry On Camping
CARLTON VISUAL ENTERTAINMENT LTD
Release Date: 9 August, 1999
Edition Details:
- Region 2 encoding (Europe, Middle East & Japan only)

- PAL, Widescreen
- ASIN: B00004CYY6
- Catalogue Number: 3711500113
- * Includes the 50-minute documentary *What's a Carry On?*

Carry On Follow That Camel
CINEMA CLUB
Release Date: 27 August, 2001
Edition Details:
- Region 2 encoding (Europe, Middle East & Japan only)
- PAL, Widescreen
- ASIN: B000051WBW
- Catalogue Number: CCD8319

Carry On Don't Lose Your Head
CINEMA CLUB
Release Date: 27 August, 2001
Edition Details:
- Region 2 encoding (Europe, Middle East & Japan only)
- PAL
- ASIN: B000051WBR
- Catalogue Number: CCD8324

Carry On Behind
CINEMA CLUB
Release Date: 27 August, 2001
Edition Details:
- Region 2 encoding (Europe, Middle East & Japan only)
- PAL, Widescreen
- ASIN: B000051WBZ
- Catalogue Number: CCD8318

Carry On Doctors and Nurses
GRANADA VENTURES LTD.
Release Date: March, 2005
Edition Details:
  Includes: *Doctor, Again Doctor, Matron, Loving, Emmannuelle* and *That's Carry On*
- Region 2
- ASIN: B0007CTKUC
- Catalogue Number: 3711507573

Carry On History
GRANADA VENTURES LTD.
Release Date: March, 2005
Edition Details:
  Includes: *Don't Lose Your Head, Up The Khyber, Up the Jungle, Henry, Dick* and *England*
- Region 2
- ASIN: B0007CTKUZ
- Catalogue Number: 3711507563

Carry On Holiday
GRANADA VENTURES LTD.
Release Date: March, 2005
Edition Details:
(Includes: *Follow That Camel, Camping, Abroad, At Your Convenience, Girls* and *Behind*)

- Region 2
- ASIN: B0007CTKUM
- Catalogue Number: 3711507583

The Complete Carry On
GRANADA VENTURES LTD.
Release Date: March, 2005
Edition Details:
    Includes all the Carlton DVDs in one set.
- Region 2
- ASIN: B0007GJ500

US REGION 1 DVD RELEASES

The Carry On Collection (NTSC)
Format: Colour, Widescreen, Box set
Rated: NR
Studio: Anchor Bay Entertainment
DVD Release Date: 22 October, 2002
DVD Features:
    Includes: *Sergeant* (1958), *Nurse* (1958), *Teacher* (1959), *Constable*(1960), *Regardless* (1961), *Cruising* (1962), *Jack* (1963), *Cabby* (1963), *Cleo* (1964), *Spying* (1964), *Cowboy* (1965), *Screaming!* (1966) and *That's Carry On* (1977)
Number of discs: 7
ASIN: B00006JDRW

Carry On Cabby/Carry On Spying
Format: Colour, Widescreen
Rated: NR
Studio: Anchor Bay Entertainment
DVD Release Date: 22 October, 2002
ASIN: B00006JDRT

Carry On Teacher/Carry On Constable
Format: Colour, Widescreen
Rated: NR
Studio: Anchor Bay Entertainment
DVD Release Date: 22 October, 2002
ASIN: B00006JDRR

Carry On Nurse/Carry On Sergeant
Format: Colour, Widescreen
Rated: NR
Studio: Anchor Bay Entertainment
DVD Release Date: 22 October, 2002
ASIN: B00006JDRQ

Carry On Cowboy/Carry On Screaming!
Format: Colour, Widescreen
Rated: NR
Studio: Anchor Bay Entertainment
DVD Release Date: 22 October, 2002
ASIN: B00006JDRV

Carry On Cleo/Carry On Jack
Format: Colour, Widescreen
Rated: NR
Studio: Anchor Bay Entertainment
DVD Release Date: 22 October, 2002
ASIN: B00006JDRU

Carry On Regardless/Carry On Cruising
Format: Colour, Widescreen
Rated: NR
Studio: Anchor Bay Entertainment
DVD Release Date: 22 October, 2002
ASIN: B00006JDRS

That's Carry On
Format: Colour, Widescreen
Rated: NR
Studio: Anchor Bay Entertainment
DVD Release Date: 22 October, 2002
ASIN: B00006JDRP

Carry On Laughing (NTSC)
Format: Colour, 5hr 25m, DVD 2-pk Set
Rated: NR
Studio: A&E
DVD Features: Interactive Menus; Scene Selection
NOTE: The complete thirteen-episode compilation of the television series. The Carlton Region 2 'Special Edition' DVDs contain twelve of the thirteen *Carry On Laughing* episodes as extras, with *One in the Eye for Harold* the only instalment not available on DVD in the UK.

Carry On Columbus was released in December 2004 by Jef Films (catalogue no. B00064AMAS). Jef Films has also released *Camping* and *Matron* on Region 1 DVD (catalogue nos. B0006Q93W4 and B0006Q93VU respectively) in February 2005.

VIDEO

UK RELEASES

NB: *Carry On* titles with an * denote the title has been deleted.

UNKNOWN RELEASE DATES:

Laugh With the Carry Ons (Volume 1)*
Deleted in the UK since 11 June 1996
Lumiere LUM2139

Norbert Smith – A Life*
Deleted in the UK since 19 September 1995
1. Polygram Video 083 388 3
2. Universal Pictures Video
Release Date: 8 July, 1991
Edition Details:
- PAL format
- PAL
- ASIN: B00008T393

2003

The Carry On Collection – 18 VHS Box Set
CARLTON VISUAL ENTERTAINMENT
  The *Collection* box set contains Special Edition versions of eighteen films: *Don't Lose Your Head, Follow That Camel, Doctor, Up The Khyber, Camping, Again Doctor, Up the Jungle, Loving, Henry, At Your Convenience, Matron, Abroad, Girls, Dick, Behind, England* and *Emmannuelle*. The set also includes *That's Carry On*, a celebration of twenty years hosted by Kenneth Williams and Barbara Windsor.
Edition Details:
- PAL format
- PAL, Box set
- ASIN: B0000AGVR7
- Catalogue Number: 6067061623
Note: Video releases do not contain any of the additional features included on the DVD releases

Carry On Don't Lose Your Head
Release Date: July 2003
Edition Details:

- PAL format
- ASIN: B0000AM75B
- Catalogue Number: 3037061163

Carry On Follow That Camel
Release Date: July 2003
Edition Details:
- PAL format
- ASIN: B0000AM762
- Catalogue Number: 3037061193

Carry On Doctor
Release Date: July 2003
Edition Details:
- PAL format
- ASIN: B0000AM759
- Catalogue Number: 3037061143

Carry On Up The Khyber
Release Date: July 2003
Edition Details:
- PAL format
- ASIN: B0000AM75F
- Catalogue Number: 3037061213

Carry On Camping
Release Date: July 2003
Edition Details:
- PAL format
- ASIN: B0000AM764
- Catalogue Number: 3037061363

Carry On Again Doctor
Release Date: July 2003
Edition Details:
- PAL format
- ASIN: B0000AM75A
- Catalogue Number: 3037061153

Carry On Up the Jungle
Release Date: July 2003
Edition Details:
- PAL format
- ASIN: B0000AM75E
- Catalogue Number: 3037061203

Carry On Loving
Release Date: July 2003
Edition Details:
- PAL format
- ASIN: B0000AM75H
- Catalogue Number: 3037061233

Carry On Henry
Release Date: July 2003
Edition Details:
- PAL format
- ASIN: B0000AM75D
- Catalogue Number: 3037061183

Carry On At Your Convenience
Release Date: July 2003
Edition Details:
- PAL format
- ASIN: B0000AM75G
- Catalogue Number: 3037061223

Carry On Matron
Release Date: July 2003
Edition Details:
- PAL format
- ASIN: B0000AM757
- Catalogue Number: 3037061123

Carry On Abroad
Release Date: July 2003
Edition Details:
- PAL format
- ASIN: B0000AM758
- Catalogue Number: 3037061133

Carry On Girls
Release Date: July 2003
Edition Details:
- PAL format
- ASIN: B0000AM75L
- Catalogue Number: 3037061453

Carry On Dick
Release Date: July 2003
Edition Details:
- PAL format

- ASIN: B0000AM75C
- Catalogue Number: 3037061173

Carry On Behind
Release Date: July 2003
Edition Details:
- PAL format
- ASIN: B0000AM75I
- Catalogue Number: 3037061243

Carry On England
Release Date: July 2003
Edition Details:
- PAL format
- ASIN: B0000AM75J
- Catalogue Number: 3037061253

Carry On Emmannuelle
Release Date: July 2003
Edition Details:
- PAL format
- ASIN: B0000AM75X
- Catalogue Number: 3037061263

That's Carry On
Release Date: July 2003
Edition Details:
- PAL format
- ASIN: B0000AM75K
- Catalogue Number: 3037061373
All these videos are part of the 18-film box set.
Also available individually.

2000
Carry On Columbus
WARNER HOME VIDEO
Release Date: June 2000
Edition Details:
- PAL format, Dolby, Surround Sound
- ASIN: B0000574CV
- Catalogue Number: S035579

Carry On Follow That Camel / Carry On Don't Lose Your Head*
CINEMA CLUB
Release Date: September 2000
Edition Details:
- PAL format, Box set
- Number of tapes: 2
- ASIN: B00005224X
- Catalogue Number: CC7572

Carry On Emmannuelle / Carry On Girls*
CINEMA CLUB
Release Date: September 2000
Edition Details:
- PAL format, Box set
- Number of tapes: 2
- ASIN: B00005224Z
- Catalogue Number: CC7574

Carry On Doctor / Carry On Again Doctor*
CINEMA CLUB
Release Date: September 2000
Edition Details:
- PAL format, Box set
- Number of tapes: 2
- ASIN: B00005224U
- Catalogue Number: CC7569

Carry On Up the Jungle / Carry On Up The Khyber*
CINEMA CLUB
Release Date: September 2000
Edition Details:
- PAL format, Box set
- Number of tapes: 2
- ASIN: B00005224W
- Catalogue Number: CC7571

Carry On Loving / Carry On Behind*
CINEMA CLUB
Release Date: September 2000
Edition Details:
- PAL format, Box set
- Number of tapes: 2
- ASIN: B000052250
- Catalogue Number: CC7575

Carry On Abroad / Carry On England*
CINEMA CLUB
Release Date: September 2000
Edition Details:
- PAL format, Box set
- Number of tapes: 2
- ASIN: B00005224Y
- Catalogue Number: CC7573

Carry On Matron / Carry On At Your Convenience*
CINEMA CLUB
Release Date: September 2000
Edition Details:
- PAL format, Box set
- Number of tapes: 2
- ASIN: B000052251
- Catalogue Number: CC7576

Carry On Dick / Carry On Henry*
CINEMA CLUB
Release Date: September 2000
Edition Details:
- PAL format, Box set
- Number of tapes: 2
- ASIN: B00005224V
- Catalogue Number: CC7570

1999
Carry On Again Doctor
CINEMA CLUB
Release Date: September 1999

Edition Details:
- PAL format
- ASIN: B00004D059
- Catalogue Number: CC7865

Carry On Loving
CINEMA CLUB
Release Date: September 1999
Edition Details:
- PAL format
- ASIN: B00004D05N
- Catalogue Number: CC7874

What a Carry On!*
CARLTON VISUAL ENTERTAINMENT LTD
Release Date: March 1999
Edition Details:
- PAL format
- PAL
- ASIN: B00004CYFX
- Catalogue Number: 3037050793
NOTE: the VHS edition contains approx. 30 mins more footage than on TV and DVD versions of this documentary.

Carry On Matron
CINEMA CLUB
Release Date: September 1999
Edition Details:
- PAL format
- ASIN: B00004D05U
- Catalogue Number: CC7875

Carry On Behind
CINEMA CLUB
Release Date: September 1999
Edition Details:
- PAL format
- ASIN: B00004D05B
- Catalogue Number: CC7861

Carry On Abroad – Collector's Edition*
CINEMA CLUB
Release Date: September 1999
Edition Details:
- PAL format
- ASIN: B00004D058
- Catalogue Number: CC7860

Carry On Don't Lose Your Head – Collector's Edition*
CINEMA CLUB
Release Date: September 1999
Edition Details:
- PAL format
- ASIN: B00004D05E
- Catalogue Number: CC7871

Carry On Henry
CINEMA CLUB
Release Date: September 1999
Edition Details:

- PAL format
- ASIN: B00004D05M
- Catalogue Number: CC7870

Carry On Dick
CINEMA CLUB
Release Date: September 1999
Edition Details:
- PAL format
- ASIN: B00004D05D
- Catalogue Number: CC7864

Carry On Emmannuelle
CINEMA CLUB
Release Date: September 1999
Edition Details:
- PAL format
- ASIN: B00004D05I
- Catalogue Number: CC7867

Carry On England
CINEMA CLUB
Release Date: September 1999
Edition Details:
- PAL format
- ASIN: B00004D05J
- Catalogue Number: CC7868

Carry On Up the Jungle – Collector's Edition*
CINEMA CLUB
Release Date: September 1999
Edition Details:
- PAL format
- ASIN: B00004D05W
- Catalogue Number: CC7872

Carry On At Your Convenience – Collector's Edition
CINEMA CLUB
Release Date: September 1999
Edition Details:
- PAL format
- ASIN: B00004D05A
- Catalogue Number: CC7863

Carry On Up The Khyber – Collector's Edition*
CINEMA CLUB
Release Date: September 1999
Edition Details:
- PAL format
- ASIN: B00004D05X
- Catalogue Number: CC7873

Carry On Christmas Capers – Collector's Edition*
Release Date: September 1999
Edition Details:
- PAL format
- ASIN: B00004D05A
- Catalogue Number: CC7867

Carry On Emmannuelle – Collector's Edition*
CINEMA CLUB
Release Date: September 1999
Edition Details:
- PAL format
- ASIN: B00004D05X
- Catalogue Number: CC7873

Carry On Doctor – Collector's Edition*
CINEMA CLUB
Release Date: September 1999
Edition Details:
- PAL format
- ASIN: B00004SPVH
- Catalogue Number: CC7866

Carry On Girls – Collector's Edition*
CINEMA CLUB
Release Date: September 1999
Edition Details:
- PAL format
- ASIN: B00004D05L
- Catalogue Number: CC7869

1998
Carry On Doctor / Carry On Matron / Carry On Again Doctor
CINEMA CLUB
Release Date: September 1998
Edition Details:
- PAL, Box set
- ASIN: B00004CXFY
- Catalogue Number: CC7678

Carry On Laughing – The Very Best In Carry Ons and Capers
VIDEO COLLECTION INTERNATIONAL LTD
Release Date: May 1998
Edition Details:
- PAL format
- ASIN: B00004CWHY
- Catalogue Number: VC6700

1997
Carry On Screaming!
WARNER HOME VIDEO
Release Date: August 1997
Edition Details:
- PAL, HiFi Sound
- ASIN: B00004CS2F
- Catalogue Number: S038039

Carry On Cowboy
WARNER HOME VIDEO
Release Date: August 1997
Edition Details:
- PAL, HiFi Sound
- ASIN: B00004CIG3
- Catalogue Number: S038034

Carry On Cruising
WARNER HOME VIDEO
Release Date: August 1997
Edition Details:
- PAL, HiFi Sound
- ASIN: B00004CIG5
- Catalogue Number: S038035

Carry On Nurse
WARNER HOME VIDEO
Release Date: August 1997
Edition Details:
- PAL, HiFi Sound, Black & White
- ASIN: B00004CIG9
- Catalogue Number: S038037

Carry On Regardless
WARNER HOME VIDEO
Release Date: August 1997
Edition Details:
- PAL, HiFi Sound, Black & White
- ASIN: B00004CSFA
- Catalogue Number: S038038

Carry On Jack
WARNER HOME VIDEO
Release Date: August 1997
Edition Details:
- PAL, HiFi Sound
- ASIN: B00004CIG6
- Catalogue Number: S038036

Carry On Spying
WARNER HOME VIDEO
Release Date: August 1997
Edition Details:
- PAL, Black & White
- ASIN: B00004CSF8
- Catalogue Number: S038041

Carry On Sergeant
WARNER HOME VIDEO
Release Date: August 1997
Edition Details:
- PAL, HiFi Sound, Black & White
- ASIN: B00004CIGA
- Catalogue Number: S038040

Carry On Cabby
WARNER HOME VIDEO
Release Date: August 1997
Edition Details:
- PAL, HiFi Sound, Black & White
- ASIN: B00004CSFB
- Catalogue Number: S038031

Carry On Teacher
WARNER HOME VIDEO
Release Date: August 1997
Edition Details:
- PAL, HiFi Sound, Black & White
- ASIN: B00004CIGB
- Catalogue Number: S038042

Carry On Cleo
WARNER HOME VIDEO
Release Date: August 1997
Edition Details:
- PAL, HiFi Sound
- ASIN: B00004CS2G
- Catalogue Number: S038032

Carry On Constable
WARNER HOME VIDEO
Release Date: August 1997
Edition Details:
- PAL, HiFi Sound, Black & White
- ASIN: B00004CSF9
- Catalogue Number: S038033

Carry On Camping*
CARLTON VISUAL ENTERTAINMENT LTD
Release Date: June 1997
Edition Details:
- PAL format
- ASIN: B00004CIG1
- Catalogue Number: RCC3059

1996
Carry On England*
CINEMA CLUB
Release Date: January 1996
Edition Details:
- PAL format
- ASIN: B00004T8SO
- Catalogue Number: CC1076

Carry On Girls*
CINEMA CLUB
Release Date: January 1996
Edition Details:
- PAL format
- ASIN: B00004T8SQ
- Catalogue Number: CC1072

Carry On – Orgy and Bess*
4 FRONT VIDEO
Release Date: July 1996
Edition Details:
- PAL format
- ASIN: B0000574CR
- Catalogue Number: 6390823

Carry On At Your Convenience*
CINEMA CLUB
Release Date: January 1996
Edition Details:
- PAL format
- ASIN: B00004T8SI
- Catalogue Number: CC1066

Carry On Cabby / Carry On Nurse*
WARNER HOME VIDEO
Release Date: Uncertain

Edition Details:
- PAL format
- ASIN: B0000574CU
- Catalogue Number: S038322

Carry On Christmas [1973]*
CINEMA CLUB
Release Date: November 1996
Edition Details:
- PAL format
- ASIN: B0000574CO
- Catalogue Number: CC1168

Carry On Stuffing*
NOTE: This was replaced with the *Christmas Capers* video – same content.
CINEMA CLUB
Release Date: Uncertain
Edition Details:
- PAL format
- Catalogue Number: CC7059

Carry On Loving*
CINEMA CLUB
Release Date: January 1996
Edition Details:
- PAL format
- ASIN: B00004T8SS
- Catalogue Number: CC1074

Carry On – Kitchener*
4 FRONT VIDEO
Release Date: July 1996
Edition Details:
- PAL format
- ASIN: B0000574CQ
- Catalogue Number: 6390803

Carry On – The Prisoner Of Spenda*
4 FRONT VIDEO
Release Date: July 1996
Edition Details:
- PAL format
- ASIN: B0000574CS
- Catalogue Number: 6390843

Carry On – The Screaming Winkles*
4 FRONT VIDEO
Release Date: July 1996
Edition Details:
- PAL format
- ASIN: B0000574CT
- Catalogue Number: 6390863

Carry On Christmas Capers*
CINEMA CLUB
Release Date: November 1996
Edition Details:
- PAL format
- ASIN: B00004T8T2
- Catalogue Number: CC7059

Carry On Again Doctor*
CINEMA CLUB
Release Date: January 1996
Edition Details:
- PAL format
- ASIN: B00004T8SH
- Catalogue Number: CC1067

Carry On Dick*
CINEMA CLUB
Release Date: January 1996
Edition Details:
- PAL format
- ASIN: B00004T8SK
- Catalogue Number: CC1075

Carry On Behind*
CINEMA CLUB
Release Date: January 1996
Edition Details:
- PAL format
- ASIN: B00004T8SJ
- Catalogue Number: CC1069

Carry On Follow That Camel*
CINEMA CLUB
Release Date: January 1996
Edition Details:
- PAL format
- ASIN: B00004T8SP
- Catalogue Number: CC1170

1995
Carry On Up The Khyber*
CINEMA CLUB
Release Date: April 1995
Edition Details:
- PAL format
- ASIN: B00004T8SV
- Catalogue Number: CC1073

Carry On Abroad*
CINEMA CLUB
Release Date: September 1995
Edition Details:
- PAL format
- ASIN: B00004T8SG
- Catalogue Number: CC1079

Carry On Emmannuelle*
CINEMA CLUB
Release Date: October 1995
Edition Details:
- PAL format
- ASIN: B00004T8SN
- Catalogue Number: CC7017

Carry On Up the Jungle*
CINEMA CLUB
Release Date: April 1995
Edition Details:

- PAL format
- ASIN: B00004T8SU
- Catalogue Number: CC1071

Carry On Doctor*
CINEMA CLUB
Release Date: September 1995
Edition Details:
- PAL format
- ASIN: B00004T8SL
- Catalogue Number: CC1068

Carry On Matron*
CINEMA CLUB
Release Date: April 1995
Edition Details:
- PAL format
- ASIN: B00004T8ST
- Catalogue Number: CC1070

1993
Carry On Regardless / Carry On Cowboy
WARNER HOME VIDEO
Release Date: April 1993
Edition Details:
- PAL format
- HiFi Sound, Black & White, Colour
- ASIN: B00005LW3U
- Catalogue Number: S038325

Carry On Screaming! / Carry On Teacher
WARNER HOME VIDEO
Release Date: April 1993
Edition Details:
- PAL format
- HiFi Sound, Black & White, Colour
- ASIN: B00005LW3V
- Catalogue Number: S038326

Carry On Spying / Carry On Cruising
WARNER HOME VIDEO
Release Date: April 1993
Edition Details:
- PAL format
- HiFi Sound
- ASIN: B00005LW3W
- Catalogue Number: S038324

Carry On Constable / Carry On Jack
WARNER HOME VIDEO
Release Date: April 1993
Edition Details:
- PAL format
- HiFi Sound, Black & White, Colour
- ASIN: B00005LW3T
- Catalogue Number: S038323

Carry On Cleo / Carry On Sergeant
WARNER HOME VIDEO
Release Date: April 1993

Edition Details:
- PAL format
- HiFi Sound, Black & White, Colour
- ASIN: B00005LW3S
- Catalogue Number: S038327

Carry On – Special Collector's Box Set*
ITC HOME VIDEO (UK)
Release Date: October 1993
Edition Details:
- PAL, Box set
- Number of tapes: 4
- ASIN: B00008T51X
- Catalogue Number: ITC8144
Containing . . .
The Screaming Winkles
Orgy and Bess
The Prisoner of Spenda
Kitchener
Also available individually.

1992
Carry On Laughing – Hilarious Holidays*
VIDEO COLLECTION INTERNATIONAL LTD
Release Date: March 1992
Edition Details:
- PAL format
- ASIN: B00008T313

Carry On Don't Lose Your Head*
CINEMA CLUB
Release Date: March 1992
Edition Details:
- PAL format
- ASIN: B00004T8SM
- Catalogue Number: CC7000

Carry On Laughing – Hysterical History*
VIDEO COLLECTION INTERNATIONAL LTD
Release Date: March 1992
Edition Details:
- PAL format
- ASIN: B00008T314

Carry On Laughing – Medical Madness*
VIDEO COLLECTION INTERNATIONAL LTD
Release Date: March 1992
Edition Details:
- PAL format
- ASIN: B00008T312

1991
Carry On Henry*
CINEMA CLUB
Release Date: July 1991
Edition Details:
- PAL format

- ASIN: B00004T8SR
- Catalogue Number: CC1065

That's Carry On*
WEINTRAUB
Release Date: July 1991
Edition Details:
- PAL format
- Catalogue Number: WTB38 320

2005
Carry On Christmas Specials 1 and **Carry On Christmas Specials 2** are being released by Fremantle Home Entertainment during October 2005. No further details are available at date of writing.

US RELEASES

2003
Carry On At Your Convenience
Format: Colour, NTSC
Studio: Jef Films
Video Release Date: August 2003
ASIN: B000065FSM

2002
Carry On Screaming!
Format: Colour, NTSC
Studio: Jef Films
Video Release Date: April 2002
ASIN: B000060MXY

Carry On Follow That Camel
Format: Colour, NTSC
Studio: Jef Films
Video Release Date: February 2002
ASIN: B00005V1YS

Carry On Regardless
Format: Colour, NTSC
Studio: Jef Films
Video Release Date: April 2002
ASIN: B000060MY2

2001
Carry On Up the Jungle
Format: Colour, NTSC
Studio: Jef Films
Video Release Date: June 2001
ASIN: B00005M2HK

Carry On Loving
Format: Colour, NTSC
Studio: Jef Films
Video Release Date: June 2001
ASIN: B00005M2HM

Carry On Dick
Format: Colour, NTSC
Studio: Front Row Video, Inc.
Video Release Date: June 2001
ASIN: B00005M2HN

Carry On Matron
Format: Colour, NTSC
Studio: Front Row Video, Inc.
Video Release Date: June 2001
ASIN: B00005M2HL

1998

Carry On Cleo
Format: Colour, HiFi Sound, NTSC
Studio: Jef Films
Video Release Date: August 1998
ASIN: 6305119309

Carry On Up The Khyber
Format: Colour, HiFi Sound, NTSC
Studio: Jef Films
Video Release Date: August 1998
ASIN: 630511739X

Carry On Camping
Format: Colour, HiFi Sound, NTSC
Studio: Jef Films
Video Release Date: August 1998
ASIN: 6305119325

Carry On Henry
Format: Colour, NTSC
Studio: Jef Films
Video Release Date: August 1998
ASIN: 6305119295

Carry On Spying
Format: Colour, NTSC
Studio: Jef Films
Video Release Date: August 1998
ASIN: 6305112150

Carry On Teacher
Format: Black & White, HiFi Sound, Colour,
NTSC
Studio: Jef Films
Video Release Date: August 1998
ASIN: 6305119244

Carry On Loving
Format: Colour, HiFi Sound, NTSC
Studio: Jef Films
Video Release Date: August 1998
ASIN: 630511742X

Carry On Cowboy
Format: Colour, HiFi Sound, NTSC
Studio: Jef Films
Video Release Date: August 1998
ASIN: 6305112169

Carry On Abroad
Format: Colour, HiFi Sound, NTSC
Studio: Jef Films
Video Release Date: August 1998
ASIN: 6305117403

Carry On Dick
Format: Colour, HiFi Sound, NTSC
Studio: Jef Films
Video Release Date: August 1998
ASIN: 6305117438

Carry On Cruising
Format: Colour, HiFi Sound, NTSC
Studio: Jef Films
Video Release Date: August 1998
ASIN: 6305112142

Carry On Behind
Format: Colour, HiFi Sound, NTSC
Studio: Jef Films
Video Release Date: August 1998
ASIN: 6305112177

Carry On Emmannuelle
Format: Colour, NTSC
Studio: Jef Films
Video Release Date: August 1998
ASIN: 6305112134

1994

Carry On Girls
Format: Colour, NTSC
Studio: Palm Beach Entertainment
Video Release Date: April 1994
ASIN: B00005KHLT

Carry On at Your Convenience
Format: Colour, NTSC
Studio: Palm Beach Entertainment
Video Release Date: April 1994
ASIN: 6303059848

Carry On Henry
Format: Colour, NTSC
Studio: Palm Beach Entertainment
Video Release Date: April 1994
ASIN: 6303059872

Carry On Camping
Format: Colour, NTSC
Studio: Palm Beach Entertainment
Video Release Date: April 1994
ASIN: B00005KHLU

1988

Carry On at Your Convenience
Format: NTSC
Studio: Krypton International
Video Release Date: February 1988
ASIN: 6300130398

Carry On Doctor
Format: NTSC
Studio: Paramount Home Video
Video Release Date: November 1988
ASIN: 6301160363

CARRY ON SERGEANT

by John Antrobus

OPEN WITH STOCK FILM OF TERRIFIC BATTLE SCENE:

COMMENTATOR: Action. Tanks churning into battle . . . smashing shellfire . . . shrapnel and bullets . . . death the only companion . . . but today's National Serviceman faces all this without so much as flinching.

The camera tracks back and shows that the battle scene is in fact being shown in a cinema, with soldiers everywhere staring vacantly at the screen. Collars are pulled open, berets on the back of heads. One is eating ice-cream . . . one is asleep . . . one is necking with his girl friend.

1. EXT. PARADE GROUND. DAY. TITLE OF FILM OVER SCENE.

A passing out parade of about sixty soldiers is taking place.

COMMAND FROM THE PARADE GROUND: Carry on, Sergeant!!!

The credit titles are shown while the parade is in progress. As the titles and the parade is just finishing, the SQUADS march off the square and out through the main gate. PRIVATE HERBERT BROWN is sweeping up leaves at the edge of the parade ground. He is under close arrest and CORPORAL COPPING, wearing insignia of the regimental police, is standing near him. HERBERT is wistfully watching the SQUADS march past him. He is so absorbed by the parade that while sweeping, he backs into COPPING and nearly knocks him over.

COPPING: Watch what you're doing!

HERBERT: I'm sorry Corp.

COPPING: You nasty thing . . . you was watching parade weren't you?

HERBERT: They're real soldiers now ain't they . . . not recruits any more now they passed out . . . I'll miss 'em . . . I had some good mates in that lot.

COPPING: You've had some good mates in the last eight squads that have passed out of here.

HERBERT: Over a year now – I been on me six weeks' training. Won't I ever turn into a soldier?

COPPING: We ain't even turned you into a recruit yet . . . get on with sweeping up them leaves.

COPPING shakes a tree near them and leaves shower down.

HERBERT: I'm gonna be lonely . . . without no mates.

COPPING: Don't worry . . . you got some more little mates coming in today . . . some more little mates comin' in the Army . . . to keep you company.

FADE.

2. EXT. TRAIN STEAMING INTO STATION. DAY.

A general shot of a passenger train steaming into Cogton Halt station.

3. EXT. PLATFORM IN STATION. DAY.

FLANGE, holding a board with sheaf of papers pinned on it, is standing at the end of the platform as the train steams in. He has a LANCE CORPORAL with him. Then out to a shot of the carriages coming into the platform.

As the carriages go past, the faces of our characters (the RECRUITS) are seen at the windows in various expressions of despair and apprehension. When the train halts there is the general hustle of people getting out and in.

FLANGE: (TO L.CPL) May the Lord have mercy on their souls . . . (SHOUTS) All recruits for Cogton Training Camp over here . . . over here all recruits . . . over here all you lot . . . come on . . . look sharp . . . ETC.

The eighteen RECRUITS scamper over to the SERGEANT and CORPORAL who push them into some semblance of a squad, shouting at them all the time. Just as they get them more or less organised, a PORTER comes out of a big door behind them pushing a big trolley and comes through the ranks from the back.

The SERGEANT and LANCE CORPORAL re-form the RECRUITS. Just as they finish, the PORTER comes back and pushes through the ranks with his trolley. With a lot of shouting orders, the LANCE CORPORAL and the SERGEANT move the RECRUITS up the platform and reform the SQUAD. Just as they finish, the PORTER comes out of another door which is behind them with his trolley and breaks the ranks again.

The NCO's move the SQUAD well clear of all the doors with a lot of shouting. The SQUAD re-form. A shower of mailbags descends on them from a chute above them and several PORTERS come on the scene and start manhandling the mailbags. The NCO's move the squad again to a place that looks well clear of anything. Just as the SQUAD are about to be re-formed the idle portion of the squad sink into the ground. They have been standing on a lift. FLANGE shouts down the well of the lift, calling them all sorts of horrible names. The lift comes up again but not with the RECRUITS . . . with a couple of PORTERS and a barrow.

The RECRUITS appear running up some steps that lead from below platform level. The NCOs finally re-form the squad near the engine.

FLANGE: Now pay attention all you . . .

His voice is drowned as a steam valve on the engine is released. The steam envelopes the SQUAD like a heavy fog. Shot of SERGEANT FLANGE feeling his way blindly. He bumps into the LANCE CORPORAL.

FLANGE: Where are they?

The steam clears and they find they are standing in the middle of the SQUAD. They elbow their way out.

FLANGE: Now pay attention all of you.

His voice is drowned by the station tannoy announcing the train's departure. FLANGE goes on shouting at the top of his voice but can't be heard at all. The tannoy stops. FLANGE'S voice suddenly becomes audible again.

FLANGE: . . . have you got that? Right, answer your names. Mervin.

MERVIN: Sergeant.

FLANGE: Rogers.

ROGERS: Here, Sergeant.

FLANGE: Smith.

Three RECRUITS in various parts of the squad answer.

THREE SMITHS: Here, Sergeant. ETC.

FLANGE: I said Smith.

THREE SMITHS: Here, Sergeant. ETC.

FLANGE looks at them hard then studies his roll.

FLANGE: Smith J.

THREE SMITHS: Here, Sergeant. ETC.

FLANGE rubs his forehead wearily.

FLANGE: McAndrew.

McANDREW: Aye, Sergeant.

FLANGE: Ross.

ROSS: Sergeant.

FLANGE: Bailey.

BAILEY: What?

FLANGE looks as though he can't believe his ears. He goes up to BAILEY.

FLANGE: What?

BAILEY: That's what I said . . . what?

FLANGE: Look laddy . . . I called out your name.

BAILEY: I know you did . . . what do you want?

FLANGE: I want to know if you're here . . . that's what I want to know.

BAILEY: Well, if I'm standing here talking to you I 'spect it's very likely I am here, don't you?

FLANGE turns to the LANCE CORPORAL.

FLANGE: I always get *one* like this. (HE TURNS BACK TO BAILEY) Look son, I didn't invent the army and I didn't call you up, but here you are, so let's make the best of it, eh?

L.CPL: There's one missing.

FLANGE: I wish they were all missing.

Cut to C.U. of THORPINGTON. He is still in the train. He is tapping on the window trying to attract attention. FLANGE glances round and notices him.

FLANGE: Come out of there.

THORPINGTON mouths a reply that FLANGE can't hear because all the windows are shut.

FLANGE: Get off the train you horrible thing.

THORPINGTON tries to explain something

by gestures. Finally he fumbles with something, his hands out of view, then holds a bit of paper up to the window with these words scrawled on it: 'The door is jammed.' FLANGE tries to pull the door open but it's stuck.

FLANGE: Open the window . . . open the window.

THORPINGTON tries to open the window but can't. FLANGE steps back, exhausted. THORPINGTON fumbles, his hands out of view again, then holds another note up to the window: 'I'll have to make the best of it.' FLANGE nearly goes mad when he sees it.

FLANGE: Go out and in the door . . . go in the other compartment . . . out that way.

FLANGE points and makes violent gestures of explanation. At last THORPINGTON seems to get the gist of it. He fumbles again, his hands out of view. The whistles start blowing for the train to start. THORPINGTON produces another note with 'I understand' scrawled on it. He disappears from view. FLANGE starts tugging on the door. It comes open suddenly.

FLANGE: Ah. Where is he?

FLANGE steps into the compartment. Immediately he does so, a PORTER, as before, comes along making sure all the doors are shut. He slams the door shut after FLANGE then blows his whistle. THORPINGTON steps out of the next compartment door, slamming it after him.

4. INT. COMPARTMENT OF RAILWAY CARRIAGE. DAY.

FLANGE is alone inside compartment. He rushes back to the door, tries to open it again but it is stuck.

FLANGE: Here, hold on . . . open the door.

5. EXT. PLATFORM. DAY.

The whistles are blowing. Shot of GUARD waving his flag. The LANCE CORPORAL is trying to open the door.

6. INT. COMPARTMENT OF RAILWAY CARRIAGE. DAY.

FLANGE beats desperately on the door. He can't get the window open either.

FLANGE: It's stuck . . . hold on.

FLANGE rushes across the compartment to try and get into the corridor but finds that the door into the corridor is jammed shut. He tugs frantically then rushes back to the window.

7. EXT PLATFORM. DAY.

The LANCE CORPORAL is still trying to tug the door open. The train starts moving. Cut back and forth to alternate shots of the interior of the carriage, with FLANGE trying to get out and the LANCE CORPORAL

running along the platform, trying to open the door. Then, as the LANCE CORPORAL is at last forced to let go, cut back to . . .

8. INT. COMPARTMENT OF RAILWAY CARRIAGE. DAY.

FLANGE, completely frantic, manages to open the door leading into the corridor.

9. INT. CORRIDOR OF RAILWAY CARRIAGE. DAY.

FLANGE rushes down the corridor, pushing anyone in the way clear.

10. INT. ANOTHER CORRIDOR OF RAILWAY CARRIAGE. DAY.

FLANGE appears at one end and rushes through . . . upsetting people everywhere.

11. INT. ANOTHER CORRIDOR OF RAILWAY CARRIAGE. DAY.

FLANGE appears at the far end and rushes through again.

12. EXT. PLATFORM. DAY.

The last of the carriages of the train pull away from the platform. As the train gathers speed going out of the station . . . the door on the back of the last carriage opens (the door that would lead to another carriage). FLANGE leaps out and falls in a heap. He gets up painfully and hobbles along the track towards the platform.

Suggest a long shot with FLANGE approaching. He climbs on to the platform. There is silence as he walks along the platform and straight up to THORPINGTON. THORPINGTON holds out his hand.

THORPINGTON: The name's Smith, Sergeant.

FLANGE just stares at him. C.U. of the hairs on FLANGE'S neck as they rise.

FADE

13 EXT. SIGNPOST. DAY.

The signpost is the type with the arms ending in a hand with a finger pointing. One of the arms has 'NAAFI' written on it. On the hand at the end of the arm has been put an old glove.

14. EXT. OUTSIDE FRONT OF NAAFI. DAY.

General shot of NAAFI building. Shot of faded sign 'NAAFI'. Then shot of main entrance. There is a path leading up to it. Beside the door to one side there is a very muddy patch of ground. Displayed prominently on the patch is the sign 'Keep off the grass'. An army bicycle comes skidding to a halt on the patch of ground. The POST CORPORAL dismounts, whistling tunelessly. He has lance corporal rank but about six long-service stripes upside down on his sleeve. He has a delivery bag slung over one shoulder. A few feet from the main entrance is an ordinary door marked 'Private'. To one side of this door are several dustbins. The end dustbin is in the way of the main entrance. The POST CORPORAL finds it in his way when he tries to go in. He has to move all the dustbins along . . . so that the main entrance is now clear but the dustbin on the other end of the line is now in the way of the private entrance. The POST CORPORAL goes inside.

15. INSIDE NAAFI. DAY.

The canteen is deserted except for JOSEPHINE (the NAAFI manageress), who is sitting behind the counter knitting. She is a formidable-looking woman of about thirty-five. The POST CORPORAL comes in.

POST CPL: Here, those dustbins out there . . . they're in the way of the door . . . blocking the way in.

JOSEPHINE sniffs and goes on knitting. The POST CORPORAL goes up to the counter.

POST CPL: Them dustbins is right in the way of the door.

JOSEPHINE: How did you get in then?

POST CPL: I shifted them out of the way.

JOSEPHINE: They're not in the way then, are they?

She pours a cup of tea for him and pushes it across the counter.

POST CPL: Ta.

He takes a loud swig of his tea. Then reflects.

POST CPL: They was in the way though, weren't they?

EMILY, who helps run the NAAFI, comes in from room behind counter. She is pretty but obviously has no idea how to dress or make up.

EMILY: Hello Posty, any letters?

POST CPL: Here we are Emily, my love.

POST CPL takes a letter out of his bag and reads the envelope.

POST CPL: Miss Emily Brown, esquire.

EMILY: Ta.

EMILY disappears into the back room again with the letter.

JOSEPHINE goes on with her knitting. The POST CPL takes loud swigs of his tea, searching his mind to keep the conversation going.

POST CPL: Hmmmm . . . yes . . . mm. I was IC dustbins in Catterick you know . . . and never a one was left in the way . . . empty and tidy, hundreds of 'em. And it was in the war when all them . . .

JOSEPHINE and the POST CORPORAL are suddenly interrupted by the sound of EMILY bursting into hysterical tears. They look at each other in surprise.

JOSEPHINE: It's Emily.

JOSEPHINE hurries through into the back room. The POST CORPORAL follows her.

16. INT. NAAFI KITCHEN. DAY.

EMILY is sitting at the table, collapsed across it, sobbing. In her hands she is holding the crumpled letter. JOSEPHINE and the POST CORPORAL come in.

EMILY: (SOBBING) Oh no, it can't be true . . . Oh no . . .

JOSEPHINE rushes over and puts her arms round EMILY.

JOSEPHINE: Emily . . . there, there . . . what is it dear?

EMILY: (SOBBING) Oh . . . ooooh . . . it couldn't happen . . . it couldn't happen.

JOSEPHINE: What is it, luv?

EMILY: (SOBBING) The letter.

JOSEPHINE: What's happened, dear?

EMILY: Ooooh . . . ooh, it's my sister.

JOSEPHINE: What's happened to her?

EMILY: Oh . . . oooohhhh . . . she's . . . she's . . .

JOSEPHINE: What, dear?

EMILY: She's . . . she's . . .

The POST CPL takes his beret off and bows his head.

POST CPL: May she rest in peace.

EMILY: She's going to get married. (RENEWED SOBS)

POST CPL: Eh?

EMILY: She's going to get married and . . . she's asked me to be a bridesmaid at her wedding. (BURST INTO TEARS AGAIN)

The POST CPL puts his beret on again.

JOSEPHINE: There, Emmy . . . there, there . . . it won't be that hard for her . . .

EMILY: For her? . . . What about me? . . . What am I going to do? . . . I can never go home again. I can't look them in the face . . .

JOSEPHINE: But . . .

EMILY: I'm an old maid. (SOBS AGAIN)

JOSEPHINE: Emily . . . Emily . . . you're only eighteen . . .

EMILY: I'm an old maid . . . sixteen . . . sixteen, that's all she is . . . and she wants me to be her bridesmaid . . . I'll drown meself.

JOSEPHINE: Emmy . . . don't go on so . . . you've got years in front of you to get married.

EMILY: What after . . . after her . . . I couldn't . . . I'll drown meself . . . two years younger than me . . . I couldn't get married after her. I'd never live it down . . .

POST CPL: Well, get married before her.

EMILY: (HALF AWARE OF THE IDEA) Eh?

POST CPL: When's she getting married?

EMILY: In six weeks . . .

POST CPL: That's time enough to find a husband, ain't it? . . . long as you ain't too fussy . . .

EMILY: But . . .

POST CPL: Better that 'n drowning yourself ain't it? . . . getting married . . . and if it ain't better you can still drown yourself later on . . . you can't lose either way . . .

JOSEPHINE wipes EMILY'S eyes with her hanky.

JOSEPHINE: Oh, don't be silly with those ideas . . . when she's upset like this . . .

EMILY: (SNIFFING AND BRIGHTENING A BIT) I . . . if I could do that, that'd show her . . . if could get married I'd like to and then . . . (STARTING TO CRY AGAIN) Who'd marry me?

POST CPL takes his beret off again and goes up to EMILY.

POST CPL: My money's not very good . . . but it's regular, and I've clean habits and . . .

EMILY: (TURNS AWAY FROM HIM WITH A SOB) I'll have to drown myself.

POST CPL looks a bit disconcerted.

JOSEPHINE: Go away, you old fool, upsetting her.

POST CPL: I'm helping, I'm offering, that's all . . . she don't have to have me if she ain't got sense enough . . . not with sixty strapping well-set-up young fellahs passing through here every month.

EMILY: Them?

POST CPL: Well, only one of them . . . I shouldn't marry more 'an that for a start . . .

EMILY: (WITH SUDDEN DETERMINATION) I'll do it . . . I will . . . I'll find a husband . . . I'll show she won't get married before me . . . she won't. Where's my compact?

EMILY takes her compact out and starts making up.

EMILY: Yes . . . I'd never thought about finding a husband here . . . but they're passing through all the time, aren't they . . . there must be one of them I could make happy for life.

CUT TO:

EXT. ARMY LORRY DRIVING ALONG ROAD. DAY.

The RECRUITS are in the back of the lorry. It is passing through a small village. THORPINGTON is by the tailboard beside BAILEY.

THORPINGTON: Well . . . two years, eh . . . I must say I'm rather looking forward to it. They say that nowadays everyone's jolly decent in the army.

BAILEY: (SARCASTICALLY) Do they? Yes . . . I think it will be quite a little romp, don't you?

THORPINGTON: Of course, we are expected to do what we're told you know . . . but then, how else could the army function?

BAILEY: Of course . . .

The lorry stops at some traffic lights. BAILEY starts to climb out.

BAILEY: Well, I'm off . . .

THORPINGTON: I say . . . where are you going?

BAILEY: Have a nice time.

THORPINGTON: I say . . . you're not . . . you're not deserting?

BAILEY ducks off and into a shop. In the driving cab FLANGE is talking to the driver.

FLANGE: Hang on . . . I'm just getting some fags.

He gets out and goes into the shop where BAILEY is. He doesn't notice at first who BAILEY is.

FLANGE: 'Scuse me . . . I'm in a bit of a hurry . . . (BAILEY takes out a handkerchief quickly and blows his nose so that most of his face is covered)

FLANGE: Ten woods please . . . oh and a box of . . . (HE SUDDENLY REALISES WHO HE SPOKE TO. HE WHEELS ROUND) Bailey!

BAILEY stares back and manages to think of something to say.

BAILEY: Just getting some fags, Sarge.

FLANGE: Eh . . . Well you'd better be careful the lorry might have gone off without you. You'd be right in trouble . . . no right at all . . . Come on.

They both hurry out and get back in the lorry.

The lorry drives on. THORPINGTON turns to BAILEY.

THORPINGTON: Thank goodness you thought better of it. The life of a man on the run is not to be envied I assure you . . . and think of the family shame . . .

In the driving cab, FLANGE pricks up his ears.

FLANGE: Can you hear knocking?

DRIVER: What's that, sarge?

FLANGE: Can you hear knocking?

DRIVER: Eh?

FLANGE: (SHOUTING LOUDER ABOVE THE NOISE OF THE ENGINE) I said can you hear something knocking?

DRIVER: What's that?

FLANGE: (FED UP) It doesn't matter.

They drive on for a little. Then the DRIVER'S ears prick up.

DRIVER: Can you hear something knocking, Sarge?

FLANGE: (LOOKS AT THE DRIVER PITYINGLY) Pull up . . .

The lorry pulls up. BAILEY immediately climbs out. THORPINGTON looks surprised.

THORPINGTON: I say . . . you haven't changed your mind . . . I beg you to reconsider the trouble you're getting yourself into.

BAILEY ignores THORPINGTON and ducks round the side of the truck, where he bumps straight into FLANGE.

FLANGE: Where are you going?

BAILEY: (COMPLETELY SURPRISED) Eh . . . Did you hear knocking?

FLANGE: I'm glad someone's awake . . .

They both examine quickly a couple of wheels.

FLANGE: No?

BAILEY: No.

FLANGE: I'll have it checked when we get back.

They both get in the lorry and it goes on its way again. THORPINGTON looks as though he is welcoming a lost sheep back to the fold.

THORPINGTON: Good man . . . You've thought better of it – I know it's hard to overcome the temptation but you're doing the right . . .

BAILEY just looks back at THORPINGTON glumly. The lorry goes on a bit. Then BAILEY spots a heavy-goods truck, which is about to overtake the lorry. He elbows THORPINGTON out of the way so that he gets to the side of the lorry.

BAILEY: 'Ere . . . watch out the way.

THORPINGTON: Steady on.

As the truck starts to overtake, BAILEY climbs on the tailboard and gets ready to leap.

THORPINGTON: I say . . . what are you doing . . . wait a minute . . . You'll regret this . . . a lifetime hiding and misery . . . don't . . . the family shame . . .

BAILEY jumps onto the passing truck and quickly hides under the tarpaulin, grinning in triumph. The truck overtakes the lorry and pulls away. The truck goes on a bit then comes up the road to the barracks and turns in the main gate pulling up on the parking lot. The lorry with the RECRUITS comes in the gate a little behind it. All the RECRUITS pile out of the lorry and line up. BAILEY peeps out from under the tarpaulin, doesn't realise where he is and hops out of the truck. He creeps round the edge of the truck. Suddenly comes into view of the RECRUITS lining up. In horror he dodges back. Then he tries to creep from the truck to the cover of some huts. THORPINGTON spots him.

THORPINGTON: I say . . . We're over here . . .

FLANGE hears THORPINGTON and catches sight of BAILEY.

FLANGE: What are you skulking over there for . . . I didn't say fall out . . . come here . . . double.

BAILEY doubles to the squad and up to FLANGE.

FLANGE: What were you doing over there, eh? Come on. What was you doing?

BAILEY: Eh . . . well . . . ermm . . . You know that knocking we 'eard . . . I was having another look.

FLANGE: Oh . . . Mmmm . . . (SEEMS SATISFIED WITH THE EXPLANATION) . . . Well you never do anything in the army less your told to do it, got it . . . But at least you're on your toes . . . Watch your cheek, you'll be alright – get in the squad.

BAILEY joins the squad. He stands next to THORPINGTON.

THORPINGTON: (WHISPERS) So you've changed your mind after all . . . Good man . . . I knew you'd realise the ignominy of desertion . . .

FADE.

EXT. OUTSIDE NAAFI. DAY.

Somebody tries to open the private door from the inside but can't because of the dustbin in the way. The door shuts again. A moment later, EMILY comes out of the main door carrying a bucket of slops. She goes up to the private door and tries to move the dustbin out of the way. Finds she can't unless she moves all the dustbins along. She puts the bucket down and moves all the dustbins along, so that the private door is clear but the main door is again blocked. She goes in the private door, shutting it behind her. Comes out again having forgotten all about her bucket. She empties it and goes in.

24. INT. NAAFI KITCHEN. DAY.

No one is in the kitchen. EMILY comes in with the bucket. She puts it down, goes to the sink, and carries on peeling potatoes that are in the sink. As she peels a potato, she stares dreamily into the sink. We hear the voice of her mind.

EMILY: (ON SLIGHT ECHO) He'll be in one of the new squads . . . handsome, young . . . with golden hair. The man I'm going to marry . . . and he'll see me standing behind the counter.

As EMILY stares into the sink of muddy water and potato peelings, the image her mind sees gradually forms until we see the dream scene. EMILY is standing behind the counter pouring tea. She is dressed in a wedding gown and hat with veil. There are several SOLDIERS at the counter.

EMILY: (VOICE ON ECHO) Yes – I'll be standing there . . . when suddenly the door will burst open.

The door is flung open and a handsome, golden-haired, flashing-teeth RECRUIT in immaculate uniform steps in. EMILY looks up in awe.

EMILY: (VOICE ON ECHO) His first words . . . will you marry me?

DREAMBOY strides up to the counter and takes her hand. Immediately the POST CORPORAL, dressed as a parson, steps in from the kitchen. He is carrying a Bible, and start the service.

EMILY: (ON ECHO) We'll be married and have babies.

Dissolve the NAAFI scene, into the next scene where EMILY is rocking her baby in a cradle. The door is flung open and in steps the DREAMBOY, teeth flashing, immaculate and with sergeant's stripes. He strides up to the cradle and looks proudly in. Inside is the BABY. It is the POST CORPORAL again.

EMILY: (ON ECHO) Then he'll go off to war . . .

Dissolve into scene of battle. DREAMBOY, immaculate as ever, is laughing as he leads a charge into a dugout. His MEN all fall dead around him. But he leaps gaily into the dugout and kills all the ENEMY. The last enemy he kills is the POST CORPPRAL.

EMILY: (ON ECHO) And he'll get lots of medals.

Dissolve to scene of GENERAL, with some important-looking people behind him . . . The GENERAL is pinning a medal on to DREAMBOY'S chest. The GENERAL shakes his hand. The GENERAL takes another medal out of his pocket and pins it on DREAMBOY'S chest. He shakes hands with him again. The GENERAL takes another medal out and does the same again. Then he takes a row of medals out and pins them on and shakes hands. Then the GENERAL starts taking off his own medals and pinning them on DREAMBOY'S chest. Finally the GENERAL takes his hat off and puts it on DREAMBOY'S head, hands him his baton and walks off. EMILY with six children, all looking like the POST CORPORAL, steps up to her DREAMBOY and puts her arms round him.

EMILY: (ON ECHO) Then he'll look down at me and say . . .

JOSEPHINE: (VOICE INTRUDING INTO DREAM) Aren't those chips ready yet?

The dream dissolves. JOSEPHINE is standing at the sink by EMILY. EMILY comes back to earth.

EMILY: What?

JOSEPHINE: Now look Emily . . . I'm not going to have you day-dreaming and moping about the place just because you've got some silly idea about getting married. Fifteen years I've worked in NAAFI's and I haven't noticed no romance in it.

While JOSEPHINE is talking, the sound of SERGEANT FLANGE with his squad becomes louder as they approach the NAAFI. EMILY hears the squad approaching. She looks excitedly out of the window.

EMILY: Oh . . . it's Sergeant Flange with his new squad.

She nervously pats her hair to tidy it.

EMILY: It could happen . . . it could . . .

EXT. OUTSIDE NAAFI. DAY.

FLANGE halts the squad of RECRUITS outside the NAAFI.

FLANGE: You ain't got long . . . so make it snappy . . . Diiiiss – miss!!

The SQUAD falls out and rushes to the door. They have to struggle with the dustbins to get in.

CUT TO:

INT. NAAFI CANTEEN. DAY.

EMILY and JOSEPHINE are standing behind the counter. The RECRUITS burst in. A couple of dustbins get pushed in as well with the rush. They rush up to the counter and all start ordering and jostling in chaos. Before EMILY and JOSEPHINE get a chance to serve any of them properly, FLANGE shouts from outside.

FLANGE: Outside . . . Let's be having you!! Come on . . . chop-chop, out you come!!

They all rush out again in panic. EMILY and JOSEPHINE stand there until the last one has disappeared to a noise of dustbins being upset.

EMILY: I couldn't even see which was which.

CUT TO:

INT. STORES. DAY.

In the stores there is general confusion. The STOREMAN, a LANCE CORPORAL, has a couple of ASSISTANTS, and they are issuing kit over the counter as quickly as they can. MCANDREW stands opposite the STOREMAN.

STOREMAN: Size boots and collar.

McANDREW: Aye . . . well, that would be fifteen collar and eight boots.

The STOREMAN bangs a big pair of boots on the counter.

STOREMAN: Fifteen boots.

He turns, grabs a couple of shirts and throws them on the counter.

STOREMAN: Eight collar, two shirts khaki . . . next.

McANDREW: But . . .

STOREMAN: Move down, hurry up . . . it ain't Saville Row . . . next come here.

The STOREMAN beckons two more RECRUITS over. They have both tried on battledress. One RECRUIT is short the other is tall. On the SHORT RECRUIT the trousers are miles too long and flap down over his feet. On the TALL RECRUIT the trousers are much too short. But their tunics fit them perfectly. The STOREMAN looks at them critically.

STOREMAN: Mmm . . . that won't do . . . (THINKS AGAIN) Change tunics.

The RECRUITS change tunics.

STOREMAN: OK. Next . . .

FLANGE: Come on . . . come on . . . hurry up, we ain't got all day.

CUT TO:

INT. ARMOURY. DAY.

The armoury is a small room with a rack of rifles down one side of it. It has two doors, one at each end of the hut. The RECRUITS crowd in one door then pass down one side of the hut. A rifle is thrust into their hands by one STOREMAN, who says 'One rifle' . . . They pass on to another STOREMAN who hands them a bayonet and calls out 'Bayonet'. They pass on to another STOREMAN, who hands them an oil bottle and pull through and says 'One oil bottle and pull through'. Then they pass on to the door at the other end of the hut, which has a partition to keep the draught out. It also hides the doorway from view. At this end of the hut, a LANCE CORPORAL sits behind a table taking the rifle numbers as the RECRUITS come to him. The RECRUITS then pass out of the door his end. THORPINGTON passes down the line being handed a rifle, bayonet, oil bottle and pull through. He comes to the table.

L/CPL: (NOT LOOKING UP) Rifle number?

THORPINGTON: I beg your pardon.

L/CPL: Rifle number?

THORPINGTON: Oh, I see, rifles have numbers, have they?

L/CPL: (STILL NOT LOOKING UP) Rifle number?

THORPINGTON: Oh, let's have a look then shall we . . .

THORPINGTON examines his rifle in various places without success. The queue grows behind him.

THORPINGTON: (EMBARRASSED) Where would you suggest I looked?

L/CPL: (STILL NOT LOOKING UP) On the butt.

THORPINGTON: I beg your pardon.

L/CPL: On the butt.

THORPINGTON: On the butt, I see yes . . . right-ho . . .

He examines his rifle clumsily again without success, having no idea where the butt is.

THORPINGTON: Where is the butt?

L/CPL: (STILL WITHOUT LOOKING UP . . . IN CONTINUED MONOTONOUS VOICE) Bottom of the stock.

THORPINGTON: I beg your pardon.

L/CPL: Bottom of the stock.

THORPINGTON: The stock? Ah . . . I see, yes . . . the stock . . .

He looks over his rifle again with the same vagueness, then enquires hopelessly.

THORPINGTON: Which would you say the stock was?

The L/CPL looks up for the first time and studies THORPINGTON. THORPINGTON is holding the rifle with the butt towards the L/CPL, who suddenly reaches forward, catches hold of the end of the butt and pulls it down sharply onto the table so that THORPINGTON gets his fingers caught.]missing text[same emotionless voice.

L/CPL : T.Z. 1937 . . . Next . . .

THORPINGTON, instead of going out of the door behind the partition, elbows his way back along the queue towards the door he came in. As he jostles his way back he bumps into BAILEY.

BAILEY: That's not the right way out.

THORPINGTON: Oh . . . thanks . . .

THORPINGTON turns and finds himself next to the man giving out rifles again. Without looking up, the MAN hands him another rifle.

MAN: One rifle . . .

THORPINGTON: I say.

He is carried on by the queue. He gets handed another bayonet, an oil bottle and pull through and finds himself front of the table again.

L/CPL: (WITHOUT LOOKING UP) Rifle number?

THORPINGTON: No . . . you see, I've . . .

L/CPL: Rifle number?

THORPINGTON: Look, you see, I was trying to get out when by mistake . . . if you could tell me . . .

L/CPL: (STILL WITHOUT LOOKING UP) Rifle number?

THORPINGTON gives up and reads off the rifle number.

THORPINGTON: B.E. 7989 . . . If you could tell me the way out.

L/CPL: Right, next.

THORPINGTON: Right? Thank you . . .

In complete confusion he goes right, which is back into the hut, and manages to get himself between the rifle-rack and the wall. He pushes his way along flustering]missing text[He gets free of the rack at the other end and tries to squeeze through the door that the RECRUITS are coming in. He can't get out and gets carried along by the tide of the queue to the MAN giving out rifles. He hands him another rifle without looking up. THORPINGTON continues to try and explain but gets pushed around again and is given a third bayonet and oil bottle and pull through as well. He finds himself back at the table.

L/CPL: (WITHOUT LOOKING UP) Rifle number?

THORPINGTON: But . . .

L/CPL: Rifle number?

THORPINGTON gives up and starts reading out his rifle number.

CUT TO:

EXT: ARMOURY. DAY.

SERGEANT FLANGE barking at the RECRUITS as they come out of the armoury with their rifles. They quickly line up.

FLANGE: (TO NOUGHTON, HIS LANCE CORPORAL) Is that the lot?

NOUGHTON: I think so, Sergeant . . .

THORPINGTON staggers out of the hut carrying about five rifles and bayonets, draped with pull-throughs, and with oil bottles sticking out of his pockets.

THORPINGTON: (BREATHLESSLY) I tried to explain . . .

A hand from inside the armoury reaches out of the door and jerks him back inside.

INT. BARBERS' SHOP. DAY:

The RECRUITS are sitting waiting while, behind a partition, three barbers are cutting hair. They cut each recruit's hair very short by just running the clippers right over it. As each RECRUIT is finished he comes out from behind the partition looking very shorn and forlorn. At the same time, one of the BARBERS with a lovely mass of wavy hair pokes his hair round the partition and calls out 'Next'. BAILEY is fourth in the queue. When it comes to his turn he goes meekly behind the screen. There is a pause and he walks out again still with all his hair. The BARBER pokes his head round and calls out 'next'. His hair is closely cropped.

FADE:

INT. NAAFI CANTEEN. NIGHT.

There are a few SOLDIERS and recruits in the

NAAFI. THORPINGTON, BAILEY and MCANDREW come in.

McANDREW: Right, gentlemen . . . now the teas are on me.

BAILEY: Eh?

McANDREW: I said, the teas are on me, lads . . . the whole round . . . I want you to understand right from the start that the McAndrews are noted for their generosity . . .

BAILEY: It's OK. Jock . . . we'll all get our own.

McANDREW: No, no, I insist . . . McAndrew will pay . . . I know down in this country there's a wild myth about we Scots being rather tight on the purse strings.

BAILEY: No, Jock . . . nobody cares mate . . . we'll all get our own.

McANDREW: Not after a McAndrew has placed his generosity at your feet . . . I'm paying for the teas.

He turns to JOSEPHINE at the counter.

McANDREW: Three teas Miss . . . fill them right up please.

THORPINGTON: That's very kind of you

JOSEPHINE fills three cups and pushes them forward.

McANDREW: Are they sugared, Miss?

JOSEPHINE: They're all sugared.

McANDREW: Right ho . . . (HE TAKES A PURSE OUT) Now how much will that be?

JOSEPHINE: Ninepence.

McANDREW: (HORRIFIED) How much?

JOSEPHINE: Ninepence I said . . . three pence a cup.

McANDREW: Three pence a cup . . . we're not paying threepence a cup.

BAILEY: Look, let's all pay for our own.

McANDREW: McAndrew's paying . . . Now see here Missy, you can't tell me that a few tea leaves and a bit of hot water cost threepence a cup . . .

JOSEPHINE: (WITH BORED PATIENCE) Ninepence please.

McANDREW: Sixpence my limit. Take it or leave it.

THORPINGTON: Look, really old chap . . . let me pay.

McANDREW: McAndrew's paying. (TO JOSEPHINE) Look, sixpence I'll give you . . . and you can keep the spoons yourself.

He takes the spoons off the saucers and gives them to her.

JOSEPHINE: Do you want this tea or don't you?

McANDREW: Seven pence! There you are . . . I'll come half way.

JOSEPHINE: It's ninepence . . . take it or leave it.

McANDREW: Sevenpence . . . and a halfpenny: There now . . . you'll not say me no that.

BAILEY: Look Jock, we can all pay . . .

MCANDREW turns on him.

McANDREW: McAndrew's paying! That's my last offer Missy . . . seven copper pennies and a copper half penny . . . that's my last offer . . . think well, my lass, think well . . . there's money can be yours if you'll say the word.

JOSEPHINE: Look I'm very busy . . . the regulation prices are on the board . . . Ninepence . . . Nine copper pennies.

MCANDREW turns proudly and takes the others by the arm.

McANDREW: We'll not drink here.

BAILEY: But Jock . . .

THORPINGTON: I say . . . look if you'll allow me . . .

MCANDREW walks out, dragging the other two with him.

McANDREW: We'll not drink here . . .

They go out. There is a pause and they all three come back in again and up to the counter. THORPINGTON puts a half crown down on the counter.

THORPINGTON: Three teas please, Miss.

McANDREW: And two of those jam tarts please . . . (HE LOOKS HESITANTLY AT THORPINGTON) By your leave of course . . .

THORPINGTON: Of course . . . Thorpington's paying.

JOSEPHINE takes the money and gives THORPINGTON the change. They all sit down. There are cubicles all along one wall and they sit in one of these. At the same time, EMILY comes out of the kitchen and starts going from cubicle to cubicle wiping the tables. BAILEY swigs his tea.

BAILEY: I needed that . . . what a day . . . pushed around like a bit of dirt . . . I'll have me razor on some of them stripeys . . . I'll cut em . . .

THORPINGTON: Oh, I wouldn't cut them . . . I can't see any reason for barring them from social intercourse.

BAILEY: From what? I've had enough, that's all.

THORPINGTON: Now you promised me . . . you said you'd stay for a week to see if you liked it, you promised . . . I'm sure I can convince you the . . .

BAILEY: I know I know . . . (MOCKINGLY) The life of a man on the run is not to be envied . . . a lifetime of misery and hiding . . .

THORPINGTON: And the shame of the family name . . .

BAILEY: Aaah . . .

THORPINGTON: It's true . . . you don't know the shame it can bring on a family. I've never told anyone this before but I know what I'm talking about . . . you see one of my ancestors ran away at Agincourt.

BAILEY: There's no need to blush . . . it won't go any further than me . . . was he caught then?

THORPINGTON: No, he was knighted and the family made their fortune . . . but it doesn't make any difference . . . the principle's the same.

BAILEY: Well, I'll stay a week . . . but that's me lot.

MCANDREW has been sitting, steadily eating and swigging his tea.

McANDREW: What's that book you got there?

THORPINGTON: It's *The Seven Loves of Vanola Mitch-Count* by Bronogorious Telstenitch. Have you read it?

MCANDREW returns to his other jam tart.

McANDREW: (VAGUELY) I expect I have somewhere . . . very likely . . .

THORPINGTON: There are some beautiful pieces of dialogue in it . . . (OPENS THE BOOK) Take this piece. It is an impassioned speech by Boris Ivanovitch to a friend about his loneliness . . .

As THORPINGTON starts to read, EMILY reaches the cubicle next to the RECRUITS. She doesn't realise THORPINGTON is reading from a book and thinks he is talking personally. Her ears prick up in interest.

THORPINGTON: (READS OUT) My dear friends, how can I tell you the secrets of my heart that even to myself shelter half unknown. The aching loneliness that fills me with its emptiness . . . I am alone . . . unloved . . . undesired . . . Oh for the love of one sweet girl to sooth my troubled soul. We laugh and near at marriage with our thoughtless jokes . . . yet I tell you that could I find the woman capable of mating my desires and hunger then I would readily take her for my wife.

EMILY looks completely moon-struck. THORPINGTON closes the book.

BAILEY: Yer . . . well, personally, I think I'll stick to woodwork.

THORPINGTON: Well those words mean a lot . . . (HE STANDS UP) We'd better get back.

They all get up.

McANDREW: Aye . . . there's a lot to do . . .

They all go out. EMILY steps out of the cubicle and hears and sees THORPINGTON make his last remark. She watches him dreamily as he goes out.

FADE.

EXT. GENERAL VIEW OF CAMP. NIGHT.

The lights in all the huts and buildings are shining. There is the sound of somebody going round shouting 'Lights out'. His voice gets fainter and fainter as all the lights go off one by one. His voice fades away as the last light goes out. There is a short pause then all the lights start coming on again.

FADE.

INT. RECRUITS HUT. DAY.

It is early morning. The RECRUITS are all fast asleep. A trumpet blowing reveille can be heard. The RECRUITS sleep on. The door bursts open and LANCE CORPORAL NOUGHTON, who was with FLANGE at the station, comes in.

NOUGHTON: Let's be having you!! Come on, come on, up you get . . . show a leg . . . you got four minutes, washed, shaved, dressed and outside.

NOUGHTON goes out again. The RECRUITS tumble out of bed, grab their toilet kit and rush out of the room. Except for THORPINGTON, who sits up in bed and stretches as the others rush past him, then feels under his bed for his slippers.

THORPINGTON gets up and ambles towards the door. On the way he passes BAILEY'S bed. BAILEY is still fast asleep. THORPINGTON gives him a tentative shake.

THORPINGTON: I say old chap . . . are you getting up for breakfast?

BAILEY mumbles something unintelligible.

THORPINGTON: Oh . . . right ho, old boy.

THORPINGTON leaves him to sleep on and goes out.

INT. ABLUTIONS. DAY.

There is only an old sink in one of the corners. The RECRUITS are all jostling each other round it. Someone turns on the hot tap but there is only a gasp from the tap and no water. They turn on the cold tap and all press round trying to use the sink and look in the speckled, cracked mirror above it while they shave. THORPINGTON wanders in behind them. He goes through a door which leads into another room. It is beautifully tiled with six neat sinks and accessories. THORPINGTON leaves the door open behind him but the rest of the RECRUITS are all too busy struggling to wash and shave in the one sink to notice the other room. THORPINGTON turns on the hot tap and hot steaming water gushes out. We cut back and forth from THORPINGTON casually shaving to the RECRUITS struggling to wash and shave. Then THORPINGTON walks out of the room, through the other room and out.

The RECRUITS carry on fighting.

EXT. OUTSIDE RECRUITS HUT. DAY.

The LANCE CORPORAL is standing outside shouting at the RECRUITS in the hut.

LANCE CPL: Come on, come on, let's be having you!! Outside for breakfast! Come on!! Bring your plates, mugs, knife, fork and spoons . . . hurry up, you horrible things!!

THORPINGTON strolls out and stands in front of the LANCE CORPORAL. The other RECRUITS all tumble out in a panic trying to finish dressing, each clutching their two plates, a mug and knife, fork and spoon. They form up, all standing at ease.

LANCE CPL: Come on, come on . . . get formed up . . . I want my breakfast as well . . . right . . . Plate and mugs in the right hand, knives, forks, spoons firmly in the left . . . hurry up . . .

The RECRUITS hold their things in the right hand.

LANCE CPL: Right . . . Squaaad . . . Shun!

The SQUAD come vigorously to attention. There is a crash of falling and breaking crockery and cutlery as the RECRUITS drop things executing the movement. The LANCE CORPORAL looks at them as if daring them to move.

LANCE CPL: Move to the right in threes . . . Riiight . . . Turn!!!

The SQUAD turns to the right. There is another crash as more things drop.

LANCE CPL: By the right . . . Double march!!!

The SQUAD go off at the double. As they run, they leave a trail of broken crockery and cutlery behind them.

CUT TO:

INT. RECRUITS HUT. DAY.

BAILEY is breathing heavily, sound asleep. There is the sound of someone approaching the hut whistling.

CUT TO:

EXT. OUTSIDE RECRUITS HUT. DAY.

FLANGE comes walking along whistling.

CUT TO:

INT. RECRUITS HUT. DAY.

The shrill whistling wakes BAILEY. He opens his eyes and sees FLANGE going past the windows. BAILEY leaps out of bed in a panic, grabs a broom and starts sweeping the floor. FLANGE comes in whistling. He spots BAILEY.

FLANGE: What are you doing?

BAILEY: Oh . . . er . . .

FLANGE: Why aren't you at breakfast? Eh?

BAILEY: The hut . . . I decided to stay behind to clean it up . . .

FLANGE takes the broom from him patiently.

FLANGE: Now Bailey . . . I can tell how much you want to get on, and it does my heart good to see someone so keen . . . you're not a regular, are you?

BAILEY: No, sergeant . . . I didn't know it was going to be so nice in the army.

FLANGE: I'll get you the forms then . . .

BAILEY: (HASTILY) No, I . . .

FLANGE: But you mustn't miss your breakfast, it's not allowed . . . and it sets you up for the day anyway . . . and you want to be set up, don't yer?

BAILEY: (RESIGNED) Yes, sergeant.

FADE.

INT. HUT CLASSROOM. DAY.

The RECRUITS are sitting on benches facing one end of the hut where there are a couple of blackboards. HERBERT is sitting in the front row. FLANGE, out at the front of the class, is pacing up and down. Every time he passes HERBERT he stops and looks at him painfully, then continues walking. He does this several times. Finally HERBERT, who has been looking back at him without any expression on his face, speaks.

HERBERT: Are you looking at me, Sergeant?

FLANGE: I'd give the world to say no. This is the fourth squad of mine you have been in.

HERBERT: I like coming in your squads best . . . you're much kinder to me than most of 'em.

FLANGE: Well I hate having you cos you're horrible . . . a horrible thing.

HERBERT: I don't mind you calling me names, Sergeant Flange, cos you don't really mean it.

FLANGE: I do mean it, Brown.

HERBERT: Not really, sergeant . . . not underneath.

FLANGE: I do mean it, Brown . . . from the bottom of my heart. I'm telling you, Brown, I hate that horrible loathsome face of yours.

HERBERT: No you don't, sergeant.

FLANGE: I do, Brown.

HERBERT: No . . .

FLANGE: Yes . . .

HERBERT: (TO THE PERSON BESIDE HIM) He don't mean it really.

FLANGE: Shut up!

FLANGE walks away over to the window. HERBERT turns to MERVIN, who's sitting next to him.

HERBERT: See, him and me been in the depot longer than anyone else and . . .

FLANGE: Shut your face, Brown! Your horrible nasty face!

HERBERT gives him an understanding smile. FLANGE looks sick and turns back to the window. He sees someone coming.

FLANGE: Right . . . here comes Lieutenant Smiley, your platoon officer . . . I warn you keep on your toes with him . . .

SMILEY appears in the doorway.

FLANGE: Hut shun!

Everyone stands up to attention.

SMILEY: Not quick enough, that's not quick enough.

He points to several RECRUITS.

SMILEY: You were late . . . you were late standing . . . and you. I'm coming in again . . .

SMILEY exits.

FLANGE: Sit down . . . Hurry up, you horrible things . . . that's a very good first impression, isn't it?

SMILEY appears in the doorway again.

FLANGE: Hut shun!

They all leap up.

SMILEY: No . . . (POINTS TO SEVERAL RECRUITS) You . . . and you . . . too late again . . .

He exits again.

FLANGE: Hurry up. . . sit down . . .

They all go to sit down. As they are sitting down, SMILEY appears again.

FLANGE: Hut shun!

They try and get up quickly.

SMILEY: Shocking.

He goes out again and reappears almost immediately.

FLANGE: Sit down! Hut shun!!

In complete confusion half of them are sitting, half standing. Chairs are knocked over in the chaos. SMILEY walks to the front of the class.

SMILEY: Terrible . . . terrible . . . complete state of unreadiness . . . enemy in . . . finished.

FLANGE: Sit down, sit down, come on, come on . . . and pay attention to your platoon officer.

They sort themselves out and sit down.

SMILEY: Right. Good afternoon. My name is Smiley, spelt . . . (TO FLANGE) Have you got the blackboard ready?

FLANGE: Yessir.

FLANGE turns a blackboard around. It has 'SMILEY' written in big letters on it. SMILEY points at it.

SMILEY: Thus . . . got it . . . right . . . Eyes . . . (POINTS TO HIS OWN EYES) . . . See and hear . . . Use of most senses (POINTS TO HIS OWN MOUTH) Smiley . . . (POINTS

TO BLACKBOARD) Smiley . . . Most senses lectures when giving . . . there you've learnt something already . . . what's your name? (HE POINTS AT SOMEONE IN THE FRONT ROW WHO GETS UP EMBARRASSED AND GOES TO SPEAK) Too late! Next! (HE POINTS AT THE NEXT MAN WHO GETS UP AND GOES TO SPEAK) . . . Too]missing text[Name? Sit down, too late . . . Two men here don't even know their names . . . not good enough . . . In the army must be on your toes all the time.

HERBERT stands up, twisting his cap a little shyly in his hands.

HERBERT: My name's Brown, sir.

SMILEY looks a little surprised but takes it all in his stride.

SMILEY: Splendid. Sit down. (SAYS TO OTHER TWO) There you are, he remembers his name, why shouldn't you . . . very easy . . . Now, to continue . . .

HERBERT, who has sat down, stands up again.

HERBERT: Well, my names a colour Sir, which makes it easier, perhaps . . . although I've always been quick on names . . .

SMILEY stares at him.

FLANGE: Sit down Brown . . . Keep quiet!

HERBERT sits down, looking a little hurt.

SMILEY: Today's army rapidly shrinking . . . must realise every man on his toes doing the work of two men. (POINTS AT SOMEONE) What did I say? Too late . . . I said every man must do the work of two men . . . Touch your left toe cap with the second finger of your right hand, quick!

Half of them just sit there. The others make some confused movements.

SMILEY: Too late . . . German up . . . stab in the back . . . dead . . .

HERBERT stands up looking puzzled.

HERBERT: What Germans? I thought we'd won that war, Sir.

SMILEY: It was an illustration.

HERBERT: Not a German?

FLANGE: It doesn't matter, Brown . . . sit down.

HERBERT: But if someone's going to stab me, Sergeant . . .

SMILEY: No ones going to stab you, Brown.

HERBERT: (RELIEVED) Oh good . . . cos I couldn't see how touching me left toe cap was going to stop 'em . . .

SMILEY stares at HERBERT in disbelief, then turns and looks at FLANGE appealingly.

FLANGE: I could send him on an errand, Sir.

SMILEY: Thank you, Sergeant.

FLANGE: 'Ere, get me ten woods . . . off you go . . .

FLANGE gives HERBERT some money.

HERBERT: OK. Sergeant.

He goes out.

CUT TO:

EXT. PATH TO NAAFI. DAY.

HERBERT walks along the path towards the NAAFI. He comes to the NAAFI, moves a dustbin out of the way and goes in.

CUT TO:

INT. NAAFI CANTEEN. DAY.

It is deserted except for EMILY behind the counter.

HERBERT: Hello Emmy . . . I'm out again . . . I been put in Sergeant Flange's new squad this time.

EMILY: (INTERESTED) What . . . with that tall boy with a book and black hair . . . is he in that squad?

HERBERT: (PROUDLY) He sent me on an errand, Emmy.

EMILY: That boy with the black hair . . . straight . . . on his forehead . . . he's in that squad isn't he . . . what's his name?

HERBERT: Out of all the others he chose me to go, Emm.

EMILY: Where?

HERBERT: On an errand.

EMILY: I asked you, is that boy in his squad?

HERBERT: What boy?

EMILY: (EXASPERATED) Never mind . . . what do you want 'Erbert?

HERBERT: Eh?

EMILY: What have you come for?

HERBERT: I come on an errand . . . I told you . . . I got chosen.

EMILY: Yes, but what for?

HERBERT: Well . . . cos he could trust me more than anyone else . . .

EMILY: 'Erbert . . . what have you come on an errand for?

HERBERT: Cos he sent me, Emm.

EMILY: Look, 'Erbert . . . when he sent you on this errand . . . what did he ask you to get him?

HERBERT: Oh. yer . . . Now what was it . . . (PUZZLES) What was it he said?

FADE.

INT. HUT CLASSROOM. DAY.

SMILEY is well on with his lecture.

SMILEY: Every man does work of two men . . . effort terms . . . one man equal two men, got it . . . Now training here divided . . . six

weekly effort weeks . . . you progress from one week to week following . . . got it . . . right what did I say? (POINTS – MAN GOES TO GET UP) Too late . . . progress from one week to next, Roger so far . . . wake up . . . Further instruction reference weapon training . . .

HERBERT comes in and walks right in front of SMILEY, who stops in surprise. HERBERT goes up to FLANGE.

HERBERT: What was it you wanted, Sergeant?

FADE.

INT. NAAFI CANTEEN. DAY.

The RECRUITS come into the NAAFI and swarm round the counter. They are served by EMILY and JOSEPHINE. BAILEY and THORPINGTON sit in a cubicle together. HERBERT comes up to them.

HERBERT: Can I sit with you?

BAILEY glances at him.

BAILEY: Hop it.

HERBERT sits down with them.

HERBERT: Thanks . . . it's nice to have some mates again.

Jostling at the counter, MCANDREW is talking to ROGERS, a spotty-faced, simpering looking lad.

McANDREW: McAndrew buys the teas! I insist lad . . . McAndrew pays!

EMILY comes out from behind the counter with a tray for dirty crocks. She is looking round for THORPINGTON. When she spots him, she goes up to their cubicle.

EMILY: 'Scuse me.

She starts wiping the table and keeps glancing at THORPINGTON, trying to look as sexy as possible. THORPINGTON smiles back in a vaguely embarrassed manner.

EMILY: (TO THORPINGTON) Are you training to be an officer?

THORPINGTON:(LOOKING A BIT FLATTERED) Huh . . . no . . . actually I'm only a recruit . . . only just joined . . .

EMILY: I thought you would be training to be an officer . . . I thought *you* would . . .

THORPINGTON: No . . . huh . . . I'm just a recruit here . . .

EMILY: Ooooh . . .

She gives him another sexy glance, but realises she can't prolong the conversation any longer by wiping the table and moves on. She goes back past MCANDREW, who is holding a plate of jam tarts and a cup of tea. ROGERS is paying over the counter.

McANDREW: (TO ROGERS) That's very kind of you . . . very kind . . . I won't forget this.

Back at the cubicle THORPINGTON is talking to BAILEY.

THORPINGTON: Have you got your weapon training kit ready, Harry?

BAILEY: No . . . I'm not bothered . . .

THORPINGTON: Now come on . . . you promised to have a go . . .

BAILEY gets up.

BAILEY: Alright, Mr Conscience.

HERBERT: Here hang on, I'll come with yer . . .

BAILEY: What do you want to come with me for?

HERBERT: Well . . . I just want to . . . it's a free country, I can go where I like . . .

HERBERT gets up and follows him out. EMILY at once rushes over to the table and gathers their dirty crocks. She looks at THORPINGTON and gives him another intimate smile.

EMILY: Clear up the crocks . . .

THORPINGTON: Oh yes . . . jolly good . . .

EMILY: I'll wipe the table for you . . .

She starts wiping it.

THORPINGTON: You've just wiped it.

EMILY: I don't mind wiping it again . . . for you . . . that's if you want me to . . .

THORPINGTON: Oh . . . (EMBARRASSED) jolly good . . .

EMILY: Don't think I'm nosy . . . but I think I know you better than you realise.

THORPINGTON: I beg your pardon.

EMILY: Inside I mean . . . where it really counts . . .

THORPINGTON: Oh . . .

EMILY: You see I have a void of loneliness that fills me with its emptiness as well . . .

THORPINGTON: (PUZZLED AND EMBARRASED) Oh . . . really . . .

EMILY: So if your soul aches . . .

Without thinking she is rubbing THORPINGTON'S arm that rests on the table with her wiping up cloth. THORPINGTON gets up . . .

THORPINGTON: Duty calls . . . goodbye . . .

As he hurries out a piece of paper falls from his pocket.

EMILY: Oh have you got to go . . . wait a minute you've dropped something . . .

In his hurry, THORPINGTON doesn't hear her and he disappears out of the door. EMILY picks up the bit of paper and starts to read it.

CUT TO:

EXT. RECRUITS HUT. DAY.

The RECRUITS are lined up looking very dismal.

FLANGE: Right . . . inoculations . . . something to cheer you all up a bit . . . a shot in the arm so to speak. (LAUGHS AT HIS OWN JOKE)

He marches the squad to the MI room. During the march, THORPINGTON whispers to BAILEY.

THORPINGTON: I say . . . you haven't seen a piece of paper around have you?

BAILEY: What paper?

THORPINGTON: Well, it was something I wrote out . . . from that book I showed you . . . a piece of prose that took my fancy . . .

BAILEY: Eh?

THORPINGTON: The character Boris Ivanovitch, he proposes. It's a lovely passage I had to copy it out.

FLANGE: Stop talking.

BAILEY: (WHISPERS) I ain't seen no paper.

THORPINGTON: Oh, it's not important.

CUT TO:

INT. NAAFI KITCHEN. DAY.

EMILY is standing looking dreamy with the piece of paper clutched to her bosom.

FADE.

INT. M.I. ROOM. DAY.

The MO is in the MI room with his ORDERLY CORPORAL. They are both wearing white coats. The MO is young and looks very nervy. He is standing looking out of the window. The CORPORAL puts down a tray then crosses over to the MO.

ORDERLY: All ready Sir?

MO: Eh?

ORDERLY: All ready for the injections Sir? . . . Sergeant Flange's squad . . . they're waiting outside.

The MO frowns.

MO: Oh, very well . . . I suppose we'd better get it over.

The ORDERLY crosses to the door.

ORDERLY: First three.

THORPINGTON, MCANDREW and BAILEY come in, in that order. They have a sleeve rolled up and look a bit pale.

ORDERLY: Over there . . .

The ORDERLY shepherds them over to where the MO has picked up a needle. THORPINGTON tries to go back so that he won't be first. The ORDERLY grabs his arm and swabs it.

ORDERLY: You're first.

THORPINGTON stands in front of the MO in a state of suppressed panic. The MO holds the needle and looks at him.

MO: This won't hurt.

THORPINGTON: (GULPING) I know, Sir.

MO: It won't hurt a bit.

THORPINGTON: I know, Sir.

MO: I know exactly how you feel . . . put your arm out.

THORPINGTON holds the arm out with the sleeve rolled down.

MO: The other one.

THORPINGTON very gingerly holds it out. The MO hesitates then goes to put the needle in. THORPINGTON jerks away.

THORPINGTON: It makes me feel faint, Sir.

MO: I don't like doing it myself . . . now come along.

THORPINGTON puts his arm out again tenderly. As he moves the needle towards THORPINGTON'S arm, he edges it away. When he moves his needle away again, THORPINGTON edges his arm forward again. They sway backwards and forwards with sweat breaking out on both their foreheads.

MO: Steady . . .

They sway for a little longer. Then the MO passes a hand across his forehead as though he is feeling faint.

MO: (WEAKLY) Open a window, Corporal.

ORDERLY: Sir.

The orderly quickly opens a window. THORPINGTON by this time is looking deathly white.

MO: We mustn't be silly . . .

They try again, both swaying. The ORDERLY has to steady both of them. Then a look of determination comes to the MO's face. He pauses, then lunges forward with the needle. THORPINGTON jerks his arm away and the MO jabs his needle straight into the Corporal's arm, who gives a yell. The MO sees what he has done, stares, then collapses in a faint. THORPINGTON collapses after him. BAILEY and MCANDREW try and revive them.

FADE.

INT. RECRUITS' HUT. NIGHT.

The RECRUITS are sitting around cleaning their kit. THORPINGTON is in bed, tossing and turning as though with a fever. HERBERT is standing at the bottom of his bed looking concerned. BAILEY comes up.

BAILEY: How is he?

HERBERT: Still a bit feverish.

BAILEY: He'd have been in a real bad way if we'd had the injections.

BAILEY goes over to his bed and sits down on it. He picks up a boot, spits and starts polishing the toe. HERBERT has followed him to his bed.

HERBERT: Here I'll get my boot and sit on your bed with you . . .

HERBERT gets his boot and brings it over and sits with BAILEY. BAILEY'S boot is shining like a mirror. HERBERT'S boot looks terrible. HERBERT looks carefully at both boots, studying them critically.

HERBERT: My boot's not as good as yours.

BAILEY just spits on his boot without answering. HERBERT spits on his boot but can't make any progress.

HERBERT: How long you been doing that toe cap?

BAILEY: Ten minutes.

BAILEY spits. HERBERT spits.

HERBERT: Oh . . . (HE REFLECTS FOR A MOMENT) I been doing mine two hours.

BAILEY: Oh yer . . .

BAILEY spits. HERBERT follows suit.

HERBERT: Yer . . .

BAILEY: Any change?

HERBERT: Yers . . . it was shiny.

BAILEY takes the boot from him and starts polishing it.

BAILEY: Oh come on . . . let's have it . . . why don't you worry someone else?

HERBERT: (A BIT DISCONCERTED) Well . . .

BAILEY: Why don't yer? Eh?

HERBERT: Well . . .

BAILEY: Ever since you joined the squad you been hanging around me . . . why d'you keep hanging round me, eh?

HERBERT: Well . . .

BAILEY spits again. HERBERT spits forgetting he isn't holding a boot.

BAILEY: Where you spitting?

HERBERT: Oh . . . I forgot I didn't have a boot to spit on . . . Ha . . .

He picks up BAILEY'S shiny boot to work on it. BAILEY snatches it away.

BAILEY: No thank you. Well, why do you?

HERBERT: Why do I what?

BAILEY: Keep hanging round me.

HERBERT: Well . . . see I'll tell you . . . now everyone in the army's got a mate . . . as you know.

BAILEY: I don't know nothink about the army . . . and I don't want to know nothink about it.

HERBERT: Well, it's true . . . everyone's got a mate in the army . . . it's very important.

BAILEY: Well, I ain't got a mate for a start . . . and I don't want one . . .

HERBERT: Well, you got to have a mate . . . I think there's a rule about it . . . Well . . . how about me being your mate?

BAILEY: Look . . . I ain't got no time to make no mates, it's not worth it . . . I'm taking off very shortly . . . if it weren't for old killjoy over there I'd have scarpered ages ago.

HERBERT: Scarpered?

BAILEY: Deserted . . . scarpered . . . 'opped it . . .

HERBERT: Stop pulling my leg . . . you can't tell me a mate of mine would be a deserter.

BAILEY: I'm not a mate of yours . . . and I'm going to hop it . . . it's only a promise keeping me here now . . . Look, why do you want me for a mate? There's plenty of others?

HERBERT: Well, 'cos you're so quick and sharp . . . and Sergeant Flange is very pleased with you, isn't he? An' I need someone who can show me things, and things, and look after me a bit . . . 'cos I know I'm a bit slow. It's not all one sided . . . I got big muscles . . .

BAILEY: Look, I'm no good for you, mate . . . I think the army's horrible . . . I only clean me kit to pass the time . . . an' I only put me uniform on cos I'm cold . . . I can't help if it looks smart can I?

HERBERT: Exactly . . . you're a natch in the army . . . why don't you sign on for twenty-two years like me? It's just the life for me and you.

BAILEY: Look 'Erbert, go to bed, go on . . . I'll clean your kit . . . just go away . . . go on . . . go to bed . . .

HERBERT: No . . . I'll help . . .

BAILEY pushes him away.

BAILEY: Go away, go on . . . for Gawd's sake . . . go to bed.

FADE.

EXT. RANGES. DAY.

The ranges look cold, bleak and desolate . . . There is a misty persistent rain.

Some bedraggled SHEEP graze here and there. There is a big sign, 'Seaview Ranges'. Along the muddy track to the range come two large three-tonners. Further up the track and a few yards from it, there is an ARTIST busy at work. A big umbrella is strapped to the top of his easel and he is wearing oilskins, sou'wester and sandals. He is painting an abstract of the landscape. He is so intent on his work, he doesn't notice the lorries pass. As the first lorry passes, he is bending down putting some more paint on his palette. The lorry goes through a puddle and a big deluge of mud spatters his painting. He stands up and goes on working without noticing the difference. The second lorry comes past and spatters mud all down his neck and back. He goes on working without noticing. The first

three-tonner goes on up the track to the butts. The second three-tonner turns off and pulls up at the hundred-yard firing point. FLANGE and his squad jump out the back of the truck. The squad huddle together, looking very dejected as the rain pours down on them. SERGEANT FLANGE goes to the driving cab. Inside, SMILEY is sitting beside the driver. SMILEY is drinking from a steaming flask. He quickly puts it away when FLANGE opens the door.

FLANGE: We're here, Sir.

SMILEY looks out at the pouring rain distastefully.

SMILEY: So we are, Sergeant . . . splendid, well done.

FLANGE: They're all a bit fed up sir, the lads . . . all this rain . . .

SMILEY: Really? Won't do, sergeant . . . get them busy . . . ammunition unloaded . . . guns oiled . . . standby complete state of readiness . . . little rain doesn't stop army . . . any weather on the go.

FLANGE: Right'ho Sir.

FLANGE salutes and goes back to the RECRUITS. He leaves the cab door open. A gust of rain blows in. SMILEY shuts the door. He turns to the DRIVER as if to make some casual remark. The DRIVER looks him in the eye. SMILEY tries not to look guilty, then gives up and gets out, slamming the door behind him. He has a second thought and opens the door again to speak to the DRIVER.

SMILEY: Check the tyres, Hopkins.

DRIVER: I haven't got a groundsheet, Sir.

SMILEY: I realise that, Hopkins.

SMILEY slams the door. HOPKINS reluctantly gets out the other side. A few SHEEP have wandered up. They walk in amongst the RECRUITS, who are unloading the boxes of ammunition. As SMILEY goes round the back of the truck, he trips over a particularly big black SHEEP. The SHEEP baas at him maliciously. SMILEY goes round to where the RECRUITS are working, and getting soaked to the skin.

BAILEY: (SARCASTICALLY) Mornin' Sir . . . nice day . . .

SMILEY: Splendid . . . splendid spirit . . . That's it, lads, good cheer, determination . . . all the best . . .

He has a shooting stick. He opens it, sticks it in the ground and sits on it. He folds his arms and watches the RECRUITS working, cheering them on.

SMILEY: That's the way lads . . . work away . . . work away regardless . . . remember . . . every man must do work of two men . . . effort terms, one man equals two men, what did I say? (*POINTS TO BAILEY*)

BAILEY: (FED UP) One man equals two men, Sir.

SMILEY: Right . . . on your toes good man, what's your name? (BAILEY GOES TO ANSWER). Too late, half asleep, wake up slackin'. Very necessary all of you realise importance, three rules . . . work hard effort . . . companionship all comrades, bags of guts . . . dig in, never retreat . . . Touch your left ankle with little finger right hand quick! Half asleep, too late, as you were . . .

The RECRUITS have put down their boxes and tried to do what was ordered, all completely fed up with the weather.

SMILEY: Keep alert all times . . . observe . . . (POINTS AT THORPINGTON) How many trees did we pass on way up track? You.

THORPINGTON straightens his back.

THORPINGTON: Well err . . .

SMILEY: Too late . . . unobservant . . . thirteen trees seven bushes . . .

BAILEY: (MURMURS TO OTHERS) Ruddy dog is he?

SMILEY: Use of senses . . . all times . . . observation . . . Quick, stand on your left leg, right hand on head.

In the pouring rain the RECRUITS do this with a look of resignation as though they are humouring a halfwit. SMILEY points at the slow ones.

SMILEY: You were late . . . and you . . . and you . . . very bad . . .

HERBERT is still trying to work it out, standing first on one leg then the other.

HERBERT: (TO HIMSELF) Right leg fourth finger . . . No, left ankle right thumb . . . No, right leg on head . . .

SMILEY points at him.

SMILEY: What's your name . . . (BEFORE HE HAS TIME TO ANSWER) Too late . . . lazy, idle . . . take his name . . . what's your name . . . (BEFORE HE HAS A CHANCE TO ANSWER) . . . Too late, take his name . . .

HERBERT: (COMPLETELY CONFUSED) Eh?

FLANGE: (WRITING IN NOTEBOOK) Private Brown, Sir . . . idle . . .

HERBERT: What's that Sarge . . . d'you want me?

SMILEY: Take his name, answering back.

FLANGE: Private Brown – answering back, Sir. Get on with your work, Brown.

HERBERT turns and helps BAILEY with a box.

HERBERT: (TO BAILEY) What did they want?

BAILEY: Oh nothing . . . just wanted to know the time I think.

HERBERT: Oh . . . (HE TURNS TO SMILEY) It's about half past ten, Sir . . . our break time.

SMILEY stares at HERBERT for a moment, surprised.

SMILEY: Take his name, Sergeant . . . Insolence . . .

HERBERT: But . . .

FLANGE: Private Brown, Sir . . . insolent . . .

HERBERT, looking completely bewildered, goes back to work.

FLANGE is talking to SMILEY as the RECRUITS finish off unloading the ammo.

FLANGE: He gets bewildered sir . . . when someone abouts at him . . . he don't mean anything . . .

SMILEY: Oh . . . I see, well, if you recommend a good talking to, Sergeant.

FLANGE screws up the paper he's been writing on.

FLANGE: Yes Sir . . . I don't think we can shoot yet Sir. Not clear enough . . . I think we should wait in the shelter Sir . . .

SMILEY: Roger . . . get them under cover Sergeant . . . No reason to get wet.

SMILEY steps back and trips over the same black SHEEP.

SMILEY: Get away!

The SHEEP baas back again maliciously.

FLANGE: Right lads . . . over to the hut . . . Double.

They all double over to a tin shelter. As SMILEY goes to double with them he trips over the same SHEEP again.

SMILEY: Will you leave me alone!

The SHEEP baas back at him. SMILEY doubles over to the hut. They are all crowded round the entrance. Sitting in the entrance blocking the way in is an OLD SHEPHERD stolidy sucking a pipe.

SMILEY: What's wrong?

He pushes through the RECRUITS to the door. FLANGE points at the SHEPHERD.

SMILEY: This is army property . . . you and your sheep trespassing . . . Necessary you move immediately . . . at once . . . (THE SHEPHERD JUST SITS THERE SUCKING ON HIS PIPE . . . SMILEY TRIES AGAIN) Regulations definite . . . must move . . . Authority Army Council.

The rain is pouring down as every one stands around getting wetter. The SHEPHERD just sits in the way without answering.

SMILEY: All your sheep off range . . . at once . . . leave with sheep now no trouble . . . must go . . .

The SHEPHERD just sits there as SMILEY stands in front of him.

FLANGE: We could shelter in the truck, Sir.

SMILEY: Splendid idea . . . much warmer.

FLANGE: Double lads!

They all double back to the truck . . . When the RECRUITS go to climb in the back of the truck it is full of SHEEP sheltering from the rain. SMILEY goes to climb in the driving cab. The big black SHEEP is sitting in his seat . . .

FADE.

SAME SCENE.

The heavy rain has turned to an overcast drizzle. Six of the RECRUITS are lying on the hundred-yard firing point. The other six are standing behind them, waiting for their turn.

SMILEY: Right . . . phone butts targets up ready to fire Corporal.

NOUGHTON at one end of the firing point has a range phone. He turns the handle to ring the bell and speaks into receiver.

NOUGHTON: Hello butts . . . hello butts . . . firing point here . . . hello butts.

CUT TO:

EXT. BUTTS. DAY.

SOLDIER is on the phone at the butts end.

SOLDIER: Hello . . . hello . . .

He speaks to a CORPORAL who is standing beside him.

SOLDIER: I can't hear 'em, Corp.

CUT TO:

EXT. 100-YD FIRING POINT. DAY.

NOUGHTON: Hello . . . butts . . . hello.

He rings the bell again vigorously.

NOUGHTON: Damn these wires, all mixed . . . hello butts . . .

CUT TO:

INT. AN OLD COTTAGE. DAY.

An old-fashioned telephone on the sideboard in the sitting room rings.

An OLD LADY in the kitchen making pastry wipes her hands and goes to answer it.

CUT TO:

EXT. FIRING POINT. DAY.

NOUGHTON is ringing the bell vigorously.

NOUGHTON: Hello . . . butts . . . can you hear me . . . butts.

CUT TO:

EXT. BUTTS. DAY.

The SOLDIER is shouting into the phone.

SOLDIER: Hello . . . hello firing point . . . hello . . .

CPL: Ring the bell man.

The SOLDIER rings the bell.

CUT TO:

INT. COTTAGE. DAY.

The telephone rings again. The OLD LADY picks it up.

OLD LADY: Hello . . . hello . . .

CUT TO:

EXT. FIRING POINT. DAY.

NOUGHTON: Hello . . . hello . . .

CUT TO:

EXT. BUTTS DAY.

SOLDIER: Hello . . .

CUT TO:

INT. COTTAGE. DAY.

OLD LADY: Hello . . .

CUT TO:

EXT. FIRING POINT DAY.

SMILEY: Where's the megaphone . . .

SERGEANT FLANGE hands him the megaphone . . . SMILEY shouts towards the butts.

SMILEY: Targets up butts!

The targets come up.

SMILEY: Steady aim, lads . . . straight at the bull . . . good shooting . . . carry on . . .

SMILEY looks towards the targets. The RECRUITS all fire one round.

CUT TO:

EXT. A COUNTRY LANE. DAY.

The SHEPHERD is walking down the lane with his SHEEP . . . There is a sudden whine and ricochet of bullets. The SHEEP scatter and the SHEPHERD leaps into the ditch. He lifts his head and peers through the hedge. About three miles away he can see the range . . .

CUT TO:

EXT. FIRING POINT. DAY.

SMILEY is looking through his binoculars towards the targets.

SMILEY: No . . . can't see any holes in the targets. Maybe all in black of the bull . . . well done lads . . . Phone butts . . . firing again . . . carry on . . .

NOUGHTON on the phone turns the bell handle vigorously again.

NOUGHTON: Hello butts . . . hello butt . . .

CUT TO:

INT. COTTAGE DAY.

The phone starts ringing again. The OLD LADY who has gone back to her pastry comes back to the phone.

OLD LADY: (INTO PHONE) Hello . . . hello . . .

CUT TO:

EXT. FIRING POINT. DAY.

The RECRUITS all fire another ragged salvo.

CUT TO:

EXT. FURTHER ALONG THE COUNTRY LANE. DAY.

The SHEPHERD is with his SHEEP, walking along again. There is the whine and ricochet of bullets. The SHEPHERD dives for cover again as his SHEEP scatter.

CUT TO:

EXT. BUTTS. DAY.

The SOLDIER is on the phone, ringing vigorously.

SOLDIER: Hello . . . hello . . . firing point . . .

CPL: Tell them there's no holes in the targets.

SOLDIER: Hello . . . hello firing point.

CUT TO:

INT. COTTAGE. DAY.

The phone is ringing again. The OLD LADY comes out of the kitchen to the phone.

OLD LADY: Hello . . . hello . . .

CUT TO:

EXT. FIRING POINT. DAY.

NOUGHTON: Hello . . . hello . . . zeroing brens . . . . . . zeroing brens.

CUT TO:

INT. COTTAGE. DAY.

OLD LADY: Hello.

CUT TO:

EXT. SHALLOW FORD OVER STREAM. DAY.

The SHEPHERD and his SHEEP are crossing the ford. There is the sudden rattattat of bren bullets. They hit the water and banks. The SHEPHERD throws himself down in the shallow water in the shelter of the bank as the SHEEP scatter in panic again.

FADE.

EXT. MORTAR RANGE. DAY.

The three-tonner with the RECRUITS pulls up by a big sign 'Mortar Range'. The RECRUITS jump out handing the mortars out.

CUT TO:

INT. COTTAGE. DAY.

The SHEPHERD is sitting at the table with the old lady eating dinner. The cottage is suddenly shaken by explosions of mortar bombs landing in the garden. The couple dive under the table. The door is blown open and the frightened SHEEP come walking in, baaing their heads off. The phone starts ringing.

CUT TO:

EXT. MORTAR RANGE FIRING POINT.

The smoke is clearing from the several mortars that have been fired. NOUGHTON is on the phone vigorously ringing.

NOUGHTON: Hello . . . hello . . . shoot completed . . . everything satisfactory . . . hello . . .

CUT TO:

INT. COTTAGE. DAY.

The couple under the table with the SHEEP bustling them and the phone ringing away.

FADE.

FRAMED SHOT OF NOTICE.

It is an order pinned to a board about a SERGEANT MAJOR'S inspection the following day, Saturday. RECRUITS that pass the inspection are to be allowed out of the barracks during the weekend.

CUT TO:

EXT. COMPANY ORDER BOARD. DAY.

BAILEY and HERBERT are looking at the order, BAILEY is reading the notice, HERBERT is puzzling. He points at the notice.

HERBERT: Here, Harry . . . what's that word?

BAILEY: (STILL READING) Mmmmm?

HERBERT: What's that word . . . that one there?

BAILEY: (IRRITABLY) Where?

HERBERT: There . . . (HE POINTS)

BAILEY: There . . .

HERBERT: Yes, there.

BAILEY: That's the word . . . there . . .

HERBERT: Oh . . . (HE STUDIES THE BOARD AGAIN) Here, what's that word.

BAILEY: (TRYING TO READ WITHOUT INTERRUPTION) Eh?

HERBERT: That word there . . .

BAILEY: (IMPATIENTLY) Will . . .

HERBERT: Oh thanks . . . there . . . will . . . (HE PUZZLES A BIT MORE) Mmmmm . . . here . . . what's that word?

BAILEY: (STILL READING) Shut up, will you?

HERBERT: What's this word here, Harry?

BAILEY: Be . . .

HERBERT: There will be . . . what's the next . . .

BAILEY: (ANGRILY) Why don't you just ask me to read it out for you?

HERBERT: (OFFENDED) I can read, thanks very much, it's just that I have trouble with some of the words . . .

BAILEY: Look, there's a Sergeant Major's

inspection tomorrow, that's what it says . . . now are you satisfied?

HERBERT: I know, I know, it's on that notice isn't it? I can see it . . . (POINTS AT PART OF THE NOTICE) Sergeant Major's inspection tomorrow . . .

BAILEY: That's the wrong paragraph.

THORPINGTON comes on the scene. He is reading a letter.

HERBERT: What are you reading?

THORPINGTON: Oh . . . it's a letter.

HERBERT: Want some help with it?

THORPINGTON: It's from that girl, Emily . . . just a note . . . be sure to meet her tomorrow afternoon outside the N.A.A.F.I. . . . signed . . . your own sweet love, Emily.

BAILEY: Yer? You mean she's fallen for you?

HERBERT: I think she's smashing . . . have you seen her washing hanging out?

The other two ignore HERBERT.

THORPINGTON: Well . . . I mean I've hardly spoken to her.

BAILEY: That's alright, you're on to a good thing. I'd meet her if I was you . . .

THORPINGTON: (DOUBTFULLY) Yes . . . still seems rather . . . still, I mean, she's quite pretty, I can't see any harm . . .

FADE.

EXT. BARRACK SQUARE. DAY.

FLANGE is marching his squad wearing BD for the first time (instead of denims) onto the square. He halts them and stand them at ease, then they wait for the appearance of the SERGEANT MAJOR. The RECRUITS look reasonably smart.

FLANGE: If you let me down in front of the Sergeant Major . . .

He sees the SERGEANT MAJOR coming, calls the SQUAD up to attention, and marches up to the SM.

FLANGE: Number fifteen training squad ready for your inspection, Sir!

SM: Where?

FLANGE: (A BIT DISCONCERTED) Over there, Sir.

SM: (FEIGNING SURPRISE) Ooh . . . they're soldiers are they? Right . . . let's have a look at em.

FLANGE and the SM walk to the first in the rank.

SM: You can get your boots better than that.

RECRUIT: Yes Sir.

He passes on to the next man.

SM: Turn your toes out . . . keep that hair short.

He passes on to the next man. It is MERVIN. His strained position of attention is very bad.

SM: (MILDLY) Are you deformed?

MERVIN: No Sir.

SM: (STILL QUIETLY) You are, you're deformed,

MERVIN: No Sir . . .

SM: You are deformed . . . anyone can see that.

MERVIN: No Sir . . .

SM: (SHOUTING) . . . The hunchback of Notre Dam was a specimen of perfection compared to you . . . Get your chest out. Get it out.

MERVIN sticks his chest out in an exaggerated manner.

SM: I said get it out, not take it for a walk.

The SM goes suddenly quiet and looks closely at MERVIN again.

SM: (QUIETLY) You are, aren't you?

MERVIN: What Sir?

SM: Deformed.

MERVIN: No sir.

SM: (LOSING HIS TEMPER) You *are* deformed. Don't pretend you're not deformed when anyone can see you're deformed . . . Take his name Sergeant . . . deformed.

FLANGE: Private Mervin. Deformed, Sir.

SM: (PASSING ON) We'll have to have him looked at.

He passes a couple more RECRUITS then comes to a recruit with his hat much too big for him.

SM: Am I right in presuming there's someone underneath that hat?

RECRUIT: Yes Sir . . .

SM: Well come out then. It's not raining. Put him down for a smaller hat, Sergeant.

He passes a couple more with minor comments. Then comes to ROGERS, the pimply, weak-faced recruit.

SM: What's your name then?

ROGERS: (SIMPERING) Rogers, Sir.

SM: That's a very nice name, isn't it?

ROGERS: Yes Sir . . .

SM: Tell me Rogers . . . did you by any chance happen to shave this morning?

ROGERS: Oh . . . no sir . . . I don't shave . . .

SM: (INTERESTED) Oh . . . you don't shave?

ROGERS: No sir . . . I don't need to . . .

The SERGEANT MAJOR starts plucking hairs from the region of ROGERS' Adam's apple. ROGERS winces each time.

SM: Oh, you don't need to shave, eh Rogers? Well, eight hundred thousand soldiers shave

every morning in this army . . . that is all bar you Rogers . . . and as I have had no notification from the war office about you not shaving . . . (SHOUTS) You will shave . . . do you understand?

ROGERS: Yes Sir.

SM: As soon as you get off parade . . . do you know how to use a razor without cutting yourself?

ROGERS: No Sir.

SM: Good . . . In the book, Sergeant.

FLANGE: Private Rogers . . . unshaven, Sir.

Next to ROGERS is BROWN.

SM: Brown.

HERBERT: Yes, Sir.

SM: The adjutant told me to tell you, Brown, that if you don't leave the depot with this intake . . . then the depot's packing up and leaving you . . . understand?

HERBERT: Mmmmm . . . quite smart for a change.

He suddenly spots HERBERT'S boots and sees one of them done up with string.

SM: (WEARILY) Brown.

HERBERT: Yes Sir.

SM: Why have you got one of you boots done up with string?

HERBERT: To keep it on, Sir.

ROGERS standing next to HERBERT gives a little snigger. The SM looks at him.

SM: What are you laughing at?

ROGERS: About the string, Sir.

SM: (MILDLY) . . . Oh, you think that's funny, do you?

ROGERS: (NERVOUSLY) Well . . . err . . . yes Sir . . . (SNIGGERS FROM NERVES)

SM: Well I don't.

ROGERS' snigger freezes on his face.

SM: You're a proper little bundle of joy, aren't you?

ROGERS is uncertain whether the SM is being amusing or not.

SM: You're a proper little giggler, aren't you?

ROGERS gives a tight smile, uncertain how to take the remark.

SM: Go on . . . have another little giggle . . . go on . . .

ROGERS starts to giggle nervously.

SM: Go on . . . don't let us stop you . . . don't mind us.

ROGERS sniggers more uncontrolled.

SM: (TO FLANGE) Look at him Sergeant . . . having a lovely time.

ROGERS' snigger becomes even more uncontrolled.

SM: Shut your nasty mouth.

ROGERS freezes in terror.

SM: You pimply faced, little hairy necked half pint. There's only one time when you laugh in the army. That's when you've been wounded. And then not till you've been given permission.

The SM moves on. He comes to THORPINGTON. His battle dress is smartly pressed. In the button hole is a carnation. The SM stares disbelieving then slowly takes it out.

SM: No . . . I don't think so . . .

There is a shout from a little way off. It is the Adjutant.

ADJUTANT: Sergeant Major.

SM: Sir.

The SM turns away from the squad and marches quickly up to the Adjutant. He has forgotten that he is still holding the carnation in his hand.

ADJUTANT: Sergeant Major, there's been an amendment to the . . .

He suddenly notices the carnation. He looks at it in surprise, then looks at the SM questioningly. The SM realises something is wrong and looks down and sees the carnation he is holding. He looks slowly up again at the Adjutant. They stare at each other for a long moment without saying anything.

ADJUTANT: (QUIETLY) You know I don't like carnations.

EXT. OUTSIDE NAAFI. DAY.

THORPINGTON is standing around waiting for EMILY. He looks rather apprehensive. EMILY tries to come out of the private door, but the dustbins are in the way. THORPINGTON hears the dustbins rattle and sees her trying to get out.

THORPINGTON: Hang on . . . wait a minute.

He hurries over to the private door . . . but EMILY has not heard him and has gone in again. He hurriedly moves the dustbins along clear of the private door. Then he knocks on the private door.

THORPINGTON: (CALLS OUT) I say . . . it's alright, I've cleared the way.

There is another rattle of dustbins from the main door, as EMILY tries to get out that way, but can't because THORPINGTON has moved the dustbins along. He rushes back to the main door and starts pulling the dustbins clear.

THORPINGTON: Oh Emily . . . you see I'd moved them along . . . hang on . . .

EMILY: (PEEVED) Why did you move them along?

THORPINGTON: Oh, well, you see they were in the way.

EMILY: I know they're in the way . . . Why'd you have to move them on over here?

THORPINGTON pulls the last dustbin clear and EMILY steps out.

THORPINGTON: There . . . you see the dustbins were . . .

EMILY: Dustbins, dustbins, dustbins . . . why don't people leave our dustbins alone. (SHE SEES HE IS A BIT PUT OFF BY HER BAD TEMPER AND QUICKLY PULLS HERSELF TOGETHER) Never mind, it's not your fault.

She puts her arm through his.

EMILY: Come on.

THORPINGTON: Oh yes . . . where?

EMILY: Did you get my note . . . ?

THORPINGTON: Oh yes . . . I . . .

EMILY: I felt shy . . . it's so sudden . . . I mean, you don't waste time but I know what you mean if fate throws us together.

THORPINGTON: You see I couldn't quite . . .

EMILY: I know, you don't have to tell me . . . Sir . . . you knew what I'd do . . . I mean right from the start didn't you . . . ?

THORPINGTON: Well . . . you know . . . I would like to take you out . . .

EMILY: I should hope so . . . come on . . .

THORPINGTON: Where are we going?

EMILY: You'll see . . . curiosity killed the cat, come on.

CUT TO:

EXT BARRACK SQUARE. DAY.

BAILEY is walking along the edge of the square, whistling happily. He is obviously off out for the afternoon. HERBERT appears about fifty yards behind him. He spots BAILEY and starts hurrying to catch him up.

HERBERT: (CALLING OUT) Harry . . . Harry hang on . . . it's me . . . it's me, Erbert . . . hang on . . . Harry.

A frown crosses BAILEY'S face as he recognises the voice . . . He doesn't look round but quickens his pace.

HERBERT: I'm going into town too . . . hang on.

BAILEY turns a corner out of sight from HERBERT. HERBERT chases after BAILEY, but when he turns the corner BAILEY is nowhere to be seen. HERBERT calls him a couple of times, then gives up and goes unhappily on his way. When he's well clear, BAILEY'S head appears over a hedge and catches HERBERT'S disappearing.

CUT TO:

INT. CAFE. DAY.

It is a very crumby cafe. In the corner sit MR & MRS SPILLER (EMILY'S parents) and GLADYS, her sister. Next to GLADYS sits a MASSIVE SAILOR (GLADYS' FIANCEE), meekly holding her hand. MRS SPILLER looks very formidable. MR SPILLER looks downtrodden. They sit there in silence till MRS SPILLER breaks it.

MRS SPILLER: (SHARPLY) Blow your nose.

MR SPILLER quickly takes his handkerchief out.

MRS SPILLER: Not you Arnold . . . Gladys.

MR SPILLER puts his hanky away again. GLADYS, looking a bit sulky, blows her nose hard. Then they sit there in silence again.

MR SPILLER tries to break the silence as pleasantly as possible. He puts his hand on the tea pot and turns to his wife.

MR SPILLER: More tea dear . . . I'll be mother, shall I?

MRS SPILLER looks hard at him.

MRS SPILLER: This is no time to be frivolous, Arnold.

MR SPILLER quickly takes his hand off the pot.

MRS SPILLER: If that boy's toying with our girl's affections, he's got another thing coming . . . (SHE SNIFFS)

Nobody ventures to comment and they lapse back into silence.

CUT TO:

EXT. OUTSIDE CAFE. DAY.

EMILY and THORPINGTON go in.

EMILY: Here we are.

CUT TO:

INT. CAFE. DAY.

EMILY and THORPINGTON come in. She spots her parents.

EMILY: (WAVING) Oo-oo Mum . . .

A look of horror creeps over THORPINGTON'S face. EMILY pulls his arm.

EMILY: Come on.

They go over to the table. Nobody gets up.

EMILY: Hello Dad.

MR. SPILLER: Hello Emmy.

EMILY: Hello Glad.

GLAD: Hello Emm . . . (SAYS VERY PROUDLY) This is Arthur, my fiancee . . .

EMILY: Oh . . . is it? (AS THOUGH GETTING HER OWN BACK ON HER SISTER) Well this is Henry, *my* fiancee.

THORPINGTON grips a back of a chair faintly. Then protests weakly.

THORPINGTON: Wait a minute Emily, I . . .

MRS. SPILLER: (BUTTS IN) Sit down young man . . . Sit down Emily.

THORPINGTON: But you see, I . . .

THORPINGTON dries under the glare of MRS SPILLER. He sits down as if needing the chair. EMILY sits down. MRS SPILLER waits till everyone is quite still.

MRS SPILLER: Right . . . are your means assured?

THORPINGTON: Look . . . I . . . (HE CRUMBLES UNDER HER GLARE) Yes . . . but . . .

MRS SPILLER: First obstacle overcome . . . Blow your nose.

THORPINGTON automatically reaches for his handkerchief. So does GLADYS.

MRS SPILLER: I mean you, Arnold.

ARNOLD hurriedly blows his nose. The others put their hankies away again.

THORPINGTON: Now look . . . Emily . . . I mean . . . I never said . . .

EMILY: You never had to say dearest . . . you wrote the sweetest note . . .

She takes the proposal note from her handbag. MRS SPILLER immediate snatches it before THORPINGTON, who has a go at taking it.

MRS SPILLER: I'll have that.

She examines it while the others await her verdict.

MRS SPILLER: That's definite enough in any court.

She puts the note in her handbag. THORPINGTON protests.

THORPINGTON: Now look . . . really I must insist . . . there's been some terrible mistake . . .

EMILY: (HEARTBROKEN) Henry?

MRS SPILLER: (TO EMILY REASSURING) It's alright dear . . . leave him to me . . . blow your nose.

EMILY blows her nose. MRS SPILLER turns squarely on THORPINGTON.

MRS SPILLER: Now . . . I don't have to tell you that a written contract to a single girl promising marriage and many children cannot be made and broken at leisure. It was you who lured my daughter in the first place . . .

FADE.

EXT. STREET. DAY.

HERBERT is wandering up the street, scuffling his feet, looking like a lost soul. The houses have little front gardens. As HERBERT passes one, he hears a dog whining. He sees, poking his nose through a gate, a big dog looking very harmless and friendly. But it has a muzzle on and is chained to a post.

HERBERT: Ain't you got no mates either?

HERBERT goes to walk on, but the dog whines pathetically. HERBERT looks back.

HERBERT: What's wrong then . . . why are you all done like that . . . are you a bad dog . . . (THE DOG WHINES. . . HERBERT GOES BACK TO THE GATE) You look nice and friendly . . . (HE PATS THE DOG AND GOES TO WALK AWAY AGAIN, BUT THE DOG WHINES AGAIN) What's the matter then? (HERBERT GOES BACK AND GIVES THE DOG ANOTHER PAT) You wouldn't bite anyone, would you? (THE DOG WHINES AND WAGS ITS TAIL) Why have the nasty people tied you up like that so that you can't go and play with your mates . . . (THE DOG WHINES) That nasty muzzle. (THE DOG WHINES PLEADINGLY. HERBERT LOOKS ROUND MAKE SURE NO-ONES AROUND) 'Ere, I'll take it off for you . . . (HE TAKES IT OFF. THE DOG WAGS ITS TAIL) There . . . you wouldn't hurt a flea would you . . . cheerio then. (HERBERT GOES TO WALK AWAY BUT THE DOG WHINES AGAIN) What's the matter then . . . is that horrible chain making you unhappy ? (HE LOOKS ROUND) It's not right, a nice friendly doggy like you being chained up . . . . . . (HE OPENS THE GATE AND TIPTOES FURTIVELY UP TO THE POST, FOLLOWED BY THE DOG WAGGING ITS TAIL. HE UNDOES THE CHAIN FROM THE POST) There . . .

The DOG immediately snarls viciously and leaps on HERBERT, knocking him over. The front door opens and A MAN comes out angrily.

MAN: What do you mean by letting that savage brute go . . .

HERBERT is struggling to get free.

HERBERT: Get him off . . . let go of me . . . Oohh . . .

HERBERT rushes out of the garden and up the street while the MAN wards the dog off with a broom.

CUT TO:

EXT. MAIN STREET. DAY.

BAILEY is wandering up the main street, looking pensive. We hear his thoughts on echo.

BAILEY: (THOUGHTS) Why haven't I scarpered I don't know . . . the week was up yesterday . . . That Herbert can't do a thing without me . . . and Thorpington . . . Why don't they all get off my back . . . I could hop it now . . . I don't know . . . I don't know what to do . . . heads or tails?

He has taken a penny out. He flips it up in the air. As he goes to catch it, someone bumps into him and the penny rolls down a drain. It is SMILEY who knocked into him.

SMILEY: I'm terribly sorry . . . great hurry . . . (RECOGNISES FACE) Wait a minute . . . name? Too late . . . err Bailey.

BAILEY: That's right Sir . . . it's alright.

Salutes and goes to pass on his way, but SMILEY stops him.

SMILEY: One moment . . . going back myself . . . give you lift, come on . . .

BAILEY: But sir, I wasn't going back . . .

SMILEY: Wanted to talk anyway . . . this way . . .

He leads BAILEY into a car park, to his car.

SMILEY: By the way . . . you dropped a coin?

BAILEY: Er . . . oh two shillings sir.

SMILEY gives him half a crown.

SMILEY: My fault . . . take it . . . observe . . . see where going . . . wouldn't bump into anyone . . . here we are . . . get in . . .

BAILEY hesitates then, resigned to going back, gets in. SMILEY jumps in. The car park is very crowded and the car is in an awkward position for getting out. An OLD CAR-PARK ATTENDANT comes up.

ATTENDANT: OK Sir . . . OK . . . I'll see you out . . . don't worry . . . Right hand down sir . . . forward you come.

SMILEY lets the car come forward it bangs into another car. Without batting an eyelid, THE ATTENDANT goes on giving instructions.

ATTENDANT: Now back a bit . . . go back, left a bit, go on, go on . . . go on back . . . you're alright.

SMILEY backs under the instructions and bangs into a car behind him.

ATTENDANT: Right . . . right hand down and forward, very easy . . . easy does it . . . come on, right hand down, come on . . .

The car bumps into another vehicle.

ATTENDANT: Back a bit now . . . just a bit . . . now come right forward, right hand down.

They bump into another vehicle and at last come clear. SMILEY feels into his pocket and hands THE ATTENDANT a tip. The attendant touches his cap.

SMILEY: Thank you.

ATTENDANT: Thank you Sir . . . thank you very much, Sir . . . thank you . . .

FADE.

EXT. COUNTRY ROAD. DAY.

SMILEY and BAILEY are in the car driving back to the barracks.

SMILEY: Lovely countryside.

BAILEY: Yes Sir . . . very pretty.

SMILEY: Ideal for defence . . . Now Bailey, personal talk.

BAILEY: Well sir, if it's about me I might as well tell you from the start that . . .

SMILEY: Very pleased with you. Excellent report. Sergeant Flange . . . natural soldier . . . NCO material . . . Private Brown . . . a friend of yours?

BAILEY: Well, sir . . . sort of . . .

SMILEY: Always together . . .

BAILEY: Well . . .

SMILEY: By the way . . . saw you drop coin my fault how much?

BAILEY: Eh . . . oh . . . actually . . . half a crown Sir . . .

SMILEY hands him half a crown.

SMILEY: Nearly forgot . . . wouldn't do. About Brown, your friend . . . eleven months in depot . . . must pass out this time . . . Much attached to you . . . could help him a great deal . . .

BAILEY: Well sir, the thing is . . .

SMILEY: Yes?

BAILEY: (RESIGNED) Yes Sir.

CUT TO:

EXT. STREET DAY.

HERBERT is walking back up the same road. He hears a clock strike four.

HERBERT: I'm going to be late for tea.

He goes to pass the same house that had the DOG. The DOG is at the gate. HERBERT steps out into the gutter to go past. As he walks past, the DOG whines plaintively. It is muzzled and chained again.

HERBERT: Traitor . . . Don't talk to me, you rotter. (THE DOG WHINES . . . HERBERT STOPS) I don't want to know . . . I know your game . . . (THE DOG WHINES AND LOOKS REPENTANT) It's no good being sorry . . . you deserve to be locked up. (HERBERT HAS GONE UP TO THE DOG ABSENT-MINDEDLY AND STARTED PATTING IT. THE DOG WAGS ITS TAIL) Don't you, eh . . . What would the world be like if we were all like you, untrustworthy . . . (DOG WHINES) Well, you might be sorry, I'm no saying you're not . . . You got to turn over a new leaf . . . And be a good dog from now on, alright . . . (DOG WHINES) Alright, just your muzzle, you don't deserve it . . . (HE TAKES OFF THE MUZZLE . . . THE DOG JUMPS UP AND LICKS HIS FACE) Well, if you're really sorry . . .

HERBERT looks round to see he isn't observed, slips the gate open and goes in and up to the post. The DOG follows him, tail wagging. As soon as he releases the chain, the same thing happens . . . The DOG jumps on him wildly. The MAN comes out of the door.

MAN: Didn't I tell you . . . leave that dog alone . . . what's your game, eh?

HERBERT rushes out to the garden, followed by the barking DOG and the MAN, who comes to the gate and shakes his fist after them.

MAN: Bring that ruddy dog back! I'll have the law on you . . .

FADE.

INT. RECRUITS HUT. DAY.

THORPINGTON is sitting on his bed with his head buried in his hands. BAILEY comes in the hut. He goes up to THORPINGTON.

BAILEY: I got something to tell you

THORPINGTON: (MOANS) What can I do . . .

BAILEY: Eh? Listen . . . it was you that got me to promise to stay, wasn't it . . . for a while . . .

THORPINGTON: (PAYING NO ATTENTION TO BAILEY BUT WRAPPED UP IN HIS OWN PROBLEMS) . . . I don't know . . .

BAILEY: Listen. Cos of that promise I gave you . . . I ain't deserted and got into trouble . . . an' I been thinking . . . the army ain't so bad after all . . . I mean Herbert is right . . . you get a few mates and that makes the difference, don't it?

THORPINGTON notices BAILEY properly for the first time.

THORPINGTON: What?

BAILEY: Well what I mean is, I'm going to have a real go now.

THORPINGTON: What at?

BAILEY: (GIVES UP) What's wrong with you?

THORPINGTON: It's Emily . . . she . . . you see its all arranged.

BAILEY: What is?

THORPINGTON: Our marriage.

BAILEY: What? Well that's quick . . . you must have fancied her . . .

HERBERT has just come in. BAILEY calls out to him.

BAILEY: Hey . . . he's asked Emily to marry him . . .

THORPINGTON: No . . . you don't understand . . .

HERBERT: Congratulations old man . . . when's the happy event . . .

THORPINGTON: I don't want to marry her.

HERBERT: Well get a divorce.

BAILEY: They're not married yet.

HERBERT: Well, they'll have to wait, won't they . . . cos it's no good – if they want to get divorced they'll have to get married first . . . it's the law, in't it . . .

THORPINGTON picks up the book that has caused so much trouble.

THORPINGTON: That's to blame . . . I'll never read another book!

He throws it across the room. HERBERT picks it up.

HERBERT: Here . . . don't do that . . .

THORPINGTON: Burn it . . . anything . . . take it out of my sight!

HERBERT: Don't you want it, then? Well, I'll have it then . . . an' read it . . . I like books . . . I'm always reading, you know . . . specially the classicals.

BAILEY: You couldn't read a teacup.

HERBERT: Eh?

BAILEY: You can't read . . . you know you can't . . . I even had to read that notice for you . . .

HERBERT: Only cos I didn't have me glasses.

BAILEY: You ain't got no glasses.

HERBERT: Who ain't . . .

He goes over to MERVIN, who has always worn glasses.

HERBERT: 'Ere . . . give me my glasses . . .

He snatches them from MERVIN'S face and puts them on. MERVIN protests weakly.

MERVIN: I say . . . wait a minute . . . they're mine . . . (BUT WITHOUT HIS GLASSES, MERVIN CAN'T SEE) Where is he . . .

HERBERT goes back to his bed, putting the glasses on. He has left the book on his bed. With the glasses on he can't see properly and feels all over the bed for his book.

HERBERT: That's better . . . I can't see a thing without these you know . . . don't know why I lend 'em out.

Finally he has to pull the glasses down his nose and look over]missing text[moment now that he can see where the book in. He tries to do it surreptitiously so that others don't notice. He picks up the book. Holding it upside down he opens it.

HERBERT: Now if you would kindly leave me . . . I can have a quiet read . . .

INT. GUARDROOM. DAY.

LANCE CPL. COPPING is sitting at a table with his feet up. He is reading a children's comic. The SERGEANT in charge of the regimental police comes in. He is a very mean-looking man. He snatches the comic from COPPING.

SERGEANT: What do you think you're doing?

COPPING: (HURT) Only reading.

SERGEANT: Get up.

COPPING stands up sulkily

SERGEANT: Why aren't you working?

COPPING: Well, you know we ain't got no prisoners under close arrest . . . even Brown's out . . .

SERGEANT: What do we get paid for then?

COPPING: Well . . .

SERGEANT: We get paid to keep this guardroom nice and full . . . that's our job, you know that.

COPPING: But . . .

SERGEANT: Now get out there . . . and get busy!

COPPING slinks out. The SERGEANT watches him go. Then he settles himself down at the table with his feet up and starts reading the comic.

CUT TO:

EXT. PATH IN CAMP. DAY.

BAILEY and HERBERT are walking to the NAAFI.

CUT TO:

EXT. ANOTHER PART OF THE PATH. DAY.

COPPING is skulking around looking for someone to get into trouble

CUT TO:

EXT. ANOTHER PART OF THE PAT.H DAY.

BAILEY and HERBERT are walking along.

HERBERT: Well, I'm glad you've changed your mind about the army.

Cut back to COPPING, still looking around. He suddenly spots the other two coming up the path. A gleam of satisfaction comes to his eyes. He steps off the path behind a tree. The other two come up the path, unsuspecting. When they get abreast of COPPING, he steps out on to the path.

COPPING: Come 'ere.

They both turn surprised and go up to COPPING.

COPPING: Where do you think you're going, all dirty and scruffy?

HERBERT: Well, we're just going to the NAAFI . . .

COPPING: Stand up straight! (THEY STRAIGHTEN UP) Brown, eh . . . might have guessed . . . you don't walk around the camp like dustmen . . . what's your name?

BAILEY: Bailey.

COPPING: 'Bailey, Corporal'! Stand up straight! Where are you going?

BAILEY: (AS THOUGH TRYING TO EXPLAIN TO A HALFWIT) He told you . . . we're going along the path over there to the building called the . . .

COPPING: Stand up straight! Where you going?

BAILEY: I was just telling you.

COPPING: Running on the spot commence!! Left right left right left right left . . .

The RECRUITS start doubling on the spot

COPPING: (TO BAILEY) Now, where is it you're going?

BAILEY: We're going . . .

COPPING: Keep 'em up . . . left right left right left right left . . . where you going?

BAILEY: We're going to the . . .

COPPING: Don't flag, Brown . . . left right left right left right left . . . (TO BROWN) Now where was you both going then . . .

HERBERT: (GETTING BREATHLESS) We're . . . we're . . . going to the . . . NAAFI.

COPPING: Eh? . . . Where you going?

HERBERT: (SO WINDED HE CAN HARDLY GET THE WORDS OUT) We're . . . we're . . . going . . .

COPPING: Speak up lad . . . and keep 'em up . . . left right left right left right left . . .

HERBERT: We're . . . we're going . . . going to . . .

COPPING: Speak up!

HERBERT: We're going . . . to . . . to . . .

COPPING: Louder!

HERBERT: We're going to . . . to . . . to . . . to the N . . . AA . . . FI . . .

COPPING: Where . . . speak up! Ain't yer got a tongue in yer head!

HERBERT makes a final effort and manages half a shout.

HERBERT: We're . . . going to the NAAFI.

COPPING: Don't shout at me, you'll be right back inside! And keep 'em up . . . left right left right left right left . . .

HERBERT: (PANTING AND GASPING) What . . . what's the use of this . . . running . . . on the spot, Corp . . . it don't get you nowhere.

COPPING: It's very useful when you ain't got nowhere to go though, isn't it . . . it's very good practise for that . . . keep those knees up! Besides which, it gives me a little pleasure to watch yer . . . and you wouldn't deny me my little pleasures, would you . . . keep up! Keep up!! Left right left right left!! I ain't got much in this world to live for . . . you wouldn't deny me the little joy I can get, would yer . . . faster, don't lag! Left right left right left right left . . . Now where was it you were going?

HERBERT: (CAN HARDLY GET THE WORDS OUT) To . . . to . . . to the . . . the . . .

COPPING: (TO BAILEY) Where is it he's trying to tell me you're going . . .

BAILEY stops running and puts his hand on HERBERT'S arm.

BAILEY: (PANTING) Alright Herbert . . . stop . . . stop Herbert.

They both stop running.

COPPING: Keep going . . . left right left right

left right left . . . double I said . . . left right left right left right left . . .

COPPING stops when he sees that his commands are having no effect. He stares at them hatefully. BAILEY looks at him with contempt, then deliberately punches his face and knocks him out.

FADE.

INT. CELL. DAY.

BAILEY is sitting on his bunk without any expression on his face.

CUT TO:

INT. GUARDROOM. DAY.

The SERGEANT is sitting with his feet up on the table, reading a comic again. COPPING comes in. He has a big black eye. The SERGEANT looks up at him benignly and COPPING smirks. The SERGEANT hands him a bit of the comic and COPPING sits down, puts his feet up and starts to read as well.

FADE.

EXT. SLIT TRENCH. DAY.

THORPINGTON and HERBERT are standing together in a slit trench in battle kit. HERBERT is talking earnestly to THORPINGTON.

HERBERT: It's not right . . . it's not justice properly . . . I was there . . .

THORPINGTON: Look, Herbert . . . he assaulted an NCO . . . I'm as sorry as you are . . . especially after he decided to really make the best of things . . . but he's done what he's done . . . and he must pay for it . . .

HERBERT: He lost his temper . . . Copping made him do it.

THORPINGTON: It doesn't alter what happened . . . he'll have to face the court martial and take what comes

While the two are talking, FLANGE walks up to the trench behind them without them noticing.

FLANGE: Halt! Who goes there?

THORPINGTON: Friends.

They turn startled.

THORPINGTON: (CONFUSED) Wait a minute Sergeant . . . we should have said that to you, surely?

FLANGE: Course you ruddy well should! You're guarding the whole line of defence . . . and all you can do is chatter while anyone strolls right up to you . . .

HERBERT: We wanted to see the whites of your eyes first, Sergeant . . . 'fore we said anything.

FLANGE: You don't have to count the hairs on me chest as well. Now I'm warning you. Keep awake and don't talk!!

FLANGE walks away.

HERBERT: Right ho sarge . . .

THORPINGTON: Alright sergeant . . .

They watch him till he's gone. Then HERBERT goes on.

HERBERT: It's not right, that's all . . . he's been a good soldier . . .

THORPINGTON: He assaulted an NCO.

HERBERT: I know that Corporal Copping . . . He got me the day before I passed out once . . .

They don't notice FLANGE reappear again. He walks up to the trench. He has a thunder flash in his hand.

THORPINGTON: The regimental police serve a function . . . the don't get on to someone for the sake of it . . . you don't think it gives them any pleasure to lock a man up, do you ?

HERBERT: It's the only pleasure in life old Copping has got . . .

THORPINGTON: Well, I hope Harry gets off the same as you . . . you know that . . . (DESPAIRINGLY) I'd rather be in his shoes though I think.

FLANGE casually strikes the thunder flash behind them. They don't hear it or notice it fizzing. FLANGE drops it in the trench and retires a little way and watches with a pleasant smile of anticipation. The two RECRUITS go on gossiping.

HERBERT: What do you mean?

THORPINGTON: You know what . . . I can't do a thing . . . the date's even been fixed . . . I've got to go with her on Sunday while they read out the bans . . .

HERBERT: Can you hear fizzing?

THORPINGTON eases the helmet strap from under his chin.

THORPINGTON: It's the pressure I think . . . this strap . . .

HERBERT: Oh . . . oh yer . . .

HERBERT eases his helmet strap. Then pokes a finger in his ear.

HERBERT: Hasn't gone off yet . . . anyway . . . he might have assaulted an NCO. . .but I still think.

The thunder flash explodes. They leap out of the trench, yelling.

FADE.

INT. BELFREY. DAY.

Church bells ringing.

CUT TO:

INT. CHURCH. DAY.

The SEXTON, a doddery old boy, is solemnly pulling the bell rope. Each time the rope goes up it carries the SEXTON about six inches off the ground. But the SEXTON carries on

pulling the rope without a change of expression as if years of bell pulling have made him oblivious of what's happening.

CUT TO:

EXT. OUTSIDE NAAFI. DAY.

THORPINGTON is waiting for EMILY.

CUT TO:

INT. EMILY'S ROOM. DAY.

EMILY, almost ready for church, is powdering her face.

CUT TO:

EXT. OUTSIDE NAAFI. DAY.

Along the path towards the NAAFI come HERBERT and MCANDREW. HERBERT has the book he got from THORPINGTON with him.

HERBERT: Now you promise not to tell no-one.

McANDREW: Not a word from my lips, Herbert.

HERBERT: An' what you learnt me is all on this page.

Shows MCANDREW the page.

McANDREW: That's the page lad, that's it . . . it's got the number on the top you see . . .

HERBERT feels in his pocket and takes out half a crown.

HERBERT: Oh yer . . . well here's that half dollar I promised you.

McANDREW: Oh no, no . . . a McAndrew won't accept payment for helping one of his friends.

HERBERT: Oh.

HERBERT goes to put the coin back in his pocket, but McAndrew quickly takes it from him.

McANDREW: But if it's in the nature of a gift, it would be churlish to refuse . . .

They come up to THORPINGTON.

McANDREW: Good morning to you, Thorpington . . . a bonny morning for the banns, is it not . . . (LAUGHS) Excuse my humour . . . rather sharp . . .

MCANDREW goes on into the NAAFI. HERBERT fidgets as he stands with THORPINGTON. He is trying to think of a natural way to start talking about the book.

HERBERT: Quite cold in't it?

THORPINGTON: (PREOCCUPIED WITH HIS OWN WORRIES) Yes.

HERBERT: It's summertime in this book though.

THORPINGTON: Eh?

HERBERT: This book . . . you gave me to read . . . remember?

THORPINGTON: Look Herbert . . . we all know very well that you . . .

HERBERT: Very good it is, very good to read . . . very good bloke what writ it as well . . . one of his best I think, don't you?

THORPINGTON: He only wrote the one book.

HERBERT: It's his best though, in't it?

THORPINGTON: Look Herbert . . . why pretend . . .

HERBERT: By chance I happen to have been reading page seventy-three here . . . one of his best pages, don't you think . . .

THORPINGTON looks away trying to ignore HERBERT.

HERBERT: This bit here . . . all these words . . . (PEERS CLOSELY AT THE PAGE) No not that lot . . . (PUZZLES AGAIN) Yes that lot . . . beautiful lot of words, that lot is . . . and arranged in very good order . . . wouldn't you say so?

THORPINGTON pointedly doesn't answer him.

HERBERT: It's where Ivan Vano . . . Vanino . . . Valinino . . . it's where Ivan confronts his friend with the accusation that he is deceiving his lover . . . Here . . . I'll read it to you . . . (PRETENDING HE IS READING FROM THE BOOK) Aaah . . . So I've found you at last . . . in the orchard . . . as well it is as well . . . No wait a minute . . . (STOPS AND PUZZLES NOT LOOKING AT BOOK HE TRIES TO REMEMBER) Oh yer . . . by the well . . . it is well we are alone . . . for I am confronting you with your own evil desires . . .

CUT TO:

EXT. PATH BESIDE NAAFI. DAY.

EMILY is walking along the path to the NAAFI. The RECRUITS are round the corner. As she comes up to the corner she hears HERBERT and pauses.

HERBERT: I speak of your fiancee and the treacherous nature of your over . . . er . . . hang on . . . tures. Yer overtures . . .

THORPINGTON: Look, I'm not interested, Herbert.

HERBERT: You will hear me, I insist . . . for I know that you are already married and have five children who you have cruelly deserted . . .

Keep cutting from the RECRUITS to EMILY to get her reactions.

THORPINGTON: Please Herbert . . . Emily will be here soon . . . just go away will you?

HERBERT: Yes. . . a family . . . and now you have proposed again. How can you bring such shame to one so fair and innocent? You will not . . . not while I have breath in my body. For I will tell her of your wickedness and offer instead my love and devotion, which she will

surely take . . . and we will be married happily
. . . and forget you ever lived.

We see EMILY'S expression of hurt fury turn
to one of calculation.

FADE.

INT. CAFE. DAY.

Exactly the same scene as before. MR and
MRS SPILLER are sitting with GLADYS and
her FIANCEE at the same table as before.
There is the same silence as before, till it is
broken by MRS SPILLER.

MRS SPILLER: Blow your nose.

GLADYS and MR SPILLER take their hankies
out quickly

MRS SPILLER: You I meant, Arthur.

Shamefaced, the SAILOR takes out a hanky and
gives his nose a massive blow. The door opens
and HERBERT comes in with EMILY. She drags
HERBERT by the hand over to her family.

EMILY: Here we are, Mum.

MRS SPILLER looks HERBERT up and down
without saying anything. MR SPILLER
forgets himself for a moment.

MR SPILLER: Well he's bigger than the last one
. . . if you're going in for size.

MRS SPILLER turns and stares at him
threateningly. The smile dies on MR
SPILLER'S lips.

FADE.

INT. BAILEY'S CELL. TWILIGHT.

BAILEY is lying on his bunk fast asleep.

CUT TO:

EXT. BACK OF GUARDROOM. TWILIGHT.

HERBERT comes creeping along. He stands
under the barred window of BAILEY'S cell.
The window is too high up for him to see in,
but by reaching up he would be able to pass
things through the bars. HERBERT looks
round to make sure no one is watching, then
starts to try and attract BAILEY'S attention.

HERBERT: Pssst . . . Pssst . . .

CUT TO:

INT. BAILEYS CELL. TWILIGHT.

BAILEY doesn't stir. COPPING comes
walking along outside BAILEY'S cell. As he
goes to walk past it, he hears HERBERT'S
'Pssst'. COPPING stops and looks at BAILEY,
as if thinking the noise came from him.

CUT TO:

EXT. BACK OF GUARDROOM. TWILIGHT.

HERBERT: Hoi . . . Pssst . . .

CUT TO:

INT. BAILEYS CELL. TWILIGHT.

COPPING, outside the cell, realises the noise
is coming from someone outside.

COPPING: Hello.

*CUT FROM COPPING TO HERBERT AS
NECESSARY*

HERBERT: (WARNINGLY) Sssshh . . .

COPPING: Who is it?

HERBERT: Not so loud or the guard will hear
you.

COPPING: The guards have gone to get the
suppers . . . Who is it?

HERBERT: Your voice is strained . . . you get
a cold?

COPPING: Who is it then?

HERBERT: Not so loud . . . you'll have old
chicken head along . . .

COPPING: Chicken head?

HERBERT: Copping . . . you know . . .

COPPING: (SWALLOWS) Who is it then?

HERBERT: It's me . . . Herbert . . . Browny . . .

A look of malicious pleasure comes over
COPPING'S face.

HERBERT: Can you come to the bars . . . I got
some things for you.

COPPING: Yer . . . hang on . . .

COPPING unlocks the cell door and crosses
over to the window. BAILEY sleeps on.

HERBERT: Here y'are . . . some fags . . .

HERBERT reaches up and pushes a hand
with a packet of cigarettes through the bars.
COPPING takes out a pair of handcuffs.

COPPING: Got any matches?

HERBERT feels in his pocket with his free
hand and takes out a box of matches. He
thrusts his other hand through the bars.
COPPING snap the handcuffs on his wrists.
The noise wakes BAILEY up.

HERBERT: Here . . . what you doing?

BAILEY: What's that?

COPPING hurries out of the cell and slams it
shut locking it.

COPPING: A bit of company for yer.

FADE.

SAME SCENE. BUT IT IS DAY.

HERBERT and BAILEY are sitting side by
side on one of the bunks

HERBERT: Well, I didn't know did I?

BAILEY: Alright . . . we know you never know
nothing . . . I wish I'd known he was in me cell
. . . I'd have blacked his other eye and been out
like a shot . . .

HERBERT: The other boys pass out in a few
days . . . and I'll be left behind again.

BAILEY: No you won't . . . we're going to pass
out before any of 'em.

HERBERT: Eh?

BAILEY: We're breaking out . . . scarpering . . .

HERBERT: That's not allowed . . .

BAILEY: Look . . . the trouble you're in, you
can't stay here . . . soon as they let you out
you're right in the church with Emily.

HERBERT: Yer . . . I didn't really want to start
a family this soon . . .

BAILEY: You're coming with me,

HERBERT: No . . . we can't desert . . . it
wouldn't be right.

BAILEY: (WILDLY) We'll join the navy . . .
anything . . . but we're going to scarper.

HERBERT: Join the navy?

BAILEY: Eh? Yer . . . that's it, we'll join the
navy. That's not deserting, that's transferring
. . . transferring to another branch of the
services . . . that often happens . . . transfers.

HERBERT: Well I don't know . . . I'd like to get
away . . . join the navy, eh? But breaking out
isn't the right way to transfer, is it?

BAILEY: It's the thought that counts. Listen . . .
we'll do it tonight . . . all we got to do is get
the guard . . . the one that stands outside our
cell during the night. Now look this is what
we'll do . . .

FADE . . .

EXT. SQUARE. DUSK.

The SQUAD of six men is drawn up. They are
wearing overcoats. COPPING stands in front
of them.

COPPING: Guard party, shun!

The SQUAD comes to attention. The camera
pans down the SQUAD. Last in the line are
ROGERS, then THORPINGTON.

FADE.

EXT. GUARDROOM. NIGHT.

General shot of guardroom at night. All the
rest of the camp is asleep.

CUT TO:

INT. GUARDROOM. NIGHT.

Four of the GUARD PARTY are lying on
beds. They are fully clothed but asleep. At the
table COPPING sits smoking, trying to keep
awake. The clock on the wall is at half past
twelve.

CUT TO:

EXT. GUARDROOM ENTRANCE. NIGHT.

ROGERS, holding a truncheon, is standing
outside the entrance on guard. He looks
wretchedly miserable and is shivering with
the cold.

CUT TO:

INT. GUARDROOM. NIGHT.

COPPING slumps off to sleep. His lighted
cigarette falls in the wastepaper basket.

CUT TO:

INT. CELLS. NIGHT.

THORPINGTON, looking bewildered, is standing in the cell gripping the bars. HERBERT stands outside the cell wearing Thorpington's overcoat and beret and holding his truncheon.

CUT TO:

INT. GUARDROOM NIGHT.

The paper in the wastepaper basket is burning merrily and beginning to set light to the things around it. COPPING snores gently.

CUT TO:

INT. CELLS. NIGHT.

ROGERS (minus his overcoat and beret) stands beside THORPINGTON in the cell. BAILEY and HERBERT have disappeared.

CUT TO:

INT. GUARDROOM NIGHT.

The wall and table have caught fire, but everyone sleeps on.

CUT TO:

EXT. PATCH OF SHRUBBERY ABOUT THIRTY YARDS FROM GUARDROOM. NIGHT.

HERBERT and BAILEY are slipping through the shrubbery. BAILEY shows HERBERT some keys.

BAILEY: They won't get out of that cell in a hurry.

He throws key away.

HERBERT: Off to Chatham, eh?

BAILEY: Eh . . . well I just want to pop home first.

CUT TO:

EXT. GENERAL SHOT OF THE GUARDROOM. NIGHT.

Smoke is coming from one part of it.

CUT TO:

INT. GUARDROOM. NIGHT.

The fire is blazing away, but everyone sleeps on. There is the sound of THORPINGTON and ROGERS shouting from their cell.

CUT TO:

INT. THE CELL. NIGHT.

THORPINGTON and ROGERS are shouting out for help.

CUT TO:

INT. GUARDROOM. NIGHT.

The noise of the shouting half wakes COPPING.

COPPING: (DROWSILY) Mmmm . . . eh . . . (SEES FIRE) Fire! Quick! Come on! Fire! Hey wake up! Wake up! Come on! All out!

He wakes the rest of the GUARD up and they tumble out of the guardroom in panic.

CUT TO:

INT. THE CELL. NIGHT.

THORPINGTON and ROGERS, forgotten in the panic, are still shouting for help. Thorpington gives up shouting.

THORPINGTON: I don't know what's wrong with them . . . sound asleep . . . we're wasting our breath . . .

They stop shouting to regain their breath. Clouds of smoke start filling the passage. They stare at it in horror and start shouting again.

CUT TO:

EXT. OUTSIDE THE GUARDROOM. NIGHT.

One of the GUARDS is ringing a fire bell. A couple of the GUARD are hurrying to the fire with buckets of water. The lights in the huts come on as the CAMP is woken by the din. COPPING shouts orders.

COPPING: Come on, hurry up with them buckets! Hurry up!

One of the guards comes running up to COPPING breathlessly.

COPPING: Did you wake the orderly office?

GUARD: Yes . . . and phoned the fire brigade.

COPPING: I'd like to know who's responsible for this . . . there'll be hell to pay . . . get some more water hurry up.

SMILEY comes hurrying up in a complete panic. He is still dressing. He is wearing trousers, but has still got on his pyjama jacket. He is buckling his Sam Brown belt over it. SOLDIERS are hurrying to the fire. SMILEY gives orders to the half-dressed SOLDIERS as he pushes his way through them.

SMILEY: Don't panic . . . no panic . . . perfect calm . . . hoses out, sand extinguishers . . . call the roll . . . effort terms one man equals two . . . don't stand around what's your name . . . too late . . .

The SOLDIERS are bemused by SMILEY'S orders and not sure what to do.

SMILEY: Put the fire out . . .

The SOLDIERS rush off to join the fire fighting. SMILEY comes to COPPING.

COPPING: Everything under control, Sir.

SMILEY: Splendid no panic . . . perfect control fire out . . .

SMILEY: Enquiry – no loss of life – recommendation promotion . . . all safe . . .

COPPING: All safe yes Sir . . . (SUDDENLY REMEMBERS THE PRISONERS) . . . the prisoners!

SMILEY: What?

COPPING points at the blazing building in horror.

COPPING: The prisoners . . . (LOOKS ROUND WILDLY) the keys . . . who's got the keys?

CUT TO:

C.U. of keys thrown away in shrubbery.

CUT TO:

EXT. QUIET SPOT A FEW HUNDRED YEARS FROM THE GUARDROOM. NIGHT.

BAILEY and HERBERT are hurrying away.

HERBERT: The noise . . . what's all that noise

BAILEY: Come on . . .

HERBERT looks back and sees the fire.

HERBERT: Blimey, the guardroom's on fire.

BAILEY: Eh . . . (LOOKS ROUND) You're right . . . well that's a piece of luck . . .

HERBERT: Eh . . .

BAILEY: Keep everyone busy, they won't notice we've gone . . . come on . . .

HERBERT: Shouldn't we go back and give a hand to put it out . . .

BAILEY: Oh come on . . . they'll be alright . . . hurry up.

BAILEY stops in his tracks horrified.

BAILEY: Rogers and Thorpington.

CUT TO:

INT. THE CELL. NIGHT.

ROGERS and THORPINGTON, as the fire spreads around them, are crying out for help.

CUT TO:

EXT. OUTSIDE TOWN FIRE STATION. NIGHT.

FIREMEN tumble out and into fire engines, dressing as they leap in. With the bell clanging the fire engine speeds off. A FIREMAN hurries out late just in time to see it go. He tries to signal to it . . . but uselessly. He flags a taxi that comes along, points at the engine disappearing in the distance and gets in.

CUT TO:

EXT. SCENE OF FIRE. NIGHT.

SMILEY is standing by a group of SOLDIERS who are holding a big hose.

SMILEY: Right . . . turn on . . . (TURNS TO COPPING) Haven't you found those keys yet . . .

COPPING: In a minute sir . . . just a minute . . .

He rushes off. SMILEY'S order 'Turn on' is repeated down the line of men who are connected to the hose. FLANGE crouches by the hydrant. The MAN who finally shouts the order to him is rather a long way off and it is hard to hear.

MAN: (SHOUTING TO FLANGE) Turn on.

FLANGE: (FROWNING) What's that?

Without thinking, the other MAN passes the question 'What's that' back up the line. They shout the question back up the line till the MAN next to SMILEY shouts.

MAN NEXT TO SMILEY: What's that?

SMILEY: I said turn on . . .

MAN NEXT TO SMILEY: (PASSING ORDER DOWN LINE) . . . Turn on!

The order 'turn on' is passed down the line again till it reaches FLANGE.

FLANGE: Oh . . . turn on . . . right . . .

FLANGE tugs one way then another, trying to shift the water cock but he can't budge it.

FLANGE: Which way does it turn?

The message is passed back along the line.

FADE.

EXT. STREET. NIGHT.

The fire engine, pursued by the taxi, is rushing through the street. There is a bang and the engine skids to a halt, punctured. Everyone jumps out, dismayed, and look at the punctured tyre. The taxi draws up and the FIREMAN gets out and goes up to the other firemen. They all turn and look at the taxi. The FIREMAN who came in it points at it. They all start unloading their buckets and hoses and piling them in the taxi, to the distress of the TAXI DRIVER.

CUT TO:

EXT. PATCH OF BUSHES WHERE THE KEYS WERE THROWN AWAY. NIGHT.

BAILEY and HERBERT are down on their knees searching for the keys.

HERBERT: We'll never find those keys . . .

BAILEY: Hold on . . . I've got an idea . . . come on. . . down to the REME workshop.

CUT TO:

INT. CELLS. NIGHT.

THORPINGTON and ROGERS are still shouting, but coughing with the smoke.

CUT TO:

EXT. SCENE OF FIRE. NIGHT.

A trickle of water is coming out of the hose and splashing on the feet of the man holding it.

SMILEY: The bucket chain . . . what's happened to the bucket chain . . .

CUT TO:

EXT. THE BACK OF A BUILDING. NIGHT.

A line of MEN stretch along the back of the building and around the corner. We follow the course of a bucket along the line. The line

goes right round the building forming a circle. A few buckets are passed continually round it. FLANGE hurries them up.

FLANGE: Come on, come on . . . hurry up . . . hurry up.

CUT TO:

EXT. STREET SCENE. NIGHT.

The taxi crammed with FIREMEN and equipment is speeding along. Passing in through one of the back windows and out of the other is a ladder.

CUT TO:

EXT. PATCH OF SCRUB. NIGHT.

Up the hill to it comes one of those big vehicles with an electromagnet driven by BAILEY and HERBERT. BAILEY is driving. He pulls up. HERBERT is in charge of the magnet control.

BAILEY: OK . . . let it down . . .

HERBERT pulls a lever. The magnet starts to rise.

BAILEY: Down . . . down . . .

HERBERT fumbles at the levers and the magnet begins to descend over the bushes. BAILEY jumps out and watches closely. There is a clang as the keys spring out of the bushes on to the magnet. BAILEY pulls them off and gives the thumbs up sign to HERBERT.

CUT TO:

EXT. SCENE OF FIRE. NIGHT.

COPPING is rushing around like a thing possessed.

COPPING: Those keys . . . the keys . . . who's got the keys . . .

BAILEY pushes through the mob and knocks into COPPING.

COPPING: (AMAZED) Bailey!

BAILEY hesitates a second, then plunges into the burning building. HERBERT comes through the mob. Once more COPPING is the only one to notice the prisoner.

COPPING: Brown!

HERBERT just sees BAILEY disappear into the building and hurries after him. The word is passed round the mob. 'Someone's gone in . . . someone's gone in to get the prisoners out.' There is a pause, then out through the smoke comes BAILEY carrying HERBERT. He puts him down and goes back in. The crowd gather round HERBERT.

CUT TO:

INT. CELLS. NIGHT.

BAILEY comes through the smoke to the cell where the other two cling to the bars coughing, nearly suffocated. BAILEY, with the keys, unlocks the cell door.

CUT TO:

EXT. SCENE OF FIRE. NIGHT.

BAILEY staggers out of the blazing building supporting ROGERS and THORPINGTON. There is a ragged cheer from the crowd.

FADE.

EXT. SAME SCENE. DAWN.

The guardroom is burnt to the ground. A few wisps of smoke at 11 come from it. One or two weary SOLDIERS stand around.

CUT TO:

EXT. MAIN GATE OF A RAF CAMP. DAWN.

The taxi is drawn up by the gate. One of the FIREMEN has got out and is talking to the RAF guard on the gate.

RAF: No mate . . . not here . . . we ain't had no fire . . .

The FIREMAN turns despondently back to the taxi. The TAXI DRIVER sticks his head angrily out of the window.

TAXI DRIVER: There's five pound six on the meter already . . . you'd better make up your mind where you're going . . .

FADE.

INT. ADJUTANTS OFFICE. DAY.

SMILEY is talking to the adjutant.

SMILEY: Yes George . . . I know . . . lot to be explained, no doubt . . . but my boys . . . excellent behaviour . . . guards and prisoners alike . . .

ADJUTANT: The electromagnet vehicle . . . why on earth . . . Copping's report . . . claims to have seen the prisoners before they . . . But I think we can dismiss that . . . the enquiry definitely establishes his responsibility for causing the fire . . . and endangering lives . . .

SMILEY: Bailey and Brown, Sir . . . ?

ADJUTANT: CO's recommendation . . . under the circumstances . . . heroic behaviour. Anyway, we haven't got a guardroom to keep them in, have we . . .

FADE.

INT. RECRUITS HUT. DAY.

The RECRUITS are sitting around. BAILEY comes in and hands HERBERT a letter.

BAILEY: Letter for you.

HERBERT makes a big thing of opening it and pretending to read it.

HERBERT: Oh . . . taa . . . mmmm . . . yes . . . huh . . . oh that's interesting . . .

BAILEY: What is?

HERBERT: (DISCONCERTED) Er . . . well . . .

BAILEY snatches it from him.

BAILEY: Come one . . . I'll read it . . . (READS OUT) Dear Herbert, I don't want to break your heart but I no longer wish to marry you. For one reason, my sister isn't getting married now, her fianceship having been broke, and for another reason, I like someone else more than you . . . Try not to take it too hard Herbert . . . Love Emily . . .

HERBERT: (FED UP) Cor . . . well that's a bit of hard luck, ain't it . . .

BAILEY: But you didn't want to marry her, Herbert.

HERBERT: Oh no . . . I didn't, did I? (CHEERS UP) Well that's a stroke of luck, isn't it?

FADE.

EXT. PARADE GROUND. DAY/

A passing-out parade with band (same as at opening of the film) is in progress. FLANGE is leading his RECRUITS on a march past.

CUT TO:

INT. CAFE. DAY.

MR and MRS SPILLER with YOUNG DAUGHTER sit as before in silence. The noise of the band can be heard. MR SPILLER ventures a remark.

MR SPILLER: The soldiers passing out.

MRS SPILLER: Don't soil your lips with that word. *This* young man had better not be toying with my daughter's affections . . . I've had just about enough . . .

The YOUNG DAUGHTER sniffs and goes to cry.

MRS SPILLER: That's enough from you . . . you should choose more carefully.

CUT TO:

EXT. OUTSIDE CAFE. DAY.

EMILY comes along. She is holding ARTHUR (the sailor) by the hand. He looks a bit apprehensive.

EMILY: Come on . . .

CUT TO:

EXT. PARADE GROUND. DAY.

The RECRUITS march off the square, towards the main gate. SMILEY is standing beside the CO.

SMILEY: Splendid . . . good sorts all . . . sorry to see them go . . . excellent material . . . each worth two . . . effort terms one man equals

two men . . . Use of senses, sir, impresses them from the start – observation – one instance – trees – how many round square?

CO: I beg your pardon? . . . I'm going to give you a spot of leave, Mr Smiley . . .

CUT TO:

EXT. NEAR MAIN GATE. DAY.

The RECRUITS disappear out of the main gate. Just by it are HERBERT and COPPING. COPPING is sweeping up leaves, and HERBERT, now a Lance Corporal, is standing guard.

HERBERT: I had a lot of mates in that lot . . .

COPPING: So did I . . .

HERBERT: Get on with your work.

He gives the tree a shake. Leaves shower down. So does a nest that tips out of the tree. There were several eggs in it. One lands on COPPING'S head and one on HERBERT'S. They stare at each other as the sound of the band fades up for the caption 'THE END'.

CARRY ON ESCAPING

by Talbot Rothwell

To the accompaniment of the dramatic beating of a single drum, SLOW PAN over the entire area. It is a square compound with a high double barbed-ire fence all around it, with the usual guard towers at each corner. There are half a dozen long huts for the 'Kriegies', grouped well away from the wire, and a separate Latrine and Ablutions hut between them and the main gates. There is a group of trees close to these gates, inside the compound. The guard towers are manned by Grman soldiers with mounted machine guns, and there's a couple of 'Goons' on guard at the main gates. The block of administrative offices known as the Kommandantura is immediately outside the main gates, by the side of the rough track which serves as a road. It is, all in all, a pretty bleak and dreary sight.

After a moment or two to take it all in, an ANNOUNCER's voice is heard over . . .

ANNR: Germany, September 1944! And of all the prison camps built to house Allied prisoners-of-war, none was more notorious – or more hard to bear – than Koldtitz!

Over the Tannoy system, a klaxon horn starts to blare out, interrupted by a guttural voice.

VOICE: Appel! Appel! Raus! Raus!

Dramatic sombre music as the KRIEGIES start to emerge slowly from the huts and amble towards the parade ground area in front of the main gates. They are a scruffy and dejected-looking bunch.

CU OF COLONEL TISSPOT, as he comes out of one of the huts. TISSPOT is the Senior British Officer, a bumbling, vague and uninspiring character, who makes a brave attempt to dress correctly always. He is followed by his Adjutant, MAJOR RHODES, a stuffy, bumptious, over-jocular nit. As they make their way to the parade ground . . .

EXT. THE KOMMANDANTURA. DAY.

The two GOONS on guard at the main gates snap to attention as the KOMMANDANT and his party come out of the block.

KOMMANDANT FOKKER is a stiff-necked, extravagantly uniformed martinet of the old school, grim-faced and steely-eyed. He is accompanied by KAPITAN BINDER, his second-in-command, a younger 'career' officer; and FELDWEBEL NUTZ, in charge of camp security – an amiable-looking, craggy-faced moron. Behind them, half a dozen SOLDIERS, armed with rifles, run out of the hut. FOKKER nods to BINDER, BINDER nods to NUTZ, and NUTZ shouts a command in German.

As the party moves off towards the compound . . .

EXT. THE COMPOUND. DAY.

The KRIEGIES are formed up in hut squads, with the S.B.O. and his ADJUTANT in front of them.

CU OF LIEUTENANT FRED PARKIN, in the front rank of one of the squads. He is a tough-looking Cockney, who probably organised his commission just as easily as he now runs most of the camp rackets. He looks towards the approaching KOMMANDANT's party, coming through the now-open main gates, and mutters to 'DUMDUM' DODDS, a rather gormless-looking individual alongside him.

PARKIN: Aye aye! Look who's coming. The Kommandant himself. (AS DUMDUM LOOKS IN THAT DIRECTION, PARKIN LOOKS DOWN AT DUMDUM'S FRONT AND ADDS WARNINGLY) Better put it away quick!

DUMDUM: Eh? (HE LOOKS DOWN AT HIS FRONT) It's not out!

PARKIN: That!

Points to an obvious map sticking out of the front of DUMDUM's battledress tunic. As DUMDUM hastily stuffs it back inside . . .

The KOMMANDANT's party arrives at a position in front of the KRIEGIES, and, as he comes to a halt, NUTZ yells a command and the GERMAN SOLDIERS come to a ragged halt.

FOKKER stands stiffly to attention in front of the KRIEGIES, waiting for something to happen.

CU OF TISSPOT seems to have fallen into a bit of a daze. RHODES moves forward and hisses to him.

RHODES: Sir?

TISSPOT: Oh . . . yes, what is it, Major?

RHODES nods meaningly at the KOMMENDANT's party before them.

TISSPOT: Oh. Beg your pardon. Yes.

He draws himself up to attention and starts the word of command.

TISSPOT: British officers . . . British officers!

And then appears to go completely blank. RHODES hisses the operative word to him.

RHODES: Attention!

TISSPOT: Oh yes. Atten – shun!

The squads of KRIEGIES come to attention and TISSPOT throws up a salute.

CU OF FOKKER, as he coldly returns the salute, then turns and nods at NUTZ. NUTZ salutes him, then turns to yell at the SOLDIERS a word of command in German, which sends them running to conduct the count of the prisoners.

FOKKER addresses the KRIEGIES in English, with a strong German accent.

FOKKER: Gentlemen! As you, in your latest unsuccessful escape attempt, have used the cover of the trees in the compound here to reach the wire, I have decided in the interests of security, to remove the wire! (EVERYONE LOOKS FAINTLY SURPRISED, THEN A RAGGED CHEER GOES UP FROM THE KRIEGIES. AS FOKKER LOOKS PUZZLED, BINDER LEANS FORWARD TO WHISPER SOMETHING TO HIM) Correction! To remove the trees! (THERE IS A GROAN OF DISAPPOINTMENT FROM THE KRIEGIES) That is all. Heil Hitler!

As he throws up the arm salute . . .

CU of PARKIN, as he covers his nose with a handkerchief, and blows a very definite raspberry.

CU of FOKKER, as he reacts with hysterical fury.

FOKKER: Who was that? Who did it? Who is blowing the gooseberry?

Suddenly there is a hoarse scream from the KRIEGIE SQUADS, and everyone reacts, startled.

CU of an unshaven, wild-eyed KRIEGIE, as he stumbles out from his squad.

KRIEGIE: I can't stand it any more! I can't stand it, I tell you! I've got to get out of here! I've got to get out!

And, to everyone's horror, yelling crazily, he runs across to the first wire fence, and starts trying to climb it. FOKKER finds his voice.

FOKKER: Vos is das? Stop that man! Stop him!

BINDER: Jawohl, herr Kommandant! (HE YELLS AT THE KRIEGIE) Halt! Halt or you will be shot!

The KRIEGIE goes on trying to climb over, and BINDER turns to yell up at the nearest guard tower.

BINDER: Shutzen! Shutzen!

CU of the GUARD in the Tower, as he suddenly springs into action, grabs the machine-gun handles and swivels it around to point at the KRIEGIE. He is just about to depress the trigger, when the complete barrel falls off the machine gun with a thump. As he looks stupidly at it . . .

Medium CU of FOKKER and BINDER, as the latter raises his eyes to heaven, and the former screams . . .

FOKKER: Dumkopf!

NUTZ yells at another GOON to follow him and they run over to the KRIEGIE and drag him off the wire.

BINDER: Bring him here!

NUTZ and the GOON lead the whimpering KRIEGIE over to them and BINDER looks at him coldly.

BINDER: So! You are wishing to get out. We can arrange it. Ten days in the cooler!

FOKKER: Nein nein, Kapitan!

BINDER: As you wish, herr Kommandant. Nine days in the cooler!

FOKKER: Nein, nein, nein! Can you not see this man is at the end of his tethers?

He gives the KRIEGIE what he fondly imagines to be a compassionate look.

FOKKER: We are not inhuman monsters. We understand what it is like to be shut up like an animal, my poor fellow.

KRIEGIE: Do you, Kommandant? Do you really?

FOKKER: Of course. Tell me, how long have you been a prisoner?

KRIEGIE: Since last Friday.

FOKKER: Ja ja . . . since last . . . Since last Friday?!

KRIEGIE: That's right. Three days now.

FOKKER: (SCREAMING IT) Scheissen! Twenty days in the cooler! (AND THEY DRAG THE HELPLESS KRIEGIE OFF) Carry on with the count!

As the GOONS jump to it . . .

Medium CU of one GOON, as he goes along behind the rear rank of a squad, counting them very carefully. He suddenly does a 'take' and looks back at a section he has just counted.

As from his P.O.V., we see what looks like the backs of three KRIEGIES. CAMERA PANS DOWN a bit to show that the centre one of the three finishes at the end of its tunic, and its boots and trousers lie in a crumpled heap on the ground.

CU of the GOON, as he scratches his head, decides that something's not quite right, and turns and calls for help.

GOON: Feldwebel!

NUTZ hurries towards him.

NUTZ: Vas ist? (THE GOON POINTS TO THE IRREGULARITY AND NUTZ REACTS, THEN DECIDES IT'S BEYOND HIM AND CALLS FOR A BIT OF HELP HIMSELF) Herr Kommandant!

CU OF FOKKER, as he starts towards NUTZ, followed by BINDER.

FOKKER: Now what is it? What is wrong? We should be able to have a simple count without trouble!

NUTZ: Yes, herr Kommandant. But . . .

FOKKER: But? But what? We don't wanting any buts, just say how many mens!

NUTZ: Yes, herr Kommandant.

FOKKER: Well? How manys?!

NUTZ: (SWALLOWS) Thirty two and a half, herr Kommandant.

FOKKER: So! Was this so difficult? Thirty two and a . . . and a half?! How can we be having halfs?!

NUTZ indicates the problem and FOKKER looks at it and reacts appropriately.

FOKKER: Vas ist dass?

He goes to the group of three in the rear rank and peers over at the half KRIEGIE.

Shooting from the front, we can now clearly see that the middle one is a dummy,

supported on either side by two rather embarrassed KRIEGIES. Shaking with fury, FOKKER turns to shout at TISSPOT.

FOKKER: Colonel Tisspot!

CU of TISSPOT, as he jerks into life.

TISSPOT: Herr Kommandant?

FOKKER: Here please!

TISSPOT goes round the back of the squad to him.

TISSPOT: Sir?

FOKKER: What is the meaning of this?

TISSPOT: What's that, Kommandant?

FOKKER: This! This!

He gets hold of the dummy's shoulder to turn it round and the head falls off into his hands.

TISSPOT: I say, steady on, sir. I mean, that sort of thing's hardly in the spirit of the Geneva Convention . . .

FOKKER: Colonel, this is a dummy! A dummy!

TISSPOT: Oh. So it is. Extraordinary thing.

FOKKER: Where is the man who should be here, Colonel?

TISSPOT: Oh . . . er . . . I . . . er . . . I refuse to answer that on the grounds that it might . . . er, yes.

FOKKER: On the grounds that it might what, Colonel?

TISSPOT: Exactly. Just what I was about to say.

FOKKER gives a frustrated exclamation.

FOKKER: It's no use, Colonel. If he has escaped, he won't get far. (HE STRIDES OFF, YELLING AS HE GOES) Get the dogs!

NUTZ yells in German towards the gates.

RESUME FOKKER, as he rejoins BINDER.

FOKKER: This camp is escape-proof. He cannot be far away!

BINDER looks highly sceptical of this and looks towards the main gates. Suddenly his eyes narrow.

As from his P.O.V., we see that one of the trees in the compound is moving. It isn't a very good model of a tree and any fool could spot it.

CU of BINDER, as he smiles knowingly.

CU of the 'tree'. Part of the bark has been cut out to provide vision, and inside we can clearly see the rather idiotic face of 'FRIGGER' PHIPPS, the enthusiastic but not very practical Escape Officer. He looks towards the main gates and beams with delight.

As from his P.O.V., we can see why. The gates are being opened by the GUARDS. Chuckling, he starts to move towards them, but comes to an abrupt stop as a couple of GOONS with guard dogs come running out of the Kommandantura.

PHIPPS freezes, looking dead worried, as one of the dogs makes directly for him. The dog goes straight up to the tree and sniffs at it suspiciously. PHIPPS closes his eyes and prays. Then the dog lifts its leg to the tree, much to PHIPPS relief and disgust, and, having done it, he moves off.

PHIPPS starts to back off towards the still-open gates, keeping a cautious eye on the dogs in the compound.

CU of BINDER as he smiles and shakes his head, then speaks quietly to FOKKER.

BINDER: Excuse me, Kommandant . . .

FOKKER: Well, what is it, Kapitan?

BINDER: The tree, sir.

FOKKER: What? What tree?

He points in that direction and FOKKER looks across and reacts.

We see the TREE moving slowly towards the main gates.

FOKKER: (OVER) Mein gott, is he mad?

By now everyone is watching the cautious approach of the tree towards the main gates.

Resume FOKKER and BINDER.

FOKKER: (SIGHS) All right, go and get him, Kapitan.

BINDER: If I may suggest an alternative, sir . . .

He leans forward to whisper something to FOKKER. FOKKER chuckles happily.

FOKKER: Oh yes. Yes, an excellent idea, Binder.

BINDER: Thank you, sir.

He turns and gives an order to NUTZ, who also laughs.

NUTZ: Yes, herr Kapitan.

And he runs off.

CU OF PHIPPS in the tree. He looks worried and 'freezes' as NUTZ runs towards him. But NUTZ runs right past the tree and out of PHIPPS' sight.

PHIPPS breathes a sigh of relief and starts moving backwards again.

We see NUTZ behind him by the Latrines shed. He bends down and opens back a large trapdoor in the ground.

CU OF PARKIN and DUMDUM.

PARKIN: Oh blimey, he's opening up the cesspit!

And we see NUTZ open the other half of the cover and then stand quickly back.

Then the whole parade watches fascinated as PHIPPS, in the tree, moves cautiously back towards the cesspit.

CU of PARKIN and DUMDUM.

DUMDUM: Six to four he misses it.

PARKIN: Done!

And PHIPPS doesn't of course. He reaches the edge and disappears from sight with a yell and a nasty-sounding plop.

CU of PARKIN as he guffaws and holds out his hand, and DUMDUM miserably hands over some fags.

CUT TO:

INT. PARKIN'S ROOM. DAY.

The usual prison-camp-type room with five or six double bunks in it, and a cupboard for each kriegie. Each bunk area is plastered with personal photos of girlfriends and wives and pin-ups culled from German newspapers and magazines. There's a bare wooden mess table centre. It is noticeable that PARKIN's area has more girlie photos and home-made 'home comforts' that anyone else's. It is a lower one (of course) and DUMDUM's is immediately above his.

As PARKIN and DUMDUM come in from Appel . . .

DUMDUM: Poor old Frigger.

PARKIN: What do you mean – poor old Frigger?

DUMDUM: Well . . . getting caught like that.

PARKIN: What do you expect? Trying to get out disguised as a flippin' tree. That's just about the daftest idea yet!

DUMDUM: I thought it was a pretty good one.

PARKIN throws himself onto his bunk.

PARKIN: Oh yes, brilliant! Brilliant! He only overlooked one small point. Trees don't move!

DUMDUM: I dunno. What about that one called Virginia Creeper?

PARKIN: Oh blimey. But it doesn't walk about, does it? And it certainly don't dive into cesspits!

DUMDUM: Well anyway, I wish I'd thought of it.

PARKIN: What for? I keep telling you – escaping's a mug's game. What the hell do you want to get home for anyway?

DUMDUM: Well . . . for a start, a bit of crumpet.

PARKIN: Oh no! Don't you ever think about anything else?

DUMDUM: No. Do you?

PARKIN: Course I do!

DUMDUM: What?

PARKIN: Higher things!

DUMDUM: Oh, you mean . . . ?

And he cups his hands to his chest to indicate boobs.

PARKIN: No, I don't mean them!

DUMDUM: What do you mean then?

PARKIN: Higher things! Things like . . . (ECSTATICALLY) Steak and kidney pud. With lashings of lovely steamy suet.

And he closes his eyes, savouring it in his imagination.

DUMDUM: What – before a bit of crumpet?

PARKIN: Listen, Dumdum. When you've had as much of both as I have, you'll realise that a steak and kidney pudding will *always* satisfy you.

DUMDUM: Maybe, but after being stuck in here for three years . . .

PARKIN: Oh blimey, we're all in the same boat, aren't we?

DUMDUM: No. Some of us are more highly sexed than others.

PARKIN: What? You mean *you*?

DUMDUM: Yes!

PARKIN: Highly sexed?

DUMDUM: Yes!

PARKIN: You're not even Highly Selassie!

DUMDUM: I can't help being the way I am, you know.

PARKIN: All right, tell me. How often? Before you came here, I mean. How often?

DUMDUM: (UNCOMFORTABLE) Well . . . as often as I could.

PARKIN: How often? On an average? Come on!

DUMDUM: Well . . . once a month maybe. Depended . . .

PARKIN: Once a month?! Blimey!

DUMDUM: But I was *thinking* about it all the time!

PARKIN: Oh shut up and give us a cigarette.

DUMDUM fumbles a pack out of his pocket and extends it to PARKIN, who grabs one. The last one. DUMDUM looks at the empty pack in dismay.

DUMDUM: Here, that was my last one until next parcels issue.

PARKIN: Well, why didn't you tell me? (HE GETS UP AND OPENS HIS CUPBOARD AND ON THE TOP SHELF WE SEE A GREAT STACK OF PACKETS OF FAGS. HE TAKES ONE PACK AND HANDS IT TO DUMDUM) Here.

DUMDUM goes to take it gratefully.

DUMDUM: Oh thanks, Fred.

PARKIN holds it back.

PARKIN: Ah ah! It'll cost you two chocolate bars.

DUMDUM: Two? It was only one last time!

PARKIN: I wasn't so hungry then.

And he chuckles as DUMDUM miserably turns to his locker to get them.

CUT TO:

EXT. KOMMANDATURA. DAY.

As FOKKER approaches it and gets a ringing salute from the GUARD on the door.

GUARD: Heil Hitler!

FOKKER winces slightly, but returns the salute.

FOKKER: Heil Hitler.

And goes in.

INT. THE KOMMANDATURA. DAY.

FOKKER crosses to his office door, labelled 'KOMMANDANT', opens it and comes to an abrupt stop.

INT. KOMMANDANT'S OFFICE. DAY.

It is comfortably furnished with desk and chair, large leather sofa and drinks cabinet. There is another door in the side wall leading to an outer office. As from FOKKER's P.O.V., shooting into the room, we see BINDER bent back over the sofa, shoulders pinned to the seat, legs waving in the air, under the onslaught of an Amazonian-built woman of about 30 – Fraulein GRETA GOBBLER, his secretary. Her magnificent muscular body is encased in a tight-fitting sort of tracksuit.

From this P.O.V., we can't at first see that the man is BINDER.

FOKKER: Fraulein Gobbler!

GRETA immediately releases BINDER and snaps to attention, saluting.

GRETA: Heil Hitler, Kommandant!

Meanwhile, BINDER, released unexpectedly, falls off the front of the sofa and flounders to his feet, straightening his uniform, embarrassed.

FOKKER: Kapitan Binder!

BINDER: Heil Hitler, herr Kommandant!

FOKKER: (IMPATIENTLY) Heil Hitler. May I request an explanation of this extraordinary conduct in my office during working hours?

BINDER: Naturally, herr Kommandant . . . naturally.

He looks towards GRETA hopefully and she obliges.

GRETA: I was just showing herr Kapitan a wrestling hold, Kommandant.

FOKKER: Oh?

GRETA: It is the defence recommended in the event of an attempted rape, herr Kommandant.

BINDER: Ja ja, herr Kommandant.

FOKKER: Good of you, I am sure, fraulein, but I hardly think herr Kapitan will be threatened with anything like that.

GRETA: No no, Kommandant. The defence is for me – the woman.

FOKKER: Even less likely. However, I am delighted to learn that you would defend your honour if such a situation arose, fraulein.

GRETA: (ARCHLY) Well of course, it depends who is trying the rape, Kommandant.

She obviously fancies him.

FOKKER: Naturally, fraulein.

GRETA: I would not dare practise such an immodest counter-move on a superior officer.

FOKKER: Immodest, fraulein? How so?

GRETA: Well, it's a little difficult to explain, Kommandant . . .

FOKKER: But you would use it on privates?

GRETA: That is it exactly!

FOKKER: What? Oh yes, I see. I think. (CLEARS HIS THROAT IN EMBARRASSMENT AND GOES TO HIS DESK) Well, I will not detain you, fraulein. You have your physical training class, I think.

GRETA: Yes, herr Kommandant. (SHE GOES TO DOOR AND TURNS FOR A VERY HEARTY) Heil Hitler!

FOKKER, almost seated, jumps and is forced to his feet again.

FOKKER: Heil Hitler. (SHE GOES OUT AND HE SITS TESTILY) I'm sure it isn't necessary to do that every time.

BINDER: Do what, herr Kommandant?

FOKKER: Heil Hitler!

And BINDER snaps to attention.

BINDER: Heil Hitler!

FOKKER controls himself with an enormous effort.

FOKKER: Kapitan Binder, I . . .

BINDER: Herr Kommandant?

FOKKER: Never mind. Is the escaper here?

BINDER: Jawohl, herr Kommandant!

FOKKER: Bring him in.

With much heel-clicking, BINDER goes to door of the communicating office and opens it.

BINDER: Feldwebel, Nutz!

NUTZ: Jawolh, Kapitan!

BINDER: Bring in the escaper!

NUTZ: Jawohl, herr Kapitan!

Everything is done at a shout.

FOKKER winces and covers his ears.

NUTZ: Escort, forward march! Left right left right left right . . .

In come two Germans with FRIGER PHIPPS between them, right up to FOKKER's desk. PHIPPS has obviously had no attention since falling into the cesspit.

NUTZ: Halt! The escaper, herr Kommandant!

FOKKER: I know that! (CONTROLLING HIMSELF AGAIN, HE TURNS HIS ATTENTION TO PHIPPS) Now then, Lieutenant Phipps, I . . .

He stops, brings out a handkerchief and jams it to his nose. Then turns to BINDER.

FOKKER: Moin gott, hasn't he had a shower or something?

BINDER: No, herr Kommandant. He refused to.

FOKKER looks at PHIPPS in amazement.

FOKKER: So! And why did you refuse to take a shower, Lieutenant Phipps?

PHIPPS: Sir, under the terms of the Geneva Convention, I am obliged under interrogation only to give name, rank and number.

FOKKER: Oh, don't waste time, Phipps. We know that you are the Escape Officer of the camp, that you have tried thirty-three escapes, all spectacularly unsuccessful, THAT YOU HAVE A WIFE LIVING IN EALING, A MOTHER LIVING IN WORTHING, A BASTARD IN BARKING, AND A MOLE ON YOUR LEFT CHEEK! (AS PHIPPS' HAND GOES TO HIS LEFT CHEEK . . .) *Not* your face! (PHIPPS LOOKS SULKY) Now then, I will ask you again. Why did you refuse to take a shower?

PHIPPS: I refuse to answer on the grounds that it might incriminate me!

FOKKER gives an exclamation of rage and bangs his desk.

BINDER leans forward towards PHIPPS and speaks deliberately and menacingly.

BINDER: We have ways of making you talk, you know!

FOKKER: Yes! (THEN, TO BINDER) Have we?

BINDER: Of course, herr Kommandant.

FOKKER: What ways?

For answer, BINDER goes up to FOKKER, and, bending to whisper, describes the ways, using a wealth of hand illustrations of a most alarming nature. It is too much for FOKKER, who turns white, nearly gags on his handkerchief, then, moaning, totters to his feet, and rushes out of the room.

EXT. PRISON COMPOUND. DAY.

There is a crowd of KRIEGIES lined up at the wire, apparently waiting for something, tensely expectant. After a moment, a cheer goes up and they all smile in relief. Now we see why: FRAULEIN GOBLER leads her P.T. class, consisting of half a dozen shapely German girls, out into the space in front of the Kommandantura, and starts exercising them. As they bend over, touching their toes, they present an enticing view of taut bottoms to the KRIEGIES.

CU of PARKIN and DUMDUM in the crowd.

DUMDUM: Cor, I couldn't half do with a bit of that.

PARKIN: Rubbish. You couldn't even touch your toes.

DUMDUM: I don't mean that. You know what I mean. That one on the end there, for instance . . . cor!

PARKIN: You wouldn't know what to do with it!

DUMDUM: Wouldn't I just!

PARKIN: All right, suppose she was to come to your room, stripped off and ready for action, what would you do?

DUMDUM: Don't be silly, Fred . . .

PARKIN: What would you do? Come on!

DUMDUM: Well . . . same as you would, I suppose.

PARKIN: Oh no, I *know* what I'd do.

DUMDUM: I bet!

PARKIN: Make a pot of tea and get out the draughtboard.

DUMDUM: What? Go on, you wouldn't.

PARKIN: Oh yes, I would, mate. Because I *know* what happens to Kriegies who are found consorting with German women! (HE MAKES AN EXPRESSIVE GESTURE OF SOMEONE SHOOTING) Bang, bang!

DUMDUM, looking the other way, smiles broadly.

DUMDUM: Yes, that's what I'd do!

PARKIN: I mean, you'd be stuck up against a wall!

DUMDUM: Why? What's wrong with using one of the bunks?

PARKIN: You'd be shot, dummy!

DUMDUM: What – just for that?

PARKIN: Just for that. Now you know what they mean by dying for a bit.

He chuckles dryly. There is a ragged cheer from the KRIEGIES and he looks towards the Kommandantura.

PARKIN: Hello, here comes the ruddy hero back.

We see a couple of GOONS with PHIPPS between them, marching from the Kommandantura. PHIPPS acknowledges the homage of the KRIEGIES with a broad smile and a wave. There are shouts of 'BAD LUCK, FRIGGER' – 'BETTER LUCK NEXT TIME' etc.

Medium CU of PHIPPS and the GOONS as they approach the main gate and come to a

stop. The GUARD on the gate inspects the paper one of the GOONS holds out, nods, then brings out a large key and tries to unlock the large padlock. After he has fumbled for a while, PHIPPS steps forward.

PHIPPS: Here, let me have a shot.

Without thinking, the GUARD lets him take the key.

PHIPPS puts it in the padlock and opens it quite easily.

PHIPPS: There. Nothing to it, old boy.

The GUARD, delighted, swings the gate open, and PHIPPS walks through into the compound, still carrying the key. After several paces, he appears to notice it, turns back to the GUARD, who now has the gate closed again, and is looking worriedly through his pockets.

PHIPPS: I say, is this what you're looking for?

The GUARD takes the key.

GUARD: Ja ja, danker, danker!

PHIPPS: Not at all, old man.

He watches as the GUARD relocks the gate, and the smile fades from his face.

PHIPPS: Oh. Perhaps I shouldn't have done that.

And, shaking his head worriedly goes back into the compound.

CU of PARKIN and DUMDUM, who have watched this little episode.

PARKIN: (DISGUSTEDLY) Escape Officer! Blimey!

INT. TISSPOT'S ROOM. DAY.

It is a smaller room than the usual, with just one double bunk. There is a small desk and chair and the walls are covered with graphs. TISSPOT is standing at one of them labelled 'ESCAPE RECORD'. It has two sub-headings:

NO. OF ESCAPES ATTEMPTED: 146.

As we watch, he crosses out the 146 and makes it 147. Then looks rather sadly at the other sub-heading:

NO. OF SUCCESSFUL ESCAPES:

TISSPOT: Not a bad record. Could be better, I suppose.

We now see that RHODES, who shares the room with him, is standing by the desk.

RHODES: I fancy luck has been a bit against us, sir.

TISSPOT: Yes, must have been.

He looks at another graph headed 'TUNNELS' and its two sub-headings:

No. OF TUNNELS CONSTRUCTED: 60.

NO. OF TUNNELS FOUND: 61.

TISSPOT: Never could understand how they found one more tunnel than we actually built.

RHODES: Ah, one of 'em turned out to be a fox's, sir.

TISSPOT: Really! A German fox?

RHODES: I presume so, sir.

TISSPOT: Bad show. Can't have that sort of thing going on, Rhodes. Bad for morale.

RHODES: Yes, sir.

There is a smart rap at the door.

TISSPOT: Yes, come in!

The door opens and PHIPPS comes in and snaps smartly to attention.

PHIPPS: Lieutenant Phipps reporting back, sir!

TISSPOT: Ah yes. Good show, Freddy. Better luck next time.

PHIPPS: Thank you, sir.

TISSPOT shakes him warmly by the hand, then catches the pong.

TISSPOT: Yes, well, I won't detain you. You'll be wanting to wash off or something.

PHIPPS: Oh, no hurry for that, sir.

TISSPOT: No. Quite. (BUT HE TAKES A FEW STEPS BACK TOWARDS THE WINDOW AND OPENS IT WIDE) Bit stuffy in here.

PHIPPS: I wanted to talk to you about Dick, sir.

TISSPOT: Oh, I hardly think that's a suitable subject for officers under these circumstances, Freddy.

PHIPPS: I mean 'Big Dick', sir.

TISSPOT: Big Dick?

PHIPPS: You know, sir. Big Dick! The . . . Stops cautiously, then goes to window and closes it. The T – U – N – N – E – L!

TISSPOT: Oh yes of course, the Tunnel. Yes of course. (AND OVERCOME BY THE STENCH, OPENS THE WINDOW AGAIN.) Yes . . . why? They haven't found it, have they?

PHIPPS: Oh no, sir. Rather not.

TISSPOT: Thank heaven!

PHIPPS: But on the other hand, neither have *we*.

TISSPOT: What? I don't follow you, Freddy.

PHIPPS: Well, if you recall, sir, we went to enormous pains this time to hide the entrance to it from the Goons . . .

TISSPOT: Yes, and you succeeded, didn't you?

PHIPPS: Yes sir, too well. That's what we've lost.

TISSPOT: Oh dear, dear. Dear me.

RHODES: That's tough, Freddy! How far did the tunnel go?

PHIPPS: Oh, all the way, sir!

TISSPOT: (MUSING) Really? Used to know a girl like that back home. Connie her name was . . . or was it Bessie? No, Bessie was the one with the big . . .

PHIPPS: Yes, yes, sir. But we were talking about Dick.

TISSPOT: Yes, that's about all she ever did. Talk about it. No patriotism, that was her trouble.

RHODES: Excuse me, sir. But this is serious!

TISSPOT: Oh yes, I agree. If a girl can't do her bit for the fighting men, what're things coming to, eh?

RHODES: I mean, about losing the entrance to the tunnel, sir!

TISSPOT: Ah yes, well, I agree. Well . . . there's only one thing to do about that, eh?

PHIPPS: What's that, sir?

TISSPOT: Find it again!

He is inordinately proud of this idea. He beams at them and PHIPPS beams back enthusiastically.

PHIPPS: By Jove, sir, that's clever. I don't know what we'd do without you for a Senior British Officer!

TISSPOT: (MODESTLY) Oh please, Freddy. Only doing the best I can.

PHIPPS: I'll get cracking on it right away, sir!

TISSPOT: Yes, yes. But first of all – far more important, Freddy . . .

PHIPPS: Yes, sir?

TISSPOT: Get a shower first, will you?

PHIPPS: Yes, sir!

He salutes smartly and goes. TISSPOT has gone back to his memories again.

TISSPOT: Extraordinary thinking of old Connie again after all these years. Cracking little girl, Rhodes. Cracking! Bosom on her like a couple of melons. Firm waist . . . long legs . . . and . . . as for. . . (HE FINISHES WITH A GROAN OF FRUSTRATION, VISIBLY AFFECTED BY THE MEMORY. THEN . . .) Leave me alone now, will you, old man. Something I have to do.

And, as RHODES discreetly goes . . .

EXT. THE COMPOUND. DAY.

FELDWEBEL NUTZ is moving slowly about an open area of the compound, probing for tunnels. This is done with a long, thin, six-foot steel rod, about three feet of which is stuck straight down into the ground at regular intervals.

PARKIN and DUMDUM, crossing the compound towards the hut which is the Camp Theatre, come to a stop and watch him with some amusement.

PARKIN: Mornin', Feldwebel. Doing some gardening?

NUTZ takes it quite seriously.

NUTZ: Nein, nein, captain Parkin. I am probing for tunnels.

PARKIN: Get away! (HE'S HAVING HIM ON) How does it work then?

NUTZ is more than ready to explain the devilish ingenuity of the master race.

NUTZ: Ven zis is pushed into der ground, ven it comes to a tunnel, you vill feel it suddenly go free, no?

PARKIN: As easy as that? Go on, I don't believe it.

NUTZ: Ya ya! I show you! (HE PICKS ANOTHER SPOT AND SLOWLY PUSHES THE PROBE DOWN INTO THE GROUND ABOUT THREE FEET) So! (HE SMILES TRIUMPHANTLY AT THEM, AND SUDDENLY THE PROBE IS WHISKED OUT OF HIS HAND, DISAPPEARING INTO THE GROUND. NUTZ IS HORRIFIED) Vos is das? (HE GETS DOWN ON HIS HANDS AND KNEES AND SCREAMS INTO THE LITTLE HOLE LEFT BY THE PROBE) Give me back mein probe! (HE BEATS ON THE GROUND) You hear me? I know you are down there! (PARKIN CACKLES GLEEFULLY. NUTZ LOOKS UP AT THEM) You saw that! They have taken my probe!

PARKIN: Maybe it was worms.

NUTZ: Verms? Nein, nein! Das is Kriegies tunnelling! (HE BANGS ON THE GROUND AGAIN) I come back, you hear? With digging party! I vill get you out! (HE GETS TO HIS FEET AND IS ABOUT TO GO, BUT PARKIN STOPS HIM)

PARKIN: Hang on a minute! Don't you think you'd better mark the spot? You might not find it again.

NUTZ: Ya, ya! Is gut. Danker, Captain Parkin. Danker.

PARKIN: You're welcome.

NUTZ brings out a little flag on a stick from his pocket and sticks it into the ground, then runs off towards the main gates.

DUMDUM looks at PARKIN in dismay.

DUMDUM: What did you want to do that for?

PARKIN: No point in fetching a digging party if you don't know where to dig, is there?

He gives DUMDUM a big wink, then goes to NUTZ' marker, pulls it out of the ground, walks off about twenty paces and carefully sticks it in the ground again.

PARKIN: That should keep 'em busy for a while.

And they resume their walk towards the Camp Theatre.

EXT. THE CAMP THEATRE. DAY.

This is a hut just like the others, but with a hand-painted notice across the front: 'CAMP THEATRE'.

PARKIN and DUMDUM approach it and go inside.

INT. CAMP THEATRE. DAY.

It is the empty shell of one of the living huts, with a stage and curtains at one end, and rows of seats made out of old Red Cross crates. A rehearsal is in progress, and the stage is set for a drawing room scene, rather crudely and sparsely furnished. The play is being directed by Lt. CYRIL GAYE, who obviously had something to do with the theatre in peace time. A rather querulous temperamental type with an affected manner, and, considering he's in a prison camp, a rather flamboyant style of dress. Capt. BAGSHOT, wearing a makeshift camp-constructed dinner suit, is on the stage, giving a rather heavy-stilted amateur performance, shouting dramatically off into the wings.

BAGSHOT: Cynthia! If you leave me now, I shall kill myself! I swear it! I have a gun! (AND HE GOES TO A DESK AND OPENS ONE OF THE DRAWERS, PRETENDS TO TAKE SOMETHING OUT, THEN DRAMATICALLY POINTS HIS EMPTY HAND TO HIS TEMPLE) There!

GAYE: Well, where is it? Where is it?

BAGSHOT: They haven't been able to get a proper gun yet.

GAYE: But this is the dress rehearsal! We're on tonight! Harry!!

HARRY, the hard-pressed, scruffy-looking STAGE MANAGER, comes on from the wings, carrying a wooden mock-up of an automatic and a knife.

HARRY: I'm making one, Cyril. How's that?

He shows the model rather proudly.

GAYE: How can he shoot himself with that? Will it go off?

HARRY: Well, I thought he could just go . . . (HE PUTS IT TO HIS TEMPLE) Bang!

GAYE: Just go bang!? This is a *drama*, Harry! We're not playing for laughs, you know!

HARRY: (TRUCULENT) Well, I'm doing the best I can.

GAYE: Well, there's no need to get all uppity about it!

PARKIN comes forward, followed by DUMDUM.

PARKIN: Why not change it to a knife?

GAYE: What?

PARKIN: He says, 'I've got a knife, you know'. Then when the time comes, he stabs himself and goes 'Bang!' (GUFFAWS)

GAYE: Very amusing, I'm sure! All right, Harry, put the knife in the drawer, and let's try it again. (AS HARRY DOES SO, HE TURNS TO PARKIN AND DUMDUM) And for heaven's sake, go and get changed, you two. You're on in a few minutes.

PARKIN: Okay, okay. Keep your pants dry.

He and DUMDUM go through a door beside the stage, leading (presumably) to the dressing room.

GAYE: All right then, are you ready, Clive?

BAGSHOT takes up his starting position again.

BAGSHOT: Yes, just about. (LAUNCHES INTO HIS LINES AGAIN) Cynthia, if you leave me now, I shall kill myself! I swear it! (TO DESK) I have a gun! (TAKES OUT KNIFE) There!

GAYE: No, no, no, no, no! It's a knife, for heaven's sake!

BAGSHOT: I know it is!

GAYE: Then you must change your line to, 'I have a knife, you know!'

BAGSHOT: Well damn it all, I've been saying gun all through rehearsals! It's asking a bit much to expect me to change at the drop of a hat!

GAYE: (APPEALS TO THE HEAVENS) Oh dear God, is it worth it? All right, go on, go on!

BAGSHOT: Forgotten where I was now.

GAYE: 'Cynthia, I'm giving you one last chance'!

BAGSHOT: Oh yes. (BACK TO THE ACTING) Cynthia, I'm giving you one last chance! Tell me now that it's not all over! (PAUSE) Cynthia?

They look expectantly towards the wings. Nothing happens.

GAYE: Cynthia! That's your cue! You're on!

DUMDUM appears from the wings, wearing a woman's wig, a singlet, a woman's skirt, and army socks.

DUMDUM: Someone's swiped me boobs!

And, as GAYE gives a despairing cry . . .

EXT. THE COMPOUND. DAY.

As NUTZ marches a half a dozen GOONS into shot, all armed with shovels, looks around for the marker, spots it, and put the GOONS to work digging.

INT. THE CAMP THEATRE. DAY.

DUMDUM is appealing helplessly to GAYE.

DUMDUM: Well, it's not my fault. I left 'em with me other clothes.

PARKIN comes on, wearing black trousers and a parson's dog collar, and carrying a pair of home-made stuffed falsies.

PARKIN: Is this 'em?

DUMDUM: Yeh! Where were they?

PARKIN: Stuffed into your knickers!

He helps DUMDUM put the falsies on.

PARKIN: You should be wearing your knickers, you know. You're a big girl now!

DUMDUM: Not the ones they gave me. They tickle.

PARKIN: So what? It should improve your performance.

GAYE: Doddsy, I don't care if they *strangle* you! You'll have to wear some tonight!

DUMDUM: I am wearing some now!

And he lifts his skirt to expose rough woollen army issue pants. GAYE gives a wail of anguish.

PARKIN: Phew! You sexy beast, you!

EXT. THE COMPOUND. DAY.

The digging party is down to about head height now, with a great mound of earth and sand beside the hole. NUTZ, standing on the edge of the hole, is beginning to look a bit worried.

INT. THE CAMP THEATRE. DAY.

The stage is clear again, except for BAGSHOT, who is striding up and down, trying to memorise his new line.

BAGSHOT: I have a *knife*, you know. I have a knife, you know . . . I have a knife, you know. (HE TURNS TO THE LONG-SUFFERING GAYE) Yes, I think I've got it now.

GAYE: I'm so absolutely *thrilled*!

BAGSHOT: Right. (BACK TO THE ACTING) Cynthia! If you leave me, I shall kill myself! I swear it! I have a knife, you know! (HE GOES TO THE DESK, OPENS THE DRAWER, AND LOOKS LOST) Where is it? (SEARCHES FEVERISHLY, THEN LOOKS SHAME-FACED) Oh. Must've put it in my pocket after the last go. Sorry about that.

He produces it from his pocket, goes to put it in the desk drawer.

GAYE: No! Just carry on, *please*!

BAGSHOT: Oh, all right. Cynthia, I'm giving you one last chance! Tell me now that it's not all over! Cynthia?

As before, they look expectantly towards the wings and, after a slight pause, PHIPPS comes on.

PHIPPS: I say, anyone seen the entrance to big X?

GAYE: What?!!

PHIPPS: The tunnel. You know. Should be somewhere around here.

GAYE: Are you mad? Don't you know there's a dress rehearsal going on here?

PHIPPS: Sorry, old lad, but this is rather important. See, I rather think there's a couple of chaps down there digging.

GAYE: *I'm* mad! We're all mad!

And starts laughing hysterically.

PHIPPS: I say, steady on, old chap. That's not very helpful.

PARKIN, DUMDUM, and HARRY come on from the wings. DUMDUM has now added a large pair of army boots to his female get-up.

PARKIN: But look, if there's a couple of blokes down there, surely you'll find the entrance when they come *up*?

PHIPPS: Ah, *if* they come up. Actually, we were supposed to have relieved them a couple of days ago.

PARKIN: Then why the hell didn't you?

PHIPPS: Don't be silly, old man. I told you, we can't find the entrance.

GAYE: I give up! I wash my hands of this entire production! I'm leaving, do you hear? I'm leaving!

And, laughing hysterically, he dashes towards the front of the theatre, and, with a horrible shriek, disappears through a trap which gives way in the floor. They all rush to the opening and peer down.

PHIPPS: Oh I say, jolly good show. He's found it!

CUT TO:

EXT. THE COMPOUND. DAY.

A few days have passed. A SLOW PAN around the compound shows us that the KRIEGIES are engaged in their normal time-passing activities – walking around the circuit, kicking a football about, messing about with their rather pitiful little gardens, and so on.

We PICK UP FELDWEBEL NUTZ walking around with his probe. He stops to watch the MAD KRIEGIE (who tried to climb over the wire in the earlier scene), who is busy constructing a giant catapult near to the perimeter wire. It consists of a long plank which pivots centrally on an upright post, with a seat on one end (facing towards the wire) and a platform on the other. As NUTZ watches, puzzled, the MAD KRIEGIE (whom we shall call MUGGINS) tests pushing down the platform end and tracing visually the possible flight of somebody from the seat end over the wire. He is apparently not quite satisfied. NUTZ'S curiosity can stand it no longer.

NUTZ: Vot are you making there, please?

MUGGINS: What . . . this?

NUTZ: Ya ya.

MUGGINS: Well, it's what we call a see-saw.

NUTZ: Zee-zaw? Vos ist das – zee zaw?

MUGGINS: Well, two people get on it and go up and down.

NUTZ: Up and down? Ah, like zig-zig!

MUGGINS: Oh no, nothing like that. Just for amusement, you know.

NUTZ: Ach so! For amusements. Little zings please little minds, no?

MUGGINS: That's right. And little trousers fit little behinds.

Both laugh heartily and NUTZ wanders off, apparently satisfied.

We PICK UP PARKIN leaning against one of the legs of one of the guard towers, reading a letter from home. DUMDUM squats in the grass near him.

PARKIN: Blimey! Listen to this! 'I have met a smashing American pilot and he is having parcels of cigarettes and food sent to you.'

DUMDUM: That's nice. Who's it from?

PARKIN: My girlfriend! The two-timing little bitch! You can't trust any of 'em these days.

DUMDUM: Which girlfriend's that?

PARKIN: What does it matter which one it is?!

DUMDUM: It'd matter to me.

PARKIN: All right. It's . . . (AND HAS TO LOOK AT THE END OF THE LETTER TO FIND OUT) Kathy. Oh well, that's all right. He's welcome to her.

BINDER, passing on the other side of the wire, comes to a stop, regarding PARKIN sardonically.

BINDER: Good morning, Capitan Parkin.

PARKIN looks round over his shoulder.

PARKIN: Oh, morning, Kapitan Binder.

BINDER: You are holding the guard tower up, no doubt?

PARKIN: That's right.

BINDER: Very amusing. You will move away please.

PARKIN: Blimey, I'm not doing any harm.

BINDER: Zat is an order!

PARKIN: Okay!

He moves away from the guard tower. There is an ominous creaking of wood, then the whole tower collapses to the ground, GUARD and all.

As BINDER starts shouting hysterically . . .

EXT. THE KOMMANDANTURA. DAY.

A covered pick-up truck draws up in front of it and a couple of GOONS leap out of the back.

GOON: Raus! Raus!!

Three new PRISONERS-OF-WAR climb out. Two of them are army officers, looking as if they'd been in a fight someplace, but the third, wearing a Lieutenant's uniform, is rather small and effeminate-looking. In fact, it is a woman,

as we can probably see from the rather unnatural fullness of her battle-dress tunic.

As they are chivvied inside, with much shouting . . .

INT. KOMMANDANT'S OFFICE. DAY.

GRETA, now wearing a semi-uniform two-piece, which does nothing to hide her full figure, is approaching FOKKER's desk with a couple of files.

GRETA: Here are the files you wanted, herr Kommandant.

FOKKER, sitting at the desk, as dapper as ever, gives her a formal smile.

FOKKER: Thank you, fraulein Gobbler. And the Senior British Officer's complaining letter?

GRETA: On the top there.

She leans over him and opens the top file to show it. FOKKER becomes conscious that her costume top is stretched to its limits and she's showing a hell of a lot of cleavage. He moves uncomfortably.

FOKKER: Yes. Good. Well, we will check the regulations on this.

He brings out from the file a book of regulations and starts to shuffle through it, still very conscious of the nearness of GRETA.

GRETA: You will find what you want on page sixty-nine, herr Kommandant.

FOKKER: Sixty-nine?

GRETA: Sixty-nine. If you like I will show you.

She goes to take the book.

FOKKER: No no, I can manage, I think, thank you. Let me see . . . ah, here we are. (HE DOES A QUICK READ AND MAKES AN EXCLAMATION OF SATISFACTION) Ah! It is as I thought. The regulations are quite explicit. I quote: 'The issue of toilet paper to prisoners-of-war shall be limited to two sheets per man per day'. (HE GIVES HER A TRIUMPHANT LOOK) And how much does the Senior British Officer request?

GRETA: Six sheets, herr Kommandant.

FOKKER: Six!

GRETA: It is what they are used to at home.

FOKKER: Gottmin Himmel! How can they expect to win the war with such wastefulness!

He comes to a decision.

FOKKER: You will take my answer please, fraulein Gobbler.

GRETA: Of course, herr Kommandant.

She moves to a chair opposite the desk, hitching her tight skirt to expose a generous amount of leg. FOKKER goggles at the display.

GRETA: (NOTEBOOK AND PENCIL POISED) Now, herr Kommandant?

FOKKER: What? Oh yes. Yes, now. (HE TEARS HIS EYES AWAY FROM THE SPECTACLE AND DICTATES FAST) From the Kommandant to the Senior British Officer. Dear Colonel Tisspot. Your request for the ration of toilet paper to be tripled is denied. I can suggest only two courses for you. Either – (a) go only every three days . . . or (b) every one and a half days and use both sides.

GRETA gives him an admiring look.

GRETA: Oh. That is brilliant, herr Kommandant. Brilliant!

FOKKER: Yes, I thought so. (THERE IS A KNOCK AT THE DOOR) Komm!

The door is opened and NUTZ marches in and throws up the usual salute.

NUTZ: Pardon, herr Kommandant, but three new kriegsgefangener have arrived!

FOKKER: Ah. Very well, I will come. (HE STANDS UP, STRAIGHTENS HIS TUNIC AND PUTS ON HIS CAP) Get that off, will you, fraulein.

GRETA: Get what off, herr Kommandant?

FOKKER: The reply!

GRETA: Oh yes, of course, herr Kommandant.

As FOKKER marches out, past NUTZ, who follows him . . .

INT. THE OUTER OFFICE. KOMMANDANTUR. DAY.

The three new PRISONERS are standing in a line between the two GOON GUARDS. FOKKER comes out of his office, followed by NUTZ.

NUTZ: Attention!!

The three KRIEGIES slouch to attention. FOKKER gives them what he fondly imagines to be a warm welcoming smile.

FOKKER: Good morning, gentlemen. I am the Kommandant of this camp – Colonel Fokker. Believe me, it is no pleasure for me to have to welcome you here. But – c'est la guerre. To coin a phrase – for you the war is over, no? And he gives a thin titter. (THIS IS OBVIOUSLY HIS STANDARD LITTLE JOKE. THE KRIEGIES ARE NOT AMUSED) Yes. Their papers please, Feldwebel. (NUTZ HANDS OVER SOME PAPERS) You will please answer to your names. (REFERRING TO THE PAPERS) Snide, Alec, Lieutenant, 13682.

SNIDE: That's me.

FOKKER: No no, that's me, *sir.*

SNIDE: No, it's me.

FOKKER: You are a soldier, Lieutenant, and I am your senior officer. You will at all times address me as 'sir'!

SNIDE: Oh, I see what you mean. Yes, sir.

FOKKER: Thank you. (BACK TO PAPERS) Cooker, James Henry. Captain. 2743.

COCKER: Yes, sir!

FOKKER: Gut. And Coles, Pat, lieutenant. 7923.

This is the small effeminate-looking one and his voice comes out rather high-pitched.

PAT: Yes, sir!

FOKKER looks at him rather sharply.

FOKKER: There is something wrong with your voice, Lieutenant?

PAT: No, sir.

FOKKER exchanges a suspicious look with NUTZ, then turns back to PAT.

FOKKER: Ah . . . perhaps you have been . . . *wounded* . . . somewhere?

PAT: Oh yes, that's right, sir. At the Front.

FOKKER: Ach so. Very painful. I am sorry.

PAT: Yes, sir. We came up against the 5th Puffter Division.

FOKKER: Puffter Division? (TO NUTZ) Vos is das? Puffter?

NUTZ: Perhaps he means *Panzer* Division, sir.

FOKKER: Ach so? Panzer Division!

PAT: Oh yes, that's it, sir.

FOKKER: It is different, no?

PAT: Oh very, sir.

FOKKER: Yes. Well, gentlemen, I vish to tell you now that we are not inhuman monsters here. Behave yourselves and you will be well treated. But try and escape and it may be necessary for us to try and shoot you. And I have no wish for this, gentlemen. I am a kind man – I *love* everyone . . . (HIS VOICE STARTS TO BREAK) and the mere thought of one of you nice young boys . . . lying across the wire . . . riddled with machine-gun bullets . . . I . . . I . . . excuse me!

He turns away, trying to hide his emotions, choking back the crocodile tears. NUTZ, affected himself, spontaneously goes to him and pats his shoulder.

NUTZ: There there, sir. It's all right. Here.

And offers him a handkerchief.

And, as FOKKER takes it and blows his nose . . .

EXT. THE COMPOUND. DAY.

Watched rather curiously by some KRIEGIES, MUGGINS is just completing his giant catapult. He has erected a tall post with a platform atop, and a ladder up to it at the platform of the see-saw. Now he signals to the watching KRIEGIES.

MUGGINS: All right, chaps. Up you go then. (THE KRIEGIES CLIMB THE LADDER UP ONTO THE PLATFORM AND MUGGINS

GOES TO THE OTHER END AND SEATS HIMSELF IN THE CHAIR THERE) Right, now!

In L.S., we see about half a dozen of the KRIEGIES jump down onto the platform at the other end and MUGGINS (DUMMY) is shot up into the air in a big arc over the perimeter wire and . . .

INT. OUTER OFFICE, KOMMANDANTURA. DAY.

FOKKER has recovered his composure now, and, returning the handkerchief to NUTZ, turns back to the new KRIEGIES.

FOKKER: Because, you see, gentlemen, this camp is escape-proof. It is quite impossible to get over the wire.

With which there is a tremendous crash above, pieces of roof shower down, and MUGGINS lands in a heap on the floor.

And, as FOKKER screams hysterically in German and draws his revolver and fires it wildly off in all directions . . .

CUT TO:

INT. THE S.B.O.'S ROOM. DAY.

As PHIPPS bursts in rather excitedly on the S.B.O.

PHIPPS: I say, sir, I thought you'd like to know. We've found the entrance to Big Dick!

TISSPOT: Big Dick?

PHIPPS looks across at the open window, goes quickly to close it, then . . .

PHIPPS: The T – U – N – N – E – L, sir!

TISSPOT: Oh yes, good show, Freddy. Big Dick, yes. Where was it?

PHIPPS: In the Camp Theatre, sir. I should have remembered, actually.

TISSPOT: The Theatre, eh? Funny place.

PHIPPS: No, sir. Actually they're doing a drama this week.

TISSPOT: What? Oh no, I meant funny place for a tunnel actually.

PHIPPS: Oh I see, sir. Sorry. But, in fact, sir, it was *your* idea, if you remember.

TISSPOT: What, doing a drama? Oh, I don't think so, Freddy.

PHIPPS: No, sir. It was *your* idea to start a tunnel from there.

TISSPOT: Oh well, I don't want to take *all* the credit, Freddy. But, even if I so say so myself, it was rather a wizard idea.

PHIPPS: Terrific, sir!

TISSPOT: Jerry would never dream of looking there for one, would he?

PHIPPS: Never in a million years, sir.

TISSPOT: (BIG DECISION) Right, Freddy. I'll give it my blessing. I suggest you start it as soon as possible.

PHIPPS: What? But it's dug, sir. Practically finished.

TISSPOT: Oh. Then what's the problem?

PHIPPS: No problem, sir. Course I was a bit worried about the two chaps who'd been stranded down there for a couple of days . . .

TISSPOT: Oh yes, I remember. How are they?

PHIPPS: Oh fine, sir! Fine! At least they will be. Had to give them the old Kiss of Life of course.

TISSPOT: (FROWNS WORRIEDLY) Oh dear, dear. I don't like that, Freddy. Kissing could raise problems in an all-male camp like this, you know.

PHIPPS: I know exactly what you mean, sir. But it couldn't be helped, I'm afraid.

TISSPOT: Well, let's hope it won't lead to anything. There is a knock at the door. (TISSPOT GIVES PHIPPS A WARNING SIGNAL. THEN, CAUTIOUSLY) Yes? Who is it?

RHODES' voice heard from outside.

RHODES: Major Rhodes, sir!

TISSPOT: Oh yes, come in, Major.

The door opens and RHODES comes in and salutes.

RHODES: Sorry to interrupt anything, sir, but I have three new arrivals.

TISSPOT: Oh well, wheel them in, Major.

RHODES: Thank you, sir. (HE TURNS TO OPEN THE DOOR) Come in please, gentlemen.

The three new KRIEGIES come in and RHODES makes the formal introduction.

RHODES: Gentlemen, this is the Senior British Officer, Colonel Tisspot.

All three snap to attention, with a 'Sir!'

TISSPOT: At ease, gentlemen. Well . . . er . . . have you done the . . . er . . . whatsitsname, Major?

RHODES: Screening? Yes, sir. They're all okay.

TISSPOT: Good show. Well . . . er . . . that's about it then, I think.

RHODES: (PROMPTING) The pep talk, sir?

TISSPOT: What?

RHODES: Your usual pep talk.

TISSPOT: Oh yes. (TRYING TO LOOK STERN) Well, gentlemen. I don't want you to think that this is a . . . er . . . a . . .

RHODES: Holiday camp, sir.

TISSPOT: Holiday camp, yes. Oh dear me, no. Even though you are prisoners-of-war, you still have a major duty to perform. And that duty is to . . . er . . .

RHODES: Escape, sir.

TISSPOT: Exactly. To escape! We can still be of service to our country, gentlemen, by hitting the enemy where it hurts most! In the . . . er . . .

RHODES: Heart of the Fatherland, sir.

TISSPOT: Exactly. Yes . . .

PHIPPS: With your permission, sir?

TISSPOT: Oh yes, carry on, Freddy. Er, this is Captain Phipps. Our Escape Officer.

PHIPPS: Hello, chaps. I just wanted to say, if you have any wizard ideas for getting out of here, just come and tell me, eh? Co-ordination, that's the thing. Can't have a mass of chaps going it alone, can we, what? Besides, we can fix you up with all the necessary papers.

TISSPOT, who seems to have dozed off during this, now starts wake.

TISSPOT: Oh yes, I've just sent a request off to the Kommandant for an increased allowance.

PHIPPS: Beg pardon, sir?

TISSPOT: Of paper.

PHIPPS: Oh no, I was talking about forged papers, sir. Passes and all that.

TISSPOT: Oh yes. But they'll need the other as well, won't they.

PHIPPS: Yes, I suppose so, sir.

TISSPOT: Right. Well, that's settled then. Major Rhodes will tell you where to bunk down. Goodbye, gentlemen, and . . . er . . .

RHODES: Good luck, sir.

TISSPOT: Thank you, and the same to you, Major.

RHODES: If you'll follow me, gentlemen . . .

He goes towards the door, but PAT steps forward towards TISSPOT.

PAT: May I speak to you privately, sir?

TISSPOT looks at her in amazement, only really seeing her for the first time.

TISSPOT: Yes? What is it, er . . .

PAT: Coles, sir. Pat Coles.

TISSPOT: Yes . . . well, what is it, Coles?

PAT: I'd prefer to speak to you *alone*, sir.

TISSPOT is plainly embarrassed.

TISSPOT: I don't think that's necessary, Coles. You can trust everyone here, I think.

PAT: No, sir. I must be alone with you.

TISSPOT looks uncomfortably at the others.

TISSPOT: I'm sorry, Coles, but one has to be careful about that sort of thing in a place like this, you understand . . .

PAT: Yes sir, but perhaps you'll know why if I show you something.

She starts to unbutton her tunic and steps forward to face him, back to us and the others.

She opens her top wide and TISSPOT reacts goggle-eyed to her chest. This is a big moment for him. He hasn't seen a pair for years.

TISSPOT: Good gad!

He is hypnotised by them. Involuntarily, his shaking hands reach out to touch them, see if they're real, when . . .

RHODES: What is it, sir? What's the trouble?

He snatches his hands back.

TISSPOT: What? What are you all standing about here for? Get out! Leave us alone, can't you!

RHODES: (STAGGERED) Yes, sir!

And he, PHIPPS and the other two KRIEGIES make a hasty exist. TISSPOT turns back to PAT, who has done her battledress blouse up again.

TISSPOT: Forgive me. It's . . . er . . . been such a long time since I . . . er . . . er . . .

PAT is amused.

PAT: Saw a pair like that. I know.

TISSPOT: (STILL IN WONDER) Fantastic!

PAT: Oh come on, sir. I'm only 38.

TISSPOT: No no, I meant . . . a woman . . . here . . . in uniform . . . you *are* a woman, aren't you?

PAT: Oh yes, sir. You don't want any further proof, do you?

TISSPOT: Yes! I mean, no! No, of course not.

He totters across to the window, looks fearfully out, then turns back to PAT.

TISSPOT: Look . . . er . . . Coles. We must keep this to ourselves, understand? (THROUGH THIS SPEECH, HE GRADUALLY GETS MORE AFFECTIONATE, PUTTING HIS ARM AROUND HER SHOULDERS, PATTING HER, ETC) In a camp like this . . . over a thousand men . . . haven't seen a woman for years . . . we'd have a riot on our hands in no time . . .

PAT: Yes, I do understand what you mean, sir.

TISSPOT: Yes . . . trouble is, my dear . . . they haven't all got the self-control that I have, if you know what I mean . . .

PAT: Oh you don't have to worry, sir. I know how to look after myself.

TISSPOT: (OBVIOUSLY DISAPPOINTED) Oh, do you?

PAT: (SQUIRMING FREE OF HIM) Yes, sir. You see, I was an agent.

TISSPOT: Really? Used to be in that line meself before the war. Travelled in ladies' underwear, you know . . .

PAT: I mean, a secret agent, sir.

TISSPOT: Oh, I see . . . yes.

PAT: I was dropped from an aircraft over France.

TISSPOT: Tut-Tut! Damned careless these RAF wallahs!

PAT: Purposely, sir. I was working with the French underground, you see.

TISSPOT: Oh yes, I understand. Have your tickets ready, mind the doors! All that, eh?

PAT: Well not quite, sir. In the Resistance.

TISSPOT: Ah! Yes of course. Knew all the time really. Just having a little joke.

But he wasn't of course.

PAT: Of course, sir. Anyway, our group got betrayed to Jerry, and, if they hadn't found this uniform for me, I'd have probably been shot.

TISSPOT: Ah, I see. Good for the old French Resistance, eh?

PAT: Oh, it wasn't them found it for me, sir. It was this nice young German captain. (GIGGLES) Good-looking too.

TISSPOT: I see . . . yes. But why are you wearing nothing underneath it?

PAT: Oh well, you know how it is, sir. I mean, he's been kind enough to do something for me . . .

TISSPOT: Uh? Yes . . . well perhaps we'd better not go into all that.

PAT: That's not what he said.

TISSPOT: But it's going to be dashed tricky keeping your sex a secret, Coles. I mean, what about the weekly shower parties? We go in groups of twenty, you know.

PAT: Yes, that will be tricky, sir.

TISSPOT: Course I'll make sure you're in *my* party.

PAT: Thanks, sir, but it may not be necessary. I want to escape as soon as possible.

TISSPOT: What? Oh, there's no hurry for that, me dear. You must stay and relax for a while, eh?

PAT: But there is a hurry, sir. I have information which I should get back home.

TISSPOT: Oh, I see. Well, in that case, I'll have a chat to Phipps. Get you out on the next one, what?

PAT: Thank you, sir. I'd be tremendously obliged.

PAT: Yes . . . in the meantime, I can let you have some underclothes. (HE GOES TO HIS CUPBOARD AND TAKES OUT PYJAMAS, UNDERWEAR, AND ARMY SHIRT) Shirt, pyjamas . . . undies . . . I mean, underwear . . .

PAT: Thank you, sir. You've been very kind.

He leers at her.

TISSPOT: Yes . . . well, aren't you going to give me what you gave that nice young German captain, eh?

PAT: Oh, I don't think you'd like me to do that, sir.

TISSPOT: Oh, I don't know. What was it, eh? Eh?

PAT: A knife in the stomach!

And, as TISSPOT reacts, and PAT makes her escape . . .

INT. PARKIN'S ROOM. DAY.

The five occupants of the room are there. PARKIN is at the table with DUMDUM, playing poker. CYRIL GAYE, the theatre director, is lying on his bunk, sulking. BAGSHOT, the 'Heavy' in the play rehearsal, is sitting on his bunk, reading. 'TRUB' TRUBSHAW is at the other end of the table, carefully carving a ration of German 'brown' rye bread into slices. The sixth bunk – the upper one to PARKIN's – is unoccupied.

There is a pile of dried beans between PARKIN and DUMDUM in the 'pot', an even bigger pile in front of PARKIN, and half a dozen in front of DUMDUM, who is looking worriedly at his hand.

PARKIN: Well, come on! What are you going to do?

DUMDUM: (UNHAPPILY) I'll see you.

He shoves his remaining beans into the centre.

PARKIN: Right. (SHOWING HIS HAND) Full house – jacks and threes.

DUMDUM: Oh no. (SHOWING HIS) I've only got two pairs.

PARKIN: (LAUGHS) There's a lucky girl. (HE SWEEPS IN THE POT) Your deal.

DUMDUM: No, I think I've had enough for now.

PARKIN: Right. (HE CALCULATES ON A PIECE OF PAPER, ENTERING THE LATEST DEBT) I make it you now owe me . . . two million, six hundred and forty two thousand and . . . two.

DUMDUM: Much as that? It can't be.

PARKIN: We've been playing for three and a half years, you know.

DUMDUM: Even so.

PARKIN: What are you worrying about? You've got the rest of your life to pay!

DUMDUM: I think I'll go and have a wash.

He gets up, starting to take off his battledress top, and goes to his bunk, out of shot.

PARKIN: You do that. We can't have Cynthia coming onto that stage stinking of de-lousing powder tonight.

GAYE: *If* there *is* a show tonight. I'm so furious I'd a jolly good mind to cancel it!

PARKIN: Why?

GAYE: *Why?* Using *my* theatre to dig a wretched tunnel! It's . . . it's *disgusting*!

PARKIN: *Our* theatre.

GAYE: *Mine*! Whose idea was it in the first place? Mine! I've given my *life* to it! It's like my own child. I gave *birth* to it!

PARKIN: Don't tell us. We had to put up with you during the pregnancy!

GAYE: Oh, you just don't under*stand*!

PARKIN: I'll tell you this: if anyone puts you in the family way again, I'm moving out!

TRUB: Dash it all, they've got to dig tunnels *some*where.

GAYE: Why?

PARKIN: He's right, you know. Why?

TRUB: Well, damn it all, we are supposed to escape.

GAYE: Oh . . . pish!

PARKIN: I couldn't have put it better myself. What do you want to get home for? So they can send you to do some more fighting? No thanks.

DUMDUM comes into shot, naked, except for a towel wrapped around his middle.

DUMDUM: No, but it would be nice to have a bit of crumpet again.

PARKIN: Oh blimey, he's off again.

DUMDUM: Well . . . I'm going to have that wash.

PARKIN: Yeh, and the way you're feeling, you'd better make it a nice *cold* one!

DUMDUM goes out. TRUB finishes the slicing of the bread, and starts counting.

TRUB: There, that's lunch. One . . . two . . . three . . . four . . . five . . . oh damn, I've made a cock of it.

PARKIN: Why?

TRUB: There's six slices and there's only five of us.

PARKIN: So we'll cut for the extra one.

BAGSHOT looks up from his book.

BAGSHOT: Huh! What's the point? *You* always win!

PARKIN: He's right. In that case, I may as well have it.

And he takes two of the slices, much to TRUB's disgust.

TRUB: I say, that's hardly fair.

PARKIN: Don't try and blame me, mate. You're the one who cut too many and put us in this embarrassing position!

TRUB is trying to work out the logic of this when RHODES pops his head through the door.

RHODES: Oh, Parkin . . .

PARKIN: Yes, Major?

RHODES: (CONSULTING PAPER) You've got a spare bunk in here, haven't you?

PARKIN: Yes, but we're saving it for Lili Marlene.

RHODES: Oh, very amusing. (HE TURNS AND CALLS INTO THE CORRIDOR) All right, Coles. You can bunk down in here.

And PAT comes in, carrying the clothing that the S.B.O. gave her, and smiles rather shyly at them.

RHODES: Look after him, won't you, chaps. He's just arrived.

And he goes. The others stare interestedly at PAT. It is GAYE who makes the effort to be pleasant.

GAYE: Oh hallo. I'm Cyril Gaye.

PAT: I'm Pat Coles.

As they react to her high voice . . . . . .

PARKIN: Blimey, another one!

PAT: What?

PARKIN: Nothing. I'm Fred Parkin. This is Peter Trubshaw . . . and that's Bill Bagshot. There's another one – Dumdum – but he's out having a cold wash-down.

PAT: I see.

PARKIN: Yeh . . . he was feeling a bit hot around his dickey.

PAT: (SMILES) Yes, I think I understand.

PARKIN: I hope you're not crumpet-mad?

PAT: I wouldn't know. I've never tried it. (AS THE OTHERS REACT TO THIS RATHER SURPRISING STATEMENT, SHE COOLLY LOOKS AROUND AND SPOTS THE VACANT UPPER BUNK) Is that my bunk?

PARKIN: That's it. Right over mine. I hope you don't snore.

PAT smiles at him sweetly.

PAT: I don't think I do anything that would bother *you*, Fred.

PARKIN reacts in surprise. It looks like he's met his match at last.

TRUB: Well, that solves the old bread problem anyway. Excuse me . . .

And he takes one of PARKIN's two slices.

PARKIN: Hey? What're you doing?

TRUB: Fair's fair, old boy. (TO PAT) Here, catch.

He chucks the slice to PAT, who catches it and looks at it curiously.

PAT: What's this for?

TRUB: Dinner.

BAGSHOT: But there'll be a mug of turnip soup to go with it.

PAT: Big deal! (TO TRUB) Thanks anyway.

GAYE suddenly gets up from his bunk and goes over to PAT.

GAYE: I say, have you ever been on the stage?

PAT: Me? Oh no.

GAYE: Pity. You'd have made a lovely woman!

PAT: (STARTS) Just what do you mean by that?

GAYE: (TAKEN ABACK) Nothing. (TO THE OTHERS) For heaven's sake, what have I said?

PARKIN: All right, Cyril. I'll explain it to him.

GAYE: Some people are so *touchy*!

PARKIN gets up and goes over to PAT.

PARKIN: Look, mate. I don't know whether it's going to be a disappointment to you, but we don't have any females in this camp.

PAT: (HIDES A SLIGHT SMILE) No? I wouldn't bet on that.

PARKIN: If it's bets you want, you've come to the right room, mate.

PAT: All right, so you've got no women here. What about it?

PARKIN: So, when Cyril here does one of his plays, he has to get blokes to dress up as birds. Get it?

PAT: Oh, I see.

PARKIN: All you need is to put on a wig, stuff a couple of falsies down your front, strap up your thingummy, and Bob's your auntie!

PAT: (TO GAYE) I'm sorry. I didn't realise what you meant.

GAYE: Oh, that's perfectly all right. Would you like to have a go at it sometime?

PAT: Well frankly, I don't think I can manage the strapping up bit, but all right.

PARKIN looks very obviously down at his trouser front.

PARKIN: Don't worry. It won't show anyway.

And turns and guffaws to the others.

PAT: (TO GAYE) But it'll have to be pretty soon. I'm not going to be in here for long.

PARKIN: Oh blimey, another escape enthusiast! That's all we needed!

And goes back to the table in disgust. The door opens and DUMDUM comes back in, with the towel wrapped around his middle, shivering.

DUMDUM: Oooh! I hope they don't let any brass monkeys near that water!

He undoes the towel and rubs at his lower middle briskly, then realises that PAT is in the room.

DUMDUM: Oh, hullo.

PARKIN: This is our new room-mate, Dumdum. Pat Coles. This is the one I was telling you about – Dodds.

DUMDUM crosses to PAT, a big grin on his face.

DUMDUM: Pleased to meet you.

And, standing in front of her (down-to-waist shot?) he chucks the towel onto his bunk and sticks his hand out.

CU of PAT. She is frozen, looking down at him in horror. DUMDUM looks down at himself, puzzled, then up at her.

DUMDUM: What's up?

PAT tears her eyes away and steps back towards the door.

PAT: Nothing! Nothing at all. I just remembered. I have to see the S.B.O.

And gets out quickly.

DUMDUM looks at the others in amazement.

DUMDUM: What's he so scared of?

GAYE: Well really, Dumdum! Need you ask? It's enough to frighten *anyone*!

EXT. THE COMPOUND. DAY.

The mound of earth beside the hole is even greater, and NUTZ and the GOON DIGGERS are out of sight. We can see the top of a ladder sticking up out of the hole, and hear the sounds of energetic digging, with spadefuls of earth chucked up periodically.

A few KRIEGIES, stand around watching apathetically. We see the S.B.O. approaching. He comes to a stop, seeing the activity.

TISSPOT: What's going on here? (NOBODY BOTHERS TO ANSWER HIM, SO HE KNEELS DOWN TO CALL DOWN INTO THE HOLE) Freddy? Is that you down there? Freddy? I say, Freddy!

The sounds of digging have stopped. After a moment, NUTZ's face appears at the top of the ladder.

NUTZ: You wanted something, Colonel?

TISSPOT: (EMBARRASSED) Oh sorry. Thought it was one of ours.

And straightens up and beats a hasty retreat.

INT. THE TUNNEL FACE. DAY.

Not that it makes much difference day or night down here. It's the chamber at the end of the tunnel – just about big enough for a chap to stand up in, shored up with bits of wood here and there, and lit by an electric light bulb on the end of a piece of flex that disappears into the tunnel proper. The actual face wall is just bare earth, and here PHIPPS and another tunneler, PADDY FIELDS, are having a very serious conference, studying something in one of the freshly-dug spade holes in the face.

PHIPPS: Yes, it's a snag all right, Paddy me boy.

PADDY: Could we not move 'em?

PHIPPS: Oh no. No, we can't do that. No . . . half a tick. (HE TURNS AWAY FROM THE FACE AND PICKS UP A LARGE PLAN OF

THE TUNNEL AND STUDIES IT) Yes . . . we can make a small detour to the left here. We'd still break out into the copse here.

PADDY: Aye, but a bit nearer the edge.

PHIPPS: Can't be helped, old lad. It's the only way. Right, let's get cracking. (THEY PICK UP SMALL SPADES AND ARE JUST ABOUT TO ATTACK THE WALL TO THE LEFT WHEN THE ELECTRIC LIGHT STARTS BLINKING. PHIPPS IS IMMEDIATELY ALERT) Hello. Something's up at the other end!

He quickly picks up an open-ended old tin-can attached to a length of string, which disappears into the tunnel, pulls it tight and speaks into it. (Yes, it's the simple 'telephone' we used to make as kids.)

PHIPPS: Phipps here. What's up? Over!

And puts it to his ear.

INT. THE THEATRE. DAY.

The trap at the entrance of the tunnel is open and another TUNNELER stands in it, head and shoulders just above the floor, with another tin can in hand. TISSPOT squats on the floor beside the trap. The TUNNELER – MICK – puts the can to his mouth.

MICK: It's me, Freddy. The S.B.O. wants to have a word with you.

He hands the can on the end of the string to TISSPOT, who admires it.

TISSPOT: Dashed ingenious!

MICK: The latest model, sir.

TISSPOT speaks cautiously into the tin.

TISSPOT: Is that you, Freddy? (AND PUTS THE CAN TO HIS EAR) Can't hear anything!

MICK: Over, sir.

TISSPOT: What is?

MICK: You have to say 'over', sir.

TISSPOT: Oh yes, I see. (TO MOUTH AGAIN) Is that you, Freddy? Over!

INT. TUNNEL FACE. DAY.

PHIPPS switches from his ear to his mouth.

PHIPPS: Yes, sir. Over!

INT. THE THEATRE. DAY.

TISSPOT switches from his ear to his mouth.

TISSPOT: How're things going? Over!

INT. TUNNEL FACE. DAY.

PHIPPS switches from ear to mouth.

PHIPPS: Not too badly thank you, sir. Over!

INT. THE THEATRE. DAY.

TISSPOT puts the can to his mouth.

TISSPOT: Good show! Over.

INT. THE TUNNEL FACE. DAY.

PHIPPS, pleased, puts the can to his mouth.

PHIPPS: Thank you, sir. Er . . . is that all? Over.

And puts it to his ear.

INT. THE THEATRE. DAY.

TISSPOT puts the can to his mouth.

TISSPOT: Oh, there was something important . . . what was it now? . . . Just a minute . . . (AS HE THINKS, PAIR OF OBVIOUS GERMAN JACK BOOTS WALK INTO SHOT AND COME TO A STOP BESIDE HIM) I'll think of it in a minute . . .

MICK notices the jack boots, looks up, and CAMERA PANS UP to show KAPITAN BINDER looking grimly down at them. MICK plucks furiously at TISSPOT's sleeve.

TISSPOT: Ah yes, I know what it was. Now listen to this carefully, Freddy . . . (HE BECOMES CONSCIOUS OF MICK'S WARNING, TAKES THE CAN FROM HIS MOUTH, TO ASK IRRITABLY) What is it? MICK points up and TISSPOT looks up to see BINDER. Oh. How do you do?

BINDER: What exactly are you doing, Colonel Tisspot?

TISSPOT: Me? Er . . . what am I doing? . . . er . . .

MICK: The Colonel's rehearsing, Captain!

TISSPOT: Oh yes . . . that's right. Rehearsing.

MICK: It's the best we can do for a microphone, you understand.

TISSPOT: That's it . . . microphone.

BINDER: I see. Perhaps you will demonstrate for me?

TISSPOT: Certainly . . . yes . . .

He puts the can to his mouth again and starts singing, rather quaveringly . . .

TISSPOT: I love you dearly . . . dearly, my dear . . . I love you dearly . . .

INT. TUNNEL FACE. DAY.

As PHIPPS, horrified, takes the can from his ear and gawps at it. Then turns to PADDY.

PHIPPS: I think the old man's going round the bend!

INT. THE THEATRE. DAY.

TISSPOT is still singing, but BINDER cuts him short.

BINDER: All right, Colonel! (TISSPOT STOPS) I think I get the idea. But would it not be better to do this from ze stage?

TISSPOT: From the stage . . . yers . . . should be an answer to that . . .

MICK: It's for 'voices off', captain. It's supposed to be coming from the cellar, you understand.

BINDER: I see. Very well, carry on, Colonel.

They watch as he struts off and out of the nearest exit.

MICK: That was a near thing, sir.

TISSPOT: Yes. If it hadn't been for my quick thinking, it might have been a disaster.

MICK: I agree, sir.

The can in his hand squawks unintelligibly, and he puts it to his mouth.

TISSPOT: Listen, I can't risk talking like this any more, Freddy. I'll come down! (HE PUTS THE CAN DOWN, LOOKS ROUND, THEN AT THE TRAP) Er . . . this way?

MICK: That's right, sir.

And, as MICK helps him down into the trap . . .

INT. THE TUNNEL FACE. DAY.

PHIPPS puts his can down and turns to PADDY, amazed.

PHIPPS: Good God, the old man's actually coming down here!

PADDY: Has he never done it before?

PHIPPS: Never! He *must* be round the bend.

PADDY: Better get ready on the rope.

He gets hold of the end of a stout piece of rope, which comes out of the tunnel, and waits. The rope twitches twice in his hands.

PHIPPS: That's it. Heave ho, Paddy!

PADDY starts pulling in the rope. It's obviously tough going.

PADDY: Phew! I've never known it so hard going!

PHIPPS: Let me give you a hand.

And together they quickly pull the rope in – seemingly, about a hundred yards of it. Then we hear muffled cries of protest, a cloud of dush appears at the mouth of the tunnel and, after it, TISSPOT, holding onto the end of the rope and sliding along on his stomach, absolutely covered in dirt and dust.

PHIPPS and PADDY help him anxiously to his feet and he stands there, gasping for breath.

PHIPPS: I say, are you all right, sir?

TISSPOT: Yes, I think so . . . but I must say . . . you ought to think up a better method of getting here than that.

PHIPPS: But you should have been lying on that little cart, sir!

TISSPOT: Oh, that's what it was for, was it? I wondered. Oh well, I'll be able to use it going back, won't I.

PHIPPS: Well no, sir, because it's at the other end still.

PADDY: (SIGHS) All right, I'll crawl back and get it.

And, disgustedly, he gets down and disappears into the tunnel, grumbling and swearing away to himself.

TISSPOT frowns after him.

TISSPOT: You'll have to watch that fellow. Doesn't sound quite with it to me.

PHIPPS: Oh, I will, sir. That's Paddy Fields. He's Irish, you know.

TISSPOT: Ah well, that explains it. Trouble with the Irish . . . not *positive.* Know what I mean?

PHIPPS: Oh yes, sir. You had something important to tell me?

TISSPOT: Yes! Er . . . what was it now? Come to me in a minute . . . er . . . you carry on with what you were saying.

PHIPPS: I wasn't saying anything, sir.

TISSPOT: Something to do with fires . . . ? Hose? No . . . It'll come back to me.

PHIPPS: Yes, sir. Er, how do you like the tunnel?

TISSPOT: What? (LOOKS ROUND) Oh yes, very nice. Bit *cramped*, mind you. But I suppose that's inevitable.

PHIPPS: I'm afraid it is, sir.

TISSPOT: Where are we now?

PHIPPS eagerly picks up a map to show him.

PHIPPS: Right here, sir.

CU of the map. It is hand-drawn of course, and shows the theatre block, the line of the tunnel under the wire, the copse . . . and the Kommandantura. We see PHIPPS' finger pinpointing their position.

PHIPPS: (OVER) Bang under this copse. By my reckoning, exactly one hundred and seventy two and a half yards from the Kommandantura here.

And he points out the Kommandantura block.

RESUME TISSPOT and PHIPPS.

TISSPOT: Really! Excellent, excellent. So you're ready to break out?

PHIPPS: Well, not quite, sir. Actually we've hit rather a major snag.

TISSPOT: Oh? What's that?

PHIPPS beckons him across to the face.

PHIPPS: I'll show you, sir. Look!

He points into the spade hole.

TISSPOT: By jove! What are they?

PHIPPS: Worms, sir.

TISSPOT: Good gad, so they are. (SMILING) Funny little things, aren't they?

PHIPPS: (SMILING SOPPILY) Well, I like them, sir, yes.

TISSPOT: Yes . . . intelligent-looking too.

PHIPPS: Yes, sir. The snag is – they're right where we were going to start digging the shaft to the surface.

TISSPOT: Oh, I see. Yes . . . tricky. Couldn't you . . . er . . . move them? Gently, I mean?

PHIPPS: Oh no, sir. Didn't you notice?

TISSPOT: What?

PHIPPS: Look, they've just had a family. (PUTS HIS FINGER IN AND GENTLY MOVES SOMETHING ASIDE) Four little ones!

TISSPOT: Oh! Aren't they absolutely *sweet*!

PHIPPS: (LIKE A PROUD MUM) I think so, sir.

TISSPOT: Oh yes. Quads! Marvellous!

PHIPPS: I thought you'd like them, sir.

TISSPOT: Oh yes, adorable. You know, I've never quite understood how worms actually . . . er . . . well, you know . . . I mean, they don't seem to *have* anything, do they?

PHIPPS: I quite agree, sir. It's a . . . well, miracle really.

TISSPOT: Yes. Well, I quite understand your reluctance to move them now. After all, that's what this war's all about. The survival of the weak and all that.

PHIPPS: I'm glad you understand.

TISSPOT: Still, it seems a pity after coming all this far. You'll have to start digging another tunnel, I suppose.

PHIPPS: Oh no, sir. We can break out on side here.

He indicates the left wall.

TISSPOT: Oh well, that's all right then.

PHIPPS: I know some people would think it's rather like taking coals to Newcastle, but there . . .

TISSPOT: Coals! That's it, Freddy!

PHIPPS: What, sir?

TISSPOT: Coles! Young lieutenant who just came in. I want you to take her out with you!

PHIPPS: *Her*, sir? I don't understand . . .

TISSPOT: I meant *him*. Damn it, Freddy, don't confuse the issue. I want him to go out on the break tonight.

PHIPPS: But he's only just arrived, sir! There's hundreds of other with more right . . .

TISSPOT: That's an order, Freddy! He's got vital information to get home.

PHIPPS: Yes, sir! I understand, sir!

He snaps to attention and throws up a salute which TISSPOT acknowledges.

TISSPOT: Good man. Well, that's it then . . . (TURNS TO GO, THEN TURNS BACK TO THE WORMS' NEST) Bye bye, little wormies. You can sleep happily tonight.

With much puffing and panting, PADDY arrives back through the tunnel, pushing the wheeled cart in front of him.

PHIPPS: Oh good show, Paddy. Just in time. (PADDY IS SO OUT OF BREATH, HE CAN ONLY NOD GRIMLY) Your carriage awaits, sir!

TISSPOT: Ah, thank you.

PHIPPS: Just lie down on it . . . on your tummy. That's it. (AS TISSPOT LIES DOWN ON IT) Now then . . . (HE PICKS UP THE HEAP OF ROPE, THEN REALISES) Oh. Didn't you bring the other rope, Paddy?

PADDY: What?

PHIPPS: There should be one attached to the other end to pull it back with.

PADDY: Oh no!

With a murderous look, he squeezes past TISSPOT and starts crawling back into the tunnel, his curses fading into the distance.

TISSPOT looks after him, then looks up at PHIPPS thoughtfully.

TISSPOT: Yes . . . I'm afraid he's definitely over the top!

CUT TO:

EXT. THE CAMP. NIGHT.

In L.S. we can see the perimeter lights illuminating the area along the wire fence, and the spotlights from the tower searchlights travelling slowly over the area of the compound. On the outside of the wire, the GERMANS are changing guard.

In the compound, it is noticeable that although KRIEGIES are moving about between the huts, and particularly in the direction of the theatre block, none of them venture into the clear area between the huts and the perimeter wire. It is in this area that the searchlights play mainly.

CU of MUGGINS, the 'mad' Kriegie. He is peering around the end of one of the huts, looking towards the wire, watching closely the movements of a particular white searchlight spot over the ground.

From his P.O.V., we see a searchlight spot travel slowly over the open ground towards the wire, go past the wire, into the area towards the copse outside, then return to the compound.

CU of MUGGINS, as he smiles maniacally. He turns back behind the cover of the hut, and we see that on the ground there is a circle of cardboard or ply or something, about twelve feet in diameter (roughly the same as one of the searchlight spots) which has been half-painted white. Enthusiastically, MUGGINS picks up brush and paint-pot and continues with the white-washing.

EXT. THE KOMMANDANTURA. NIGHT.

BINDER approaches it at his usual formal stiff walk and goes in.

INT. THE KOMMANDANTURA. NIGHT.

As BINDER comes briskly in, NUTZ and GRETA, still working at their desks, spring to attention.

NUTZ: Heil Hitler!

BINDER returns the salute.

BINDER: You did not find the tunnel, Feldwebel?

NUTZ: No, Kapitan. I don't understand it. We went down thirty feet!

BINDER: Perhaps you were digging in the wrong place.

NUTZ: Oh no, Kapitan. I marked it very carefully. The Britisher – Captain Parkin – he saw me do it. He'll tell you!

BINDER: So! And then you went away to get the digging party, no doubt?

NUTZ: That's correct, Kapitan.

BINDER: Leaving Captain Parkin to move your marker.

NUTZ: That's . . . cor . . . oh. (HE LOOKS PITEOUSLY TOWARDS GRETA) He wouldn't do that, would he?

BINDER looks at him contemptuously.

BINDER: Feldwebel Nutz. You may not realise it, but the Russian Front is getting nearer.

NUTZ: Oh really? Is that the latest news, Kapitan?

BINDER: (A ROAR) For *you* it's getting nearer!

As NUTZ swallows hard, he goes briskly to a door at the rear, smartens his appearance, then knocks.

We hear FOKKER's voice from inside.

FOKKER: Yes? Who is it?

BINDER: Kapitan Binder, herr Kommandant.

FOKKER: (OFF) Oh. Well, come in, Kapitan.

BINDER opens the door and goes in.

INT. FOKKER'S PRIVATE ROOM. NIGHT.

It is very comfortably, even opulently, furnished, with a large, comfortable canopy bed, a chaise longue, easy chairs, and a drinks cabinet. FOKKER, at the drinks cabinet, is out of uniform and wears very gay lounging pyjamas, with a smoking jacket over them. A long cigarette holder with cigarette completes the ensemble.

BINDER closes the door behind him, clicks his heels together, and barks as . . .

BINDER: Heil Hitler!

FOKKER: (CHOKES ON HIS DRINK) Please, Kapitan! We are off duty now. We can dispense with all that nonsense. Relax, have a drink.

BINDER: (STIFFLY) Thank you, no.

FOKKER: Please yourself. (HE TURNS BACK TO THE CABINET AND PICKS UP A LARGE ROUND BOTTLE HALF-FILLED WITH DARK BROWN LIQUID AND REPCHARGES HIS OWN GLASS) I have some rather interesting captured British liquor here . . . (READING OFF THE LABEL) 'Syrup of Figs'. You heard of it?

BINDER: No, Kommandant.

FOKKER: Nor I. A bit on the sweet side, but goes down well.

BINDER: I do not indulge in alcohol, Kommandant.

FOKKER: Oh well, you know how it is. In these days, you've got to have something to keep you going.

And tops up his glass again.

BINDER: Herr Kommandant, I suspect the British are building another tunnel.

FOKKER: Oh? What makes you think that?

BINDER: Firstly, the business of Feldwebel Nutz's prodder.

FOKKER: (NEARLY CHOKES AGAIN) Why? What on earth has happened to it?

BINDER: It was pulled off him, Kommandant.

FOKKER: Poor fellow. That must have been very painful. But there, if he goes around exposing it . . .

BINDER: He was only pushing it into the ground.

FOKKER: What? Oh, you mean his *probe*. Oh yes, I heard about that. But we only have *his* word for that, Kapitan.

BINDER: True. But I have a *feeling* . . .

FOKKER: Oh come now, you worry too much, Binder. This camp is escape-proof! It is quite impossible to get away, you know that.

BINDER: All the same, sir . . .

FOKKER: Stop worrying, Binder. You will feel better after a good night's sleep.

BINDER: Perhaps so, Kommandant.

FOKKER: Or better, still, go and look up Fraulein Gobbler, eh? Eh? (NUDGE, NUDGE)

BINDER: (STIFFLY) No thank you, Kommandant. Anyway, she is still working.

FOKKER: Really? Extraordinary woman. She's always at it, you know.

BINDER: So I have been given to understand, sir.

FOKKER: Be a good chap. On your way out, tell her she can have tonight off.

BINDER: Yes, herr Kommandant. (FOKKER REPLENISHES HIS GLASS, AS BINDER GOES TO THE DOOR, TURNS AND . . .) Heil Hitler! (WHICH MAKES FOKKER JUMP AGAIN)

INT. KOMMANDANTURA OFFICE. NIGHT.

As BINDER comes out of FOKKER's room. NUTZ has gone, and only GRETA is at her desk.

BINDER: Oh, fraulein Gobbler. I have a message for you from the Kommandant about tonight . . .

GRETA: Yes, Kapitan?

BINDER: He wishes you to have it off!

GRETA smiles and her eyes light up with Germanic fervour.

GRETA: I shall be happy to be of service to the Kommandant, herr Kapitan!

BINDER looks faintly surprised, but goes on out.

INT. CAMP THEATRE. NIGHT.

The curtains are closed, the auditorium is lit, and it is a full house. From a loud-speaker, music is playing.

It is noticeable that PHIPPS, MICK and PADDY are seated right by the now-closed trap entrance to the tunnel.

PADDY: Now, Freddy?

PHIPPS: No. Wait till the show starts. He looks past them along the row and we see PAT sitting there. All right, Coles?

PAT: Yes. Fine, thanks.

PHIPPS: Good show. Won't be long now.

He gives PAT a reassuring smile.

INT. BACKSTAGE, THEATRE. NIGHT.

GAYE is peering through the crack of the curtains, looking at the 'house'.

He turns from them, smiling broadly, and speaks to PARKIN, lounging in one of the home-made easy chairs of the set, dressed incongruously as a parson.

GAYE: It's a full house! Not a seat to spare!

PARKIN: (SURPRISED) Get away! (LOOKS UPWARDS) He must have heard my prayers.

GAYE gives him a filthy look, then turns to the wings, calling.

GAYE: All right, everyone! Places please! Come along now!

BAGSHOT comes on as LORD BUMFREY and takes up a position in front of the painted fireplace.

GAYE: Where's Cynthia? Cynthia!

And DUMDUM comes on, fully-dressed and made up now. He looks anything but glamorous and moves very awkwardly.

PARKIN: (WOLF WHISTLE) Here, what are you doing after the show, ducks?

DUMDUM: Oh knock it off!

PARKIN: Ta, I might take you up on that?

And guffaws dirtily.

GAYE: Quiet everybody, *please*!

DUMDUM: Have you got a pin?

GAYE: We've no time for *that*! Get into your place!

DUMDUM: Yes, but . . .

The music stops.

GAYE: That's it! (AS HE RUSHES OFF INTO THE WINGS) Curtain! Curtain!

INT. THE THEATRE. NIGHT.

There is a cheer from the audience as the curtain goes back.

DUMDUM, who has been grasping his middle with one hand, now stands in front of PARKIN.

DUMDUM: Oh, reverend, there is only one way I can express my willingness to do what you want!

He holds out both hands appealingly towards PARKIN, and his army-issue underpants fall neatly around his ankles.

As the AUDIENCE whistle and fall about, laughing . . .

INT. THE THEATRE WINGS. NIGHT.

CU of GAYE, as he screams despairingly . . .

GAYE: Curtain! Curtain!

And, as the curtain comes quickly across on DUMDUM wrestling with his underpants, and PARKIN cackling like mad . . .

EXT. THE COMPOUND. NIGHT.

MUGGINS has finished painting his white disc, and now lifts it up, showing that there are a couple of handles on the underside, and, between them, a cut-out portion, permitting him (when underneath) to peer up through it. He now puts the disc on top of his head, white side uppermost, and goes cautiously to the end of the hut. He looks carefully around, sees one of the searchlight spots travelling over the open ground towards him. As the spot reaches the end of the hut, he moves quickly out so that his white disc fits neatly into the searchlight spot, and starts moving with it towards the wire.

EXT. A GUARD TOWER. NIGHT.

Shooting past the GOON manipulating the searchlight, down towards the compound. We can see MUGGINS' white disc moving along with the searchlight spot – a little erratically, to be truthful, but getting there.

EXT. THE COMPOUND. NIGHT.

CU of MUGGINS under the disc, looking up and smiling happily. It' s actually working!

EXT. THE COMPOUND. NIGHT.

In L.S. we watch as MUGGINS' disc moves slowly in the searchlight spot towards the perimeter wire. But, instead of crossing over the wire, the spot comes to a stop just before it.

CU of MUGGINS, frozen to the spot, looking up worriedly.

Then, in L.S. again, we see the spot start to travel back into the compound again, with

MUGGINS' following it, even more erratically.

EXT. GOON TOWER. NIGHT.

It is obvious that the GOON on the searchlight has cottoned on to what is going on and has decided to have a game with MUGGINS. He chuckles nastily and starts to move the searchlight all over the place.

EXT. THE COMPOUND. NIGHT.

We see MUGGINS trying to desperately follow the path of the spot. He's eventually led right up to the wire again, and he smiles in relief again. This time? No, back into the compound goes the spot.

INT. THE CAMP THEATRE. NIGHT.

The performance is under way again.

(NOTE: It is a straight play, not well acted of course, which goes on all through the action in the auditorium. I'll do a script for it as and when we know roughly how much time is needed. It is the action in the auditorium which is of more importance at this stage.)

We see GAYE standing right at the back of the auditorium, watching the stage as if it were at least a performance of the Bolshoi.

CU of PHIPPS, MICK and PADDY, seated beside the gangway about half-way down the auditorium. He gives them a nod and they move quietly out of their seats, open the trap door in the gangway leading down to the tunnel. MICK and PADDY disappear down it. PHIPPS goes back to PAT and whispers . . .

PHIPPS: Right, move out at regular intervals! Pass it along!

PAT reaches down and picks up a bundle between her legs, whispers to the next KRIEGIE, then moves quietly out after PHIPPS. The rest of the row also pick up bundles, creep quietly out, and disappear into the tunnel.

EXT. THE COMPOUND. NIGHT.

MUGGINS, panting heavily now, is still zig-zagging about under the searchlight spot.

CU of the GOON in the box. He is clearly enjoying all this. As another great idea occurs to him . . .

In L.S. we see the spot and MUGGINS move slowly towards one of the blocks. Is it going to go right over the block? To MUGGINS' horror – yes. At the last moment, we see the disc detach itself from the spot, move rapidly around the end of the block, and join up again with the searchlight spot on the other side.

CU of the GOON, nearly in hysterics.

INT. THE THEATRE. NIGHT.

We are just approaching the end of the first scene. The curtain comes across and the

houselights come up, and GAYE, still standing at the back and obviously delighted with his masterpiece, looks around the auditorium. His jaw drops.

Now we see why – the auditorium is practically empty.

CU of GAYE. He just can't believe it.

GAYE: What? Where *is* everybody? I don't believe it!

He tears round to the far gangway and starts down it, yelling hysterically and, with a shriek, disappears down the still-open trap.

EXT. THE COMPOUND. NIGHT.

To resume – and terminate – the Muggins story.

MUGGINS can hardly keep up with the spot now, he's so worn out.

Perhaps the GOON realises this, because . . .

IN L.S., we see the spot slow up and move towards the wire once more, but directly towards the huge mound of earth and the hole beside it dug by NUTZ's party earlier.

With a hoarse yell, poor MUGGINS disappears into the hole and the white disc settles over the top of it.

INT. THE KOMMANDANT'S ROOM. NIGHT.

FOKKER is at the drinks cabinet again, just finishing the syrup of figs. As he breaks out another bottle . . .

There is a gentle tap at the door.

FOKKER: Yes? Who is it?

The door opens and GRETA comes in.

Gone is the Teutonic martial super-woman. She has come to make seduction pleasant and easy, wearing a very feminine see-through outfit and matching make-up and hair-do.

FOKKER is slightly surprised by her appearance, but pleasantly so.

FOKKER: Oh, fraulein Gobbler. I didn't recognise you at first.

GRETA: I received your message, Kommandant, and dressed accordingly.

FOKKER: Oh well, that's good. Life cannot be all work, no? One must relax and enjoy oneself occasionally.

GRETA: I must tell you that I have been waiting for this moment for a very long time.

FOKKER: Well, now that it's here, what do you intend to do with it?

GRETA: I would prefer you to suggest something, Kommandant. (COMING NEARER) You will find me very . . . *amenable.*

FOKKER: (SLIGHTLY DISCONCERTED) Well, I don't know. I mean, it's not so much

what one does, as where one does it, don't you think?

GRETA: I don't understand . . .

FOKKER: Well, personally, I like to get out in the open air.

GRETA: The open air?

FOKKER: Yes . . . the town park is very pleasant at this time of the year.

GRETA: But there will be many people about.

FOKKER: Oh, I don't mind that, fraulein. You might think it vain of me, but I rather enjoy being *seen.*

GRETA: In *uniform*?

FOKKER: Yes! People say 'There goes the Kommandant. On the job again!'

GRETA: No! I am sorry, Kommandant, but I cannot do this. Not for the first time anyway.

FOKKER: But there has to be a first time for everything, fraulein.

GRETA: Then it must be here, in this room!

FOKKER: What? What must be?

GRETA: That we make love!

FOKKER: Make love? You must be mad! I can't make love!

GRETA: Of course you can. I will show you. It is not difficult!

And before he can do anything, she lifts him up bodily and carries him across to the chaise longue.

FOKKER: Fraulein, what are you doing? Put me down! Put me down, I say!

GRETA: Do not worry, mein liebchen. I will do everything.

FOKKER: But I don't want to do everything!

As she plonks him down onto the chaise longue . . .

INT. THE TUNNEL FACE. NIGHT.

PHIPPS, MICK, and PADDY are working on the up-shaft to the surface. They have their faces blacked-up already, and the line of KRIEGIES stretching back into the tunnel are blacking their faces using boot polish. All hold escape bundles.

PHIPPS: That's enough, chaps. We're close to the surface now. Remember, we are just six and a half feet into the copse. As soon as you get out, keep low and head north! (THERE IS A MURMUR OF ASSENT FROM THOSE PRESENT) Right, this is it then. Good luck, chaps. See you in Blighty!

With which he picks up a hefty pick-axe and starts swinging it into the up-shaft above him. As the earth starts to fall . . .

INT. THE KOMMANDANT'S ROOM. NIGHT.

GRETA has the struggling FOKKER pinned

down to the chaise longue and half undressed now.

GRETA: Relax, mein liebchen . . . relax . . . I will do it . . .

FOKKER: I don't want you to do it!

GRETA: Just think of the beautiful male child we shall make! With your brains and my body . . .

FOKKER: Yes, but supposing it has *your* brains and *my* body!

GRETA: Now the trousers . . .

She sits back on his legs, pinning them down and starts to undo the trousers.

FOKKER: No, no, no!

There is a great splintering of wood and the portion of the floor under the chaise longue gives way and, with a yell, FOKKER and GRETA disappear with it. There is a great cloud of dust into the room, a lot of confused shouting from below. Then the faces of FOKKER, PHIPPS, MICK and PADDY appear out of the abyss. PHIPPS looks around in dismay.

PHIPPS: Oh, I say, something seems to have gone wrong.

FOKKER: What is this? What are you doing here? What is the meaning of this?

PHIPPS and the others look at him perplexed for a moment, then as one put their heads together and start belting out a Negro spiritual . . .

ALL: See them shuffle along . . . ETC.

CUT TO:

EXT. THE COMPOUND. DAY.

It is some days later. NUTZ and a party of GOONS are entering the compound, calling 'Appel! Appel! Raus!'

INT. PARKIN'S ROOM. DAY.

As the OCCUPANTS stir from their bunks, cursing and grumbling, we can hear the shouts of 'Appel! Raus' continuing outside.

PARKIN, in long underwear, swings his legs out and draws on his trousers, then stands up to put his battledress tunic on. He stops, looking up puzzled at the top bunk, where PAT is making extraordinary movements under his blankets (obviously getting dressed). PAT completes the operation, then climbs down, fully dressed now. PARKIN gives him an old-fashioned look, and, as PAT goes out of the door, shakes his head.

EXT. THE COMPOUND. DAY.

KRIEGIES are emerging from the huts and forming into their squads.

The main gates are opened for FOKKER and BINDER, immaculately uniformed as usual, and they march to their position facing the

'parade', which is now formed into squads, standing at ease and yawning heavily.

There is a pregnant pause, then RHODES gives a meaningful little cough at TISSPOT.

RHODES: Sir?

TISSPOT: What? Oh yes. British officers! British officers – atten . . . . . .

And goes blank. RHODES quickly hisses at him.

RHODES: Shun!

TISSPOT: Shun! And they come to attention.

FOKKER nods at NUTZ and he and some GOONS move off quickly to start the count, whilst FOKKER addresses the parade sternly.

FOKKER: Pay attention please, gentlemen! I have decided – because of the abortive attempt to escape by means of a tunnel – to punish the entire camp. And so – until further notice . . . (HE CONSULTS A SLIP OF PAPER IN HIS HAND) One! There will be no more issue of Reich turnip soup!

A great cheer goes up from the parade. FOKKER looks furious.

FOKKER: Two! The camp theatre will be closed!

Another great cheer.

CU of GAYE, as he looks round at the others angrily.

GAYE: Beasts!

FOKKER: And three! There will be de-lousing parties for everyone today!

This gets a great 'Boo!' and he smiles nastily.

CU of PAT, but she's looking dead worried.

INT. PARKIN'S ROOM. DAY.

As they all troop back into the room, grumbling.

GAYE: I knew it would happen! I *knew* it! That wretched tunnel! They just don't deserve to have a theatre!

PARKIN: Well anyway, we'll have a rest from old Dumdum driving us all mad in his falsies.

DUMDUM: Oh knock it off, Fred.

PAT: (WORRIED) This de-lousing business . . . what does it entail?

PARKIN: What do you mean – what does it entail?

PAT: Well . . . what happens exactly?

PARKIN: We're marched over to the Kommandantur and put under this special shower.

PAT: (EVEN MORE WORRIED) What . . . separately?

PARKIN: No. Two at a time.

PAT: Oh no!

PARKIN: Why? What's wrong with that?

PAT: I have to see the S.B.O.

And he goes out quickly.

PARKIN: What's the matter with him?

GAYE: I must say, he does act rather peculiarly!

BAGSHOT: Maybe he just doesn't like showers.

PARKIN: He can't do. I haven't seen him take one yet. Have you?

BAGSHOT: Come to think of it, no.

PARKIN: And all that business of dressing and undressing underneath the bedclothes!

GAYE: Well, some of us do like our little bit of privacy, you know.

PARKIN: Why? What's he got that's so remarkable? Two of 'em?

GAYE: Oh don't be disgusting.

PARKIN: Well, I tell you I'm getting a bit fed up with his prissy ways.

DUMDUM: I wish I had.

PARKIN: Wish you had what?

DUMDUM: Two of 'em.

PARKIN: Blimey, you can't even use one properly!

DUMDUM: Not here I can't!

GAYE: Oh, for heaven's sake! Can't you two ever stop talking about it? It's not the only thing in life, you know.

PARKIN: No, but it'll do till something else comes along.

We hear NUTZ's voice off, shouting.

NUTZ: (OFF) Hut ten! De-lousing! Raus, raus!

PARKIN: Such as that! Let's go.

They all get up and start undressing.

The door opens and PAT comes in with the S.B.O.

BAGSHOT: Atten-shun!

They all come more or less to attention, DUMDUM with his trousers at half-mast.

TISSPOT: Oh, at ease, men. I – er – I'm joining your de-lousing party today. (AS THEY ALL LOOK SURPRISED, HE SMILES AT PAT AND GIVES HER AN AFFECTIONATE LITTLE SQUEEZE) Don't worry. I'll look after you.

And, as they look even more surprised . . .

EXT. DE-LOUSING HUT. DAY.

A double-line of KRIEGIES are waiting at the entrance, watched over by BINDER and a couple of GOONS. The 'uniform' for this is just a greatcoat, a pair of shoes, and a towel.

As a couple of KRIEGIES come out, freshly de-loused, and the line moves forward a bit . . .

INT. DE-LOUSING HUT. DAY.

The double line of KRIEGIES extends towards the 'De-lousing' chamber doors, two of them side by side. TISSPOT and PAT are the front pair with PARKIN and DUMDUM right behind them. We can hear the noise of the showers inside the chambers.

At this moment, BINDER's voice is heard from the door.

BINDER: Colonel Tisspot?

TISSPOT: Oh damn. Er – yes, Kapitan?

BINDER: Here please!

TISSPOT: Oh darn it. (GIVES PAT A REASSURING SMILE) Don't worry. I'll be right back.

He goes quickly out of shot. At this moment the noise of the showers ceases, the two doors open and a pair of freshly washed KREIGIES come out from each, shrugging into their greatcoats.

NUTZ, in charge of the de-lousing procedure, shouts.

NUTZ: Next two!

PAT, left on his own at the front, looks round worriedly for TISSPOT.

NUTZ: Come on! Next two, next two!

And pushes PAT and DUMDUM towards one of the doors.

PAT: But . . .

NUTZ: No buttings! Go, go, go!

And pushes DUMDUM and PAT firmly in. As the door closes behind them . . .

PARKIN: Here, what about the S.B.O.?

NUTZ: He can go with you. In, in, in!

And pushes PARKIN into the other cubicle.

EXT. DE-LOUSING HUT. DAY.

TISSPOT is arguing with BINDER just outside the door, and casting worried looks back into the hut.

BINDER: But it is the Kommandant's order, Colonel!

TISSPOT: Maybe, but I don't *want* to be excused from de-lousing!

BINDER: You don't *want* to be excused?

TISSPOT: No, I love it! Mad about it!

BINDER: (SHRUGS) Very well, Colonel.

TISSPOT, relieved, hurries back inside.

INT. DE-LOUSING HUT. DAY.

NUTZ is waiting by the door of the cubicle which PARKIN went into, as TISSPOT hurries back.

NUTZ: Ah! In here please, colonel!

TISSPOT: Oh thank you.

As he goes in . . .

INT. PARKIN'S CUBICLE. DAY.

PARKIN is just turning on the shower, which works from a bar in the ceiling, as TISSPOT closes the door. There is quite a bit of steam in the cubicle.

TISSPOT: Phew! That was a near . . . (SEEING ITS PARKIN) What? Where's Coles?

PARKIN: He's in the next one with Dumdum, sir.

TISSPOT: Oh no!

Horrified, he looks towards the wall of the partition.

INT. DUMDUM'S CUBICLE. DAY.

PAT is standing miserably against one of the walls, her greatcoat still on, as DUMDUM shrugs out of his. PAT reacts to his nakedness and turns quickly away.

DUMDUM: Right. Here goes!

He turns the shower on.

DUMDUM: Hey! Take your coat off or you'll get it all wet!

DUMDUM starts washing under the shower.

DUMDUM: It's not so bad once you get used to the pong.

PAT, still keeping her back to him, takes off her greatcoat, hangs it up and gets under the shower, carefully keeping her back to him.

DUMDUM: It's the chemical they put in it, see.

INT. PARKIN'S CUBICLE. DAY.

PARKIN, under the shower, is looking worriedly at TISSPOT, who has his ear pressed to the partition.

PARKIN: Something the matter, sir?

TISSPOT: What? Oh no . . . not yet. Er . . . don't think so anyway. (CALLING) I say! Are you all right in there!

INT. DUMDUM'S CUBICLE. DAY.

DUMDUM stops washing and looks towards the partition.

DUMDUM: What's that?

TISSPOT: (OFF) Are you all right in there?

DUMDUM: Oh yes, thanks, sir. Fine! (OVER HIS SHOULDER, TO PAT) Fancy the old S.B.O. worrying about us! (AND, REACHING BEHIND HIM WITH THE SOAP . . .) Here, do my back, will you?

PAT, startled for a moment, takes the soap, then turns around behind him and starts soaping his back. DUMDUM starts to giggle.

DUMDUM: Steady . . . I'm very ticklish . . . no, steady . . . not too hard . . . oh no . . . no, no, no, that's enough! (HE SUDDENLY TURNS ROUND) Now I'll do yours.

PAT is too late to turn. She just stands there, arms trying to cover her breasts. Slowly it dawns on DUMDUM. The smile leaves his

face, his jaw drops, his eyes slowly travel downwards.

DUMDUM: Crikey!

PAT: Please don't tell anyone!

DUMDUM's head shakes vaguely, his jaw wags feebly, then he passes out in a dead faint.

CUT TO:

INT. PARKIN'S ROOM. DAY.

PARKIN is sitting at the table, playing a game of patience. DUMDUM is stretched out on his back on his bunk, staring into nothingness, and BAGSHOT is at the other end of the table, concocting some sort of dish out of crushed hard tack biscuits and spam.

PARKIN sighs and looks at the mixture in disgust.

PARKIN: What's that?

BAGSHOT: Spam a la Bagshot!

PARKIN: Blimey!

BAGSHOT: You don't have to eat it.

PARKIN: No. I could fill in the cracks in the wall with it.

BAGSHOT, huffy, pounds away at the gruesome-looking mixture on the table, complaining as he does so.

BAGSHOT: Look, I didn't ask to be room cook, you know. I've got far better things to do with my time than look after you lot!

PARKIN: All right, all right. Skip it. (HE GOES BACK TO HIS PATIENCE GAME, GOES TO PUT A CARD OUT, THEN STOPS) Hey! Where's that king of spades gone? It was right there!

BAGSHOT: Well, I'm sure I haven't tou . . . oh. (HE COMES ACROSS SOMETHING IN THE MIDDLE OF THE GOO, AND GINGERLY EXTRACTS IT) It's the king of spades. There you are.

PARKIN: Thank you! (PARKIN CLEANS THE CARD OFF AS BEST HE CAN) Oh, sod this. Come on, Dumdum, let's have a game of poker. (NO RESPONSE FROM DUMDUM) Dumdum!!

DUMDUM: Yes?

PARKIN: Let's have a game.

DUMDUM: Oh . . . no thanks. I'm too tired.

PARKIN: Oh, I'm sorry. It's an exhausting business of course, sitting at a table holding onto five bleeding cards!

The door opens and PAT comes in, carrying a Red Cross parcel.

PAT: I've just been issued with this Red Cross parcel. What do I do with it?

PARKIN: Who's going to tell him?

DUMDUM, with a smile, fairly leaps off his bunk.

DUMDUM: Here, I'll take it.

PAT: Oh, thanks.

She returns DUMDUM's smile and gives him a conspiratorial wink.

DUMDUM: It goes in the food cupboard here.

And he stows it away. PARKIN has watched this in some amazement. PAT smiles pleasantly enough at him, then looks at the patience lay-out.

PAT: Playing patience?

PARKIN: No, taking a driving test.

PAT: Umm. You won't pass like that.

And puts a dark ten onto a red knave. An action not calculated to make PARKIN like her any better.

PARKIN: I'd *seen* that!

And puts the dark ten back again where it was.

PAT: Oh, pardon me!

And walks away. As soon as she's clear, PARKIN sneaks the dark ten back to where she's placed it again.

PAT: Gosh, my bunk's a mess.

DUMDUM: Here, let me give you a hand!

And eagerly goes across to help PAT straighten her bedclothes. Again PARKIN watches in amazement.

PAT: Thanks, Dumdum.

DUMDUM: You're welcome. (HE'S LIKE A BASHFUL YOUNG BOY WITH HIS FIRST DATE) It's a lovely day.

PAT: Not bad.

DUMDUM: Sun was shining just now.

PAT: Was it?

DUMDUM: Yeh!

PARKIN exchanges a stupefied look with BAGSHOT.

DUMDUM screws his courage up.

DUMDUM: Would you . . . like to come for a walk round?

PAT: Yes, that'd be nice.

DUMDUM: Good oh!

And, immensely pleased, they go out.

PARKIN: What the bloody hell's come over him!

INT. TISSPOT'S ROOM. DAY.

TISSPOT is working on his escape charts. They don't show any improvement. There is a knock at the door.

TISSPOT: Yes?

The door opens and PHIPPS comes in and salutes smartly.

PHIPPS: Captain Phipps, sir. Reporting back from the cooler.

TISSPOT: Ah yes. At ease, Freddy.

PHIPPS: Thank you, sir.

TISSPOT: Yes, it was damned bad luck with that tunnel. Damned bad luck.

PHIPPS: Very disappointing, sir. But there, you can't win them all.

TISSPOT looks ruefully at his Escape Chart.

TISSPOT: No. So it seems. Any idea what went wrong?

PHIPPS: Oh yes, sir, definitely!

TISSPOT: Oh? What was it?

PHIPPS: Well sir, the tunnel came up bang under the Kommandant's room!

TISSPOT: Oh yes, I knew that, Freddy. But . . . er . . . why?

PHIPPS: Why, sir?

TISSPOT: Yes . . . I understood it was supposed to come up in the copse?

PHIPPS: Ah, yes, sir. That's easily explained. Compass error!

TISSPOT: Compass error? I don't understand . . .

PHIPPS: Well sir, I don't want to get too technical, but, as you probably know, our compass was constructed out of part of a Red Cross jam tin . . .

TISSPOT: Yes, yes, I know.

PHIPPS: Well sir, we have since discovered that the needle had got stuck on a lump of jam!

TISSPOT: Great Scott, that was bad luck, Freddy. What sort was it?

PHIPPS: Oh, the usual, sir. A couple of watch hands stuck together and magnetised at one end . . .

TISSPOT: No, no, not the needle. The jam.

PHIPPS: Oh, damson, sir.

TISSPOT: Ah, that explains it. Rotten stuff. Don't know why they send it to us.

PHIPPS: I quite agree, sir.

TISSPOT: Yes . . . well, we mustn't let a little thing like that deter us, Freddy. We must press on, keep the Hun on the run, eh?

PHIPPS: Oh yes, definitely, sir.

TISSPOT: Any more ideas?

PHIPPS: Well sir, Muggins has come up with another extraordinary idea . . .

TISSPOT: Yes? What's that?

PHIPPS: Well sir, it's a bit difficult to explain. I think you ought to see him . . .

TISSPOT: Yes of course. Lead on, lead on . . .

INT. PASSAGEWAY, KREIGIE HUT. DAY.

It is the passageway running the length of the prison hut. PHIPPS has just put a table under a hatch in the ceiling, and is now putting a chair on top of the table. TISSPOT stands by, watching curiously.

PHIPPS: Excuse me, sir.

He climbs up onto the table and chair, and cautiously raps a signal on the hatch.

We hear MUGGINS' voice.

MUGGINS: Who is it?

PHIPPS: Only me! Freddy!

The hatch is removed and MUGGINS' mad face peers down from it.

MUGGINS: What do you want?

PHIPPS: I've brought the S.B.O. along to have a look at it.

MUGGINS: Oh, well come on up!

He disappears from the open hatch and PHIPPS starts climbing up.

INT. THE ROOF. KRIEGIE HUT. DAY.

As PHIPPS clambers through the open hatch, then bends to help TISSPOT.

PHIPPS: That's it, sir. Easy does it . . . That's fine.

He hauls him up into the roof, and TISSPOT turns to MUGGINS.

TISSPOT: Well now, Muggins, what's this great idea of yours, eh?

MUGGINS: There it is, sir!

He proudly points to one side and TISSPOT looks.

As from their P.O.V., we see that MUGGINS is constructing a very Heath Robinsonish affair that looks remarkably like a miniature submarine. It is made out of Red Cross crates, tins, etc., and there are plenty of materials lying around.

TISSPOT: Oh yes. Very interesting . . . very . . . er . . . very well made too.

MUGGINS: Thank you, sir. Course, it's not *perfect*, but I reckon it'll get me out of here all right.

TISSPOT: Yes, yes . . . I dare say. But . . . er . . . will it fly?

MUGGINS: Fly?

TISSPOT: Yes . . . without . . . well . . . er . . . wings?

MUGGINS: Oh gracious me, sir, it's not an aeroplane!

This strikes him as a real hoot. TISSPOT joins in the laughter, a bit uncomfortably.

TISSPOT: Course not. I was only joking.

MUGGINS: I should hope so, sir. A bloke'd have to be a right nutcase to try and *fly* out of this place.

TISSPOT: I'm glad you realise that, Muggins.

MUGGINS: Oh yes, sir. An aeroplane! That's a hoot!

And more laughter.

TISSPOT: Yes well . . . er . . . What is it, Muggins?

MUGGINS: Can't you see? A miniature submarine!

And this is where the audience should be able to see that it could possibly be one.

TISSPOT: A miniature submarine?

MUGGINS: Yes, sir! You see, the propeller will go on here. I thought I'd make that out of an old electric fan. You haven't got one by any chance?

TISSPOT: No, but . . . dash it, Muggins, why a miniature submarine?

MUGGINS: Can you think of a better way of getting out of here, sir?

TISSPOT: No, no, it's ingenious enough. Very ingenious. But . . .

PHIPPS: I think the S.B.O. is worried about the fact that there's no *water* around here.

TISSPOT: Yes, that's it, precisely. No use without water, eh?

MUGGINS: Good God, you don't think I hadn't thought about that, sir? Good gracious, no! (AND LAUGHS AGAIN) How stupid can other people be? First thing I thought of!

TISSPOT: Then . . . what exactly is your plan?

MUGGINS: It's so simple, it's almost incredible, sir. First of all, we build a tunnel under the wire . . .

TISSPOT: Yes?

MUGGINS: *Then* we fill the tunnel up completely with water, put the old sub in, and . . . woosh! We're away!

TISSPOT and PHIPPS just look at him.

PHIPPS: See what I mean, sir?

TISSPOT: Yes . . . Yes, I see . . .

He walks up and down, thoughtfully.

MUGGINS: Well sir? What do you think?

TISSPOT comes to his decision.

TISSPOT: I like it! Carry on, Muggins, and good luck!

MUGGINS: Thank you, sir!

As TISSPOT starts to climb down again, followed by a rather worried PHIPPS . . .

INT. PASSAGEWAY, KRIEGIE HUT. DAY.

PHIPPS: You can't really mean that, sir?

TISSPOT: Course not, Freddy. But may as well keep him happy. Oh no, there's one major snag in the scheme. Spotted it immediately.

PHIPPS: Oh? What's that, sir?

TISSPOT: Where's he going to get an electric fan, eh? Eh? Answer me that!

And chuckles craftily.

EXT. THE HUT. DAY.

As TISSPOT and PHIPPS come out, an open cart is passing, laden with tree trunks, driven by a GOON wearing very thick pebble glasses and pulled by a couple of horses.

TISSPOT: Oh, I see they've started to cut the trees down, then.

PHIPPS: Yes, I'm afraid so, sir.

TISSPOT: Bad show.

They watch as the cart nears the main gates. It is stopped by the two GOONS on guard who give it a thorough search, both on top and underneath, before opening the gates to let it drive through.

CU of TISSPOT and PHIPPS.

PHIPPS: Not much chance of getting out in that, sir. They search every load.

And we hear BINDER's suave voice . . .

BINDER: I am glad you realise that, Captain.

They start and turn to see BINDER smiling nastily at them.

INT. PARKIN'S ROOM. DAY.

PARKIN is sitting moodily by himself as DUMDUM bursts in, looks round eagerly, then appears disappointed.

DUMDUM: Oh. Pat's not here then.

PARKIN: No, he's not.

DUMDUM: You don't know where he is?

PARKIN: No, and I don't care. (AS DUMDUM TURNS TO GO) Just a minute! I want to talk to you!

DUMDUM: What about?

PARKIN: You know perfectly well. What's going on with you two?

DUMDUM: I don't know what you mean.

PARKIN: Oh yes you do! All this whispering in corners, going for regular walks together . . . it's not healthy!

DUMDUM: Oh don't be silly.

PARKIN: Who's being silly? I tell you, people are beginning to talk!

DUMDUM: Well, you can all just mind your own blooming business!

PARKIN: Blimey, it is my business when a mate of mine starts making a damn fool of himself.

DUMDUM: I'm not making a fool of myself! I just happen to like her, that's all!

PARKIN: That's all very well, but . . . (SUDDENLY REALISING WHAT DUMDUM SAID) Her? Did you say 'her'?

DUMDUM: No . . . I meant him.

PARKIN: But you said *her*!

DUMDUM: Crikey, well anyone can make a mistake, can't they?

PARKIN: Not *that* sort of mistake!

DUMDUM: Look, Fred, if I tell you something promise you won't tell anyone else?

PARKIN: What?

DUMDUM: Promise?

PARKIN: All right! Promise!

DUMDUM: See that wet, see that dry, cross my heart and hope to die?

PARKIN: All right, all right! See that wet, see that dry, cross my heart and hope to die!

DUMDUM goes all conspiratorial.

DUMDUM: Well . . . the fact is . . . she's a woman!

PARKIN: Yes, I know all ab . . . she's a what?

DUMDUM: Pat! She's a woman!

PARKIN: A woman?

DUMDUM: Yes!

PARKIN: A woman . . . one of those things with . . .

And he makes motions indicating breasts and so on.

DUMDUM: Yes, that's right.

PARKIN: In a prison camp.

DUMDUM: Yes!

PARKIN, under the impression that he's going round the bend, starts humouring him.

PARKIN: Yes, yes of course. I should have known, Dumdum.

Puts his arm around his shoulders and pats him gently.

DUMDUM: Don't forget you promised not to tell anyone.

PARKIN: I wouldn't dream of telling anyone, Dumdum.

DUMDUM: Only she'd never forgive me, see.

PARKIN: Oh, I understand that, Dumdum, don't you worry now.

DUMDUM: I'm glad I told you, though. I couldn't have kept it to myself much longer.

PARKIN: Course you couldn't have. Now look, why don't you just lie down for a bit?

DUMDUM: I don't want to lie down for a bit!

PARKIN: Blimey, you *have* changed!

DUMDUM: You . . . you don't believe me, do you?

PARKIN: Course I believe you, son. Course. I just wondered how you found out, that's all?

DUMDUM: Well, it was that day we went on the de-lousing party. I asked her . . . only I thought it was a him then . . .

PARKIN: Yes, yes, I know.

DUMDUM: Well, I asked her to do my back, see. And she tickled me and made me turn round suddenly . . . and, well, I saw.

PARKIN: (MAKING MOTIONS AGAIN) What he'd got, you mean?

DUMDUM: Yes. And what she hadn't got!

PARKIN: Yes, yes. Now listen, Dumdum, I don't want you to worry about a thing, okay?

DUMDUM: I'm not worried.

PARKIN: Course you're not. Now you just lie back on your bunk and take it easy . . .

And he forces him down onto the bunk.

DUMDUM: What for?

PARKIN: Because I'm asking you to. A little bit of rest never did anyone any harm, did it?

DUMDUM: But I don't need a rest!

PARKIN: Just to please me. There, there . . . everything's going to be all right. I'll be back in a jiffy.

And he goes quickly out.

DUMDUM looks after him, puzzled.

DUMDUM: Poor old Fred. He's going round the bend!

INT. TISSPOT'S ROOM. DAY.

TISSPOT is in there alone, as there comes a knock at the door.

TISSPOT: Yes?

The door opens and PARKIN comes in.

PARKIN: Excuse me, sir, but I'd like to have a confidential talk with you.

TISSPOT: Oh well, what's it all about, Captain . . . er . . .

PARKIN: Parkin, sir.

TISSPOT: Yes, well, go ahead, Parkinsir.

PARKIN: I understand there's a possibility of repatriation for permanently sick prisoners, sir . . .

TISSPOT: A rather remote one, I'm afraid. Why?

PARKIN: Well sir, I'd like you to put Lieutenant Dodds' name at the top of the list.

TISSPOT: Dodds? But why?

PARKIN: He's gone doo-lally, sir.

TISSPOT: Doo-lally?

PARKIN: Bonkers, crackers, nuts!

TISSPOT: Oh dear, dear, dear. What makes you think so?

PARKIN: Well sir . . . he's convinced that one of his room-mates is a woman!

TISSPOT: Good gracious! Which room-mate is that?

PARKIN: One that came in recently, sir. Coles.

That brings TISSPOT to his feet.

TISSPOT: Good God, this is terrible.

PARKIN: I thought you'd think so, sir.

TISSPOT: Yes, yes . . . terrible!

Worried, he crosses to the window and peers out.

PARKIN: Of course, he's been inside for nearly four years, and thinks about nothing else but crumpet, but still . . .

TISSPOT: (TURNING BACK) Yes, yes, but I want to know just one thing . . . er . . .

PARKIN: Parkin, sir!

TISSPOT: Yes, Parkinsir . . . er . . . what was I saying?

PARKIN: You wanted to know just one thing, sir.

TISSPOT: Ah yes, that was it. (GOES ALL CONFIDENTIAL) How the devil did he find out, eh?

PARKIN: (LOST) Find out *what*, sir?

TISSPOT: That Coles was a woman!

It is PARKIN's turn to be shaken.

PARKIN: Blimey! Not you too!

TISSPOT: What? What about us two?

PARKIN: No, I mean – well blimey sir, he didn't find out. He just *imagines* he's one!

TISSPOT: One what?

PARKIN: He just imagines Coles is a woman!

TISSPOT: Ah! Well, that's more like it. Ah yes. (PUTS HIS ARM AROUND PARKIN'S SHOULDERS AND LEADS HIM WOARDS THE DOOR) Well, listen . . . er . . .

PARKIN: Parkin, sir.

TISSPOT: Yes. Well, listen . . . or . . . I understand your concern, but I don't think there's any cause to worry. Oh no, these things happen, you know. Yes indeed. I want you to forget this conversation ever took place, right?

PARKIN: That won't be difficult, sir!

TISSPOT: (OPENING DOOR) Good man! Good man!

He gives him a final pat and pushes him through the door, and closes it.

EXT. KRIEGIE HUT. DAY.

As PARKIN, still rather bemused, comes out.

PARKIN: They're *all* bleedin' barmy!

And as he strides off purposefully towards his own hut . . .

INT. THE CAMP THEATRE. DAY.

BAGSHOT, dressed in a makeshift Romeo costume – unfortunately still with his army boots on – is on the stage, looking rather fed up. GAYE is in front of the stage, throwing one of his tantrums.

GAYE: For heaven's sake, Baggy! Just because they've closed the theatre doesn't mean we shouldn't rehearse!

BAGSHOT: Yes, but I just don't see the point in it!

GAYE: We want to be ready when they open it again, don't we? Now for goodness' sake, let's get on with it!

BAGSHOT: Oh, all right then.

GAYE: Thank heaven! Scene two!

BAGSHOT takes up a position looking up towards the flies on one side and starts declaiming.

BAGSHOT: He jests at scars that never felt a wound. But soft! What light through yonder window breaks? It is the east and Juliet is the sun!

The theatre door slams open and PARKIN strides in purposefully.

PARKIN: Where's Coles?

GAYE: Oh for heaven's sake! We're rehearsing!

PARKIN: I don't give a damn about that! Where is he?

GAYE: If you must know, he's getting changed!

PARKIN: Right!

He strides towards door leading to backstage.

GAYE: All right, go on, Baggy please!

BAGSHOT: Arise fair sun and kill the envious moon, who is already sick and pale with grief . . . (ETC)

INT. DRESSING ROOM CORRIDOR. DAY.

DUMDUM is very obviously on guard at one of the doors, in a makeshift LADY MONTAGUE costume, as PARKIN strides in and looks around.

PARKIN: Oh, so there you are. Coles in there?

DUMDUM: Yes, but you can't go in. She's dressing.

PARKIN: You mean *he's* dressing!

DUMDUM: I'm sorry, I meant he.

PARKIN: That's better. Right, out of the way!

DUMDUM: No, you mustn't!

PARKIN: Out of the way!

He shoves DUMDUM aside, opens the door, and goes in.

INT. THE DRESSING ROOM. DAY.

As PARKIN comes in, looks around and apparently spots PAT.

PARKIN: All right, now you listen to me, mate . . .

And comes to a stop, staring unbelievingly.

REVERSE SHOT to show PAT. What has caught PARKIN's attention is her obviously red toe-nails. CAMERA PANS SLOWLY UPWARDS to show that she is wearing only a pair of knickers and holding a flimsy piece of chiffon across her chest. It is quite obvious now that she is indeed a woman, in spite of her cropped hair.

Resume PARKIN, still looking goggle-eyed, as DUMDUM comes in quickly behind him, closing the door.

DUMDUM: I told you not to come in!

PARKIN: Blimey, it's true! She is a woman!

DUMDUM: I *told* you!

PAT: If you don't mind, I'm dressing!

DUMDUM: I'm awfully sorry, Pat, but he just bust in!

PAT: Well, I'd be very grateful if he'd just bust out again!

PARKIN suddenly snaps out of his goggle-eyed admiration and becomes most apologetic.

PARKIN: Oh, I'm terrible sorry. I didn't know. But don't worry, miss . . . your secret's safe with me, I promise . . . (HE BACKS TOWARDS THE DOOR, BUMPING INTO DUMDUM, AND TURNS ON HIS FURIOUSLY) Well, don't stand there gawping when a lady's dressing! Get out!

And pushes him out through the door again.

INT. DRESSING ROOM CORRIDOR. DAY.

As DUMDUM and PARKIN come out of the dressing room and PARKIN closes the door and leans against it wonderingly.

PARKIN: I just don't believe it! A real woman!

DUMDUM: You won't tell anyone, will you, Fred? You promised, you know!

PARKIN: Course I won't tell anyone! If I did, there'd be a bleeding riot!

DUMDUN: I'm glad, because she's awfully nice.

He's got a soppy smile on his face when he says this and PARKIN looks at him sharply.

PARKIN: Here, you and her. You haven't been . . . ?

DUMDUM: What? Certainly not! I wouldn't dare!

PARKIN: Yeh, well there's plenty of bods around here who would! (AND IT'S OBVIOUS BY HIS EXPRESSION THAT HE WOULD POSSIBLY BE ONE OF THEM) Blimey!

DUMDUM: What?

PARKIN: I was just thinking – to think that that's been lying in the bunk above me for two weeks!

DUMDUM: Fred! You're not thinking of . . . ?

PARKIN: Course not! I mean, I wouldn't hesitate if I was home . . . but here? Well, it just wouldn't be right! (HOPEFULLY) Would it?

And behind him, PAT pops her head out of the door to say very firmly . . .

PAT: No, it definitely would not!

PARKIN gives her an embarrassed smile.

PARKIN: No, that's what I was just saying.

And we hear HARRY, the Stage Manager's voice bellowing from somewhere.

HARRY: Juliet! Where are you? You're on!

PAT: Excuse me, that's me.

And she comes out of the dressing room, dressed in her Juliet costume.

PARKIN watches her walk down towards the stage and growls.

PARKIN: She'll have to go!

And he and DUMDUM hurry after her.

INT. THE CAMP THEATRE. DAY.

BAGSHOT is still on the stage appealing to where the balcony should be normally.

GAYE, out in front, is appealing hysterically for some action.

GAYE: Well, where is he, for heaven's sake! We're waiting!

HARRY: (COMING INTO VIEW) Just coming, Cyril.

PAT stomps onto the stage. She is plainly trying not to walk like a woman would, and is rather overdoing it.

PAT: Sorry if I've kept you waiting. I'm not really used to women's clothes.

GAYE: Well, none of us are, dearie!

PAT: Do you want me to start?

GAYE: No, let's have a look at you first. Walk up and down a bit.

PAT does so.

GAYE looks disappointed.

GAYE: Well, I suppose it will do, but we definitely can't have those ridiculous bosoms.

PAT: Why? What's wrong with them?

GAYE: They're enormous! We're not trying to get laughs in this, you know!

PAT: (COLDLY) Well, I didn't think they were so bad.

GAYE: *Far* too much padding! You're not playing a cow, you know. (HE STARTS CLIMBING UP ONTO THE STAGE) Oh, I suppose I'll have to do it. (AS HE APPROACHES HER) We need half of that out at the least!

And he is definitely going to reach into the neck of her gown and start hoiking the padding out. PAT steps back quickly.

PAT: Here, what do you think you're doing?

GAYE: I only want to take some of the padding out.

PAT: Oh no you don't!

GAYE: Well, for heaven's sake *you* do it then!

PAT: No, I won't!

GAYE: Well, I'm certainly not allowing you to appear on the stage like *that*!

And he starts for her again.

PARKIN and DUMDUM rush onto the stage and forestall him.

PARKIN: You leave him alone!

GAYE: I *beg* your pardon?

PARKIN: Leave him alone! His bust's okay!

GAYE: (OUTRAGED) Huh! And what, if I may ask, do *you* know about it?

PARKIN: A ruddy sight more than you, mate!

GAYE: Well, I happen to be directing this show and *I* say it's positively grotesque!

PARKIN: Grotesque! What are you talking about? It's a smashing pair! I tell you, *I* wouldn't mind warming my ears with 'em!

PAT: Do you mind!

PARKIN: Well, you know what I mean. Course I realise it's only padding . . .

GAYE: Oh for heaven's sake! *I* am directing this play. And if I say they've got to be smaller, that's final!

PARKIN: And I say they stay as they are!

GAYE: Not in this show!

PARKIN: Right, that's it then. We resign! Come on, Pat, let's go.

And, to GAYE's astonishment, puts his arm protectively around PAT's shoulders and leads him off.

BAGSHOT: Well! Since when did they become bosom friends?

GAYE: Never mind that! Where am I going to find another Juliet? Where, for heaven's sake!

He looks wildly around and his eyes light on HARRY speculatively. HARRY gets the message.

HARRY: Oh no! No bloody fear!

And runs for it.

CUT TO:

INT. TISSPOT'S ROOM. DAY.

A meeting of the Escape Committee is in progress. TISSPOT, PHIPPS and MICK seated behind a table, with paper and pencils before them. RHODES stands to one side, and Lt. BRIGGS stands at attention before the table. BRIGGS wears the usual Kriegie attire but has a mock-up German officer's cap on his head. He looks remarkably like KOMMANDANT FOKKER (in fact, he is played by the same person).

PHIPPS: Now let's understand this clearly, Captain Briggs. You wish to try and escape *as* the Kommandant?

BRIGGS: (ENGLISH ACCENT) That's right, sir.

PHIPPS: Hmmm . . . what do you think, sir?

TISSPOT: Well . . . he certainly *looks* like him. Remarkably so, in fact. Yes . . . (TO PHIPPS) Does he speak German?

PHIPPS: The Kommandant, sir? Oh yes, I think so.

TISSPOT: No, no, I meant Captain Briggs.

PHIPPS: Oh, I do beg your pardon, sir.

BRIGGS: Yes sir, I'm confident I could speak enough.

PHIPPS: Exactly how would you go about it?

BRIGGS: Well, I'd wait till the Kommandant paid a visit to the compound, and then, as soon as he was out of sight, put on the old uniform and just walk out.

TISSPOT: Ummm . . . sounds almost too simple. There must be a snag somewhere . . .

PHIPPS: Ah yes! He'd need a pass of course sir, to get through the gate.

TISSPOT: Aha! Yes, how about that, Briggs?

BRIGGS: Oh, the forgers can supply that all right, sir.

TISSPOT: Oh really? Good show. Yes, splendid. Forgers, eh?

He looks interrogatively at PHIPPS.

PHIPPS: The chaps who make all our false papers, sir.

TISSPOT: Yes, yes, yes, I know. Well . . . seems foolproof . . . doesn't it?

MICK: One moment, sir. What happens when he's through the gate, that's what I'd like to know?

BRIGGS: Simple, sir. I'll go into the toilet in the Kommandantura, take off the uniform, and just walk out.

TISSPOT: Ah! But what happens if the toilet happens to be engaged?

And he looks round at the others triumphantly, the only man who's thought of the big snag.

BRIGGS: I'll just wait till it's free, sir.

TISSPOT: Hmmm . . . yes, well, you could do that, I suppose. Yes, well . . . any other questions, gentlemen? (THE OTHERS SHAKE THEIR HEADS) Yes . . . well, I can't see much wrong with that, Briggs. I think as soon as the opportunity presents itself, you can give it a go.

BRIGGS: Thank you, sir!

He whips off the cap, stuffs it into his pocket, salutes smartly, and goes.

TISSPOT: Yes . . . well, any more, Major?

RHODES: Just one, sir. Captain Parkin.

He goes to the door.

PHIPPS: Parkin? What on earth does he want?

RHODES: (AT DOOR) Captain Parkin?

PARKIN: (OFF) Sir!

RHODES: You can come in now.

PARKIN marches in, followed by PAT and DUMDUM, in Kriegie attire once more. They come to attention and salute.

TISSPOT: At ease, gentlemen. You . . . er . . . asked to see the escape committee?

PARKIN: That's right, sir!

TISSPOT: For what reason?

PARKIN: For permission to escape, sir!

This causes something of a sensation.

PHIPPS: *You*?

PARKIN: That's right. Why not?

PHIPPS: Well . . . I thought you were so dead against it, that's all.

PARKIN: I can change my mind, can't I?

PHIPPS: Yes, of course . . . but why?

PARKIN: Well sir, for one thing, it's important for Lieutenant Coles to get safely out of here and back to England. The S.B.O. knows *why*.

TISSPOT: Yes, that's very true, Phipps. Er . . . important information to get back and all that sort of thing . . .

PHIPPS: Well, if you say so, sir. But as I said before, plenty of chaps have been here longer. I don't see what's he got to lose by waiting a bit.

PARKIN: You'd be surprised!

TISSPOT: Yes . . . well, any idea how you're going to get out?

PAT: Yes, sir. There's a cart comes in every day to collect the trees they chop down . . .

PHIPPS: Oh yes, but they search that very thoroughly every time it goes out.

TISSPOT: That's true. I've watched 'em myself.

PARKIN: Sure! The cart yes, but there's one thing they don't even look at!

TISSPOT: What's that?

PARKIN: The horses!

TISSPOT: By Jove! Do you mean . . . ? Good heavens! What do you think, Phipps?

PHIPPS: It's absolutely brilliant, sir! Terrific! I might have thought of it myself! Well done, chaps!

PARKIN: Right, here's how we do it, sir. It's going to need four of us, with civvy clothes and railway passes. We'll be a family of Polish workers . . .

And, as they bend excitedly over his plans . . .

CUT TO:

EXT. THE COMPOUND. DAY.

The cart with the two horses is standing where they are felling the trees. It is nearly completely loaded and a couple of GOONS are lifting another tree trunk onto it. 'FOUR-EYES', the short-sighted GOON DRIVER, is standing by the cart.

INT. A HUT ROOM. DAY.

PARKIN, DUMDUM, PAT and PHIPPS are standing at the hut window, watching the loading from a distance. It's all very tense and we gather that this is 'it'. They are all dressed in slacks and sweaters and are holding parcels containing civvy clothes and passes.

PARKIN: That's just about the full load! Where the hell's the S.B.O.?

PAT: He can't do it there. He has to wait until the cart's out of sight of the other goons.

PARKIN: I know that! But where is he?

DUMDUM: It's moving off now!

They look back through the window.

EXT. THE COMPOUND. DAY.

As from their P.O.V., we see that FOUR-EYES is indeed driving the cart down the track which passes between the hut they're looking from and the next one. As it reaches a point between the two huts, we see TISSPOT step out into its path.

PARKIN: Thank god for that!

TISSPOT holds up his hand to stop the cart.

EXT. TRACK BETWEEN HUTS. DAY.

As FOUR-EYES pulls the horses up and strains to peer through his pebble glasses.

FOUR-EYES: Who is that? What do you vant?

TISSPOT: Actually, I was wondering. Would you like to come to my room for a while?

FOUREYES: Vot? Vos is das?

TISSPOT: Don't say a word! Make it well worth your while! Cigarettes! Soap! Chocolates! Just follow me!

And he starts off towards hut.

FOUR-EYES looks after him, puzzled. Then greed gets the better of him and he looks round to see that he's unobserved, then gets down from the cart and follows TISSPOT.

As soon as he goes into the hut, MICK and three other KRIEGIES appear as if from nowhere and start quickly unharnessing the horses.

INT. THE HUT ROOM. DAY.

PARKIN and the others turn from the window, jubilantly.

PARKIN: That's it! Let's go!

And, as they rush out . . .

EXT. THE MAIN GATES. DAY.

As FOKKER strolls up to them and the GOON GUARDS quickly open them to allow him into the compound. He seems to be in rather a good mood today and shows them his pass with an affable smile.

INT. A HUT ROOM. DAY.

CAPTAIN BRIGGS (the one who looks remarkably like FOKKER) is lying on his bunk reading as another KRIEGIE dashes excitedly in.

KRIEGIE: Briggs! The Kommandant has just come into the camp!

BRIGGS: Good-oh! (HE LEAPS OFF HIS BUNK) Tail him and don't let him out of your sight, Ron!

KRIEGIE: Right!

And, as BRIGGS takes up a floor board and brings out a German uniform from below . . .

EXT. TRACK BETWEEN HUTS. DAY.

As FOUR-EYES comes out of the hut with the S.B.O., grinning happily and stuffing cigarettes and chocolate into his pockets.

TISSPOT: Good, eh?

FOUREYES: Ya, ya, danker, danker.

TISSPOT: Good show.

He gives him a final friendly pat and watches him walk back in the direction of his cart.

In CU, we see FOUR-EYES climb up onto the driving seat, take up the reins and give a cry to start the horses.

Now we see the horses as they start off. They are of course cunningly fashioned skins, with presumably the four ESCAPERS inside them. (They should look reasonably like horses).

We see KRIEGIES stop to watch the progress of the cart and horses towards the main gates. Music or drum-beats accentuate the tenseness of the operation.

EXT. THE MAIN GATES. DAY.

To see the two GOON GUARDS standing watching the approach of the cart and horses.

It reaches the main gates and FOUR-EYES halts the horses.

The two GUARDS don't give the horses a glance, but go back to the cart and look at FOUR-EYES pass and carefully inspect the cart and the load of trees.

ENT. THE COMPOUND. DAY.

We see various groups of KRIEGIES watching the inspection tensely.

EXT. THE MAIN GATES. DAY.

The GOONS are satisfied and one of them waves FOUR-EYES on as the other opens the gates.

As the cart drives through . . .

INT. HUT ROOM. DAY.

CAPTAIN BRIGGS puts on the made-up German officer's tunic, just as RON comes running in.

RON: He's on the other side of the compound, by the theatre!

BRIGGS: Good oh. (PUTTING ON THE HAT) How do I look?

RON: (SMILING) Revolting! Just like him!

BRIGGS: Well . . . here goes then!

RON: Good luck, Briggsy!

BRIGGS: Thanks, Ron.

And, as he goes out . . .

EXT. THE HUT. DAY.

BRIGGS appears in the doorway, smartens himself, and starts walking casually towards the main gates. He passes some KRIEGIES, who come to a rather sloppy attention.

KRIEGIE: Good morning, Kommandant.

BRIGGS smiles at them and gives the usual salute.

BRIGGS: Heil Hitler, gentlemen!

And strolls on.

KRIEGIE: (SOURLY) Big poof!

EXT. THE KOMMANDANTURA. DAY.

As FOUR-EYES drives the cart up to it and comes to a stop, climbs down, and goes into the Kommandantura.

CU of one of the HORSES. We see PARKIN's face peering out of a spy-hole in the front of it. He looks cautiously around, then . . .

PARKIN: That's it! Everybody out!

They unzip the horse-skins (from inside), get quickly free of them, and, carrying their bundles, run quickly into a nearby shed, leaving the horse skins in a heap on the ground.

EXT. THE MAIN GATES. DAY.

As BRIGGS strolls up to them. The GOONS snap to attention and give the Hitler salute, which BRIGGS returns.

GOON: Your pass please, herr Kommandant?

BRIGGS: Oh yes of course.

And produces his pass. We get a CU of his face, watching tensely as the GOON examines the pass. The GOON hands it back.

GOON: Thank you, herr Kommandant.

BRIGGS gives him a smile, then, as they rush to open one of the gates, strolls through.

As the GOONS close the gate behind him . . .

EXT. THE SHED. DAY.

As PARKIN and PHIPPS peer cautiously out of the doorway. PARKIN is now dressed as a Polish worker, with a big droopy Russian-style fake moustache. PHIPPS in similar gear, with a beret. They look carefully around, then back towards the main gates and 'freeze'.

PHIPPS: It's the Kommandant!

PARKIN: Back, quick!

And he pulls PHIPPS back inside.

CU of BRIGGS, strolling towards the Kommandantura. He is smiling happily. The plan is working wonderfully.

He comes to a stop between the Kommandantura and the shed, looks carefully around, then decides on the shed. As he turns towards it . . .

INT. THE SHED. DAY.

CU of PARKIN and PHIPPS, just inside.

PHIPPS: He's coming this way!

PARKIN signals him quickly and they take up positions either side of the doorway.

EXT. THE SHED. DAY.

BRIGGS nears it, comes to a stop, looks cautiously around again, then nips quickly inside.

INT. THE SHED. DAY.

BRIGGS and PHIPPS are standing, looking at each other rather foolishly.

BRIGGS: Phipps! What on earth are . . . ?

But that's as far as he gets. PARKIN, with a fair-sized lump of timber, crowns him smartly from behind, and as he collapses, grabs him and gently lowers him to the ground.

PHIPPS: I say! Was that necessary?

PARKIN: Another second and he'd have given the alarm! 'Sides, I've been wanting to do that ever since I've been in here. (HE LOOKS CAREFULLY OUT OF THE DOOR) Okay, its all clear! Get the others!

PHIPPS: Coles! Dodds!

PAT and DUM-DUM appear from the back of the shed somewhere. PAT is now dressed as a peasant girl and looks rather stunning, in spite of the poorness of the clothes. DUMDUM is dressed as a peasant woman. PHIPPS is lost in admiration, seeing PAT.

PHIPPS: I say! Doesn't he make a smashing bit of stuff!

PARKIN: Never mind that! Come on!

EXT. THE SHED. DAY.

As PARKIN leads the others out, and they start down the road away from the Kommandantura and the camp.

EXT. THE MAIN GATES. DAY.

The two GOONS are slouched on guard, yawning. One of them looks around the compound and suddenly freezes, a horrified look on his face.

GOON: Otto! Look!

He points into the compound and the other GOON looks in that direction and reacts in disbelief.

R.S. as from their P.O.V. we see the KOMMANDANT strolling towards the main gates.

RESUME the two GOONS. They look at each other, thoroughly bewildered, then look around towards the Kommandantura, but there's no sign of the 'other' Kommandant. They look back at each other and OTTO puts it into words.

OTTO: It's a trick!

And, as they turn to face the oncoming figure grimly, rifles at the ready . . .

EXT. THE KOMMANDANTURA. DAY.

FOUR-EYES comes out of the building, finishing a large salami sandwich. He wipes his mouth, belches, then strolls to the cart, climbs up into the driving seat, picks up the reins and makes the usual 'giddup' noise. Then he realises something's not quite right. He peers short-sightedly towards where the horses should be, climbs down again, and goes and picks up one of the horse skins curiously. Baffled, he looks around for help.

EXT. THE MAIN GATES. DAY.

As the KOMMANDANT strolls up to the two grim-faced GUARDS, smiling benignly.

OTTO: (A SCREAM) Halt!

The KOMMANDANT is rather taken aback.

FOKKER: Good, good . . . but there is no need to be quite so officious.

OTTO: Who are you?

FOKKER: What? Why, I'm the Kommandant! Colonel Fokker!

He puts his hand into his tunic to bring out his pass, but the other GOON threatens him with his rifle.

GOON: Do not move!!

FOKKER: But this is ridiculous!

OTTO: The Kommandant went out of the compound five minutes ago!

FOKKER: But he can't have done! I *am* the Kommandant! I can prove it!

And again he goes for his inside pocket.

GOON: Look out, he's got a gun!

OTTO throws himself on FOKKER and they wrestle him to the ground, where OTTO sits on him.

OTTO: Call the guard!

GOON: Guard! Guard!!

EXT. THE KOMMANDANTUR. DAY.

We hear the GOON calling for the guard as BINDER appears in the doorway, followed by NUTZ. He looks towards the main gates and raps out an order.

BINDER: Get the guard, Feldwebel!

NUTZ: Yes, sir!

Binder starts quickly towards the main gates, passing the cart and poor FOUR-EYES.

FOUREYES: Oh, Kapitan, something funny's happened here . . .

BINDER: Not now, corporal! I am busy!

And goes on towards the main gates.

EXT. THE MAIN GATES. DAY.

Inside the gates, OTTO and the other GOON are still sitting on the struggling FOKKER.

FOKKER: Let me up! Let go of me! ETC.

We hear a shout from BINDER . . .

BINDER: Let me in!

OTTO turns round and sees BINDER at the gates.

OTTO: Go and let the captain in!

The GOON straightens up and lets BINDER in, as FOKKER goes on raving . . .

FOKKER: You'll pay for this! I'll have you shot, do you hear? Shot!

BINDER runs into shot with the other GOON.

BINDER: What is going on here? (RECOGNISING FOKKER) Herr Kommandant!

OTTO: What? It *is* the Kommandant?

BINDER: Of course it is, you fool! Let him up!

OTTO scrambles up, and together they help FOKKER to his feet. He is shaking with fury.

OTTO: I beg your pardon, herr Kommandant. A mistake, I assure you . . .

FOKKER: It's a mistake all right! One that you'll regret!

OTTO: But, who was the other one?

BINDER: What other one?

OTTO: The other Kommandant we passed through the gates, Kapitan?

FOKKER: You passed another one through?

OTTO: Yes, herr Kommandant.

FOKKER: Fool! Imbecile! Idiot!!

BINDER: Herr Kommandant, I think we'd better look into this immediately.

FOKKER: Yes, yes, immediately! (TO OTTO) Well don't just stand there! Let us out, let us out!

OTTO: Yes . . . have you a pass, sir?

FOKKER: Yes of course. I . . . (HE STARTS LOOKING FOR IT, THEN SUDDENLY STOPS) What am I doing! Let us out!

OTTO rushes to do so. And, as they go through . . .

EXT. THE KOMMANDANTURA. DAY.

FOUR-EYES is still peering at the horse-skins, trying to puzzle out what happened, as FOKKER and BINDER hurry up to the Kommandantura. FOKKER is almost past the cart when he freezes and turns back, aware that something is not quite right.

FOKKER: What are you doing, corporal?

FOUR-EYES: Oh. Er, trying to puzzle out where these horses've gone, Kommandant.

FOKKER: What?

FOUR-EYES: (SHOWING SKIN) They were in these when I went in for my lunch.

FOKKER: Am I going mad?!

BINDER takes a quick look at the skins and guesses it.

BINDER: I think there has been another escape, herr Kommandant.

FOKKER: Another Escape?! Excuse me. I must lie down for a while.

And he totters into the Kommandantura. BINDER turns on FOUR-EYES.

BINDER: You! Come inside and bring those ridiculous skins with you!

He turns and goes into the Kommandantura.

INT. THE KOMMANDANTURA. DAY.

As BINDER comes in, he is nearly knocked down by NUTZ leading a party of about six GOONS out.

BINDER: Feldwebel, there has just been an escape! Search all the buildings!

NUTZ: Jawohl, herr Kapitan!

And, as BINDER makes for FOKKER's office . . .

INT. FOKKER'S OFFICE. DAY.

The floor has been repaired of course. FOKKER is stretched out on the chaise longue, gibbering quietly to himself.

FOKKER: The camp is escape-proof! Nobody can get out! It's escape-proof! It's impossible to get out! (AND, AS BINDER COMES IN, HE JUMPS UP) How did they get out, captain? How?

BINDER: I am not quite sure, herr Kommandant . . .

And FOUR-EYES comes in, carrying the horse's skins. He is the bearer of good news.

FOUR-EYES: Herr Kommandant, it's all right! They've found the horses!

BINDER: Where were they?

FOUR-EYES: In the compound, Kapitan . . . in the Latrines!

BINDER: Well, now we know how they got out!

FOUR-EYES: Through the latrines, Kapitan?

FOKKER: No, you fool! In there! (HE POINTS TO THE HORSE'S SKINS) In those skins!!

He turns away, almost crying.

FOKKER: Russian front, here I come!

And falls into a chair, burying his face in his hands. There is a commotion at the door and we hear NUTZ's voice.

NUTZ: Gently with him! Easy now! (BINDER TURNS AND WE SEE NUTZ LEADING IN THE PARTY OF GOONS, GENTLY CARRYING BRIGGS IN THE KOMMANDANT'S UNIFORM STILL. HE'S HAD A NASTY KNOCK) Put him on the sofa there . . . gently . . .

BINDER: What's this, feldwebel?

NUTZ: The poor Kommandant, Kapitan. Someone's clobbered him good. I . . . (HE SUDDENLY SEES FOKKER, WHO HAS GOT TO HIS FEET, HARDLY BELIEVING THIS CAN BE HAPPENING) Oh! (HE LOOKS BACK AT THE INERT HEAP LYING ON THE CHAISE LONGUE, THEN BACK TO FOKKER) I . . . I don't understand . . .

FOKKER: (DOING HIS NUT) Don't you? It's perfectly simple, Feldwebel! We're all raving mad! Mad! Ha ha ha!

With which there is a great crashing of woodwork and part of the floor splits open, water pours out of the hole, closely followed by the nose of MUGGINS' submarine. A moment later, MUGGINS himself pops his head up, looks around, and with an insane grin, says . . .

MUGGINS: Oh, terribly sorry. Wrong place!

FADE OUT.

FADE IN.

EXT. RAILWAY STATION. NIGHT.

It is a fairly small station, with a notice identifying it as:

COLDTITZ RAILWAY STATION.

But in German of course.

A few CIVILIANS are going in and out, as PARKIN, PHIPPS, DUMDUM, and PAT approach in a group and go inside.

INT. BOOKING OFFICE, STATION. NIGHT.

There is one window open and a lugubrious-looking old TICKETMAN is dispensing tickets to a queue of four or five German CIVILIANS.

PARKIN, PHIPPS, DUMDUM and PAT come in, look round cautiously, and PARKIN spots a railroad map of Germany on one wall and signals the others across.

As they look at the map, PHIPPS traces the route, with his finger . . .

CU of the map. As he points out the route . . .

PHIPPS: (OVER) We're here . . . Coldtitz. It is in the Cottbus area. We go through to Berlin, change there, and then straight through to Lubeck.

PARKIN: Blimey, that's a long way. What's wrong with Switzerland?

PHIPPS: Too risky. That's exactly where they'd expect us to make for.

PAT: That makes sense. What happens when we get to Lubeck?

PHIPPS: Pick up a boat across to Sweden. Then Stockholm – England!

DUMDUM: I used to know a girl before the war who said she lived in Berlin.

PARKIN: (SARKY) Really? We must look her up.

DUMDUM: Oh, I don't know whether she'd remember me.

PARKIN: Not like that she wouldn't!

DUMDUM looks down at his woman's get-up.

DUMDUM: Oh yes . . . I forgot.

PARKIN: Oh come on!

They turn away from the map and come to a stop, seeing a RAILWAY POLICEMAN, who is eyeing them very suspiciously. They take their place at the Booking Office window, very conscious of the POLICEMAN's stare.

PARKIN: Don't panic! Just smile back at him!

They all give very artificial smiles at the POLICEMAN, who just looks grimly back.

DUMDUM: Why's he looking at me like that?

PARKIN: Maybe he fancies you!

The CIVILIAN before them at the window gets his ticket and moves away.

PHIPPS: Better let me do this. I've had far more experience at this sort of thing.

As he steps up to the window . . .

PARKIN: Blimey, he's never got out of the camp!

The TICKET CLERK appears at the window.

CLERK: Yes?

PHIPPS: Oh . . . heil Hitler!

CLERK: Who?

PHIPPS: Er . . . Hitler?

CLERK: Oh yes, him. What do you want?

PHIPPS: Excuse my German not being very good, but we are Polish workers . . .

He ferrets out an official-looking piece of paper from his pocket, but the CLERK just waves it aside.

CLERK: Yes, yes, all right. Where do you want to go to?

PHIPPS: Oh, er . . . England.

CLERK: What?

PARKIN: Oh blimey! Excuse me . . . (HE ELBOWS PHIPPS ROUGHLY ASIDE) Pardon my friend here. He means Lubeck.

CLERK: Oh, I was going to say. You can't go to England, you know. There's a war on.

PARKIN: Get away! (TO THE OTHERS) I told you we should have got a newspaper

to-day. (HE SNATCHES THE PAPER FROM PHIPPS AND SHOVES IT THROUGH) There's the travel voucher.

CLERK: Uh-huh. Four of you, is there?

PARKIN: That's right. (INDICATING PHIPPS) My son . . . (INDICATING PAT) Daughter . . . (INDICATING DUMDUM) And my wife.

CLERK: Your wife, eh?

He looks through at DUMDUM, then laughs.

PARKIN: Who said they hadn't got a sense of humour?

CLERK: Well, we've all got our problems. (HE HANDS PAPER BACK WITH FOUR TICKETS) There you are.

PARKIN: Thank you very much.

He grabs the tickets and paper and leads the way through to the platform.

Before going through, DUMDUM looks back and sees the POLICEMAN still eyeing them suspiciously, and fairly bolts through.

EXT. STATION PLATFORM. NIGHT.

As DUMDUM joins the others, waiting on the platform, PHIPPS smiles round triumphantly.

PHIPPS: Well, that went smoothly enough.

PARKIN: Yeh, no thanks to you! Four singles to England please . . . blimey!

PHIPPS: Well, anyone can make a mistake.

PAT: How long do we have to wait for the train?

PHIPPS: (LOOKS AT WATCH) Should be along any minute now.

DUMDUM looks around and spots a slot machine at the back of the platform.

DUMDUM: Look, a slot machine!

PARKIN: So what?

DUMDUM: Maybe we can get something to eat out of it?

PARKIN: Well, all right. Long as you can do it without attracting too much attention to yourself.

DUMDUM: Don't worry.

Track back with him, as he goes back to the slot machine, peers at it, then brings out a coin and selects a slot and puts it in. Nothing happens. He gives it a slight tap. Still nothing happens. Annoyed, he gives it a kick and all hell breaks loose. Mechanism whirrs loudly, drawers bang open and closed, and the whole thing positively shudders with the effort, completely out of control. DUMDUM tries to pacify it, but it's hopeless. All the other PASSENGERS are looking at it in amazement.

The POLICEMAN comes out of the Booking Office and starts towards DUMDUM.

Fortunately at this moment the train comes into the station and draws to a halt.

PARKIN rushes back to DUMDUM and drags him away from the machine.

PARKIN: Never mind that! Come on!

And hurries him to the nearest train door and gets in after the others.

We hear a whistle shrill and the train starts off.

INT. TRAIN COMPARTMENT. NIGHT.

It is empty. PHIPPS, PAT, DUMDUM and PARKIN appear in the corridor, look in, see it's empty, open the door, and come in, closing the door after them. As they all sink gratefully into seats . . .

PARKIN: Phew! (TO DUMDUM) What on earth did you do to that machine?

DUMDUM: Search me. I just put sixpence in and it went berserk!

PARKIN: Sixpence!

DUMDUM: Yes! I don't know what went . . . oh. I suppose it should have been German money.

PARKIN: Oh no! Germany's full of slot machines that take English tanners, didn't you know!

PHIPPS: Well, never mind. Anyone can make a mistake.

PARKIN: Oh blimey, if he says that once more I'll strangle him!

PHIPPS: Well, anyway, we made it!

PAT: There's a long way to go yet!

PHIPPS: Oh, mustn't look on the gloomy side, old lad.

PARKIN: Look, will you stop calling her old lad! She's supposed to be a woman!

PHIPPS: All right all right! There's no need to be so huffy!

PAT gives PARKIN a mischievous smile.

PAT: Perhaps it's my fault. Don't I look enough like a woman?

PARKIN: (LEERING) Not half. You make a right little smasher.

And he starts to put his arm around her to cuddle her.

PAT: Thank you. That's very nice of you to say so . . . *father!*

PARKIN gets the message and removes his arm again.

PARKIN: Something told me that was a mistake!

PHIPPS: Well, two hours till Berlin. I suggest we all get a bit of the old shut-eye, eh?

And settles down. We hear a sort of stifled groan from DUMDUM.

PARKIN: What's up with you?

He turns to see DUMDUM squirming uncomfortably.

DUMDUM: I don't half want to spend a penny.

PARKIN: Oh blimey!

DUMDUM: Well, I can't help it. It's all the excitement.

PARKIN: Well, go on then, but for God's sake, be careful!

DUMDUM: Oh, I will.

He gets up, opens the compartment door and goes out.

INT. TRAIN CORRIDOR. NIGHT.

DUMDUM comes out, closes the door behind him and turns to go down the corridor, and comes to a sudden stop.

From his P.O.V., we see that the RAILWAY POLICEMAN is standing further down the corridor.

DUMDUM gives an embarrassed little smile, turns and goes quickly along the corridor the other way. And, as the POLICEMAN starts to follow . . .

We see DUMDUM reach an obvious lavatory door, push it open and go in quickly.

The POLICEMAN reaches the door and reacts to the notice on it which reads 'HERREN'.

There is a bellow of rage from inside in a very manly voice and DUMDUM comes quickly out again, followed by an irate GERMAN GENTLEMAN, adjusting his dress.

GERMAN: What are you doing in here? Can't you read the notice, woman?

DUMDUM: I . . . I'm terribly sorry. No speak German very good . . .

POLICEMAN: Now then, what's going on here?

And, as they all start speaking at once . . .

INT. TRAIN COMPARTMENT. NIGHT.

As PARKIN reacts horrified to the babble of voices outside.

PARKIN: Blimey, that sounds like Dumdum! He jumps to his feet and opens the door, just in time to let DUMDUM through, hotly pursued by the clamouring POLICEMAN and the GERMAN CIVILIAN. Just a minute, just a minute! What is the trouble here please?

DUMDUM: Don't ask me!

The POLICEMAN and the CIVILIAN turn on him with a furious stream of explanations (in English).

PARKIN: Excuse me, excuse me! But we talk very little German! You'll have to talk much slower! Understand? Slower!

Again the gabble of words from them both.

PAT gets to her feet and comes forward to confront the irate GERMANS, a charming smile on her face.

PAT: Excuse me. Can I help?

Both GERMANS come to a sudden stop, appreciating her looks.

POLICEMAN: I am sorry for this inconvenience, fraulein, but the lady here went into the gentlemen's toilet . . .

GERMAN: I was just sitting there peacefully reading!

PAT: Oh, I do understand and I am most awfully sorry, but she is not understanding German very well, you see. We are Polish.

POLICEMAN: Ah! Polish!

PAT: Yes. We have been transferred from one labour camp to another, you see.

GERMAN: I understand, fraulein. And please, think no more of it. There is no harm done.

PAT: Oh thank you. It's most awfully sweet of you to take it so well.

The GERMAN and the POLICEMAN pat her comfortingly, completely won over.

GERMAN: It's all right, fraulein. Please forgive the intrusion.

POLICEMAN: Of course. My apologies also.

PAT: Oh, but you did quite right, gentlemen. I promise you it will not happen again.

GERMAN: Thank you, fraulein. (TO POLICEMAN) Come! We need not disturb them any more.

POLICEMAN: Yes . . . a natural mistake. Goodnight, fraulein.

PAT: Goodnight.

And they back out, all smiles. PAT closes the door after them.

PHIPPS: I say, that was a near thing!

PARKIN: Too bloody right! (TO PAT) But where the hell did you learn to speak German like that?

PAT: I spent four years at a girls' school in Munich before the war.

PHIPPS: At a *girls'* school?

PAT realises her mistake and is momentarily at a loss for words. PARKIN quickly steps in.

PARKIN: Yes. He was a physical training instructor, weren't you?

PAT: That's right!

And, as they sit back and exchange a secret smile and a wink . . .

EXT. THE TRAIN. NIGHT.

As it rushes through the night – purely to denote the passing of some time.

INT. THE COMPARTMENT. NIGHT.

PARKIN and PHIPPS are slouched back in opposite seats by the window, having a kip.

DUMDUM is in a corner by the door, cradling PAT's head on his shoulder, who is also fast asleep.

We hear the train slowing down and PHIPPS stirs and peers out of the window. As the train comes to a stop . . .

DUMDUM: Not Berlin, is it?

PHIPPS: No, not for another hour yet.

He turns and sees DUMDUM and PAT and looks disapproving.

PHIPPS: I say, steady on, Dodds!

DUMDUM: Eh? (HE LOOKS DOWN AND REALISES HE IS CUDDLING PAT) Oh. Well, he was rather tired, see.

PHIPPS: Yes, but just remember you're a chap too.

DUMDUM tries to ease his arm away gently, but PAT wakes up.

PATT: Oh sorry. Have I been sleeping on you?

DUMDUM: Oh that's all right. I didn't mind at all.

PAT: You're sweet.

They smile at each other and PHIPPS looks even more disapproving. DUMDUM sees his look and frees himself from PAT. Fortunately at this moment, PARKIN starts awake.

PARKIN: Where are we?

PHIPPS: Just a stop. Not there yet.

We hear the whistle shrill outside and the train starts off again. They are just settling down again, when there's a heavy tramp of boots outside in the corridor and a couple of GERMAN SOLDIERS look in, grin, then shove the door back. One is young and the other middle-aged and both are carrying full kit.

The four ENGLANDERS exchange anxious glances. They could clearly have done without this intrusion.

The two GERMANS sling their kit up onto the rack and settle into the two seats opposite DUMDUM and PAT, and give them openly appreciative smiles, then turn and give each other congratulatory winks. Then look back at DUMDUM and PAT and eye them up and down very frankly indeed. DUMDUM and PAT look suitably embarrassed and DUMDUM tries to pull his skirt lower down.

The middle-aged GERMAN, whom we shall call FRITZ, chuckles and whispers something to the younger one, EMIL, and they both chuckle dirtily. FRITZ then leans forward and addresses DUMDUM.

FRITZ: Good evening, fraulein. And how far do you go?

DUMDUM takes it the wrong way.

DUMDUM: Eh?!

He looks helplessly at PAT, who comes to the rescue.

PAT: As far as Berlin.

FRITZ: Ah, Berlin, eh? That is good! Plenty of night life, schnapps . . . love, eh?

PAT: Oh no, nothing like that. We are just polish workers.

FRITZ: Ah! Polish workers! (GIVES EMIL ANOTHER BIG WINK) That also is good!

EMIL: Yes. We have just come from the Russian front!

PAT: Is that so? You must be very tired.

EMIL: (ROGUISHLY) Not too tired!

They chuckle dirtily.

FRITZ: No no. We haven't seen a woman for months. (BRINGS OUT A BOTTLE OF SCHNAPPS) We'll have a little drink, eh? Have some fun!

PAT: Oh no, I don't think we'd better. We're with those gentlemen there, you see.

FRITZ: Ah, so.

He and EMIL look at PARKIN and PHIPPS, who give nervous smiles back.

PARKIN: How do you do.

The GERMANS nod coolly back and EMIL leans over towards the two 'women'.

EMIL: Don't worry. We'll get rid of them.

And winks.

PAT: Oh no! No, I don't think you'd better do that.

FRANZ: It's all right. Leave it to us! (HE WHISPERS SOMETHING TO EMIL, WHO GRINS AND NODS, AND THEN TURNS TO PARKIN AND PHIPPS, WHO HAVE BEEN STRAINING VAINLY TO OVERHEAR THE CONVERSATION) You speak German?

PHIPPS: Er . . . very little.

FRITZ: I understand. (HE BECKONS THEM TO FOLLOW HIM, GETS UP AND OPENS THE DOOR) Come!

PARKIN and PHIPPS look at each other, wondering what to do.

PARKIN: Don't go! Stay put!

FRITZ: Some!

PARKIN: No thank you, I . . .

He comes to a stop, looking at EMIL who has brought out a wicked-looking pistol, and, whistling casually, is waving it around in their direction, pretending to examine it.

PHIPPS: Better see what he wants!

PARKIN: That's the trouble, I know what he wants! (BUT, UNDER THE TACIT THREAT OF THE PISTOL, THEY GET UP) Well, just for a moment perhaps.

They follow FRITZ out and EMIL gets up and follows behind them.

INT. CORRIDOR. NIGHT.

FRITZ goes to the 'HERREN' door, opens it, and stands aside and gestures them to go in, smiling. PARKIN and PHIPPS exchange a worried look.

PARKIN: In there? What for?

FRITZ shows the bottle.

FRITZ: It will be more peaceful. Away from the women, eh?

Laughs jocularly. PARKIN and PHIPPS look back and see EMIL behind them, still playing with the automatic.

PARKIN: Well . . . perhaps a quick one.

They go in, and as PHIPPS passes, FRITZ gives him a push, slams the door on him, and, producing a T-key, locks it. FRITZ and EMIL chuckle.

FRITZ: Now then . . . !

He starts back towards the compartment, ignoring the muffled bangs on the door from inside the toilet.

EMIL: A moment, Fritz. I can have the young one, eh?

FRITZ: Why not? Old fiddles make the sweetest music!

And, laughing, they go back into the compartment.

INT. THE COMPARTMENT. NIGHT.

As FRITZ and EMIL come back in, PAT and DUMDUM look distinctly worried.

PAT: Where are the others?

FRITZ: They will be back in a moment.

And, smiling, pulls the blinds down on the compartment door and side windows. DUMDUM looks even more worried. Even more so when EMIL plonks himself down beside PAT and puts his arm around her.

FRITZ: First we will all have a little drink, eh? Just to loosen us up.

And, as he starts pouring . . .

INT. THE 'HERREN' TOILET. NIGHT.

PARKIN is banging on the door still and shouting. They are in the wash-room part of the toilet, with the loo at the rear.

PARKIN: Hey! Let us out of here! (ETC)

PHIPPS tries to restrain him.

PHIPPS: Stop it! We don't want that damn policeman coming back!

PARKIN: That's true, damn it. But we've got to get out somehow! I'm worried about the others!

PHIPPS: Good gracious me, they can look after themselves all right. After all, they're grown men!

PARKIN: One is!

PHIPPS: What do you mean – one is?

PARKIN: Pat's a woman!

PHIPPS: What?! You mean . . . a woman . . . with . . . ?

PARKIN: Well, there is only one sort!

PHIPPS: Good God! But even so, I'm sure those Germans wouldn't really try anything.

PARKIN: Don't you believe it! As far as they're concerned, Polish workers are *always* in season!

PHIPPS: Great Scott!

And, horrified at the thought, he starts working feverishly to get the door opens.

INT. THE COMPARTMENT. NIGHT.

DUMDUM, looking distinctly worried, is holding a bottle-top of schnapps.

FRITZ: Come on, drink up, drink up!

DUMDUM screws up his courage and knocks the drink back and nearly chokes.

FRITZ roars with laughter, then reaches over, grabs DUMDUM's hand and pulls him over onto his knees, much to DUMDUM's horror.

DUMDUM: No, no, you mustn't! I . . . (AND FINISHES WITH A SQUEAL AS FRITZ ENCIRCLES HIS WAIST AND GIVES IT A HEFTY SQUEEZE) Ow! No please . . . you mustn't take liberties! I'm a married woman!

FRITZ: Good, good! Married is better!

And swings DUMDUM backwards to lie on the seat.

DUMDUM: No! No please . . . stop it!

And desperately fights his wandering hands off.

Across on the other seat, PAT is having nearly as much trouble as EMIL tries to kiss her.

PAT: No, I don't want to kiss you!

EMIL: Oh come on, just a little one.

PAT: And I certainly don't want a little one!

And, as she continues to struggle against his advances . . . FRITZ has poor DUMDUM really pinned down now.

DUMDUM: No please . . . you must stop it . . . ow! (AS HE JUST MANAGES TO STOP FRITZ' HAND GOING UP UNDER HIS SKIRTS) Stop that! Somebody might see us!

FRITZ: Oh, I'll fix that!

And he reaches up and switches the compartment lights off. In the darkness, we hear muffled yelps from DUMDUM and PAT.

INT. THE HERREN TOILET. NIGHT.

PHIPPS is working at the door with a very small penknife, trying to lever it open.

PARKIN: Oh for goodness' sake, you'll never do it that way! Get out of the way!

He goes back into the loo as far as possible while PHIPPS stands aside, then takes a running charge at the door with his shoulder. It doesn't give an inch and he goes rigid with the pain and shock of it.

INT. THE COMPARTMENT. NIGHT.

The struggle is still going on, with the loudest protests coming from DUMDUM.

FRITZ: Do not fight it, liebchen! Your temerity surprises me . . .

DUMDUM: Not half the surprise you'll get if I stop fighting!

FRITZ: No, no . . . I insist . . . !

DUMDUM: No, stop it . . . take your hand away . . . I . . . oh!

We finishes with an outraged squawk as we hear a rending of cloth. For a moment there is silence, then FRITZ gives a bellow of real outrage.

FRITZ: Godammerung?!!!

And the lights come on again. FRITZ is standing by the switch, looking down at DUMDUM in horror. DUMDUM is trying to gather his torn skirt together.

EMIL: What is it? What's the matter?

FRITZ: It's a man!

EMIL: What?!

He lets go of PAT and jumps to his feet, pulling out the automatic again.

EMIL: A man? Why are you disguised as a woman? Answer me!

PAT sees her opportunity, brings her leg up, plants her foot against EMIL's rear and shoves hard, sending him hurtling across the compartment.

FRITZ gives a cry of rage, tries to grab her, but she grabs his hand and uses a judo throw to send him hurtling across EMIL.

PAT: Let's get out of here!

And, as she grabs DUMDUM . . .

INT. THE CORRIDOR. NIGHT.

Shouts and bangs are still coming from the 'HERREN' toilet as the RAILWAY POLICEMAN comes along the corridor.

He looks at the door, tries it, then fishes in his pocket for a key.

INT. THE HERREN TOILET. NIGHT.

PARKIN: It's no damn use. Here, let's give it one more try!

And he goes back into the loo and takes a running charge at the door . . .

INT. THE CORRIDOR. NIGHT.

As the POLICEMAN opens the door, just in time to receive the full force of PARKIN's charge in his stomach. He goes back against the side of the corridor like a deflated balloon.

PAT and DUMDUM tear into shot, with FRITZ and EMIL yelling behind them, as PARKIN and PHIPPS appear.

PAT: Run for it!

And they all tear off down the corridor, hotly pursued by FRITZ, EMIL and eventually the POLICEMAN, all shouting 'Stop'. In CU we see PARKIN pull the emergency stop.

EXT. THE TRAIN. NIGHT.

Shooting towards the rear platform of the last coach. There is a great squeal of brakes as the train grinds to a halt. PARKIN, PHIPPS, PAT and DUMDUM appear on the platform and leap off to one side, disappearing into the darkness.

We see the PURSUERS run onto the rear platform and come to a stop, looking round helplessly.

CUT TO:

EXT. FARMLAND. DAY.

Fairly open countryside with a cow barn in the foreground.

INT. THE COWBARN. DAY.

SLOW PAN along the sleeping forms of PARKIN, PHIPPS, PAT and finally DUMDUM. A big fat pig is gently nosing and snuffling at his face. A pleased smile appears on his face and he murmurs in his sleep . . .

DUMDUM: No, don't . . . no, stop it, Pat . . . don't be naughty now . . . . . . no, it tickles . . . stop it . . .

And he opens his eyes, sees the pig and gives a horrified squawk.

The others immediately start awake, ready to fight for their lives.

PARKIN: What is it? What's up?

DUMDUM: That bloomin' pig!

PARKIN: Blimey, is that all?

DUMDUM: Is that all! How would you like to be woken up with a morning kiss from that?

PARKIN: It's the best offer you're likely to get!

PAT: I don't know. He wasn't doing so badly in the train last night!

She chuckles at him.

PHIPPS: Yes. Just think though, if he hadn't have made such a fuss, we might have been in Lubeck by now.

DUMDUM: Well, what did you expect me to do? He was trying to make love to me!

PARKIN: You shouldn't have looked so willing!

DUMDUM: Crikey, that's nice, that is! I tell you . . .

He is interrupted by the roar of an aircraft engine starting up somwhere outside.

PARKIN: Blimey, what's that?

He and the others run to the door of the barn and peer cautiously out.

EXT. COUNTRYSIDE. DAY.

As from their P.O.V. the noise seems to be coming from behind a tall hedge about a hundred yards from the barn.

PARKIN signals the others to follow him and starts across at a crouching run.

EXT. THE HEDGE. DAY.

It is about head height. We see their heads peer cautiously over the top and react.

EXT. SMALL AIR FIELD. DAY.

As from their P.O.V. there is a twin-engined, civilian aircraft about fifty yards off, capable of carrying half a dozen or so passengers. A pick-up truck is drawn up near to it, and a couple of MECHANICS are running up the engines, one inside the cabin at the controls and the other standing outside. As we watch, the MECHANIC outside gives the 'thumbs up' to the one inside and the engines are cut. As he climbs out . . .

EXT. THE HEDGE. DAY.

PARKIN and the others bob back down behind it, grinning.

PARKIN: How's that for service?

We hear the pick-up start up and they peer over the hedge again.

EXT. THE AIRFIELD. DAY.

The pick-up is just starting off towards the hangars on the other side of the field.

EXT. THE HEDGE. DAY.

PARKIN: Let's go!

As they start scrambling over it . . .

EXT. THE AIRFIELD. DAY.

They run towards the plane, open the door, and climb in.

INT. THE AIRCRAFT. DAY.

PARKIN leads the way into the pilots' compartment, sits in one of the seats and looks feverishly at the jumble of switches.

PARKIN: How do you start the ruddy thing?

PAT: Try those switches!

He indicates a bank of switches, labelled in German.

PAT: It says 'engine'. (PARKIN PUTS THEM ALL ON AND WE SEE A COUPLE OF IGNITION LIGHTS COME ON) Now try pressing these buttons! (PARKIN DOES SO AND ONE OF THE ENGINES STARTS TURNING OVER AND BURSTS INTO LIFE) Now the other one!

He presses the other button and the second engine bursts into life.

PARKIN laughs triumphantly.

PARKIN: What a little beauty! Right, who's

going to fly? (THE OTHERS LOOK AT EACH OTHER HELPLESSLY) What? You don't mean to say none of you knows how to fly? (SHAME-FACEDLY, THEY SHAKE THEIR HEADS) Well, now's a nice time to tell me!

PHIPPS: Can't you?

PARKIN: Course not!

PAT: (LOOKING OUT FRONT) Well, you'd better try! The pick-up's coming back!

PARKIN looks out . . .

EXT. THE AIRFIELD. DAY.

As from their P.O.V., we see that the pick-up has just completed its turn and is coming back towards them fast.

INT. THE AIRCRAFT. DAY.

PARKIN: Oh blimey! Where's the brake? (HE LOOKS FEVERISHLY AROUND THE CABIN, SPOTS WHAT LOOKS LIKE A HAND-BRAKE, PUTS IT OFF, THEN LOOKS DOWN AROUND THE FLOOR) Where's the accelerator! There's no ruddy accelerator!!

PHIPPS: There must be!

He leans forward to look and pushes against the throttle levers, pushing them right forward. The engines roar and PARKIN grips the control column frantically as the aircraft starts to move forward, gathering speed quickly.

As PARKIN see-saws madly at the control wheel . . .

EXT. THE AIRFIELD. DAY.

L.S. to show the very erratic progress of the aircraft, more or less in the direction of the fast-approaching pick-up.

CU of the PICK-UP DRIVER's face, as he realises that the aircraft is heading in his direction. He takes dramatic avoiding action, turning completely around to get as far away from it as possible, but finds it following up fast. Too damn fast. He does a tight turn which gets him out of the way of it, just in time.

INT. THE AIRCRAFT. DAY.

As it bounces along, swerving crazily from side to side.

PARKIN: Where's a map? Where's a map?

PAT: Let's get it off the ground first!

EXT. THE AIRFIELD. DAY.

The pick-up has come to a stop and the DRIVER is wiping his perspiring face. His PASSENGER points fearfully ahead and the DRIVER looks that way. The aircraft is swinging around in a huge turn and . . . yes, heading back his way. He flings it into gear and, turning around, tries to get out of its way, but it seems to follow every swerve and turn . . . and always getting nearer and nearer.

Finally, they give up, screech to a halt, scramble out of the pick-up and throw themselves flat on the ground.

INT. THE AIRCRAFT. DAY.

As DUMDUM points ahead at the stopped pick-up. It seems to be rushing towards them at an alarming speed. Instinctively, PARKIN pulls back on the control column.

EXT. THE AIRFIELD. DAY.

As the aircraft takes off, jumps the pick-up with only inches to spare, and thuds back onto the ground again.

We see the MECHANICS get up and shake their fists after it.

INT. THE AIRCRAFT. DAY.

PAT: No, keep the stick back! Keep it back!

PARKIN jerks the stick right back and the others sprawl backwards in a heap as the aircraft stands on its tail.

EXT. THE AIRFIELD. DAY.

To see the result of this manoeuvre, as the aircraft seems to go straight up, teeter a moment, then level out and start a more or less normal climb.

INT. THE AIRCRAFT. DAY.

The others are back on their feet as PARKIN turns to them triumphantly.

PARKIN: We did it! We're in the air!

PHIPPS: Fine. But we still have to get back onto the ground sometime!

PARKIN: We'll worry about that when the time comes.

DUMDUM: Where're we going?

PARKIN: West of course! Switzerland!

PAT: I wonder what they're doing back in the camp right now?

CUT TO:

EXT. THE PRISON CAMP. DAY.

The KRIEGIES are standing around in groups, listening to the muffled sounds of a war going on, apparently all around them.

EXT. THE KOMMANDANTURA. DAY.

As BINDER, looking very grim, runs into it.

INT. FOKKER'S OFFICE. DAY.

FOKKER is standing at the window as the door opens and BINDER tears in, excitedly.

BINDER: Herr Colonel! The Americans have broken through! We are kaput!

This scene should be all very stiff upper-lip, with the noises of warfare going on in the background.

FOKKER: I see. Is there anything we can do?

BINDER: I'm afraid not, Colonel. We are by-passed and completely surrounded.

FOKKER: So. It is the finish. There is only one honourable thing left for me to do.

BINDER: I understand, Herr Colonel.

FOKKER: Then . . . I will say goodbye, Kapitan.

BINDER: Goodbye, Colonel! (SPONTANEOUSLY, HE SHAKES FOKKER'S HAND, CHOKES BACK A SOB, THEN TURNS AND GOES QUICKLY TO THE DOOR, OPENS IT AND, TURNING) Heil Hitler!

FOKKER winces as BINDER goes out, closing the door behind him.

FOKKER: I wish he wouldn't do that!

He sighs, squares his shoulders, goes to his desk, gets out a gun, looks at it, then carefully places it on the desk. Then he crosses to a wall mirror, inspects himself carefully, putting on his cap and adjusts it to the correct angle. Then he pours himself a stiff drink, toasts himself grimly in the mirror, knocks it straight back, then, straightening his tunic, goes back to the desk, picks up the gun and carefully checks that it is loaded. He has just shot the magazine back in when the door suddenly flies open and an AMERICAN GENERAL backed up by a couple of G.I.s with automatic rifles burst in.

GENERAL: Hold it!

FOKKER jumps and the gun goes off in his hands, sending him into a fury.

FOKKER: What on earth do you think you're doing!

GENERAL: Gee, I'm terribly sorry . . .

FOKKER: That's all very well, but I could have *killed* myself!

EXT. THE CAMP COMPOUND. DAY.

The KRIEGIES are all drawn up in squads as the GENERAL and his STAFF stride in through the open gates. The GERMAN GOONS are all gathered in a sorry-looking group to one side, watched over by a couple of armed G.I.s.

TISSPOT: British officers! British officers – atten . . . .

RHODES: Shun, sir!

TISSPOT: I know! Why do you always have to spoil everything!

The GENERAL comes to a stop before him and takes the salute.

GENERAL: Men! It is my privilege to tell you that this prison camp has been liberated!

(THERE IS A CHEER FROM THE KRIEGIES) The Kommandant, Colonel Fokker, has surrendered it to me as of 12.33 this morning! (ANOTHER CHEER) As of now you are free men. You have nothing more to worry about!

The noise of approaching aircraft engines is heard and he looks up at the sky.

As from his P.O.V. We see a twin-engined aircraft approaching at about 2000 ft.

INT. THE AIRCRAFT. DAY.

PARKIN is still at the controls, with the others gathered beside him, poring over the maps.

DUMDUM: I can't even find Switzerland. Are you sure we haven't gone past it?

PARKIN: How the hell would I know? Look . . . (AND BREAKS OFF AS THE AIRCRAFT ENGINES SPLUTTER OMINOUSLY) What's happening? What's wrong?

He fiddles with the throttle levers. PAT spots the trouble and points at one of the dials.

PAT: We've run out of petrol!

As the engines die completely.

PARKIN: Oh no! Now what do we do?

PAT: Land!

PARKIN: Obviously! But where?

He has put the aircraft into a gliding dive. The others peer out of the windows.

PHIPPS: There's a fairly clear space just to the right there!

PARKIN: Okay. Hang on and pray!

He increases the dive.

EXT. THE CAMP COMPOUND. DAY.

Now everyone is looking at the approaching aircraft and getting a bit worried.

As from their P.O.V., it appears to be making straight for the compound at a fast speed.

CU of GENERAL, as his nerve breaks.

GENERAL: It's a Jerry! Run for it!

And he and his STAFF run for it.

The KRIEGIES stand firm, TISSPOT apparently mesmerised by the aircraft.

RHODES: Sir, don't you think we'd better . . . ?

TISSPOT: What? Oh yes, perhaps so. British officers . . . dis–

RHODES: Miss!

And that's enough. The KRIEGIES break ranks and run for it.

INT. THE AIRCRAFT. DAY.

They are looking ahead, horrified.

EXT. THE COMPOUND. DAY.

As from their P.O.V., in the aircraft. They are very low and the compound, with the Kommandantura beyond it seems to be approaching at an alarming speed.

PAT: Level off! Level off!

EXT. THE COMPOUND. DAY.

The GENERAL, making for the Kommandantura, stops and looks back in horror, then throws himself flat on the ground, burying his face in his arms.

We hear a screech of rubber tyres, a tremendous rending of woodwork, several crashes, a pause, and finally a gigantic crash. Then silence. The GENERAL looks up.

Now we see the trail of havoc left by the aircraft. It has gone completely through two of the huts, the perimeter fence, and finished up somewhere in the heap of ruin that once was the Kommandantura.

INT. THE KOMMANDANTURA. DAY.

Or rather, what remains of it. Part of the wreckage on top of the aircraft stirs, is flung back, and PARKIN climbs out, followed by the others, and looks around curiously.

DUMDUM: Where are we? Switzerland?

PARKIN: I don't know, but I have a funny feeling . . . (SOME MORE OF THE WRECKAGE STIRS AND A VERY BEDRAGGLED FOKKER EMERGES, COUGHING AND SPLUTTERING) Oh no! It couldn't be!

FOKKER sees him, and, shaking with rage, starts bawling him out.

FOKKER: You! Look what you've done to my beautiful stalag! You've ruined it! I'll make you pay for this, do you hear? I'll make you pay!

PARKIN sighs and looks straight into camera . . .

PARKIN: I think this is where you came in!

And turns back to FOKKER as he continues with his tirade.

FOKKER: The only completely escape-proof camp in Germany! Ruined! Ruined!

CAMERA TRACKS BACK swiftly from the scene of devastation and we bring in . . .

CLOSING MUSIC.

And SUPERIMPOSE:

'DAS ENDING'

BIBLIOGRAPHY

The following publications have proved useful sources of information whilst writing this book.

Barrie, Amanda: *It's not a Rehearsal,*
Headline, London,
ISBN: 075531123X

Bright, Morris and Ross, Robert: *Mr Carry On –*
The Life and Work of Peter Rogers,
BBC, London,
ISBN: 0563551836

Hayward, Anthony: *Who's Who on Television,*
Boxtree, London,
ISBN: 075221067X

Hibbin, Sally and Nina: *What A Carry On,*
Hamlyn, London,
ISBN: 0600558193

McFarlane, Brian: *The Encyclopedia of British Film,*
Methuen, London,
ISBN: 0413773019

Parsons, Nicholas: *The Straight Man – My Life in Comedy,*
Weidenfeld and Nicolson, London,
ISBN: 0297812394

Ross, Robert: *The Carry On Companion,*
Batsford, London,
ISBN: 0713479671

Sims, Joan: *High Spirits,*
Partridge, London,
ISBN: 1852252804

Snelgrove, Kevin: *The Carry On Book of Statistics,*
KAS Publications, Frome,
ISBN: 0954420004

Webber, Richard: *The Complete A-Z of Dad's Army,*
Orion, London,
ISBN: 075284637X

Webber, Richard: *The Complete A-Z of Only Fools*
and Horses,
Orion, London,
ISBN: 0752847317

Whitfield, June: *. . . and June Whitfield, The Autobiography,*
Bantam Press, London,
ISBN: 0593045823

The excellent website, www.imdb.com, was a valuable tool when it came to adding meat to the bones of some of the actor and production team profiles. Also, of course, Andy Davidson's informative and extensive site, www.carryonline.com, the official *Carry On* website, a must for all fans of the film series.